THINKER, FAILURE, SOLDIER, JAILER

THINKER, FAILURE, SOLDIER, JAILER

AN ANTHOLOGY
OF GREAT LIVES
IN 365 DAYS

The Telegraph

Edited by Harry de Quetteville

Aurum
Press

First published in Great Britain
2012 by Aurum Press Ltd
74–77 White Lion Street
London N1 9PF
www.aurumpress.co.uk

This paperback edition first published in
2014 by Aurum Press Ltd

Picture Credits: Courtesy of the Kasanka Trust: 560; Courtesy of Mrs Rendell: 423;
Sebastian O'Kelly: 267; Getty Images: 11, 22, 35, 49, 76, 107, 109, 149, 152, 178, 205, 209,
240, 269, 291, 305, 308, 309, 331 348, 351, 352, 378, 391, 403, 413, 416, 421, 423, 433,
445, 457, 502, 505, 517, 532, 547, 549

A catalogue record for this book is available from the British Library.

ISBN 978 1 78131 309 1

3 5 7 9 10 8 6 4 2
2014 2016 2018 2017 2015

Text design by carrdesignstudio.com
Typeset in Berling
Printed and bound by CPI Group (UK) Ltd, Croydon, CR0 4YY

CONTENTS

INTRODUCTION

⟶◆⟵

'How do you choose?'

This, I have discovered in my years editing *The Daily Telegraph* obituaries page, is the question that most strikes the curious-minded when they discover what I do.

'I mean,' my inquisitor will add, leaning in and whispering confidentially, as if asking after a tip for the 3.30 at Plumpton, 'how do you decide who goes in?'

It is a question which at first makes me fizz with pride. What an honour, the implication is, to make that decision. What judgment, the inquiry seems to suggest, must be required to make the right call.

But then I grasp that the query might not necessarily be entirely hypothetical. Those young enough to have a reasonable expectation of lasting a while longer will add that a treasured uncle, who built really quite extraordinary model boats, has just died. Those a touch older might drop a hint about their own service in the Armed Forces. Suddenly, I become aware that I am being viewed not as the lucky incumbent of one of the great jobs on Fleet Street, but as journalism's equivalent of the man behind the velvet rope at an exclusive club, haughtily weighing up prospective entrants.

This realisation is a great reminder, if any were needed, of the reputation that the *Telegraph* obituaries page has acquired in the last quarter of a century. Deservedly, and entirely through the efforts of my predecessors, it has become a much-loved institution. And when I am buttonholed with 'How do you decide who goes in?' in a tone that conveys more than the benign spirit of inquiry, I realise that it is an institution to which access is keenly contested. All this even though successful 'applicants' know full well that they will not be around to see the results of their efforts in print.

At such times the fizz of pride gives way to the low murmur of humility – for how does one explain whose life shall make a great obituary? How can one possibly tell?

In truth, the answer is not straightforward. There are, of course, the obvious selections. You would be right to assume that prime ministers, archbishops and generals glide effortlessly onto the page. But not even all-out war between Downing Street, Lambeth Palace and the MoD could furnish us with enough candidates to publish day after day on that basis alone.

High Court judges and peers of the realm certainly stake their claim, as do those oozing that most cherished quality of the new Establishment: celebrity. Scientists and artists of renown take their place. The odd academic. MPs expect their due. But then ...

It took the genius of Hugh Massingberd, who revolutionised *Telegraph* obituaries when he launched the daily obits column in 1986, to appreciate that accomplishment is a concept that encompasses very much more than a position on the green benches (or the red) at Westminster. After he took over, his genial, broad-minded view of the world was blissfully expressed in such opening paragraphs as:

> Denisa Lady Newborough, who has died aged seventy-four [21 March], was many things: wire-walker, nightclub girl, nude dancer, air pilot. She only refused to be two things – a whore and a spy – 'and there were attempts to make me both ...'

Whole new vistas of delight opened up to readers. Gone were the dry as dust recitations from *Who's Who*; in their place were character portraits, sketches, anecdotes and tales of the unexpected.

Adventurers, opium smokers, shark fishermen and members of the criminal fraternity were soon every bit as welcome on the obituaries page as the Bishop of Bath and Wells. Fire and brimstone preachers took their place alongside con men. As often as not it turned out that the fire and brimstone preachers were con men. If they were it was all one to those lucky enough to be working on the obits desk – this was the stuff of life.

And life, not death, is what obituaries are all about – every barmy, uplifting scrap of it.

To illustrate my case, allow me to point to just a few of the lives that have crossed my desk. One chap had traversed the Himalayas in a hovercraft. Another was a spy who had saved Churchill at Tehran. Yet another provided the voice for the puppet George (a 'shy, pink and slightly camp hippopotamus') on the children's television programme *Rainbow*.

Witness too the extraordinary feats of derring-do that grace the page: acts of courage of men and women such as Tommy Gould (d. 6 December), who crawled along the outside of his submarine to retrieve two bombs stuck there and haul them over the side, knowing that the sub might have to dive at any moment and drown him. ('What were you thinking,' he was later asked by the Marquess of Donegal, 'while you were busy with the bombs'?' 'I was hoping,' Gould replied with admirable restraint, 'that the bloody things would not go off.') Then there is Nancy Wake (d. 7 August), the 'White Mouse' who led Maquis fighters against the Nazis in Occupied France. Or Norman Jackson (d. 26 March), who attempted to put out a fire on the wing of his Lancaster bomber by crawling out of the cockpit at 22,000ft with a extinguisher stuffed into his jacket.

Hugh Massingberd certainly cherished the glorious. But he also cherished the vainglorious. And he positively celebrated the ludicrous, the absurd, and the frankly ridiculous.

So room was made for comedies and calamities, military ones included. Prominence was given to the exploits of such figures as Brigadier Ted Hughes (d. 31 March), who took part in the siege in 1919 of Spin Baldak, in Afghanistan, and wrote about it in 'a richly sarcastic memoir that was enjoyed more by his contemporaries than by his senior officers'. The siege was the last occasion when a British Army unit used scaling ladders. And as Hugh himself recounted in 2000, its tactical idiosyncrasies, despite the requirement for total silence, 'could only have succeeded if the enemy had been chloroformed'.

'A sound as of corrugated iron being dropped from a great height denoted that the scaling ladders were being loaded on the carts,' the obit noted. Apart from this, 'no one would have had an inkling that several thousand armed men were pressing forward to the fray'.

It was thus that while the great and the good earned their places on the *Telegraph* obits page, they were, on occasion, joined by the ham-fisted and inept. Sometimes, if readers were very lucky indeed, there would be an appearance by the bad or the positively wicked.

Still, this enlightened and inclusive approach to obituaries, instituted by Hugh and enshrined by his successors, hardly helps whittle down the list of potential subjects. With rogues and reprobates, failures and frauds, every bit as welcome as Wing Commanders and Baronets, Nobel Prize Winners and Fellows of the Royal Society, the question can be posed with more justice than ever:

'How do you choose?'

After all, space dictates that we cannot include everyone who might wish to feature (not everyone does). The *Telegraph* usually publishes three or four obits a day, six days a week. That amounts to more than 100 each month – perhaps 1,250 a year. But while this may seem a lot, it is a pitifully small number compared with the avalanche of submissions and suggestions which we receive. For every life we publish, there are many worthy alternatives that do not make it into print.

As a result, it is not easy to settle on which characters to include on any given day. How much harder, then, to select those who appear in the pages of this book – a digest of the quarter of a century in which obits at the *Telegraph* have become famous.

In a way the calendar format which these pages take has helped – providing a framework around which to shape my wilder flights of fancy. I also hope that the diary layout will prove fun to read – enabling idle perusers to flick through and pick out the celebrated deeds of a life that came to its end on any given day of the year. For the obits contained herein are entered not on the date of publication, nor the subject's date of birth, but on the date that whichever hero (or villain) slipped away. Which seems appropriate to the form: obituaries are concerned with achievement – virtuous or otherwise – and few of us achieve much of note on our first day.

All of the lives featured – all but one – came to an end after 1986. Of course, obituaries did appear in the *Telegraph* before Hugh Massingberd took over. But these were usually arid recitations of achievements, and appeared intermittently. There was nothing comparable to the regular section of recent years. If readers today call and ask if we might point them to the obit of a long-dead architect, say, we are obliged to inform them, to almost universal surprise, that the obits page they consider as old as print itself, is in fact a relatively new creation. The resultant disbelief is the greatest compliment to Hugh's art there is: people simply can't imagine that things were ever different.

But they were, and to illustrate the fact, I have included in this book a single pre-1986 obit: Winston Churchill, who died on 24 January 1965. In truth, his was a life into which so much incident was packed that even in the modern obits format there would be little room for anecdote amid the lists of events and honours. Still, its style stands out.

When great figures died in the old, pre-1986 days – Picasso, say, or Louis Armstrong – an article might appear on the news pages under the byline: By Our Obituaries Staff. Oddly enough, such an event seems to have eclipsed Hugh on the very day slated for the inauguration of his new-style obituaries section – which in its earliest configuration claimed a column or two on the Court and Social page.

Monday 1 September 1986 was to have been the day that the obits butterfly emerged from the rather gloomy chrysalis which it had inhabited for so many years. But then, on Sunday 31 August, the great sculptor Henry Moore died, and for one last day, the old formula was adopted: Spin Baldak would have to wait.

But in its way, Henry Moore's death was an indication of an imperative that still exists today. If a famous name dies, we do our absolute best to make sure that there is a suitably glorious obit ready to read the next day. Or, in this internet age, sooner than that. This fact inevitably prompts the second most asked question after: 'How do you choose?' This is: 'How many people do you have prepared?'

At least on this score I can be more precise. The answer is a great many. Several thousand at least, in various stages of readiness. Some files contain nothing but redundant, archived scraps of news cuttings decades old; others are filled with up-to-the-minute, ready-to-print pieces. It is delicate but true to disclose that prominent subjects in the latter group are the famous and sick (think Steve Jobs – d. 5 October); the famous and hunted (Osama bin Laden – d. 2 May); or, curiously, the old and the active.

I hope that it is not revealing too much of the anonymous obituarist's art (*Telegraph* obits are not bylined) to note that most people achieve those things for which they become known in the early or middle parts of their lives. But by the same token, there are few people who go on to do radically different things, or rise dramatically to prominence, at a very advanced age. Of such aged achievers, there can only be a handful of global prominence, and of those, I can only really think of one or two who make significant decisions at a time in life when the most fateful choices of their contemporaries are to write ungrateful godsons out of wills. Such a combination of advanced age and ongoing, ever-changing influence, keeps the obits writer in a state of constant fret. Updates are required almost daily. Does the Pope realise he is the cause of such angst?

Sometimes, however, the roles are reversed, and obits writers begin to scribble pen-portraits that might, by their very existence, cause disbelief and, no doubt, disquiet in their subjects – if only they knew. I confess to wondering whether, as we mull potential pieces to prepare on the desk, and the name of a youthful but addled talent is suggested, it would have any effect on the subject's self-destructive trajectory if they knew that we were getting ready. Would Amy Winehouse have changed her ways had she known that we – and, I bet, every other paper in the obits business – had long readied a piece in advance of her death, at the absurdly young age of twenty-seven? Of course not, it would be vanity to pretend so. But still. It would surely have given her pause, no? To imagine that writers who were neither friends nor foes, but simply objective observers, had weighed the balance of probabilities, and decided that there was a serious risk of her not seeing thirty. Sadly, some deaths are all too predictable.

On the other hand, many come utterly out of the blue. And even though we prepare a great number of obituaries in advance, we sit on a stockpile much smaller than some people suspect. Occasionally I get the impression that even a few colleagues at the *Telegraph* believe that the obits team simply twiddles its thumbs until the telephone rings and a demise is reported, at which point one among us trudges to a cabinet and pulls out a magically prepared article. If only it were so ...

Many are the obits editors, on this and other papers, whose nerves have been frazzled by the limitless potential for getting caught out. Scenes of potential devastation, where every casualty is a youthful, unobituarised hero of the pop charts, play in the mind's eye, causing the palms of otherwise lantern-jawed Fleet Street stalwarts to sweat. Millions of television viewers tune in each week to watch the football on *Match of the Day*. Only the obituarist wonders how the managers are dealing with the stress – it can't be healthy, after all. We are by nature worriers.

So, finally, how do we decide who to include, from all of brimming humanity?

The answer, in total honesty, is that we are led by you, dear reader. Despite the sparks of pride and pleasure that the obit of a loved one might bring a grieving family, it is not for them that we publish. An article does not appear in the hope that it might offer a surviving widow, or children, a modicum of consolation, though we surely hope that it does. In the end we publish the selected obituaries because we believe that they will be of the greatest interest to the newspaper's readers.

So we try to obituarise the fantastically talented, and the fantastically entertaining. Hopefully you will find plenty of each on these pages.

That is not to suggest that this book is simply a roll call of the most famous names of the last twenty-five years. Of course, there are plenty of celebrated figures here, from Jane Russell (d. 28 February) to Henry Cooper (d. 1 May). But if you are left wondering why Ronald Allen ('sixteen years in the role of David Hunter, the debonair motel manager in the legendary television soap opera *Crossroads*' – d. 18 June) appears at the expense of, say, Marlon Brando, it is no reflection on their relative merits as actors. It is not because I feel, deep down inside, that Allen's masculine frame would have been better in *Streetcar Named Desire*, or offered a more harrowing Kurtz in *Apocalypse Now*. It is primarily because Allen's obit contains the immortal description of his character in *Crossroads*. Hunter, the obit recalls, was 'the most famously dull character in the history of soap operas' with what Hilary Kinglsey called 'the charisma of an ashtray and all the life of Sooty without Matthew Corbett's hand ... To describe him as wooden would bring a libel suit from the Forestry Commission.'

Or take Emmanuel de Margerie (d. 2 December), the late French ambassador to London. It would have been easy to omit 'Bobby' de Margerie, and leave the way clear for the soldier and actor Richard Todd, or the wrestler Big Daddy, who both died on the same day. But in the end they all had to go in, because de Margerie's obit contains the splendid tale of the visit of President Mitterrand to London – when one of his bodyguards 'took it upon himself to test the efficacy of the security services by planting two lumps of dynamite in the embassy garden, and then inviting the British police to search for them', continuing:

> The wheeze, presumably, was to complain when the officers failed to find the explosive. But it never does to underestimate the British dog. Olive and Lucy, two labradors, effortlessly sniffed out the ruse, and the President's bodyguard was hauled off to Scotland Yard.
>
> The British put on a fine display of outrage … Eventually the Quai d'Orsai announced that it 'regretted the misunderstanding', which was reckoned to be as close to an apology as a French government is capable.

Such gems abound. For *Telegraph* obituaries are not just about substance, they are also about style. It has always been the privilege of obits editors, from Hugh onwards, to work with contributors who combine great expertise and a way with words. On my desk at work is a rather tattered list of names and contact numbers for an array of specialists who can deliver articles of real insight on every conceivable topic – from big-game hunting to ballroom dancing, mountaineering to movie moguls.

On one occasion I was called by the thrill-seeking correspondent who tends to concentrate on obits of those with a fondness for extreme sports (of the kind which shape fascinating lives, but all too frequently lead to untimely deaths). Would I be interested, he asked, in a piece about Chris Dale (d. 19 February), a hell-raising climber. I said I might. Good, he replied, because Chris was an unusual figure. The subsequent obit began:

> Chris Dale, who has died aged forty-nine, was a 6ft 6in mountaineer with a passion for solo climbs among the hardest peaks of Scotland, Wales and the Alps. He was also an equally enthusiastic cross-dresser who went by the name of Crystal.

Obits editors are lucky indeed to have submissions comprising such insider knowledge and journalistic verve. Understated turns of phrase combine to form elegant paragraphs that are a pleasure to edit and, I hope, to read.

So this book is, in its way, a tribute to all those who have written for the obits page over the years. I will not attempt to mention them all – to do so would only end with the accidental omission of a crucial contributor. But it has been an enormous pleasure and honour to have worked with so many in the time since I joined the obits desk in 2008.

I can, however, mention by name my fellows on that desk, without whom the job would be impossible, and life a duller place. They are Roger Wilkes, Katharine Ramsay and Jay Iliff. My sincere thanks are due to them. Before he retired, David Twiston-Davies also provided a vital education about the world of obituaries. We tend never to name the authors of individual obits, but I will bend a rule this once to reveal that Ronald Bailey (d. 14 May) was a typical Twistonian composition. It details a diplomatic life which involved being near-eviscerated by a deranged attacker, and denying a visa to a bearded man whose passport bore the name 'Jesus Christ'. The piece began:

> Ronald Bailey, who has died aged ninety-two, enjoyed a wide variety of postings during his 35-year diplomatic career, of which the most striking was Taiz in the Yemeni Highlands, once described as 'hastening at full speed into the fourteenth century'.

Such obits are diverting. But they can be enlightening too. After all, obits contain more facts per line than any other form of journalism (which means more things to get wrong – another source of worry for the eternally fretful editor). For pub quiz fans there is a boundless seam of trivia to mine. Dates, names and places are all there for fans of the old 'who, when, why, where, what?' school of history. And for devotees of miscellanea, tips, and barmy factoids, this book is a repository of the wisdom of many lives well lived to explore with a drink at hand.

Here, for example, is just one obscure but possibly valuable nugget of information, which I heartily recommend to every gardener. It comes from the obit of Ernie James (d. 5 July), who lived his whole life on the land as one of the last 'Fen Tigers'. It's about doing away with pesky moles.

> The secret of setting mole traps, he explained, is to ignore the molehills, which merely indicate where the moles have been digging for worms, and look instead for small depressions in the ground indicating a mole run underneath. To tell whether a run is still in use, he advised pressing a heel into the ground, then looking at the indentation the following day; if the heel mark shows any signs of disturbance, the moles are still using the run.'

Which leaves just one other point. On the day that a distinct section emerged, headed and underlined OBITUARIES, the very first obit that appeared was that of Lady Fisher of Lambeth. Occasionally, since then, we have received the odd complaint that we do not feature enough women on the page.

To this I always reply: obituaries are not a reflection of society as it is now, or of how we might like it to be, but rather as it was when our subjects were in their prime, often many decades ago. To lament that not enough women feature is like complaining that too few of the photographs that illustrate our obits are in colour. Over time both these things will change.

There is no doubt, however, that over the years, women have provided just as many truly great obits as men. So, though I have not totted up an exact count, the articles in this book are split almost equally between the sexes.

One notable obituary of a woman is that of Jade Goody (d. 22 March), the reality television star who died of cancer in 2009. For some reason a decision was taken then not to publish the piece in the paper, which was a shame because it was one of the best pieces of writing it has been my pleasure to oversee. Though it was published online, this book is the first time that it appears in print. It makes quite astonishing reading.

Just six editors have overseen *Telegraph* obituaries since Hugh Massingberd waved his wand over the page in 1986: Hugh, David Jones, Kate Summerscale, Christopher Howse, Andrew McKie, and now me. I recognise that this book is as much their achievement as my own, and to them, as to our writers, I offer my thanks. It is a cause for genuine sorrow that one of the obits between these covers is that of Hugh, who died on Christmas Day 2007. I hope that his obituary will give readers who never knew him an elegant, entertaining, true portrait of the man – for that is what he felt obituaries are meant to do and, because of him, that is what the writers of *Telegraph* obituaries continue to do better than anybody else.

Harry de Quetteville
April 2012

JANUARY

⚜ 1st ⚜

Margot Bryant, b. 1897, d. 1988

Margot Bryant, the actress who has died aged ninety, became one of the most familiar faces on television in the late 1960s and 1970s through her portrayal of the simpering, cat-loving Minnie Caldwell in 560 episodes of Granada TV's interminable serial, *Coronation Street*.

The diminutive old dear, who always had a faintly flyblown look and a distracted manner, was the put-upon member of that formidable coven which held sway in the snug of the Rovers Return. Delicately supping her milk stout, Minnie would be subjected to acid tongue-lashings by the other occupants of this moral crow's nest, Ena Sharples and Martha Longhurst, for her vague incomprehension of the finer points of the latest gossip.

The verbal interplay between the three yielded some of the Street's richest moments, delighting John Betjeman and all other fans of the serial's earthy Northern humanity.

Minnie Caldwell's life tended to revolve around her ginger tom-cat, Bobby (once a permanent fixture on the rooftops in the programme's opening sequence), and his various vicissitudes. At one stage in the early 1960s she had a lodger, the cheeky Jed Stone (played by Kenneth Cope), with whom she enjoyed a maternal relationship; he called her 'Ma', she called him 'Sunny Jim'.

Later she toyed with the affections of the miserable old codger, Albert Tatlock; marriage was in the offing, but when Minnie discovered that their union would have a deleterious effect on her pension she cancelled the match.

Having appeared in the third episode of *Coronation Street* in 1960, Moaning Minnie stayed on until 1976. According to the storyline, the character left the Street to keep house for her old school friend, Handel Gartside, in Derbyshire.

Margot Bryant, a doctor's daughter, was born at Hull in 1897 and began her career as a chorus girl in pantomime. She went on to dance in the Fred Astaire show, *Stop Flirting*, in the 1920s, and her other West End roles included Lucy in *Gay's the Word* at the old Saville.

Quite unlike Minnie Caldwell in real life – the only thing they had in common was a preference for the feline species to the human – Miss Bryant was outspoken, caustic and sophisticated with a love of travel.

'She always had a twinkle in her eye,' recalled the Street's only survivor from the original cast, William Roache (who plays Ken Barlow), 'and liked to shock people.'

Eugene Wigner, b. 1902, d. 1995

Eugene Wigner, the nuclear physicist and Nobel laureate who has died aged ninety-two, played an important part both in building the atomic bomb and in persuading Albert Einstein to back the project.

The latter proved difficult, not because of any reluctance on Einstein's part but because in 1939 no one knew where to find him.

Fearing Nazi assassins, the great man was living in Long Island under the assumed name of 'Dr Moore'.

One day in July, Wigner and Leo Slizard, his colleague and fellow Hungarian, set out in a car to find 'Dr Moore's' isolated cabin. They soon became hopelessly lost.

'Perhaps I misunderstood on the telephone,' said Wigner. 'I thought he said Patchogue.'

'Could it have been Cutchogue?' asked Slizard irritably.

They drove into Cutchogue, but no one there had heard of Dr Moore. 'Maybe fate never intended this,' said Wigner. 'Let's go home.'

'Wait,' said Slizard. They stopped at the kerb and asked a small boy if he knew Professor Einstein.

'Sure,' replied the child, 'want me to take you to him?'

Einstein duly wrote a letter to President Roosevelt which resulted in the Manhattan Project to build the bomb. On 2 December 1942 Wigner was present when Enrico Fermi started the first nuclear chain reaction, in a squash court at Stagg Field, Chicago. 'The Atomic Age,' declared Wigner, 'has arrived.'

⊰ 2nd ⊱

George Carman, b. 1929, d. 2001

George Carman, the barrister who has died aged seventy-one, possessed such a fearsome reputation that whenever the rich and famous faced a libel action they hurried to send for him – before the other side did.

A succession of politicians, sportsmen and soap stars were humbled by Carman's forensic skills. Jonathan Aitken, Ian Botham and Gillian Taylforth were among those who were – as Mr Aitken put it – 'Carmanised' in the witness box.

Another was Jani Allan, the South African columnist who failed to convince a High Court jury that she had not had an affair with the neo-Nazi leader Eugene Terre Blanche. 'Whatever award is given for libel,' she told Carman during the case, 'being cross-examined by you would not make it enough money.'

Carman's standing was established long before libel actions became fashionable. When the comedian Ken Dodd was charged with tax fraud in 1989 he vetted a string of barristers before eventually telling his solicitor: 'I want to see George Carman. I ought to see George Carman.'

For many years, Carman practised out of the limelight on the Northern Circuit. But in 1971, shortly after Carman took silk, the solicitor Sir David Napley saw him at the Old Bailey defending a manager of Battersea Funfair. The man was charged with the manslaughter of four children after the Big Dipper collapsed. Carman secured a verdict of Not Guilty, having, in Napley's opinion, 'mesmerised' the jury. Napley determined to make use of him.

In 1978 Napley telephoned Carman to tell him that the leader of the Liberal Party, Jeremy Thorpe, was probably going to be committed for trial on charges of conspiracy to murder and that he was going to retain him.

The Thorpe trial in May 1979 caused a sensation. Carman pulled off a succession of masterstrokes – not least his decision not to put Thorpe in the witness-box. He ended his closing speech with a flourish that Perry Mason might have been proud of. Thorpe, said Carman, had won millions of votes from the people of this country, but now came the twelve most precious votes of all. Directing his gaze and a finger to each member of the jury in turn, he then repeated the word 'yours' to each one. 'I thought for a very long time about doing that,' he later admitted.

Thorpe's acquittal thrust Carman into the first rank of the Bar. He moved his practice to London where he took on a series of high-profile criminal cases: Dr Arthur, the paediatrician accused of murdering a Down's syndrome baby, whose acquittal gave Carman the greatest pleasure of all his cases; Geoffrey Prime, the GCHQ spy; and Ken Dodd, freed from his embarrassment with the Inland Revenue.

The Dodd case bore many of the hallmarks of a typical Carman performance: a famous defendant, seemingly incontrovertible evidence and a sensational acquittal. The result owed much to Carman's deftness at arguing that comic genius and careful accounting were strangers. He encapsulated the hypothesis in a phrase that he rightly judged would strike a chord with the jury: 'Some accountants are comedians,' he said. Then, after a pause: 'But comedians are never accountants.'

George Alfred Carman was born in Blackpool on 6 October 1929. He recalled his father, who ran a furniture shop, as 'a very different kind of man from myself: calm, tranquil, content. I've never had the pleasure of enjoying any of those qualities in abundance.'

George went to St Joseph's College, Blackpool, and, after National Service in the Army, went up to Balliol to read Jurisprudence. After taking a First in 1952, he was called by Lincoln's Inn in 1953 as the King George V Coronation Scholar, then did his pupillage in London. But with neither money nor connections, he decided to practise from chambers in Manchester.

The early years were hard. 'After five years I was earning as much as a Manchester bus driver without overtime,' he recalled. 'I almost left the Bar three times.' His concern about his fees was compounded by his marriage in 1955 to the daughter of a Manchester brewer. To make ends meet, his wife took a job as the manageress of the canteen at Great Universal Stores, and regularly pawned her wedding ring. The marriage did not last; nor did his next two.

Away from work, Carman was a reasonably enthusiastic guest on the party circuit, but essentially lived a quiet life. Although not universally popular among his peers – some of whom gave him the nickname 'Gorgeous George' – he was refreshingly friendly and unstuffy to younger barristers making their way. Retirement, he admitted, scared him. 'People say "Write a book" but I'm not a writer. I don't play golf, I don't play bridge, I don't garden, so what would be left? If you could find me an adequate substitute, I might eventually be attracted to it. But there is no adequate substitute for work.' Last autumn he was forced to retire when he became ill with cancer.

⋈ 3rd ⋈

Will Eisner, b. 1917, d. 2005

Will Eisner, who has died aged eighty-seven, was the American strip cartoonist who did the most to develop the genre from a formulaic children's entertainment into a sophisticated, arresting way of presenting dramatic stories rich in humour, irony and pathos.

He was one of a generation of comic artists, predominantly Jewish, that flourished at the end of the 1930s and on into the 1950s – a golden age brought to an end by the Senate's investigations into the links between comics and juvenile delinquency. It was an era celebrated in the novel *The Amazing Adventures of Kavalier and Clay* (2000), by Michael Chabon, who based aspects of his hero on Eisner. When Chabon was working on the book, Eisner told him that he always saw comic strips as art, and discussed how much he owed to the Jewish story-telling tradition.

His two greatest creations were The Spirit, a detective who faked his own death in order to combat crime in Central City; and, debatably, the graphic novel itself – his sequence of four stories, *A Contract with God* (1978), is considered to be the first example of the form. It evokes the Bronx tenements Eisner knew as a child. As he commented: 'My interest is not the superhero, but the little man who struggles to survive in the city.'

William Erwin Eisner was born in Brooklyn, on 6 March 1917, the son of a furrier. By the age of seven his natural talent for drawing was already obvious. He attended De Witt Clinton High School in New York, and in his youth wanted to become a stage designer. His fascination with architecture and perspective would permeate his urban landscapes later.

Eisner's first comic strip, entitled 'Captain Scott Dalton', appeared in 1936 in a publication entitled *Wow, What a Magazine!* This work brought him into contact with other comic artists and writers, in particular S.M. 'Jerry' Iger. When others were selling their creations to big houses – Jerry Siegel and Joe Shuster parted with the rights to Superman for $130 in 1938 – Eisner and Iger had the acumen to form their own company. They produced more than twenty original strips per week for major comics publishing houses, including Fiction House, Fox and Quality Publications.

The first Spirit story appeared on 2 June 1940, and there was a lot of room for the character to develop – the vigilante's costume amounted to nothing more than a mask and gloves. He was a criminologist named Denny Colt – who was supposedly dead, but was actually living in a hideout in Wildwood Cemetery.

The strip became Eisner's masterpiece, with splendid imagery, exotic locales, and a mosaic of intricate characterisations. Eisner looked deep into the nature of cruelty and plotted his tales with taste, conviction and brilliant craftsmanship. His character no longer faced super-criminals but rather a gallery of losers and hoodlums. The reader was thrust into a heavily atmospheric world of streets, sewers and skylines in an advanced state of decay. Despite the epic lengths and variety of stories, 'The Spirit' maintained an underlying thematic unity, to become one of the few really adult strips in the history of comics.

As Eisner's plots grew more elaborate, so his graphic virtuosity increased. He turned comic pages into film storyboards, using cinematic effects, angles and perspective to evoke pace and timing. Short silent panels interjected power and speed, long shots were contrasted with close-ups.

Many of the Spirit's deadliest foes were women, and Eisner's females were the sexiest ever to slink across a comic page. The crueller the villainess, the more attractive Eisner made her. With names like 'Silk Satin', 'Plaster of Paris', and 'Powder' ('like in gun powder – I blow up just as quick and I'm twice as deadly'), Eisner endowed his women with wasp-waists, sensuous lips and doe-eyes. They were exaggerated versions of Jane Russell, Lauren Bacall, Joan Crawford and other stars of the 1940s.

In 1978 he published *A Contract with God*, the graphic novel that showed the full extent of his innovations. The Jewish themes that had been implicit in his previous work became more evident in these tales of morality and sexuality, spritzed with the Yiddish that was by now better appreciated throughout the States. From then on he produced a book a year; the last, called *Plot*, deals with the Protocols of the Elders of Zion and the anti-Semitism that document fomented.

⊰ 4th ⊱

Harry Helmsley, b. 1909, d. 1997

Harry Helmsley, who has died aged eighty-seven, made himself a billionaire and bought the Empire State Building, but his success as a property dealer was overshadowed by his wife's imprisonment on tax evasion charges.

Although Helmsley was a virtual recluse prior to his second marriage, in 1972, to Leona, the Helmsleys thereafter became known for an extravagant lifestyle on one hand and penny-pinching on the other. Even by American standards, they were conspicuous consumers and party-givers, and controlled a property empire said to be worth more than $5 billion, but they fell foul of the law for writing off against tax $4 million-worth of personal expenses – including redecoration of their weekend home, underwear and jewellery.

In 1988, when Leona went on trial for extortion and falsifying records as well as tax fraud, the press christened her 'Queen of Mean'. Even Donald Trump felt moved to write to Helmsley to tell him that his wife was 'a disgrace to the human race'.

Mrs Helmsley was sentenced to four years in prison, fined $7.1 million, and ordered to pay back taxes of $1.7 million and to carry out 750 hours of public service. She served eighteen months of her sentence.

Helmsley himself did not have to stand trial, on the grounds that his brain had been damaged by a series of strokes.

If the trial turned public opinion against the Helmsleys and made them a symbol of 1980s greed, it did not mar their close relationship. Leona referred to her husband as 'my pussy-cat, my snooky, wooky, dooky' and each year gave a birthday party for him, at which the guests were encouraged to wear badges with 'I'm just wild about Harry' written on them.

Harry Brakmann Helmsley was born in New York City on 4 March 1909, the son of a buyer for a dry goods wholesaler. He went to Evander Childs High School in the Bronx, and started work at sixteen to support his family.

Inspired by his maternal grandfather, who had rented out flats, Helmsley took a job as an office boy in the property firm, Dwight, Voorhis & Perry, for $12 a week. After cutting his teeth by collecting rents in the Hell's Kitchen area of New York, Helmsley was rapidly promoted and became a partner in 1938.

Two years earlier he had bought his first building for $1,000 and, although he sold it for a profit, his policy was to buy buildings and keep them. 'Why sell the corner of 58th and Park Avenue,' he once pondered. 'They're not making them any more.'

In 1949 he formed a partnership with a lawyer, Lawrence Wien. It was Helmsley's job to find buildings and negotiate their purchase while Wien set up syndicates of investors to raise funds.

It was a successful formula and they set about acquiring chunks of New York and holdings all over America, including Detroit, Chicago, Los Angeles, Houston and Washington, DC.

Their crowning achievement was the purchase, in 1961, of the Empire State Building. The price was reported to be between $65 and $85 million. Typically, Helmsley immediately set about reducing the building's costs and increasing its profits: he automated the lifts, cut overtime for employees and put up rents. The cleaning of the building – its largest cost – was taken over by Helmsley's own company, Office Maintenance Corporation.

In the 1960s he moved into building skyscrapers. During the 1970s he began to buy hotels, and installed Leona to run them. When Leona went to prison, Helmsley ordered the lights on the Empire State Building to be dimmed. The same thing happened to mark his death.

⊰ 5th ⊱

Alfred Hinds, b. 1917, d. 1991

Alfred Hinds, who has died aged seventy-three, proved himself, in the course of a prolonged struggle to establish his innocence of a shop-breaking charge, the most successful prison escaper in English history and also one of the shrewdest legal minds never to have been called to the Bar.

His troubles began in September 1953, when, along with four others, he was charged with stealing some £30,000 in jewellery and £4,700 in cash from Maple's store in Tottenham Court Road. That December Hinds, pronounced by Lord Goddard to be 'a most dangerous criminal', was jailed for twelve years.

Yet, though it took the jury only half an hour to make up their minds, the evidence against him was essentially circumstantial. The prosecution claimed that traces of a fuse used to blow the safe had been found on Hinds, together with material from the lining of the safe.

Hinds had eight previous convictions, some of them involving safe-breaking. Nevertheless, in recent years it had appeared that he was going straight, living in a house near the Thames at Staines, where he helped his brother in a building and demolition business.

From the very first he protested his innocence, but in December 1953 the Court of Criminal Appeal dismissed his appeal application. Next year Hinds published a pamphlet in which he demanded an inquiry or a retrial. This was ignored, and in November 1955 Hinds escaped from Nottingham prison.

He took a hacksaw blade out of an electrician's toolbag, made a copy of the prison workshop key from brass after memorising its shape, purloined some planks which he used to climb the prison wall, and made off in a lorry provided by a friend.

He was already a seasoned escaper.

Alfred George Hinds had been born at Newington Butts, in south London, in 1917. His father, described variously as a labourer, street betting agent and pugilist, was sentenced to seven years as a consequence of a bank raid at Portsmouth in 1935; he also received ten strokes of the cat-o'-nine-tails which, Hinds believed, contributed to his early death.

At the age of seven Alfred found himself in Pentonville remand home, from which he made his first break. Subsequently he was brought up by foster parents in the Midlands, where he acquired his considerable skills at metalwork and machine-turning.

In the Second World War he was in the Royal Tank Corps, until he decided to desert. Subsequently, he arranged for friends to create a disturbance while he was being transported in an Army truck at Clapham Junction; with the guards distracted, he made his getaway in a car supplied by another accomplice.

In 1945 Rochester Borstal afforded the next opportunity for Hinds to demonstrate his escaping skills. But the escape from Nottingham prison in 1955 was an altogether more ambitious project, and one that he combined with sustained literary endeavour.

Several papers were bombarded with letters. 'I made this escape,' he wrote to one, 'because it was the only way now left open to me in my fight to obtain justice. I am entirely innocent of the crime for which I was sentenced for twelve years.'

The letters were all postmarked SW1, as was the parcel containing the musical boxes which Hinds sent his children for Christmas; nevertheless rumour was endlessly fertile, placing Hinds in Turin, in France, in Ireland, in America. Not until he had been free for 245 days, on 31 July 1956, was the absconder finally caught, in Dublin: he had been living in a cottage which he had bought for £750 at Greystones, Co. Wicklow.

Hinds was charged with prison-breaking and, acting in his own defence, proved himself more than a match for learned counsel – and also for the judge. 'My Lord, I think I can help you there,' he would helpfully intervene; and indeed the judge was forced to admit that the accused knew more about some aspects of the law than anyone else in court.

Hinds managed to get himself acquitted of prison-breaking, and he received only eleven days extra sentence for escaping from custody before returning to serve his longer sentence.

He seemed to have acquired a taste for the law, and soon reappeared before the Queen's Bench Division to argue a point in an action against the prison commissioners for his illegal arrest.

Hinds contacted accomplices who were instructed to smuggle him a padlock into the Law Courts. Once there he asked to go to the lavatory, whither he was accompanied by two guards. When they removed his handcuffs Hinds and a friend succeeded in bundling the guards into the lavatory and padlocking the door.

He was quickly recaptured, and Rab Butler, the Home Secretary, remained deaf to all demands for a retrial. Hinds was sent to Chelmsford prison where, in June 1958, he fashioned a key that gave him entry into the bathhouse and thence escaped by way of a skylight on to the roof and over the wall into a waiting Morris Minor.

This time he eluded his pursuers for almost two years, again in Ireland, where, under the name William Herbert Bishop, he established himself as a flourishing second-hand car dealer. It was customs officials who finally caught him, in January 1960, for possessing cars that had been smuggled across the border, an offence for which he received six months in Belfast prison.

On his return to his native land to continue his sentence for the Maple's robbery Hinds settled into a prolonged series of battles with the English legal establishment. But appeal after appeal was dismissed, and Hinds' legal manoeuvres seemed to have got him nowhere, until in 1964 he successfully sued Superintendent Herbert Sparks for libel, gaining £1,300 in damages and costs.

This civil victory forced a reconsideration of the criminal sentence, and Hinds was released. Even so, in November 1965 the Court of Criminal Appeal decided that the original conviction had been correct, and once again refused him leave to appeal.

Hinds retired to Jersey, where he established a property business, and in 1973 reached the semi-finals of a contest to discover the most intelligent person in the island. With an IQ of 150 he made an admirable secretary of the Channel Islands Mensa Society.

❧ 6th ❧

Fred Francis, b. 1919, d. 1998

Fred Francis, who has died aged seventy-eight, invented Scalextric, the children's racing car set said to be the toy most often hijacked by adults on Boxing Day.

Francis founded Minimodels, his toy business, in 1947. It originally produced tin-plate toys, but later began making clockwork cars with metal bodies, under the trade name Scalex.

Production soared, and in 1952 Francis built a new factory in Havant, Hampshire. But by 1956, with plastic becoming the main material for toys, and clockwork seeming out of date, demand for Scalex cars suddenly collapsed. Francis desperately sought some way of saving the company.

That summer, at a London Toy Fair, he saw a metal roadway around which electric-powered toy cars ran. Francis understood at once that what this concept lacked was any opportunity for the players to control each car. He realised that if he could adapt the idea, the toy might save Minimodels.

There followed three months of intense activity with everyone sworn to secrecy as Francis and his team developed their prototype. To save time and money, the new toy used the same bodies as the Scalex models of Ferrari and Maserati racing cars. The Scalex name was well established, so it was decided simply to add '-tric', to show that the cars were now electrically powered.

The launch of Scalextric at the Harrogate Toy Fair in January 1957 was a triumph. Scalextric layouts were lent to major retailers so that customers could try them out. A Scalextric Owners' Club was formed, with public competitions at Goodwood and Gamages.

Scalextric was a hit. The American market, so long impervious to British toys, was soon demanding more kits than Minimodels could supply from their Havant factory.

Bertram Frederick Francis was born at Hampstead on 15 October 1919 and educated at Finchley Catholic Grammar School. Showing little academic ability, except in mathematics, he left school at fourteen and took a job with a local tool-making company.

In 1939, with money borrowed from his father, he founded his own tool-making business, at Mill Hill. The company prospered, supplying tools vital to the war effort and providing Francis with the capital he needed to found his toy-making business.

Apart from his toy-making, Francis was a keen sailor. While working in Havant, he lived aboard his motor yacht, the *Yvalda*, moored in Chichester, and used it to travel to work.

⊰ 7th ⊱

Sir Atholl Oakeley, b. 1900, d. 1987

Sir Atholl Oakeley, 7th Bt, who has died aged eighty-six, was a champion wrestler, an impresario of giants, master of a former Bristol pilot cutter offering rugged holiday cruises and an authority on *Lorna Doone*.

A veteran of nearly 2,000 bouts, he described his career as a wrestler in an engaging autobiography, *Blue Blood on the Mat* (1971). He was heavyweight champion of Great Britain from 1930 to 1935, of Europe in 1932 and remained unbeaten on a seventeen-bout tour of America.

Although only 5ft 9in tall, Oakeley was broad in the beam. He started wrestling seriously after being beaten up by a gang of louts and built up his body by drinking eleven pints of milk a day for three years. This regimen had been recommended by the giant wrestler Hackenschmidt, who later told Oakeley that the quantity of milk prescribed had been a misprint.

Giants always held a particular fascination for Oakeley. He liked to recall how he had bent a man of 9ft with a half-nelson which it took several other wrestlers sitting on his opponent to untangle. He received his distinctive cauliflower ear in a bout in Chicago when, as he recalled, Bill Bartuch 'got me in a scissors grip between his knees'.

His active career came to an end in 1935 when he broke his shoulder. He then acted as manager to Jack Sherry, the world heavyweight champion, for four years, and later promoted championship wrestling at the Harringay Arena. Among the wrestlers he staged was Gargantua, a 50-stone German with a 90in chest measurement, for whom special travelling arrangements had to be made with British Railways.

Edward Atholl Oakeley was born in 1900, the grandson of Sir Charles Oakeley, 4th Bt, a Bengal Cavalryman who was also an amateur heavyweight prize fighter. The baronetcy was created in 1790 for an ancestor who was Governor of Madras.

Oakeley was educated at Clifton and Sandhurst and commissioned in the Oxfordshire and Buckinghamshire Light Infantry. He was Army marathon and 10-mile track champion shortly after the First World War.

His interest in wrestling had first been aroused by reading *Lorna Doone* as a boy. The novel and its background remained a lifetime interest and in 1969 he published *The Facts on which R. D. Blackmore based Lorna Doone*. He mounted a lengthy and ultimately successful campaign to persuade the Ordnance Survey to change the map of Exmoor, showing that the Doone Valley was sited at Lank Combe rather than Hoccombe.

Ginnie James, b. 1940, d. 2008

Ginnie James, who has died aged sixty-seven, was a feisty yet warm-hearted figure, equally at home in the bullrings of Portugal and the racing villages of the Lambourn Valley.

Aged twenty-one she took herself to Portugal, immersing herself in the largely closed world of Portuguese bullfighting (which differs from the Spanish version in that the bull is killed away from the ring). Determined to become a *rejoneadora* (the *rejoneador* fights on horseback and plants rosettes in the bull's back), she spent the next three years training.

She became famous in Portugal, fighting in bullrings across the country under the name of Virginia Montesol. When she was invited to fight in Mexico, an American director asked to make a film about her – but with typical modesty she declined both offers, fearing it might embarrass her parents.

⇚ 8th ⇛

Colonel David Smiley, b. 1916, d. 2009

Colonel David Smiley, who has died aged ninety-two, was one of the most celebrated cloak-and-dagger agents of the Second World War, serving behind enemy lines in Albania, Greece, Abyssinia and Japanese-controlled eastern Thailand.

After the war he organised secret operations against the Russians and their allies in Albania and Poland, among other places. Later, as Britain's era of domination in the Arabian peninsula drew to a close, he commanded the Sultan of Oman's armed forces in a highly successful counter-insurgency.

After his assignment in Oman, he organised – with the British intelligence service, MI6 – royalist guerrilla resistance against a Soviet-backed Nasserite regime in Yemen.

During the Second World War he was parachuted four times behind enemy lines. On one occasion he was obliged to escape from Albania in a rowing boat. On another mission, in Japanese-controlled eastern Thailand, he was stretchered for three days through the jungle with severe burns after a booby-trap meant for a senior Japanese officer exploded prematurely.

Smiley's exploits led some to suggest that he was, along with several other candidates, a model for James Bond. It was also widely mooted that John le Carré, albeit unconsciously, had taken the name of his hero from the real-life Smiley.

Born on 11 April 1916, David de Crespigny Smiley was the youngest son of Major Sir John Smiley, 2nd Bt, and Valerie, youngest daughter of Sir Claude Champion de Crespigny, 4th Bt, a noted jockey, balloonist, all-round sportsman and adventurer, also famed for his feats of derring-do.

After Pangbourne Nautical College, David went to Sandhurst in 1934. He served in the Blues from 1936 to 1939, leading the life of a debonair man-about-town, owning a Bentley and a Whitney Straight aircraft.

In 1940 Smiley persuaded General Wavell, a family friend, to recommend him for the newly formed Commandos, in which he became a company commander with the rank of captain. Sneaking from Sudan into Abyssinia, Smiley operated for the first of many times behind enemy (in this case Italian) lines.

After training at a school for secret agents in Haifa and taking a parachuting course with his friend David Stirling and his Special Air Service (SAS) near the Suez Canal,

Smiley joined the Special Operations Executive.

For eight months in Albania he organised fractious partisans in a series of ambushes and acts of sabotage (bridge demolition, sometimes by climbing under them at night while German troops were patrolling above, became a Smiley trademark). After leaving Albania, where his activities brought him an MC and Bar, he was transferred to the Siamese section of SOE, known in the Far East as Force 136, where he liaised with guerrillas operating against the Japanese. It was then that he was injured by the premature explosion of a booby-trap meant for a Japanese officer.

The pinnacle of Smiley's post-war career was his three-year tenure as commander of the Sultan of Muscat and Oman's armed forces during a civil war which threatened to bring down one of Britain's more reactionary allies in the Gulf.

By now in his early forties, Smiley ran a gruelling counter-insurgency which gradually drove the guerrillas back from the scorching plains into their mountain retreat, the 10,000ft-high Jebel Akhdar, which had never been successfully assaulted. With two squadrons of the SAS under his command, Smiley planned and led a classic dawn attack on the mountain fastness, finally crushing the enemy.

After leaving Oman in 1961, Smiley was offered the command of the SAS, but chose to retire from the British Army and file occasional reports for Raymond Postgate's *Good Food Guide*.

Smiley moved to Spain, where, for nineteen years, he grew olives, carobs and almonds, and continued to advise Albania's surviving anti-Communists, by now all in exile.

⊰ 9th ⊱

Sir John Harvey-Jones, b. 1924, d. 2008

Sir John Harvey-Jones, who has died aged eighty-three, was a flamboyant chairman of ICI who later turned himself into a television celebrity as 'The Troubleshooter', dispensing pungent advice on the art of management.

Troubleshooter was the first 'how-to' business documentary to catch the imagination of the viewing public: in a Gallup poll in 1992, one in five respondents named Harvey-Jones as the person they would most like to see in No. 10 in place of John Major.

Harvey-Jones's trademarks were his shoulder-length hair, his dizzying selection of abstract ties and an approach which combined blokeish bonhomie with penetrative and often unpalatable home truths. 'This strategic plan is a load of bloody cobblers,' he told the South Yorkshire police force in one episode, to the evident discomfort of the chief constable. At Norton Motorcycles he recommended liquidation.

'Everyone thinks I'm a smartarse who can solve any bloody problem,' he observed. 'I'm not. I'm just a very old businessman and a very experienced businessman who made every mistake in the book and can recognise one when I see one.' He believed that successful corporate leaders were resented rather than admired in Britain, and set out consciously to fill what he perceived to be a need for 'management heroes'.

Troubleshooter, watched by an audience of more than three million, won a Bafta award for originality. Part of its success lay in the communication of Harvey-Jones's genuine love of factories and manufacturing processes, and his patriotism – he claimed to wear Union Flag underpants. His belief in the vital importance of a healthy industrial base (the subject of his 1985 Dimbleby lecture) placed him radically at odds with Thatcherite thinking: he once described the then prime minister as 'British industry's greatest handicap'.

John Henry Harvey-Jones was born at Hackney on 16 April 1924. His father was guardian and minister of state to an Indian princeling, the Maharajah of Dhar, and the first years of John's life were spent in a world of palaces and tiger-shoots, surrounded by servants and complete with his own caparisoned elephant for state occasions.

At six, however, he was dispatched to a bleak prep school at Deal, Kent, where he was so miserable that he considered suicide. He conceived an ambition to be a lawyer, but his father told John bluntly that he would not support him financially for long enough to enable him to qualify. Instead he opted for the Navy, entering Dartmouth as a cadet in 1937.

Life at the naval college was more congenial, despite its rigid discipline. In 1940, still only sixteen, Harvey-Jones went to war as a midshipman in the light cruiser *Diomede*. His next two ships, the destroyers *Ithuriel* and *Quentin*, were sunk by enemy action, but he went on to specialise in submarines, receiving his first command at the age of twenty-four.

After the war Harvey-Jones qualified as a Russian interpreter and worked in naval intelligence, rising to lieutenant-commander. In later years he remained reticent about the precise nature of his intelligence duties, but admitted to having been several times in Russia. He was seconded to the Cabinet Office, and awarded a military MBE in 1952.

He would have stayed in the Navy, but his only daughter had contracted polio, and in 1956 he resigned his commission in order to be able to spend more time with her.

He joined ICI on Teesside as a work study officer, and rose through the management ranks of the heavy organic chemicals division, becoming commercial director in 1967. He became chairman of the petrochemicals division in 1970 and joined the main board in 1973.

His tenure as chairman, from 1982 to 1987, was marked by controversy. He was voted Britain's most admired industrialist several years running and was credited with turning the company around from its first ever quarterly loss – in 1982, at the bottom of the industrial cycle – to profits of more than £1 billion. But many of his former colleagues felt that the credit should have been more widely distributed and the former cabinet minister Cecil (now Lord) Parkinson once observed that the best way to cause a silence at the ICI lunch was to say something nice about Harvey-Jones.

Sensitive to criticism and prone to self-analysis, Harvey-Jones attributed the uncomfortable edges of his personality to an unhappy childhood, in which he strove in vain to win the approval of a cold Victorian father, and was bullied mercilessly at school. He felt himself to be much misunderstood. 'I'm a pussycat, actually,' he insisted.

⊰ 10th ⊱

Sir Edmund Hillary, b. 1919, d. 2008

Sir Edmund Hillary, who has died aged eighty-eight, made his name in 1953 as the first conqueror (with Tenzing Norgay) of Everest.

By his own admission, Hillary had been quite determined that he himself would be chosen for the final ascent. Together he and Tenzing climbed from Base Camp to Camp III and back again in a day – a pointless effort, as Hillary himself admitted, save that it showed that he and Tenzing were ultra-fit.

Hillary followed up by putting in mighty efforts as a load-carrier, first from Camp VII to the South Col, and then up to Camp IX at 27,900ft. James (now Jan) Morris, who covered the expedition for *The Times*, wrote of Hillary working in the half-light,

'huge and cheerful, his movement not so much graceful as unshakably assured, his energy almost demonic. He had a tremendous, bursting, elemental, infectious, glorious vitality about him, like some bright, burly diesel express pounding across America.'

Hillary and Tenzing spent the night of 28/29 May at Camp IX; rose at four o'clock in the morning, with the temperature at -27 centigrade; proceeded to the South summit; and cut steps cautiously along the left-hand side of the summit ridge until they reached the 40ft rock face now called the Hillary Step. Hillary managed to wriggle his way up a narrow crack.

They spent a quarter of an hour at the peak. Turning in typical Anglo-Saxon manner to shake Tenzing's hand, Hillary was enveloped in a bear hug: 'with a feeling of mild surprise I realised that Tenzing was perhaps more excited at our success than I was'.

Hillary remained determinedly low-key. 'Having paid my respects to the highest mountain in the world,' he recalled forty-six years later in his autobiography *View from the Summit* (1999), 'I had no choice but to urinate on it.'

The 7th Marquess of Bristol, b. 1954, d. 1999

The 7th Marquess of Bristol, who has died aged forty-four, multiplied his inheritance in a series of shrewd business investments and then threw it away – together with his health and dignity – as he descended into drug addiction.

The representative of a line which had been seated at Ickworth, Suffolk, since the Middle Ages, he numbered among his forebears some of the most notorious addicts, philanderers, profligates and bullies of their day. He showed early that he too was capable of waywardness.

At sixteen, he inherited £1 million and two years later a further £4 million. By the time he was thirty he had multiplied his fortune more than threefold by investing in oil, farming and property.

But already Lord Jermyn, as he then was, had fallen foul of the law. At twenty he was fined for stealing 'No Waiting' signs from outside the Rolls-Royce garage at which he worked. By thirty-one he had twice been disqualified for driving while drunk.

At one of his own soirees, frustrated by his inability to open a fridge for some champagne, he blew the door off with a shotgun. At another party, he demolished a 500-glass champagne fountain by tying a piece of cotton thread between it and a duchess's chair. On another occasion he lent an American woman a rubber dinghy to fish in the lake at Ickworth, and then fired at it until it sank. The more she screamed, the more he laughed.

John Jermyn succeeded to the marquessate in 1985, but his life thereafter rapidly disintegrated. His marriage foundered and in 1987 was dissolved. In 1988 it was reported that he had offered an American male stripper $6,000 for a sexual liaison, but in the event he had been too debilitated by drugs to go through with it. The episode brought to mind Lady Hester Stanhope's opinion of Lord Bristol's kin, that there are three genders – male, female, and Hervey.

Frederick William John Augustus Hervey was born on 15 September 1954, the eldest son of the then Earl Jermyn and his first wife Pauline Mary (nee Bolton).

The family had been raised to the peerage in 1703 when John Hervey, the former MP for Ickworth, was created Baron Hervey of Ickworth. The earldom of Bristol was created for him in 1714.

The 1st Earl's son, pilloried by Alexander Pope as 'that milk-white curd of asses milk', was addicted to tea. The 3rd Earl boasted of deflowering a dozen Portuguese nuns and his Countess was accused of holding up a bank in Rome at gunpoint.

The 4th Earl, Bishop of Derry, was notably ghastly. He once treated a group of fat clergymen to a splendid dinner, and then enjoined them to run a race through the grounds of Ickworth; he promised the winner a rich living which was vacant. To the Bishop's great mirth, all fell floundering in the boggy ground to which he directed them and none completed the course.

It was the 4th Earl who began the building of Ickworth House, a rotunda connected by two corridors to flanking wings and modelled on a 'Temple of the Winds'. He had intended to house his family in the drum, but after his death the Herveys lived in the east wing.

Ickworth had passed to the National Trust in 1956 in lieu of death duties, but the family continued to lease the sixty-room east wing as their home. In 1996 Lord Bristol moved out and sold its contents; he said he was glad to have shed a responsibility that he had felt since birth. Last year, the National Trust bought out the remainder of the lease from him.

⊰ 11th ⊱

Prince Dado Ruspoli, b. 1924, d. 2005

Prince Dado Ruspoli, who has died in Rome aged eighty, was one of the leading figures of Italy's 'Dolce Vita' – the circle of beautiful people immortalised by Federico Fellini in his film about high society in 1950s Rome – and a byword for aristocratic dissipation, extravagance and charm.

In his handsome prime, the Maserati-driving prince was the toast of his haunts on the Via Veneto, at St Tropez and on Capri. His friends were all the right people; he shared a villa with Roger Vadim and Jane Fonda, while Brigitte Bardot came to the baptism of his son. He knew Truman Capote, Willem de Kooning and Balthus, and took lessons in hypnotism from Orson Welles. Ruspoli developed a lifelong interest in magic and the occult after witnessing a demonstration of Welles's powers.

While sitting in a café, Welles asked him what he would like to see happen. Ruspoli told him that nothing would please him more than that a pretty girl at a neighbouring table drop her Bloody Mary down the front of her shirt. The glass duly obliged.

This taste for the exotic naturally led Ruspoli in the 1960s to Asia, where he became a student of yoga and transcendentalism. His travels in the region also nurtured his taste for opium (the first of several scandals concerning him had come in 1953 when he was caught with 5lb of the drug hidden in his car).

He had first become hooked at seventeen, but had been rescued by Jean Cocteau. The respite, however, was only temporary. His other weakness was for women. Ruspoli, claimed his sometime fellow orgiast, Salvador Dali, had 'the biggest limousine in Europe'. His first two marriages were ruptured by his unabashed infidelity. The first, in 1947, to another aristocrat, Francesca Blanc, ended after six years. A decade later she took her own life. The second, in 1964, to a French painter, Nancy de Girard de Charbonnières, also failed, though it produced an heir. He was not brought to heel until his seventies, when he married a French model forty years his junior.

He fathered his second child by her at the age of seventy-three, and by then was content in the role of family man. Nonetheless, he was proud of his continued vitality. 'I am a tree still full of fruit,' he liked to say, 'when all around me I see so many withered vines.'

Alessandro (Dado) Maria Galeazzo Ruspoli, 9th Prince of Cerveteri, 9th Marquis of Riano and 14th Count of Vignanello, was born in the family palazzo by the Via del Corso, Rome, on 9 December 1924. His father wrote poetry, while his Neapolitan mother was the heiress to the largest industrial fortune in Latin America.

'Haven't you ever worked?' he was once asked. 'No,' came the riposte, 'I've never had time.'

❧ 12th ❧

William Rees-Davies, b. 1916, d. 1992

William Rees-Davies, who has died aged seventy-five, was for thirty years one of the most colourful MPs in the House of Commons, where he sat as Conservative Member for the Isle of Thanet from 1953 to 1974, and then for Thanet North from then until 1983.

Affectionately known as the 'One-armed Bandit' (he lost an arm in action with the Welsh Guards) 'Billy' Rees-Davies was celebrated for his mental agility and wit. A convivial bon vivant, he was the subject of many anecdotes, and throughout his career as a barrister and MP was dogged by scrapes and misadventures.

At Westminster he was capable of pungent contributions to debates, although he was apt to act the shy violet when the division bell rang: in one session of 1969, for instance, he was absent from 198 votes.

In 1983 he failed to be re-selected as a parliamentary candidate. It was a bitter blow, as three years earlier he had given up his law practice and become a 'full-time politician'.

A devotee of the Turf, Rees-Davies had also fought a valiant battle, both at Westminster and in the courts, on behalf of gamblers everywhere. At Marylebone Court in 1958 he successfully defended John Aspinall and others from gaming charges, when the prosecution was unable to establish that chemin de fer was an unlawful game; later that year he played a hand of 'chemmy' in court while defending another three players, and won his case after a speech lasting a day and a half.

In 1963 he sponsored a Bill to allow greyhound racing on substitute days (though not on Sundays); and in 1966 he attempted to exclude bets with bookmakers on approved racecourses from the general betting duty.

The son of Sir William Rees-Davies, a former Liberal MP and Chief Justice of Hong Kong, William Rupert Rees-Davies was born on 19 November 1916 and educated at Eton and Trinity College, Cambridge, where he won a cricket Blue in 1938.

At the beginning of the Second World War, Rees-Davies was commissioned into the Welsh Guards; he served until 1943, when he was disabled.

He stood unsuccessfully as a Conservative candidate for South Nottingham in the general elections of 1950 and 1951 before being returned for the Isle of Thanet at a by-election in 1953. At Westminster he also acquired the sobriquets 'Swashbuckling Billy' and (for his cloak) 'Count Dracula'.

His career at the Bar was somewhat erratic. Suspended for the first time in 1954, he was fined and reprimanded ten years later by his Benchers for failing to turn up at the Old Bailey to make a speech for his client. In 1970 he again neglected to appear to make a final speech in mitigation on behalf of his client, who was sentenced to six years. And in 1980 he was suspended from the Bar for six months for professional misconduct – after another absence from court.

Rees-Davies never seemed put out by these setbacks, and took silk in 1973.

Lorna Wishart, b. 1911, d. 2000

L orna Wishart, who has died aged eighty-nine, was a ravishing beauty who broke the hearts of both Laurie Lee and Lucian Freud and inspired some of their best work.

Lorna Wishart had two brothers and six almost equally striking sisters. Of these, Kathleen became the mistress and later wife of Jacob Epstein and Mary the wife of the South African poet Roy Campbell.

Another sister married a French fisherman – 'like Jean Marais, only better looking' – while another managed to seduce her idol T.E. Lawrence before retiring to a cottage with a lady named Philip de Winton.

But Lorna was loveliest of all; tall, lean and feline, with dark hair and enormous deep blue eyes, she exerted an extraordinary seductive power over men. She was, as her daughter Yasmin later described her, 'a dream for any creative artist ... savage, wild, romantic and completely without guilt'.

The writer Laurie Lee, who met her in 1937 on a beach in Cornwall, never stood a chance. He was playing his violin and Lorna beckoned him over, saying: 'Boy, come and play for me.'

Lee soon found himself caught up in a delirium of passion and, to impress her, went to fight in Spain as a Republican volunteer, albeit briefly – Lorna soon engineered his return. She then left her husband, Ernest Wishart, and her children and set up home with Lee in a small flat in Bloomsbury.

She returned to her husband in 1939, after bearing Lee's daughter, Yasmin, who was brought up as part of the Wishart family; Yasmin only learned Lee was her real father when she was twenty-one.

Lorna's affair with Lee continued nonetheless. Hunched in a caravan or the back bedroom of a Bognor semi, Lee would wait in for her to roll up in her Bentley, showering him with gifts of champagne, goose eggs and 'an eddying fragrance of irresistible passion' – only for her to race back hours later to her life of domesticity and chic.

They continued to see each other until 1943, when she fell for the painter Lucian Freud, then twenty, whom Lawrence Gowing described as 'fly, perceptive, lithe, with a hint of menace'. 'This mad, unpleasant youth appeals to a sort of craving she has for corruption,' Lee wrote in his diary. 'She goes to him when I long for her.' In time Freud too disappeared from the scene.

Bizarrely, with Lorna Wishart's encouragement, Laurie Lee later married one of her nieces, while Freud went on to marry the other.

She was born Lorna Garman on 11 January 1911, the daughter of a wealthy, brutal doctor and his Irish wife. Strictly brought up and unhappy at boarding school, she jumped over the school tennis net with glee when she realised – aged twelve – that the death of her father meant she had to leave.

At fourteen she met Ernest Wishart, a Cambridge law student. Wishart was a Communist, but a rich one. His father, Colonel Sir Sidney Wishart, had extensive estates in Sussex. Lorna married at sixteen and had her first son, Michael, at seventeen.

Despite her affairs, it was Wishart to whom Lorna always returned and who ultimately gave her the stability she needed.

After leaving Lucian Freud, Lorna Wishart converted to Roman Catholicism and returned for good to her husband's Sussex home where she sculpted and cultivated a garden.

⊰ 13th ⊱

Sir Dai Llewellyn, b. 1946, d. 2009

Sir Dai Llewellyn, 4th Bt, who has died aged sixty-two, became famous as a playboy and darling of the gossip columns, his reputation reflected in sobriquets such as 'Seducer of the Valleys', 'Conquistador of the Canapé Circuit', or simply 'Dirty Dai'.

He was celebrated for his serial seductions of 'It' girls, models and actresses, his relentless appetite for partying and his outrageous indiscretions.

Good-looking in his youth, with dark Welsh curls, his success with women was famous. He claimed, in his heyday, to be in the habit of going through Queen Charlotte's Balls 'like a dose of salts'. He insisted, though, that he 'never got up in the morning and thought, "I'm going to screw three girls today"'. But: 'If it happened, it happened.'

His seduction methods were direct and somewhat lacking in refinement: 'I am not one of these oily Italian method-pullers,' he said. 'Thirty years, and I still can't undo a bra. The only trick is that I do not waver. I know what I want and so do they.'

Stories of Llewellyn's priapic exploits, mostly gleefully retailed by the Don Juan himself, proved irresistible to the tabloid press. The journalist Peter McKay, who became a friend, was once having lunch with him at San Lorenzo when Llewellyn suddenly leapt from the table and disappeared for half an hour. 'What happened?' asked McKay when his host returned, looking flushed. 'Oh, I just remembered,' said Llewellyn. 'I left my secretary tied up in the bath.'

Quite what Llewellyn did by way of a career was never entirely clear. He once described himself as a 'a kind of upper-class redcoat' who 'earned his living out of being Dai Llewellyn'. In practice this seemed to involve a bit of PR work, organising the odd celebrity party, and a lot of schmoozing of rich toffs in jet-set nightclubs such as Tramp and Annabel's. 'Dai Llewellyn's London,' wrote one interviewer, 'is a web of reciprocal favours, backhanders and feuds which require all his reputed Machiavellianism to manage.'

David St Vincent Llewellyn was born at Aberdare on 2 April 1946. His father, Sir Harry Llewellyn, 3rd Bt, would win a gold medal for showjumping at the 1952 Olympics on his horse Foxhunter. Dai was sent to prep school at Hawtrees, and then to Eton and went to study Philosophy at the University of Aix-en-Provence. There he lost his virginity to an older, American woman 'who smelt so disgusting that it put me off doing it again for several months'.

Llewellyn claimed to have fallen in love three times, firstly with Lady Charlotte

Curzon, to whom he claimed to have proposed 100 times in a single evening (she turned him down). In the 1970s he was engaged to Beatrice Welles, daughter of Orson, but their relationship became so tempestuous that people stopped inviting them to parties. Inevitably, he broke it off.

In 1980 he married Vanessa Hubbard, the convent-educated niece of the Duke of Norfolk. Signalling his determination to go on as if nothing much had happened, he reportedly rolled up at the wedding, reached out of the car and handed a near-empty bottle of champagne to a group of gawping youths. The couple had two daughters but divorced seven years later.

He never grew up. On a visit to South Africa aged sixty, he claimed to have fallen through a bedroom floor into a cellar while 'attempting to roger a girl called Nettie', the girlfriend of a friend. 'I wish I could tell you this was an isolated incident,' he told a journalist.

⤟ **14**th ⤞

Air Vice-Marshal John 'The Baron' Worrall, b. 1911, d. 1988

Air Vice-Marshal John 'The Baron' Worrall, who has died aged seventy-six, led a Hurricane fighter squadron throughout the fall of France and in some of the fiercest fighting of the Battle of Britain.

The desperate predicament of Worrall – at twenty-nine somewhat older than most of his pilots in No. 32 Squadron – as they fought to protect their Biggin Hill base and other No. 11 Group airfields in the summer of 1940, can be gauged from a typical exchange:

Controller:	'24 bombers with 20 plus more behind them.'
Worrall:	'Got it.'
Controller:	'20 plus more bombers and 20 fighters behind and above.'
Worrall:	'All right.'
Controller:	'Now 30 more bombers and further 100-plus fighters following.'
Worrall:	'Stop. No more information please. You are frightening me terribly.'

In fact Worrall's courage was such that he became known as 'the Baron', a sobriquet recalling the First World War ace 'the Red Baron' von Richthofen.

John Worrall was born in 1911 and educated at Cranleigh and Cranwell. In 1954 he returned to Fighter Command as Commander, Eastern Sector. Other staff appointments followed before he retired in 1963 when he was appointed CB.

❧ 15th ❧

Olivia Goldsmith, b. 1949, d. 2004

Olivia Goldsmith, who has died aged fifty-four after complications following plastic surgery, was the author of the best-selling novel *The First Wives Club* (1992), the tale of ex-wives wreaking revenge on their rich husbands; in 1996 it became a hit film starring Goldie Hawn, Diane Keaton and Bette Midler as the vengeful trio.

Olivia Goldsmith had been inspired to write the book when her own 'extremely nasty' divorce left her broke and bitter. Her husband had come away from the marriage with an apartment in Manhattan, a beach house in the Hamptons and a Jaguar; she received $300,000 and spent the entire sum on lawyers. 'I hate divorce lawyers and judges more than I ever did my ex,' she said in 1996, adding, 'no, that's not right. I hate them all, and I want them dead.'

The success of *The First Wives Club* and subsequent books earned Olivia Goldsmith some $4.5 million in royalties and, having acquired houses, cars, money and even affairs with younger men, she vowed never to marry again. As Ivana Trump, making her cameo appearance as the patron of *The First Wives Club*, explained: 'Don't get mad – get everything.'

Olivia Goldsmith was born Randy Goldfield in New York in 1949. One of three daughters of a civil servant and a teacher, she grew up in Dumont, New Jersey, and attended New York University. Having changed her name to Justine Olivia Rendal, she became a successful businesswoman and was one of the first women to be a partner at the management consultant firm Booz Allen Hamilton before she married and decided to write children's books. But the marriage collapsed after five years and she found herself homeless and jobless.

In a recent interview Olivia Goldsmith joked that after her death she would have cosmetic surgery so that her friends would be able to say that she 'never looked better'. She died on Thursday after falling into a coma following a face-lift.

Father Sean Breen, b. 1937, d. 2009

Father Sean Breen, who has died aged seventy-one, was one of the best-known priests in Ireland for his delight in, and prowess on, the Turf; a canny tipster and a lucky racehorse owner, he was a familiar face at the Cheltenham Festival for more than forty years.

His definition of the spiritual dimension was comprehensive, allowing him to recommend to punters in 2005 that Cardinal Ratzinger was a hot bet to be the next Pope. 'A few of the lads got on at 13–2,' he revealed after the white smoke had filtered out of the Vatican chimney, 'but I did not back him myself out of reverence.'

He first attended the Cheltenham Festival in 1964, witnessing the first of Arkle's three triumphs in the Gold Cup. Thereafter, only the imperative of a funeral would keep him away, and he was wont to say: 'It's very inconsiderate of people to die just before Cheltenham.'

As an owner, the priest was considerably more fortunate than most. With two friends he formed the Heavenly Syndicate, which raced a horse called One Won One, winner of twelve races (including a Group 3 sprint at the Curragh and five Listed races) and some £500,000 in prize money.

Sean Macarius Breen was born on 9 March 1937 at Cavan, where his father was a schoolmaster. As a boy Sean was a gifted tennis player, reaching the semi-finals of the under-18s competition held at the Fitzwilliam Club in Dublin.

After St Patrick's College, Cavan, he went on to Clonliffe College in Dublin to study for the priesthood. He was ordained in 1962 and served in several parishes in Co. Dublin, including fourteen years at Glencullen. After a spell at Eadstown, Co. Kildare, he became priest at Ballymore Eustace, also in Kildare and sandwiched between Punchestown and Naas racecourses. This was to be his final parish, and he could often be found holding court at the Ballymore Inn.

⊰ 16th ⊱

Auberon Waugh, b. 1939, d. 2001

Auberon Waugh, who has died aged sixty-one, was the most controversial, the most abusive, perhaps the most brilliant journalist of his age – an acerbic wit, a traveller, a farceur, an epicure; above all, a hater of humbug in all its forms and of politicians in most of theirs.

His forte, displayed in his Way of the World column in *The Daily Telegraph*, was to express, with pellucid and succinct brilliance, ideas and prejudices of which many people were subliminally aware, but which they would never have dared to articulate, or even consciously think. Waugh's courage was equalled only by his extraordinary intellectual energy.

The *succès d'animosité* which he achieved as a journalist made him at once greatly admired and greatly feared. Yet he had begun his professional life as a novelist, in emulation of his father, Evelyn Waugh. The fact that he eventually gave up writing fiction may have been due to the complicated involvement with the memory of a father in whose shadow he had inevitably once stood. But not even his worst enemy – a title for which there was hot competition – could deny that he had successfully stepped out of that shade.

Auberon Alexander Waugh, Evelyn Waugh's second child and first son (there would be two more sons and two more daughters), was born on 17 November 1939 at Pixton, a house belonging to his mother's family on the borders of Devon and Somerset. His mother was Laura Herbert, a shy and gentle woman who had married the enfant terrible – soon to be angry old man – of English fiction.

'Bron' – as he was known to family and friends – was born just as Evelyn Waugh joined the Army, so father and son saw little of each other for six years. Even after that, Evelyn Waugh preferred to visit his children no more than 'once a day for ten, I hope, awe-inspiring minutes'.

Bron won an exhibition to Christ Church, Oxford. Before going up, he joined the Royal Horse Guards (The Blues) as a National Service cornet. While serving in Cyprus he underwent an experience which he was later to describe, as only he could, in an immortally funny piece.

Trying to unjam a Browning machine-gun in his armoured car, he managed to set it off and to fire, at point-blank range, four bullets through his chest and shoulder, one through his arm and one through his left hand before he noticed what was happening 'and got out of the way pretty quick'. Horribly injured, he was still alert enough to say 'Kiss me, Chudleigh' to his troop sergeant, on whom the allusion was lost and who treated him afterwards with suspicion.

His survival was miraculous; and for the rest of his life he was often in pain (the chest wounds required disagreeable treatment from time to time) and was conscious of the closeness of death. But he always made light of his physical troubles.

After a spell on the Peterborough column of *The Daily Telegraph*, he moved to the *Daily Mirror*. During the Six-Day War, the paper sent Waugh to Israel where Miss Mandy Rice-Davies was said to be working as a nurse at the front. In fact, she was still to be found in her Tel Aviv nightclub, but Waugh had her dressed up and photographed as a nurse.

That year he joined *The Spectator*, but in 1970 Waugh was working at the magazine's printers when on a whim – and to settle a score – he altered the name of George Gale in the list of contents to 'Lunchtime O'Gale'. For this, he was sacked by Nigel Lawson, then editor.

A spell as columnist on *The Times* also ended with the sack, but not before he had written a column including an old Army joke about the curious trousers worn by men in certain parts of the Near East. This caused outrage in Islamic countries. When the British Council library in Rawalpindi was burned down by a mob, Waugh was, he said, 'naturally proud to have caused such devastation'.

Vendettas were a characteristic of his journalism. Some of his targets were inherited from his father – Sir Stephen Spender ('-Penny'), Cyril Connolly, Lord ('Trimmer') Lovat – and some he acquired for himself: 'Dame' Harold Evans, the late Charles Douglas-Home ('Charlie Vass, the well-known female impersonator') and many politicians.

From 1970 to 1986 he wrote a column for *Private Eye* which was in some ways his most characteristic achievement. As it developed, the *Eye* Diary was a dazzling mixture of fantasy and frightful abuse. It was hard to know how far Waugh was being serious, and whether he really intended the offence he sometimes gave.

In 1990 he began on the Way of the World column in *The Daily Telegraph*, having launched what he described as a 'necessarily bleak and tortuous, sometimes crab-like, campaign to take over the column [from Christopher Booker, author of a perceived slight]. Six months later it had all been settled. On Monday, 7 May 1990, I wrote my first piece under Peter Simple's old banner: Way of the World.' He would continue to write the column until shortly before his death.

Waugh himself was impossible to classify, least of all politically. As with his father's fictional alter ego Gilbert Pinfold, his idiosyncratic Toryism seemed to some more sinister than Socialism. Many of his passions – his dislike of the police, his contempt for most laws (notably that against drinking and driving), his opposition to the Falklands War, his disgust at the Gibraltar shootings in 1988 – scarcely placed him on the right, but rather made him a liberal individualist of the most extreme cast. If Auberon Waugh was a reactionary, it was in the best sense of reacting against the folly and cruelty and oppression of his own age. Brought up a Roman Catholic, he was disgusted by the course which the Church had taken in the last generation, and largely gave up church-going. But the best traditions of humane Christianity never left him. In the tradition of Dean Swift, he served human liberty through the laceration of folly.

⁓ 17th ⁓

The Lord Kagan, b. 1915, d. 1995

The Lord Kagan, who has died aged seventy-nine, arrived in Britain as a refugee in 1946 and went on to become a multi-millionaire, an acolyte of Harold Wilson, a life peer, and an inmate of Rudgate open prison.

Kagan made his fortune with Gannex cloth, in which air was sealed between nylon and wool linings to create a lightweight, waterproof and warm fabric for jackets and coats.

He partly owed his business success to Wilson, who first wore a Gannex raincoat on a visit to Russia in 1956, the year the fabric was patented. By the time Wilson became Prime Minister, in 1964, his Gannex mac was as much a part of his persona as the celebrated pipe. Other world leaders, including Chairman Mao, soon took up the style.

To capitalise on Wilson's patronage Kagan became a major contributor to Labour Party funds, and helped to finance Wilson's private office. But at times he seemed a sinister figure, and this impression was reinforced by his friendship with Richardas Vaigauskas, who was expelled for espionage in 1971. The security services were naturally alarmed at the possibility of a Soviet contact in the Downing Street entourage. Nonetheless Kagan was created a life peer in the Wilson resignation honours list of 1976.

When sales of Gannex began to dwindle Kagan tried to carve a niche in the growing market for denim. But his business acumen inclined to short cuts rather than steady endeavour, and in 1978 he was charged with the theft of indigo dye and with defrauding the public revenue. After two years on the run Kagan was tried and convicted in 1980.

A textile manufacturer's son, Joseph Kagan was born in Lithuania on June 6 1915. When the Nazis invaded in 1941 Kagan was interned in the Jewish ghetto at Vilijampole, where in 1943 he married Margaret Stromas.

Kagan managed to escape with his wife and mother, and they hid in a factory until the Nazis retreated in 1944. At the end of the war Kagan travelled to Bucharest and persuaded the British mission to allow him in to England.

Although Kagan was stripped of the knighthood conferred on him in 1970, annulling his life peerage proved too complicated. Having served a 10-month sentence he quickly returned to the House of Lords. 'I certainly do not feel discredited or disgraced,' he declared.

⚜ 18th ⚜

Neville Crump, b. 1910, d. 1997

Neville Crump, who has died aged eighty-six, trained the winners of three Grand Nationals.

He was known for his booming voice and Chaucerian humour. At Liverpool once Crump was asked about the suitability of a stand-in steward. 'Oh, he'd be perfect,' he said. 'He's deaf, he's blind, and he knows sod-all about racing.'

Beneath the bluster, though, he was the kindest and most loyal of men, an exceptional judge of horses and a genius at training staying steeplechasers.

Neville Franklin Crump was born at Beckenham on 27 December 1910. His father, a cheese manufacturer, was a Master of Foxhounds and a superb horseman, and young Neville learned to ride almost as soon as he could walk.

Crump was educated at Marlborough and Balliol, where he scraped a pass, and was commissioned in the 4th Hussars, only to resign in 1935. By this stage he was already making a name for himself as a jockey at point-to-points, and he soon started riding as an amateur under Rules.

He spent two years as a paying assistant to Sonny Hall near Lambourn, before taking out a licence to train a small string at Upavon on Salisbury Plain. He won his first race, an optional seller worth £58, at Torquay in 1938.

During the Second World War, Crump served as a captain in the North Somerset Yeomanry in Palestine and then as a tank trainer at Barnard Castle, where his friends included John Le Mesurier.

On demobilisation, Crump returned to training and soon moved to Middleham. He sent out the first of his Aintree Grand National winners in 1948. Sheila's Cottage, under his stable jockey Arthur Thompson, came home at 50–1.

A year earlier, the same mare – a moody, reckless animal given to biting and kicking – had been first past the post, but riderless. Next, she had attempted the Scottish Grand National, then held at Bogside on the Ayrshire coast.

Again she unseated Thompson, this time proceeding to gallop into the Firth of Clyde and swim across an inlet. She was eventually retrieved by Crump from Irvine police station at midnight.

In 1952 he had his second Aintree winner with Teal, at odds of 40–1. The victory paid rich dividends for its owner, a hard-betting builder named Harry Lane. Crump had earlier told Lane that Teal was a 'good thing' for the National, but the horse first had to run in a preliminary race at Kelso.

Lane had not yet had his bet, however, and not wishing to see Teal's odds shorten unduly for the National, he telephoned Crump and, to the trainer's horror, threatened to remove his horse from the stable unless he was 'stopped' in the Kelso race.

When the race started, Teal set off at a gallop, and was a jump ahead of the rest of the field by halfway, at which point Arthur Thompson dismounted, ostensibly to look for a stone in the horse's hoof, then remounted and finished second. It was the nearest Crump ever came to saddling a non-trier, and on several occasions in later years he threw out good horses whose owners wanted them to be given 'an easy race'.

Crump's third and most convincing Grand National winner was Merryman II, who overcame an interrupted preparation to romp home by fifteen lengths in 1960, the first year that the race was televised and the last to feature the old-style fences at their most forbidding.

Crump enjoyed hunting – he was Master of the Aldershot Draghounds before the war – but regretted that he had never learned to shoot: his father had told him that 'shooting is just for shits'.

He hated wearing jackets, finding them too tight under the armpits, and would refuse dinner invitations unless allowed to wear a sweater. He was also reluctant to go out if *Emmerdale Farm* was on television.

❧ 19th ❧

Bhagwan Shree Rajneesh, b. 1931, d. 1990

Bhagwan Shree Rajneesh, who has died aged fifty-eight, was the notorious 'guru' who drew thousands of followers from all over the world by preaching a bizarre blend of Eastern religion, pop psychology and free love.

The Bhagwan, known as Osho Rajneesh in recent years, had a dedicated following in his heyday. His enigmatic *aperçus*, encouraging the guilt-free enjoyment of wealth and sexual licence, were apparently taken as gospel by more than half-a-million 'Orange people', many of them prosperous Europeans – including a not insignificant group of expensively educated Britons.

Among the events organised by the Bhagwan's British followers was 'an explosion of energy and consciousness' at the Napoleon Room of the Café Royal in Regent Street.

But after the Bhagwan abruptly decamped from his original commune in Poona in mysterious circumstances in 1981 – there was talk of smuggling, drug-trafficking and prostitution, not to mention tax problems – it seemed increasingly clear that 'the Bagwash' was a charlatan.

The saying was coined: 'Jesus saves, Bhagwan spends'. Certainly he managed to accumulate such items as a Lear jet, thirty-five jewel-encrusted watches and ninety-three Rolls-Royces.

He transplanted his operation to 'Rajneeshpuram' in Oregon where, together with several thousand of his red-robed followers, he set about constructing a self-sufficient utopia. The Bhagwan would drive around the site in one of his Rolls-Royces past lines of chanting, clapping fans, but the allegedly paradisiacal atmosphere was somewhat offset by his escort of helicopter and armed guards; indeed the supposedly loving community was riddled with paranoia and internecine feuds.

The crash came in 1985 when several of the movement's leaders were jailed. The Bhagwan's principal aide, Ma Anand Sheela, left the commune with the parting shot: 'To hell with Bhagwan.'

⇜ 20th ⇝

Bill Werbeniuk, b. 1947, d. 2003

Bill Werbeniuk, who has died aged fifty-six, loomed large over the professional snooker scene during the late 1970s and early 1980s; although never ranked higher than eighth in the world, Werbeniuk's colossal girth – he was the first man to split his trousers during a televised match – and his consumption of fifty pints of lager a day made him one of snooker's most recognisable figures.

Werbeniuk's 25-stone bulk, and his intake of alcohol, became – unfairly – his most prominent characteristics in the minds of the public. But those were, by any standards, extraordinary. Werbeniuk suffered from an hereditary nervous disease (or so he and his doctors claimed) which caused his hands to shake. The only solution which allowed him to participate in his trade was drink.

Werbeniuk's condition, as he argued towards the end of his career, could have been stabilised under the influence of beta-blockers. Unfortunately, the only such drug recommended by his own consultant, Inderal, was banned by the World Professional Billiards and Snooker Association. He acquired a medical certificate which approved his beer-drinking, and became the envy of every armchair viewer when it was explained that he could offset the cost of beer against income tax.

Werbeniuk would have outclassed any amateur drinker, however. 'I'd down six to eight pints of lager before I started,' he said. 'Then I'd have one pint a frame.' In one match, against the British player Nigel Bond, in January 1990, Werbeniuk downed twenty-eight pints of lager and sixteen whiskies over the course of eleven frames. (Bond won 10–1.) After the match, Werbeniuk went home and drank a bottle of Scotch to drown his sorrows. 'I have got to think seriously if I'm going to bother playing any more,' he said a day or two later. 'I drank twenty-eight pints of lager and eight double scotches during the day and was only starting to feel comfortable at the table in the final couple of frames. Now I know that I can only play if I'm totally drunk, and that's not fair on me.'

William Werbeniuk was born on 14 January 1947 at Winnipeg, Manitoba. His father owned Pop's Billiards, on the town's Logan Avenue, and by the age of nine his son had demonstrated his abilities at the table.

After his defeat by Bond, Werbeniuk realised that the game was up. A bankruptcy notice was filed against him in 1991, and later that year he was severely reprimanded and fined £5,000 for refusing to take a drugs test. He threatened to take the WPBSA to court over his beta-blockers, but eventually retired to Canada. There he was out of work and lived on disability benefits. 'I live with my mother and brother and watch sport on the TV. You have to make the most of whatever situation you find yourself in.'

⊰ 21st ⊱

Jack Dupree, b. 1910, d. 1992

Champion Jack Dupree, who has died aged eighty-one, owed his sobriquet to his prowess in the ring, but gained wider renown as a blues singer and barrelhouse pianist.

The keyboard style he developed might have been crude and harmonically inaccurate, but there was no denying its insistent force, achieved by a steady, rhythmic bass, and a treble that chopped in and out in staccato patterns.

As a singer Dupree evolved a style that was an amalgam of rural and city blues – the voice earthy, the delivery pungent, and the emotion straight from the heart. The title of one of his albums, *Blues from the Gutter*, summarised the kind of experience he evoked. His appearance – teeth filled with gold, fingers thickly bejewelled – matched his colourful character. There was also half a heart tattooed on his arm, a relic of a spell in jail – unhappily the tattooist was executed before he could finish the design.

Jack Dupree was born at New Orleans on 4 July 1910, and was still a baby when his home was attacked by the Ku Klux Klan; both his parents perished.

In the aftermath of this outrage the infant was cared for by the whores of the city's Storyville District, before being admitted to the Home for Coloured Waifs and Strays – an orphanage which also sheltered Louis Armstrong.

Dupree was introduced to the piano by an Italian priest, and taught by a character known as 'Drive-Em-Down'. He soon came to know the authentic black bluesmen – Tampa Red, Jazz Gillum, Big Bill Broonzy and Blind Lemon Jefferson. For a time he was an itinerant musician, walking huge distances to gigs or proceeding from St Louis to Chicago as a hobo, riding on the carriage couplings of the railroad trains.

Back in New Orleans, Dupree tended to play with jazzmen who had not – like Louis Armstrong – hearkened unto the siren voices of the North. But times were hard for blacks, and before long he himself drifted north again to Chicago, where he encountered Al Capone.

He was not the only musician to speak well of Capone – who, he recalled, delivered food to the poor. This was the stage at which Dupree earned his crust as a boxer, starting out in fairground boxing booths and amusements arcades, where three-minute challenges would bring a purse of $10.

Later, he graduated to Kid Green's boxing gym. A welterweight with a southpaw style, he engaged in nearly 200 professional contests and fought exhibition bouts with Joe Louis, Jack Dempsey, Gene Tunney and Tommy Farr. His career in the ring, though, left Dupree with markedly slurred speech, which, combined with his pronounced Southern drawl, made him difficult to follow in conversation.

In 1940 he abandoned boxing and began to record for the Okeh label. The titles of his songs reflected his varied career – 'Gamblin' Man Blues', 'Warehouse Man Blues', 'Chain Gang Blues', 'New Low Down Dog', 'Bad Health Blues', 'Heavy Heart Blues', 'Weed Head Woman' and 'Junker Blues'.

But shortly after his recording debut Dupree was drafted into the Navy as a cook, in which capacity he fed the future president John F. Kennedy aboard the *Roosevelt*. When the *Roosevelt* was sunk in the Pacific, Dupree was captured and interned by the Japanese.

On demobilisation Dupree resumed his career in music. By this time there was a resurgence of interest in old-time jazz, so that he was able to make a fair living out of singing the blues. He moved to Greenwich Village, New York.

Still, though, Dupree encountered racial prejudice – there was a shooting incident – and after a European tour in 1959 he decided to move to Britain. He met his wife, Shirley, when she was working in a London club; they lived in Zurich for a while and then settled at Halifax, Shirley's birthplace, where their council house became a haven for touring American blues artistes.

Dupree found plentiful work in clubs throughout England, and played with the Rolling Stones, Eric Clapton and the Beatles, as well as continuing to record for a variety of labels.

In his old age he chuckled over his hobo days, but retained bitter feelings about the Ku Klux Klan.

'All my life, from six years old, I wanted to work and save up enough money and get enough ammunition to catch them at a Klan meeting and spray them, and let them spray me. As long as I could lay down dead in the field with a few of them I'd be happy.'

≋ **22**nd ≋

Rose Fitzgerald Kennedy, b. 1890, d. 1995

Rose Fitzgerald Kennedy, President John F. Kennedy's mother, who has died aged 104, knew the extremes of triumph and disaster but neither ever broke her stoic Catholic will.

She married for love, and soon had every cause to repent. Instead, she supported her brutal husband in the creation of a great political dynasty, only to see her achievement destroyed by the assassination of President Kennedy in 1963 and of his brother Robert five years later.

These were the culminating horrors in a long litany of grief. Of her other seven children, her eldest boy, Joseph Jr, a naval lieutenant and pilot, was killed in 1944 when his plane exploded over the English Channel; her eldest daughter, Rosemary, was mentally retarded; the second daughter, Kathleen, died in an air crash in 1948 (her husband, the Marquess of Hartington, had been killed in action four years before).

In this context, it seemed only a minor misfortune that Rose Kennedy's youngest boy, Edward ('Ted'), should have blighted his presidential prospects by failing immediately to report his having driven off the side of a bridge at Chappaquiddick in 1969; his passenger, Mary Jo Kopechne, was killed.

'Kennedys don't cry,' was Mrs Kennedy's reaction to misfortune. 'I would much rather be known as the mother of a great son than the author of a great book or the painter of a great masterpiece.'

Angela Culme-Seymour, b. 1912, d. 2012

Angela Culme-Seymour, who has died aged ninety-nine, was a dazzling feature of smart society before and after the Second World War, changing husbands and lovers with bewildering regularity; they included, but were not limited to, Churchill's nephew, an English peer, a French count, an Army major and a professor of atomic physics who was married to her half-sister.

She was disarmingly frank in admitting that she preferred promiscuity to monogamy. Interviewed in her eighties, she said: 'I've never been married long enough to know for how long monogamy is realistic. I imagine about seven years.' But she never waited that long.

Her maternal grandmother, Trix Ruthven, was said to have been the model for Nancy Mitford's 'Bolter' – hence the title of Angela's memoir, *Bolter's Grand-daughter* (2001). When it came to skipping out on romantic attachments, however, she put her grandmother in the shade. Despite this apparently selfish lifestyle she continued to charm those who met her until the end of her life.

As the diarist James Lees-Milne noted, Angela Culme-Seymour had camellia-like skin, large glowing dark eyes and long bewitching lashes which gave her an air of complete innocence. But 'commonplace codes of behaviour simply did not apply to her. Loyalty to one partner even at the start of a love affair appeared not to concern her.

'And yet she could not be accounted scheming, because her amours seldom brought her particular happiness and never material gain. She was like a ravishing cat with sheathed claws, a cat which happily settles on whatever cosy cushion presents itself.'

Angela Mary Culme-Seymour was born on 3 August 1912. Her father, a captain in the Rifle Brigade, was killed at Ypres in 1915. At the end of the war her mother Janet married his friend Geoffrey Woolley, VC, who took Holy Orders and went to Rugby school as assistant master, then to Harrow as chaplain. Angela enjoyed a liberal education at Bedales and Dartington Hall, both co-educational and the most progressive schools in the country.

Her introduction to affairs of the heart began at the age of fifteen, when she received a letter from her reverend stepfather announcing that he was in love with her. She then went to southern Spain where she became friendly with the writer and Hispanophile Gerald Brenan, who would sometimes take her hand and put it into his trouser pocket, and once crept into bed with her.

Johnny Churchill, artist nephew of Winston Churchill, was her first husband. They married in Portofino in 1934, and a daughter was born the following year, after which they went briefly to stay with the future prime minister at Chartwell. They then took a house in Spain, near the Brenans, shortly before the outbreak of the Civil War. But Angela soon broke out of that marriage to pursue a French count, René de Chatellus, to Paris. She did not marry him for another twelve years, and in the meantime her life continued on its eclectic path.

In 1937 she took up with Patrick Balfour, a bisexual author and journalist, and they were soon married.

She was soon taking lovers again. 'I can no longer remember when I started being unfaithful to Patrick,' she wrote in her book. But it was before Balfour became Lord Kinross on the death of his father in 1939. The new Lady Kinross recalled travelling by the night train to Edinburgh to attend her father-in-law's funeral and sharing a sleeper with 'a painter called David something'.

She went to art school in Suffolk, where she met Lucian Freud (but did not become one of his many muses). Angela exhibited her work in London and would continue to paint for many years.

When war came, she had a brief affair with a man at the Italian embassy, until Italy entered the war against the Allies and he had to leave. She joined the Women's Auxiliary Air Force, and when Kinross joined the RAF Volunteer Reserve and was posted to Cairo, the marriage came to an end. After the war he wrote a novel, *The Ruthless Innocent*, inspired by her.

A meeting in 1940 with Major Robert Hewer-Hewitt of the Royal Army Service Corps led to a five-year relationship which Angela often found unsatisfactory. No marriage took place, but two sons were born and given her maiden name.

Having escaped with the two boys, she was contacted by the Comte de Chatellus, who urged her to go to Paris and marry him. This she did, but the revival of their youthful love affair was short-lived. Angela amused herself by painting, playing the guitar, going to the Crillon Bar to meet Sam White and other journalists, and writing a column on life in Paris for *Woman's Own*. She was reunited with her daughter for the first time in ten years.

It was almost inevitable that this marriage would not last. What was surprising, indeed shocking to her friends, was that she ran off with the man who was married to her half-sister Janetta Kee.

Derek Jackson was a brilliant atomic physicist in the field of spectroscopy, who had been previously married to Augustus John's daughter Poppet and to Pamela, one of the Mitford sisters. He was initially attracted to Angela at the Travellers Club's summer ball in Paris, which they attended together at Janetta's suggestion because she was seven months pregnant.

Two months later, having taken Angela to Brittany, Jackson went to London (where his wife had just given birth), and told her he was leaving her for Angela. They lived together outside Paris, where their friends included another Mitford – Diana (then Diana Mosley). After three years, Jackson left her.

When writing her memoir years later, Angela was so ashamed of her behaviour with Jackson that she refers to the episode only in a short paragraph, omitting to mention either him or her half-sister. But she admits, with endearing and unvarnished honesty: 'I was *vache*, ungrateful, promiscuous'. On her return to London, Angela was shunned by many of her acquaintances, though not by her lifelong friend Anne Hill, wife of Heywood Hill (of the eponymous bookshop). She never saw Jackson again, and it was twenty-seven years before she met again and was reconciled with Janetta.

Angela Culme-Seymour continued her peripatetic existence, spending two years in Australia and holidays in Greece, until she embarked on the most rewarding years of her life. These came when she met and, aged sixty-five, married a Turkish aristocrat, Ali Bulent Rauf. They lived mostly in Turkey and together translated some of the writings of the twelfth-century Andalusian spiritual teacher Muhyiddin Ibn 'Arabi, which led Rauf to co-found the Beshara School of Esoteric Education, at Chisholme House, Hawick, in the Scottish borders.

The school, which promotes self-knowledge and 'the realisation of love as the prime motive in existence', gave Angela some spiritual contentment. After Rauf's death in 1987, she became honorary life president of the Muhyiddin Ibn 'Arabi Society. In her nineties she went to live at Chisholme and was looked after there until she died.

⊰ 23rd ⊱

Vasili Mitrokhin, b. 1922, d. 2004

Vasili Mitrokhin, who has died aged eighty-one, was the former KGB archivist whose defection to Britain in 1992 brought a treasure trove of Soviet secrets to the West.

Mitrokhin's archive consisted of a huge volume of material culled from tens of thousands of top-secret KGB files, which he had laboriously copied down over twelve years and hidden in tins and milk crates underneath his dacha. It contained detailed records of every operation the KGB had mounted from its inception in 1917 to Mitrokhin's retirement in 1984, demonstrating the extent to which the KGB had successfully infiltrated the West and the way in which it had oppressed the Russian people.

Among other revelations, the papers disclosed that more than half of Soviet weapons were based on designs stolen from America; that the KGB had tapped the telephones of American officials such as Henry Kissinger and had spies in almost all the country's big defence contractors. In France, at least thirty-five senior politicians were shown to have worked for the KGB during the Cold War. In Germany, the KGB was shown to have infiltrated all the major political parties, the judiciary and the police.

Also fascinating was the insight given into the absurd lengths to which the Russians were prepared to go to discredit those they regarded as ideological enemies. There was a plan to break the legs of Rudolf Nureyev, the ballet dancer, after he defected to the West in 1961. On one occasion a team of eighteen KGB operatives was dispatched to the Philippines with instructions to ensure that the Soviet world chess champion, Anatoly Karpov, was not defeated by the defector Victor Korchnoi in the World Chess Championship. The methods employed including stationing a hypnotist in the front row of the audience, who stared intently at Korchnoi throughout the matches.

The acquisition of the Mitrokhin archive was a huge coup for British intelligence, which had recognised the value of the material after it had been turned down by the Americans.

Mitrokhin's motives were the subject of much speculation. He did not defect for the money and was not being blackmailed; nor did he seem to enjoy his new life in the West. Some suggested that he had become embittered after being transferred from operational duties for the KGB to archives. But it is equally possible that his own explanation was the genuine one. He simply decided that Soviet Communism was evil and should be opposed.

The son of a decorator, Vasili Nikitich Mitrokhin was born on 3 March 1922 in Yurasovo, in the rural Rayazan province of Soviet Russia. After leaving school, he entered artillery school, then attended university in Khazakhstan, graduating in History and Law. Towards the end of the Second World War, he took a job in the military procurator's office at Kharkov in the Ukraine.

Then an idealistic Communist, Mitrokhin was recruited into the KI (the Committee of Information), the Soviet external service which was absorbed into the newly formed KGB in 1954.

During the 1950s he served on various undercover assignments overseas. In 1956, for example, he accompanied the Soviet team to the Olympic Games in Australia. But later that year, after he had apparently mishandled an operational assignment, he was moved from operational duties to the archives of the KGB's First Chief (Foreign Intelligence) Directorate, and told he would never work in the field again.

When, in 1972, the archives were moved from the Lubyanka in Moscow to a new repository on the outskirts of the city, Mitrokhin seized his chance. Given the responsibility of checking and sealing about 300,000 files, he began making notes on the documents, which he smuggled out of the building in his shoes, trousers or coat. Had he been caught, he would almost certainly have been executed.

Mitrokhin continued his clandestine activities for twelve years until his official retirement in 1984, when his boss, Vladimir Kryuchkov, congratulated him for his success in transferring the archives and his 'irreproachable service to the state security authorities'.

In retirement, Mitrokhin watched and waited, little expecting that he would ever have the opportunity to bring his archive to light. His opportunity came when the Soviet Union began to fall apart. In 1992, he obtained permission to take a holiday in Latvia. Taking samples of his archive with him, he walked into the American embassy in Riga and asked if he could defect. CIA officials at the embassy, struggling to cope with hundreds of Russian exiles trying to flee the crumbling Soviet Union, were not interested. They reasoned that Mitrokhin was not a spy, just a librarian, and the handwritten documents were probably fakes.

Mitrokhin then tried the nearby British embassy, which immediately recognised his importance and began to make arrangements to spirit him out of the country. These were initially hampered by the need to retrieve the rest of the archive, still buried under Mitrokhin's dacha. A plan was hatched involving six MI6 officers dressed as workmen, who unearthed six trunks of material and loaded them into a van. On 7 September 1992, Mitrokhin, his family and his archive arrived in Britain.

But life in exile was difficult for Mitrokhin, who lived in fear that he might be stalked by vengeful former comrades. He spoke little English, had few friends and was devastated when his wife, Nina, died in 1999. Interviewers noticed a sadness hanging over him.

The Mitrokhin archive led to resignations, arrests and a few prosecutions around the world, though there are believed to be about 300 Soviet sources still living in Britain and America who have not yet been publicly identified.

⇗ 24th ⇗

Sir Winston Churchill, b. 1874, d. 1965

If Sir Winston Churchill, who has died at the age of ninety, had never, as the architect of victory in the 1939–45 war, written such an imperishable page in the story of Britain and of civilisation, his genius, which flowered in several forms, would still have ensured him a place in history.

He was an acknowledged master of the written and spoken word, and would have been remembered in the world of literature if only for his life of Marlborough.

He held more ministerial posts than any other politician, including two memorable terms as First Lord of the Admiralty when Britain was embarking on both World Wars. He was twice Prime Minister, holding office at two critical stages of our history.

He was the only member of the War Cabinet to remain in office from 3 September 1939 until victory had been achieved in Europe. Finally, his brilliant and versatile temperament found such fluent expression at the artist's easel that he was, at the age of seventy-three, elected an honorary Academician Extraordinary of the Royal Academy.

The threads of his life story were woven, unobtrusively enough at first, in the tapestry of British history. Winston Leonard Spencer Churchill was born at Blenheim Palace, historic home of the Marlboroughs, on 30 November 1874, the son of Lord Randolph Churchill, third son of the seventh Duke of Marlborough. His mother was formerly Miss Jennie Jerome, of New York, a fact he was not slow to recall, with impish humour, when his audience was American.

His schooling at Harrow and at Sandhurst was undistinguished. He declared modestly later in life that book-learning was not his forte, and that he had had to pick up things as he went along. His commission in the 4th Queen's Own Hussars in 1895 was not achieved without difficulty in passing the necessary examinations.

But he displayed signs quite early of that restless independence, and spirit of adventure, which was later to figure so prominently not only in his military but also in his political career.

He secured permission to serve with the Spanish forces in Cuba in the Spanish–American War, and in 1897 he was attached to the Punjab Infantry with the Malakand Field Force. He subsequently served with the Tirah and Nile Expeditionary Forces and was present at the Battle of Khartoum.

In 1899 he found time to contest, unsuccessfully, Oldham in the Conservative cause before service in South Africa with the Light Horse. Here, while acting as war correspondent of the *Morning Post*, he was the central figure in an escapade of the type in which he revelled.

Captured when a troop train was ambushed by the Boers, he escaped within a month, jumped a goods train and travelled to neutral territory hidden in bales of wool. Among the officers who had interrogated him was one Jan Christiaan Smuts, later to fill his own particular niche as a great soldier-statesman and to become a firm friend of his former captive.

Sir Winston Churchill's political career began in earnest in 1900 with his success, at the second attempt, at Oldham. He retained the seat until 1906, but his differences with the party leaders on several matters of policy, including that of Tariff Reform, led him to join the Liberal Party. From 1906 to 1908 he was Liberal MP for North-West Manchester, and he had his first experience of office as Under-Secretary for the Colonies.

For the next fourteen years, in the course of which he held eight offices and saw some more active service, he represented Dundee. He was President of the Board of Trade 1908–10, and Home Secretary 1910–11.

In 1911 came the start of his initial term as First Lord of the Admiralty, an appointment for which the nation subsequently had cause to be profoundly grateful. As well aware of the German menace at that period as he was a quarter of a century later, he saw that the Royal Navy was brought to such a pitch of preparedness that at the outbreak of war it slipped quietly, but with deadly precision, into action. It was conceded on all sides that most of the credit for this was due to the foresight, vigilance and energy of the First Lord.

When in 1915 the failure at Gallipoli caused his undeserved and temporary political extinction, his desire for a more active part in the war led to his command in 1916 in France, as a lieutenant-colonel of the 6th Royal Scots Fusiliers. But he was recalled in 1917 to become successively Minister of Munitions, Secretary for War, and Secretary for Air. Colonial Secretary 1921–22, he was elected for Epping in 1924, and having returned to the Conservative fold he was appointed Chancellor of the Exchequer from then until 1929.

As Hitler loomed large on the European horizon, Sir Winston's forebodings, which he characteristically expressed on every possible occasion, began to irritate those who adhered to the policy of appeasement which culminated in Munich.

His ceaseless warnings of the wrath to come were regarded contemptuously as the meanderings of a man with an obsession, and resulted in a 'sojourn in the wilderness' which caused him grim amusement, and brought a sense of despair and frustration to his sympathisers.

The relief which accompanied his appointment in 1939 for the second time as First Lord, and the affection in which he was held in naval circles, were demonstrated by the single message which was flashed round the Fleet – 'Winston is back.' A sense of strength and confidence permeated this maritime nation at the realisation that at least one of the most important posts had been more than adequately filled.

The refusal of the Socialists in 1940 to serve in a Coalition under Mr Chamberlain, and their enthusiastic acceptance of Sir Winston as Prime Minister, led to the magnificent culmination of his career at the head of a country more closely united than ever before.

He started immediately to fulfil his onerous dual role of Prime Minister and Minister of Defence with an energy and determination that did not relax until the surrender of Germany.

That his war-time travels to conferences, often accomplished in the face of difficulties and dangers that many would have considered risks outside the line of duty, amounted to more than 40,000 miles was a striking example of the eager, almost ferocious way he set about the tasks before him.

He ranged from America, where he talked with Mr Roosevelt and drew tumultuous applause from both Houses of Congress in the United States and the Canadian Parliament, to Cairo and Moscow, where he first met Marshal Stalin, in 1941–42.

There followed visits to Casablanca, Turkey, Tripoli, Teheran and to America again in 1943. Two attacks of pneumonia, one suffered in England and the other in Carthage, created public alarm, but failed to shake the determination of this indefatigable and indomitable man.

He was back in England by January 1944, and six days after D-Day he was beaming with pleasure at the rousing welcome accorded him by the troops on the beaches of Normandy.

Two more visits to Northern France were followed by conferences in Italy with Tito, Umberto and Badoglio, and a call on the troops preparing for the invasion of southern France. Within a fortnight he flew to Quebec for another conference with Mr Roosevelt, and then on to Moscow, accompanied by Mr Eden.

On Christmas Day, a month after his seventieth birthday, he flew with Mr Eden to Athens to study the problems raised by the internecine warfare which had broken out in Greece.

At Yalta, in the Crimea, in February 1945, he met Mr Roosevelt, in company with Marshal Stalin for the last time.

The shock, and the sense of personal loss, with which the Allies received the news of Mr Roosevelt's death in April aroused its deepest echo in the heart of Sir Winston, whose unbounded admiration for 'that great and good man' was fortified by the bonds of genuine, and reciprocated, affection.

The defeat of the Conservative Party in the General Election of 1945, at which Sir Winston was first returned for Woodford, was due in no way to any diminution in the esteem in which he was personally held.

This was proved not only by the tremendous reception he received on his 1,000-mile electioneering tour of Britain, but by the many tributes which have since been paid to his war leadership by even his bitterest political opponents.

Six years were to pass before he was in office again. But no temporary setback at home could deprive him of the extraordinary influence and prestige which he enjoyed abroad.

In addition to delivering many vigorous and powerful assaults on the government in his role as Leader of the Opposition, he had worked arduously, and with a moving sincerity, for European co-operation.

His speeches to the International Council of the European Movement, and at the Congress of Europe and the Council of Europe, bore eloquent testimony to his passionate desire for unity among the Western nations.

He was no less anxious for full Anglo–American accord. In speeches at Fulton, Missouri, and in Massachusetts, he pleaded for a perfect understanding between the two countries that would perpetuate their war-time comradeship.

Much of the credit for the North Atlantic Treaty, as well as for the movement towards a united Europe, must in justice be awarded to him.

His profound warnings on the attitude and activities of Russia drew caustic comments from sympathisers with that country and allegations of warmongering. He remained unmoved by both, and waited calmly for time to prove him right, as it had done so frequently, and so painfully, in the past.

The election of 1950 left the House of Commons almost equally divided. A further eighteen months, notable for a further slide towards insolvency and for the loss of more of our hard-won prestige, had to pass before the nation once more entrusted its destinies to Sir Winston's care.

The gravity of the times, exemplified by the outbreak of war in Korea, must have made many feel that he was the man for the hour; but there is good reason to suppose that a widespread fear of war, which was unscrupulously exploited by his opponents, did much to reduce the Conservative majority in the House of Commons.

With the energy and realism that had characterised the whole of his political career, he quickly tackled the problems which lay before him on assuming office for the second time.

In Parliament he refrained from any attempt to make capital out of the parlous situation inherited by his government, and in a sombre but confident broadcast, in the course of which he warned his hearers of the rough road Britain had to travel, he appealed for an end to bitter party strife.

Overshadowing in world interest his many other important activities, however, was his arrangement to visit Mr Truman at Washington. There can be no doubt that he fulfilled his purpose of giving a new tone to Anglo–American relations.

His speech to Congress was acclaimed as fully up to his own high standard. Some observers detected signs that the physical though not the intellectual machine was running down.

He was not the type, however, to permit a decline in heath to halt the vigour of his control of the nation's affairs. On his return to England he made several personal interventions into vexed problems which displayed all his old mastery.

None felt with a greater sense of loss the death of King George VI. As Monarch and Prime Minister in the years of Britain's greatest trial, they had formed bonds of the deepest affection and respect.

In 1953, when Mr Churchill became Sir Winston as a Knight of the Garter, he played his full part in the Queen's Coronation and presided over all five plenary sessions of the Commonwealth Prime Ministers' Conference in London. When Mr Eden, as he then was, fell ill that year he also took over the Foreign Office, and he made plans for another Atlantic crossing to meet President Eisenhower in Bermuda.

Fears that all these burdens would overtax his strength were realised when his doctors ordered a month's complete rest just before he was due to sail. The Bermuda talks were postponed but not abandoned.

The following year he was off again, flying to Washington for further talks with the President and Mr Dulles. These were followed by a visit to Canada.

On his eightieth birthday in 1954 he was still at the head of affairs, after months of rumours about his impending retirement. His birthday was greeted by gifts and tributes from all over the world, among them a controversial portrait by Graham Sutherland presented to him in Westminster Hall by both Houses of Parliament.

President Eisenhower wrote: 'We Americans salute you as a world statesman, as an unconquerable warrior in the cause of freedom, as our proven friend of many valiant years.' Earl Attlee described him as 'the last of the great orators'.

With money gifts Sir Winston formed the Winston Churchill Memorial Trust, with the object, among others, of endowing his country home, Chartwell, as a museum containing 'relics and mementoes of my long life'.

From the £259,175 received he founded scholarships at his old school, Harrow, to encourage the study of English language and literature. He also gave £25,000 to assist the foundation of Churchill College, Cambridge, created for scientific studies.

Sir Winston eventually handed over the premiership to his partner for so many years in war and peace, Sir Anthony Eden, who had married his niece, Miss Clarissa Spencer Churchill, in 1952. But his retirement, announced on 6 April 1955, in the midst of a national newspaper stoppage, was not his farewell to politics. A few weeks later he was fighting his fifteenth General Election.

He did not speak, though he was in the House, during the Suez crisis in 1956. But the following May, after Sir Anthony Eden's resignation, he publicly praised his 'resolute action' and condemned the United Nations.

He was one of the two elder statesmen, the Marquess of Salisbury was the other, consulted by the Queen when Sir Anthony resigned in January 1957, and his advice was frequently sought by Sir Anthony's successor, Mr Macmillan.

In 1958 an attack of pneumonia while he was on holiday in the south of France caused worldwide anxiety. It forced him to postpone an informal visit he had planned to the United States. But he made the journey the following year and, at the White House dinner in his honour, called for new efforts to build Anglo–American unity.

In the General Election of 1959 he stood again at eighty-four as candidate for Woodford. On his return to Parliament he became Father of the House of Commons, an honour he would have achieved long before but for his two years out of Parliament, after his defeat at Dundee in 1922.

The same year his old friend, Field Marshal Viscount Montgomery, unveiled a bronze statue of him at Woodford, and in November 1959 he went to Paris to receive from Gen. de Gaulle the Cross of Liberation, one of France's highest awards.

Among the thousands of congratulatory messages he received on his eighty-fifth birthday was one from Khrushchev.

The breaking of a small bone in his back as a result of a fall at his London house in Hyde Park Gate caused further anxiety about his health in 1960, but he made a good recovery. The following spring he went for a three-week cruise to the West Indies in the yacht of his friend Mr Aristotle Onassis, the ship-owner.

In 1960–61 he drew for the first time his full annual pension of £2,000 as a former Prime Minister. Because of uncertain health he was unable to lay the foundation stone of Churchill College in the autumn of 1961, and the annual Songs of Harrow School were postponed until November so that he could attend, for the twenty-first time.

On his eighty-seventh birthday, which brought more world-wide tributes, among them one from President and Mrs Kennedy, he was applauded in the Commons, a breach of the rules of the House to which the Speaker turned a blind eye.

Sir Winston broke his thigh in a fall in Monte Carlo in 1962. Then came nearly two months of anxiety, with an emergency operation, a flight back to London and fifty-two days in the Middlesex hospital. After this he had his first outing in the following November when he dined with friends of The Other Club, which he formed with F.E. Smith, later the first Earl of Birkenhead, in 1911.

On 1 May 1963, Sir Winston announced that he was giving up his seat at Woodford at the General Election. In the previous October he had completed sixty years as an MP.

Last year he still attended the Commons and in February went to another dinner of The Other Club.

On 5 June, Prince Philip, in the presence of Lady Churchill, Mrs Christopher Soames, her daughter, Mr Randolph Churchill and Mr Winston S. Churchill, Sir Winston's grandson, paid tribute to Sir Winston in performing the official opening of Churchill College, Cambridge.

Party politics were forgotten on 28 July, when the Commons paid tribute to the Father of the House on his retirement. They gave unanimous assent to a motion which put on record their 'unbounded admiration and gratitude for his services to Parliament, to the nation and to the world'.

Sir Alec Douglas-Home, the then Prime Minister, left with a delegation of MPs to present the resolution, printed on vellum, to Sir Winston at his home at Hyde Park Gate, Kensington.

On Sir Winston's ninetieth birthday on 30 November, messages of good wishes broke all records. As a crowd outside his London home sang 'For He's a Jolly Good Fellow' Sir Winston came to the window. There were telegrams from the Pope, President Johnson, Gen. de Gaulle and other world leaders. Mr Johnson proclaimed the day 'Sir Winston Churchill Day'.

The years following Sir Winston's resignation of the Premiership saw the publication, between 1956–58, of his *History of the English Speaking Peoples* in four large volumes. This was the last of more than thirty books from his pen. The first was *The Story of the Malakand Field Force* in 1898. His other works included *Lord Randolph Churchill* (1906), a study of his famous father, *The World Crisis* (1923–29), a masterly review of the 1914–18 War and its origins, and *Great Contemporaries* (1937).

He reached the peak of his literary prowess with the publication of his history of the 1939–45 war, extracts from which were serialised in *The Daily Telegraph*.

In 1953 he received the Nobel Prize for Literature, one of a host of honours showered upon him by countries all over the world, among them honorary citizenships, some fifteen foreign decorations, gold medals of cities, and the freedom of more than forty boroughs and cities.

The knighthood conferred on him by the Queen at Windsor in 1953 when she invested him with the Insignia of a Knight Companion of the Garter was offered to him at the end of the war. He declined it on that occasion and in 1946 accepted the Order of Merit instead.

He took particular pride In his appointment in 1941 as Lord Warden of the Cinque Ports and also in the fact that he was an Elder Brother of Trinity House (1913).

In 1963 he became an honorary citizen of the United States.

A Privy Councillor since 1907, he was also a Companion of Honour (1922), a Fellow of the Royal Society (1941), an honorary Bencher of Gray's Inn (1942), honorary Academician Extraordinary of the Royal Academy (1948), and an honorary Fellow of Merton College, Oxford (1942).

In 1908 he married Miss Clementine Hozier, daughter of Col. Sir Henry and Lady Blanche Hozier. She survives him with one son, two daughters, ten grandchildren and three great-grandsons.

⇒ 25th ⇐

Fanny Blankers-Koen, b. 1918, d. 2004

Fanny Blankers-Koen, who has died aged eighty-five, was voted the greatest female athlete of the twentieth century.

The 1948 Olympics, held in London, were the first to be staged since those at Berlin twelve years earlier. Fanny Blankers-Koen arrived at the White City stadium in London as the holder of six world records, yet found herself dogged by criticism. The manager of the British team dismissed her as being too old, at thirty; while in Holland there were many who believed that she would be better employed looking after her children. Her detractors might have been even more vocal had they known that she was already in the early stages of a third pregnancy.

She secured her first victory with ease, winning the 100m by three metres in 11.9 seconds. Two days later she lined up for the final of the 80m hurdles as favourite, but hit the fifth flight as she caught up with Britain's Maureen Gardner, lost her stride and finished in a dead heat with Gardner and the Australian Shirley Strickland.

She thought that she had lost to the Briton, her training partner, and believed her fears confirmed when the band began to play 'God Save The King'. This, however, was for George VI, who was just taking his seat, and a few moments later she heard the Dutch anthem. Blankers-Koen had won in 11.2 seconds (the same time as Gardner), a new world record.

By now, however, Fanny Blankers-Koen – a strongly built yet rather shy blonde – was indeed beginning to miss her children; and when her husband went into the dressing room before the 200m semi-finals, he found her in tears. She told him that she hated the event – the distance was being run by women for the first time at an Olympics – and that she wanted to go home.

He sympathised with her, but said that she would later regret her decision if she quit. 'Jan was right,' she remarked later. 'I had a good cry and felt much better.' Indeed, so good did she feel that, in the heat, she set a new Olympic record of 24.4 seconds, a time she almost equalled when she later won the final by seven metres on a soaking-wet track.

The last of Fanny Blankers-Koen's four golds came in the sprint relay, and was claimed by her in dramatic fashion. Running the anchor leg, she received the baton in fourth place, but blasted past her opponents to snatch victory for Holland. She had won all four medals in just eight days.

Fanny Blankers-Koen, who had been nicknamed 'The Flying Housewife' by the British press, returned to Amsterdam to be greeted by vast crowds. 'All I did was run fast,' she said in some bewilderment. Her critics were silenced, and the nation showed its appreciation of her victories by presenting her with a new bicycle – so that she would not have to run so much.

The daughter of a government official, she was born Francina Elsje Koen at Baarn, Holland, on 26 April 1918. As a child she enjoyed swimming, gymnastics and fencing, and took up athletics only at sixteen, at her father's suggestion. As an eighteen-year-old at the Berlin Games, she finished sixth in the high jump and came fifth with the relay team. The highlight for her, however, was securing Jesse Owens' autograph. Almost forty years later, at the Munich Olympics, she reminded him of this, telling him: 'My name is Fanny Blankers-Koen.' 'You don't have to tell me that,' said Owens, 'I know all about you.'

'Imagine,' she recalled later with her usual modesty, 'Jesse Owens knew who I was.'

Fanny Blankers-Koen retired from competition in 1955, and lived in Amsterdam (where a statue of her was erected), enjoying tennis and getting out on her bicycle until recently, when she began to suffer ill health. She refused to be jealous of modern athletes such as Marion Jones, who secured a multi-million-dollar sponsorship contract after taking two golds at the Sydney Olympics in 2000.

'She trains twice a day,' Fanny pointed out. 'We only trained twice a week.'

⊱ 26th ⊰

The 12th Marquess of Huntly, b. 1908, d. 1987

The 12th Marquess of Huntly, who has died aged seventy-eight, was premier Marquess of Scotland and did homage on behalf of the marquesses at the Coronation of George VI in 1937.

His first marriage, by which there is a son and daughter, was dissolved in 1965. In 1977, he married Elizabeth, daughter of Lt-Cdr F.H. Leigh.

His new bride, a nurse, was more than forty years his junior. At the time his engagement was announced, he was quoted as saying: 'I'm a very fit man. I walk my dog every day. I don't have to wear spectacles. I still have my own teeth. Why should I marry some dried-up old bag?'

Douglas Charles Lindsay Gordon was born on 3 February 1908, eldest son of Lt-Col Douglas Gordon, equerry to the Duke of Connaught. He was commissioned in the Gordon Highlanders (the family regiment founded by the 5th Duke of Gordon in 1796) and served in the Second World War as a lieutenant.

Lord Huntly took his seat in the House of Lords as Lord Meldrum, a peerage of the United Kingdom created in 1815 for the 9th Marquess in the days when peers of Scotland could only be represented by certain of their number at Westminster.

Lord Huntly had great respect for the House of Lords. 'Their intelligence is far and away above that of the House of Commons,' he said. 'That is why they are there.' He was once also reported as saying that Harold Wilson 'should be suspended from the end of a long pole'.

⊱ 27th ⊰

Cecil Lewis, b. 1898, d. 1997

Cecil Lewis, who has died aged ninety-eight, led an astonishingly diverse life; a veteran of aerial combat over Flanders in the First World War, he was one of the first four members on the staff of the BBC, wrote twenty books and plays, and founded a quasi-religious community in South Africa.

In addition he won an Oscar, lived in Tahiti, flew across Africa, and seduced many hundreds of women. Even so, he accomplished rather less than he promised. His uncompromising zest for experience meant that he was doomed to what he described as a 'weather-vane life, swinging this way and that', content to taste, dabble and move on.

Cecil Arthur Lewis was born at Birkenhead on 29 March 1898. His father was a Congregationalist minister whose preaching brought him a fashionable West End pulpit, from which he eloped with a rich member of his flock.

Precociously intelligent, Cecil Lewis was educated at Dulwich, University College School and Oundle, from where, in 1915, he joined the Royal Flying Corps. A stringy beanpole of a boy, 6ft 4in tall, he celebrated his eighteenth birthday in France, and had flown only twenty hours (without any map reading, Morse or formation training), when he was posted to No. 9 Squadron. He flew BE2cs and French-built Morane 'Parasols' in preparation for the Somme offensive. 'If ever there was an aircraft unsuited for active service,' Lewis wrote, 'it was the BE2c.' As for the Morane, he remembered how bullets crackled through its spruce and linen frame.

On 1 July 1916 Lewis saw the mile-high fountain of earth thrown up by the detonation of two mines beneath the German positions. As he related in his classic account of those experiences, *Sagittarius Rising* (1936), the life of a pilot might be more comfortable than that of the men in the trenches, but it was no less dangerous. Life expectancy was three weeks, and in an era before parachutes a disabled plane could take five minutes to plunge 10,000 feet to earth.

Lewis had a series of narrow shaves; his wings were shot away and engine failure brought him down on the front line. Yet he survived eight months before being sent home during the winter of 1916–17 for a spell as a test pilot. He was twice mentioned in despatches and in 1916 awarded the Military Cross for 'continuous bravery'.

He returned to France with No. 56 Squadron, equipped with the new SE5 fighters. Lewis had been specially selected to outfly and outfight Baron von Richthofen and his 'Circus'.

In May 1917 Lewis led the squadron over the Channel to fight the world's first mass air-battle. He recalled: 'The enemy, more than double in number, greater in power, and fighting with skill and courage, gradually overpowered the British, whose machines scattered, driven down beneath the scarlet German fighters.'

Lewis was one of the five in the eleven-strong squadron to survive. He was also the last to see Albert Ball, VC, as the Allied ace disappeared into a cloud bank during the dogfight. At the Armistice, still only twenty, he was credited with the destruction of eight enemy machines.

The experience left Lewis bitter. The war, he reflected, 'deprived me of the only carefree years and washed me up ill equipped for any serious career, with a Military Cross, a Royal handshake, a £600 gratuity and, I almost forgot to say – my life.'

In 1922 Lewis answered an advertisement for a job as deputy director of programmes at the BBC. There were only five applicants, and Lewis, though he knew nothing about broadcasting, was successful. He thus became the youngest of John Reith's three employees.

Versatility was essential, and Lewis found himself producing the BBC's greatest initial success, *Children's Hour*. From 1922 to 1926 he was Director of Programmes.

Lewis pioneered the techniques of radio drama, adapting two of Bernard Shaw's plays himself. He also organised the first simultaneous transmission of the news on the various regional stations, an event introduced by a drunk but word-perfect F.E. Smith.

In 1926 Lewis resigned from the BBC in typically impulsive fashion, irritated by the growth of bureaucracy and the dilution of quality necessary to a mass medium. The microphone, he wrote later, 'clamoured daily to be fed. At first it was satisfied with simple fare and a little of it,' but it became 'a most terrible and insatiable monster'.

After an abortive attempt to interest America in radio drama, he turned to writing himself, encouraged by his friend Charles Ricketts, the artist and aesthete, and by Bernard Shaw. 'Your literary age I take to be about seven,' observed Shaw of one effort; nevertheless he allowed Lewis to film, disastrously, *Arms and the Man*.

Lewis retreated to a villa he had built on a beautiful site above Lake Maggiore on land paid for by Ricketts. There he wrote *Sagittarius Rising*, and after a brief return to the BBC, landed a lucrative writing contract with a Hollywood studio, where his slender contribution to the script of *Pygmalion* brought him a share of an Oscar in 1938.

'For the only time in my life,' he remembered, 'I had more money than I could spend.' He celebrated this predicament with a spell of beachcombing in Tahiti.

On the outbreak of the Second World War he rejoined the Royal Air Force. His first assignment was to test hare-brained ideas such as trailing cannon balls on cables from the hatch of a Wellington in order to intercept incoming bombers. Later he became a flying instructor, teaching his own son to fly, and served in Transport Command.

Soon after the war Lewis became powerfully influenced by the writings of the mystic Georgi Gurdjieff, who taught that man must learn to observe himself in order to wake from his living sleep.

Lewis's several attempts to explain Gurdjieff's teachings in print did not make for easy reading, but he had finally found an enthusiasm of which he did not tire. It dominated the remaining half of a hitherto directionless life, prompting him to set up a community in South Africa to preserve the philosophy against the expected Armageddon of the next war.

The venture was a failure, and in 1966 Lewis retired to Corfu. Although he continued to write, little of his output matched the quality or panache of his early success.

He retained his attractiveness to women, and even at ninety-five might have passed for a spry seventy. Yet he believed that Gurdjieff had cured him of conceit, and acknowledged that 'a successful seducer never makes a good husband'.

⚜ 28th ⚜

Jerry Siegel, b. 1914, d. 1996

Jerry Siegel, who has died aged eighty-one, was one of the creators of Superman, arguably the best-known comic-strip character in the world.

Siegel and his collaborator, Joe Shuster, dreamed up Superman in 1933, when they were working on science fiction fan publications. Siegel was the writer and Shuster the artist.

They offered the strip to every major comic publisher of the time, but it was not until 1938 that DC Comics, looking for some material to round out its *Action Comics No 1*, finally bought the Superman story and all rights to the character.

Action Comics was a sensation on the newsstands. Every issue sold out instantly, and Superman's popularity was such that the next year he was given his own eponymous comic – the first time a comic magazine had been devoted to a single character.

Symbolising 'Truth, Justice and the American Way', Superman became one of the most enduring comic-book characters in the world; in the 1980s he spawned a series of feature films starring Christopher Reeve which reaped profits of more than a billion dollars.

But Siegel's fate was more bleak. He and Shuster had signed away the *Superman* rights for $130, plus $15 a week each. After protracted legal battles DC Comics awarded the pair pensions of $20,000, later adjusted to $30,000, for the rest of their lives.

'How would anyone feel in our shoes?' asked Siegel. 'Everywhere we go it's Superman this and Superman that.'

Of modest background, Jerome Siegel was born at Cleveland, Ohio, on 17 October 1914. His earliest ambition was to be a newspaper reporter or a writer for pulp magazines. At seventeen he met Joe Shuster while working on the school newspaper at Glenville High School in Cleveland.

Siegel continued to contribute occasional stories to the *Superman* comics until the 1960s.

He is survived by his wife, Joanne, whom he met when she was working as Shuster's model for Lois Lane, Superman's girlfriend.

⚞ 29th ⚟

Carl Gorman, b. 1907, d. 1998

Carl Gorman, who has died aged ninety, was the oldest surviving member of the group of Navajo Indians enlisted by the US Marines to render their communications impenetrable to the Japanese during the Second World War.

Gorman was one of 400 Navajo 'code talkers' sent to the Pacific theatre of war to develop a code based on the Navajo tongue. Navajo is a language without an alphabet and has such a complex, irregular syntax that in 1942, when the Marines first sought Navajo help, it was estimated that, except for its 50,000 native speakers, no more than thirty other people in the world – and none of them Japanese – had any knowledge of it.

Equipped with a radio rather than a rifle, Gorman spent much of the war on the front line in the Pacific enabling Marine commanders to issue orders, report on troop movements, and co-ordinate complex operations without any fear that their communications would be compromised.

Japanese code breakers – who managed to crack American army, navy and air force codes – heard only an unintelligible guttural chatter when they listened in on the Marines. For instance, after the Americans planted the famous flag on the summit of Iwo Jima's Mount Suribachi, the placename was spelled out to Pacific Command as an acrostic, using in succession the words *dibeh* (Sheep), *no-dah-ih* (Uncle), *gah* (Rabbit), *tkin* (Ice), *shush* (Bear), *wol-la-chee* (Ant), *moasi* (Cat), *lin* (Horse), and *yeh-hes* (Itch).

Partly because Navajo lacked words for modern military terms, Gorman and his colleagues worked out a two-tier code in which English words were represented by different Navajo words.

Various kinds of aeroplane, for instance, were represented by Navajo words for birds, among them *tas-chizzie* (swallow) for torpedo plane, *jay-sho* (buzzard) for bomber, and *da-he-tih-hi* (humming bird) for fighter aircraft.

When the Japanese finally realised that Marine radio operators were speaking Navajo, they tortured a captured Navajo soldier to gain the key. But the soldier, unfamiliar with the code, was as bemused as his captors; he could tell them that *chay-da-gahi* meant turtle, but he could not know that turtle was the code for tank.

Although Gorman and the other code talkers became heroes to the Marine commanders – one general later said that his troops could never have taken Iwo Jima without them – the Navajo code was considered so valuable that they were not allowed to talk about it until 1969, when the code was finally declassified.

Carl Gorman was born on the Navajo reservation in Chinle, Arizona, in 1907. As a young man he was subjected to a concerted American government campaign to suppress Indian languages. When he was a student at a mission school he was once chained to an iron pipe for a week because he had insisted on speaking his native tongue.

Gorman volunteered for the Marines in 1942 when he learned that they were recruiting Navajos who were fluent in English and Navajo. He had worked as a government translator, but at thirty-four was too old for the Marines, so he lied about his age.

After the war Gorman became an artist, teaching at the University of California before settling at Fort Defiance, Arizona, where he painted horses and other subjects. He lectured on the code talkers, and a statue in his honour was erected on the campus of Northern Arizona University, at Flagstaff.

⚜ **30**th ⚜

Miles Kington, b. 1941, d. 2008

Miles Kington, who has died aged sixty-six, was a humorous columnist and the inventor of Franglais.

He began to produce his series of Franglais books in 1979; the first was *Let's Parler Franglais!* They were rapidly to become a fixture in the lavatories of middle-class households. *Let's Parler Franglais Again!* (1980) promised: 'Comme parlé par Sacha Distel, le Roi Jenkins, etc. Teach yourself dans dix minutes. C'est un walk-over.'

There were also *Parlez-vous Franglais?* and *Let's Parler Franglais One More Temps!* In 1984 Franglais transferred to the small screen in a Channel 4 programme which featured Angela Rippon, Cliff Richard, Petula Clark and Kington himself.

'We have enough people speaking French like Edward Heath already without encouraging more,' was the view of *The Daily Telegraph*, rather confirming the soundness of Kington's underlying idea.

Despite the title, *The Franglais Lieutenant's Woman* (1986) departed a little from the rest of the series, by tackling Franglais versions of the world's great books. Wilde, Hemingway, Verne, Mills & Boon, Beckett and Solzhenitsyn were among those given the treatment.

Besides being keen on jazz and trains, he was an enthusiastic cyclist. He could not abide trifle.

≈ 31st ≈

Moira Shearer, b. 1926, d. 2006

Moira Shearer, who has died aged eighty, was a strikingly beautiful leading ballerina with the Sadler's Wells (later the Royal) Ballet; she was best known for her performance in the film *The Red Shoes*, which won her the heart of the writer and broadcaster Sir Ludovic Kennedy, whom she married in 1950.

At one time in the mid-1940s Moira Shearer was compared to the great Margot Fonteyn and in 1947, when she was twenty-one, she was persuaded to take the lead role in Michael Powell and Emeric Pressburger's film *The Red Shoes*.

She was enchanting as Victoria Page, the young ballerina torn between a struggling composer and a powerful impresario. Released in 1948, it won four Oscar nominations and made Moira Shearer one of the most widely known ballerinas in history.

The daughter of a civil engineer, Moira Shearer King was born at Dunfermline, Fife, on 17 January 1926. It was her mother who pushed her into ballet. At fourteen she entered the Sadler's Wells School.

But, as she admitted later: 'I never wanted to be a dancer. When you're ten you don't have much say in the matter. I suppose I did enjoy it in a way – I don't blame Mama at all – but I think what one does should be one's own choice.'

It was through *The Red Shoes* she captured the heart of Ludovic Kennedy, who was persuaded to see it by his mother, even though he had no interest in ballet. He fell deeply in love. By good fortune, some time later he was given two complimentary tickets to the Sadler's Wells-Old Vic Ball. When he arrived he found that Moira Shearer and Ralph Richardson were presenting the prizes. Though they had not been formally introduced, Kennedy eventually plucked up courage to approach her. 'I walked boldly up, gabbled my name and said, in a rush, "Would you like to dance?"'

By the time they reached the dance floor, he was beginning to wish he was anywhere else: 'I put one hand in hers and the other round her waist (Oh, boy!). Then she said, "Before we start, I must tell you something." What could it be? "I don't dance very well." We set off, and within a step or two it was clear she couldn't dance for toffee.' So began a courtship which ended in their marriage in 1950.

FEBRUARY

⇒ 1st ⇐

The Reverend Henry Thorold, b. 1921, d. 2000

The Reverend Henry Thorold, who has died aged seventy-eight, was a splendid example of that now vanishing English country type, the bachelor antiquarian clergyman or squire, imbued with a deep love and knowledge of architecture, ecclesiology, heraldry and the classics.

An old friend of John Betjeman's and John Piper's, Henry Thorold shared their feeling for the picturesque in landscape and architecture. Like Piper and Betjeman, he was a born writer with an eye for the rare, the odd, the special and the forlorn.

There is a memorable vignette of Thorold in *A Mingled Measure* (1994), the fifth volume of James Lees-Milne's diaries: 'a profile like George III's and a stomach like George IV's. Is rather greedy and hogs his food ... Knows Lincolnshire backwards and all the families that ever were, they being to a man his relations. Is fervently right-wing and deplores all I deplore ... He motors around the country in a large old Bentley motor car and wears a dog collar, an unexpected combination ... Should be an archdeacon.'

Angelo Dundee, b. 1921, d. 2012

Angelo Dundee, who has died aged ninety, never boxed himself, but became the most famous cornerman in the world as the trainer of Muhammad Ali.

Fiercely loyal and protective towards his fighters, Dundee admitted deliberately ripping open a tear in Ali's glove to buy precious seconds after his fighter had been flattened by a Henry Cooper left hook in their famous non-title clash at Wembley Stadium on 18 June 1963.

Ali (then still Cassius Clay) was on the cusp of a world title shot against Sonny Liston when he travelled to London to take on Cooper. In the build-up he had labelled the Englishman 'a bum', a description he clearly had cause to regret when dropped by the famous left hook in round four.

What happened at the end of that round has become part of boxing folklore. 'They accused me of cutting the gloves,' said Dundee. 'Can you imagine me doing something like that? There was a rip in the gloves. All I did was make it a little bigger. They're hunting around for gloves and I'm buying my man time.' Clay went on to stop Cooper on cuts in the following round.

Describing what he looked for in a fighter, Dundee said: 'Balance is a must; so is great co-ordination of hands, feet and body. But I guess the most important ingredient is desire: the desire to be a fighter, the desire to win and the desire to be the best there is.'

Betty Parsons, b. 1915, d. 2012

Betty Parsons, who has died aged ninety-six, was childbirth guru to well-heeled mums-to-be of Kensington and Chelsea, though she enjoyed a reputation which extended far beyond the 20,000 or so women and assorted spouses who attended her studio in Seymour Street, Mayfair.

Elegant, slim and with the sort of reassuring, well-modulated voice that dispels all fears, Betty Parsons was regarded by her devoted followers as a woman who offered the recipe to stress-free childbirth; moreover, they felt that her philosophy of 'relax for pregnancy and life' was indispensable to their general wellbeing and happiness.

Quite why her advice to 'Drop your shoulders and relax' was so superior to what was available (for nothing) on the NHS was never entirely clear to those who had not met her. But no one could be in any doubt about her appeal. One profile-writer recalled her surprise when a best friend announced that, though she had been planning to start a family aged twenty-eight, she was advancing the timetable by four years because she had heard that Betty Parsons was retiring — 'So if I don't have one straight away, I won't be able to go to her classes.'

She never gave interviews, probably because the Queen and Diana, Princess of Wales, were among her 'mums' — along with sundry other members of the Royal Family. Her eightieth birthday party was held in St James's Palace.

She was, it must be said, somewhat guileless when it came to dealing with the Fourth Estate. When a journalist rang her up to verify a rumour that she had been giving private relaxation lessons to the Queen, she said: 'How extraordinary. I don't know how you could have heard. I'm sorry, but I can't talk about anyone I give classes to.'

2nd

Haroun Tazieff, b. 1914, d. 1998

Haroun Tazieff, who has died aged eighty-three, was among the world's leading vulcanologists and an intrepid adventurer whose accounts of his encounters with lava led the playwright Jean Cocteau to dub him 'the poet of fire'.

Hazardous though his volcanic researches were, Tazieff came closest to disaster while on a caving expedition in the Pyrenees in 1952. Searching for the source of an underground river, he watched as the tackle holding the expedition's leader snapped, fatally injuring the man and trapping the rest of the team almost a mile beneath the surface.

A line was lowered to them, but as Tazieff was being winched up, the machinery failed and for four hours he dangled helpless under a stream of freezing water. He was held only by a five-millimetre cable that might have given at any moment, and as his clothing got wetter the weight increased. When he finally reached the surface, after an upwards journey of six hours, he had been underground for eight days; so exhausted and beyond emotion was he that for several minutes he could not speak to his rescuers.

Haroun Tazieff was born in Warsaw on 11 May 1914. His Russian father died when he was an infant, and his Polish mother brought him up in St Petersburg and Brussels. He studied Agriculture and Geology at the University of Liege and, having worked for the Resistance during the Second World War, went as an engineer to the tin mines of the Belgian Congo.

In 1948 he was making a geological survey of the country when he was invited to watch the eruption of the Congolese volcano Kitouro. The experience altered the direction of his life.

'The only way you can understand what a volcano eruption is like is to see it for yourself,' he later said. 'Even after years of study as a geologist, and knowing in theory what it should be like, when I first saw an eruption I could not believe my eyes.'

Tazieff resolved to devote his life to studying volcanoes, and after visiting sites in Africa, as well as Etna and Stromboli, published his first book, *Craters of Fire* (1952). It told of his narrow escapes from choking mephitic gas and streams of molten lava.

From 1950 until 1952, Tazieff was an assistant Professor of Mining Geology at the University of Brussels, but after his escape in the Pyrenees, told in *Caves of Adventure* (1952), he concentrated on his writing and on making films about volcanoes to educate the public. 'To capture the beauty of an eruption,' he wrote, 'one would have to be Van Gogh.' But he was determined to record that dangerous beauty and dared to get closer than others to volcanoes.

The result was several singeings and the much-praised film *Volcano* (1961), a tour of seventeen craters in various states of excitement. Yet despite the risks, Tazieff insisted that he was not a glory-seeker: 'I am not brave,' he said, 'and I certainly have no intention of committing suicide, even for science.'

Tazieff also became interested in earthquakes, which often occur near the site of volcanoes. He undertook the seismological exploration of Tanna, a volcano on Vanuatu, and later recalled 'experiencing strong sensations, among them the fear of being eaten by cannibals'.

Tazieff predicted that several great cities of the world, including Rome, Seattle and Mexico City, were still threatened by large volcanoes. 'Those volcanoes regarded as extinct are only dead to eyes that cannot see. A thousand-year sleep is nothing to a volcano.'

Godfrey Baseley, b. 1904, d. 1997

Godfrey Baseley, who has died aged ninety-two, was the founder of *The Archers*. In a memorandum in August 1950, Baseley explained to his BBC superiors that he sought an accurate, if 'reassuring', picture of country life, drawing 'portraits of typical country people, following them at work and at play and eavesdropping on the many problems of living that confront country folk in general'. While it should be aimed at the general listener (that is, 'the townsman') it should set out to 'to keep a good balance between the factual and the more entertaining aspects of country life'.

At that time Baseley was producer of agricultural programmes for the Midland region of the BBC. At Whitsun 1950 the first 15-minute episode was broadcast in the Midland region only. The first episode broadcast nationally was on 1 January 1951. Within two years it had an audience of nine and a half million.

Godfrey Baseley was born on 2 October 1904 at Alvechurch in Worcestershire. Trained for the stage, he made his first broadcast in 1929. He became a producer in 1943.

He remained editor of *The Archers* for 22 years. In 1955 he was responsible for shocking audiences – many of whom seemed to mistake the episode for reality – by killing off Grace Archer in a stable fire.

He had no sentimentality about the characters he had invented: 'I'd kill off any character if I thought it would be of value to the programme. The only thing that worries me is the actors. You can't just tell someone who's been doing the job for twenty-one years that they're not needed any more.'

But that was precisely what Baseley was told in 1972 when he was dismissed as script editor. He was replaced by Malcolm Lynch, a former scriptwriter of *Coronation Street*.

Baseley gave lectures on *The Archers* all over Britain, but he became increasingly critical. 'They ought to take it off the air until they get it right again,' he commented in 1986. 'It's the townsman's view of life in the country and utterly phoney. Petty politics and sex have crept in, which would never have happened when I was there.'

In retirement Baseley came to look and sound uncannily like an alternative Dan Archer. He entertained some bloodthirsty fantasies for the *Archers* characters. 'I'd kill the old ones in a car crash,' he said in 1990 at a BBC party to celebrate the serial's fortieth birthday. 'I'd like to put a gun to Phil Archer's head – he's had it. As for Eddie Grundy, I'd push him down a well. He's a libel on the countryside. I've never met anyone like him in my life. When I started *The Archers* forty years ago, it changed people's lives – but it's all just gossip now, with no vision any more.'

Baseley made one of his last comments on the programme last year, when controversy blew up around the 'outing' of Sean Myerson, the fictional landlord of the Cat and Fiddle.

'I cannot understand for a moment why they should want a homosexual character. *The Archers* has completely lost its way,' Baseley said. 'Luckily, I'm nearly completely deaf and can't listen to it any more.'

⊰ 3rd ⊱

Maria Schneider, b. 1952, d. 2011

Maria Schneider, the French actress who has died aged fifty-eight, shot to fame as a twenty-year-old after starring, with Marlon Brando, in possibly the most notorious sex scene in cinema.

Last Tango In Paris (1972), directed by Bernardo Bertolucci, is the story of a young Parisienne, Jeanne (Schneider), who begins an affair with a middle-aged American businessman (Brando) who insists that their relationship should be purely sexual; the lovers do not even know one another's names. Though much of the film now seems dated, one sex scene – in which Brando finds a novel use for butter – has never been forgotten.

'Marlon had the idea, and I had a burst of anger,' she recalled of the scene. 'But I was too young [to say no]. I was no more than a baby at nineteen. So I did the scene and I cried. I cried real tears during that scene. I was humiliated. [Later] I heard that the character I played was supposed to be a boy. That maybe explained it.'

At the time, the sexual content caused outrage and the film was banned in a number of countries, including in parts of Britain. Despite the film winning Oscar nominations for both Bertolucci and Brando, its director was hauled before a court in Italy and given a two-month suspended jail sentence.

Maria Schneider, meanwhile, became a celebrity overnight, a development that propelled her on to the well-trodden path of drug addiction, suicide attempts and fractured romantic relationships. 'I felt very sad because I was treated like a sex symbol,' she complained in later life. 'I wanted to be recognised as an actress, and the whole scandal and aftermath of the film turned me a little crazy and I had a breakdown.'

In 1975 she became a voluntary patient at a psychiatric hospital in Rome, apparently to be close to her then lover, the American photographer Joan Townsend, daughter of the head of the Avis rental-car empire.

Although Schneider continued to make films, nothing she appeared in subsequently had the impact of *Last Tango*, which defined her for the remainder of her life. The film of which she was most proud, however, was Michelangelo Antonioni's *The Passenger* (1975), in which she co-starred with Jack Nicholson.

The Passenger has not had wide distribution, reportedly because Nicholson owns the rights and wanted to keep the film to himself 'like a work of art'. But many critics regard it as far more durable than *Last Tango*, some even labelling it 'a masterpiece'.

Maria Schneider was born on 27 March 1952, the product of an affair between the actor Daniel Gélin (whom she did not meet until she was fifteen) and a seventeen-year-old Romanian-born Frenchwoman who ran a Paris bookshop called Marie Christine. As a teenager she adored films, going to the cinema up to four times a week, and she left home at fifteen after an argument with her mother.

While working as an extra she met Brigitte Bardot, who knew her father and offered Maria a room in her house.

Through Bardot, Maria also met important figures in the film business. Warren Beatty introduced her to the William Morris agency, and her first break came in 1970, when she appeared in *Madly*, starring Alain Delon and directed by Roger Kahane. She had been offered a role in another film with Delon when the offer came in for *Last Tango In Paris*. Her inclination was to turn down Bertolucci, but the agency told her: 'It's a leading role with Marlon Brando — you can't refuse.'

Latterly in her spare time she had worked for The Wheel Turns, an organisation which supports actors, dancers and other performers who have reached the end of their careers. 'It's a very precarious existence,' she explained. 'My advice to young actors would be to know how to do another job.' For those women who persisted with the profession, she had another piece of advice: 'Never take your clothes off for middle-aged men who claim that it's art.'

⁓ 4th ⁓

Liberace, b. 1919, d. 1987

L iberace, the flamboyant American popular pianist who has died aged sixty-seven, was the world's highest paid performer throughout the 1960s and 1970s.

His extraordinary success as an entertainer can be credited to his peculiarly American synthesis of sentimentality, bravado and showmanship.

But as one devoted to extravagance in an age of puritanical austerity, there was bound to be a backlash. It came in peculiarly venomous form from the journalist William Connor writing as 'Cassandra' in the *Daily Mirror* in 1956, when Liberace appeared at the London Palladium.

Cassandra described the performer as 'this deadly, winking, sniggering, snuggling, chromium-plated, scent-impregnated, luminous, quivering, giggling, fruit-flavoured, mincing, ice-covered heap of mother-love'. After denying his homosexuality in the High Court in London in 1959, Liberace won libel damages of £8,000 and an apology.

Wladziu Valentine Liberace (known to his besotted public as 'Lee') was born in Milwaukee on 16 May 1919. His Italian father had enjoyed some small success as a bit-part actor in silent movies before concentrating on his career as a grocer.

His Polish mother, Frances, had been a concert pianist before her marriage, and throughout her life maintained her interest in show business, calling Liberace's younger brother Rudolph Valentino Liberace after the screen idol of the time.

A child prodigy, Liberace's career began on more formal lines than those along which it would progress. But after one tour as a soloist with the Chicago Symphony Orchestra, he found himself attracted to a less-restrained form of music and dress, much to the chagrin of his father, a musical purist.

He found much sympathy, though, from his mother, to whom he always remained devoted, later exhibiting many of her personal effects, including her knitting basket, in his own Liberace museum in Las Vegas.

This attachment to his mother was to form an important part of his stage persona: invariably in attendance at his concerts, she would happily wear furs and jewellery identical to her performing son's.

Perhaps to lend himself an air of ruggedness with which nature had not chosen to endow him, he adopted the stage name 'Walter Busterkeys' when he embarked on his early career in a dance band, but swiftly changed hats, calling himself simply 'Liberace' and playing up his already bizarre character.

'I began to disarm my audience and say what people were thinking before they could say it. I heckled myself,' he once said.

The first sign that Liberace had embarked upon a road along which reticence would never ride came when he placed a candelabra on his piano when playing for the dance band. At this, the dam of discretion appeared to burst: first came a white tail suit, followed by stage patter about his mother and his philosophy of life, then a gold lamé jacket and a diamond-studded tailcoat.

His piano playing, though unfaltering, was never rigid in its adherence to tradition: of the 153 pages of Tchaikovsky's *First Piano Concerto*, he would perform only the first twelve and the last four, adding four bars in the middle of his own creation.

As success grew, so too did flamboyance: in 1984 he was spotted wearing a $300,000 rhinestone-studded Norwegian blue fox cape with a 16-foot train; and in 1986, stepping on stage out of a Rolls-Royce painted with the Stars and Stripes, he was witnessed in red, white and blue hot pants.

Liberace's private tastes were similarly steeped in an absence of sobriety. His master bedroom was painted with a re-creation of the Sistine Chapel ceiling, his lawn was centrally heated, his swimming pool was piano-shaped and among his possessions – or 'happy-happies' as he liked to call them – was a piano made out of 10,000 toothpicks.

He is also credited with having invented a lavatory that could disappear into a bathroom floor at the flick of a switch. 'There's no reason why you should walk into a bathroom and see a toilet. It's unglamorous,' he explained.

⊰ 5th ⊱

Pamela Harriman, b. 1920, d. 1997

Pamela Harriman, the American ambassador in Paris who has died aged seventy-six, was proudly described by her second husband as 'the greatest courtesan of the century'.

From obscure, if aristocratic, beginnings in Dorset, she became in turn Winston Churchill's daughter-in-law, the lover of some of the world's richest men, a powerful Washington hostess, a multi-millionairess and, finally, a successful diplomat.

All this, and much more, Pamela Harriman achieved through the clear-sightedness with which she marked down her quarries, the ruthlessness with which she pursued them, the seeming indifference with which she shrugged off criticism, and the courage and energy with which she accepted reverses and marched on to new conquests. She was never guilty of self-pity.

Red-haired, but with a tendency to dumpiness, Pamela Harriman was far from being an overwhelming beauty – though 'the best facelift in the world' (as friends described an event which she herself refused to acknowledge), together with her undimmed vitality, made her an exceptionally stunning seventy-year-old.

Her secret lay in her ability to make any man at whom she set her cap feel that he was the sole object of her attention. Women tended to be less impressed. Yet part of her skill was to subsume her own ambitions in those of her conquests.

'She's interesting because she has fantastic taste,' Truman Capote considered, 'but she has no intellectual capacities at all. She's some sort of marvellous primitive. I don't think she's ever read a book or even a newspaper except for the gossip column. Pamela's a geisha girl who's made every man happy.'

The talent ran in her family. She was born Pamela Beryl Digby at Farnborough, Kent, on 20 March 1920, the first of four children born to Edward Kenelm Digby, who succeeded as the 11th Lord Digby two months after her birth. Pamela's mother was a daughter of the 2nd Lord Aberdare.

'Something in all the Digbys caused them to win renown by being at odds with society,' wrote the biographer of Sir Kenelm Digby (1603–65). The rogue gene was still active in the nineteenth century when a Jane Digby became one of the great adventuresses of her time, leaving a trail of husbands and lovers from Bavaria to Syria.

Pamela was sent away to Downham School in Hertfordshire, before being 'finished' in Paris – an episode later inflated into 'postgraduate work at the Sorbonne'. She also went to Germany where, she claimed, Unity Mitford introduced her to the Führer.

In 1938 Pamela Digby returned to do 'the season'. 'She was very plump and so bosomy that we all called her "the dairy maid",' one of her contemporaries remembered. 'She wore high heels and tossed her bottom around. We thought she was quite outrageous. She was known as hot stuff, a very sexy young thing.'

On coming out she was taken up by Lady Baillie, whose Leeds Castle set was a rival to that at Cliveden. Pamela Digby was delighted to be drawn into the ambit of men of power and influence.

In 1939 she met Randolph Churchill, and notwithstanding dire warnings on every side married him three weeks later. Nine years older than she, he already had a reputation as an alcoholic roustabout, and it did not help that he insisted on reading Gibbon aloud to her during their honeymoon. Fidelity he never even attempted.

Worse, his capacity for accumulating debts left her constantly short of money, breeding in her two enduring characteristics: insatiable avarice and a dislike of English men – which eventually came to embrace the entire country.

Nevertheless, she established excellent relations with her parents-in-law, Winston and Clementine Churchill, and while Randolph was away lived at 10 Downing Street and Chequers. Her alliance with the Prime Minister was sealed by the birth of young Winston in October 1940.

As Pamela Churchill's marriage deteriorated, she amused herself with American servicemen; Sir Charles Portal, the British Chief of Air Staff, was also much struck. But she did not confine herself to the military; her American admirers included William Paley, the president of CBS, Jock Whitney, who would later be American ambassador to London, and the broadcaster Ed Murrow.

Her most notable conquest was Averell Harriman, President Roosevelt's Lend-Lease envoy and twenty-eight years her senior. Their liaison was encouraged by Lord Beaverbrook, who gave her money for clothes, and condoned by Winston Churchill, who saw Pamela's potential as a conduit of information between the Allies. The affair ended when Harriman was sent as ambassador to Moscow in 1943.

By this time her attitude to Randolph had become vitriolic. 'Panto [Pamela] hates him so much that she can't sit in a room with him,' recorded Evelyn Waugh in May 1942.

They were divorced in 1946, though Pamela always remained loth to relinquish the name of Churchill. For a while she worked for Beaverbrook on the *Evening Standard*'s Londoner's Diary, but her journalistic career did not survive her conquest of Prince Ali Khan.

In 1948 she moved to Paris and pursued an affair with Gianni Agnelli, heir to the Fiat empire. But though she nursed him back to health after a serious car crash, and even joined the Roman Catholic Church (which duly produced an annulment for her), he would not contemplate marriage. When she became pregnant she had an abortion.

She became a friend of the Greek shipping magnate Stavros Niarchos, and the lover of the French banker Elie de Rothschild. But de Rothschild, like Agnelli, preferred to finance her as a mistress rather than indulge her as a wife. 'They just don't want to marry her,' Truman Capote gleefully observed.

Pamela Churchill did not repine; she turned to America, where she settled on Leland Hayward, a theatrical impresario and the producer of *The Sound of Music*. He had been married five times (though only to four women); and in 1962 the number increased to six.

Though he turned out to be less than colossally rich – and such fortune as he possessed was speedily diminished by her taste for interior decoration – the marriage was a success. Pamela Hayward looked after her husband devotedly as his health failed.

When he died in 1971, she moved speedily into action. Spurned by Frank Sinatra, that August she found herself – whether by chance or design – sitting next to her old flame Averell Harriman (now seventy-nine, recently widowed and one of the richest men in America) at a Washington dinner party given by Katharine Graham, editor of the *Washington Post*. The opportunity was not wasted; they were married at the end of September 1971. In December Pamela Harriman became an American citizen.

Averell Harriman was a pillar of the Democratic Party, to which Pamela, though instinctively conservative, now conformed. Their house in Georgetown, Washington, became the unofficial heart of the party in exile during the years of Reagan and Bush.

Pamela Harriman proved herself an incomparable hostess and fundraiser, and invitations to her parties became as prized as those to the White House. Though still no intellectual, she began to acquaint herself with foreign policy issues, and accompanied Harriman on trips to the Soviet Union. In consequence, when Raisa Gorbachev visited America in 1987 she had tea with Pamela Harriman rather than Nancy Reagan.

Harriman had died in 1986, leaving her a fortune and a leading position in the Democratic Party. Her choice for the 1988 nomination was Al Gore; in the event she had to make do with Michael Dukakis, who caused her considerable alarm on his visit to her house by threatening to slip off a narrow podium into her proudest possession, Van Gogh's *White Roses*.

In 1992 Pamela Harriman gravitated to Bill Clinton, who delighted her by picking Gore as Vice President. After his election President Clinton appointed her the American ambassador in Paris, the post once held by Benjamin Franklin and Thomas Jefferson.

Her energy and social adroitness ensured her success in Paris. But Pamela Harriman had become embroiled in controversy over the management of trusts which Harriman had left her, and from which his two daughters drew income. At first all went well, but between 1989 and 1993 $21 million of the trust money was poured into a hotel and conference centre in New Jersey that failed.

In 1994 the Harriman heirs, whom Pamela Harriman had treated with disdain, instituted a lawsuit alleging that she had squandered the family funds. A settlement was reached at the end of 1995, but the cost was evidently considerable: Pamela Harriman sold three of her paintings (a Picasso, a Renoir and a Matisse) for $11 million, as well as one of her two houses in Georgetown.

⊰ **6th** ⊱

Sir Peter Saunders, b. 1911, d. 2003

Sir Peter Saunders, the theatre manager, owner and producer who has died aged ninety-one, mastered the art of a long run with one of his earliest West End productions, *The Mousetrap*.

Under his aegis, the murder mystery by Agatha Christie opened on tour at Nottingham on 6 October 1952, and in London on 25 November 1952. It has since come to outlast everything else in the history of the theatre. The more records it broke, the more Saunders determined to break those that remained. Finally, when it had surpassed all previous runs, there was nothing left to beat and Saunders could not bear to bring it to an end.

Yet at the beginning, nobody thought that highly of the drama. Agatha Christie herself supposed it was worth 'a nice little run of six months' and gave the copyright to her teenage grandson, Mathew Prichard. When the play opened, initially directed by Peter Cotes and starring Richard Attenborough, the critics praised it for 'sustaining the curiosity', but no more. The secret of its enduring success remains wholly unfathomable.

The plot, which concerns a collection of people snowed up in a country guest house, one of them being a murderer and two his intended victims, certainly engages the sleuthing instincts of the audience. But the play is otherwise unremarkable and, as the decades wore on, began to look decidedly dated. Despite brave attempts to update the text with mentions of 'TV licences' and 'a Jeep', its references to domestic staff, retired majors and villains who wore felt hats made it resemble a live version of the board game Cluedo.

Yet still the audiences flowed in. In December 1971, it became the longest-running production the world had ever seen. Every night at the Ambassadors from 1952 until 1974, and since then next door at St Martin's, the queues formed. Certainly a high proportion of those buying tickets were tourists, and the play's run became self-generating. But Saunders was highly skilled at marketing, and ran advertisements in the newspapers on ships crossing the Atlantic, with the prices in dollars and the news that afternoon teas ('a quaint old English custom') were available at matinees.

Whatever the reason for the play's success, it mattered not to Saunders who, for much of the time, owned the leases of the two theatres in which he was putting on the play. His only difficulty came in repeating his feat. Nearly everything else he produced was more interesting, but he could never rediscover the formula. Nor, in all probability, will anyone else.

Peter Saunders was born at Swiss Cottage, north London, on 23 November 1911, and was educated at Oundle; he saw his first play as a schoolboy and it was, strangely enough, a thriller at the Ambassadors. His first job was as a film cameraman. He then directed one, unsuccessful, film before taking a job as a reporter on the *Daily Express* in Glasgow; his next job was as press agent to the bandleader Harry Roy.

In the Second World War, Saunders joined the Army, serving in the Intelligence Corps. His staff sergeant, A.P. Dearsley, had written a play; he showed it to Saunders, who liked it and promised to try to get it produced in the West End after the war. It was a promise he kept: *Fly Away Peter*, which Saunders staged with the £2,700 he had saved during his six years in the Army, marked his debut as a theatrical manager.

His autobiography, published in 1972, was entitled *The Mousetrap Man*. He perhaps took his identification with his greatest success a little too far in renaming his Hampstead home Monkswell, after the house featured in *The Mousetrap*.

⚜ 7th ⚜

Norman Thelwell, b. 1923, d. 2004

Norman Thelwell, who has died aged eighty, created some of the most recognisable images in equine art with his cartoons of freckled girls being bounced along on the backs of their recalcitrant, spherical ponies.

His first of more than twenty-five cartoon books, *Angels on Horseback*, appeared in 1957 and has never been out of print. Like those of Giles, Thelwell's books had a place in the downstairs lavatory of almost every country house. Ponies of a certain shape and temper became known as 'Thelwells'.

He claimed to have no horse sense and to have ridden only once in his life. Horses, he declared, were 'great windy things that'll grab your coat off your back as soon as look at you'.

Norman Thelwell was born on 3 May 1923 at Birkenhead, one of two sons of Christopher and Emily Thelwell. The family lived in a small terraced house which

Norman's mother kept spotless; as he recalled, she 'thought that anyone who didn't move the wardrobes once a week to dust underneath was a bit suspect'.

He went to Rock Ferry High School, which had no art room, and left aged sixteen to become a junior clerk in an office. The Second World War had already broken out and at eighteen he joined the East Yorkshire Regiment as an infantryman. Happy to carry extra weight in the form of his sketchbook and paints, he dashed off extraordinarily vivid pen-and-ink drawings of his fellow soldiers.

The first and last time he ever rode was while serving in India, when his horse bolted with Thelwell clinging on around his neck.

His clerking job in Birkenhead had been held for him post-war, but one day of it was enough; he handed in his cards and, after obtaining a government grant for ex-servicemen, enrolled at Liverpool College of Art, where he completed the five-year degree course in three years. By this time he was married to Rhona Ladbury, herself a painter, whom he had met while attending a life class in the evenings in Nottingham.

They lived next to a field which contained two fat, hairy ponies of uncertain temper. 'They were owned by two little girls about three feet high who could have done with losing a few pounds themselves,' he recalled. 'They would arrive to collect their mounts in yellow pullovers, tiny jodhpurs and velvet safety helmets. I could hear the air whisper as they tested their whips – so could Thunder and Lightning, who pointedly ignored them and went on grazing.

'As the children got near, the ponies would swing round and present their ample hindquarters and give a few lightning kicks which the children would sidestep calmly, and they had the head-collars on those animals before they knew what was happening. I was astonished at how meekly they were led away; but they were planning vengeance – you could tell by their eyes.'

Thelwell enjoyed renovating old buildings to live in. After reconstructing a derelict Cornish mill and its outbuildings – described in his book *A Millstone Round My Neck* (1981) – he moved to Heron's Mead, a cottage on the Hampshire Test, near Romsey, with seven acres, where he landscaped a garden and lake; this gave rise to another book, *A Plank Bridge by a Pool* (1978).

A contented man, he rarely left home, except to play boules in the New Forest with friends on Thursday afternoons, and to visit the pub with his wife. Otherwise he would spend hours wandering around his garden or in a small dinghy on the lake. He did not much care for things foreign, and never acquired a taste for pasta or pizza. Whenever he went on holiday he could not wait to get home.

8th

Elisabeth Mann Borgese, b. 1918, d. 2002

Elisabeth Mann Borgese, who has died aged eighty-three, was the last surviving child of the German novelist Thomas Mann and successful herself in several different fields: as an anthropologist; as a political scientist; as an environmentalist with a special interest in oceans; and as a writer of short stories.

One of her more outlandish achievements, at the end of her life, was to train an English setter to play piano duets with her. To this end she had a special piano made – with no legs and no black notes, and with keys twice as wide as normal. A visitor wrote the following account of the performance:

'Mrs Mann Borgese sat down on the floor at the left of the keyboard, and the dog took his place to the right of middle C. They performed two short duets, one by Schumann and the other by Mozart. Encouraged by praise, pats on the head and pieces of meat fed to him during unscored pauses, the dog mostly hit the right note at the right moment. Certainly he had a good sense of rhythm. He made a few mistakes, but she explained this by saying he'd gone for three weeks without practising while she was away.'

Bram van der Stok, b. 1915, d. 1993

Bram van der Stok, who has died in Hawaii aged seventy-seven, was one of only three Allied airmen prisoners of war to make the 'home run' to Britain after the 'Great Escape' from Stalag Luft III.

Of the seventy-five who made it out of the camp in Lower Silesia on the night of 24 March 1944, all but Flt Lt 'Bob' van der Stok, Sgt Per Bergsland and Pilot Officer Jens Muller were recaptured. Angered by the escape, Hitler ordered fifty of those recaptured to be shot.

For almost a year before the escape Van der Stok had helped with the construction of three tunnels, named 'Tom', 'Dick' and 'Harry'; Tom was discovered, Dick was abandoned, Harry was used.

When the great night came some 220 escapers prepared to crawl through the tunnel, but disruptions – due to its falling short and to cave-ins – restricted the escapers to seventy-five.

Van der Stok was the eighteenth to emerge from the tunnel, posing as Hendrik Beeldman, a Dutch draughtsman taking home leave from Siemens. He wore a dark blue Royal Australian Air Force greatcoat, Dutch naval trousers and a beret. His passes were lodged in an imitation leather wallet made by Flt Lt G.W. Walenn, head of the camp forgery department – and one of the fifty murdered officers.

As he walked to Sagan railway station, Van der Stok was asked by a German civilian what he was doing in the woods. He replied that he was a Dutch worker, afraid that the police might arrest him for being out during an air raid.

'It's all right if you're with me,' said the German, who escorted him to the station, where he had to wait three hours because trains were delayed by a large RAF raid on Berlin. Some thirty-six hours later he arrived at Utrecht, after changing trains at Breslau, Dresden and Halle.

His parents and other members of the family were living there, but Van der Stok resisted the temptation to go home and holed up two streets away in a friend's house. After six weeks he was fed into the Dutch-Paris Escape Line and smuggled by skiff across the Maas and into Belgium. He then bicycled to Brussels, where he was put up by a Dutch family for six weeks until the Line could send him on by train.

Van der Stok had by now changed his cover story, and represented himself as a Flemish worker in a Belgian firm. When he reached Toulouse he sold his watch to raise money towards the 10,000 francs required for guidance across the Pyrenees.

His guide, though, was shot dead in a skirmish with frontier guards. Van der Stok fell in with a maquis band which led him through the mountains to the edge of Spain. From Madrid he was passed to Gibraltar, and then flown in a Douglas Dakota transport to Bristol.

Bram van der Stok was born on 13 October 1915 on Sumatra, where his father was a Shell engineer. He spent his boyhood there, in Holland and the Dutch West Indies.

After finishing his education at the Lyceum Alpinum in Switzerland he studied Medicine at Leiden University. But rowing and ice hockey distracted him from his studies and in 1936 he joined the Dutch Air Force. Commissioned the next year, he joined a fighter squadron. After a year he transferred to the reserve and resumed his medical training, this time at Utrecht University.

He was mobilised in 1939 and in May 1940 fought as a fighter pilot until the Dutch capitulation. He was then permitted to continue his medical studies. He formed a resistance cell, and made three unsuccessful attempts to reach Britain. On the fourth attempt he reached Scotland in a boat in June 1941, and Queen Wilhelmina decorated him with the Dutch Bronze Cross.

Van der Stok was commissioned into the RAFVR and posted to No. 91, a Spitfire squadron based at Tangmere. Shortly afterwards he was transferred to No. 41 Squadron, flying Spitfires from Westhampnett.

Promoted flight lieutenant, he became a flight commander and was credited with six victories before baling out over France. 'Only six kills,' said his German captors. 'You are just a beginner.'

At Stalag Luft III his medical knowledge obtained him a job in the hospital.

After the Great Escape van der Stok rejoined No. 91 Squadron and took part in D-Day and anti-V1 operations. In 1945, following a period with No. 74 Squadron, he moved to No. 322, a Dutch squadron serving in the RAF and based in Holland.

This enabled him to visit his family and learn that his two brothers had died in concentration camps and his father had been blinded by the Gestapo.

After the war he joined the Dutch air staff at The Hague and helped introduce the new Dutch Air Force before returning in 1946 to Utrecht University, where he finally qualified as a doctor in 1951.

Later he emigrated to America with his wife, Petie, and their three small children. He specialised in obstetrics and gynaecology at Syracuse, New York, before joining Nasa's space lab research team at Huntsville, Alabama.

In 1970 van der Stok moved to Honolulu, where he practised medicine, joined the US Coastguard and took part in 162 rescues. He was appointed MBE in 1945 and received numerous other awards.

Anna Nicole Smith, b. 1967, d. 2007

Anna Nicole Smith, who has died aged thirty-nine, was a former stripper and *Playboy* centrefold and became a star of American reality television on the strength of her eye-popping figure and her brief, notorious marriage to one of the richest oilmen in Texas.

In 1991, as a penniless 22-year-old, she was pole-dancing at a seedy club in Houston when she caught the eye of J. Howard Marshall II, a Yale-educated, wheelchair-bound tycoon almost four times her age. He had a reported $1.4 billion fortune in oil stocks and 'a strong yearning', as his son later put it, 'for large breasts'.

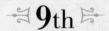

9th

Canon John Hester, b. 1927, d. 2008

Canon John Hester, who has died aged eighty, devoted his ministry predominantly to members of the entertainment professions, particularly between 1963 and 1975, when he was rector of Soho and senior chaplain of the Actors' Church Union.

He evinced a particular sensitivity to the strains and stresses experienced by thespians – ever on the move and treading the narrow line between fiction and reality. Always welcome backstage and in dressing rooms, he would give a nervous leading lady a first-night blessing, sometimes celebrate Holy Communion for the cast, and always be available for conversation and counsel.

He was therefore a natural choice for the special demands of ministry in Soho, where the parish included film studios as well as theatres and (in the days before Westminster City Council tightened its control of the area) fifty strip clubs, many pornography outlets, homosexual bars and clubs, and a large company of prostitutes.

The parish church, St Anne's, had been virtually destroyed by wartime bombing in 1940 – only its tower was left standing – and the rector worked from a tiny chapel and a meeting place known as St Anne's House.

Every day, and often late into the night, Hester's neatly bearded and becassocked figure was to be observed going in and out of establishments not normally frequented by clergymen; but he eschewed the cassock when visiting homosexual clubs after this was confused with 'drag'. His attitude to the activities of some of his parishioners was nothing if not tolerant, and surprising to many even in the liberal 1960s and 1970s.

'A striptease performance,' he declared, 'is a display of beauty, sipped and its bouquet savoured, as one might do with a rare and delightful wine.' Describing its opponents as 'puritans', he added: 'Arrested personalities might easily turn to far more vicious, anti-social behaviour if they did not find the sort of release which striptease gives.'

On pornography, his views were equally positive – 'It caters for areas of inadequacy and repression which are present in us all' – and he deplored the fact that the magazine *Penthouse* was required by law to ensure that in pictures of nude women 'their most characteristically feminine feature was obscured by pose or drapery'.

Hester sympathised with prostitutes who, he said, 'spend much of their time catering for the needs of the physically and emotionally handicapped'. Nonetheless, he recognised the serious social problems created by the unconventional and sometimes criminal elements in his parish, and he chaired the Soho Project, which brought together doctors, police, social workers and others concerned with the many human casualties. He was also chairman of the Theatre Girls' Club – a hostel for thirty-five young women working in or studying for various branches of the entertainment profession.

John Fraser Hester was born at West Hartlepool on 21 January 1927. He was educated at the local grammar school. He went to St Edmund's Hall, Oxford, on a scholarship, and after training at Cuddesdon Theological College became a curate at St George's church, Southall, in west London, from 1952 to 1955. He then spent three years as a curate at the church of the Holy Redeemer in Clerkenwell, where the possibility of a special ministry in the entertainment world was first recognised.

After Soho, Hester was for ten years vicar of Brighton which – at that point in its history – was bound to be something of an anticlimax, though Hester found some scope for the continuation of his work among the seaside entertainers.

From 1985 to 1997 he was a canon residentiary of Chichester Cathedral which, with neither a strip club nor a sex shop in sight, gave him only minimal satisfaction. Besides his other commitments, he was often away leading pilgrimages. His interest in travel started when, between National Service and Cuddesdon, he spent a year as personal assistant to the Bishop of Gibraltar, accompanying him to many places in his far-flung diocese. Later Hester led innumerable pilgrimages to the Holy Land and to various other parts of the world. Unsurprisingly, perhaps, he was well known in Las Vegas.

⊰ 10th ⊱

Giulio Bich, b. 1907, d. 2003

Giulio Bich, who has died aged ninety-five, was the last survivor of one of the most dramatic episodes in the history of Arctic exploration, the search for the survivors of the airship *Italia*, which crashed on to the pack ice while returning from the North Pole in 1928.

Two years earlier, an expedition led by Roald Amundsen and the American adventurer Lincoln Ellsworth had crossed the Pole in a dirigible piloted by an Italian engineer, Umberto Nobile. Had not Richard Byrd, three days before, made his controversial claim to have reached the Pole in an aeroplane, Nobile's would have been the first flight over it.

Encouraged by Mussolini's jingoistic regime, Nobile quickly made plans for another voyage, which he hoped would land at the Pole itself, as well as explore the still largely uncharted frozen wilderness. He made thorough preparations, including selecting a potential rescue party of nine Alpine soldiers, chosen for their expertise in the snow. Among them was Bich, then a twenty-year-old corporal in the Aosta Battalion.

The troops were sent on ahead in March 1928 to Nobile's base at Spitsbergen, part of the Norwegian territories in the Arctic. None of the mountain-raised soldiers had seen the sea before, and the voyage north in the expedition supply ship took forty days. It was, Bich recalled, 'like being crucified'.

Having started at Milan, Nobile's craft, the *Italia*, reached the Pole on 24 May. On board was a crew of eighteen, and his fox terrier, Titina. High winds prevented them from landing, and then, as they began to return to Spitsbergen, an elevator jammed, causing the dirigible to lose hydrogen. Slowly it became heavier, and 180 miles from base began to drop with increasing velocity towards the ice. The crash separated the gondola from the envelope itself which, with six men inside, drifted upwards out of sight and was never seen again.

There were nine survivors (and Titina), although most, including Nobile, had multiple broken bones. They had some provisions, a four-man tent and a radio set, but were otherwise at the mercy of the elements, and hungry polar bears. After ten days, their SOS appeal was heard by a Russian farmer listening on ham radio, and half a dozen nations – including Norway and Soviet Russia – sent out search parties. Their efforts to locate Nobile's party – by now drifting with the ice – were, however, largely unco-ordinated, and nine of the rescuers lost their own lives, most notably Amundsen, whose aircraft disappeared over the Arctic Ocean.

The Italians, meanwhile, had been slow off the mark, even though the eyes of the world were focused on the disaster. The petty jealousies of the army, navy and air ministries meant that Bich and his fellow soldiers were not permitted to scout for the survivors until 3 June, when they set out on to the ice in two-man patrols. Bich himself and two others were attached to the whaler *Braganza* and sent to investigate a possible location of the 'red tent', as Nobile's camp became known from the aniline dye he had smeared on his bivouac in the hope of making it more visible.

Bich endured a nightmarish, and fruitless, week's search on the ice. Battered by winds and snow, his party constantly had to remove their skis to cross broken floes, and it was so cold that they could not sleep. Instead, they walked across the pack for almost five days without stopping, sustained only by handfuls of pemmican. Its taste ever after haunted Bich's memories. On 12 June, much to the soldiers' frustration, a dispute between the service ministries led to their being recalled to the ship.

It was not until a week later that an Italian pilot managed to locate the tent and drop supplies. Nobile was then picked up by a Swedish flier, but the aeroplane crashed when the Swede returned for the others and he had himself to be rescued.

The remaining five survivors, by now stranded on a rapidly melting floe, were finally taken aboard a Russian ice-breaker after spending forty-nine days in the snowy wastes. Three other men had set off earlier to try to walk to Spitsbergen. Only two were later picked up, one of their number having dug his own grave in the ice before lying down to die. That the other two survived for another twelve days without food led some to believe that they had subsequently dug up their companion and eaten him.

Bich and his fellow alpinists were hailed as heroes in Italy, where the Fascist press otherwise portrayed the episode as a blow to national pride. Nobile was vilified – not least for having agreed to be rescued before his crew – and he ultimately emigrated to Russia. His reputation was not restored until after the fall of Mussolini.

Giulio Bich, the son of a tailor, was born in 1907 and grew up in Valtournenche, a mountain village in the shadow of the Matterhorn in the Italian Alps. His three brothers all became well-known guides; one was killed in an attempt on the Dent d'Herens, the neighbouring peak to the Matterhorn.

While still young, Bich worked as a porter on alpine expeditions, and after leaving the army qualified as a ski instructor in 1934 and as a guide in 1938. His expertise was soon being sought out by visiting personalities such as the Duke of Aosta, commander of Italy's forces in Africa during the Second World War. After one rescue, Bich was awarded a civil medal for bravery, and in 1942 was chosen to show the Queen of Italy, Maria Jose, the path up the Matterhorn.

Despite becoming – in what is a highly competitive profession – the best-known guide in the region, Bich always retained his innate modesty and spontaneous good humour. He retired in 1976, aged nearly seventy, and settled near Cervinia, in the Valle d'Aosta.

❧ 11th ❧

Willem Kolff, b. 1911, d. 2009

Willem Kolff, who has died aged 97, was one of the creative geniuses of twentieth-century medicine, responsible for the invention of the kidney dialysis machine and instrumental in the development of the artificial heart and the artificial eye; more remarkable still, his greatest achievements took place in the Netherlands at the height of the German occupation.

As a young physician in the Dutch city of Groningen before the war, Kolff had witnessed the death of a 22-year-old man from kidney failure. It was a miserable, painful end and Kolff had to tell the man's mother, who was dressed 'in a black dress and a little white cap like the farm women have', that her only son was going to die and that there was nothing he could do. It struck him that if only he could somehow have removed the urea that the patient was creating, then he might have had a chance.

The man died, but Kolff immediately devoted himself to research, though it was only in 1941, by which time the Netherlands was under German occupation, that he succeeded in developing a prototype machine. Materials were in short supply and much of what was available was commandeered by the Germans. Nonetheless Kolff set to work, begging and borrowing from a local factory, salvaging a cooling system from an old Ford car and metal pieces from a downed German fighter plane.

Eventually he fashioned a machine out of cellophane sausage skins wrapped around a cylinder, resting in an enamel bath of cleansing fluid. The patient's blood would be drawn through the tubing, into the bath, cleaned, and passed back into the body.

In 1943 he tested the machine on his first patient, who died, as did several others. Yet Kolff persisted, his hopes of success encouraged by fact that, despite the loss of life, his machine proved amazingly successful at replicating the effects of the human kidney.

The breakthrough came a month after the war ended, in August 1945, when Kolff was asked to treat Maria Schafstad, a 65-year-old woman who had been imprisoned as a Nazi collaborator but was in a coma due to renal failure.

Though he realised that many of his fellow countrymen 'would have liked to wring her neck', he accepted his Hippocratic duty as a doctor. After many hours of treatment, he recalled, 'she slowly opened her eyes and said, "I'm going to divorce my husband."' She did and lived for six more years before dying of causes unrelated to her kidney problems.

Willem Johan Kolff, known to his family as Pim, was born on 14 February 1911 at Leiden.

He studied at Leiden University, where he became an assistant in pathological anatomy and made his first invention – a device which helped patients with poor circulation by intermittently inflating then deflating a cuff fitted round the leg.

On the day of the German invasion, 19 May 1940, Kolff happened to be in The Hague attending a funeral. Seeing German bombers pass overhead, he made his excuses and went straight to the city's main hospital, where casualties were already pouring in, and asked if they would like him to set up a blood bank.

Provided with a car and an armed escort, he drove through the city's streets, dodging sniper bullets, and bought bottles, tubes, needles, citrate and other paraphernalia. Four days later, he was in business, storing supplies of blood, blood plasma and concentrated red blood cells. It was the first blood bank in Europe.

A month after the invasion, Kolff's mentor, the Jewish hospital director at Groningen, committed suicide and a Nazi was appointed in his place. Not wishing to work with the man, Kolff applied for a post in a small hospital in the town of Kampen, where he remained for the rest of the war.

Kolff did what he could to assist the local Resistance, providing medical 'alibis' for those wanting to avoid detection. On one occasion he was approached by a local Resistance leader who was wanted for questioning.

The man wondered if Kolff could help him to simulate so serious an illness as to require his hospitalisation, so there would be no point in the Germans arresting him. Kolff took a couple of pints of blood from the man's arm, which he then poured into his stomach through a tube. This produced the loose, black and offensive stool characteristic of severe bleeding from the gut.

He instructed his 'patient' in the symptoms of a bleeding ulcer, and sent a blood and stool specimen off to the laboratory, which confirmed that the man was both very anaemic and had a large amount of blood in his stool. The 'ulcer' failed to improve and the man was forced to prolong his stay in hospital until the danger passed.

After the war, in 1950, Kolff left the Netherlands, sensing better opportunities in America. At the Cleveland Clinic, he was involved in the development of heart-lung machines to oxygenate blood and maintain heart and pulmonary function during cardiac surgery. He also improved his dialysis machine.

In 1967 he became head of the University of Utah's Division of Artificial

Organs and Institute for Biomedical Engineering. Here he was instrumental in the development of the artificial heart, the first of which was implanted in a patient in 1982.

Kolff also carried out research which showed that the electrical stimulation of certain parts of the brains of blind people could produce the sensation of seeing points of light. His research bore fruit when in 1999 his collaborator William Dobelle fitted a Brooklyn man with the world's first artificial eye.

After sixty years, he separated from his wife, his inability to give up making things with pipes and tubes reportedly having proved too much for her.

Maurice Rickards, b. 1919, d. 1998

Maurice Rickards, who has died aged seventy-eight, founded, in 1975, the Ephemera Society, which attracted a worldwide membership of collectors and scholars as well as anorak-clad frequenters of flea markets.

The society 'devoted to the conservation, study and presentation of printed and handwritten ephemera' made an academic discipline out of things that end up in wastepaper baskets – receipts, tickets, timetables, tax demands, school reports and instruction sheets.

Sir John Betjeman was its first president, and Rickards served as chairman and later vice-president, helping to establish satellite societies in other countries including Norway, where collectors were persuaded to broaden their interests from a narrow dedication to sardine-tin labels.

12th

Screamin' Jay Hawkins, b. 1929, d. 2000

Screamin' Jay Hawkins, who has died aged seventy, was a performer whose bizarre and frenzied act caused a sensation in the early days of rock and roll; even more than Little Richard, he epitomised the wild and ungovernable aspect of the music.

Hawkins projected a crazed and dangerous persona on stage. He would be carried on in a coffin, dressed in a Dracula-style cape, and throughout the proceedings make use of such props as a rubber snake, a large plastic tarantula, various voodoo objects and a cigarette-smoking skull named Henry.

Sometimes he wore a bone in his nose. He had a penchant, too, for fire, and more than once set himself alight, causing considerable injury. His flamboyant showmanship, he claimed, derived from his love of opera and its extravagant spectacle.

Jalacy Hawkins was born on 18 July 1929 in Cleveland, Ohio. Abandoned at birth, he was later adopted by an American Indian family. He began teaching himself the piano as a child and showed promise as an amateur boxer, winning the Golden Gloves middleweight championship in 1949.

After serving in the US Army, he worked first as a pianist to the guitarist and bandleader Tiny Grimes, and later joined Fats Domino's band. Domino sacked him for insisting on appearing in a gold and leopardskin suit and turban.

By 1955, Hawkins was working as a solo act. His most famous song, 'I Put A Spell On You', dates from the following year. Although his own manic recorded version did not score a chart hit, the song itself became hugely popular and was later recorded by many other artists, among them Nina Simone, The Who and The Animals. Among his later songs were 'Alligator Wine', 'Feast Of Mau-Mau', 'I Hear Voices' and the unbroadcastable 'Constipation Blues'.

In the late 1960s Hawkins moved to Hawaii and teamed up with the singer Shoutin' Pat Newborn. The collaboration prospered until she knifed him in a jealous rage. He returned to mainland America and in 1980 opened for the Rolling Stones at Madison Square Garden. He became friends with Keith Richards, who played guitar on a Hawkins recording session in the same year.

When he was nearly sixty, Hawkins began taking small parts in movies, in particular the films of Jim Jarmusch. He appears in *Mystery Train* (1989, as the hotel desk clerk) and *Stranger Than Paradise* (1984), of which 'I Put A Spell On You' is the theme tune.

In recent years Hawkins married a Cameroonian woman (said to have been his ninth wife) and moved to Neuilly, in the suburbs of Paris. He performed infrequently, but his influence had been considerable. Apart from direct imitators, such as Screaming Lord Sutch, a whole generation of frantic rockers, like Black Sabbath, are clearly in his debt.

It is entirely typical that he should have issued elaborate instructions regarding the disposal of his ashes: 'Fly over the ocean and scatter the dust so I can be little particles in everybody's eyes. Drive everybody crazy for the rest of their lives.'

⊰ 13th ⊱

Sister Lucia de Jesus Dos Santos, b. 1907, d. 2005

Sister Lucia de Jesus Dos Santos, who has died aged ninety-seven, was the last of the three children said to have seen apparitions of the Virgin Mary outside the Portuguese town of Fatima in 1917.

On six occasions between May and October 1917, Lucia claimed, the Virgin Mary appeared to her and her cousins, Jacinta and Francisco Marto, while they tended the family sheep. She urged them to pray the rosary daily for world peace and to bear their daily hardships as a sacrifice to ensure that sinners reached heaven.

A crowd of 50,000 arrived at Fatima on 13 October 1917, the date of the final apparition – at which the Virgin had promised a 'miraculous sign so that all may believe'. Thousands claimed that they saw the sun turn red and spin violently on its axis, though others suggested they had merely witnessed an eclipse.

Exactly six months earlier, the Virgin had made her first appearance to the children as they played after lunch on a rocky slope. Seeing a flash of white light over a holm oak tree, they feared a thunderstorm, and were shepherding the flock downhill when they met a lady by the tree 'shining white, brighter than the sun', as Lucia recorded in her memoirs.

Announcing that she was from heaven, the Virgin said that she would appear to them for six successive months, at the same place and on the same day each month, revealing her identity during the final vision.

Subsequently, she confided a terrible vision of hell 'where poor sinners go', showing blackened souls floating in a fiery pool. If humanity did not repent, warned the Virgin, a second, more terrible war would break out.

This was the first of the Three Secrets of Fatima. The second predicted that Russia would return to Christianity and, in 1944, while gravely ill, Lucia sent a sealed envelope containing the contents of the Third Secret of Fatima to the Vatican, with strict instructions that it should not be opened before 1960.

The Pope in 1960, John XXIII, announced that the secret did not concern him, and it mouldered in the Vatican vaults for a further forty years. This prompted rumours that it contained an awful vision of the apocalypse or referred to problems in the Church since the Second Vatican Council. Such speculation even led a former Trappist monk to hijack an Aer Lingus plane in 1981, threatening to blow it up unless the secret was revealed.

When, in 2000, the Church finally disclosed that the secret consisted of an allegorical vision showing a bishop clad in white, who had been shot and was stumbling across a field strewn with corpses to reach the Cross, many were disappointed. Rumours of an undisclosed 'third part of the third secret' abounded; but the Church suggested that the vision was a prophecy of the assassination attempt on John Paul II in St Peter's Square by a Turkish gunman in 1982; John Paul II himself attributed his salvation to the Virgin of Fatima, declaring 'one hand fired and another hand guided the bullet away'.

The next year, he placed the bullet in the crown of the Virgin of Fatima, the image of the Virgin in the Portuguese town; and, in 2000, the Pope beatified Francisco and Jacinta Marto, thus placing them on the path to sainthood. Both had died in childhood, as predicted by the Virgin during the 1917 apparitions. But she had told Lucia that her mission was to remain on earth to spread the Fatima message of prayer, penance and life conversion.

The seventh and last child of Antonio Dos Santos and Maria Rosa e Rosa, Lucia Dos Santos was born on 22 March 1907 at Aljustrel, a hamlet of Fatima. On making her First Holy Communion at the age of seven, Lucia renounced worldly pleasures, preferring instead to meditate on spiritual matters. She had plenty of opportunity when sent, that year, to shepherd the family sheep on land in Fatima. Soon she had her first vision of an angel, a rather blurred apparition resembling, she told her family, 'somebody wrapped up in a sheet'; the description drew much teasing from her siblings.

It came as a shock when, on 13 May 1917, the Virgin Mary appeared to the children over the oak tree. Before ascending to heaven, she opened her hands towards them and, Lucia later wrote, streams of light issued from her hands and appeared to pierce the children's chests. Having announced her reappearances , the Virgin asked for a church to be built on the Cova da Iria, the spot at which she appeared. She added that the First World War, then in its penultimate year, would soon end.

News of the apparitions spread quickly. Although Lucia had urged silence, six-year-old Jacinta found it impossible to say nothing. As Lucia suspected, trouble followed: all the children were interrogated together and separately by priests and a psychologist. Lucia was severely scolded by her mother, who threatened to beat her unless she confessed that the apparitions were a lie.

Shortly before the apparition in August, the regional administrator kidnapped the children and, in a series of separate interviews, threatened to boil them alive in oil if they did not deny the apparitions. When this failed, he cast them for a night into the county jail, where Francisco led the prisoners in prayer and Jacinta danced the fandango with a thief. The children interpreted these hardships as the suffering predicted for them by the Virgin Mary.

By 1925, Lucia had entered their novitiate at Pontevedra, over the border in Spain, where she saw fresh visions of the Virgin and Child Jesus. In 1929 the Virgin Mary instructed Lucia to ask the Pope to say a special prayer, in union with every Catholic bishop in the world, consecrating the entire world – but especially Russia – to her immaculate heart. Only thus, said the Virgin, would Russia be prevented from spreading its errors (Communism).

In 1942, the Pope made the consecration. However, he failed to ask the other Catholic bishops in the world to unite with him in prayer. In 1984, John Paul II repeated the consecration in Rome, this time in union with the world's bishops. For years malcontents speculated that the consecration was incomplete; but in 1989, months after the fall of the Iron Curtain, Sister Lucia announced that 'heaven' had accepted the Pope's 1984 consecration.

Since taking her final vows in 1928 Lucia, now known as Lucia de Jesus, had tried to keep a low profile in the convent, though she was constantly besieged by visitors. She wrote four separate accounts of the 1917 visions to satisfy her bishop and spiritual director, who guessed correctly that Lucia was suppressing the full story. In a letter attached to her fourth memoir, finished in December 1941, Lucia told her bishop that she had finally told all, and felt like a 'skeleton stripped bare and put on exhibition in the museum of the world'. In March 1948 Sister Lucia transferred from the Institute of St Dorothy to the Convent of Carmel at Coimbra, Portugal, by special permission, and though never seen by the public, she would sometimes reply to written requests for prayer.

❧ 14th ❧

Yosef ben Ab-hisda Ha'abta'ai, b. 1919, d. 1998

Yosef ben Ab-hisda Ha'abta'ai, who has died aged seventy-nine, was the High Priest of one of the world's smallest and most ancient religious communities, the Samaritans.

He was, by their reckoning, the 124th High Priest in a distinguished line dating back to the biblical Ithamar, the son of Aaron and nephew of Moses.

Samaritans claim to be the remnant of the Israelite tribes of Ephraim and Menasseh, who were dispersed by the Assyrians when they destroyed the northern kingdom of Israel in 722BC. Jews regard them as the semi-pagan descendants of Assyrian settlers.

It was the shunning of Samaritans by Jews that Jesus addressed in the parable of the Good Samaritan (Luke 10:30) and in the story of the Woman of Samaria (John 4:9).

The Samaritans, however, believe themselves to be the true keepers of the ancient Israelite faith and, indeed, many of their religious standards on diet and ritual purity are stricter than those demanded by rabbinical Judaism. Samaritan men are permitted to marry Jewish women, if the bride agrees to live by their code. Samaritan women, however, are forbidden to leave the sect.

'If a Samaritan woman leaves she can be punished by stoning until she dies. But we don't have the power to impose the penalty, so she is merely excluded from the community and nobody talks to her,' the High Priest told *The Daily Telegraph* in one of his last interviews.

Yosef ben Ab-hisda Ha'abta'ai, otherwise known as Joseph Cohen, was born in 1919. He worked as a teacher of religion until he became High Priest in 1987.

The Samaritans claim to have once been a nation of more than a million people, but at the start of British rule in Palestine in 1917 the community numbered a mere 146 men, women and children. Thus every birth is vital, and in the eleven years of Yosef ben Ab-hisda's tenure, the sect grew from 529 to 604 souls.

❧ 15th ❧

Norman Parkinson, b. 1913, d. 1990

Norman Parkinson, the photographer, who has died aged seventy-six, devoted much of his life to the study of beautiful women, whom he treated with a reverence bordering on idolatry, and was an unofficial portraitist to the ladies of the Royal Family.

A man of singular charm, 'Parks' was once described as resembling 'an elegant giraffe'; sporting a twirling moustache and a Kashmiri bridal cap, he liked to deck his lean 6ft 5in frame in kaftans, loud beach shirts and heavy gold jewellery.

In the 1930s, when he first began 'snapping', Parkinson was one of a new breed of heterosexual photographers. Rather than shoot his fashion features in studios, he pioneered a slightly surrealist method, taking his models to grimy, industrial locations. 'I was one of the first to take the scent-laden atmosphere out of photographs,' he explained, 'and the first to get girls to run, to jump, to stretch, to let air through their knees.'

It was his opinion that men should be photographed only when strictly necessary, and true to this principle he concentrated upon photographing the most beautiful women.

'Being photographed', he claimed, 'is a whole section of a woman's identity. She has to be admired.' In his quest for pulchritudinous subjects Parkinson would sometimes drive round London and hand out his card to pretty girls – keeping an eye out for possessive boyfriends.

But there was no shortage of willing subjects. 'Parks has got a little bit of hypnotism about him,' his beautiful wife Wenda once commented. 'Women will do anything for him.'

If, as Parkinson claimed, 'the best photographs tell the biggest lies', then his supreme fictions were reserved for royalty. His 1971 portraits of Princess Anne, taken for her twenty-first birthday, were the first occasion on which a member of the Royal Family had been given the full treatment, with extensive professional make-up and so on – a far cry from the stiff pre-Cecil Beaton days. 'Princess Anne does look quite beautiful sometimes,' Parkinson observed as he set to work. 'We want none of that nonsense here,' growled Prince Philip.

He then made further explorations in the royal field, creating some notably romantic images of Queen Elizabeth the Queen Mother, in soft focus with every jewel a-sparkle.

There were times, though, when his ingenuity gave the impression of vaudeville, as when he posed her looking through the glass window of a door; and, least successfully of all, when he posed her for an eightieth birthday portrait with the Queen and Princess Margaret, each of them draped in a dark blue silk overall. The result recalled nothing so much as a publicity shot for the Supremes and was waggishly dubbed 'the Windsor Sisters'.

He liked to imbue his glamour photographs with a certain degree of titillation. He once explained, 'In every photographer, there is a girlie photographer waiting to get out.' His 1985 book, *Would You Let Your Daughter...?* was meant to teach 'the delights of intelligent eroticism'. It depicted a number of luscious models in pleasing states of nudity accompanied by a text in bold capitals with such memorable phrases as 'MY WILL IS STRONG BUT MY WON'T IS WEAK'.

A barrister's son, he was born Ronald William Parkinson Smith on 21 April 1913 and spent his early days in a semi-detached house in Putney. He was educated at Westminster, where he proved a popular if unacademic figure. At the bottom of one particularly dismal report his headmaster scrawled, 'This is one of the worst reports I have ever seen, but I can't help liking the fellow.'

At the age of twenty-one 'Parks' set up his own studio in Dover Street with six staff and set to work photographing debutantes, which soon led to assignments in exotic locations for *Harper's Bazaar*. Already Parkinson had developed his flamboyant style and could often be seen wearing a blood-red Harris tweed cape – though Noel Coward warned him, 'People who have talent dress like stockbrokers.' During the Second World War Parkinson combined aerial reconnaissance photography with fashion and propaganda work, while nurturing his society contacts. In 1945 he married Wenda Rogerson, a *Vogue* model discovered by Cecil Beaton.

She became one of Parkinson's favourite subjects. On one occasion he photographed her for American *Vogue* in evening dress amid the rubble of the New York Ritz, which was being demolished behind her. They were both arrested by a passing policeman, but released when a crowd of admirers proved to be on their side.

In 1963 Parkinson moved from his flower-covered house in Twickenham to Tobago. He began selling postcard views of the island, mainly to American tourists; and later had the idea of setting up a sausage factory, exporting his sausages to America under the name Star-Spangled Bangers. Fearing this might offend American patriotism, he later changed the name.

On Tobago Parkinson could enjoy his hobbies, listed in *Who's Who* as 'pig farming, sun worshipping, bird watching, breeding Creole racehorses' (he gave his telephone number as 'none, fortunately'). This idyllic existence was marred, first by the sudden death of Wenda in 1987 and, soon afterwards, by the fire which destroyed his house, said to have been one of the most beautiful in the Caribbean.

In spite of his privileged connections, Parkinson remained distinctly modest and once insisted, 'I'm quite the most downmarket man; I'm quite unposh.' He was a natural aristocrat, though, and quite grand in an insouciant way. Explaining that his remains would be interred at a private burial ground on Tobago, for example, he said, 'I couldn't bear to be buried with people that I have not been introduced to.'

⊰ **16**th ⊱

Lady Cusack-Smith, b. 1912, d. 1998

Lady Cusack-Smith, who has died aged eighty-five, was one of the most colourful figures in the world of Irish foxhunting; she was Master of the Bermingham and North Galway from 1946 to 1984, a term as MFH only exceeded in the British Isles by the late 'Master', the 10th Duke of Beaufort.

North Galway country stretches from the north of Galway city, along Lough Corrib in the west and north, and extends northwards into Co. Mayo and eastwards into parts of Co. Roscommon. Stone walls, four or five feet high, are a common feature of the landscape, and Mollie Cusack-Smith was celebrated for her fearless jumping – though if her hunter Hippo did not like the look of a wall, he would turn his back on it and kick it down.

She was born Adela Mary O'Rorke in Dublin in 1912, the daughter of Charles Trench O'Rorke, a scion of the O'Rorkes of Breffni. Young Mollie grew up at Bermingham House and aged ten was hunting to her father's hounds. After an unsuccessful spell at Sherborne School for Girls – 'They gave me two out of a hundred for "trying" in mathematics, but I told them I wasn't trying' – she was sent to be finished in Paris, where she learned to sing.

When her father fell ill in 1937, Mollie returned to Bermingham to look after him. After an uncle had said of her, 'Mollie will never be any good, she is a jack of all trades and master of none', she decided to become a Master of Foxhounds. 'My operatic contralto,' she said, 'which I knew how to project, came in very useful when controlling the field.'

After numerous spills and fractures cheerfully borne, Mollie Cusack-Smith gave up hunting at seventy-one; she had hoped to do forty seasons, 'but my old horse, Willy, could do no more'. 'I've had a gorgeous, wonderful life,' she said in 1994, 'but I have no money. I've got nothing left. And the roof occasionally blows off, which is very awkward.'

❧ 17th ❧

John Allegro, b. 1923, d. 1988

John Allegro, the controversial Semitic philologist, who has died aged sixty-five, was once aptly described as 'the Liberace of Biblical scholarship'.

Unlike most scholars in that field, Allegro was not himself a believer, having abandoned the faith after a brief period as a lay preacher and Methodist ordinand. He was, indeed, frankly hostile to the religious impulse – and particularly to what he called 'these tales of this rabbi, Jesus, and his Mum and Dad'.

In a series of increasingly fantastical books he claimed that Christianity was a cryptic version of ancient sex-cults inspired by the hallucinogenic mushroom *Amanita muscaria* or fly-agaric. By means of Sumerian etymologies he sought to establish that all the sacred rites in the Bible were mushroom rites; and that most of its leading characters, including Moses, David and Jesus, are in fact walking mushrooms. Thus Christ's final utterance on the Cross, '*Eloi eloi, lama sabachthani,*' is not a tragic appeal but 'a paean of praise to the god of the mushroom'. Such theories did not find favour with the academic establishment.

John Marco Allegro was born in London in 1923 and educated at Wallington County Grammar School. He served in the Royal Navy during the Second World War and then had a brilliant undergraduate career at Manchester University.

After a spell studying Hebrew dialects at Magdalen College, Oxford, he was invited in 1953 to join an international body of scholars working on the Dead Sea Scrolls in Jerusalem. He was personally involved in the opening and decipherment of the Copper Scroll, which was found five years after the Dead Sea Scrolls.

Allegro claimed to have found in the Scrolls references to a pre-Christian 'teacher' whose disciples were to guard 'the broken body of their Master' until Judgment Day – thus establishing 'a well defined Essenic pattern into which Jesus of Nazareth fits'. This claim caused great controversy.

In 1956 he published his theory in a book, *The Dead Sea Scrolls*, which is one of the best and almost certainly the most readable book on the subject. It was a bestseller, and having hit the jackpot he went on to write *The People of the Dead Sea Scrolls* (1958) and *The Treasure of the Copper Scroll* (1960), which, though still an original work of scholarship, carried more than passing echoes of *Treasure Island*.

He was, after all, a respected and popular lecturer in Comparative Semitics and Old Testament Studies at Manchester University. But as the 1960s wore on his theories became increasingly outré, and the obsession with mushrooms took hold.

In 1970 Allegro's theories reached their apogee with *The Sacred Mushroom and the Cross*, which, in the words of one critic, 'gave mushrooms a bad name'. It excited more derision than outrage but nonetheless enjoyed a passing popularity, for those were the days of the drug culture gurus, and Allegro's ideas, if improbable, were at least in vogue.

In 1971, unchastened and still flourishing his mushrooms, he wrote *The Chosen People*, which suggested that the Children of Israel were not so much chosen as stoned. Then followed *Lost Gods*, which as Anthony Quinton remarked in *The Sunday Telegraph*, has 'all the freshness and coherence of the conversation of a very tired man in a crowded pub rather late at night'.

Miles White, b. 1914, d. 2000

Miles White, the costume designer who has died aged eighty-five, once dressed fifty elephants in tutus for a ballet choreographed by Balanchine to music by Stravinsky.

Stravinsky took some persuading. 'All right,' he finally agreed. 'If they are very young elephants, I will do it.'

The *New York Times* reported: 'The Ballet of the Elephants was breathtaking. They came into the ring in artificial, blue-lighted dusk ... first the pink dancers, then the great beasts.

'In the centre ring, Modoc the elephant danced with amazing grace and in time to the tune, closing in perfect cadence with the crashing finale.'

Later White recalled this triumph. 'No one thought it could be done,' he remembered. 'They all thought I was crazy. So of course I was determined to do it.'

⚜ 18th ⚜

The 18th Duke of Alburquerque, b. 1919, d. 1994

The 18th Duke of Alburquerque, who has died aged seventy-four, saw a film of the Grand National on his eighth birthday, and for the next forty-eight years held fast to his dream of winning the steeplechase.

In Spain his position as head of the household of Don Juan de Borbon, the Count of Barcelona and pretender to the throne, gave him some part in the negotiations with Franco under which, in 1969, the Caudillo named the Count's son, Juan Carlos, as the future King of Spain.

But in Britain the Duke of Alburquerque was known for his magnificent obsession with Aintree. 'He's another Don Quixote,' a rival jockey observed, 'and the Grand National is his own bloody windmill.'

But the knight of the doleful countenance would have lacked the spirit to go on tilting at windmills if he had sustained more than thirty fractures: the Duke regularly started the National with his bones pinned together by metal, and ended it in Walton Hospital.

Such English as he mastered – 'Ze going? Good? Thank you' – related solely to racing. But his extraordinary courage required no translation, so that his appearance in the saddling enclosure invariably evoked hearty applause.

The dukedom of Alburquerque dates from 1464. The 18th Duke was born Don Beltran Alfonso Osorio y Diez de Rivera on 15 December 1919, and grew up in Spain and in France; his family moved to Biarritz when Alfonso XIII went into exile in 1931.

He intended to be an engineer, but his studies were interrupted by the Spanish Civil War, in which he rode with the Nationalist cavalry. By 1939 he had abandoned engineering to concentrate on racing.

Although he represented Spain in the three-day event in successive Olympic Games, and achieved steeplechase victories all over Europe, his ambition remained fixed on the Grand National. He first rode in the race in 1952 when, on Brown Jack III, he fell at sixth.

It was feared that he had broken his neck; it turned out to be only two vertebrae. The Duke could only think of his horse: 'Poor animal, it was past it.' Eleven years passed before his next attempt.

In the 1963 National he rode Jonjo, and stayed with the leaders before coming to grief at the 20th, this time suffering nothing worse than cuts and bruises. He was not so lucky in 1965; mounted on Groomsman he fell at Valentine's Brook and broke his leg. Two years later the Duke again escaped lightly when L'Empereur pulled up only four fences from home. In 1973 he made his first attempt on the Spanish-bred Nereo. A stirrup-leather broke at the start, and it was a tribute to his horsemanship that he kept his seat over eight fences before pulling up at the Canal Turn.

Next year, again on Nereo, Alburquerque recorded his only finish in the National – a remarkable achievement, given that he had broken his collar-bone the week before and had had sixteen screws taken out of his leg a fortnight previously.

Early in 1975 the Duke suffered a fall in Seville which put him into hospital with compound fractures of his right leg. But that December, on his fifty-sixth birthday, with his leg fortified by a metal pin, secured by seven screws, he achieved a double at Leicester on Heracles and Nereo.

In the ensuing Grand National he was going well on Nereo until the 13th, when he had one of his worst falls, and was badly trampled upon. It took him two days to regain consciousness, and he broke seven ribs and a wrist, besides fracturing his thigh.

Nevertheless the Duke was eager to return in 1977, and was only foiled by the Jockey Club's ruling that amateurs over the age of fifty must undergo a medical. But he went on racing in Spain up to his sixty-seventh year.

❧ 19th ❧

Chris Dale, b. 1962, d. 2011

Chris Dale, who has died aged forty-nine, was a 6ft 6in mountaineer with a passion for solo climbs among the hardest peaks of Scotland, Wales and the Alps. He was also an equally enthusiastic cross-dresser who went by the name of Crystal.

His long reach allowed him to establish several bitterly tough routes which have rarely, if ever, been repeated. Where climbers today often prepare first ascents by abseiling down a rock face and practising the moves in stages, Dale preferred to lead 'on-sight' and 'ground-up', with no preparation. He specialised in bold climbs with minimal protection and loved all forms of adventure: besides climbing, he also explored the disused mines of Wales and made solo caving excursions in France.

He was very active in Scotland, particularly in winter, soloing innumerable routes and making dozens of first ascents. In 2003 he climbed what he believed to be Britain's last unclimbed mountain, a rocky pinnacle called Dun Dubh – Gaelic for black fort – on the Quiraing mountains on the Isle of Skye. Lying two miles off the tourist path, the 1,000ft face took Dale an hour to ascend. 'If you slipped, you would fall to the bottom,' he reported afterwards. 'It's quite precipitous.'

Besides mountains, Dale's other passion was women's clothing. On one occasion he was in drag when introduced to a Frenchman as 'Chris Dale'. The Frenchman misheard 'Crystal', and the name for Dale's alter ego stuck.

As a mountaineer the name held other resonances for Dale. A keen rock hunter, he would often climb the north faces of the Aiguille du Grepon, Grand Charmoz and the Aiguille du Plan in the Alps in search of precious crystals to sell. In recent years he was proud of his transvestism and Crystal became a familiar, if always memorable, sight at parties.

Friends joked that they did not want to meet the woman he bought the clothes from. In fact, they were purchased openly, which led to one unfortunate incident in a branch of Asda. Thrown out for acting suspiciously, Dale complained in writing, citing the Sexual Discrimination Act, and received a grovelling apology and a substantial voucher. It was with no little pleasure that he returned to try on some clothes, soliciting the help of the manager who had evicted him.

His appearance in drag at an annual mountain guides' dinner, however, proved a step too far. When an inebriated member groped under his skirt, the long reach that served Dale so well on rock was put to devastating effect. The disciplinary action that followed was severe; there were many who felt he was treated harshly.

Chris Dale, known as Big Chris, was born on 14 January 1962 in Penrith and educated locally until he ran truant at sixteen. He turned up four days later having soloed the Old Man of Stoer, a 200ft sandstone sea stack off the west coast of Scotland. The achievement is all the more remarkable as he had no knowledge of the route, its grade, and carried no rope (so obliging him to solo back down). Furthermore he had only just taken up climbing.

A few years later he travelled to Australia and quickly proceeded to make an impact with a bold first ascent up a 600ft sandstone face in the Blue Mountains, which he named Big Glassy. The upper half was entirely overhanging, on soft and crumbly rock, and the feat took three days. Success owed much to Dale's unwavering commitment and optimism while leading.

In the 1980s he belonged to the group of British climbers which made its home in the makeshift campsite of Snell's Field, Chamonix, beneath Mont Blanc. This was a period before climbing and extreme sports were fashionable; the climbers were rebellious and anarchic, and viewed as borderline criminal by the French Gendarmerie, which regularly raided the campsite.

Dale put up a handful of new routes in the region, and was a keen adherent to informal rules which attached great importance to the style of ascent.

Hammering in pitons or leaving gear behind was frowned upon, while using a drill to place bolts was a sacrilege. Purist methods were best – it was felt a climber should tackle a mountain armed only with courage and skill; a rope was just for backup.

Chris Dale was less traditional, however, when it came to naming trails which he had blazed. Mountaineers studying the guides to follow in his tracks still have to contend with the following routes: 'Vive Les Unbathed Pinkos'; 'Dog Breath in the Year of the Plague'; and 'Brain Death and Bad Craziness'.

He subsequently trained as a mountain guide, but was slow to qualify in the early 1990s owing to his difficulty with skiing. Like many British guides whose backgrounds lay in rock climbing, mastering the sport was an unhappy experience. After he passed his exams the first thing he did was throw his skis away, vowing never to strap on a pair again.

As a guide he stayed true to his climbing principles, eschewing popular routes up well-known mountains in favour of more challenging objectives off the beaten track. Blessed with both enormous climbing talent and a natural instinct for route finding, Dale inspired total confidence.

In recent years injury prevented him from guiding and he found employment introducing disadvantaged children to the outdoors and in a climbing shop. He belonged to the sport's tradition of modesty and never boasted of his exploits: his Facebook page listed his interests as 'fluff, pink things, sparkly stuff and mountains'.

⚜ **20**th ⚜

Sarah Kane, b. 1971, d. 1999

Sarah Kane, the playwright who has committed suicide aged twenty-eight, made a controversial debut with *Blasted*, a play which opened in 1995 at the Royal Court Theatre Upstairs.

The play, about the nature of violence and war, was set in a Leeds hotel room that erupts into a Bosnian battlefield. In what the *Daily Mail* critic Jack Tinker described as 'a disgusting feast of filth', it featured, among other atrocities, scenes of masturbation, fellatio, micturation, frottage, defecation, homosexual rape, eye-gouging, tongue-munching and baby-eating. Sarah Kane herself declared that *Blasted* was 'quite a peaceful play about hope'.

Francis Coulson, b. 1919, d. 1998

Francis Coulson, who has died aged seventy-eight, was the founder of Sharrow Bay Country House Hotel, at Ullswater, which he ran for forty-nine seasons.

The brochure promised 'an oasis where one can escape from the world and one's own problems', largely with menus that were an unashamed celebration of Edwardian richness and plenty. Breakfast could be a banquet in itself; nursery teas presented home-made scones laden with cream; dinner eked out deliciousness over six or seven courses. 'The quickest and most pleasurable way to a coronary I know,' a doctor reported to the *Good Food Guide*.

⁂ 21st ⁂

Dame Margot Fonteyn, b. 1919, d. 1991

Dame Margot Fonteyn, the legendary ballerina who has died aged seventy-one, was the greatest dancer of her generation. A performer of incomparable grace, imagination and charm, she made the ballet more accessible than it had ever been.

It was, above all, her partnership with Rudolf Nureyev which caught the public's imagination. After their first performance together in *Giselle* at Covent Garden in 1962, which was received with twenty-three curtain calls, they made headlines wherever they went.

But famous as their partnership deservedly was, Fonteyn was an international star long before Nureyev appeared on the scene: she tackled the lead in *Swan Lake* the year he was born. Even today, Fonteyn's performance haunts every production of that ballet.

That is the price an audience must pay for having seen perfection – and for a privileged generation Fonteyn was exactly that, over and over again. She never gave a bad performance: her every appearance was unique and the magic never failed.

With a light olive complexion, long blue-black hair and a gentle face dominated by dazzling black eyes, Fonteyn was also gifted with an almost perfectly proportioned physique for dance. Where most dancers have some minor fault to overcome – and no world is more aware of tiny faults in physical symmetry – she was generally recognised as approaching the ideal.

Any photograph of Fonteyn dancing, taken at any moment in any classical work, became an instant, frozen sculpture, each part of her body in seemingly perfect relationship with every other. Nothing jarred, nothing was wrongly positioned. In motion this subtly changing, flowing set of relationships is what many trained observers find most satisfying about dance.

Born Margaret Hookham at Reigate, Surrey, on 18 May 1919, she was the daughter of an engineer with the British-American Tobacco Company and an Irish-Brazilian coffee heiress.

'Peggy' grew up in England, Kentucky and China, and was educated by governesses and at local schools; her dance training began at the age of five.

After studying in Shanghai with Goncharov and in London with Astafieva she went to Ninette de Valois's school and from there joined de Valois's company at the age of fifteen, making her professional debut as a snowflake in *The Nutcracker*. Her stage name was adapted from her own first name and her mother's maiden name.

Based at Sadler's Wells, with Frederick Ashton, Constant Lambert and Robert Helpmann as its leading spirits, she was part of what was at that time a small, experimental, struggling dance company, devoted to classical ballet in the Russian tradition. It grew into the Royal Ballet at the Covent Garden Opera House, one of the major international companies, and Fonteyn could claim a substantial share of the credit for that astonishing change.

When Alicia Markova left in 1935 Fonteyn stepped into the leading roles and remained the company's prima ballerina until – on her sixtieth birthday and final retirement – the Royal Ballet revived the title of Prima Ballerina Assoluta for her, which she held until her death.

As de Valois added to her repertory the five great ballet classics – *Swan Lake*, *Sleeping Beauty*, *Nutcracker*, *Giselle* and *Coppelia* – she little realised that Fonteyn would perform in them throughout the Western world.

Meanwhile Frederick Ashton, a choreographer of genius, created a stream of works to exploit and extend the full range of Fonteyn's remarkable gifts. This interaction between interpretive artist and gifted creator, each inspiring and stimulating the other, made for a golden epoch in British ballet.

She had luck, too, in her partnerships. Robert Helpmann, so vividly dramatic a dancer that she had to stretch every nerve she possessed to compete, was followed by Michael Somes, an impeccable aristocrat, sympathetic and technically secure.

Then, when it began to seem that there were no more worlds to conquer, Nureyev joined the company in 1962 as a permanent guest artist. Fiercely impulsive, amazingly talented, sensual to the point of narcissism, he called again for fresh qualities if she was to hold her own.

She married, in 1955, Dr Roberto Arias, a former Panamanian ambassador to the Court of St James's, whom she had first met when she was eighteen. In 1964 he was shot in Panama and completely paralysed from the neck down, leaving him so handicapped that he could talk only in a faint whisper.

For the rest of his life (he died in 1989) Fonteyn knew that she had to wake every four hours in the night to turn him, and that if she did not do so he would die. Arias retained his restless and ambitious mind, and continued to travel with her for much of the rest of her career.

The costs of maintaining him in comfort with the necessary staff were financially crippling for Fonteyn. After her retirement they lived frugally on a small ranch in South America, much too proud to accept the financial assistance so many friends and admirers would have been only too ready to give.

Gene Scott, b. 1929, d. 2005

Gene Scott, the American television evangelist who has died aged seventy-five, offered his followers all the advantages of Christianity with none of the inconveniences, and thus became immensely rich.

Scott's followers were assured that they did not have to go to church on Sunday and that such foibles as homosexuality, adultery, abortion, profanity and drinking were just fine. 'I don't ask you to change,' he told his congregation. 'I take you as you are.'

His appeal lay in his genius as an entertainer. Buccaneering, shaggy-haired and bearded under a bandana or flamboyant hat, he was by turns unpredictable, outrageous, funny and inspired, but always compelling. Fat cigar in hand, his face contorted with rage, he would mix scripture with profanity-laden monologues about the state of the world ('Nuke 'em in the name of Jesus!' he cried during the Gulf War), punctuated with demands for more money.

No gimmick was neglected. At church services a rock band would belt out such hymns of praise as 'Kill a Pissant for Jesus'. His television shows would sometimes feature 'Scott's Bunnies', a bevy of female followers in thong bikinis. (He felt he could 'probably teach Hugh Hefner a thing or two' about sex.) When he found himself under investigation by the authorities for alleged fraud, he assembled a band of wind-up toy monkeys, then proceeded to smash them to pieces on television with a baseball bat.

To qualify as a member of his Church, the main requirement was a valid credit card, Scott's aim apparently being to make it richer than the Vatican. 'A skinflint may get to heaven,' he admitted, 'but what awaits him are a rusty old halo, a skinny old cloud, and a robe so worn it scratches. First-class salvation costs money.'

When Scott was diagnosed with cancer, he decided to 'give God the first shot' before resorting to conventional medicine. By the time it became clear that the Almighty had stayed his hand, it was too late.

⊰ 22nd ⊱

Ernest Lough, b. 1911, d. 2000

Ernest Lough, who has died aged eighty-eight, made one of the most evocative – and popular – classical records of all time in March 1927 when, as a fifteen-year-old treble soloist with the Temple Church Choir, he sang 'O, For The Wings Of A Dove' from Mendelssohn's anthem *Hear My Prayer*.

The sound of Lough's ethereal voice, under perfect control in the soft resonance of the church, seems to defy the evanescence of youth and offer a moment of perfect beauty perpetuated forever. 'That wretched boy,' complained Dame Nellie Melba, 'has achieved overnight what has taken me years!' Within ten years the record had sold over a million copies; and as the decades slipped by, the surface crackle added nostalgia to the emotion of the music. Sales now stand at around five million.

'We did four or five takes,' Lough recalled sixty years later. 'One was discarded because a child was whistling outside; another because the Temple clock chimed. I wasn't aware I was making history. I was so small I had to stand on a couple of Bibles so the single microphone would pick up my voice.'

As the fame of the record spread throughout the world, fans (mainly women) would crowd to services in the Temple to hear Lough sing. He found the adulation 'a bit of a menace', not least because he had to answer so many letters when he would much rather have been playing football.

When his version of another piece was advertised as 'the last recording of the boy soprano', the rumour spread that Lough had expired. Lough remembered meeting two old ladies near the Temple Church who wanted to know where they could send their donations: 'He died, didn't you know?'

'No he didn't,' the boy replied. 'I'm Ernest Lough.' But they were not to be convinced.

Ernest Lough was born on 17 November 1911 in Forest Gate, London. Neither of his parents was musical and his early progress as a boy soprano was unpromising. Having sung in the local parish church of St Peter's, he failed his audition for Southwark Cathedral.

Across the river however, the 28-year-old George Thalben-Ball was already renowned as a trainer of boys' voices, and in 1924 he accepted Lough into the Temple Church Choir.

Lough attributed his early renown largely to the excellent training provided by Thalben-Ball. 'I don't think my voice had any special quality,' he said, though all the world disagreed. But he remained indifferent to fame. It was a relief for him when, at sixteen, his voice finally broke – or rather, as he put it, 'just slid down'. 'Thank God,' he thought, 'the pressure is off.'

At twenty Lough had taken a job making the tea and doing the packing in the advertising department of HMV. In 1937 he made another record, of Schubert's *Serenade*. He insisted, though, that he was an unexceptional baritone, and felt no regrets about never attempting a professional career in music.

During the Second World War he served in the fire service. One night he was called out to the Temple, and in the absence of water supplies had to watch helplessly as the church, struck by incendiary bombs, was gutted.

After the war, Lough joined the advertising agency Masius and Ferguson, but continued to sing Sunday services in the ruins of the Temple Church as part of the Temple Male Voice Choir.

In 1953 he sang at the Coronation and was joined by his first son Peter, a chorister at the Chapel Royal. The following year the Temple Choir was re-formed and his second son, Robin, became the youngest of the new choristers. Father and son can be heard together in several performances. A third son, Graham, was also a soloist at the Temple, where George Thalben-Ball continued to direct the choir.

❧ 23rd ❧

Sir Stanley Matthews, b. 1915, d. 2000

Sir Stanley Matthews, who has died aged eighty-five, was one of the greatest footballers of any nation and any time. The genius which he deployed for Stoke City, Blackpool and England was quite at odds with the terrier-like endeavours which have too often characterised English football.

On the field of play, Matthews was the supreme individualist, an unrivalled dribbler of the ball. He not only tormented full backs on a weekly basis but did it with a sportsmanship that emphasised the brilliance he tried to shrug off. 'The ball ran for me today,' he would tell dazed opponents after the game, as though he genuinely did not understand what all the fuss was about.

Few others were in doubt. In the days before comprehensive television coverage of soccer, Matthews' mere presence on the right wing was enough to add 10,000 to the gate. While he was at Stoke in the 1930s, the average home crowd was 66,000.

His career as a player lasted more than thirty years, beginning in 1932 and ending in 1965. His eighty-four international appearances were between 1934 and 1957.

The essence of Matthews' dominance was his unparalleled acceleration over ten yards. Full backs knew that he would feint to go inside them and then whisk by on the outside. They were still powerless to stop him.

It required rigorous self-discipline to sustain his speed for so many years. Every day during his professional career his diet was the same: carrot juice at lunch-time, steak with salad for dinner, a fast on Mondays. And every morning at Blackpool there would be a training run on the beach.

Although in one sense the perfect sportsman, Matthews took an aggressive delight in showing his mastery. He might remain stationary with his foot on the ball for ten seconds or more, daring the opposition to challenge him. The same kind of steel was evident in his attitude to opponents who tried to kick him out of the game. Such malefactors would be refused his handshake after the game – a slight that imported professional obloquy.

Despite a thousand brilliant displays, there were particular triumphs that stood out above the rest.

When England played Germany in Berlin in 1938, Goering, Hess, Ribbentrop and Goebbels assembled to witness the victory of the Fatherland and watched unsmiling as Matthews tore the German defence to pieces, even scoring himself (Matthews scored surprisingly few goals) in England's 6–3 victory. 'A fellow like Matthews risks everything and can do everything,' the German magazine *Fussball* proclaimed in wonderment.

The winger put in another astonishing display for England against Scotland at Maine Road, Manchester, in 1943, with Denis Compton on the other wing. When Matthews scored the final goal in England's 8–0 victory, even some Scottish players could scarcely forbear to cheer.

On to the Cup Final of 1953. With twenty minutes to go, Blackpool were 1–3 down to Bolton. Matthews had had a quiet game. Then, as the defence tired, he became irresistible.

Stan Mortensen netted one of his crosses and then scored again from a free kick. In injury time, Matthews ghosted past two defenders before cutting the ball back for Perry, who hammered home the winner. Outside Bolton, the entire country rejoiced.

At thirty-eight, Matthews still had twelve more years in the game. Playing against Brazil at Wembley in 1956, he made Nilton Santos, one of the greatest Brazilian defenders, look like a novice. England won 4–2. The same Brazilian side, with the not unimportant addition of Pele, won the 1958 World Cup.

The third of four sons, Stanley Matthews was born on 1 February 1915, at Hanley, one of the five towns of the Potteries. His father, a barber, would work in his shop from 8 a.m. to 9 p.m., and then train for his other career, that of professional boxer. A featherweight, notably quick on his feet, and believed to be the last professional to enter the ring with a waxed moustache, Jack Matthews fought some 350 bouts, many of twenty rounds, and lost only nine times.

Stanley first made his mark as a sprinter. He learned his football on 'Meakins' Square', a rough piece of ground alongside the local pottery and, by the time he was six or seven, the locals were making detours to watch his astonishing skills with the ball.

At Wellington School, Hanley, his team would win by embarrassing totals such as 18–0. In 1929 he was chosen to represent England Schoolboys versus the Rest, and then England Schoolboys against Wales.

On leaving school, Matthews became a bricklayer's apprentice and worked in the barber's shop in the evening, lathering customers in preparation for their shave. In 1930 he joined Stoke as a ground boy.

He had two games for Stoke reserves when he was fifteen and next season, 1931–32, turned out for the reserves twenty-two times. In 1932, he signed as a professional with a salary of £5 a week in winter and £3 a week in summer. After his first game for the first team, away against Bury, Huddersfield offered £5,000 to sign him.

By the 1933–34 season, Matthews was playing regularly for the first team. Stoke were promoted to the First Division, with Matthews scoring fifteen goals (eleven in the League), a total he would never beat. The directors of the club celebrated by giving every player a three-piece suit.

Though Matthews made his international debut against Wales in 1934 and later that year played against Italy and Germany, he did not make an auspicious beginning for England, and was dropped until 1937.

On the outbreak of hostilities the War Office decreed that leading players should continue to entertain the public. Matthews joined the RAF, was posted to Blackpool, and played in internationals against Scotland and Wales throughout the war.

In 1947 Matthews was transferred to Blackpool (where he was already living) for £11,500. At his new club, he formed a potent partnership with Mortensen, though Blackpool lost two Cup Finals – in 1948 to Manchester United, and in 1951 to Newcastle – before triumphing in 1953.

Blackpool were a major force in the First Division throughout the 1950s. Matthews remained with the club until 1961 when, aged forty-six, he was transferred back to Stoke for £3,500.

Stoke were then languishing near the bottom of the Second Division with an average home gate of 7,000. For Matthews' return, against Huddersfield, there was a crowd of 35,000. The club were able to buy new players and in 1962–63 won the Second Division championship and gained promotion to the First Division – emulating the triumph of Matthews' youth thirty years before. In 1963, Matthews was given the freedom of Stoke.

He was appointed CBE in 1957 and knighted in the New Year's Honours of 1965. It was thus as Sir Stanley that he played his last game for Stoke, against Fulham on 6 February 1965. This was five days after his fiftieth birthday and he became the oldest player ever to appear in a First Division match.

Spurning offers of international tours, Matthews became the manager of Port Vale, then a Fourth Division side. This proved a disastrous interlude. In 1968, due to a proposal to pay an illegal bonus to the players and to a failure to pay registration fees, the club was fined £2,000 and expelled from the League.

Having remarried, Matthews went to live for a while in Malta, where he managed a local club team. His skill and experience was imparted on tours of Canada, Australia and Africa but largely lost to his own country.

In 1987 a statue of Matthews was unveiled in Hanley. 'I'm no hero,' he protested. 'Doctors and nurses are heroes. We had a real hero born in Stoke, Reginald Mitchell, who designed the Spitfire. He saved Britain. Now that's what I call a hero.'

ᚼ 24th ᚼ

Pastor Jack Glass, b. 1936, d. 2004

Pastor Jack Glass, who has died aged sixty-seven, was the founder of the Zion Sovereign Grace Baptist Church in Glasgow and a pastor in the ranting, fire and brimstone tradition of John Knox.

Glass would go anywhere to anathematise the ungodly, and his targets included the Church of Scotland, Billy Connolly, religious satires, pornography, homosexuality and, of course, the Roman Catholic Church. Even Ian Paisley considered him an extremist.

Glass's finest moment was undoubtedly during the visit of Pope John Paul II to Scotland in 1982, when he led protests against the 'Antichrist' from Rome, proclaiming that the Pope had 'no right to set foot on a Protestant island' and that his visit 'violated the British Bill of Rights'. When it was rumoured that the Pope intended to visit the ecumenical community at Iona, Glass turned up one lunchtime in the abbey, mounted the pulpit, informed those present that they were 'the lickspittle of the Antichrist', then departed to catch the ferry.

Jack Glass was born in 1936 and joined the Salvation Army as a child. After studying Moral Philosophy and English at Glasgow University, he founded his Zion Baptist Church in 1967 and began his unrelenting one-man mission to lead the people of Scotland away from Satan.

Over a period of some thirty years, he picketed shows by the comedian Billy Connolly in protest at a sketch in which Connolly translated the Last Supper to the Saracen's Head pub in Glasgow's East End: 'If the Forth was lava, I would throw Connolly in.'

At the 1999 Edinburgh Festival, wearing a crown of thorns, Glass led an eighty-strong demonstration to picket the opening night of Terence McNally's play *Corpus Christi*, in which the Son of God discovers his sexuality with Judas. Protesting that the Lord had been 'spoofed as a poof', Glass confronted the actor who was playing Judas in front of the assembled television cameras and hurled a bag of money at him with the words: 'There's your thirty pieces of silver, you Judas!' When the coins were counted, there were found to be only twenty-nine.

When not bawling, and if he could be tempted off the topic of religion, Glass was said to be a charming, affable man who did not mind being told he was 'batty'. Paisley, who fell out with him over unspecified doctrinal differences, called him 'a man of great honour who had a great love of the Bible'.

'I don't hate anyone,' Glass said recently. 'I'm just trying to bring people to Christ. Glasgow has turned its back on God. Sadly, God will have to punish it.'

When he was diagnosed with lung cancer last year, he regarded the tumour as a 'personal attack' by Satan, who was trying to steal his voice 'to destroy Christ's message'. When doctors gave him the all-clear around the turn of this year, he proclaimed his recovery an 'amazing miracle'. The Devil had suffered a tremendous defeat. 'I've lived to see the Devil run away. I'm like Lazarus, who rose from the grave.'

But a few weeks later it emerged that the cancer had spread to his brain.

❦ 25th ❦

Sir Donald Bradman, b. 1908, d. 2001

Sir Donald Bradman, who has died aged ninety-two, was on any reference to averages by far the greatest batsman who has ever lived; so marked, indeed, was his preeminence that he became one of the great sporting legends of the twentieth century, standing forth not merely as a national hero in Australia, but as a phenomenon for all the cricketing world to wonder at.

When The Don walked out to bat in his last Test match, at the Oval in 1948, his average in Tests was 101.39. Applauded all the way to the wicket, and given three cheers by the English team, he was then bowled for a duck second ball by a googly from Eric Hollies.

So Bradman ended with a Test batting average of 99.94 from 52 Tests, a surprisingly small number by modern standards. (Allan Border played in 156 Test matches between 1978 and 1994.) Bradman played 338 innings in first-class matches, and made 28,067 runs with an average of 95.14.

This total included 117 centuries, so that he scored a hundred slightly more than one in every three times he went out to bat. He would have made many more had he not lost so much of his prime to the Second World War.

Among those batsmen who have completed their careers and played in more than twenty Test innings, the next best averages are those of Graeme Pollock, George Headley and Herbert Sutcliffe, who all finished with an average of 60, some 40 runs behind Bradman. It is difficult to think of any other field of endeavour in which the best is so much better than the merely excellent.

On the other hand, Bradman was never a particularly elegant player, nor a classically orthodox one. He was, after all, entirely self-taught, and had been brought up on concrete wickets covered with matting; he did not bat on a grass wicket until he was eighteen (then, of course, he made a century).

In these circumstances Bradman had developed an unusual grip, which he steadfastly refused to change. The right hand was twisted to the right so that as the palm gripped the handle it was facing nearly directly down the pitch. The left hand was turned so that its back faced the bowler.

As Bradman took up his stance the leading edge of the bat pointed almost towards the bowler, while its bottom rested between, not behind, his feet. He took the bat up at an angle of forty-five degrees to the flight of the ball. This set-up made him particularly strong in the hook, the pull and the cut. He said his grip made it impossible to lift the hook shot unless he tried to; and he was equally safe with the cut. More extraordinarily, given his grip, he also developed an effective off-drive. On the debit side, it was argued, the grip handicapped him on wet wickets where there was sharp turn. But then his footwork was so sprightly that he could usually smother spin.

It goes without saying that Bradman was quick and accurate in his judgment of length and speed, possessed the sharpest reflexes, and was gifted with perfect hand-eye co-ordination. But he was not alone in these qualities. What made him wholly exceptional were his inner confidence, his determination to dominate an attack, and his ability to sustain total concentration over a long innings.

Jim Laker used to tell how, at Lord's in 1948, he tied Bradman up for an over and was only prevented by the faintest edge from claiming him LBW. 'Well bowled, Jim,' Bradman said at the end of the over. 'Thank goodness that's over. Now we can get on with some batting.' He hit the first ball of Laker's next over for four and was never in trouble again.

On strike, Bradman would be entirely still, not even tapping his bat. Often he was grinning – cynically, as many bowlers came to feel. 'As I ran up to bowl,' Jim Laker has recorded, 'Bradman always seemed to know where the ball was going to pitch, what stroke he was going to play and how many runs he was going to score.'

Only at the start of an innings did Bradman appear vulnerable. Once he had settled, his instinct was not just to attack the bowling but to tear it to pieces. Scoring fast was almost as important to him as scoring high, and over his career he averaged forty-two runs an hour. His dominance at the crease was the more remarkable as he was only 5ft 8in tall, and used a light bat.

Off the pitch he was neither falsely modest nor arrogantly boastful. Unwilling to talk about himself, he was always ready with praise of other players. Yet he was never one of the boys. Teetotal and a non-smoker, when possible he avoided rowdy celebration, although as a talented pianist he was sometimes roped in to accompany sing-songs. After he made 309 not out on the first day of the Test match at Headingley in 1930, against an attack including Larwood and Tate, he went up to his room to listen to music and write letters.

Some of his team-mates resented this attitude. In particular, the Irish and Roman Catholic members of Australia's side in the 1930s – Jack Fingleton and Bill O'Reilly to the fore – took exception to the tight, dedicated, Empire-loving, Royalty-idolising, aristocrat-adulating genius under whose shadow they lay. E.W. Swanton noted that, when Bradman was out for nought in his last Test, 'I thought they [Fingleton and O'Reilly] were going to have a stroke, they were laughing so much.'

Donald George Bradman was born at Cootamundra, 200 miles south-west of Sydney, on 27 August 1908. He was the fifth of five children and grew up in a weatherboard bungalow, with no water supply. Often left to his own devices, he satisfied his sporting instincts by throwing a golf ball against the brick base of a water tank, attempting (and usually succeeding) to hit it with a stump as it rebounded. He practised fielding by throwing his golf ball at the bars in a gate – which meant tedious retrieval if he missed.

At Bowral High School, Don, aged twelve, played for the school team against their rivals at Mittagong, and made an undefeated 115 in a total of 155. Two years later, in 1921, he was given a chance in Bowral Town senior team. Still in shorts, and using a bat far too large for him, he went in at No. 10, and made 39 not out.

Don left school at fourteen and began work in an estate agency in Bowral. In 1923–24 he played no cricket at all, and very little in the following summer. Most of his free time was given to tennis.

It was his uncle George Whatman who lured him back to play cricket for Bowral. In December 1925 the town played their local rivals from Wingello, the match taking place on successive Saturday afternoons. The opposition had a demon bowler, nearly three years older than Bradman: Bill O'Reilly, no less. At the close of play on the first Saturday Bradman was 234 not out. In the next match he made 300 against Moss Vale.

Word of these deeds travelled to Sydney, and in October 1926 the New South Wales selectors invited the prodigy for a trial. He impressed, and in December 1927 made his debut for the state in a match against South Australia at Adelaide. Going in at No. 7, he treated Clarrie Grimmett, one of the greatest of all leg spinners, with scant respect, and duly completed his century.

His debut in Test cricket came against England at Brisbane in 1928. For once he failed to do himself justice, and was dropped for the second Test. Returning for the third at Melbourne, he made 79 and 112, and then hit another century in the fifth match of the series. In between he hammered Victoria's attack for 340 not out.

In 1930 Bradman flayed Queensland's bowlers to amass 452 not out, which for almost thirty years remained the highest score in first-class cricket.

There were seasoned English players – Maurice Tate, Frank Woolley and Percy Fender among them – who felt that Bradman's cross-batted attacking style could never succeed so well on English wickets. Bradman gave his response in the Test series of 1930, when he scored 974 runs (still a record) and averaged 139.14 without the benefit of a single not out.

He rated his 254 at Lord's that year as the best innings he ever played; every shot, he said, went exactly where intended, even the one from which he was caught; he had only forgotten that Percy Chapman was so tall. His 334 in the next Test at Headingley remains the highest score by an Australian against England.

Nemesis came in the form of the bodyline tactics employed by Douglas Jardine when England toured Australia in 1932–33. Larwood and Voce fired in short-pitched deliveries aimed at the body and head with a cluster of short legs to take the catch as the batsman tried to fend the ball off. Larwood, of course, was one of the fastest bowlers of all time, and he was reinforced by the ruthlessness of Jardine, who required his players to refer to Bradman as 'the little bastard'.

England succeeded in reducing Bradman's average for the series to 56.57, excellent for any other player who has ever lived, but a comparative failure for him. Australia lost the series 1–4.

During the tour of England in 1934, Bradman (now promoted to vice-captain) was troubled by bad health – to such an extent that he went thirteen innings without making a century, before making amends with 304, 244 and 77 in the fourth and fifth Tests.

At the end of the season an abnormally complicated appendix operation left him at death's door. He did not play cricket again for more than a year. Appointed captain of Australia for the 1936–37 season, he got off to a disastrous start, as Australia were heavily defeated in the first two Tests. But thanks to a glut of runs from the skipper, they eventually won the series 3–2.

The Australians retained the Ashes in England in 1938, with Bradman averaging 108.50 in the Tests, and 115.66 for the tour. His 103 in appalling gloom in the fourth Test at Headingley was one of his finest innings. 'Bradman is in such form,' wrote Jack Hobbs, 'that he could play by candlelight.'

Back in Australia he was more prolific than ever in 1938–39. But the war proved an unhappy time for him. Volunteering for the Royal Australian Air Force in 1940, he subsequently transferred to the Army as a supervisor of physical education. But his health broke down. He suffered from muscular trouble and, graver still, his eyesight temporarily worsened, so that his scores in 1940–41 were 0, 6, 0 and 12.

In May 1941 Bradman was discharged from the Army on medical grounds. A frozen shoulder left him unable to lift his right arm. He also lost all feeling in the thumb and index finger of his right hand; it never returned, he wrote in his book *Farewell to Cricket* (1950).

When the England team arrived in Australia in 1946, they thought Bradman looked so ill that he would be better off in a nursing home than on a cricket pitch. But, without recapturing the flair of his pre-war days, Bradman scored 187 in the first Test, and 234 in the second.

England were duly annihilated, and the next season he went on to plunder the Indians for an average of 178.75 in the Tests. Confident in his team, he set off for

England in 1948 determined to complete the tour without defeat. The mission was achieved.

In the fourth Test at Headingley he achieved one of his greatest triumphs, when Australia scored 404 for three wickets in their second innings to win a game they had looked like losing. Bradman's contribution was 173 not out.

After a final three testimonial matches in Australia, Bradman was knighted in 1949. 'I would have preferred to remain just Mister,' he volunteered.

He worked as a stockbroker until 1954 when he announced, rather curiously, that his doctor had advised him to retire. His golf handicap was quickly reduced to scratch.

Latterly Bradman avoided the limelight. 'They usually leave this sort of thing until you are dead,' he remarked when a stand was named after him at Sydney in 1974.

⊰ 26th ⊱

Roger Longrigg, b. 1929, d. 2000

Roger Longrigg, who has died aged seventy, was unmasked in 1962 as the author of novels supposedly written by Rosalind Erskine, a seventeen-year-old schoolgirl, who launched 'herself' on to the literary scene with a raunchy novel about a group of boarding-school girls who turn their school gym into a brothel.

In *The Passion-Flower Hotel*, Cordelia, captain of Hockey, is awakened to romance and Gaby de la Gallantine performs her amazing dance. On the book's dust jacket, under a photograph of 'Miss Erskine', shot from behind, readers were informed that, owing to her 'excitable and highly strung temperament', she had been educated at home by a series of governesses – 'some French, some German, some Swiss, many English, but none of whom stayed for more than eight months'.

Thereafter she had attended a series of boarding schools at one of which 'she made an impact out of all proportion to the time she spent there'. Her hobbies included practising with her 9mm Luger automatic.

Further inquiries (transmitted to Miss Erskine via her publishers Jonathan Cape) elicited the information that she had written her book without her parents' permission ('If they knew about it they'd die'); and that she intended to go to Oxford, although 'many of the things I want to learn aren't taught by dons'.

Roger Erskine Longrigg was born in Edinburgh on 1 May 1929 into a military family. He spent his early years in the Middle East where his father was serving as a brigadier. He was sent home to be educated at Bryanston and Magdalen College, Oxford, where he read History and supplemented his allowance by offering foreign tourists drinks in his rooms.

He then joined the London Press Exchange, an advertising agency. The advertising world gave him the material for his satirical first novel, *A High Pitched Buzz* (1956) and over the next decade he published several more novels under his own name and as Rosalind Erskine.

His play *The Platinum Cat* (1965), starring Kenneth Williams and Caroline Mortimer, was staged at Wyndham's Theatre.

In 1968 he gave up advertising to become a full-time writer. Under his own name, Longrigg wrote several general histories of horse racing and country sports. *The English Squire and his Sport* (1977) was a 600-year survey of country sports from falconry to the catching of pike with live frogs tied to pinioned geese.

⤧ 27th ⤠

Spike Milligan, b. 1918, d. 2002

Spike Milligan, who has died aged eighty-three, created through the *Goon Show* a new form of British humour – surrealist, inconsequential and chaotic.

By no means everyone found the Goons irresistible; nevertheless the show attracted some seven million listeners, and made Milligan a national figure. But the triumph eventually became a source of grievance. 'Wrote the *Goon Show* – died: that's how people think of me,' Milligan complained when Channel 4 ran a spoof obituary in 1991.

His career in comedy began with the outbreak of the Second World War, when Milligan joined D Battery of the 56th Heavy Regiment Royal Artillery, which was stationed at Bexhill-on-Sea.

As the leading member of the Battery band he not only found an outlet for his musical talents – 'honestly, we were the Beatles of Bexhill' – but also began to develop a reputation as a comedian. It was at this point that the name Spike began to take hold.

Music remained to the fore even after the Battery moved to North Africa in January 1943. In September 1943 the Battery – with Milligan still clutching his trumpet – crossed the Mediterranean to Salerno and marched north towards Naples. Exhausted and suffering from piles, he was wounded in the left leg by mortar fire, and reduced to a shaken, incoherent and lachrymose wreck. 'I ran out of courage,' he later explained.

The sense of failure never left him. Later in life he would express admiration for *Telegraph* obituaries – 'all those war heroes. Makes me wish I had done a bit more.'

To the end, however, Milligan remained incapable of failing to crack a joke when the opportunity presented itself, professing relief at the death of Harry Secombe with the declaration: 'Now I won't have to have him singing at my funeral.'

James Burridge, b. 1921, d. 2000

James Burridge, who has died aged seventy-eight, bred the great racehorse Desert Orchid, winner of four King George VI Chases, the Cheltenham Gold Cup, the Whitbread Gold Cup and the Irish Grand National.

Having retired from the law, Burridge spent much of his time hunting with the South Notts and Belvoir. He heard that a ten-year-old mare was for sale and went to see her, but could not at first find the horse since she had jumped into the neighbouring field, where she was standing with icicles hanging from her coat. She cost £175 and was called Grey Orchid.

Despite her delicate name, she was wild and would sometimes try to pin him by falling over backwards when he rode her, so he decided to use her for breeding. She produced a bay mare whom he called Flower Child, and in 1979 she in turn gave birth to Desert Orchid.

'Dessie', a grey, was to prove extraordinarily tough and versatile, equally at home on firm or heavy going, just as happy over two miles as over almost twice that distance, and victorious despite often carrying top weight.

Desert Orchid was immensely popular with the public at large, their admiration sparked by his exuberant front-running, his evident courage, and his taste for showmanship.

By contrast to the horse's obvious confidence, Burridge himself was extremely superstitious and feared the most unlikely disasters. He would wear the same battered trilby to every race in which the horse was running, worrying that if he changed it might prove unlucky. He would then chain-smoke through the race, longing for it all to be over.

James Dugdale Burridge was born in Lahore on 7 December 1921. His father was a major, later a lieutenant-colonel, in the Sikh Regiment. James spent his early childhood in India, where he learned to ride, and was then educated at Haileybury, the fees reputedly being paid by his father's success at the gaming table.

On the outbreak of war Burridge was commissioned into the 11th Hussars and posted to North Africa. In May 1942, while commanding a reconnaissance patrol of three armoured cars, he was – aged 21 – the first man into German-occupied Tunis. He later recounted the experience in his diary:

> As we went down the main street, the inhabitants of Tunis appeared to be caught right off guard. Germans were strolling up and down the pavements talking to their girlfriends. We reached a fairly large square, which seemed a good place to stop. As we came into it, the gendarme held us up and waved on the traffic going across us; he had no idea we weren't German. Hand grenades went off and Sergeant Lyon shot the bloke who threw them and another who was just about to. It was the essence of craziness.
>
> The crowd became impossible, swarming everywhere, cheering endlessly. Had there been a single German capable of organising anything we would certainly have been finished, but madness and confusion saved us. After about an hour, reinforcements came and I gave myself up to unrestrained singing and flirting ...

In 1946, Burridge decided not to return to Oxford and instead went to the Sudan as an Assistant District Commissioner. There he began to study law. He passed his Bar exams and in 1952 was called by Inner Temple.

He later changed to being a solicitor and eventually became a partner in the City firm Lovell White Durrant, where he headed the company law department.

He retired in 1985 and established the Ab Kettleby stud at Melton Mowbray, Leicestershire.

Desert Orchid followed his coffin at the funeral.

❦ 28th ❦

Jane Russell, b. 1921, d. 2011

Jane Russell, who has died aged eighty-nine, was a Hollywood film star of the 1940s and 50s whose acting ability attracted less attention than her vital statistics.

Her 38in bust became the bedrock on which her career was built.

Unlike modern actresses, she never unveiled it, but its fully clad charms were still enough to arouse censors worldwide. Her first film, *The Outlaw*, made in 1941, was briefly shown in 1943 but caused such controversy that it was rapidly withdrawn and not widely released until 1950.

The film is innocuous by modern standards, not to say dull. But promotion is a powerful tool. 'Mean, moody and magnificent', the publicity department called her, and many a humble GI swallowed the message. Soldiers in Korea even named two hills on the battlefield after her. The Press followed suit, reporting that her bosom 'hung over the picture like a thunderstorm over a landscape'.

Born Ernastine Geraldine Russell on 21 June 1921 at Bemidji, Minnesota, she grew up in California, graduating from Van Nuys School. In 1940, she enrolled in Max Reinhardt's Theatrical Workshop. Later, she studied with Maria Ouspenskaya, with a little modelling on the side.

That was how Howard Hughes discovered her, shrewdly placing her under long-term contract and lending her services to other studios.

Paramount, then planning a spoof Western with Bob Hope and Ginger Rogers, balked at the leading lady's terms and signed Jane Russell instead to play Calamity Jane in *The Paleface*. Hope would later introduce his co-star as 'the two and only Jane Russell'.

Her biggest success – the one memorable film of her career – was *Gentlemen Prefer Blondes* in 1953. It was blessed by a stroke of casting genius. The blonde whom gentlemen are supposed to prefer was Marilyn Monroe, leaving Russell to play the brunette they allegedly marry. The production was closely monitored by the censors and several lines had to be cut. Nevertheless, the raunchiness of the material – two gold-diggers on the make – could not be entirely suppressed.

This was the high-water mark of her career. Nothing she did later (including a 1955 sequel without Monroe, *Gentlemen Marry Brunettes*) quite matched it. She continued to film regularly until 1957 but the movies were increasingly gimmicky and ludicrous. *Underwater* (1955), for example, is remembered only as the first (and last) film to be premiered beneath the sea, off Florida. Her last film appearance was in a supporting role in the thriller *Darker than Amber* in 1970.

In real life, Jane Russell claimed to be quite different from her screen image. 'I'm the mothering type,' she admitted, when visiting England in the early 1950s to attend the Royal Command Film Performance. High on her agenda was 'to adopt a really cute little English baby boy', as she was unable to have children, possibly as a result of what she described as a botched abortion prior to her first marriage.

The quest for that 'cute' little boy opened up a long and bitter battle, involving questions in the House and impassioned pleas by Lt-Col Marcus Lipton, Labour MP for Brixton, for the actress to return the fifteen-month-old boy, Thomas Kavanagh of South Lambeth, to his rightful mother.

In the end, after an eleven-month struggle, Miss Russell did adopt Thomas Kavanagh, whose parents were discharged conditionally in London 'for unlawfully permitting the care and possession of the child to be transferred'.

MARCH

⊰ 1st ⊱

Peter Malkin, b. 1927, d. 2005

Peter Malkin, who has died aged seventy-seven, was the Mossad agent who grabbed Adolf Eichmann from a street in Buenos Aires and spirited him to Jerusalem, where he was tried for war crimes.

Eichmann, who had been in overall command of the 'Final Solution', had fled Germany after the war and had been living in Argentina under the name Ricardo Klement, working in the Mercedes-Benz factory. Each evening, he would return on the 203 bus, and walk from the stop back to his house on Garibaldi Street; on 11 May 1960, Malkin approached him, saying, '*Un momentito, senor*' – the only three words of Spanish he knew, and which he had practised for weeks.

Malkin then grabbed Eichmann by the right hand (he had been warned that the German might have a gun) and by the throat, though he had worn gloves to avoid touching him directly. He dragged him to the ground, and twenty seconds later – twice as long as he had thought it would take – had Eichmann inside a car. '*Ein Laut und du bist tot* [One sound and you're dead],' said one of his accomplices, and the Mossad squad drove off.

After ten days of interrogation, which attempted to establish, among other things, whether Eichmann knew the whereabouts of Josef Mengele (he did not), the SS officer was taken, disguised as an El Al steward and drugged to appear drunk, to Israel, where he went on trial in April. Eight months later he was hanged.

Marie-Helene de Rothschild, b. 1927, d. 1996

Marie-Helene de Rothschild, who has died aged sixty-eight, was known in the French press as 'the Queen of Paris' on account of the palaces she refurbished and the extravagant parties she gave.

She was the second wife of Baron Guy de Rothschild, the head of the French branch of the family. He was forty-seven when he married her in February 1957, an age when many men are content to settle for a peaceful life. But Marie-Helene was a force of nature who permitted no disengagement.

There were those whom she failed to captivate. 'She is admired, criticised, envied, imitated,' Guy de Rothschild admitted. 'She enchants, she subjugates, she inspires jealousy. One likes her or one dislikes her. In any case, she stirs, she disturbs, she upsets. One is for, one is against.'

Early in their marriage the Rothschilds bought a house on the rue de Courcelles in Paris that had once belonged to Napoleon's niece, Princess Mathilde. For their country seat they restored a manor house near Deauville. But Marie-Helene's eyes soon fell upon Ferrieres, a chateau twenty-five miles north-east of Paris, where Guy had been brought up.

Two evenings in particular stood out. There was the Proust Ball, given in celebration of the centenary of the writer's birth in December 1971. The winter garden was transformed into a ballroom and festooned with orchids; in the centre were gigantic *pieces montées*, edible constructions made out of the little madeleine cakes immortalised by Proust.

The next December Marie-Helene dreamed up a Surrealist Ball, attended by Salvador Dali himself. The hostess donned a red deer's mask studded with teardrops made of real diamonds; Audrey Hepburn appeared with her head in a cage; and the footmen, wearing cats' heads, were instructed to fall asleep on the stairs. The evening reached its climax when eight footmen carried in a platter on which a nude woman reclined on a bed of roses. The display was made entirely of edible spun sugar, and hacked to pieces.

In 1975 Marie-Helene embarked on a new project, which originated at a lunch with Baron Alexis de Rede, who complained that he was being evicted from his Parisian apartment in the seventeenth-century Palais Lambert. This building overlooks the Seine from the Ile de St Louis; Voltaire, who had once lived there, called it 'a palace for a philosopher-king'.

'I don't know why we don't buy it,' Marie-Helene volunteered to de Rede over the cheese. In no time she was on to her husband at the bank. 'Do you feel young enough and romantic enough to change the course of your life in the space of two hours?' she demanded.

'Why not?' the Baron nervously responded.

Furniture and painting were moved in from Ferrieres, including *The Astronomer* by Vermeer. When the dust settled Guy de Rothschild was left to reflect that, after a quarter of a century of marriage to Marie-Helene, he had entirely forgotten the colour grey.

The eldest of three children, the second Baroness Guy de Rothschild was born Marie-Helene Naila Stephanie Josina van Zuylen de Nyevelt in New York on 27 November 1927.

Her father Egmont van Zuylen, though of Dutch origin, had been a diplomat in the service of the King of Belgium. He became engaged to a princess, only to break off the match when, en poste in Cairo, he encountered the beautiful Marguerite Nametalla.

'Hers is intelligence in its purest state,' observed Andre Malraux of Marguerite, 'since it is unencumbered by any intellectual baggage.'

While still very young, Marie-Helene married the Comte Francois de Nicolay, a union later annulled by papal dispensation. She met Guy de Rothschild in racing circles; '*Notre rencontre fut un coup de foudre devastateur comme un ouragon,*' the baron vouchsafed.

In later life, despite the inexorable progress of a muscular disease, Marie-Helene's social appetite remained strong. She discovered, indeed, that travelling to parties in an ambulance was the best way to beat the Paris traffic.

⊰ 2nd ⊱

Lord St John of Fawsley, b. 1929, d. 2012

Lord St John of Fawsley, the former Conservative MP Norman St John-Stevas, who has died aged eighty-two, served as Arts Minister and Leader of the House under Margaret Thatcher and later as Master of Emmanuel College, Cambridge, and chairman of the Royal Fine Art Commission; he was also something of a work of art and national treasure himself.

The Royal Fine Art Commission, of which he served three terms as chairman from 1985 to 1999, described itself as 'the ultimate authority for consultation on matters of taste and aesthetics' – a remit which fitted Lord St John to perfection. Like Oscar Wilde, he put his genius into his life, affecting the flamboyant mannerisms of an Edwardian aesthete (proffering his hand in papal fashion, lapsing into Latin, deliberately mispronouncing modern words).

Irrepressible, witty and disarmingly immodest, Lord St John was an expert on much else besides aesthetics. In the 1990s, during the break-up of the marriage of the Prince and Princess of Wales, he became known for his frequent television appearances in which he would give the nation the benefit of his expertise on the attendant constitutional implications, a role in which he claimed extensive knowledge of the inner workings and private thoughts of the Royal Family.

It was never entirely clear how much direct access he had, though he was certainly a great friend of Princess Margaret. When criticised for his willingness to pontificate on any royal issue, however trivial, he explained that his motivation was a 'desire to do what one can to help the monarchy and help the Queen'.

In his role as Arts Minister in Mrs Thatcher's first administration, Norman St John-Stevas was said to be one of the only cabinet members allowed to tease the Prime Minister, whom he referred to as 'the Blessed One', 'the Leaderene' or (unaccountably) 'Heather'. He liked to tell the story of how he asked to be excused from a meeting because he had a reception to go to. 'But I'm going to the same function,' protested Mrs Thatcher. 'Yes, but it takes me so much longer to change,' replied St John-Stevas. Yet it seemed that Mrs Thatcher did not see the need for a licensed jester – particularly one so well known for his indiscretions with the press over lunch.

For St John-Stevas did not so much leak as gush, providing an entertaining running commentary on the foibles of his colleagues (on whom he bestowed nicknames), spiced up with fruity society tittle-tattle. 'The trouble with you, Norman,' one listener complained, 'is that you're such a compulsive name-dropper.' 'The Queen said exactly the same to me yesterday,' came the rejoinder.

Norman Anthony Francis St John-Stevas was born in London on 18 May 1929 ('the same birthday as his late Martyred Imperial Majesty Nicholas II'). He was sent to

Ratcliffe, a small Roman Catholic school near Leicester, and then spent six months in Rome studying for the priesthood before discovering he had no vocation. Instead he went up to Fitzwilliam House, Cambridge, where he became president of the Union and famous for things like jumping into the river in evening dress. After graduating with a First in Law, he went on to Christ Church, Oxford, where he was secretary of the Union and obtained a Second in the examination for Bachelor of Civil Law. He was called to the Bar by the Middle Temple in 1952.

But he 'never practised, only preached', and became a noted academic lawyer, lecturing and tutoring at Yale, at Southampton University, King's College, London, and at Oxford. He lectured all over the United States and held a visiting professorship at the University of California at Santa Barbara. From 1954 to 1959 he was legal adviser to Sir Alan Herbert's committee on book censorship. His *Obscenity and the Law* was published in 1956 and became a key work of reference during subsequent reforms.

In 1959 he joined *The Economist*, at first to edit the collected works of Bagehot, a mammoth and scholarly task that eventually saw the light of day as a series of fifteen beautifully produced and highly regarded volumes published between 1966 and 1986. He also became the magazine's correspondent on law, the Church and politics.

Having contested the hopeless seat of Dagenham in 1951, St John-Stevas won Chelmsford for the Tories in 1964, and remained its MP until his elevation to the Lords in 1987. Although generally regarded as a 'wet', he supported Mrs Thatcher for the Conservative leadership against Ted Heath and became Opposition spokesman on education, in which role he got on famously badly with his populist right-wing colleague Rhodes (later Sir Rhodes) Boyson, to whom he gave the ironic nickname 'Colossus'.

It came as a relief when, in 1978, he was made shadow Leader of the House. After the Conservative victory in 1979, he was appointed Leader of the House, Chancellor of the Duchy of Lancaster and Minister for the Arts.

Despite becoming better known for his contributions to the arts, St John-Stevas made his most enduring contribution as Leader of the House. He inaugurated the present system of parliamentary select committees, placing them on a departmental basis and ensuring that membership was not controlled by the party whips.

His dismissal by Mrs Thatcher in January 1981 was a devastating blow, but he had no shortage of friends in the arts world and took on a clutch of appointments on national bodies concerned with theatre, dance, music and the decorative arts. He was created a life peer as Lord St John of Fawsley in 1987.

His time at the Royal Fine Art Commission was not entirely uncontroversial. The Commission had been a dozy quango which, for many years, could hardly even be bothered to produce an annual report, and it was hoped that his appointment would inject a bit of panache and excitement. It did, and he changed the public image of the Commission considerably. But critics accused him of turning it into a personal publicity vehicle, and of allowing his own wayward preferences to take precedence over the views of the experts.

Problems magnified after Lord St John was elected Master of Emmanuel College,

Cambridge, in 1991. Academic politics proved highly diverting, and his frequent absences from the Commission's offices in London raised eyebrows. In 1994 the government called in the retired civil servant Sir Geoffrey Chipperfield to examine the Commission. His conclusions were devastating: the Commission acted arbitrarily and was not respected, and the chairman's office and car were over-lavish for a publicly funded body. Any other chairman would probably have had to resign, but Lord St John defied all predictions and was reappointed for a third term in 1995.

His time at Emmanuel College, which lasted until 1996, was equally tumultuous. It was said that the dons of the historically Puritan institution first had doubts about whether they had chosen the right man when several of his friends were caught naked one night in the Fellows Garden swimming pool.

Lord St John was also accused of spending an excessive amount of time with a small clique of mainly public school-educated young men who, it was alleged, were favoured with introductions to royalty and captains of industry, to dinners at White's, private theatrical performances at the Master's Lodge and long, affectionate letters. Such special privileges were extended to very few. Other undergraduates would recall the Master cutting them off in mid-sentence with some disparaging remark in Latin. To bitchy colleagues in other colleges, Emmanuel became known as 'Mein Camp'.

In *Who's Who* Lord St John described himself, somewhat superfluously, as 'unmarried'.

Serge Gainsbourg, b. 1928, d. 1991

Serge Gainsbourg, the controversial French singer, composer and film director, who has died in Paris aged sixty-two, was best known in Britain for his *succès de scandale*, 'Je T'aime Moi Non Plus', the heavy-breathing duet recorded with his then girlfriend, the English actress Jane Birkin.

'Je T'aime' achieved huge popularity in 1969, despite – or perhaps because of – being banned by the BBC and denounced by the Vatican. Peter Cook recorded a spoof version featuring 'Serge Forward and Jane Firkin'.

Having developed, with 'Je T'aime', the taste for putting a nation into shock, Gainsbourg set out – with some success – to repeat the experience. In 1979 there was outrage from French traditionalists when he recruited a group of Jamaican reggae musicians and recorded a highly idiosyncratic version of 'La Marseillaise'. The song was re-titled 'Aux Armes et Caetera', and provoked riots when concerts were disrupted by veteran paratroopers.

Six years previously there had been opposition to the release of *Rock Around the Bunker*, his collection of songs about the Third Reich. The LP included a reading of 'Smoke Gets In Your Eyes', which many listeners considered to be in questionable taste.

Record buyers who were familiar with Gainsbourg's family history, however, chose to see this and other of his more controversial releases as an indication of the singer's having been born with 'a skin too few'. As a child, Gainsbourg, the offspring of Russian Jewish refugees, had been made to wear the yellow star, and on several occasions had narrowly escaped death.

The son of a nightclub pianist, he was born Lucien Ginzburg in Paris on 2 April 1928 and brought up in Pigalle. He changed his name for one he considered to be more aristocratic while still acknowledging his Russian origins.

He trained as a painter but by the early 1950s he came under the influence of the jazz musician, Boris Vian, and began to work as a singer and pianist in the nightclubs of Saint Germain des Prés.

In the 1960s Gainsbourg, whose own recordings tended towards the cynical, specialised in writing mainstream pop for such luminaries as Juliette Greco and Petula Clark. Increasingly, however, he indulged his fondness for mischief, notably in 1966 when he wrote the highly suggestive 'Les Sucettes' ('Lollipops') for the young France Gall. Mlle Gall, only sixteen, had no idea of the song's 'hidden agenda'.

In the mid-1960s, Gainsbourg wrote 'BB' and other 'bubble-gum pop' hits for Brigitte Bardot. Then in 1968 he met the coltish Jane Birkin, who had already acquired some valuable experience of minor scandal (as a result of her nude nymphet role in Antonioni's film *Blow Up*).

Birkin lived with Gainsbourg for more than ten years before leaving him in the early 1980s. 'We were a public couple,' Gainsbourg recalled. 'We went out a lot. The trouble was, I didn't always make it back.'

As his career progressed, Gainsbourg discovered that his capacity to outrage was increasingly hindered by public tolerance. But nevertheless he achieved his aim in 1984 with 'Lemon Incest', an unusually sensual reading of Chopin's *Etude No 3 in E Major*, Opus 10. The video for the song showed Gainsbourg in bed with his fourteen-year-old daughter, Charlotte, who subsequently embarked on a successful career as a film actress.

Paul Raymond, b. 1925, d. 2008

Paul Raymond, the entrepreneur who has died aged eighty-two, amassed fortunes from nudity and property.

'The King of Porn', as Raymond was dubbed, was an avuncular figure who claimed that he was an honest entertainer. But some argued that his prurient productions and publications whetted the public's appetite for darker material, and that Britain's moral decline began in 1958, when Raymond circumvented the laws prohibiting striptease by opening a private club, the Revuebar, his flagship and life-long base.

The club could be joined at the door, and within two years it had more than 45,000 members. Businessmen and tourists mingled with politicians, shop stewards and nobility to gawp at Bonnie Bell the Ding Dong Girl and Julia Mendez the Snake Girl. Such immodesty attracted the attention of the police, who were obliged to spend much time on the premises; in its early years the Revuebar was raided several times, and in 1961 Raymond was fined £5,000 after a magistrate decided that allowing members of the audience to ring the Ding Dong Girl's bells constituted an unruly house – and that, furthermore, Julia Mendez should not have swallowed the snake in public.

⊰ 3rd ⊱

Michael Foot, b. 1913, d. 2010

Michael Foot, the former Labour leader who has died aged ninety-six, spent the latter part of his political career vainly attempting to unite a party which, during his many years as a backbench MP, he had seemed positively eager to split.

Temperamentally, Foot was far better suited to criticism than construction. In his mental universe idealistic Socialists strove heroically against the dastardly machinations of capital and privilege. While he could admire an unprincipled adventurer like Disraeli, or a self-destructive logician like Enoch Powell, he felt only withering contempt for Tories anxious to protect interests for which they had neither toiled nor spun.

For most of his life he appeared to regard with even more loathing the Labour Judases who compromised the one true faith. As a backbench zealot of the left, Foot had regularly flouted the whips, sallying forth like the Levellers or Ranters of old in defence of Socialist virtue.

His literary heroes Swift, Hazlitt and Byron were all rebels, and Foot was proud to stand beside them against the dragons of reaction. He was a fine speaker, at his best when addressing a vast meeting with the moral fervour of an Old Testament prophet, but also an accomplished performer in the House of Commons, where even opponents delighted in the wit and venom that poured from him.

Yet the ideologue who appeared in public debate to be drained of all sympathy for his enemies presented a different face in private. Foot was wholly without vanity or side. Away from the hustings he became an immensely likable man of charm and sensibility, exuding in every contact the courtesy and kindliness conferred upon him by his middle-class Methodist background.

Up until 1970, when he was fifty-six, Foot had never even put himself forward as a candidate for the shadow cabinet; on joining the front bench he remained as committed as ever to nationalisation and nuclear disarmament. Nevertheless, something changed. In 1960 Barbara Castle told Foot that he had 'grown soft on a diet of soft options because he never had to choose'. After 1970 he was subject to the shifts and compromises that political survival requires.

By October 1971 Foot was standing against the inveterate Europhile Roy Jenkins for the deputy leadership; though beaten, he was by no means disgraced. When Labour scraped back to power in February 1974, he was appointed Secretary of State for Employment.

Foot began by settling the miners' strike which had toppled the Conservative government, by the simple expedient of allowing pay rises of between 22 and 25 per cent. Next came a Trades Union and Labour Relations Act, which repealed the Conservatives' Industrial Relations Act and accorded extensive recognition to union rights.

The urge to appease the unions grew apace. A succession of ruinously high wage settlements – 31 per cent for the electricity workers, 27 per cent for the railwaymen, 37 per cent for the National Union of Seamen – produced roaring inflation.

By the time of Harold Wilson's resignation in 1976 Foot's reputation was such that he topped the first ballot to elect a new leader. Though Jim Callaghan finally emerged victorious, Foot became deputy leader.

Reality was crowding in. In the summer of 1976 Foot actively helped Denis Healey to agree plans with the unions for wage restraint and though he balked at the expenditure cuts demanded by the IMF that autumn, he did not threaten resignation. Indeed, he told Tony Benn to 'face the real problems'.

Then, believing that the limit for wage increases could be held, Foot made a fatal error in helping to dissuade Callaghan from calling an election in the autumn of 1978. In the ensuing 'winter of discontent' the government's standing collapsed.

Still Foot tried to cobble together alliances with the minority parties. But Labour lost a motion of no confidence by one vote, which meant a general election and the triumph of Mrs Thatcher. It seemed that he was now destined for a quiet literary retirement; in 1980 he published *Debts of Honour*, in celebration of various heroes.

But when Callaghan resigned as leader in 1980, Foot was the only candidate of the left with a chance of defeating Healey. This time he came second on the first ballot, but was elected after John Silkin and Peter Shore withdrew. Two days later he fell downstairs and had his leg encased in plaster.

Thereafter Foot was never able to throw off the image of an old man struggling gamely, but ineffectively, against manifold physical disabilities. It was true that, since a bad car crash in 1963, he had been obliged to walk with a stick; while in 1976 he had lost the sight of an eye after an attack of shingles. But Foot did not lack energy; his problem was that he was crippled politically.

His own past rendered him powerless to prevent the Labour Party from drifting further to the left after the defeat of 1979. The consequence was that, in 1981, the Gang of Four (Roy Jenkins, Shirley Williams, David Owen and William Rodgers) left to found the Social Democratic Party.

By the time of the general election of 1983, twenty-four Labour MPs had defected to the SDP. To add to Foot's woes, in 1981 Tony Benn insisted – against Foot's express wish – on standing against Denis Healey for the deputy leadership. For weeks on end the hopes of the extreme left were paraded before an appalled electorate. It did not help that Foot could not himself shake off accusations that he had disrespectfully worn a donkey jacket to Remembrance Sunday events at the Cenotaph that year (he claimed it was a respectable green jacket).

The Falklands War further undermined his position. He seemed to fall between two stools, at first demanding an effective riposte against Argentine aggression, and then emphasising the need to work for a peace settlement with the junta.

Labour registered but 27.6 per cent of the votes cast, a mere 680,000 more than the 25.4 per cent which the Alliance achieved. Foot immediately resigned the leadership.

The fifth of seven children, Michael Mackintosh Foot was born at Lipson Terrace, one of the best addresses at Plymouth, on 23 July 1913. Of his three elder brothers, Dingle would serve as solicitor-general in the first years of Harold Wilson's administration; Hugh became Britain's representative at the UN from 1964 to 1970 and was created a life peer as Lord Caradon; and John, who took over the family law firm, was also made a life peer. The youngest boy, Christopher, followed his elder brother into the family firm.

Isaac Foot, the father of this brood, was himself a remarkable man: a solicitor; Liberal MP for Bodmin and briefly parliamentary secretary for mines in the National Government of 1931, he was also a Methodist lay preacher steeped in the poetry of Shakespeare, Milton and Wordsworth. A radical in the seventeenth-century Puritan tradition, his children were brought up to believe that the ultimate sin was to vote Tory.

Michael was educated at Leighton Park, the Quaker School near Reading, from where he won a History exhibition to Wadham College, Oxford (only to read PPE). After coming down his first job was with the Blue Funnel Line at Liverpool, where the poverty and unemployment helped to make him a Socialist. He had also become a protégé of the Labour Cabinet minister Stafford Cripps, whose son had been a friend at Oxford.

In November 1935, only a few months after joining the Labour Party, Foot stood as a candidate in a by-election at Monmouth. Back in London, he worked briefly for the *New Statesman* before finding a more permanent berth on *Tribune*, the left-wing weekly. In 1938 Foot went to work for the *Evening Standard* as a feature writer. His pieces for the *Standard* were later developed into a book, *Armistice 1918–39* (1940).

During the war Foot, disqualified from active service by his asthma, took over as editor of the *Standard*. He was exceptionally well-off at this period, being paid nearly £4,000 a year. But in 1944 he left the paper and took up a far less well-paid post on the *Daily Herald*, to which he contributed a political column twice a week for the next twenty years.

Having been adopted as the Labour candidate for Plymouth Devonport in 1938, Foot was swept into Parliament in the Labour landslide of 1945. Typically, his maiden speech in the Commons contained a slashing attack on Winston Churchill, 'an avowed supporter of the police government of Signor Mussolini'.

Soon, though, he was turning his guns on the Labour government's foreign policy. At the end of 1945 he was one of twenty-three Labour MPs who voted against the terms imposed by an American loan: 'American capitalism,' he fulminated in *Tribune*, 'is arrogant, merciless and convinced of its capacity to dictate the destinies of the world.'

But he never blinded himself, like some on the left, to the difference between Democratic Socialism and Communism. In 1946 a visit under Bevin's auspices to Tehran and Azerbaijan left him convinced of Stalin's imperialist aims and by October 1946 *Tribune*, which he had rejoined in 1945, was reluctantly acknowledging that the defence of democracy might require help from the Americans.

Though the Conservatives won the 1951 election, Foot held on to Plymouth Devonport, aided by the choice of his friend Randolph Churchill as the Tory candidate. In 1955, however, he lost the seat to Joan Vickers.

Out of Parliament, he settled down to write *The Pen and the Sword* (1957), which gleefully described how Jonathan Swift's polemics had brought down the great Duke of Marlborough. But the advent of Hugh Gaitskell as leader was 'a galling moment' for Foot, even if it seemed at first mitigated by the appointment of Aneurin Bevan, moving force behind the creation of the NHS, as shadow foreign secretary.

Bitter disillusion was to follow. At the 1957 party conference Bevan abandoned the unilateralist disarmament policies which were at the heart of Foot's political creed. Subsequently, Foot was one of the founders of the Campaign for Nuclear Disarmament, to be seen every year in the front rank on the march to Aldermaston.

Though offered the safe Labour seat of Aberavon, he determined to fight Plymouth Devonport again, only to go down once more to Joan Vickers in 1959. After the death of Bevan in July 1960, however, he was adopted for Ebbw Vale, and returned to the House of Commons that November. Over the years he would conceive a deep affection for the constituency.

But the rift with Bevan, the greatest of Foot's political heroes, had never been completely healed. Jenny Lee, Bevan's widow, attributed her husband's death to the nuclear disarmers: 'Until their attacks began, he never had so much as a stomach ache.'

Foot, clinging fast to his belief in unilateral nuclear disarmament, had the Labour whip withdrawn after he voted against the Army Estimates in March 1961. Despite the death of Gaitskell and the succession of Harold Wilson, Foot did not regain the Labour whip until November 1964, after Labour had been returned to power. The possibility was aired that he might become number two to Frank Cousins at the ministry of technology, but no such appointment transpired.

Soon Foot was at loggerheads with the Labour government on the defence of the pound, on steel nationalisation, on the Vietnam War, on Rhodesia and on immigration. In May 1965 he unhesitatingly rejected an overture from Wilson that might have resulted in a place in the government.

The decisive Labour victory in the 1966 general election failed to produce a government more acceptable to Foot and he courted expulsion by voting against it several times.

Though Foot remained MP for Ebbw Vale (or Blaenau Gwent) until 1992, his resignation as leader in 1983 left him with more time for his books. In July 1995 he received 'substantial damages' from *The Sunday Times*, after articles had been published under the heading 'KGB: Michael Foot was our agent'.

⇥ 4th ⇤

Captain Joe Baker-Cresswell, b. 1901, d. 1997

Captain Joe Baker-Cresswell, who has died aged ninety-six, was the destroyer captain whose capture of a U-boat in 1941 led to a sensational intelligence coup which changed the whole course of the Second World War.

Late in 1940, Baker-Cresswell was appointed captain of the destroyer *Bulldog*, leading the 3rd Escort Group. On 9 May 1941, the Group was in the Atlantic, escorting convoy OB 318, outward bound from Liverpool, when it was attacked by U-110 – commanded by a notable U-boat ace, Kap. Lt Julius Lemp, the man who sank the liner *Athenia* on the first evening of the war.

Lemp sank two ships in the starboard columns of OB 318, but his periscope was sighted by the nearest escort, the corvette *Aubrieta*, which dropped a pattern of ten depth-charges.

Bulldog and the destroyer *Broadway* were about to join the attack when all eyes were caught by a sudden, violent water turbulence. The patch of strange broken water, containing eerily large bubbles, spread very rapidly and then, before anybody could react, a U-boat surfaced in the middle of it, with men already pouring out of the conning tower. The U-boat survivors (Lemp was not among them) were picked up by *Aubrietia*.

Baker-Cresswell was quick-witted enough to realise that the U-boat crew would assume their boat had been sunk. Their captain was certainly dead. The U-boat men were quickly hustled below decks. They saw, and were told, nothing.

U-110 was boarded by a party from *Bulldog* which methodically stripped the boat of all the equipment they could remove – binoculars, sextants, books, logs, charts, diaries, pictures, tools and instruments. A telegraphist noted down the tuning positions of all the radio sets in the wireless office. *Bulldog's* whaler had to make several trips, back and forth, loaded with treasures.

Baker-Cresswell realised there was a good chance of saving this U-boat and of keeping any information gained from it secret from the Germans. He decided to take U-110 in tow. This was achieved shortly after 4 p.m. and at first *Bulldog* made good progress, although the U-boat was noticeably down by the stern. But the weather worsened overnight and *Bulldog* had to heave to. Next morning, U-110 suddenly put its bows up in the air, until the hull was nearly vertical, and then sank.

Baker-Cresswell was bitterly disappointed to lose his prize, but the cryptanalytical gains from U-110 were beyond price – far more valuable than the U-boat itself. Experts from Bletchley Park went up to Scapa Flow to meet *Bulldog*, taking with them small briefcases, expecting only a few papers.

When they saw two large packing cases, they could hardly believe their eyes. They handled the contents like men in a daze. Here were items they had only dreamed of, including: U-110's Enigma cipher machine, with the settings for 9 May still on its rotors, the special code settings for high-security '*Offizierte*' (officer only) traffic, and the current code book for U-boats' short-signal (*Kurzsignale*) sighting reports.

Baker-Cresswell was awarded the DSO, and his engineer officer, Lt-Cdr Dodds, and the boarding officer, Sub-Lt Balme, were both awarded DSCs.

Addison Joe Baker-Cresswell was born on 2 February 1901, into an old Northumbrian family. He went to Gresham's School, Holt, and joined the Navy in 1919, his first ship, as a midshipman, being the battlecruiser *Tiger*. His first command, in 1940, was the destroyer *Arrow*.

After *Bulldog*, Baker-Cresswell joined the Joint Intelligence staff at Storey's Gate in London before, late in 1943, he was appointed chief of staff to the C-in-C Western Approaches, Admiral Sir Max Horton. After a volcanic clash of personalities he asked to be relieved, and went out to command the East Indies Escort Force until the end of the war.

In 1946 Baker-Cresswell commanded the cruiser *Gambia* for a two-year commission in the Far East. For his last three years in the Navy, he was deputy director of Naval Intelligence. He retired in 1951, and was appointed ADC to King George VI the same year.

In retirement, Baker-Cresswell went back to his native Northumberland. He farmed near Bamburgh, became a JP and chairman of the bench, and was High Sheriff in 1962.

The story of U-110's capture was kept secret for many years. The formal letter the Admiralty sent Baker-Cresswell on his retirement, summarising his naval career, did not mention it. But as King George VI said when he invested Baker-Cresswell with his DSO, U-110's capture was perhaps the most important single event in the whole war at sea.

⇚ 5th ⇛

Vivian Stanshall, b. 1943, d. 1995

Vivian Stanshall, who has died aged fifty-two, was a musician, satirist and all-round eccentric.

His heyday was the mid-1960s, when as the singer of the Bonzo Dog Doo-Dah Band he brought his anarchic humour to a wide audience, hitting the charts in 1968 with 'I'm The Urban Spaceman' – perhaps the only top-ten single ever to feature a hosepipe solo.

The Lord Denning, b. 1899, d. 1999

The Lord Denning, the former Master of the Rolls who has died aged one hundred, was one of the outstanding judges of the century and a fearless champion of the rights of the common man.

'Unlike my brother judge here, who is concerned with law,' he once teased at a legal dinner, 'I am concerned with justice.'

Whenever 'Tom' Denning was faced with a situation that seemed to him dishonest, unjust or wrong, all his ingenuity and erudition would be directed to finding a remedy, even if the wrongdoer appeared to have the law on his side.

This was particularly the case when some powerful institution seemed to be oppressing a smaller body or individual. Denning's devotion to justice was rooted in his strong faith. 'Without religion there is no morality,' he wrote, 'and without morality there is no law.' For many years he was president of the Lawyers' Christian Fellowship, and he liked to have the Bible close to hand when writing judgments. 'It is the most tattered book in my library,' he said.

Denning's style, whether in his judgments or in his books, was always simple, clear, vigorous and direct. He used short sentences in which adjectives, sometimes even verbs, were at a premium; and he liked to present the facts in the form of a story.

'It happened on 19 April 1964. It was bluebell time in Kent,' began his judgment in Hinz v. Berry (1970). 'In summertime, village cricket is a delight to everyone,' was the opening of his summary in Miller v. Jackson (1977).

For all his legal eminence, it was in a non-judicial role that Denning first became a household name. In June 1963 the Prime Minister, Harold Macmillan, asked him to undertake the inquiry into the security risks arising from the resignation of the Secretary of State for War, John Profumo.

'The Denning Report', published the next September, became an instant bestseller. Its chapter headings would have passed muster in any twopenny thriller: 'Christine Tells her Story', 'The Meeting of the Five Ministers', 'The Slashing and the Shooting', 'The Man in the Mask'.

Some felt that Denning's innate puritanism rendered him unfit for such an investigation. The report made unsubstantiated allegations against Stephen Ward, and a photograph of Christine Keeler, who was indeed very attractive, provoked him to comment that there was no doubt about the nature of her profession. But Mandy Rice-Davies spoke for many when she remarked that Denning was 'quite the nicest judge I ever met'.

Alfred Thompson Denning was born at Whitchurch, Hampshire, on 23 January 1899, the fourth of five sons of Charles Denning, a draper, and his wife Clara. Tom was considered by his mother to be the weakest of the brood. Nevertheless, after being educated at the local Whitchurch elementary school and at the grammar school in Andover, he served on the Western Front.

In the spring of 1918 he joined the 151st Field Company of the Royal Engineers, which was building bridges across the River Ancre under heavy fire. Denning escaped without injury, though he spent Armistice Day in hospital with the exceptionally fierce influenza that took even greater toll than the war.

He returned to take a First in Mathematics at Magdalen College, Oxford, notwithstanding his diffidence about being a grammar school boy in a rich man's college.

In 1921 he returned to Magdalen and next year gained another First, this time in Law. He was called to the Bar in June 1923. He practised on the Western Circuit and in London, and in 1938, when he was earning more than £3,000 a year, he felt secure enough to take silk. Though his salary did not actually decrease with his elevation, as often happens, he never commanded colossal fees.

On the outbreak of the Second World War, Denning immediately volunteered for service, but was rejected as too old. So he continued to practise law until December 1943, when he made his debut on the Bench as a Commissioner of Assize in Manchester for three weeks, replacing a judge taken ill. Then in March 1944 Lord Simon appointed him a High Court Judge in the Probate, Divorce and Admiralty Division.

As an Assize judge he found himself obliged on occasion to sentence men to death; it was only later in his life that he concluded that capital punishment was morally wrong. And in the case of a youth who had hit an old woman over the head in order to steal £20, he did not hesitate to order twenty-five strokes of the birch.

Promotion continued to come swiftly: in October 1948, after only four and a half years as a trial judge, Denning was elevated to the Court of Appeal. In 1957 he was made a Lord of Appeal in Ordinary, with the usual life peerage attached to that office. But five years later, he moved back to the Court of Appeal as Master of the Rolls.

The appointment reflected tensions of a personal and professional nature. Denning did not enjoy his time in the House of Lords: 'To most lawyers on the Bench,' he remarked, 'the House of Lords is like heaven – you want to get there some day, but not while there is any life in you.'

⊰ 6th ⊱

Willie Gunn, b. 1910, d. 1996

Willie Gunn, the fisherman who has died aged eighty-six, gave his name to one of the deadliest salmon flies that has ever been tied.

It was Rob Wilson, who had a tackle shop in Brora, Sutherland, who tied the original Willie Gunn fly. It was one of about twenty experimental patterns, and Wilson asked Gunn to select one.

Gunn's experienced eye fell upon one which was intended to be a hair-wing variation of another noted salmon fly, the Thunder & Lightning. 'By gum,' said Gunn, 'that one looks bonny. That's the fly I would use.'

'Well,' said Wilson, 'you must have it and we will name the fly the Willie Gunn.'

Gunn's instant judgment was rapidly vindicated. That very day he caught six fish with the black, orange and yellow fly, and four the day after. Word spread and everyone on the River Brora began to use the Willie Gunn. Now it is known throughout the salmon-fishing world.

Willie Gunn was born on 1 January 1910 at Skerray on the wild north coast of Sutherland. He spent his early years in what he was later to describe as very poor conditions. His parents were crofters at Skerray; his father fished to make ends meet.

Gunn arrived on the estate of Lord Strathnaver, the son of the Countess of Sutherland, when he was aged about eighteen, after spells with the Forestry Commission and in farming. He began by working with the gundogs and he learned quickly. A football injury put an end to his stalking. The job could mean walking many miles a day in rough terrain, and Gunn was no longer capable of that.

His life with rod and line began as a hobby. He began as a trout fisherman, but his horizons widened when he caught his first (16lb) salmon on the River Mallart. The largest fish he ever caught was a 28-pounder taken from the Bengie pool on his beloved Brora.

According to one story, the Queen Mother, a skilled and enthusiastic salmon fisher, knew the fly, though not the man himself. It is said that she turned to her ghillie on an unproductive day on the Sutherland estate and asked why they had not tried the Willie Gunn. 'Ma'am,' he said. 'I am Willie Gunn.'

❧ 7th ❧

Chelita Secunda, b. 1945, d. 2000

Chelita Secunda, who has died suddenly aged fifty-five, was a familiar and stylish figure in the rackety worlds of art, fashion and pop music during the late 1960s and 1970s; her friends included Ossie Clark and Derek Jarman, and her uninhibited sense of glamour influenced the look of such bands as T Rex and Roxy Music.

A little given to drama, and no stranger to hauteur, Chelita Secunda was above all capable of putting on a good performance. Shortly after the birth of her daughter, Tallulah, in 1986, she went on holiday to the south of France, and wandered determinedly down to the beach in a diaphanous white robe, chopsticks in her hair and her face covered with glitter.

An elderly Frenchman turned to his boules partner. '*Ça doit être les Anglais*,' he sniffed. 'Oh darling,' wailed Chelita Secunda to her friend, 'that's terrible. I thought we were so international.'

Professor William Hamilton, b. 1936, d. 2000

Professor William Hamilton, who has died aged sixty-three, was the most influential evolutionary biologist of his generation.

Bill Hamilton's paper on 'the genetical evolution of social behaviour' (1964) became the most cited paper in all science. He was responsible almost single-handedly for a revolution in the study of animal behaviour. But the full story of how Hamilton came to write his classic paper only emerged in his autobiographical sketches published in 1995. As a shy and lonely graduate student dividing his time between the London School of Economics and University College London, Hamilton was ignored at one institution and mistrusted at the other.

He later wrote of his time at University College: 'I never had a desk there nor was ever invited to give any presentation to explain my work or my occasional presence to others. Most of the time I was extremely lonely. Sometimes I came to dislike my bed-sitting room so much that I would go to Waterloo Station, where I continued reading or trying to write out a [mathematical] model sitting on the benches among waiting passengers in the main hall.'

The question that obsessed Hamilton, if none of his peers, was how altruism could evolve as an instinct. The prevailing mood in evolutionary biology saw animal behaviour as always devoted to the 'good of the species'.

Hamilton thought this made no sense, because an animal's closest competitor was often a member of its own species, so evolution should produce selfish, not altruistic individuals. Yet it plainly did not. As Darwin had been worried to observe, the extreme co-operation seen in the social insects – termites, bees and ants – seemed hard to explain.

The answer that Hamilton came up with was that animals might be selected to have altruistic instincts towards relatives, whose genes they share. So altruism will evolve in rabbit warrens if on average the rabbits are sufficiently closely related.

This was expressed in what is now known as Hamilton's rule. He illustrated his theory, which became known as kin selection or inclusive fitness, with a study of the social Hymenoptera – ants, bees and wasps – whose unusual genetics put them in the strange position of being more closely related to their sisters than their daughters and who have delegated reproduction to each colony's queen.

Hamilton's paper was rejected out of hand by *Nature* magazine. The mathematics was dense and the prose denser. It was eventually published in two parts in 1964 in the comparatively obscure *Journal of Theoretical Biology*. It was the first clear statement of what has since become known variously as the 'gene's eye view' of evolution, the 'selfish gene' school, or 'sociobiology' – the theory that sees individuals as vehicles for competing genes.

William Donald Hamilton was born on 1 August 1936 and went to Tonbridge School. He devoted his spare time to collecting insects in the countryside. He read Zoology at Cambridge, then after National Service and his lonely spell doing the work on altruism in London, made the first of many expeditions to Brazil to study bees and wasps. There he fell in love with the rich insect fauna.

On his return he got a job as a lecturer at Imperial College and published a series of important papers on genes and behaviour. He also befriended a self-taught American, George Price, an ardent atheist who became an equally ardent biblical scholar. In between, Price managed to do brilliant work to improve and expand the mathematics of Hamilton's theory, while railing against its implications.

They collaborated on a pair of important papers. When Price eventually committed suicide with nail scissors in an abandoned building near Euston Square at Christmas 1974 having given all his money to the homeless, the police contacted Hamilton, whose name they found among his few effects.

In 1977 Hamilton moved to the University of Michigan, where he experienced at first hand the controversy stirred among radical students by opponents to the sociobiological theories he had spawned, enduring protests and sit-ins.

He was a distinctive figure with his heavy shock of white hair, stooped figure, low monotone voice and unworldly air. This did not make him an inspiring lecturer, but he was fortunate that his ideas were taken up by more lively teachers, notably John Maynard Smith and Richard Dawkins, both of whom dated their conversion to gene-centred thinking to their first encounters with Hamilton's work.

He remained an active researcher, never happier than when collecting a little-known burying beetle or fig wasp deep in the rainforest. He was oblivious of risk. His last expedition, to the war-torn Congo, was to test the theory that the origin of the human Aids epidemic lay with the polio vaccine.

⊰ 8th ⊱

Joe DiMaggio, b. 1914, d. 1999

Joe DiMaggio, who has died aged eighty-four, was arguably the greatest baseball player of the twentieth century; after his retirement he compounded his fame by marrying perhaps the only person of that period to outstrip him in the affections of the American people, Marilyn Monroe.

In 1934 DiMaggio, aged nineteen, was bought from a minor Californian team by the New York Yankees. His transfer made him the most discussed rookie player in the major leagues since the advent of Ty Cobb in 1905.

Before DiMaggio arrived at the Yankees the team had been underperforming for several years. After he began to play for them, they won the World Series nine times in the twelve seasons played between 1936 and 1951, the year DiMaggio retired.

DiMaggio's game was distinguished by his powerful and, above all, consistent hitting, rooted in an unorthodox wide stance and a loose, easy swing reminiscent of 'Shoeless' Joe Jackson, which he only unleashed at the last possible moment.

In his first month as a professional, DiMaggio became one of only three players then to have hit two home runs in one inning. He went on to have a career average of .325, scoring 361 home runs, and in 1941 set a new record of 56 consecutive hitting games (in which he made 91 hits), beating the former record of 42 games, which had stood since the previous century. The mark set by DiMaggio has yet to be surpassed.

Yet these triumphs never went to his head. Asked why he seemed to give his all in every game he played, the 'Yankee Clipper' replied: 'Because out there is some kid seeing me play for the first time. I owe him my best.'

Joseph Paul DiMaggio was born at Martinez, California, on 25 November 1914. His parents were emigrants from Sicily and his father worked as a crab fisherman. The eighth of nine children, Joe had two brothers who also became professional baseball players.

Joe grew up and was educated in San Francisco, learning to play baseball on the city's wastelands. In 1932 he was recommended by his brother Vince as a fielder to a local minor team, the San Francisco Seals. In his first game he batted well but endangered the spectators with his wild throwing.

Nevertheless, he was called back by the team the next season and broke the Pacific Coast League record by hitting safely in sixty-one consecutive games.

In 1951 DiMaggio retired from baseball, working first as a television commentator and later as a representative for several large frozen food firms.

His first marriage, to the starlet Dorothy Arnold, had been dissolved after five years in 1944. Then, in 1952, he was introduced to Marilyn Monroe, who was just starting to make her name in films. He was smitten, and as her studio was keen to raise her profile, they sent her on a blind date with DiMaggio. She had little idea who he was and was two hours late for dinner. Halfway through the meal Mickey Rooney came over and asked DiMaggio for his autograph. Only then did Marilyn Monroe begin to grasp the eminence of her modest dining partner.

They were married in January 1954, but the union was not a success. DiMaggio's only real interests were baseball and television – Marilyn Monroe later revealed that he had spent most of their honeymoon watching the one on the other – and he naively believed that his wife would gladly become a housewife.

They were divorced after only nine months of marriage, the final straw being DiMaggio's rage at seeing his wife flashing her underwear at a crowd of gawping spectators as she filmed the subway grating scene for *The Seven Year Itch*.

Nevertheless, DiMaggio remained protective of Marilyn Monroe. It was he who made the arrangements for her funeral. Afterwards, he sent two roses to her grave three times a week for the rest of his life.

⊰ 9th ⊱

Terry Nation, b. 1930, d. 1997

Terry Nation, the television writer who has died in Los Angeles aged sixty-six, will be best remembered for inventing the Daleks, those mechanical monsters bent on universal domination in the long-running series *Doctor Who*.

From their first appearance in the early 1960s, with their robot-like cry: 'Ex-ter-min-ate', they went on to attract a large and enthusiastic following. Yet Nation had originally turned down the offer to write a short series of scripts for *Doctor Who* because he thought the show was destined for disaster.

'But there was a sudden need for money and so I did the series,' he recalled. 'It turned out to be the shrewdest move I've ever made.'

The first Dalek appeared on British television screens on 21 December 1963 – or at least its plunger arm did, when, at the end of the episode, Doctor Who's assistant, Barbara, screamed at the threatening approach of the mutant monster.

Nation had been inspired to design the Daleks, with their gliding motion, after seeing a performance of the Georgian State Dancers. (In a later episode, when the Doctor appeared to have reached safety by going upstairs, the pursuing Daleks displayed an unsuspected ability to levitate.)

The Daleks' first adventure was set on their home planet, Skaro, where they had been reduced to etiolated mutants supported within a mechanical shell, with a sucker and ray-gun. The exterminating was done with a 'disruptor ray'. At the end of the first story the Daleks were wiped out, but they had to be brought back for series after series.

The Daleks changed Nation's life. Sharing the royalties fifty-fifty with the BBC for toys, books and other commercial spin-offs, he swiftly became rich. He bought a beautiful Elizabethan house set in thirty-five acres, at Lynsted Park in Kent.

There, with Kate, his attractive Yorkshire wife, he loved to entertain. Her parents lived in the house with them and their two children, and another house was built in the ground for his parents.

Nation found himself at last free to write what he really wanted. This work included his children's bestseller *Rebecca's World*, named after his daughter, *The Survivors*, a television series about a group of people who survive the destruction of civilisation, and the blockbuster television science-fiction series *Blake's Seven*, which has acquired a cult following of its own.

☙ 10th ❧

Lady Read, b. 1905, d. 1996

Lady Read, the widow of the writer and art critic Sir Herbert Read, who has died aged ninety, sometimes professed to find the English antipathetic, yet her personality, talent and wit added immeasurably to the richness of English life.

She was, in fact, half German, a quarter Scottish, an eighth Irish and an eighth Italian – not at first sight an ideal mix for Yorkshire, where she lived much of her life. But her character was powerful enough and original enough to transcend all the usual categories. Not that she held English social values in contempt. When Herbert Read was offered a knighthood, all his impulses were to refuse; he was, after all, a self-proclaimed anarchist.

Margaret Read swept aside such objections – she wanted, she said, to obtain decent service at the local garage – and so in 1953 the knighthood was duly conferred. She came to bask in Yorkshire society. As hosts, she and Herbert Read complemented each other – he severely intellectual, given to silence, more than a bit intimidating to newcomers; she constantly setting the other end of the table on a roar with her outrageous and unpredictable sallies.

When her son, Piers Paul Read, became a novelist, she professed the deepest shock at his books. 'They're absolutely filthy,' she would exclaim with wide-eyed and joyous amazement – at which her husband would comment: 'He does not get that from me.'

The publication of Piers Paul Read's book *Alive* (1974), a compelling account of how the victims of an air crash in the Andes kept body and soul together by devouring slices of their dead comrades, offered his mother an irresistible opportunity. Told that some of the survivors of the crash were coming to dinner, she dispatched an alarmed enquiry: 'But, darling, what do I give them to eat?'

She was born Margaret Ludwig at Aberdeen on 27 March 1905, the third of nine children of Charles Ludwig, a shipping broker and sometime German consul. After Aberdeen High School she went on to Edinburgh University, where she read music under Sir Donald Tovey, obtaining a first-class degree.

After graduating, Margaret Ludwig went to Cologne, where she studied Music. Back in Edinburgh she played the viola in the MacNaghten Quartet and became a

Roman Catholic in 1932. A few weeks later, ironically through Catholic influences, she met the decidedly un-Catholic Herbert Read, who was Professor of Fine Arts at Edinburgh University – and married, with a son.

In 1933 Herbert Read and Margaret Ludwig bolted, creating an immense scandal in the tranquil atmosphere of Edinburgh's academe. The erring but happy couple found lodging in the Mall Studios in Hampstead. Barbara Hepworth and Ben Nicholson lived nearby; Henry Moore was in the next road. It was not until 1936, after Herbert Read's divorce had been finalised, that they were able to marry. In the interim Margaret Ludwig played at Glyndebourne under Fritz Busch.

After her marriage Margaret Read's energies were mainly devoted to bringing up three sons and a daughter. Herbert Read had been born near Kirkbymoorside, some twenty miles north of York, and after the war he returned to the area and bought Stonegrave, a beautiful house near Ampleforth. Years before, when she had given a concert at Ampleforth, one of the monks had laughed so much at her party piece – whistling the tune of 'God Save The King', while humming the harmony at the same time – that he burst his collar stud.

⚡ 11th ⚡

Paul Rising, b. 1918, d. 2002

Paul Rising, who has died aged eighty-three, worked for thirty years as a night switchboard operator at *The Daily Telegraph*; in his spare time, under the nom de guerre Paula La Dare, he was a talented and flamboyant female impersonator.

He got his break after the war in the all-male revue *Get In* as a member of the line of 'chorus girls'; he played the part of an Eastern slave girl who was carried on stage in a litter before disembarking to execute the Dance of the Seven Veils.

The experience on this highly popular show gave Rising the confidence to branch out as a solo artiste. Although not a proficient singer ('I was a dancer, really, couldn't sing a note'), 'Paula La Dare' would entertain at pubs and clubs in east London by performing well-known standards such as 'My Heart Belongs To Daddy' and 'The Lady Is A Tramp', often in the manner of Marlene Dietrich. By the 1950s he had adopted a new routine, a striptease of 'women through the ages', featuring characters such as Eve in the Garden of Eden, the Venus de Milo (this he performed with his hands behind his back), and Cleopatra.

Rising continued with his second career in cabaret after joining *The Daily Telegraph* as a night switchboard operator in the early 1950s; his department's pattern of shiftwork – long periods at work, followed by ten-day breaks – suited him, and he remained in the job until his retirement in June 1983.

He was proud of his extensive women's wardrobe, of his collection of costume jewellery (in the early years he would buy a sixpenny bracelet each week from Woolworth's), and of his skill with make-up ('I always use Estee Lauder – very good slap'). He was still attending 'drag balls' when he was more than eighty.

The 9th Earl of St Germans, b. 1914, d. 1988

The 9th Earl of St Germans, popularly known as the 'Bookie Peer', who has died aged seventy-four, was an engaging eccentric whose recreations, according to his *Who's Who* entry, were 'huntin' the slipper, shootin' a line, fishin' for compliments'.

He succeeded to the Earldom of St Germans in 1960 but made the 6,000-acre estate over to his son and heir and went into tax exile, settling in Tangier.

Calling himself the 'Tangerine Earl' and with the telegraphic address of 'Earls Court', St Germans was one of Tangier's most colourful characters. But on one occasion in 1963 – after an unfortunate incident in the Safari Bar when he apparently threatened customers with an unloaded and unauthorised gun – he found himself spending the night in a police cell.

St Germans, who enjoyed sailing in the Mediterranean, also lived in the South of France (changing the name of his villa from La Magnerie, 'as I can't pronounce that', to Sea View) and latterly in Switzerland. But he always hankered for home and his beloved racing.

He particularly missed 'the things about England that one never stops to think of when you live there', citing his club, steak and kidney pudding, treacle tart and 'a decent game of backgammon'. He recalled, however, that on one of his return visits, 'when I got back to Dover in the pouring rain, I asked the dining car attendant on the train for anchovies and toast. "The anchovies are off, sir," he said. "So is the toast." I must say I felt a little better about my exile then.'

⁓ 12th ⁓

The Lord Menuhin, b. 1916, d. 1999

The Lord Menuhin, better known as Yehudi Menuhin, who has died aged eighty-two, stood out among the great violin virtuosi of this century; his name was synonymous with his instrument, even to people who had never entered a concert hall.

By courageously playing a concerto with the Berlin Philharmonic conducted by Wilhelm Furtwängler in 1947, he enraged his Jewish brethren in America and elsewhere who could not forgive Furtwängler for his Nazi associations. Ironically, Menuhin, with Benjamin Britten as his accompanist, had in July 1945 toured the death camps, including Belsen, playing to the survivors two or three times a day for ten days.

Menuhin has been described as 'the greatest artist' on the violin, a subtle distinction from 'the greatest violinist'. He never attained the merciless technical perfection of Heifetz, nor the consistently sustained warmth and strength of tone of his friend David Oistrakh. Infallible command of technique eluded him for most of his adult career.

For a spell of several years after the Second World War, he suffered from severe hypertension in his bowing arm. His intonation and rhythm were uncertain and his tone became frail. But he largely overcame this condition through his practice of yoga; and even on bad days there would be phrases and paragraphs in his performance when the whole interpretation – of the Beethoven and Elgar slow movements especially – had an incomparable, almost spiritual, grace. At such times Menuhin was without peer in his ability to see, hear and play beyond the notes. That was the artistry.

Yehudi Menuhin was born in New York on 22 April 1916, the son of Russian-Jewish parents who originally transliterated their name as Mnuchin, a guide to its correct pronunciation.

For his fourth birthday Yehudi asked for a violin. His formal debut, aged seven, was on 29 February 1924, at the Oakland Auditorium, where he played de Beriot's *Scène de Ballet*. A year later he played Lalo's *Symphonie Espagnole* with the San Francisco orchestra.

In 1926 the Menuhins went to Europe, where Yehudi played in Brussels. Having conceived a longing to study with the Romanian violinist Georges Enescu, whom he had heard in San Francisco, Yehudi then went to Paris to become his pupil, and lifelong friend – 'the Absolute by which I judge others', he wrote. 'What I learned from him was the note transformed into vital message, the phrase given shape and meaning.'

Yehudi Menuhin's European debut took place in Paris, in a concert with the Lamoureux Orchestra conducted by Paul Paray, on 6 February 1927.

On the family's return to America, Menuhin was invited by Walter Damrosch to play at Carnegie Hall with the New York Symphony Orchestra under Fritz Busch, who, when told the ten-year-old prodigy was to play Beethoven's concerto, exclaimed: 'One doesn't hire Jackie Coogan [a child film star of the day] to play Hamlet.' But after a run-through he said to Menuhin: 'You can play anything with me, any time, anywhere.'

In Europe, Menuhin continued his studies with Adolf Busch, brother of Fritz, on Enescu's recommendation. He first appeared in Berlin on 12 April 1929, when he played concertos by Bach, Beethoven and Brahms conducted by Bruno Walter.

Such was Menuhin's fame by then that the police had to be called to control the crowds. In the audience was Alfred Einstein, who hugged the boy afterwards and said: 'Now I know there is a God in heaven.' His London debut, with the LSO conducted by Fritz Busch, followed on 4 November 1929.

Menuhin had begun to make records in 1928. What is still perhaps his most famous recording was made in London at the HMV studios in Abbey Road on 14–15 July 1932, when he played Elgar's concerto with the composer conducting. Elgar, then seventy-five, described the sixteen-year-old soloist as 'the most wonderful artist I have ever heard'.

Returning to New York, Menuhin found its music dominated by Toscanini, with whom he played on many occasions – although he much preferred, as he admitted later, to work with Bruno Walter. Menuhin toured America during this period and in 1935 completed his first world tour, performing in seventy-three cities in thirteen countries.

After America entered the war, Menuhin gave more than 500 recitals for Allied troops and relief bodies. Playing to please audiences who might never before have attended a concert took him out of his shell and in 1944, after the liberation of Paris, he was the first artist to play in the Paris Opera; he began his sonata recital with 'La Marseillaise'. In November 1945 he visited Moscow for the first time, where David Oistrakh greeted him as he stepped off the aeroplane.

In the years after the war, Menuhin gradually diversified his activities. In 1956 he established the Gstaad Festival in Switzerland, where in 1957 he made his conducting debut. He had enjoyed playing at the early Aldeburgh festivals, and Britten and Pears suggested Gstaad to him and gave two recitals in the first year.

But perhaps his most important venture was when in 1963 he founded his own school for musically gifted children. This opened in London, but in 1964 moved to Stoke D'Abernon, Surrey.

In 1965 he was appointed honorary KBE. Twenty years later he became a British citizen and so was entitled to use the prefix 'Sir'. He was appointed a member of the Order of Merit in 1987, providing another link for him with Elgar, who had been the first musical OM.

Fortunately, Menuhin leaves a large number of recordings. Once, on board an ocean liner, he heard Beethoven's concerto played as he would love to have played it – only to discover that it was his own recording made with Furtwängler in 1947.

❧ 13th ❧

John Hobbs, b. 1946, d. 2011

John Hobbs, who has died aged sixty-four, emerged from the demimonde of post-war west London to become one of the most successful antique dealers of his generation; when his restorer accused him of selling fakes, however, he faced professional disgrace and financial ruin.

John Edmund Hobbs was born on 8 May 1946, and grew up in Fulham where his father Sid was, until 1968, the proprietor of Odds & Hobbs, a junk shop at which he held court to a circle of local characters, many of a roguish stripe.

John worked with his father from the age of fourteen and was later apprenticed to a local tallyman. There he became a 'knocker' – knocking on doors to charm from the occupants furniture which could be sold on to the trade at great profit. This was a time when many grand town houses were disgorging their contents before being sliced into flats.

By Hobbs' own account, his younger self was no stranger to fencing stolen goods and housebreaking. One such foray, he claimed, was to the home of the politician and journalist Woodrow Wyatt. In the newspapers the next day, Wyatt trumpeted that he had seen off the intruders – but in reality, Hobbs asserted, he had hidden under the bedcovers shouting: 'Take what you want but don't touch me.'

Other misdemeanours included lending Nicholas Van Hoogstraten his car, which the vengeful property baron used (without Hobbs' knowledge) in a hand-grenade attack on the home of a former business associate. Hobbs also ran into trouble after a weekend in France with the gossip columnist Nigel Dempster's new wife. His cover was blown when his clothes went missing in transit, only to be mistakenly delivered by Heathrow staff to Dempster at his office. Fisticuffs followed; the marriage headed swiftly to divorce.

Meanwhile Hobbs was still 'running furniture', and had been joined by his brother Carlton, who was nine years younger. In 1974 they set up business in the newly established Kings Road Furniture Cave, supplying pieces, at a modest mark-up, mainly to the trade. The early days at the 'Cave' were perhaps Hobbs' happiest. The place had the air of a club – albeit a thoroughly disreputable one whose membership embraced an eclectic mix of dealers, housebreakers and pimps, not to mention a smattering of Old Etonians.

The brothers' ambitions eventually outgrew the 'Cave'. A crucial decision was to widen the international horizons of their buying. Carlton began to trawl Europe buying up 'stale' stock there which was still 'fresh' to the English market. Biedermeier furniture, in particular, was beginning to be appreciated, and the brothers bought boldly and well, made big profits, and met new clients.

In 1987 they managed to secure, on the flip of a coin, a lease on premises at 107 Pimlico Road in Chelsea. Soon they became major players, travelling through Scandinavia, then awash with Russian furniture, which they brought back to London. They also began to make a splash in the salerooms, outgunning established dealers to bag some notable trophy lots at auction.

But this meteoric transformation did not go unremarked. Competitors speculated about a shadowy millionaire backer or accused them of selling to undiscriminating celebrity clients. What the critics did not know about was the discreet arrangement the Hobbs brothers had made for the exclusive services of a Kent-based restorer, Dennis Buggins.

Despite their success, tensions between the brothers forced a split in 1993. Both set up successful galleries and Buggins continued to work exclusively for them even after their demerger. Then disaster struck.

In 2007 Carlton filed a multi-million-dollar suit against the restorer, claiming that some pieces had not been delivered and that others were damaged. Soon, Hobbs too was in litigation with the restorer. It was an act of professional suicide. After losing both his major clients, Buggins decided to go public with allegations against Hobbs, even if an injunction prevented him from discussing Carlton.

Buggins claimed that since 1992 his workshop had handled 1,875 items for Hobbs, more than half of which involved major alterations or outright inventions. Photographs and records provided by Buggins showed how he had transformed ordinary pieces of furniture into high-end antiques. Such had been Hobbs' demand for period wardrobes, he alleged, that it had even been necessary to rent a barn in which to store them.

The embellished items were then attributed by Hobbs to the great cabinetmakers of the past, and described as 'rare' and 'significant'. One such invention, described by Hobbs as a 'large and important gilt metal mounted mahogany pedestal partners desk, early 19th-century in the manner of Marsh and Tatham', had an asking price of £1.2 million. Buggins claimed he had designed the desk himself and the cost for labour and materials had been £100,000.

The restorer's revelations provoked great anxiety among decorators – and their clients – around the world. That June, a pair of commodes that Hobbs had sold to a Swedish businessman for £395,000 in 1997 was withdrawn from a Sotheby's sale in New York after a tip-off from a journalist. The catalogue described them as German neo-Classical, circa 1800, with a high estimate of $300,000: but Buggins produced evidence that he had made them out of a few old wardrobes and cedar from a local timber merchant.

For Hobbs, the impact was ruinous. His stock, when he could sell it, was now worth only a fraction of its previous value. He faced escalating legal bills and a large unanticipated tax demand. Worse, his health – he had been diagnosed with cancer in 2004 – was fast deteriorating. He finally reached a settlement with Buggins at the High Court in 2010, moments before he was due to be cross-examined. The agreement involved a substantial cash payment.

A tall, well-built man and snappy dresser, Hobbs always wore his hair 'over the collar'. He was charismatic and capable of attracting real loyalty. But he understood when and how to apply menace and had a self-destructive personality and a gambler's disregard for consequences. He spent most of his life battling addictions to drink and drugs and was prone to depression.

When he died he was working on his memoirs, to be titled *Honest John*.

⇒ **14**th ⇐

Empress Zita of Austria, b. 1892, d. 1989

Empress Zita of Austria, who has died aged ninety-six, was the Consort of Karl, the last Hapsburg Emperor, sharing the throne of an empire that consisted of Austria, Hungary and what is now known as Czechoslovakia, together with parts of present-day Italy, Yugoslavia, Romania, Poland and Russia.

She shared too the historic throne of the Holy Roman Empire, and was crowned Queen of Hungary in Budapest with her husband beside her wearing St Stephen's Crown as Apostolic King.

Princess Zita of Bourbon-Parma was born in 1892, fifth of the twelve children whom Duke Robert I of Parma had by his second wife, the Infanta Maria-Antonia of Portugal, having already had twelve children by his first wife.

Princess Zita had a happy childhood at her father's castle in Austria and his villa in Italy; the family moved from one to the other in a special train with fifteen or sixteen coaches to hold the children, the servants, the horses and the baggage, not to mention the scholarly Duke Robert's books.

She grew up to be a princess of exceptional beauty and intelligence; it came as no surprise when, in 1911, at the age of nineteen, she married Europe's greatest Catholic royal, the 24-year-old Archduke Karl, second in line of succession to the throne of his great-uncle, the Emperor Franz Joseph.

It was a love match and an enduring success, blessed with five sons and three daughters. For the first three years of their marriage, the young Archduke and

Archduchess lived mostly away from the limelight while he soldiered. Though it was almost certain that Karl would one day be Emperor (the son of Franz Ferdinand, the immediate heir, being excluded from the succession on account of his morganatic marriage) that day seemed a long way off. Franz Ferdinand was in the prime of life. But in 1914 Franz Ferdinand and his wife fell victims to the bullets of Sarajevo, making Karl the immediate heir to the throne. It was to Karl and to the Archduchess Zita that Franz Joseph, after hearing the news, made his famous remark: 'I am spared nothing.'

Karl's initiation into affairs of state was interrupted by frequent visits to the front; he was, after all, a soldier and the Empire was fighting a war. However much that war may be blamed on Austria-Hungary, the young Archduke was in no way responsible for its making; he loathed the conflict and on succeeding as Emperor in November 1916 lost no time in trying to bring it to an end.

The Emperor Karl's peace attempt of 1917, in which the Empress Zita's brother, Prince Sixte of Bourbon-Parma, acted as intermediary, was the only serious effort to end the fighting made by the leader of any of the belligerent powers. It failed, but only just; he had the enthusiastic support of the British Prime Minister, Lloyd George.

Had it succeeded, millions of lives would have been saved and the subsequent history of Europe would have been very much happier. At the same time as he worked for peace, the Emperor Karl set about reconstructing his heterogeneous Empire on federal lines so that he came to be known both as the 'Peace Emperor' and the 'Emperor of the People'.

In these the two objects which, as Emperor, he put before all others, Karl had the full support of the Empress, with whom he constantly discussed them. Happily married to a highly intelligent wife, who was dedicated to her husband and his subjects, it was natural that he should have initiated her into the secrets of state and sometimes taken her advice.

With the defeat of the Austrian forces in the autumn of 1918, Karl's Empire collapsed around him. For a brief while, as the outlying states of the Empire fell away in an orgy of self-determination, it seemed that Karl might at least have kept the throne of Austria; but the fall of the German monarchies brought down the monarchy in Austria as well. The Emperor, who refused to abdicate, which he felt would be to renounce a responsibility given to him by God, agreed to withdraw from all affairs of state, while remaining in Austria.

A few months later, when Austria was on the verge of a Communist takeover, and there was a real danger that the Emperor and Empress and their children might suffer a fate similar to that of the Tsar and his family, they were prevailed upon to go into exile in Switzerland.

In 1920, after the collapse of a short-lived Communist regime, Hungary was declared a monarchy once again, under the Regency of Admiral Horthy. In 1921 Karl made two attempts to regain his Hungarian throne, by going to Hungary himself; but each time he was foiled by Horthy, who on the second occasion used force against him and the Empress.

As a result of Karl's second restoration bid, which was very nearly successful, he and his family were banished to Madeira. Here, in a damp and primitive villa which was the best they could afford, the Emperor died of pneumonia early the following year, aged thirty-four.

Two months later, the Empress gave birth to their youngest child, the Archduchess Elisabeth. Later, the Empress and her family settled in Belgium; she moved to the United States during the Second World War and then, after a period in Mexico, returned to Switzerland.

She spent her long widowhood devoting herself to her family and to the memory of her husband. She travelled frequently; towards the end of her life she paid her first visit to Austria since the fall of the monarchy and was given a tumultuous reception.

She also paid two visits to Rome, being on cordial terms with Pope John Paul II, whose father had not only been a subject of the Emperor's but had been commissioned by him in the Kaiserlich und Koniglich Army.

⚜ 15th ⚜

Benjamin Spock, b. 1903, d. 1998

Benjamin Spock, who has died aged ninety-four, wrote what became a bible for a generation of young mothers; *The Common Sense Book of Baby and Child Care* (1946) long remained the world's best-selling book after Holy Scripture.

The secret of Dr Spock's success was simple; he told parents to react spontaneously to their children, to give them love, cuddles, food and discipline when they felt it was appropriate, and not according to a rigid schedule.

The famous opening of his child-care classic lifted the hearts of faltering mothers everywhere: 'Trust yourself. You know more than you think you do.'

Benjamin McLane Spock was born at New Haven, Connecticut, on 2 May 1903; he remembered his puritanical mother was 'very moralistic, excessively controlling'. Benjamin proved to be the model of a diligent, devoted son. In 1925 he enrolled at the Yale Medical School, going on from there to Columbia University College of Physicians and Surgeons. He completed residencies in paediatrics at the New York Nursery and Child's Hospital, and in psychiatry at New York Hospital.

From 1933, Spock practised paediatrics privately in New York, taught at Cornell and acted as a consultant in paediatric psychiatry. 'One of my faults as a paediatrician,' he later said, 'has always been that I whoop it up too much with children.' But it was a fault that soon won him a large clientele, who appreciated his gift of putting children at ease.

During the Second World War, Spock served in the Medical Corps of the US Naval Reserve. He worked as a psychiatrist in naval hospitals in New York and California, and by 1946 had risen to the rank of lieutenant commander. It was in his spare time during these years that he prepared the manuscript of *Baby and Child Care*.

At that period the most commonly consulted American baby-care book was Dr John B. Watson's severe treatise, *Psychological Care of Infant and Child* (1928). Typical of Watson's many stern admonitions to parents was: 'Never, never kiss your child. Never hold it in your lap. Never rock its carriage.'

Spock's *Baby and Child Care* was first published in 1946, and was an immediate success. He emphasised the importance of the differences between individual babies, and of the need for flexibility. Parents, he suggested, need not worry constantly about spoiling their offspring.

During the 1960s, Spock threw himself into opposition to America's entanglement in Vietnam and in late 1967 was charged with conspiracy to aid and abet draft-dodging. He was sentenced to two years but the convictions were quashed on appeal. By then, however, Spock's baby-care philosophy was being denounced by conservatives as the very breeding ground of the Permissive Society.

Spock's belief in demand-feeding babies – giving the baby the breast or the bottle when the baby wanted it – was now seen as the root cause of the self-indulgence associated with the 'Me Generation'. Spock was blamed for a decline in the Protestant work ethic; the Spock baby was raised, it was said by critics, to 'want it now', and grew up to live for instant pleasures, instant responses, with a low capacity for duty, self-sacrifice and responsibility.

And while his politics on peace remained radical for the rest of his life, on child-care Spock modified his earlier liberal views. He altered sections of the original *Baby and Child Care* book in later editions, gently reminding his readers that discipline also played a part in child-care.

Many child-care books would follow in Spock's wake; his very success created a market for ever more tracts in the same vein. But Spock's manual remains remarkably helpful as a practical guide. Child psychology is notoriously vulnerable to fashion, but colic and cradle-cap go on forever.

Alistair Morrison, b. 1911, d. 1998

Alistair Morrison, who has died in Fremantle, Western Australia, aged eighty-six, was the inventor of the language Strine.

In the guise of Professor Afferbeck Lauder ('Alphabetical Order'), Professor of Strine Studies, University of Sinny, Morrison identified Strine as a tongue spoken by many Australians, and reduced it to written form.

He published his first book of Strine, *Let Stalk Strine* in 1965, which caught on instantly. The flavour of Strine can be gathered from some of the simpler entries – thus: Baked Necks: a popular breakfast dish. Others include Emma Necks; Scramblex; and Fright Shops.

In 1968 Afferbeck Lauder turned to London's West End in *Fraffly* (as in 'frightfully') *Well Spoken* (1968), the clipped dialect of the English moneyed classes. Some briefer entries:

> Air, Eh: interchangeable suffixes (corresponding to the English -y), as in:
> Complittlair; extroddnerreh; etc.
> Cod: A large fish; also a small piece of stiffened paper on which may be printed
> a message, or symbols, e.g., Christmas Cods; purse cods; pleng cods, on

which appear speds, hots, dammonds and clopse.

Egg-Wetter Gree: An expression of concurrence and agreement. As in: 'Em Nogwet shorrif egg-wetter gree withol you sair, but ashel defend to may death your rate to say so.'

⊰ **16**th ⊱

Brigadier the 17th Lord Lovat, b. 1911, d. 1995

Brigadier the 17th Lord Lovat, 24th Chief of Clan Fraser, who has died aged eighty-three, was a legendary commando leader in the Second World War, playing an important part in the raids on Lofoten and Dieppe – as well as in the D-Day landings, during which he was severely wounded.

Lovat was in command of No. 1 Special Service Brigade, a force containing five commando groups, which landed at Ouistreham on 6 June 1944 and fought its way six miles inland to the Orne bridges. Accompanied as usual by his piper, Lovat marched across the Orne and took up position to repulse the advancing Panzers. He was subsequently wounded, and as he was being carried off the field on a stretcher sent a message to his men: 'I can rely on you not to take one step back.' Nor did they.

Lovat had joined the newly formed commandos in 1941, when he took part in the raid on the Lofoten Islands off Norway. The object was to destroy the fish-oil processing station there, from which Germany was obtaining glycerine for the manufacture of explosives. Lovat's commandos sank twelve ships, destroyed eighteen factories and burned some 800,000 gallons of petrol and oil. They also brought back an Enigma machine which proved vital to the Ultra deciphering operation. Before leaving for England, with Norwegian volunteers and German prisoners aboard, Lovat sent an insulting telegram to Hitler from the local post office.

Lovat went on to enjoy a rare triumph amid the otherwise disastrous Dieppe raid of 1942, when his commandos fought through heavy opposition to reach and destroy a large German battery behind Varengeville.

Lovat had expected the Germans to be waiting for them, but in the event the commandos sustained only light casualties when negotiating the barbed-wire defences, and then proceeding to the battery. Once they had reached the objective the men charged through their own smoke screen, their eyes smarting, and took the enemy by surprise; many of the Germans did not have time to put on their trousers before taking up positions and spraying the commandos with machine-gun fire. As soon as the target had been taken a flight of Messerschmitts went over, whom Lovat reassured with a friendly wave.

By the time the commandos had returned to the beach Lovat was bubbling with excitement. 'Went straight in, cut them to shreds,' he said before wading out to a landing craft.

On his return to London, Lovat reported to Mountbatten and then, penniless and filthy, made his way to the Guards' Club, where an elderly servant gave him a precious bar of soap. After bathing Lovat fell asleep in the library, wrapped in towels. He was awarded the DSO to add to his earlier MC (for a reconnaissance raid on Boulogne), and his part in the Dieppe raid became celebrated as a classic commando exercise. Lovat later discovered that the Gestapo had offered 100,000 Deutschmarks for his capture, dead or alive.

Simon Christopher Joseph Fraser was born on 9 July 1911, the elder son of the 16th Lord Lovat, a celebrated all-round sportsman who, in the South African War, had raised and commanded the Lovat Scouts, a regiment of his own clansmen.

The Jacobite 11th Lord Lovat, known as 'the Old Fox' and familiar as the mountainous grinning septuagenarian painted by Hogarth, became in 1747 the last peer to be beheaded in the Tower of London. The Master of Lovat, as Simon was styled until succeeding his father in 1933, was educated at Ampleforth and, after a period working on a coffee and cattle ranch in South America – an experience which gave rise to his love of the pampas and an abiding delight in cowboy films – went up to Magdalen College, Oxford.

On coming down he joined the Scots Guards, with whom he served from 1932 to 1937. On the outbreak of war he joined the Lovat Scouts, the yeomanry regiment founded by his father.

After frustration during the 'Phoney War' Lovat became involved in the formation of the various irregular forces out of which the commandos grew. He was promoted lieutenant-colonel in 1942 and brigadier in 1943.

In 1945 Lovat was appointed Under-Secretary for Foreign Affairs in Churchill's caretaker government – a period of office which was brief and not particularly distinguished. He then withdrew to his family seat of Beaufort Castle in Inverness-shire, where he devoted himself to forestry and bred shorthorn Aberdeen Angus and Highland cattle, which he also judged at shows all over the world.

Athletic, good-looking and with considerable presence, he was a natural leader, though he possessed a formidably autocratic streak. Winston Churchill described him as 'the handsomest man who ever cut a throat'.

⊰ 17th ⊱

Rod Hull, b. 1935, d. 1999

Rod Hull, the entertainer who has died aged sixty-three, sprang to fame on the arm of a mass of purple raffia, his irascible creation Emu.

Hull's act essentially consisted of only one joke, that he could not control the puppet he was obviously manipulating. But he overcame the apparent limitations of this ploy by endowing the bird with its own distinct, slyly malevolent personality.

Silent and aggressive, there was always the certainty that Emu would administer a vicious peck to whoever was talking to Hull, and occasionally the alluring prospect that Emu would humiliate someone who thought themselves protected because they were on television.

It was this simmering sense of the unexpected that made Hull immensely popular throughout the 1970s and 80s; children in particular seemed to adore the promise of violence.

Emu was no respecter of persons. Famously, it mauled Michael Parkinson when Hull appeared on his chat show in the early 70s, wrestling him to the ground and eating his shoe. When it met Queen Elizabeth the Queen Mother, it swallowed her bouquet, causing her to comment, with admirable if perplexed *sang froid*: 'I think your emu is rather hungry.'

Emu was born in Australia in 1968, where Hull first established himself as a children's television presenter. A viewer sent in a giant model egg, believing it had educational value. Hull, whose comedy was always of the madcap variety, placed the egg on a radiator and told his audience he was waiting for it to hatch. After three weeks, searching desperately in the props cupboard for a suitable chick, he stumbled across Emu.

Hull and Emu first toured Britain as support to the actor Warren Mitchell's one-man show, but by the early 1970s, after successful appearances in pantomime, they had been signed up by the BBC. At the height of his celebrity, Emu was receiving more than 200 fan letters a day.

But beneath Hull's outward success there appeared to be a streak of melancholy. His deeply lined face made him seem older than he was, and he remained acutely sensitive to suggestions that Emu controlled too much of his life. 'I know some ventriloquists who actually believe their dolls exist,' he said, 'but when my work's over, it's over. I can hardly bear to look at the thing.'

Rodney Hull was born on the Isle of Sheppey, Kent, on 13 August 1935. His father, Leonard, was a gentle eccentric who spent much of his time applying for jobs for which he had no qualifications.

Having worked as a shoveller in a glue works and a plumber (on the strength of having acquired a plunger from Woolworths), Leonard set himself up as a bicycle repairer. His first, and last, customer was a district nurse whose saddle was wobbly. Leonard swiftly ascertained that the problem was a missing nut, and remedied it with another taken from the handlebars. 'Then,' recalled Rod Hull, 'we all watched her cycle off, straight into a wall.'

Young Rod seemed to inherit much of his father's whimsical and childlike approach to the world. His meagre confidence was not helped by a profound stammer, which led to his being bullied at Delamark Road School, from where he went on to the County Technological College at Sheerness.

In 1961, having undertaken his National Service in the RAF and trained as an electrician, Hull emigrated to Australia. His father had moved there three years previously, in part because the fare was only £10 and he had never before left Sheppey.

In Sydney, Leonard became a door-to-door salesman of burial plots. He thoughtfully equipped his wife Hilda with an electric organ, on which she would let rip with 'Rock Of Ages' when a potential customer opened the door. The business did not prosper.

In Australia, Rod Hull found lighting jobs in television and then had an occasional part in *Skippy*, the series about a bush kangaroo. He also began to submit scripts to children's television programmes, and had his first success with *The Constable Clot Show*; Hull took the part of Clot himself.

He was then asked to host a live breakfast television programme each morning, and cleverly transformed the character of Clot into that of the caretaker of the station. Each morning Hull would be seen bringing in the milk, switching on the television mast, making himself breakfast and – since he presumed almost no one was watching – rambling on about whatever came into his head. By 1968, when Emu made his debut, the programme topped the ratings.

Once established in Britain, Hull undertook much work for charity. The later years of his life, however, were dogged by misfortune. It emerged that his financial affairs had been badly mismanaged by an adviser. He was declared bankrupt in 1994.

Hull was forced to move to a small cottage in Winchelsea, Sussex, where he lived in part on the royalties of a book of verse, *The Reluctant Pote* (1983). He was killed in a fall from the roof of the house while adjusting the television aerial to get better reception of a football match.

⊰ 18th ⊱

Norman Barclay, b. 1925, d. 1997

Norman Barclay, who has died aged seventy-one, was an intrepid amateur sportsman, whether in bobsleighs, luges (light toboggans), power-boats or motor cars; he also became the first – and last – person to water-ski from Scotland to Ireland.

His sure sense of balance and slim aerodynamic frame were ideally suited to the Cresta Run, and he won the Baron Oertzen Cup in his first season.

Back in Scotland, Barclay took up the new sport of water-skiing, and soon hit the headlines when he was arrested for violating river laws by water-skiing down the Clyde from his office in the city to his home at Helensburgh. There were no objections, though, when he water-skied from Scotland to Ireland.

After gaining his Cresta colours, Barclay pioneered British involvement in the new international winter sport of lugeing. With a few hopeful comrades he travelled to obscure ice tracks in Poland and Eastern Europe. He also led a British team to the 1963 World Championship at Imst, in Austria, and then to the 1964 Olympics at Innsbruck.

The Innsbruck course was treacherous, and the inexperienced British team were soon in difficulty. Their most experienced tobogganner, Kai Strypeski, was killed when he flew off the track and hit a tree during practice. Gordon Porteous and Barclay both had bad crashes on the second and third run and went to hospital, Barclay with a broken arm and dislocated shoulder.

Interviewed by the BBC in hospital, Barclay complained that the track was much too dangerous, and advised Keith Schellenberg, the only uninjured member of the British team, to withdraw.

However, after a few drams with the interviewer, Max Robertson, Barclay was persuaded to give a more cheerful account. This time he told the British sporting public that the run was tremendously exciting, and that he had only crashed because he was 'going for the track record'.

He urged Schellenberg not to be nervous, but to go flat out without braking and so to 'take over where I left off, and break the record for me'. Schellenberg understandably ignored this instruction and finished safely, in twenty-third place.

≍ 19th ≍

Sir Arthur Clarke, b. 1917, d. 2008

Sir Arthur Clarke, who has died aged ninety, was, for many, synonymous with science fiction, and in particular with *2001: A Space Odyssey*, Stanley Kubrick's film of his novella *The Sentinel*; his principal gifts, however, were his ability to popularise science and his genius as one of the most prophetic voices of the space age.

In the hundred or so books he wrote, co-wrote or edited, Clarke predicted, with remarkable accuracy, such developments as the moon landings, space travel, communications satellites, compact computers, cloning, commercial hovercraft and a slew of other scientific developments – though he was also, inevitably, often wide of the mark. In many cases, though, that was because he underestimated the speed of technology's advance.

The paradox of Clarke's fiction is that the writer most associated in the public mind with accurate predictions, based upon potential technology and grounded in 'real' science, returns again and again to themes of an almost mystical sort, in which advanced cultures, often benevolent, allow humanity to transcend its Earth-bound beginnings.

These were expressed in Clarke's laws, of which the best known was his dictum that 'any sufficiently advanced science is indistinguishable from magic'.

Arthur Charles Clarke was born on 16 December 1917 at Minehead, Somerset, and educated at Huish's Grammar School, Taunton. After leaving in 1936 he moved to London to take a job as a civil service auditor with the Exchequer. He was active as a fan of science fiction before the war, in which he served as a radar instructor with the RAF. After his demob in 1946 he enrolled at King's College London, from which he took a First in Physics and Mathematics in 1948.

In 1950 he advised the creators of the comic strip *Dan Dare* on technical matters before publishing two novels. But his first real success – and probably the work for which he was to be best known – came with *The Sentinel*, a short story which appeared in 1951.

It is an account of the discovery of a monolithic alien artefact on the Moon, the emanations from which come to indicate significant insights into Man's place in the universe, and into the development of the species.

Despite a steady stream of books thereafter, Clarke's primary influence on science fiction was as a prophet, rather than a stylist. Many of his essays (unfailingly entertaining) were collected in *Greetings, Carbon-based Bipeds!* and offered more insight and interest than much of his prose fiction.

The most recent edition of his *Collected Stories* was published in 2001; the final piece, 'Improving the Neighbourhood', became in 1999 the first science fiction story to be published in the scientific journal *Nature*. In it, humanity blows itself, the Earth and the Moon to pieces, much to the relief of more advanced and civilised aliens in a nearby part of the galaxy.

Clarke did not rule out the prospect of resurrection – cloning by highly advanced aliens being, predictably enough, his favoured method. In the late 1990s he donated a few of his remaining strands of hair to be launched into space as part of the AERO Astro Corporation's 'Encounter Project' which, after a boost from Jupiter, was intended to travel deep into the solar system.

Clarke hoped that 'maybe a million years from now, some super-civilisation will capture this primitive artefact from the past. Recreating its biological contents might be an amusing exercise for their equivalent of an infants' class.'

<hr />

Lady Mary Clive, b. 1907, d. 2010

Lady Mary Clive, who has died aged 102, was an author, a sister of the late Lord Longford and for more than sixty years the widow of the Herefordshire landowner Meysey Clive, a descendant of Clive of India.

Her autobiography, *Brought Up and Brought Out*, was published in 1938, when she was in her early thirties. It describes her childhood and experiences as a debutante in the 1920s and provides an excellent antidote to those who tend to sentimentalise, or who, like the family friend Evelyn Waugh, glamorised that world.

As she recalled: 'In my day all the debutantes were dowdy unless they wanted to be branded as unpresentably fast, but the actual year that I came out was a bumper dowdy year.'

For her, the boredom of an endless round of luncheon parties at which one was always served the same food was matched only by the limitless potential for humiliation at the dances in the evenings: 'Soon there is nobody left but yourself and two monstrously ugly girls. Your hostess catches sight of you three and looks quickly away.' Even if you secured a partner, it was unlikely that he could dance. After all, she recalled: 'It was considered very vulgar for a man to dance well, like talking French with a French accent.'

Of the so-called debs' delights, Lady Mary was to observe: 'They were practically deformed. Some were without chins. Some had no foreheads. Hardly any of them had backs to their heads.'

⊰ 20th ⊱

Dorothy Young, b. 1907, d. 2011

Dorothy Young, who has died aged 103, was the last surviving stage assistant to Harry Houdini, the master showman, illusionist and escapologist.

She was born on 3 May 1907 at Otisville, New York, the daughter of a Methodist minister. While studying at Beaver College, Pennsylvania, she saw Anna Pavlova perform and determined to become a ballet dancer.

But while visiting New York with her parents aged seventeen she saw an advertisement in the stage paper *Variety* for a vaudeville dancer to join a Broadway show, followed by a tour of the United States. When she arrived for the audition, she sat at the back, too shy to step forward.

But she was spotted by Houdini and his manager, who asked her to dance the Charleston; she signed a year's contract and was sworn to secrecy about the mysteries of Houdini's act. She then had to persuade her parents that joining the great illusionist was a suitable career move.

During her spell with the 'World-Famous Self-Liberator', she played the role of the scantily clad 'Radio Girl of 1950', a 1920s impression of what radio would be like several decades later.

Houdini's wife, Bess, fitted her silk stage costume. In the show the two women performed a stately minuet before the great man made his entrance and introduced the 'Radio Girl'.

In one illusion, The Slave Girl, Houdini would tie Dorothy Young from throat to ankles to a pole, before causing a curtain to fall to the floor. She would then emerge in a beautiful butterfly costume en pointe and dance a ballet number.

Houdini's finale was his famous Chinese Water Torture Cell, which he had performed in England to great acclaim. Clad in bathing trunks, his feet padlocked into mahogany stocks, he would be lowered upside-down into a glass-fronted tank filled with water.

A curtain would then be drawn across the tank. Although Dorothy Young knew how he escaped, she never revealed his secret.

⁑ 21st ⁑

Pamela Hill, b. 1917, d. 2000

Pamela Hill, who has died aged eighty-three, lived a life dominated by a single love affair, elevated by her indomitable will into one of the most romantic stories to emerge from the Second World War.

She was born Pamela Seely Kirrage at Tunbridge Wells on 16 February 1917, the eldest of three daughters, and given an education largely devoted to learning to dance and to play tennis at Hamilton House, a school 'for the daughters of gentlemen'.

When in March 1939 she met Donald Hill, a good-looking RAF pilot, Pamela Kirrage was a model, and, in her own words, 'interested in nothing but having fun'. Hill was more serious, but their first dance proved a *coup de foudre* for them both.

That summer of 1939, they were together for every moment that could be spared from Hill's flying duties. In July they exchanged rings; and they were planning their marriage when Hill was ordered to the Far East.

Almost seven years were to pass before they saw each other again. The war put an end to Pamela Kirrage's plans to fly out to join her fiancé. In December 1941, the Japanese invaded Hong Kong; when the colony surrendered on Christmas Day, Flight Lieutenant Donald Hill was taken prisoner. For eighteen months, Pamela Kirrage did not even know whether he was alive. She continued, however, to write to him every week.

She found work first in the Red Cross, later for the Political Warfare Executive, responsible for black propaganda. At their headquarters at Woburn Abbey, there was no shortage of unattached, glamorous men interested in a beautiful and seemingly unattached girl.

Among the most persistent suitors was the songwriter and SOE officer, Eric Maschwitz, who wooed her by taking her to the Mirabelle and singing to her his hit song 'A Nightingale Sang In Berkeley Square'. But she resisted all her admirers. 'I know that today it must seem silly being in love like that,' she said years later, 'but Donald was the one person who made me feel complete.'

It was not until the summer of 1944 that an answer came to her letters. 'My darling,' Donald Hill wrote, 'Last week a miracle happened. I received a letter from you, dated 11th July 1942. My first letter, darling, and what a difference it made. I was so excited that I started reading it upside down. I just live for the day when I shall see you again, my darling. I shall probably be struck dumb.'

At the outbreak of war he had started to keep a diary. To conceal an activity punishable by torture or death, he encrypted the entries and disguised the rows of figures as mathematical tables.

After the war, he was decorated for his conduct during the battle and for maintaining morale in camp. However, the effects of malnutrition and maltreatment were severe, and on release he was sent to recuperate in New Zealand. Not until January 1946 were he and Pamela re-united.

Ten days after his return they were married, and over the next decade had three children. But Hill, like so many former prisoners of the Japanese, had suffered deep psychological scars.

Increasingly, Pamela found her husband becoming more withdrawn, and prone to violent swings of mood. He would not talk about what had happened in camp, nor would he decode the diary he had brought back. 'I can think of more enjoyable things to read,' he would reply, brushing the subject aside.

They began to quarrel. For Pamela, the diary became a symbol of the locked-away part of his personality that she could no longer reach. Their estrangement grew, and eventually the marriage broke down. In 1978 they were divorced.

Donald re-married, but away from Pamela his mental state deteriorated rapidly. In a violent flashback, he assaulted his second wife, and was remanded to a mental hospital. There Pamela found him again. She began to visit and help to look after him. Gradually their old intimacy returned. On her 65th birthday, he bought her flowers.

'Darling,' he declared, 'you know you're the only woman I've ever loved.' Although still legally married to his second wife, he insisted they have an unofficial wedding ceremony. The ring he slipped on to her finger was the engagement ring she had given him in 1939. When he died in 1985, she was holding his hand.

Among his few possessions was his coded diary. It became Pamela's mission to decipher it. Over the next decade she sent it to institutions like the Imperial War Museum and the RAF Museum, but each time it was returned, the code unbroken.

Finally, it arrived on the desk of Dr Philip Aston, a mathematician at Surrey University. With the university's resources, he felt the puzzle might be solved in a weekend or two. But Donald had buried his secret deep in layers of code.

For five months, Dr Aston ran endless permutations through a computer, gradually breaking through each layer, but at the heart of the puzzle Donald had placed a final keyword. It defeated all logical attempts at solution until one night, lying sleepless in bed, Dr Aston suddenly understood that it could only be what was most important to the prisoner.

Putting together the two names – Donald Samuel Hill Pamela Seely Kirrage – in a single word, he applied it to the diary's code, and all at once the chaos resolved itself into coherence.

When the decoded diary was given to her in 1996, Pamela found that his fear of betraying to his captors his deepest feelings had driven him to hide them. 'Thank God for you, Pammy darling,' he had written, 'your memory is ever with me.'

'It feels as though the man I first loved has been restored to me,' Pamela said after reading it.

Denisa Lady Newborough, b. 1913, d. 1987

Denisa Lady Newborough, who has died aged seventy-four, was many things: wire-walker, nightclub girl, nude dancer, air pilot. She only refused to be two things – a whore and a spy – 'and there were attempts to make me both', she once wrote.

She was also a milliner, a perfumier and an antiques dealer; but her real metier, in early life at least, was what she called 'profitable romance'. Her opinions on the subject of presents from gentlemen would have done credit to the pen of Anita Loos: 'I have never believed that jewels, any more than motor cars, can be called vulgar just because they are gigantic.'

Her admirers included the Kings of Spain and Bulgaria, Adolf Hitler (whose virility she doubted), Benito Mussolini (whom she described as 'a gigolo') and Sheikh ben Ghana (who gave her 500 sheep). When she lived in Paris, she had no fewer than five protectors – all 'shareholders' as she termed them – and persuaded each, who was ignorant of his fellows, to part with a flat or a house.

Denisa Josephine Braun was born on April Fool's Day, 1913, in Suborica, Serbia. In her early teens she ran away to Budapest, where for a time she slept under bridges with tramps. Then, styling herself 'Baronne de Brans', she became a nude dancer and mistress of boyars, including a pair of twins. A decade of adventures followed, in Sofia, Bucharest, Paris, St Moritz and Berlin.

She served as a transport officer with the Red Cross at the beginning of the Second World War but was dismissed in 1941 because she was not of British birth.

In 1958, she published an autobiography, *The Fire in My Blood*, the flavour of which may be surmised from such chapter headings as 'Gipsy Love', 'Elegant Sin in Bucharest' and 'On the Trail of the White Slavers'.

She was convicted in 1964 of permitting her maisonette in Davies Street to be used for the purpose of habitual prostitution, though her conviction was quashed on appeal.

Lady Newborough was a great beauty and she was charming and funny. By conventional standards, her morality matched her flaming red hair, but she remained as proud of the one as of the other.

22nd

Jade Goody, b. 1981, d. 2009

Jade Goody, who has died aged twenty-seven, was catapulted into the limelight in 2003 by the apparently none-too-glittering achievement of coming fourth on *Big Brother*, so began a roller-coaster career that made her the poster girl of the curious contemporary cult of talentless celebrity.

Although she was frequently vilified, Jade Goody's final days as a victim of cancer saw her transformed into a serious figure whose frankness about her illness was deemed by some to be beneficial to the wider community.

The first time she was mentioned in the press, in May 2002, Jade Goody was described as a 'pretty dental nurse, twenty, from London'. But twenty-four hours later, as she began her gobby, ignorant trajectory in the *Big Brother* house, the *People* went on the attack under the headline: 'Why we must lob the gob'. Before long it was open season. The *Sun* called her a hippo, then a baboon, before launching its campaign to 'vote out the pig'. The *Sunday Mirror* rejected porcine comparisons on the ground that it was 'insulting – to pigs'.

Inside the '*BB*' house, Jade Goody found herself in bed with her male housemate, PJ, who ran away, shrieking. Her drunken striptease in a drinking game rigged by the male contestants ('Me kebab is showing!') forced even Channel 4 to blank the screen. 'Here she is: fat-rolled, Michelin girl Jade in all her preposterous lack of glory,' thundered the *Daily Mirror* the next day. 'Naked as the day Dr Frankenstein made her.'

Jade Goody's main function, as she put it herself, was to be an 'escape goat' – a pressure valve for the vindictive rage of the mob and their tribunes in the red tops. Polls suggested that she was more unpopular even than Saddam Hussein (a boxer, said Jade). Such was the public venom it was feared that things might get dangerously out of hand.

But, no sooner had she hit rock bottom then she bounced back up again. The tabloid campaign had developed into such an orgy of hate that it inspired a retaliation in her defence. Viewers, it seemed, warmed to her malapropisms, guilelessness and obvious vulnerability.

Told by their readers that they had gone too far, journalists began back-pedalling furiously. Finding they had struck gold, promoters and advertisers came flocking to her door. For the next four years it was impossible to turn on the television without seeing Jade Goody on some reality show or other.

She even had her own scent, Shh! ('Not actually a smell of me, like. It's not my BO or my feet cheese or nothing'), which became a best-seller. There were also Jade Goody fitness DVDs. Along the way, she acquired, cheated on and discarded several boyfriends, gave birth to two sons (the romances, break-ups, pregnancies and births all sold to magazines on an exclusive basis), changed from blonde to brunette and shed three stone.

By 2007, when she made her second visit to the Big Brother house on *Celebrity Big Brother* (alongside her surgically enhanced mother Jackiey), Jade Goody had become, by her own account, 'the twenty-fifth most inferlential person in the world'. She was said to be worth £2–4 million, was the proud owner of three 'footballers' wives' style homes, a £60,000 turbo-charged Range Rover and was the 'author' of a best-selling autobiography.

But what should have been a triumphant return to the scene of past glories soon turned to disaster, when Jade Goody became embroiled in a row over an Oxo cube with the Bollywood star Shilpa Shetty. Days of tension, during which Jade called her nemesis 'Shilpa Poppadom', ended in a foul-mouthed tirade. Booted out of the house, Jade Goody was branded a racist bully. In India she was burned in effigy.

Retribution was swift. 'Jade, We Hate You – The Nation Turns On Thick Racist Bully!' ran one headline.

But a career nosedive was not part of the script. *Big Brother*'s producers, Endemol, had recorded a new chat-show pilot with her as host. There followed a well-orchestrated campaign of rehabilitation, featuring a public plea for forgiveness and a 'goodwill visit' to India, where she visited a children's charity, apologised (again) and made a donation.

Jade's rehabilitation was crowned by an invitation by the makers of *Bigg Boss*, India's equivalent of *Big Brother*, to take part in their show. She did so in August 2008 and was seen learning to dance to Bollywood songs. But she was forced to leave abruptly after being told she had cervical cancer.

To most people, the prospect of eight weeks' confinement in the exhibitionistic surroundings of the Big Brother house would be the closest thing to hell. Jade Goody seemed to regard it as a vision of paradise. When she went in through the sliding door, she explained, 'It was like no one could get me or hurt me in there ... I was safe.' Her life story reveals why.

Jade Cerisa Lorraine Goody was born in Bermondsey on 5 June 1981. Her father, of mixed-race parentage, was a heroin addict and small-time pimp turned career criminal who spent most of his life behind bars, eventually dying of an overdose in the lavatory of the Kentucky Fried Chicken in Bournemouth. Her paternal grandmother, who once ran a brothel, had a crack habit. Her mother, Jackiey, the daughter of a market trader, was described in her daughter's autobiography as a petty thief and 'clipper' – a woman who pretends to be a prostitute but runs off with the money instead.

Jackiey threw Jade's father out of the house when Jade was eighteen months old, after discovering that he had hidden guns under her cot. To add to the confusion, Jackiey herself later came out as a lesbian.

Jade rolled her first joint for her mother when she was four and she took her first puff aged five, an event celebrated by her mother in a family photograph. At about the same time Jackiey was seriously injured in a motorcycle crash and lost the use of her left arm, as a result of which Jade spent much of her childhood in the role of carer.

Jade's schooling, not surprisingly, was chaotic. She was expelled from one school after her mother hit another mother, and from a second when her mother hit a teacher. It was not long before Jade began dishing out the bullying herself, once biting off a chunk of another girl's earlobe ('It wasn't a huge part of her earlobe or anything, just the tip').

As her performance on *Big Brother* made clear, her years of formal education had left Jade Goody with little knowledge. She thought that a ferret was a bird and abscess a green French drink; that Pistachio painted the *Mona Lisa*; that Sherlock Holmes invented the flush lavatory; that East Anglia ('East Angular' in Jade-speak) was abroad; and that Rio de Janeiro was 'a bloke, innit?'

After leaving school, Jade eventually found employment as a dental nurse. When she applied for a place in the *Big Brother* house, however, she was up to her ears in debt, had recently been evicted from a flat in Rotherhithe and was facing jail over an unpaid council tax bill.

Given Jade Goody's status as a media creation, it was perhaps inevitable that when stories began to circulate of a 'cancer scare', some assumed it was just another tasteless publicity stunt. That did not prove to be the case. After her initial diagnosis, it quickly became clear that her cancer was at an advanced stage. Radical surgery failed to stem its progress and she was told it was terminal.

There was time for one more twist however, as, on 22 February, in a blaze of publicity which was said to have earned her close to £1 million, Jade Goody married a 21-year-old carpet fitter, Jack Tweed. In order that the couple could spend their wedding night together, he was allowed to ignore the 7 p.m. curfew which was a condition of his early release from an eighteen-month prison sentence imposed for assaulting a sixteen-year-old boy with a golf club.

⇥ 23rd ⇤

Donald Swann, b. 1923, d. 1994

Donald Swann, the composer and entertainer who has died aged seventy, was the musical and comedy partner of the late Michael Flanders; in their revues they epitomised English nonsense humour in the good-natured tradition of *Punch*.

'The Hippopotamus Song', with its chorus 'Mud, mud, glorious mud', was their most celebrated number and was translated into eighteen languages; Swann himself sometimes sang the chorus in Russian.

The entertainment rested on Flanders' monologues and the comic rapport between the pair. Swann appeared as the boyish subordinate who would listen with lively interest while his partner conversed with the audience, and then occasionally go 'slightly berserk' as he tried to hog the stage with a turn at the piano.

'It is an astonishing entertainment,' commented the late W.A. Darlington in *The Daily Telegraph*. 'When the curtain rises, your natural reaction is to wonder how they will keep things going for the whole evening. But once their insidious brand of lunacy gets hold of you, you believe they might easily keep things going for a week if they wanted.'

Jim Edwards, b. 1935, d. 2009

Jim Edwards, who has died aged seventy-three, was the co-founder of the World Elephant Polo Championships, which are held in Nepal each year.

Although there is some evidence that the game may have been played in India in the early twentieth century, the idea took off in 1981 when Edwards met the Scottish polo player and tobogganist James Manclark in a club at St Moritz. Manclark suggested that an obvious way to expand Edwards' tourist business was to introduce elephant polo, and over a drink the pair devised some provisional rules. But Edwards thought no more about it until he received a telegram from Manclark some months later: 'Arriving Kathmandu April 1. Have long sticks. Get ready elephants.'

24th

Maurice Flitcroft, b. 1929, d. 2007

Maurice Flitcroft, who has died aged seventy-seven, was a chain-smoking shipyard crane-operator from Barrow-in-Furness whose persistent attempts to gatecrash the British Open golf championship produced a sense of humour failure among members of the golfing establishment.

In 1976 the 46-year-old Flitcroft bought a half-set of mail-order clubs and set his sights on finding 'fame and fortune' by applying to play in the Birkdale Open 'with Jack Nicklaus and all that lot'. He prepared by studying a Peter Allis instruction manual borrowed from the local library, honing his skills by hitting a ball about on a nearby beach.

He obtained an entry form from an unsuspecting Royal and Ancient, which organises the championship, and, having no handicap to declare as an amateur, he picked the other option on the form: professional.

Invited to play in the qualifier at Formby, he put in a performance which one witness described as a 'blizzard of triple and quadruple bogeys ruined by a solitary par', achieving a total of 121 – 49 over par, the worst score recorded in the tournament's 141-year history. In fact, this was only a rough estimate, his marker having lost count on a couple of holes.

His playing partner, Jim Howard, recalled his suspicions being aroused almost from the word go: 'After gripping the club like he was intent on murdering someone, Flitcroft hoisted it straight up, came down vertically and the ball travelled precisely four feet,' he said. 'We put that one down to nerves, but after he shanked a second one we called the R&A officials.' Under the rules of the tournament, however, nothing could be done. 'It wasn't funny at the time,' said Howard.

Others demurred, and Flitcroft's performance dominated the next day's sports pages, while stars such as Jack Nicklaus found themselves relegated to the small print. Flitcroft was interviewed endlessly. The score, he maintained, 'weren't a fair reflection' of his play. He blamed the fact that he had left his four-wood in the car: 'I was an expert with the four-wood, deadly accurate.'

Furious that their game had been held up to ridicule, the R&A tightened the entry rules. Flitcroft was banned from R&A tournaments for life.

Refusing to be beaten, in 1978 he posed as an American professional named Gene Pacecki ('as in pay cheque', he explained helpfully) and blagged his way into the qualifier at South Herts, where he was detected after a few holes and bundled unceremoniously off the course.

At a qualifier at Pleasington in 1983, he tried disguise, dyeing his hair, donning a false moustache and masquerading as Gerald Hoppy, a professional golfer from Switzerland. He fared rather better this time, playing nine holes and sixty-three strokes before officials realised that they had 'another Maurice Flitcroft' on their hands. 'Imagine their surprise when they discovered they had the actual Maurice Flitcroft,' he said.

In 1990 he entered the qualifier at Ormskirk as James Beau Jolley (as in Beaujolais), an American golf professional. He hit a double bogey at the first hole and a bogey at the second; he claimed to be 'looking at a par' at the third when he was rudely interrupted by an R&A golf buggy which screeched to a halt in front of him. He remonstrated with the driver, asking to be allowed to finish the hole, but officials were not in the mood to show mercy. Nor did they return his £60 entry fee.

Flitcroft never understood why the R&A was so upset. 'I never set out to belittle them. Golf's just a game and I tried my best. What did they need to get so uptight about?'

Maurice Gerald Flitcroft was born in Manchester on 23 November 1929 and claimed to have been a talented schoolboy athlete. After leaving school he joined the Merchant Navy, then made a living as a high-diving comedy stunt man with a travelling theatre group. After his marriage he moved to Barrow-in-Furness, where he became a crane operator at the Vickers Armstrong shipyard. He retired in the 1970s.

Flitcroft's entryist assaults on the Open made him a cult figure in some golfing circles. He received mail from around the world addressed simply to Maurice Flitcroft, Golfer, England.

A club in New York State named a trophy after him, and another in Michigan named a tournament in his honour, the event featuring a green with two holes to give the truly hopeless a sporting chance. In 1988, when Flitcroft was flown in as an honorary competitor at the event, he explained that it was the first time he and his wife had been out of the house together 'since our gas oven exploded'.

⊰ 25th ⊱

John Snagge, b. 1904, d. 1996

John Snagge, the broadcaster who has died aged ninety-one, was one of the best-loved voices of the BBC.

He was most familiar for his annual commentaries on the Boat Race, which he covered from 1931 to 1980. In 1938 his sound commentary accompanied the first televising of the race. In 1949 he was heard to say: 'Oxford are ahead. No, Cambridge are ahead. I don't know who's ahead – it's either Oxford or Cambridge.' In a career lasting from 1924 to 1965, Snagge's imperturbable tones were broadcast from almost every kind of public event. After the Coronation in 1953 he received an apology from the Archbishop of Canterbury. 'He said he turned over two pages at once,' Snagge remembered, 'and that I must have had a heart attack when, instead of introducing "All People Who On Earth Do Dwell", he said: "Let us pray". I told him that nobody in the Abbey was praying half as hard as I was.'

⊰ 26th ⊱

Norman Jackson, b. 1919, d. 1994

Norman Jackson, who has died aged seventy-four, was one of ten Lancaster aircrew awarded the Victoria Cross during the Second World War and the first RAF flight engineer to be so honoured: he won his decoration for an exploit described in the citation as 'almost incredible'.

By April 1944 Jackson had flown thirty missions and, although not obliged to fly further, volunteered to accompany his crew, who still had operational sorties to complete. On the night of 26 April, shortly after receiving news of the birth of his youngest son, he took off for a raid on Schweinfurt.

The Lancaster dropped its bombs over the target but was then lacerated by cannon-fire from a Focke-Wulf 190; a fire erupted on the upper surface of the starboard wing, adjacent to a fuel tank.

Jackson, despite being wounded by shell splinters in the right leg and shoulders, immediately tackled the potentially catastrophic blaze. Pushing a small fire-extinguisher inside his jacket, he clipped on his parachute pack and jettisoned the escape hatch above the pilot's head. With the Lancaster still flying at 22,000ft and 200mph, he climbed on to the top of the fuselage and began to inch towards the blazing wing.

Almost immediately his parachute opened and the canopy and rigging spilled back into the cockpit. The pilot, bomb aimer and navigator gathered the parachute together and held on to the rigging lines, paying them out as Jackson crawled aft. But he slipped and fell from the fuselage on to the starboard wing.

He held on by grasping an air intake on the leading edge. The extinguisher fell from his jacket and was lost; the flames burned Jackson severely. Then the Germans strafed the Lancaster once more. Jackson was hit, lost his grip and was sucked through the fire and off the trailing edge of the wing, dragging his parachute behind him.

For a while Jackson hung in the slipstream; then his surviving comrades released the parachute and he fell towards earth, his canopy in flames. The remaining crew baled out; four landed safely, but the captain and rear gunner perished with the aircraft. Jackson's parachute canopy was two-thirds burned and he was fortunate to sustain only a broken leg on landing; but his right eye was closed through burns, and his hands were horribly burned and useless.

At daybreak he crawled towards a village on his knees and elbows. He knocked on the door of a cottage, whose occupant spat at him and shouted: 'Churchill gangster!' The man was then pushed aside by his two beautiful daughters, who bathed Jackson's wounds. 'I was lying there like a lord,' recalled Jackson. 'I began to think I was pretty lucky.'

After ten months in hospital he was sent to a prison camp. He made two attempts to escape; the second time he succeeded in penetrating the German lines, and met the Americans near Munich.

He was decorated by George VI at Buckingham Palace. Jackson's mother was delighted: 'The only other outstanding thing he ever did,' she told reporters, 'was to ride in a procession through Twickenham on the smallest bicycle ever made.'

Alex Comfort, b. 1920, d. 2000

Alex Comfort, who has died aged eighty, made his name across the world with *The Joy of Sex* (1973).

'Before my book,' he wrote, 'writing about sex gave the impression of being written by non-playing coaches. Dear old Freud probably never witnessed an act of sex except in a mirror.'

Written in two weeks with his first wife, *The Joy of Sex* was illustrated by drawings of a bearded man and his inamorata. Subtitled *A Gourmet Guide*, the book was coyly arranged in three sections: 'Starters', 'Main Courses' and 'Sauces & Pickles'. Couples who staggered, exhausted, to the end were almost immediately hit with *More Joy of Sex* (1974).

In the early 1970s Comfort was inclined to dismiss the dangers of venereal diseases as a puritan scare. But in revised editions, after the advent of Aids, he conceded the dangers of promiscuity. Accordingly, in *The New Joy of Sex* (1991), 'Fidelity', formerly featured at the end under 'Problems', was moved to the beginning under 'Ingredients'.

Comfort married twice: first, in 1943 (dissolved 1973), Ruth Harris; and secondly, in 1973, Jane Henderson, who died in 1991. The son of his first marriage, Nicholas Comfort, writes obituaries for *The Daily Telegraph*.

⊰ 27th ⊱

Irene Thomas, b. 1919, d. 2001

Irene Thomas, who has died aged eighty-one, was the former chorus girl who became an omniscient panellist on television and radio quiz programmes from the 1960s onwards.

Witty and charming, she exuded an air of erudition. Lord Quinton, sometimes the question master on *Round Britain Quiz*, was astounded by her knowledge: 'I thought she must go home every night to read *Encyclopaedia Britannica*.'

In fact, far from being well educated, Irene Thomas had left school at fifteen. She attributed her success to a highly retentive memory and to a magpie's instinct for 'jewels of information which lie about everywhere'.

She was born Irene Roberts Ready at Feltham, Middlesex, on 28 June 1919, the only child of a former bandsman in the King's Royal Rifles who had entered the Army as a nameless orphan. Her mother, a former court dressmaker, was the daughter of a village blacksmith.

Little 'Reen' was greedy to learn and taught herself to read long before she went to school; by the age of ten she was absorbing everything she could find, from *Jane Eyre* to her grandfather's copy of *Diseases of the Horse*.

At the County School, Ashford, she loved exams and was assured by her teachers that she was certain to win a scholarship to Oxford; but there was no question of her going to university at all, since her upkeep would have been far beyond her parents' means. Instead, at fifteen she joined the Inland Revenue as a clerk.

Having had singing lessons, in 1946 she was taken on as a member of the embryonic opera company at Covent Garden. For three years she sang in the chorus, and took a small solo role in *The Magic Flute*. She absorbed the atmosphere of the Opera House and left with a phenomenal knowledge of music which was to prove invaluable to her in her quiz career.

Later she joined the chorus of the ice pantomimes at Wembley, which in turn led to fifteen years' work as a session musician with George Mitchell. She provided the backing for films and detergent commercials, and appeared as a sequinned chorus girl in *Saturday Night at the London Palladium*.

In 1959 she took an IQ test and scored 159. This encouraged her to take part in the radio programme *What Do You Know?* (later *Brain of Britain*), which she won in 1961. She then applied for the *Round Britain Quiz*, but was turned down. Undeterred, the next year she defeated two other Brains of Britain to take the title 'Brain of Brains'.

She then began to make appearances on television and radio quizzes, including *Ask Me Another* (on which she won enough kitchen cupboards to equip a barracks), and *Sale of the Century*, on which she won prizes worth more than she had ever earned in a year.

But it took seven years of patient letters to the BBC before she was allowed to appear on *Round Britain Quiz* in 1967. 'I had almost lost hope of disturbing the monastic calm of the Quiz with the presence of an ex-chorus girl,' she recalled.

From 1973, when the programme returned after several years off the air, she became a permanent member of the London panel. By the time the programme finally came to an end in 1995, she was, with John Julius Norwich, its most senior contestant.

⊰ 28th ⊱

Baroness Maria Augusta von Trapp, b. 1905, d. 1987

B aroness Maria Augusta von Trapp, who has died in Vermont aged eighty-two, was the inspiration for the popular musical play and film *The Sound of Music*.

She said that she was much wilder as a girl than Julie Andrews' film portrayal – 'not so goody-goody' – and preferred Petula Clark's more tomboyish version in the 1981 revival of the Rodgers and Hammerstein musical.

As an unruly twenty-year-old novice nun in the Tyrolean Alps she was temporarily assigned as governess to the family of a local nobleman, Baron Georg von Trapp. She fell in love first with the seven children and then with their father. They were married a year later, in 1927, and had three more children.

The Baron, who his wife said was by no means the martinet portrayed in the film, was a fierce opponent of the Nazis, and his feelings were shared by his wife. She once called Hitler 'someone you would not want to have in your living room'.

The von Trapps fled when the Germans invaded their country. They crossed the Alps on foot and travelled to the United States on visitors' visas, arriving with $4 between them.

At home in Austria, the family had sung in concerts for friends around Salzburg. They decided to turn professional in America, where they soon became famous. Dressed in Tyrolean costume and armed with flutes, recorders, cellos and a spinet, they performed Austrian folk songs, old English madrigals, operatic arias, Gregorian chant and hymns on tours throughout the United States and South America.

After three years' touring, the family bought a ramshackle house near Stowe in Vermont, where the scenery reminded them of the Tyrol. They continued to tour as the Trapp Family Singers until 1957, by which time the ramshackle house had become the Trapp Family Lodge – a skiing hotel and musical centre.

The Baroness wrote five books, one of which, *The Trapp Family Singers*, was the source for Rodgers and Hammerstein's 1959 musical and the Oscar-winning film in 1965 (which made about £100 million). Having sold the film rights to a German company for £1,500, the Baroness made very little from the phenomenal success of her story. 'But I have never felt sorry. I have seen how destructive riches can be to the human character,' she said.

In 1980 the Trapp Family Lodge was destroyed by fire, but the Baroness began anew with a good humour and built a rather grander hotel in its place. She retired from active life in 1985, after two strokes.

Lockwood West, b. 1905, d. 1989

L ockwood West, who has died aged eighty-three, was one of the most engaging and experienced character actors of his time.

Recently he created a gem of characterisation as the eccentric and sexually obsessed old chaplain in the television adaptation of Tom Sharpe's novel *Porterhouse Blue*. Many will cherish the memory of his dialogue with Zipser (played by John Sessions) when, in order to facilitate the deaf confessor's hearing, the undergraduates' intimate problems are discussed by means of a loud hailer.

'Is it SELF-ABUSE?' enquires the chaplain, his amplified tones reverberating round the college court, before proceeding to issue his standard recommendation about female foreign language students.

29th

David Hicks, b. 1929, d. 1998

D avid Hicks, who has died aged sixty-nine, was a very grand and successful interior decorator – still more grand and successful after his marriage in 1960 to Earl Mountbatten of Burma's daughter Pamela.

Yet Hicks's first appearance in Mountbatten's diaries was less than auspicious. 'Walked with Pammy barefoot on the lawn for one hour hearing about David Hicks,' Mountbatten recorded for 13 September 1959. 'As a result had blood blisters on both feet. Very painful.'

Certainly interior decorators did not feature at the peak of Mountbatten's vision of the social hierarchy. But Hicks was not only talented; he was impossible to put down. 'I enjoy being me,' he once remarked, and no one ever succeeded in undermining that delight.

David Nightingale Hicks was born on 25 March 1929 and brought up at Coggeshall in Essex. Both his father (a real Victorian, born in 1863) and his maternal grandfather were stockbrokers. His father's ideal of painting, he remembered, was a series of coloured hunting prints by John Leech.

At Charterhouse the boy did not sit his school certificate, because his master considered he would never pass. He was more at home at the Central School of Art, but hated his first job, in an advertising agency.

His breakthrough came after he had redecorated his mother's house in South Eaton Place. *House and Garden* ran a feature on it, and suddenly Hicks found himself in demand as an interior decorator. In 1956 he went into partnership with the antiques dealer Tom Parr, and three years later set up his own business, specialising in the redecoration of houses in both London and the country.

At home he worked at Windsor and Buckingham Palace; abroad he decorated hotel chains in Japan and offices for Aeroflot. His nightclub for the *QE2* had walls covered with grey flannel edged with silver, and featured bright-red screens to be drawn across the windows at night.

He designed the library for the British Embassy in Washington, a yacht for King Fahd, and two restaurants for the Barbican. He acted as a consultant on car interiors for BMW. In the 1970s he branched out into fashion accessories for the Japanese market, producing everything from umbrellas to bedroom slippers.

His ideas caught on because he spoke as one having authority. 'This house is a marriage of Inigo Jones, Palladio and myself,' he declared of a building he had designed for some Iranians in the Algarve. Such a manner annihilated his clients' indecision – albeit at considerable expense.

◄ 30th ►

Sir Ranulph Bacon, b. 1906, d. 1988

Sir Ranulph Bacon, otherwise 'Rasher of the Yard', who has died aged eighty-one, sparked a controversy in the mid-1960s when as Assistant Commissioner of 'the Met' he advised the public to 'have a go' against criminals.

Tall, convivial, popular with colleagues and earning respect, even affection, among opponents in the underworld, 'Rasher' Bacon was always ready to speak his mind. Even now his urging of bystanders not to stand still or get out of the way but to 'have a go' remains the subject of lively debate.

After retiring from the Yard as Deputy Commissioner in 1966, he was appointed to the newly established Gaming Board and quickly asserted himself as the strong man of the club scene, policing London's gambling jungle. Bacon had already distinguished himself in that field in the Bahamas, where he investigated gambling scandals and sent Mafia operators scuttling back to New York.

'A shotgun is part of the adult Englishman's equipment,' he told one crime conference.

◄ 31st ►

Aileen Plunket, b. 1904, d. 1999

Aileen Plunket, who has died aged ninety-four, was the eldest of three sisters – the others were Maureen (later Marchioness of Dufferin and Ava) and Oonagh (Lady Oranmore and Browne) – collectively known as the 'Golden Guinness Girls'.

Aileen was considered the most beautiful of the trio. But as chatelaine of Luttrellstown Castle, near Dublin, she came to be known chiefly for her parties.

Though apparently frail, with only one kidney for much of her life, Aileen Plunket invariably outlasted her guests, even in old age. She was stern with those who went to bed before the evening reached its climax in her 'nightclub' in the castle basement. 'I can't understand why the young people go to bed,' she would say, 'when we're still up.'

Rooms were kept ready for those incapable of driving home. These would be supremely comfortable, with open wood fires in the bedroom and bathroom, kept alight throughout the night. At eleven in the morning, a footman in livery would appear with a 'Pink Special' (Aileen's name for a Bloody Mary) to aid recovery.

Aileen Sibell Mary Guinness was born on 16 May 1904, the eldest daughter of Ernest Guinness, younger son of the 1st Earl of Iveagh. During the Great War, Ernest Guinness accused a British officer he saw bicycling through the lines of being a German spy. No one so young, he reasoned, could have amassed so many decorations. The 'spy' turned out to be the Prince of Wales.

Aileen and her sisters grew up at Glenmaroon, an Edwardian house near Dublin. After coming out, Aileen was photographed by Cecil Beaton. In 1927 she married Brinsley Plunket, the younger son of the 5th Lord Plunket. They had three daughters, one of whom died in infancy. The Plunkets divorced in 1940, and some months later Brinsley Plunket was killed while on active service in the RAF Volunteer Reserve.

In 1956 she married the Yugoslav-born designer Valerian Stux-Rybar, who specialised in opulence, earning the description 'the world's most expensive decorator'. They divorced in 1965. 'He was a mistake,' Aileen later conceded, 'but we're still good friends.'

At Luttrellstown, meanwhile, she filled the castle with beautiful furniture – including a commode from Louis XV's bedroom at Fontainebleau – and paintings by Stubbs and Vernet. She thought it impossible to find decent flowers in Ireland. Before parties, the Duchess's secretary would fly in from Paris with bouquets.

The extravagance eventually took its toll and, towards the end of her life, Aileen Plunket imagined herself poor. Luttrellstown had eighteen indoor staff, and she began to find paying their wages a strain. In 1983, at the age of seventy-nine, she was persuaded to sell the castle, along with its contents. 'Even the picnic baskets had a lot number on them,' the *Telegraph*'s sales correspondent reported. 'It was one of the saddest sights I have seen.'

Thereafter she dispensed hospitality at Ballyconneely, her 'cottage' (which slept twenty) in Connemara.

To the last she was faithfully looked after by her butler Jerry Higgins, who had been with her for forty-six years.

APRIL

⊰ 1st ⊱

Martha Graham, b. 1894, d. 1991

Martha Graham, the American dancer and choreographer, who has died aged ninety-six, made a profound and exhilarating impact on modern dance.

In the course of a career spanning seventy years Graham choreographed some 180 pieces and collaborated with such composers as Aaron Copland and Samuel Barber. She retired as a dancer in the early 1970s, but continued to create new pieces well into her tenth decade.

Founder of the Martha Graham Centre of Contemporary Dance – where her principal dancers included Merce Cunningham, Paul Taylor and Twyla Tharp, and her more recent students the pop star Madonna – Graham developed a revolutionary technique of movement which has been copied by companies all over the world.

As the choreographer Agnes de Mille put it, 'She created a new system of leverage, balance and dynamics ... She found an original way of communication.'

The essentials of Graham's technique were based on a new and exciting approach to the back – as the place in the body where movement originates – which she understood in terms of 'contraction and release'.

The two other major aspects of the technique were spirals and falls; and great attention was paid to different kinds of walks and travelling steps. In all her works she offered a rigorously fresh interpretation – frequently related to the contemporary conflicts of women's lives. Men invaded her company – and her life – from time to time; but in her choreography they had a tendency to remain as sex objects, often scantily clad and explicitly animal. More human roles were largely reserved for heroines.

Never afraid of controversy, she created gripping depictions of lust, greed, jealousy and love. Her virgins, goddesses and madwomen disturbed and mesmerised audiences with a raw emotion as they whirled across bare stages in bare feet to relentlessly dissonant scores.

Petite and fragile-looking, with arched eyebrows, a vividly painted mouth and a tightly wound chignon, Martha Graham was as vibrant and ruthlessly perfectionist off stage as she was on it. 'I know that I'm vain and arrogant,' she once said. 'All artists are vain. I want to be vain, and I try to teach the girls in my company to be vain. It's essential.' She certainly took herself very seriously, and in this respect has much to answer for.

Daughter of a psychiatrist of Scottish extraction, Martha Graham was born on 11 May 1894. Her father disapproved of her desire to become a dancer, and it was not until the year of his death in 1916 that she entered the Denishawn School in Los Angeles.

Her progress was rapid, and in 1920 she made her professional debut as the female lead in Ted Shawn's *Xochitl*, based on an Aztec legend. Three years later Graham joined the Greenwich Village Follies in New York and spent two seasons dancing in Moorish and Oriental works before taking up a teaching post at the Eastman School.

In 1929 she founded her dance troupe, and evolved an increasingly independent style. She aimed, she said, to create dances which freed the body to 'make visible the interior landscape' – a maxim amply borne out in works such as *Lamentation* (1930), in which the body moves as if obsessed with grief.

In the 1930s she introduced several dances inspired by a visit to New Mexico, but it was Greek mythology which dominated the 1940s. Besides *Cave of the Heart*, she produced *Errand into the Maze* (1947), a transformation of the Minotaur myth, and *Night Journey* (1947), which told the story of Oedipus through the eyes of Jocasta.

By now Martha Graham's company was touring all over the world. After a successful visit to Europe in 1954 it performed in the Near and Far East, and in 1957 she danced Judith in Berlin.

As a teacher she gradually came to terms with the balletic technique she had earlier rejected at the Denishawn School, and during the 1940s and 1950s her dancers gained impeccable line and control. All was not sweetness and light, however, when she was hard at work. She toiled with a demonical intensity, taking little account of the feelings of her dancers.

When she had to cease dancing herself, she continued to appear on stage at the beginning of performances to deliver pithy, and invariably instructive, inaugural speeches.

After a serious physical breakdown at the age of seventy-five she was jealously cared for by Ronald Protas, a former photographer. Protas increasingly became the shield between her and a demanding world, sitting in on press interviews, reading her mail, organising her social life.

Occasionally flashes of the real Graham broke through: she refused one interview with a magazine because she thought its dance critic 'an evil spirit' who might 'put a curse on the new work'.

Jewell New, b. 1945, d. 1998

Jewell New, who has died aged fifty-two, excelled in persuading lions to ride motorcycles.

He took six months coaxing his favourite lion, Kenneth, to join him on his bike. 'At first the cat wouldn't go near the bike,' he said. 'Then he wouldn't get off.'

Kenneth showed a natural sense of balance as New roared round the ring, but his master sometimes complained of back strain after supporting the thirty-stone beast's head and paws on his shoulders.

New was able to pull off stunts that would have made orthodox lion-tamers think twice. 'No one told me what couldn't be done,' he said, 'so I just went ahead.' This came home to him at a ticklish moment with another lion, Buddy. Although Buddy had been bottle-fed by New from the age of two days, he turned awkward at the climax of the act, when New put his head inside his jaws.

'He just kept it there,' New recalled. 'He didn't bite me, he just held me in place with his teeth. When he decided at last to let me go, my groom just asked me why I'd kept my head in there for such a long time.' New decided in future to use a different lion for that particular trick.

⊰ 2nd ⊱

Linda Lovelace, b. 1949, d. 2002

Linda Lovelace, who has died aged fifty-three, was the star of *Deep Throat* (1972), the pornographic film which challenged the American obscenity laws and became the first of its kind to be shown in mainstream cinemas; she later wrote a book, *Ordeal*, about her experiences and became an outspoken opponent of the porn industry.

Linda Lovelace was introduced to the world of adult entertainment in 1970 after meeting Chuck Traynor, who was to become her husband and manager. She was introduced to the seedy world of 'skin flicks', and appeared in a few sex 'shorts' before *Deep Throat*.

The plot of *Deep Throat* was, in the tradition of porn films, unchallenging. Linda Lovelace goes to the doctor complaining that she is having trouble finding sexual satisfaction. After a thorough examination, the doctor discovers that she has sexual organs in her throat and advises her to pursue pleasure accordingly – which she duly does for the rest of the film.

Deep Throat, which took two weeks to make and cost a few thousand dollars, might easily have joined the ranks of thousands of other cheap porn films had it not been released at a time when 'porno chic' was becoming fashionable. Suddenly porn was not only for old men in raincoats, and Linda Lovelace, a sweetly pretty, innocent-looking and unthreatening brunette, seemed to appeal to mainstream audiences.

Traynor lost no time in cashing in on Linda Lovelace's charms. Soon she was appearing at Hollywood parties in the company of celebrities such as Sammy Davis Jr. She was touted as 'the first superstar of erotic entertainment' and although the film was banned in a number of states (and in Britain) she became something of a celebrity.

She also claimed that the film was educational. 'I get letters,' Linda Lovelace said in 1973, 'about a hundred a day – a lot of them from reverends and psychologists. They say that *Deep Throat* definitely has redeeming social value.'

But in *Ordeal* (1981), Linda Lovelace revealed that her career had been a catalogue of violent physical and sexual abuse and that every interview and public appearance had been scripted by the sadistic Traynor. She claimed that he had forced her at gunpoint into a life of prostitution and pornography. 'When you see the movie *Deep Throat*,' she told an interviewer that year, 'you are watching me being raped. It is a crime that movie is still showing; there was a gun to my head the entire time.' The film grossed $600 million. Linda Lovelace made $1,250.

Linda Boreman was born in the Bronx on 10 January 1949, the daughter of a New York policeman. She was educated at Catholic school but her childhood was not happy. Her mother beat her and was appalled when she gave birth to an illegitimate child at the age of nineteen (the child was adopted).

Linda Boreman saw Traynor as an escape from her family, and ultimately, *Deep Throat* was her escape from Traynor: 'a low point and a salvation'. In 1975 she left him for David Winters, who produced her in *Linda Lovelace for President* (1976), an abysmal sex comedy which saw her on the campaign trail following a cross-country bus route mapped out in the shape of a penis. Her career as an actress did not flourish.

After *Ordeal* was published she toured the country for real, giving lectures on abuses within the pornographic industry. She also testified before several commissions on the effects of pornography on women and children. 'I'm not ashamed of my past or sad about it,' she said. 'I look in the mirror and I know that I've survived.'

But *Deep Throat* dogged her life. 'Deep Throat' was even the codeword for the undercover source used by the reporters Woodward and Bernstein, who revealed the Watergate scandal. Linda Lovelace has featured in pop songs and countless jokes. But all she ever dreamed of, she said once, was 'a little home, kids, a decent husband'.

⊰ 3rd ⊱

Lionel Bart, b. 1930, d. 1999

Lionel Bart, the composer and lyricist who has died aged sixty-eight, was one of the most tuneful songwriters in the post-war theatre; his most enduring success was the musical *Oliver!* (1960).

Oliver!, based on Charles Dickens' novel *Oliver Twist*, ran in London for 2,618 performances. On Broadway, Bart won a Tony award for his score, and when Carol Reed's film version (1968) starring Harry Secombe and Oliver Reed was awarded six Oscars, Bart's reputation soared.

Success tempted him into buying very large houses in London, New York and Malibu – and a castle-like property in Tangiers. He hobnobbed with Brian Epstein, John Lennon and Jimi Hendrix, and became one of the most prominent – and popular – personalities of London's so-called Swinging Sixties.

When in Hollywood, he was chauffeured about in the company of a giant teddy-bear named Spencer Tracy; and his name was romantically linked with Judy Garland and Alma Cogan. Noel Coward said he would 'rather spend five minutes in a four-ale bar with Lionel Bart than a year's yachting cruise with the Oxford Debating Society'.

But before the end of the 1960s, in order to fund his extravagant way of life – and his heroic consumption of alcohol – Bart had been persuaded to part with the rights of *Oliver!* (for £15,000); and in the 1970s his career crashed.

Nemesis came in 1975, with the musical *Twang!!*, a burlesque of Robin Hood (described by Bart as 'an adult satire on the Crusades, definitely not for family trade'). So many people walked away from it before it reached London that Bart felt obliged to finance the production himself, and as a result was bankrupted. After that, his fortunes never recovered.

He was born Lionel Begleiter, in Whitechapel, east London, on 1 August 1930, the son of a tailor. His work would show the strong influence of the Yiddish theatre he saw on youthful expeditions with his mother to the Grand Palais in the East End. *Oliver!*, he said years later, was 'a strange marriage of the Jewish music of my bar mitzvah and the street cries of my childhood. Fagin's music was like a Jewish mother-hen clucking away.'

He showed an early talent for drawing and at thirteen won a scholarship to St Martin's School of Art, where Quentin Crisp was his first life model. On leaving St Martin's, he worked as a graphic artist and scene painter.

His involvement with the theatre began in 1953, in a production at the Unity, the left-wing London theatre, where he collaborated with Alfie Bass. 'There was a satirical review about the Coronation,' Bart recalled, 'for which I was painting scenery. Alfie put up a notice on the board asking people to do songs, and I wrote a couple for a lark. Alfie told me to stop painting scenery.'

For the Unity Theatre, Bart composed 'Wally Pone', a cockney version of Ben Jonson's *Volpone*. At the same time, he was also busy writing lyrics for the successful opening show at Bernard Miles' Mermaid Theatre, *Lock Up Your Daughters* (1959).

Bart (who had no musical training) then wrote both score and lyrics for an even bigger success, *Fings Ain't Wot They Used T'Be*, directed by Joan Littlewood and starring Barbara Windsor. Set in Soho with a cast of pimps, prostitutes and small-time criminals, the show had two separate runs at the Theatre Royal, Stratford East, before transferring to the West End, where it ran for two years.

By then Bart had written 'Living Doll', which was to be Cliff Richard's first No. 1 hit, and had become one of the first writers of his generation to introduce politics, albeit mildly, into his lyrics.

In 1963 he wrote the theme to the James Bond film *From Russia With Love*, sung by Matt Monro. The next year he wrote the music and lyrics for *Maggie May*, Alun Owen's story about dockers, sailors and a prostitute in pre-war Liverpool. Judy Garland recorded four songs from it.

But the 1970s were not to prove so kind. Critics called *Twang!!* dank, bedraggled, feeble and a shambles, and after forty-three performances in the West End it closed. Despite writing several other musicals in the years that followed, including *Lionel* (about his own career), Bart never again achieved consistent success.

He overcame alcoholism, but by the 1980s was reduced to living above a shop in Acton, west London. Looking back, Bart reflected, without rancour, on his golden period: 'We had too much. Sometimes – often – limitations can be your best asset.'

⊰ 4th ⊱

Kenny Everett, b. 1944, d. 1995

Kenny Everett, who has died aged fifty, was a disc jockey and television comedian with an engaging line in coarsely satiric comic sketches in disconcertingly bad taste.

'Cuddly Ken,' as he liked to be known, first came to public attention in the 1960s, when his manic broadcasts for pirate radio won him a large following among adolescents. Snapped up by BBC Radio 1, Everett pioneered the role of disc jockey as popular entertainer, with nonsensical jingles, scatological extemporisations and wild lunges at figures of authority.

Nervous and unconfident in company, he found that the seclusion of the radio studio allowed him to escape from his own neuroses into a world of fantastic invention. 'Radio is a good place to work,' he said, 'if you are not really a jolly person, but want to appear to be one.'

From the late 1970s he was much in evidence on television. Diminutive and bearded, with receding hair and wildly rotating eyes, he presided over an hysterical melange of music and fustian lampoon, laden with innuendo. His zenith in this line came with *The Kenny Everett Video Show* and *The Kenny Everett Television Show*.

He created a gallery of memorable grotesques, the foremost of which were Sid Snot (a filthy Hell's Angel), Mr Angry of Mayfair, Marcel Wave (a fastidious French hairdresser), the Thora Hird-inspired Verity Treacle and the pneumatic American starlet Cupid Stunt, for whom Everett coined the catchphrase 'all in the best pahssible taste!', as 'she' crossed her legs with an extravagant lack of discretion.

In 1970 Everett was sacked by the BBC for making a jibe about Mary Peyton, the wife of the then Minister of Transport, after she had taken her driving test – 'She only passed because she slipped him a fiver – I know these people'.

The BBC took him back, but in 1984 he made another unfortunate joke, albeit one handed him on a piece of paper by his producer: 'When England was an empire,' he gurgled, 'we had an emperor, when we were a kingdom, we had a king, and now we are a country, we've got Margaret Thatcher.' This was inconsistent of Everett, as in the previous year he had 'come out' as a Tory at a Young Conservatives' rally attended by the Prime Minister, at which he jovially yelled (to the embarrassment of the assembled faithful): 'Let's bomb Russia!'

The son of a tugboatman, Kenny Everett was born Maurice Cole into a working-class family of Liverpool Roman Catholics on Christmas Day 1944; he was educated at St Bede's Secondary Modern and St Peter Claver College. A spindly, sensitive child, he recalled his schooldays with distaste: 'Most kids thought the best way to get on top was to punch someone in the mouth – usually me.'

After leaving school, he had a brief flirtation with the priesthood and spent a year at a missionary college. 'I'm no longer Catholic,' he later said. 'I'm freelance.' His first job was 'scraping gunk off sausage-roll trays' in a Liverpool bakery, before moving on to an advertising agency.

Having acquired an ability to impersonate everything from the Goons to the opening of the airlocks in *Journey into Space*, he bought two tape-recorders and began to make his own programmes, interspersing music with bouts of silliness.

He changed his name to Kenny Everett, and in 1964 became a disc jockey for Radio Luxembourg; before long he moved to the pirate ship Radio London, where he teamed up with Dave Cash. When the government cracked down on the pirate stations Everett switched to Radio 1. Sacked from the BBC for the second time, he joined the new Capital Radio, where he was reunited with Cash.

For twelve years Everett was married to a spiritualist known as Crystal Clear. When they parted his wife revealed that the main obstacle to nuptial bliss had not been Everett's homosexuality but his profound depressions. 'Even the plumber would leave our house feeling depressed after talking to Ev,' she wrote.

Latterly Everett lived alone in a flat he kept obsessively tidy, even vacuuming the plastic grass on the balcony. He was fond of animals, and at one stage had a chihuahua-Yorkshire terrier cross, two cats, a parrot and several horses. His companion in his last years was a cat called Pussy Cat.

By way of recreation, he enjoyed needlework.

Rixi Markus, b. 1910, d. 1992

Rixi Markus, who has died aged eighty-one, was the first woman in the world to become a bridge grandmaster, and with the late Fritzi Gordon made up the most formidable women's bridge partnership in the world.

They were an excitable, argumentative pair, and their habit of venting their frustrations in public earned them the sobriquet 'Frisky and Bitchy'.

Rixi certainly had a voluminous ego, and thought nothing of confiding that a team-mate was 'a selfish bitch'. At the same time, away from the competitive baize, she was a loyal and warm-hearted personality. She always regretted the aggressive image she gained in the game.

'At the bridge table I had to be a killer,' she would recall with a sigh. 'Well, no, a tiger.'

As for romance, Mrs Markus quickly learned the value of discretion. 'I preferred to choose my romantic affairs outside bridge,' she declared. 'I don't have too much respect for the bridge male.'

⊰ 5th ⊱

The 1st Viscount De L'Isle, b. 1909, d. 1991

The 1st Viscount de l'Isle, who has died aged eighty-one, was the senior Knight of the Garter, Secretary of State for Air and the last Englishman to be Governor-General of Australia – though his place in history rests on the Victoria Cross he won at Anzio in 1944.

Then a major in the Grenadier Guards, Bill Sidney (a collateral descendant of the heroic sixteenth-century soldier-poet Sir Philip Sidney) showed a gallantry which recalled that of his Grenadier father-in-law, Field Marshal Viscount Gort, VC, to whom he was personally devoted.

During the Anzio battle Sidney engaged the Germans at point-blank range with his tommy-gun, and drove them out after they had penetrated his post. They counter-attacked and Sidney was hit in the face by a grenade. Single-handed and badly wounded in the thigh, he kept the enemy at bay until the arrival of reinforcements and only then retired for the dressing of his wound. Once again the Germans attacked and Sidney returned to his post, fighting for another hour until the position was consolidated.

Weakness from loss of blood then compelled him to retire once more, but the close proximity of the Germans made evacuation impossible for another day. During the whole of that day, states the citation, Sidney 'continued to act as a tonic and an inspiration to his men'.

He was decorated with a piece of the Victoria Cross ribbon, cut from Lord Gort's tunic, at Anzio beachhead, on 2 April 1944, and was presented with the Victoria Cross by His Majesty King George VI at Buckingham Palace on 10 October 1944.

William Philip Sidney was born on 23 May 1909, the only son of W.S. Sidney, a barrister and former mayor of Chelsea. The male line of the Sidneys died out in the eighteenth century and the present line is by male descent Shelleys, of the same family as the poet Percy Bysshe Shelley.

Bill Sidney was educated at Eton and Magdalene College, Cambridge. He then qualified as a chartered accountant and worked for a time for Barclays Bank. In 1929 he was commissioned into the Supplementary Reserve of the Grenadier Guards and, on the outbreak of the Second World War ten years later, he joined the regiment with the rank of captain.

In June 1940 he married Jacqueline Vereker, daughter of Lord Gort, the C-in-C of the British Expeditionary Force. After a variety of postings Sidney was promoted to major and posted to the 5th Battalion of the Grenadier Guards in North Africa as company commander.

After recovering from the wounds incurred at Anzio, Sidney was transferred to the Regular Army Reserve of Officers for Parliamentary Duties. He was elected Conservative MP for Chelsea in 1944 and a few months later was appointed parliamentary secretary to the Ministry of Pensions.

In 1945 his father succeeded to the Barony of De L'Isle and Dudley but died a few weeks later, whereupon Bill Sidney inherited the title, becoming the 6th Lord De L'Isle and Dudley. So his career in the Commons was short-lived.

In 1951, when the Conservatives returned to power, Winston Churchill appointed De L'Isle Secretary for Air, a post he held until the end of 1955. There were some who thought, with an element of justification, that his appointment was due to Churchill's well-known predilection for war heroes.

In 1956, after leaving the Air Ministry, he was created Viscount De L'Isle. Five years later Sir Robert Menzies submitted his name to the Queen for the office of Governor-General of Australia. He was, as it turned out, the last Englishman to be appointed to the post.

He was sworn of the Privy Council in 1951, elected an honorary Fellow of Magdalene in 1955, appointed GCMG and KStJ in 1961 and GCVO in 1963, and installed as a Knight of the Garter, at the same time as the Prince of Wales, in 1968.

Thus De L'Isle became the second man in history – the first was Lord Roberts – to place the proud letters 'KG' in second place after his name: for the Victoria Cross takes precedence over even the oldest order of chivalry in Europe.

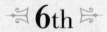

6th

Isaac Asimov, b. 1920, d. 1992

Isaac Asimov, who has died in New York aged seventy-two, was best known for his works of science fiction, a genre in which he reigned supreme, but he could also claim to have written more books about more subjects than any other author.

Of his 467 works, many were non-fiction. They included a two-volume guide to Shakespeare's plays, and an investigation into the authorship of the Book of Genesis. 'I write as a result of some inner compulsion,' he once remarked, 'and I'm not always in control of it.'

A bearish, messianic figure with mutton-chop whiskers, Asimov was stoically resigned to his own eccentricity. He liked to attribute his success to a 'lucky break in the genetic sweepstakes'. Asked if he had been a child prodigy, he would answer: 'Yes I was – and I still am.'

Isaac Asimov was born at Petrovichi, Russia, on 2 January 1920, the son of a rabbi who brought him to America at the age of three. As a student at Columbia University, New York – where he took a degree and a doctorate – and subsequently as a teacher of biochemistry at Boston University, he wrote in his spare time. By the mid-1950s his growing reputation enabled him to concentrate on a literary career.

For the next thirty-five years, almost without a break, Asimov produced ninety words a minute, eight hours a day, seven days a week, first on a typewriter and later on a word processor; he invariably wrote three books at once.

His only respite was in travel. Curiously, for a man who wrote so much about spaceships, he detested flying, and went everywhere on cruise liners, usually paying his way by giving popular science lectures to the passengers.

A master of spontaneous oratory, Asimov could hold forth on almost any subject with brilliant lucidity – as in his much-cited off-the-cuff description of how human life depends on the sun: 'All of us are living in the light and warmth of a huge hydrogen bomb, 860,000 miles across and 93 million miles away, which is in a state of continuous explosion.'

His most celebrated science fiction work was *The Foundation Trilogy*, published in instalments in the early 1950s. Set far in the future, it told of the fall of a mighty

Galactic Empire, and of the efforts of Hari Seldon, a great social scientist, to build a new and better empire out of the ruins of the old.

It was the fruit of one of the most dynamic imaginations in the sci-fi business. Long before the advent of robots and personal computers, Asimov invented a race of super-intelligent robots. Many of these machines were indistinguishable in appearance from human beings, but not all – one of his stories described a race of intelligent motor-cars which, once parked for the night, would zoom away to sex orgies.

Besides the *Foundation* stories, Asimov's best-known book was probably his second, *I, Robot* (1950), in which he promulgated three unalterable 'Laws of Robotics' – first, that a robot may not harm a human being, or, through inaction, allow a human being to come to harm; secondly, that a robot must obey the orders of a human being, except when this would conflict with the first law; and thirdly, that a robot must protect itself, except when this would conflict with the first and second laws. His kindly robots succeeded in transforming the image of the conscienceless marauders which had long dominated the pages of pulp sci-fi.

Asimov's extraordinary output of ten books a year did not let up, even after he suffered a heart attack in 1977 and triple bypass surgery two years later. But the operation marked a turning-point.

Formerly he had been prone to pessimism, full of gloomy prognoses about over-population and wars, which would prevent mankind from ever fulfilling its dream of colonising other planets. After the surgery, told to lose fifty pounds, he duly transformed himself into a jogging optimist. 'If I can pull myself up by my own bootstraps,' he declared, 'then so can the human race.'

In contrast to his fiction, Asimov took nine months to write his autobiography, which was considerably longer than *War and Peace*. 'I wanted to show the reader what it was like to be me. A genius, maybe, but also a schmuck. It's a big effort for me to behave like other people.'

⊰ 7th ⊱

Cecile de Brunhoff, b. 1903, d. 2003

Cecile de Brunhoff, who has died in Paris aged ninety-nine, made up a story in 1930 about an orphaned elephant to tell her young children at bedtime; they were so enchanted that they told their father, who turned it into a picture book.

It was published as *The Story of Babar* in 1933, soon to be followed by *The Travels of Babar, Babar the King, Babar and His Children*, and so on. The latest in a series of more than thirty-five books was *Babar's Yoga for Elephants*, published by Cecile de Brunhoff's son, Laurent, and a departure from the established format of Babar and family encountering a problem, solving it, and living happily ever after.

One of four children, Cecile de Brunhoff was born Cecile Sabouraud in Paris on 16 October 1903. Her father was a dermatologist.

After graduating from the Ecole Normale de Musique in Paris, Cecile Sabouraud worked as a piano teacher. In 1923 she married Jean de Brunhoff, a painter from

Montparnasse four years her senior. They set up home at Neuilly, near the Bois de Boulogne, and had three sons.

During the summer they would repair to her family's manor house in Ile-de-France, outside Paris, and it was there, one fine evening in 1930, that five-year-old Mathieu complained of a stomach-ache. To distract him, Cecile de Brunhoff made up a story about a little elephant who was happily playing in the jungle when a cruel hunter came along and shot his mother.

The little elephant ran off and, after several days, arrived, tired and footsore, in a town. There he found a purse, which enabled him to buy clothes. After an enjoyable spree and various other adventures, the elephant was eventually persuaded by his cousins to return to the jungle, where he was crowned king.

In Jean de Brunhoff's first hand-written draft, Babar is referred to simply as Bébé Elephant (as Cecile de Brunhoff had called him in her story), and in later years no one in the family could remember quite how his name came about.

The book began: 'In the Great Forest a little elephant was born. His name was Babar. His mother loved him dearly and used to rock him to sleep with her trunk, singing to him softly the while ...'

The tale was originally intended simply for the enjoyment of the de Brunhoff boys, but Jean de Brunhoff was soon persuaded by his brother to publish it. It was an immediate success, and is still in print.

≈ 8th ≈

Joan Wyndham, b. 1921, d. 2007

Joan Wyndham, who has died aged eighty-five, came from an eccentric upper-class family and as a young woman led a disreputable life which she unflinchingly chronicled in four volumes of memoirs.

An aspiring actress, heroic drinker, jitterbugger and Benzedrine-fuelled bohemian, she enjoyed an outrageous reputation; later she held court in 'Swinging London', where her circle included jobbing rent boys, April Ashley, Michael Foot, Christine Keeler ('rabbity teeth'), assorted acid-trippers and Jeremy Beadle.

To social historians she was gold-dust, being one of the few women happy to go on the record – and on camera – to discuss sex in general and her virginity in particular, which she shed early in the war after renting an artist's studio in Redcliffe Road, Chelsea. 'One night there was a really bad raid and the whole shelter was shaking, and I thought: 'Ah well! The opposite of death is life so I might as well go and get myself devirginised!'' she explained on television.

Only in her sixties did Joan Wyndham turn to writing. Her younger daughter came across her diaries in a trunk in the attic and convinced her mother that she should publish them. They chronicled the adventures of a young woman on the loose in wartime London, living it up with the likes of Quentin Crisp ('hair down to his shoulders'), Philip Toynbee ('sick on the sofa'), Dylan Thomas, Julian MacLaren-Ross and David Tennant, her cousin who owned the Gargoyle Club.

When she was twenty-one she had an affair with the 'so unbearably attractive' 17th Lord Lovat, commando leader, hero of the Dieppe beaches and 25th Chief of the Clan Fraser, whom she had met during a mess party at his house, Beaufort Castle. In describing their assignation over partridge at the Ritz, she not only kissed but told all, unsparingly, in another memoir, *Love Is Blue* (1986).

In July 1943, in a taxi in Soho, Dylan Thomas, who had pinched her bottom in a pub, 'smothered me in wet beery kisses'; later she had to bolt and bar her bedroom as the poet repeatedly hurled himself against the door. Only at war's end did she come to the conclusion that the black depression she felt – 'an unidentifiable cafard lying in wait for me like a vast cloud of poisonous blue gas' – was the result of 'too many men'.

Joan Olivia Wyndham was born on 11 October 1921 at Clouds, the Victorian sandstone house in Wiltshire built by her great-grandfather, the dandy Percy Wyndham. She spent her first three years there, hazily remembering that it had forty bedrooms and a kitchen so far from the dining room that food was transported on a miniature railway track.

Her parents divorced when she was two and she was sent to be educated at two convent schools. Aged fifteen she fell in love with the young John Gielgud; having seen him in *Hamlet*, she 'sometimes followed him home so that I could kiss his doorknob'. She later transferred her affections to 'the totally gorgeous' Laurence Olivier and the dancer Robert Helpmann ('gosh, what a bottom!').

In 1937 Joan went to RADA, but left after a year. Nearly seventy years later she published a witty account of her time there in her memoir *Dawn Chorus* (2004). Her wartime diaries, *Love Lessons* (1985) and *Love Is Blue* (1986), described her service with the WAAFs, which started at 9 Group Fighter Command near Preston, where she was a filter room plotter.

After being commissioned Joan Wyndham was posted to Fighter Command headquarters at Stanmore, which she described as 'living in some wonderful dream' compared with the dreariness of Lancashire. She spent her first week's leave with a bearded Czech artist who had picked her up in Wigmore Street, and who had rented a room in a former brothel in Oakley Street, lived in by Dylan Thomas and owned by a woman with the telegraphic address Chastity, London.

Despite being appraised as 'a very peculiar type of officer, not amenable to discipline and a bad example to other ranks', Joan Wyndham was promoted to flight officer, and in January 1945 was posted to Watnall, near Nottingham. It was, she complained, 'ugly and squalid – but it has one great advantage, a mixed Mess!' At one point she was taken up for a spin by the youngest squadron leader in the Polish Air Force, and recorded that it was 'the first time I've ever had my bottom pinched at 3,000 feet'.

After the war she met and married her first husband, Maurice Rowdon, the son of a docker who admired his new daughter-in-law turning up for the wedding 'all dolled up like a tallyman's ink bottle'. Joan and her new-born daughter Clare followed Rowdon to Baghdad, where he had landed a teaching job; but the marriage was dissolved on their return to England.

Meanwhile, Joan's father had been shot dead by a sniper while covering the Arab–

Israeli war for *The Sunday Times*, and she used her legacy to buy a small cottage in Kent. She was startled to learn from Cyril Connolly that Dick Wyndham had been 'one of Europe's great flagellists', and had been known as 'Whips' Wyndham.

Joan's affair with her Russian lodger, Shura Shivarg, produced another daughter, Camilla. After spells as a horoscope writer, working in a theatre and as a publisher's reader, Joan moved to Oxford to open the city's first espresso coffee bar, complete with jukebox.

In 1957 she divorced Rowdon and married Shivarg, buying a scruffy five-storey Georgian house in Wellington Square, off the King's Road, and landing a job on *Housewife* magazine. She stuck this for a couple of years before becoming a prominent figure in the King's Road set in the mid-1960s. In the 1970s she and Shura visited Russia and the United States, where she met Andy Warhol and looked up her Aunt Olivia, who lived with a black actress in Harlem.

By the time she turned to writing in the 1980s, Joan Wyndham had moved back to the Fulham Road. In later life she came to dislike cooking, but nursed passions for whisky, cigarettes and the television programme *Blind Date*. Although her memory faltered in old age, she managed to produce a further two volumes of memoirs: *Anything Once* (1992) and *Dawn Chorus* (2004).

9th

Jess Yates, b. 1918, d. 1993

Jess Yates, who has died aged seventy-four, was celebrated as the presenter of *Stars on Sunday*, a phenomenally popular religious programme on British television in the early 1970s.

Yates, a cherubic figure known as 'The Bishop', would introduce the show seated at an electric organ placed in front of a stained-glass window. He was prone to make such observations as 'We can't see round the bend in the road, but God can'.

His own avuncular persona, however, proved unsustainable. In the summer of 1974 the *News of the World*, under the headline 'THE BISHOP AND THE ACTRESS', revealed that Yates was carrying on a relationship with Anita Kay, a showgirl thirty years his junior who had recently 'starred in Paul Raymond's nude revue *Pyjama Tops*'.

Amid the ensuing furore Yates had to be smuggled from Yorkshire Television's studio in Leeds in the boot of a motor-car. His attempts to resuscitate his career were not helped by continuing press interest in his personal life – fanned by the celebrity of his daughter, Paula, who married Bob Geldof.

He always disliked being introduced as Paula Yates's father: 'I have a great yearning not to go to my grave as "Bob Geldof's father-in-law".'

Editor's note: Paula Yates's biological father was subsequently revealed to be the broadcaster Hughie Greene.

Paola Borboni, b. 1900, d. 1995

Paola Borboni, who has died aged ninety-five, was the grande dame of the Italian stage, whose willingness to shock earned her the sobriquet 'Paola of the scandals'.

In 1925 she stunned the audience at one production by flagrantly baring her breasts, causing, a journalist noted, 'the use of more binoculars than at the San Siro [the Milanese race course] in fifty years'.

⋙ 10th ⋘

André Deutsch, b. 1917, d. 2000

André Deutsch, who has died aged eighty-two, was perhaps the most remarkable of that extraordinary generation of central European émigrés which reinvigorated, and to some extent dominated, British publishing from the 1950s to the 1980s.

A small, dapper figure with a shrewd but benevolent gaze and a handsome head topped with a quiff of grey hair, Deutsch retained a distinctive Hungarian accent. 'Dear boy,' was his usual mode of address to men, while 'love' was bestowed irrespective of sex. A natty dresser, he favoured well-pressed suits, often of corduroy, and pink shirts.

As with all the best publishers, his life was his work. Skiing provided a diversion until he was well into his seventies, but when a fellow publisher took him to watch Arsenal at Highbury he arrived with the proofs of his firm's forthcoming catalogue and never looked up from its pages.

André Deutsch was born in Budapest on 15 November 1917. His Jewish father was a dentist; his mother was allegedly of French, Turkish and Hungarian stock.

Egged on by an uncle who had translated H.G. Wells into Hungarian and thought England the only civilised country, Deutsch made up his mind to live there and aged twelve began learning English. He finally arrived in Britain in June 1939, having worked in a tyre factory and trained as a photographer.

His first job in England was as a bird-scarer in Shropshire, which he once described as the most congenial employment he ever found. He was working as a floor manager in the Grosvenor House Hotel when, in late 1941, Hungary entered the war on the wrong side.

Deutsch found himself interned as an enemy alien, initially in the parrot house at Manchester Zoo and then on the Isle of Man. Among his fellow-internees was Arthur Koestler's cousin, a dubious Hungarian publisher called Ferenc Aldor. When, three months later, Deutsch was released, Aldor asked him if he would look after his business – for £8 a week and the loan of Aldor's mistress and his Mayfair flat.

This gave Deutsch an entrée into publishing. He soon moved to the more respectable firm of Nicholson and Watson, where he learned about every aspect of the trade. To supplement his income he wrote reviews for *Tribune*, where George Orwell was literary editor.

Orwell was having trouble finding a publisher for *Animal Farm* – Victor Gollancz and T.S. Eliot at Faber were among those who had turned it down for fear of affronting the Russians – and Deutsch was amazed when his superiors refused it as well.

Orwell then suggested that Deutsch should set up on his own and publish *Animal Farm*. But Deutsch, in a rare failure of nerve, turned down a chance to make his fortune. The episode, though, hardened his resolve to be his own master.

It was Norman Mailer's *The Naked and the Dead* in 1949 which provided Deutsch with his first and most spectacular bestseller. Denounced in *The Sunday Times* as a book that should not be left around to contaminate innocent 'womenfolk', it inevitably went on to sell 150,000 copies in hardback.

But this success brought problems. Deutsch had to take on new shareholders and new directors to raise the money to finance reprints, and lost control of his firm in the process. The new arrivals wanted to publish books of a rather different kind, precipitating Deutsch's departure.

In 1952 he started all over again, this time trading under his own name, soon establishing himself as one of the most exciting and energetic publishers in the country. His authors included Laurie Lee, Philip Roth, John Updike, Mordecai Richler, J.K. Galbraith, and Arthur Schlesinger.

Fiction and memoirs were particular fortes. More specialised lines included a series on librarianship, cookery books, and a list of children's books.

In 1969 Deutsch sold 40 per cent of his firm to Time Inc., but finding the demands of corporate life irksome, bought back the shares after a couple of years and resumed his life of independence.

André Deutsch never married, but for decades 'shared his life' with a married woman, always referred to, enigmatically and with Hungarian gallantry, by her first name, Gwen.

⊰ 11th ⊱

Joan Jackson, b. 1915, d. 2008

Joan Jackson, who has died aged ninety-two, was in her earlier life Joan Hunter Dunn, the inspiration for Sir John Betjeman's most popular poem, *A Subaltern's Love-song*, which hymned her red-headed beauty as 'furnish'd and burnish'd by Aldershot sun'.

Betjeman first saw her in a canteen while walking down a corridor at the Ministry of Information at London University in December 1940. 'Gosh, look!' he remarked to a friend. 'I bet she's a doctor's daughter from Aldershot.' He discovered that she was, indeed, a doctor's daughter – though from nearby Farnborough, Hampshire – and conjured up his reverie about them being affianced and playing tennis together:

> What strenuous singles we played after tea,
> We in the tournament – you against me!
> Love-thirty, love-forty, oh! weakness of joy,
> The speed of a swallow, the grace of a boy,
> With carefullest carelessness, gaily you won,

I am weak from your loveliness, Joan Hunter Dunn.
Miss Joan Hunter Dunn, Miss Joan Hunter Dunn,
How mad I am, sad I am, glad that you've won,
The warm-handled racket is back in its press,
But my shock-headed victor, she loves me no less.

After composing the 44-line poem Betjeman wrote seeking her permission to publish. On being introduced to her early the following year he went down on his knees – at which she burst out laughing. 'My first impression was one of extreme humour,' she later recalled. 'I thought anybody who got down on his knees to say "How d'ye do" to me must be mad.

'I must say I was absolutely overwhelmed,' Joan Jackson continued. 'It was such a marvellous break from the monotony of the war. It really was remarkable the way he imagined it all. Actually, all that about the subaltern and the engagement is sheer fantasy, but my life was very like the poem.'

Tex Geddes, b. 1919, d. 1998

Tex Geddes, who has died aged seventy-nine, was successively a lumberjack, smuggler, commando and Laird of Soay, the tiny Hebridean island from which, in the 1940s, he operated a shark hunting business with Gavin Maxwell, the author of *Ring of Bright Water* (1960).

Geddes and Maxwell first met in 1942, when Geddes was an instructor on amphibious warfare at Arisaig, the SOE training centre on the West Highland coast. Maxwell was also a lecturer at the base, specialising in fieldcraft and small arms. The two men soon formed a rapport. Geddes, who by the age of twenty-one already had a lifetime's adventuring under his belt, was the personification of the man of action that Maxwell idolised.

Fond of playing darts with throwing-knives, he was as lean and quick as a whippet, and possessed a mercurial temperament that was composed in equal measure of charm, confidence and cheek. For his part, Geddes admired Maxwell's sense of noblesse oblige, ease with money and love of wildlife.

When the war ended, Maxwell, who yearned to test himself against the elements, bought the isle of Soay, which lies close to the south coast of Skye. The waters of the Minch, and Soay Sound itself, are the seasonal home of large numbers of basking sharks, which can grow up to thirty-five feet and weigh five tons.

Maxwell planned to harvest the sharks for the oil in their vast livers. He built a factory to process his catch, bought a boat, and hired Geddes as his harpoon-gunner.

The venture was not a success. Maxwell and his crew were hampered by their own inexperience; to begin with they even used the wrong sort of harpoons. Yet there was no doubting the courage of the shark hunters, or the exhilaration of the chase once their quarry was sighted; but in the end the fish proved too unpredictable, and their hunting too unprofitable.

By 1948, Maxwell had spent his entire inheritance of £11,000 on the shark scheme. Having failed to become a society portrait painter, he began to turn his experiences into a book, *Harpoon at a Venture* (1952). The book was an instant success, and established Maxwell's reputation as an observer of the natural world.

Geddes, meanwhile, became a freelance shark hunter, but after the publication of *Harpoon* he was summoned to London to give evidence on behalf of Maxwell. A rival shark fisherman wanted an injunction against Maxwell, having written a book about his own adventures. The rival was represented by Melford Stevenson (later celebrated as a trenchantly old-fashioned judge), and he and the plain-speaking Geddes did not see eye-to-eye.

Geddes later gave his version of events to Maxwell's biographer, Douglas Botting. 'We had a hell of a carry-on,' he recalled. 'I told Melford Stevenson that he didn't know a thing about sharks and couldn't tell his arse from his elbow. When he suggested I was a liar, I told him I'd take his trousers down and wallop him if he said it again.' The case was settled out of court.

Tex Geddes was born in Peterhead, Fife, in 1919. He was the youngest son of a fisherman; his mother died giving birth to him.

He later gave out – not least to the impressionable Maxwell – several colourful versions of his early years. He claimed that when he was two, he and his father emigrated to Newfoundland after an altercation between the police and Tex's father resulted in the constabulary taking an unexpected swim in Port Gordon harbour.

His father found work as a lumberman. But five years later he was killed blowing up a log-jam, and young Tex was brought up by his father's foreman. When, said Geddes, he was expelled from school at the age of twelve, he fled to the woods rather than face his foster-father.

More plausible was his claim that he had worked in a lumber camp as a monkey boy, receiving the princely rate of £1 a day. The job entailed climbing to the tops of trees and sawing them off; the pay was so high because the work was so dangerous.

In his mid-teens, Geddes turned for his livelihood to the sea, working the straits between Newfoundland and Quebec. His trade, however, was not fishing but the more profitable one of rum-running.

When the authorities instituted a crackdown on the smugglers, Geddes fled back to Scotland. There, in a Glasgow pub, he was in 1939 persuaded to enlist in the Seaforth Highlanders. After he had injured his leg in commando training, he was posted as a course instructor to Arisaig.

In 1953, Soay was evacuated of all of its small population, except for Geddes and his family. Life there was demanding, but Geddes was infinitely resourceful. He thrived for more than forty years ploughing what he called 'the fields between Scotland and America'. He also bred sheep and ponies. His memoirs, *Hebridean Sharker*, came out in 1960.

Geddes's willingness to spin a yarn made him much in demand throughout the isles as a story-teller. He also possessed a rich streak of eccentricity, being a staunch supporter of landowners but a fierce enemy of non-resident landlords. One such, a

German, was surprised to be told by Geddes that if he gave his tenants any trouble, Geddes would eat him.

Tex Geddes died while returning from a bagpiping competition in the Outer Isles.

❧ 12th ❧

Colonel Albert Bachmann, b. 1929, d. 2011

Colonel Albert Bachmann, who has died aged eighty-one, was Switzerland's best-known and most paranoid spymaster, in a country that traditionally has no enemies and refrains from foreign entanglements.

Mustachioed, pipe-smoking and blessed with an ability to wreak havoc within his own organisation, Bachmann's resemblance to Inspector Clouseau was striking; by the time his plots and schemes were uncovered by an astonished commission of inquiry, he had reduced the Swiss military intelligence agency, in which he had mysteriously managed to rise to a senior role, to a state bordering on chaos, not to mention bankruptcy. So catastrophic was his impact that, when he was finally unmasked, many assumed he must be a double agent. He was not.

His most controversial, some would say delusional, acts occurred between 1976 and 1979, when he took charge of top-secret operations for Switzerland's military intelligence force, the Untergruppe Nachrichtendienst der Armee (UNA). Though Bachmann had flirted with communism in his student days, he was by then a fanatical Cold Warrior, and brought the zeal of the convert to the fight against the Soviet Union.

His first significant move was to buy a country estate in Ireland for use by a Swiss government-in-exile in the event of a Soviet invasion. His second bold step was Projekt-26 (P-26), the creation of a clandestine army of Swiss guerrillas trained in weaponry, bombing and assassination techniques to repel the dreaded Soviets.

The problem was that neither the Irish venture nor the secret anti-Soviet army had been officially authorised, and were the fruits of what Bachmann called his 'initiative'. Others would come to call it insubordination or even fantasy.

But neither plan stalled Bachmann's rise. Indeed, his intelligence career was curtailed only after a top-level investigation into an operation he sanctioned in 1979 that deeply embarrassed Switzerland and Austria – friendly neighbours with the same neutral status and few if any military secrets to hide from one another.

In November that year, Austrian troops on manoeuvres in the city of St Pölten tapped on the window of a parked car at 2.30am and were surprised to find inside not a courting couple but a Swiss management consultant called Kurt Schilling. He had been ordered there, he was happy to recount, by Bachmann, his case officer. His arrest on charges of spying for information freely available to Swiss and other foreign observers at the manoeuvres was portrayed in the press as worthy of a comic opera.

The press mocked Schilling as 'the spy who came in from the Emmenthaler', after Switzerland's famous cheese. But it was Bachmann's career that never recovered. In the wake of the Schilling debacle, it became clear that Bachmann and his department were out of control. His boss was forced to resign, and Bachmann himself – exposed as a loose cannon, unchecked and unregulated – was consigned to early retirement.

Albert Bachmann was born in Zurich on 26 November 1929, the son of a house painter, and grew up in humble circumstances. While employed as a printer, he enrolled in the youth wing of the PDA, the Swiss communist party. But in 1948, following the communist coup in Prague, he renounced his left-wing sympathies, became staunchly pro-West and began his National Service with the Swiss grenadiers.

His military career blossomed, and against expectations (he had completed only eight years at school) Bachmann successfully applied to the officer training academy, where he specialised in intelligence gathering.

After sparking a furore by encouraging Swiss citizens to spy on each other in the event of a Soviet invasion, he headed to Biafra, which was seeking to secede from Nigeria. There he operated undercover as a pipe-smoking upper-crust Englishman called Henry Peel and cultivated an air of mystery, hinting at links to secret arms deals involving the Shah of Iran.

On his return Bachmann was promoted to the rank of colonel in the intelligence and defence section of UNA. The post gave him authority over three units of secret military intelligence, including a special service (Spec D) set up to respond to invasion by an occupying power.

Under Bachmann's eccentric command, its remit grew extensively, and agents were trained as sharpshooters, bomb-makers, code-breakers and even mountain guides who were to lead key government and administration figures to safety over the Alps in the event of an attack. Projekt-26 was born.

Meanwhile, using government funds, Bachmann bought the imposing 200-acre Liss Ard country estate near Skibbereen, in west Cork. Intended for use by a Swiss government-in-exile, its Georgian manor houses were among the first properties in Ireland to be fitted with hi-tech computer equipment, when most Irish homes possessed, at best, black-and-white televisions. Furthermore, the basement of one was designated as a secret depository for Switzerland's massive gold reserves.

After news of this emerged, Bachmann was obliged to retire in 1980. An official investigation criticised P-26 as an illegal paramilitary programme. When Bachmann's secret army was finally dismantled, its war chest – gold worth six million Swiss francs – was donated to the Red Cross. But he always insisted that it served a vital function. 'How vital,' Bachmann told the reporters who sought him out, 'I cannot tell you.'

He remained in Ireland and ran a riding school, and in retirement became a familiar figure in the bars and restaurants of Skibbereen. Wary of being photographed, he would duck out of pictures taken in pubs. But he did not regret his actions, or the notoriety they brought.

'I am not bitter,' he said. 'I accept the judgment of others, but have enough confidence in myself to know what I am capable of.'

⧉ 13th ⧉

James 'Jimmy the Gent' Burke, b. 1931, d. 1996

James 'Jimmy the Gent' Burke, who has died aged sixty-four, was a notorious New York gangster whose criminal exploits and colourful character formed the basis of Martin Scorsese's film *Goodfellas*.

Nicknamed for his dapper appearance and charming manner, Burke's activities ranged from gambling, bookmaking, loan-sharking and extortion rackets to drug trafficking and murder.

His speciality was hijacking. In 1978 he masterminded the biggest cash heist in American history, when six men stormed the Lufthansa Airlines cargo terminal at New York's Kennedy Airport and made off with $5 million in cash and $850,000 in jewellery. Despite an intensive investigation, the FBI was unable to recover the haul, or to pin the crime on Burke. Later, a dispute among the robbers resulted in several deaths. Burke, known for his psychopathic temper when crossed, was presumed responsible.

His career was detailed by the crime writer Nick Pileggi in his book *Wiseguys*, later adapted for the film *Goodfellas* (1990). Burke's character, Jimmy Conway, was played by Robert de Niro.

Henry Hill, a co-conspirator whose testimony eventually helped to convict Burke, noted that the mobster loved stealing so much that 'if ever you offered Jimmy a billion dollars, he'd turn you down and then try to figure out how to steal it from you'.

James Burke was born on 5 July 1931. He was abandoned as a baby at a hospital in Queen's, New York, and placed in foster care, where he was abused. By the age of fourteen he was burgling and by sixteen he was in a reformatory. In the course of his subsequent career he would spend more than twenty-five years in prison.

Burke's connection with organised crime began when he was sentenced to an adult prison at the age of eighteen. The criminal fraternity considered him tough, smart and, above all, reliable.

He became an associate of the Lucchese crime family, one of New York's five largest. But, being Irish, he was unable to join the Mafia officially, and so established his own mob of tough guys; this band of hoodlums earned him the title of 'the Irish Godfather'.

Burke ran his operations from Robert's Lounge, a bar in Queen's, until he was arrested and jailed for a parole violation in 1982. While in jail he was convicted of a college baseball point-shaving scheme, and later received a life sentence for the murder of a rival drug dealer, whose body was found trussed-up and frozen in a camping trailer.

Known as a devoted family man, Burke had two sons, Frank James Burke and Jesse James Burke – named after the outlaws of the Old West – and one daughter. Frank was killed several years ago in a shoot-out. Burke is survived by his wife, his daughter and Jesse, who enjoys the quiet life.

⊰ 14th ⊱

Barbara Robertson, b. 1915, d. 2002

Barbara Robertson, who has died aged eighty-six, was chairman of the Bath Music Festival from 1970 to 1976; before that she had gained a reputation as a colourful and inventive hostess, described on one occasion as being responsible for more jolly social occasions in the city than anyone since Beau Nash.

Under her aegis a series of outdoor picnics, colourful pageants and glittering balls added glamour and spectacle to the annual programme of music. In 1960 she launched the first in a series of grand social events, during Yehudi Menuhin's era at the helm of the Bath Festival, that were designed to prick the stuffy exterior of his concerts.

Her most infamous effort came in the form of a Roman orgy held at the city's Roman baths in 1961. Guests, many of them from high society, were forced to wear togas as they joined in the celebrations. They later described a menu that was a tribute to the Roman diet: fried dormice, nightingales' tongues and sows' udders. Across the waters floated a boat with slave girls bearing guests' meals. When the last revellers refused to leave at 4 a.m., the city authorities drained the Roman baths.

Barbara Robertson, though, was unrepentant: 'Bath tends to be a bit stodgy,' she said, 'so we felt we should liven it up.'

⊰ 15th ⊱

Sir Clement Freud, b. 1924, d. 2009

Sir Clement Freud, who has died aged eighty-four, experienced the fullest and most public of lives as a gourmet, gambler, restaurateur, nightclub owner, lover of cricket, pétanque and the Turf, humorist, broadcaster and for fourteen years a Liberal MP; for four decades he was also a witty and well-loved participant on the radio panel show *Just a Minute*.

Most men with such varied interests could be said to have enjoyed them, but Freud, having ruthlessly marketed himself as a celebrity, was unable to conquer a dyspeptic nature. This manifested itself in a lugubrious manner which made him less popular with those who knew him – even in that most tolerant of clubs, the House of Commons – than with those who heard him on the radio.

Freud's near-lifelong estrangement from his artist elder brother Lucian was not of his making, however. When the then Clemens Freud looked like winning a boyhood race round a Vienna park, Lucian called out: 'Stop thief!' and Clemens was seized by passers-by.

He lived by his wits, not least at the backgammon table. He was – until sacked for betting illegally in his own casino – a director of the Playboy Club in London and of Playboy International. Yet despite his involvement in the racy side of life, he said of Soho strip clubs: 'As a piece of eroticism I prefer kipper fillets with brown bread.' A jockey in his youth and the owner of more than forty racehorses, he was an accomplished pilot and once sailed from Cape Town to Rio.

Freud ('Clay' to his colleagues) strove to be a serious politician but was never accepted as one. Never at his best in the chamber, he was a victim of his reputation as a funny man, which got in the way of determinedly serious performances.

But despite his unfortunate manner with colleagues and staff – he got through nine secretaries in eight years – Freud was revered in his Isle of Ely constituency. They re-elected him to his seat (from 1983 North-East Cambridgeshire) at four general elections.

A grandson of Sigmund Freud, Clemens Raphael Freud was born in Austria on 24 April 1924 to the architect Ernst Freud and his wife Lucie. He escaped with his family to Britain after the Anschluss of 1938 and earned an immediate reputation for bumptiousness at The Hall, Hampstead. He completed his education at Dartington Hall and St Paul's.

He worked at the Dorchester until called up for war service with the Royal Ulster Rifles; his introduction to Army life was, inevitably, bizarre. Apprised of Freud's origins, his CO sent for him and observed: 'Mr Freud, I don't quite know how to put this, but are you sure you're on the right side?' By 1946 he was serving as a liaison officer at the Nuremberg war crimes trials.

On demobilisation he headed for the continent in search of haute cuisine, before becoming catering manager of the Arts Theatre Club.

In 1952 he became proprietor of the Royal Court Theatre Club, making it a highly successful avant-garde dinner-and-dance venue in still-drab post-war London. When, early in 1963, the Royal Court reclaimed the premises for its own use, Freud ran a succession of restaurants – one at the Open Air Theatre in Regent's Park – and wrote and broadcast prolifically.

He was at his best writing on food and drink. Once, having waited twenty-five minutes for turtle soup, he told the waitress: 'If you are making fresh turtle soup it is going to take two days, and we do not have the time. If it is canned turtle soup, I do not wish to eat here if it takes you twenty-five minutes to open a can.'

He was, unsurprisingly, an award-winning after-dinner speaker, despite, or perhaps because of, his rudeness toward other guests.

⇜ 16th ⇝

Professor Edward Lorenz, b. 1917, d. 2008

Professor Edward Lorenz, who has died aged ninety, was a mathematician and meteorologist who was one of the early exponents of chaos theory and in particular of the 'butterfly effect' – the notion that a tiny event, such as the movement of a butterfly's wings in Brazil, can have enormous effects, such as a tornado in Texas.

In 1820 Pierre Laplace had suggested a deterministic universe in which prediction would be possible if one knew exact details of all the laws of Nature and had both the ability to plot the position of all physical elements, and an intellect which could submit this data to analysis. 'Laplace's demon', as this theory became known, came to be used to explain why 'noise' (or unknown background factors) made it difficult to establish 'true' scientific values in complex systems.

Lorenz discovered quite how dramatic this effect could be when, in 1961, he re-entered data into his computer from a weather simulation he had previously run. Having retyped the numbers from the printout of the first experiment, he found that it produced wildly different results.

He realised that the reason was that the original computer had entered numbers to six decimal points, but the printout provided only the first three. Entering 0.506, rather than 0.506127 – though a margin of error of less than 0.1 per cent over the experiment, regarded then as utterly trivial – resulted in huge changes and made prediction all but impossible.

Chaos theory became enormously influential in a host of fields besides weather forecasting. But despite its name, chaos theory does not imply randomness. Indeed, as Lorenz was at pains to point out, chaos theory enables us to improve our knowledge of apparently unstable systems such as the weather, and thus describe and analyse them, and improve our forecasts.

☙ 17th ❧

Colonel Maurice Buckmaster, b. 1902, d. 1992

Colonel Maurice Buckmaster, who has died aged ninety, led the French section of the Special Operations Executive for most of the Second World War, almost certainly the hottest seat in SOE.

For three years from 1941 he masterminded the training and dispatch of agents to France. These agents were to provide a roll of honour second to none in the story of British wartime undercover operations. Their stories inspired a host of books, films and television series.

Some agents, such as Violette Szabo, were tortured and shot. Others, like Odette Churchill, suffered at the hands of the Gestapo, but survived.

Perhaps the most telling tribute of all came from Hitler, whom Buckmaster quoted as saying: 'When I get to London I am not sure who I shall hang first – Churchill or that man Buckmaster.'

Maurice James Buckmaster was born on 11 January 1902. He went to Eton, but it was touch and go in his last year whether the fees could be found. When his father was made bankrupt the school recognised his prowess by giving young Maurice a scholarship.

After school he was sent to France where he perfected his command of the language working as a journalist on *Le Matin*. There followed six years with the merchant bank, J. Henry Schroder & Co. Then, in 1929, he joined Ford, first as assistant to the chairman and thereafter as manager in France and then the whole of Europe.

Buckmaster's European contacts and linguistic abilities inevitably led, on the outbreak of the Second World War, to a job in the Intelligence Corps. He claimed, aged thirty-seven, to be the oldest second lieutenant in the Army. His task was to arrange suitable French billets for 50 Division, a job which led to a lifelong friendship with Paul Krug, head of the celebrated champagne house.

At Dunkirk in 1940 Buckmaster was ordered by the future Field Marshal Templer to stay behind with the rearguard on the grounds that when the Germans arrived Buckmaster would have only to divest himself of his uniform to pass himself off as a native Frenchman for the duration.

In the event, he managed a spectacular escape, and in the autumn of 1940 secured attachment to 'Operation Menace', an ill-fated Anglo-French enterprise designed to wrest Dakar, capital of French West Africa, from the Vichy government and hand the port over to the Free French under de Gaulle. Buckmaster recalled this fiasco as 'sitting in the Bay of Rifisque and being bombarded and dive-bombed for twenty-four hours, and torpedoed'.

In 1941, 50 Division was posted to North Africa, where Buckmaster reasoned that his French would be of little use, so he presented himself at the War Office, hoping to find more relevant employment. There he bumped into Templer again.

'Ah, Buckmaster,' he said, 'You speak French. Got a job for you. Start this afternoon. No. 64 Baker Street.'

Once in the hot seat Buckmaster, ably assisted by Vera Atkins, worked up to eighteen hours a day. He would occasionally give himself a break by bicycling home to Chelsea for an early dinner before returning at 8 p.m. to Baker Street, where he would remain until 4 a.m.

He was acutely aware of the loneliness of his agents and of their doubts about those such as himself understanding or even caring about their problems. So he made a point of presenting them, as they were leaving for France, with personal gifts – for instance, gold cufflinks or cigarette cases for the men, powder compacts for the women – carefully manufactured to disguise their origin. 'You can always hock it,' he used to say, 'if you run out of money.'

By the end of the war he had been responsible for the training and dispatch of some 500 people. He was devastated by the loss of men and women whom he regarded as close personal friends and felt keenly the responsibility of sending them, however unwittingly, to their deaths.

He was always fiercely loyal to his operatives, who included men like Richard Heslop, codenamed 'Xavier', who sent a fusillade of boulders on to a Panzer division on the Route Hannibal, delaying its arrival in Normandy until a crucial seventeen days after D-Day.

Then there were the two schoolmasters, Francis Cammaerts and Harry Ree. By the summer of 1944 Cammaerts had been so successful in the south of France that Buckmaster could claim that he had 10,000 men under his orders – at least half of whom had been armed by his efforts.

Ree immobilised the tank turret production factory at the Peugeot works at Sochaux. It was his demolition exploit which gave Buckmaster the satisfaction of calling on 'Bomber' Harris at Bomber Command HQ with photographic evidence. Harris had hitherto been sceptical of SOE's ability to blow up targets which, he maintained, were better left to his air crew.

Buckmaster found it intensely frustrating that he himself was not allowed to go into enemy territory. Nonetheless, this did not prevent him on one occasion – so the story went – from flying to France in a Lysander in order to make essential voice-to-voice contact with George Starr, one of his agents in the Gers.

As they approached the rendezvous Buckmaster's pilot remarked crisply: 'Look at those bloody awful lights.'

At which Starr's inimitable Staffordshire accent cut in over the plane's radio: 'Your lights would be bloody awful too, if you had the Gestapo less than a mile away.' Starr merged into occupied France so successfully that he became mayor of his local village.

Perhaps the most characteristic story of Buckmaster was his reaction to General de Gaulle's post-war attempt to expel Starr on the grounds that he did not hold a French passport. Starr replied that he only answered to his Colonel and asked Buckmaster for orders. Buckmaster cabled: *'Tu y es, tu y restes.'* This rather impressed de Gaulle who relented at once and appointed Starr to the Legion d'honneur instead.

In 1945 Buckmaster returned to Ford, first in his old job as head of Europe and subsequently as director of public relations.

Then, in 1960, he went freelance. He was best known in the field of public relations as an appropriately effervescent PR officer for the wines of Champagne. A trip to Champagne with Buckmaster was a privileged opportunity to see a rare example of the Entente Cordiale in action – as the various houses vied with each other in doing honour to the legendary Colonel Buckmaster and his friends.

⁂ 18th ⁂

Thor Heyerdahl, b. 1914, d. 2002

Thor Heyerdahl, the Norwegian anthropologist who has died in Italy aged eighty-seven, was propelled to fame by his remarkable crossing of the Pacific Ocean aboard a balsa-log raft, the *Kon-Tiki*, in 1947.

Against all prevailing expert opinion, Heyerdahl's researches had convinced him that ethnological traits common to Polynesia and South America were the result of pre-historic transoceanic migration by Peruvian Indians, perhaps around 500BC.

Academic orthodoxy held that Polynesia had been colonised from Asia, not South America, and that the journey of almost 5,000 miles central to Heyerdahl's heretical theories was beyond the navigational skills of a primitive people such as the Peruvians. The features common to the two cultures were said to be coincidental.

Since no publisher would print his thesis, Heyerdahl decided that only a recreation of such a voyage could give his ideas the necessary credibility. With five friends as crew, he constructed a 60ft-long raft with sails, its design based on ancient pictures of Indian ocean-going vessels. The craft was named *Kon-Tiki*, after the mythical Polynesian hero Tiki, who was said in oral tradition to have led the ancestors of the islanders there from the east.

On 28 April 1947, the *Kon-Tiki* pushed off from the Peruvian port of Callao. For 101 days it drifted across the Pacific, pushed towards Polynesia – as Heyerdahl had predicted – by warm currents and the south-east trade wind. The crew supplemented their US Army issue rations with freshly caught shark. Almost 4,500 nautical miles later, the raft grounded itself on the Raroia reef, and Heyerdahl waded ashore on Tuamotu Island, the southernmost tip of Polynesia. His story of the intrepid voyage eventually sold more than 30 million copies and was translated into sixty-seven languages.

Thor Heyerdahl was born at Larvik, Norway, on 6 October 1914. His father ran a mineral water plant and a brewery while his mother ran the town museum. He was schooled locally and made expeditions into the mountains by sledge with his pet husky. Despite his taste for adventure, he remained terrified of water after twice almost drowning as a boy, and did not learn to swim until he was twenty-two.

At the University of Oslo, Heyerdahl read Zoology and Geography, but he had already become fascinated by Polynesia. Thus on Christmas Eve 1936, he and his new bride, Liv, set off for a year-long honeymoon on Fatu-Hiva, in the Marquesas chain. The experiment proved not wholly successful. Liv was struck down by disease, and Heyerdahl had to call on modern medicine to save her.

He was excavating sites in British Columbia in search of evidence to support his theories of transoceanic cultural pollination, when he was stranded, almost penniless, by the outbreak of the Second World War. After a variety of labouring jobs, he eventually made his way to England and joined the Free Norwegian Army, where he was trained as a saboteur and wireless operator, although several aborted missions meant that he never saw action.

After *Kon-Tiki* his conviction in the existence of links between ancient peoples did not diminish, and in the late 1960s he began to make plans for another sea voyage after seeing Inca pottery which depicted reed ships resembling those of Pharaonic Egypt. Other parallels between the two civilisations included stepped pyramids, mummification, calendars and hieroglyphs, and Heyerdahl began to wonder if Mediterranean culture had arrived in America before Columbus.

Chad was the only African country where traditional boat-making skills had survived, and accordingly local shipwrights were hired to construct a 50ft sloop from Ethiop papyrus. The vessel, named *Ra*, left the Moroccan port of Safi on 25 May 1969. Having covered 2,800 miles in two months, it was struck by a storm 600 miles off Barbados and, because of a fault in the design, became waterlogged. Despite the protests of his crew, Heyerdahl abandoned the boat, but in July 1970 successfully crossed the Atlantic in another reed boat, *Ra II*.

His voyages had also convinced him of the essential unity of mankind ('The ocean does not separate us – it unites us,' he said), as well as of the need for Europe to be modest about its role in civilising the globe; Heyerdahl was fond of pointing out that the continent was the last, apart from Australia, to have become civilised, and that architecture, astronomy and even religion all began elsewhere.

⇥ **19**th ⇤

Frankie Howerd, b. 1922, d. 1992

Frankie Howerd, the comedian who has died aged seventy, was a master of the lubricious leer and the outraged double-take, and over the decades perfected a classic music-hall persona – genteel, portly and camp.

With his Humpty-Dumpty appearance – shiny-apple face, wig perched like a squashed dead stoat on top – Howerd belonged body and soul to the variety stage. With his gift for innuendo and suggestive bluster, he contrived to raise the status of low comedy. He gave his whole expressive personality over to the defence of propriety, turning into something like an exasperated camel, the mouth pouting and bursting with lugubrious disgust at mankind's dirty-mindedness.

As the gales of laughter blew about him, he would interrupt himself with desperate denials: 'No, missus, oooh, aahhh, I mean, the very idea, no.' When Howerd was on a run, it seemed that nothing could touch him. But, like all stock acts, his brand of provocative indignation went in and out of fashion; beneath the bombastic exterior, he remained profoundly susceptible to critical slights.

Cripplingly nervous in his youth, he later became prone to bouts of devilish depression and never learned to weather the swing between acclaim and rejection.

Francis Alix Howard (he later adopted the spelling Howerd) was born at York on 6 March 1922, the son of a Royal Artillery sergeant and a Scottish mother. He lived at Eltham, south-east London, from the age of two, and won a scholarship to Shooters Hill Grammar School, Woolwich.

Francis's early ambition was to be a saint. He became interested in acting in his early teens as a result of an attempt to cure a stammer. His Sunday School teacher offered him a part in the nativity play and he doggedly stuttered through his few lines. He was a surprise success: 'My fate was sealed.'

At seventeen, Howerd auditioned at RADA. In the audition room, clutching a packed lunch, he was told to read the soliloquy from *Hamlet*. He was so scared that his left leg began to tremble and continued to twitch throughout his speech. ('To be, or um, not to be, that's the, well, that's the question isn't it?') Desperate to stop his leg 'oscillating', Howerd hit his knee. He was still holding the packet of sandwiches. The bag split and showered everyone with bread and cheese. He was not accepted.

He took the disaster as a sign from God that he was meant to be a comic. Having started work as a clerk, which he hated, he spent his days learning comedy scripts he had hidden in office files. In desperation he had changed his name to Ronnie Ordex and did a 'turn' at Lewisham Hippodrome as a stand-up comic.

He recalled being in such an advanced state of nerves that the spotlight hit him 'gaping and shaking and squinting', and he retreated tearfully from the stage without saying a word.

The comedian then repeatedly tried to join ENSA but to no avail. Instead he enlisted in the Army and became a sergeant in the Royal Artillery. Howerd recalled that he often went AWOL with a couple of friends so that they could perform concert party 'turns' dressed as three ATS girls.

After the war, Howerd was 'talent spotted' while giving a free show at the Stage Door Canteen in Piccadilly. He made his professional debut in *Just For The Fun Of It* at the Sheffield Empire in 1946, billed as 'Frankie Howerd, The Borderline Case', at the bottom of the bill. By 1948, he was top of the bill at the Palladium and earning £85 a week.

During the early 1950s, Howerd was a huge success: after going to Korea to entertain the troops, he starred in his own television show. He made his film debut as a courier in *The Runaway Bus* (1953), opposite Petula Clark and Margaret Rutherford, and went on to star in Bernard Delfont's topless revue *Pardon My French*, with a contortionist and the Four Congaroos ('an alarmingly energetic black dance group').

But in 1957, he suffered a breakdown. An ill-fated bid to extend his range as a serious actor as Bottom in *A Midsummer Night's Dream* was followed by several other flops before he went on to suffer one of his most spectacular failures ever, in *Mr Venus*, a surreal work about a visitor from another world, in which he played opposite Anton Diffring – dressed in 'sequinned jock strap and a pair of wings'. By the time the show reached London – it had opened in Manchester – Howerd claimed he was 'ready for the padded cell'.

Between 1959 and 1963 he was again prone to depressions. Then, in 1963, he scored a sensational hit as a surprise guest on Ned Sherrin's cult television revue *That Was The Week That Was*. Suddenly he was everybody's favourite comic again.

Morale almost entirely restored, Howerd took on a part in the British version of the Sondheim musical *A Funny Thing Happened On The Way To The Forum*. It enjoyed great acclaim and Howerd found himself top of the bill for two years, until 1965.

At the beginning of the 1970s, Howerd appeared for the second time in a toga: on this occasion playing Lurcio in the BBC's *Up Pompeii* (1971). It was vintage Howerd: his asides, loaded with innuendo, were followed by howls of disgust that his 'innocent remarks' should have been misinterpreted.

Following its success Howerd appeared regularly on television but, towards the end of the decade, and despite having been voted TV Personality of the Year, his popularity began to wane once again.

He spent five years suffering from lack of confidence before, in 1985, his fortunes began to rise again. He took the part of Frosch, the drunken jailer, in *Die Fledermaus* and returned to the West End in a revival of *A Funny Thing Happened* (1987). The second run was as successful as the first, coming as it did after a re-screening of *Up Pompeii* in 1986.

⊰ **20th** ⊱

Sebastian Snow, b. 1929, d. 2001

Sebastian Snow, who has died aged seventy-two, was one of the last amateur gentlemen adventurers.

He carried out his explorations and wanderings in the jungles of South America with a minimum of support and the smallest of parties. Mildly eccentric in the manner of the traditional Victorian explorer, Snow was also charmingly impractical.

As a result, all his travels had a flavour of Evelyn Waugh, but this did nothing to diminish his achievements. His trip down the Amazon at the age of twenty-two was described by his friend Chris Bonington as 'one of the great solo adventures of the post-war years'. Braving ferocious rapids, snakes, head-hunters and pirates, Snow safely navigated the 3,505 miles from the source in the Peruvian Andes to the Atlantic on canoes and balsa log rafts.

On his arrival back in Liverpool, the *Daily Mirror* hailed Snow as a 'a six-foot live hero, straight from the Bumper Book for Boys'. And sure enough, in 1954, a strip cartoon about his adventures did appear in a boys' paper.

Sebastian Edward Farquason Snow was born at Midhurst, Sussex, on 21 January 1929, the son of a local director of the National Provincial Bank. He was educated at Eton, where he broke his thigh so badly playing football that he was later rejected by the Army.

Having wanted to be an explorer since he was a small boy, Snow instead began a series of adventures with a solo trip by motor-cycle from Oslo to Stockholm via Norwegian and Swedish Lapland, living among the Lapp herdsmen and visiting the north Cape and Soviet frontier.

In the same year, he made a lone overland expedition from Istanbul to Karachi, much of the way on foot. His enduring attachment to South America began in April 1951. After answering an advertisement, he joined an expedition to Peru to try to establish the 'true' source of the Amazon from a hydrological survey of its headwater areas.

Snow and his companion John Brown eventually confirmed the source of the Amazon as the glacial lake of Ninococha, 15,000ft up in the central Peruvian Andes.

By using a powerful dye, uranin, which progressively changed the colour of the water in the adjacent lakes, Snow established that Ninococha has an outlet via underground channels to Lake Santa Ana, and from there to Lake Lauricocha. Thus he calculated that the length of the Amazon – hitherto given variously up to a maximum of 4,000 miles – was in fact 3,505 miles, making it the world's second longest river (after the Mississippi-Missouri).

During the course of the expedition Snow spent nine weeks alone on the Maranon glacier above Lake Ninococha, taking soundings. It was while there that he began to contemplate his journey from the source of the Amazon to its mouth. 'I was not sufficiently prepared,' he recalled in his book *Half a Dozen of the Other* (1972). 'I was not prepared at all – but I would try!'

Accompanied by a resilient Peruvian named Pacchini, he covered the first stage on foot, relying for food 'on the goodness of the local Indians', and sleeping in the open.

After being delayed by malaria and flooding, Snow was eventually built a balsa raft by Indian hillmen, one of whom agreed to accompany him. Occasionally, he was forced to take to hills, and to build another raft on his return to the river. But he did not shirk many of the rapids.

In the treacherous canyon known as the Pongo de Mansariche – 'Gateway of Parrots' – Snow recalled being 'thrown about like a bagatelle ball'. At least two of his rafts were wrecked, but each time he managed to swim ashore. Rapids and snakes were not the only hazards: a pirate canoe once came alongside. 'I immediately started gibbering nonsensical Spanish,' recalled Snow, 'using the word "pistola" with great frequency.' Snow did not in fact carry a gun, holding that it was 'better to be friendly'.

He eventually arrived in Iquitos on 25 July 1952, and from there he went by riverboat to Para, the mouth of the Amazon.

The Amazon trip only increased his appetite for adventure. The next year, he returned to Britain from Ecuador with severe frostbite after climbing two of the highest peaks in the Andes, and the year after that he set off to southern Peru to search for the lost Inca city of Paititi.

He took with him presents and a pair of dental forceps to relieve hostile Indians of toothache and win their confidence. On his return he announced that he and his companions had discovered not one but three lost cities.

When, in 1957, Snow married Contessina Letizia Bizzarri, he declared: 'My roaming days are over. Now we're going to raise broiler fowls.' But although they soon had a son and three daughters, it was not long before he was off again (the marriage was dissolved in 1970).

By 1965, he was back in South America, travelling 4,500 miles through unknown fever jungles from the River Amazon to the Plate. The next year, with Bonington, he penetrated the jungle of Ecuador to the lip of 17,450ft Mount Sangay, the world's most active and inaccessible volcano.

In 1968, he made an unsuccessful attempt to retrace the steps of Francisco de Orellana across South America; he almost died after his raft overturned.

Snow laid no claim to any skill in his chosen occupation, claiming to have 'no talent for survival'. His trips were often, by his own admission, attended by a fair amount of chaos. His personal motto was 'Bash on, regardless.'

Christopher Milne, b. 1920, d. 1996

Christopher Milne, who has died aged seventy-five, spent much of his life in embarrassed retreat from his identification with Christopher Robin, the protagonist of his father A.A. Milne's children's books.

He even thought, in bitter moments, 'that my father had got to where he was by climbing upon my infant shoulders, that he had filched from me my good name and left me with nothing but the empty fame of being his son'.

The first literary effort that Christopher inspired in his father was the poem *Vespers*, which has the lines: 'Hush! Hush! Whisper who dares! / Christopher Robin is saying his prayers.' This work, he said, brought him 'more toe-curling, fist-clenching, lip-biting embarrassment than any other'.

⇜ 21st ⇝

Gay Kindersley, b. 1930, d. 2011

Gay Kindersley, who has died aged eighty, was one of the most engaging figures on the Turf; a former champion amateur jump jockey who later turned to training, he made his mark less for his professional achievements than for his extra-curricular exploits as a drinker, gambler and serial womaniser.

Most men of that stripe earn disapproval, even enmity. Kindersley largely escaped censure thanks to his being blessed with a barrel-load of charm; he was also utterly without malice.

In a foreword to Robin Rhoderick-Jones's biography *Flings Over Fences – The Ups And Downs Of Gay Kindersley* (1994), Kindersley's friend Lord Oaksey wrote: 'Whether riding, singing, drinking, or succumbing to what the author calls "his incurable tendency to infidelity", my old friend has been a source of more pleasure and amusement than sorrow and disappointment to his innumerable friends.'

These friends extended well beyond the racecourse, and included Peter Cook and Dudley Moore, Peter O'Toole and Albert Finney. Another was Queen Elizabeth the Queen Mother, who, on a visit to Kindersley's home at East Garston in Berkshire, asked if she might see round the house. As Gay opened the door to one of the guest bedrooms, he and his visitor were confronted by the sight of a couple *in flagrante*. 'How nice,' murmured Queen Elizabeth. 'But I think perhaps we should not go further.'

Kindersley's engaging naivety is illustrated by an incident in 1985, when he took the writer Graham Lord as his guest to a lunch at the Savoy Hotel that was being given to welcome the Australian Test side to England. Spying the Aussies in a corner of the River Room, the two went over to greet them: 'Hello, folks,' said Kindersley breezily. 'I'm Gay and this is my friend Graham.'

'Jeez!' said one of the Aussies. 'Backs to the wall, mates.'

More recently, in 2004, Kindersley went into his local branch of Waitrose. Asked by the checkout girl if he would like some cash back, Kindersley (who was unfamiliar with this transaction) replied: 'That's really awfully sweet of you, how kind.'

He suggested £50, which he took across the road to the betting shop, investing it on a 10–1 shot which duly came in. He then returned to the store to tip the checkout girl £10 for her kindness. For good measure, he gave £10 to the other girls on the tills as well. It was only when his bank statement arrived that he understood the nature of 'cash back'.

Gay Kindersley was born on 2 June 1930. His father was Philip Leyland Kindersley, son of the 1st Lord Kindersley; his mother was Oonagh Guinness, who would later marry the 4th Lord Oranmore and Browne. By the time Gay was at prep school his parents' marriage was in trouble.

After Eton and Oxford he joined the 7th Hussars, serving in Germany, but aged twenty-one he announced that he wished to marry. To cure him of this ambition, he was sent to Canada, where he worked as a roughneck on an oil rig and took the opportunity to ride in the Calgary Stampede and compete in rodeos – once being thrown and lying unconscious for four hours.

On returning to England he embarked on his career as an amateur jockey. His mother (by now Lady Oranmore and Browne) was kept informed of his progress by her butler, Patrick Cummins, who one night at dinner proffered her a rissole and, in his thick Irish accent, gave her news of her son's latest race: 'Mr Gay's turd.' The strait-laced guest seated next to Lady Oranmore was horrified.

As a married man he would have many affairs, his lovers including Ann, Marchioness of Queensberry; the zither player Shirley Abicair; a White Russian known as 'the Volga Boatwoman'; and a lady master of foxhounds with a pilot's licence nicknamed 'the Flying Fornicator'. He once declared: 'I've got this infidelity thing, I've always had to be chasing.'

Aged twenty-five Kindersley inherited £750,000 from his grandfather's estate – a colossal sum in those days. He would often say that 'the way to a small fortune is to start with a large one'.

In 1959–60 Kindersley won the amateur jockeys' championship after riding twenty-two winners from a hundred rides – all but five of those had been on his own horses. During his career as a jockey Kindersley twice broke his back, in 1955 at Stratford and seven years later at Hurst Park; on the second occasion his doctor told him his days as a jockey were over, but he returned to the saddle. He rode in the 1965 Grand National, but came to grief at the third.

He retired as a National Hunt jockey in the same year, though he continued to ride in Flat races until 1969. Meanwhile, he set up as a trainer at East Garston, enjoying mixed success. He never abandoned his quest to win a National, and in 1984 he trained Earthstopper to finish fifth, although the horse collapsed and died after the race.

Gay Kindersley, who retired from training in 1985, had part-owned Carrickbeg who, ridden by Lord Oaksey, was caught by Ayala only in the final strides of the 1963 Grand National. To add insult to injury, Ayala's owner (the hairdresser 'Teasy Weasy' Raymond) did not appear at the traditional post-National party at the Adelphi Hotel in Liverpool, and as owners of the runner-up Kindersley and Oaksey had to foot the bill for the festivities.

⊰ 22nd ⊱

Alex Madonna, b. 1918, d. 2004

Alex Madonna, who has died aged eighty-five, was the proprietor of the Madonna Inn, a 108-room pink hotel on the Californian coast which boasts themed bedrooms, a café made entirely from copper, and a rock waterfall urinal; the Inn was immortalised in Umberto Eco's collection of essays *Travels in Hyperreality* (1991), in which the Italian scholar analysed the American love of grotesque fakery.

'The poor words with which natural human speech is provided,' wrote Eco, 'cannot suffice to describe the Madonna Inn ... Let's say that Albert Speer, while leafing through a book on Gaudi, swallowed an overgenerous dose of LSD and began to build a nuptial catacomb for Liza Minnelli.' But that, he reiterated, could not convey its true ghastliness.

Jack Best, b. 1912, d. 2000

Jack Best, who has died aged eighty-seven, took part in one of the most audacious escape attempts of the Second World War, the plan to build and fly a glider out of Colditz.

The idea was dreamed up by Tony Rolt, a naval officer, who had noticed that the roof of the castle's chapel was hidden from sight of the guards below. He convinced Bill Goldfinch, a Sunderland flying boat pilot, to draw up a design for a glider which could be flown from the roof, and with Best erected a false wall in an attic of the chapel to form a workshop.

In this, the glider was painstakingly constructed over nine months using tools improvised from bedsteads, iron window bars and gramophone springs, which were turned into makeshift saws.

Best made the wingspars from floorboards and parts of the fuselage from bed slats, while the control wires were electric cable torn from unused parts of the castle. The aircraft's skin was made from cotton sleeping bags stiffened with the prisoners' ration of boiled millet.

On the day of the flight, a hole was to have been made in the wall of the attic and the glider hauled out on to the roof of the chapel. The wings, measuring 32ft across, would then have been attached to the body, and the glider launched by a catapult system, the counterweight of which was an earth-filled bathtub dropping five storeys from the roof to the ground below.

In the event, however, the war ended too soon for them to discover whether the plan would have worked, and the glider is thought to have been broken up for firewood during the bitter winter of 1946 by occupying Russian troops.

But almost fifty years later, Best and his fellow PoWs did get the chance to see if their ingenuity would have been rewarded. In 1993, they returned to Colditz and successfully flew a one-third scale model from the chapel roof. Then, in February 2000, Best was at RAF Odiham in Hampshire to see a full-size replica of the original glider take to the skies.

Its maiden flight was almost half a century late, but there no longer could be any doubt that it would have made possible yet another break-out from the supposedly escape-proof fortress.

John William Best, known as Jack, was born on 6 August 1912 at Vivod, near Llangollen in North Wales, and grew up on the family estate. He was educated at Stowe, took part in a public schools' tour to Kenya, and in 1931 became an apprentice farmer there.

When war came in 1939, he was training for a civilian pilot's licence and accordingly joined the RAF, gaining his wings at No. 4 Flying Training School, at Habbaniyah in

Iraq. He then became a ferry pilot, flying aircraft from Takoradi in Ghana across Africa to Egypt.

He transferred to No. 69, a Maryland bomber reconnaissance squadron, and on a flight in 1941 ran out of fuel over the Mediterranean. He was forced to land in the sea off southern Greece, where he was captured by the Germans.

He was sent to a camp at Biberach and in the winter of 1941–42 on to Stalag Luft I at Barth. Best was later moved to Stalag Luft III, at Sagan, near the Polish border. Here he made several attempts to escape and in June 1942 he, Goldfinch and Henry Lamond tunnelled 80ft out under the wire. They had pilot's notes for a Ju52 transport and so headed for an airfield with the intention of stealing such an aircraft.

They watched German air cadets undergoing glider training, but as they could not find a suitable aeroplane they walked instead by night to the banks of the Oder, staving off hunger with some potatoes which they had dug up.

There Best and the two other escapers found a skiff and so set off for the Baltic, intending to stow away on a ship bound for Sweden. But they made the mistake of failing to obey the rule of the sea and rowed up the wrong bank, against the river traffic. They were sleeping under the upturned boat when they were rumbled by the police, who gave them bread and cheese and beer before returning them to Sagan. From there they were dispatched to Colditz.

Best was liberated in May 1945 and demobbed as a flight lieutenant. He later farmed in Kenya and served with the reserve police during the Mau Mau troubles. Eventually he returned to Britain and farmed in Herefordshire.

❧ 23rd ❧

Denis Compton, b. 1918, d. 1997

Denis Compton, who has died aged seventy-eight, was one of the greatest and most dashing of all English batsmen.

He was at his zenith after the Second World War, when in four summers and two overseas tours – to Australia in 1946–47 and to South Africa in 1948–49 – he scored 14,641 runs and made sixty centuries. But statistics tell little of a player whose genius was born of daring and improvisation.

Compton used a light (2lb 2oz) bat – though a tendency to leave his equipment behind meant that he was sometimes obliged to pick up whatever he could find – and he wielded it as a rapier rather than a bludgeon.

His trademark was the sweep, which he did not hesitate to play off balls that would have hit the middle stump. He relished the opportunity to hook bumpers. On one occasion, having slipped and fallen flat on his back in mid-stroke, he managed to execute a one-handed late cut that sent the ball winging to the boundary.

In the late 1940s Compton became a national idol, his Brylcreemed form staring down from posters all over the land. Sir Neville Cardus perfectly caught the manner in which he irradiated a drab post-war Britain. 'Never have I been so deeply touched on a cricket ground,' Cardus wrote, 'as I was in this heavenly summer of 1947 when I went to Lord's to see a pale-faced crowd, existing on rations, the rocket-bomb still in the ears of most – and see this worn, dowdy crowd raptly watching Compton.

'The strain of long years of anxiety and affliction passed from all heads and shoulders at the sight of Compton in full sail, sending the ball here, there, and everywhere, each stroke a flick of delight, a propulsion of happy, sane, healthy life. There were no rations in an innings by Compton.'

The Corinthian image created when playing for Middlesex and England in the summer was fortified in the winter when Compton turned his attention to football. He was good enough to hold his place in the great Arsenal sides before and after the war, collecting both a League and a Cup medal. He also won fourteen wartime international caps for England.

By 1950, when he appeared in the Cup Final against Liverpool, he was already into his thirties, inclined to run out of puff, and troubled by a notorious knee injury. In the first half, in his own words, he 'played a stinker'; in the second, fuelled by a mammoth slug of whisky administered by Alex James, he put in a dazzling performance.

His excised knee cap, incidentally, is now kept at Lord's. 'It's a revolting thing,' Compton observed, 'looks as if rats have been nipping at it. I can't imagine why anyone would want to look at it.'

Denis Charles Scott Compton was born on 23 May 1918, the son of Jessie and Harry Compton, who ran a painting and decorating business in Hendon. There was a sister, and an elder brother, Leslie, who would be centre-half for Arsenal and England, and wicketkeeper for Middlesex.

Denis was educated at Bell Lane School, and learned his cricket up against the lamppost in Alexandra Road, Hendon. At fourteen he made his first appearance at Lord's, captaining the Elementary Schools and duly making a century.

The innings caught the eye of Sir Pelham Warner, and the next summer Compton was recruited to the MCC groundstaff at Lord's. He started at the foot of the ladder as a one of the 'Nippers' or 'Roller boys' who were put to various ground duties and received net practice and tuition. His salary was twenty-five shillings a week, the same amount as he was paid in the winter by Arsenal.

Compton had little need of formal tuition, for the basic principles of batting came naturally to him. At fifteen he scored a century for the MCC against Suffolk at Felixstowe.

A few days after his eighteenth birthday he was promoted to the full Middlesex side for the Whitsuntide match against Sussex at Lord's. Three weeks later he scored his maiden first-class century, at Northampton. By the end of 1936 he had passed the 1,000-run mark, won his county cap, and only narrowly missed being selected for the England tour of Australia. Emphatically, he was on his way.

He was only twenty when, in 1938, with all the poise and coolness of an old hand, he saved England from probable defeat against Australia at Lord's with an innings of 76 not out. A fortnight earlier, in his first Test against Australia at Trent Bridge on a perfect wicket, he had made the fourth hundred of the innings, following those of Barnet, Hutton and Paynter.

He had been chosen first for England in the third and last Test of the 1937 summer against New Zealand, making 65 before, as the non-striker, being run out from an accidental diversion by the bowler. That was pure ill-luck, but prophetic in that the one flaw in his batting was running between wickets.

His great friend and partner, W.J. Edrich, is credited with the remark that Denis's initial call was no more than a basis for negotiation. This happy-go-lucky approach – banished only at the crease when things really mattered – occasionally tested the patience of his captains. Hence J.J. Warr's remark that Compton took 415 catches in the course of his career 'when he was looking'.

The annus mirabilis was 1947, when Compton made 3,816 runs (easily topping Tom Hayward's record 3,518, made in 1906). His eighteen hundreds that year exceeded the record sixteen of Sir Jack Hobbs, made in 1925; his average was 90. It was a gloriously hot, dry summer during which the South Africans suffered most from his bat, to the tune of six hundreds, four of them in Tests.

Perhaps his two greatest innings were those against Bradman's all-conquering Australians in 1948: 184 at Trent Bridge in an eerie, yellow light with Lindwall and Miller at their fastest, and 145 not out at Old Trafford. This was the time when, within a few minutes of going in, he was obliged to retire for stitches to a cut eyebrow, sustained in hooking at a no-ball from Lindwall.

We saw now, in the words of Neville Cardus, the Ironside breastplate as well as the Cavalier plume. Bandaged but indomitable, Compton returned to play an innings which laid the foundation of what would likely have been an England victory had the weather not interfered.

At this point, he had made eight hundreds in the last ten Tests, a sequence which only Bradman had achieved. But now, at his peak, an old football injury to Compton's right knee began to give out danger signals. For a while the surgeons and 'physios' contrived to keep him on the field, and in the spring of 1950, in his last game of football, with the knee heavily bandaged, he helped Arsenal to victory in the Cup Final. Within a few weeks he was hobbling off the field at Lord's, and W.E. Tucker, the famous orthopaedic surgeon, was performing the first of numerous operations, which culminated in 1955 with the removal of his knee cap.

In the tour of Australia in 1950–51, with English batting at its weakest, Compton had an utter failure, his only one in a Test series. He never touched again the brilliance of his golden period.

Nevertheless, handicapped in mobility as he was, he was still an automatic choice for England, and in the following three rubbers against Australia was batting at the moment of victory.

In 1956, at the Oval, shortly after a rigorous surgical manipulation and still with a limp, Compton faced the old enemy for the last time. Showing many glimpses of his best, he made 94, the highest score of the match, and 35 not out. Sir Donald Bradman described his 94 as the best innings of the series.

When one considers the loss of six wartime summers from the age of twenty-one onwards, and the later physical handicap, Compton's achievements, numerically speaking, are marvellous indeed. His 38,942 runs, including 123 hundreds, were made at an average of 51.85; his 5,807 Test runs, including seventeen hundreds, at 50. His slow left-arm bowling yielded 622 rather expensive wickets.

Retiring before his fortieth birthday, Compton made successful careers in advertising and in journalism with the *Sunday Express*, for which he wrote about cricket (generally not unaided) from 1950 to 1988. He also commentated over many years on television, often with unexpected force.

⫸ 24th ⫷

Margaret Gelling, b. 1924, d. 2009

Margaret Gelling, who has died aged eighty-four, transformed our understanding of the derivation of English place-names.

When she began her career as a research assistant at the English Place-Name Society in 1946, the field was dominated by scholars such as Sir Frank Stenton, who, as she put it, 'empathised with the ruling classes' and were more interested in place-names designated by members of the elite, such as Kington or Knighton ('royal manor' and 'estate of the young retainers'), than by names with a popular origin.

Margaret Gelling, by contrast, revealed the extent to which Anglo-Saxon names were invented by ordinary people and noted the myriad connections between place-names and features of the local landscape.

She established, for example, that the Anglo-Saxon peasant farmer had as many words for 'hill' and 'valley' as the Inuit has for 'snow'. Just as importantly, by going out and actually looking at the landscape, she established that none of these was a synonym. Each of the forty-odd different terms which can be translated as 'hill', for example, referred to a different size and shape of mound.

The topographical vocabulary of the early Anglo-Saxon settlers was highly nuanced and exact, she argued, because in an age without maps or signposts, the distinctions between a 'knoll' and a 'creech', a 'don' and a 'brough', or an 'ofer' and an 'ora' would have been very important navigational concepts.

Margaret Gelling's work offered an insight into the Anglo-Saxon imagination, and provided an invaluable reference tool for archaeologists looking for previously unknown sites indicated by place-name references to, say, farming or ancient routes. She also showed how a study of place-names can help historians gain a more accurate picture of early history.

For example, she challenged the view – based largely on the writings of the sixth-century historian St Gildas – that the ancient Britons were forced out to the 'Celtic fringe' by Anglo-Saxon invaders. If that were true, she asked, why do so many place-names in southern England have Celtic origins? 'If you believe Gildas, the Anglo-Saxons would have been chasing the ancient Britons, catching up with one who wasn't fast enough and saying, "Look here, before I cut off your head, just tell me the name of this place".'

In 2001 new genetic research confirmed that far from being purged when the Anglo-Saxons arrived in the fifth century, many ancient Britons remained in England.

Margaret Joy Midgley was born in Manchester on 29 November 1924. Her father worked in insurance, and the family moved to Sidcup when she was a child. From Chislehurst Grammar School, she became the first member of her family to win a place at university and went on to read English at St Hilda's College, Oxford, which she found a 'waste of time'.

In 1952 she married the archaeologist Peter Gelling and moved to Birmingham, where he had a post at the university. She accompanied him on many expeditions, including, in the 1960s, to the Alto Plano in Peru to investigate the history of potato use, including freeze-drying at altitude.

As a result she became experienced at cooking over a fire of dried llama dung in a cave. In July 1974 she was in Cyprus sorting finds in the castle at Kyrenia when the Turks invaded – she and her colleagues were forced to spend several uncomfortable hours cowering in the castle's lavatories.

❧ 25th ❧

Sir Hugh Rankin, b. 1899, d. 1988

Sir Hugh Rankin, 3rd Bt, an eccentric remarkable even by the rarefied standards of the baronetage, who has died aged eighty-eight, was variously a riveter's mate in a Belfast shipyard; a trooper in the cavalry; a sheep shearer in Western Australia; president of the British Muslim Society; vice-president of the World's Buddhist Association; and a campaigner for 'an independent Red Republic of all Scotland, excluding Orkneys and Shetland'.

Born in 1899 in the middle of the Tunisian desert, the elder son of the traveller and big-game hunter Sir Reginald Rankin (who searched for the extinct giant sloth in Chile), he was christened Hubert Charles Rhys Rankin but later changed his first name to Hugh. At one stage he adopted the surname of Stewart-Rankin and during his Muslim period also briefly assumed the forename of Omar.

He was educated at Harrow but ran away to work in a Belfast shipyard before joining the 1st Royal Dragoon Guards as a trooper. In 1921 he was broad-sword champion of the cavalry, but the following year, while serving in Ireland during the Troubles ('on the wrong side, I'm afraid'), he was shot by a sniper and invalided out of the Army.

Rankin, who wrote articles on agricultural stock, then devoted himself to the study of sheep, being elected president of the Clun Forest Sheep Breeders Association in 1928. Ten years later he represented British sheep breeders in petitioning the government on the problems of the industry. At the time he succeeded to the baronetcy in 1931 he was a 'piece-work' shearer in Western Australia, covering the area between Bunbury and Broome.

During travels in the Middle East, Rankin came under the influence of the Muslim peer, the 5th Lord Headley, whom he succeeded in 1935 as president of the British Muslim Society. But a few weeks later he resigned after a rowdy meeting: 'They were very rude ... and knew nothing of law and order or methods of procedure. I was disgusted with the whole lot of them.' He then formed a new society along orthodox and non-sectarian lines and in 1937 was the British representative to the first all-European Muslim Congress in Geneva.

During the Second World War he served as a captain in the Royal Army Service Corps in India but on being demobilised, 'realised what an awful fool I had been to fight for Britain. If a revolution comes – and come it must after the next world war – I'll do my damnedest to see it succeeds.'

He said that he had 'always hated and loathed the Christian religion. The Muslim religion is a fighting one, so I dropped it and became a Buddhist.' From 1944 he was a practising non-theistic Theravda Buddhist and claimed to be the second 'Britisher' to perform the Holy Buddhist Pilgrimage.

In 1959 he declared it was 'no news' that Abominable Snowmen existed: 'It is part of our known belief that five Bodhisattvas ("Perfected Men") control the destiny of this world. They meet together once a year in a cave in the Himalayas to make their decisions. One of them lives permanently on the higher Himalayas. One of them lives in the Scottish Cairngorms.' Sir Hugh said that he and his wife had clearly seen the latter Bodhisattva in the Lang Ghru Pass.

Rankin's political affiliations were equally varied: he joined the Labour Party in 1939 and was subsequently a Dominion Home Ruler for Scotland, a Scottish Nationalist, a Scottish Communist and a Welsh Republican Nationalist. In *Who's Who* he stated that he held 'extreme political views' and was 'now left-side Labour'.

In 1965 he claimed to be 'the only baronet in the United Kingdom who is living on national assistance' and added that his title had always been a hindrance. Asked what job he might like, he replied: 'Anything. Anything except being a butler. I hate snobbishness.'

Baron Rolf Beck, b. 1914, d. 1991

Baron Rolf Beck, the Czechoslovakian-born industrialist, who has died aged seventy-seven, bought Layham Hall, in Suffolk, where his first wife kept exotic pets.

In the Baron's frequent absences on business, she found solace in the company of a white rat. Guests at Layham, initially alarmed by this rodent, were generally won round by its docile character. The rat, when not sleeping on the Baroness's sleeve, would sit on her shoulder or nibble at titbits from her hand.

The Baroness also kept cats, Labradors, guinea fowl, Pekingese, several horses and a wallaby. Less successfully, she adopted an Indian sloth bear, named Bear. In 1964 this animal suddenly went berserk and mauled its owner. The Baron, after stalking it through the mansion, felled it with eight blasts from his shotgun.

After this experience he and his wife vowed that they would never again offer hospitality to wild animals; nevertheless, four years later his wife accepted a homeless 5ft-tall Malayan sun bear called Yogi.

This time the Baron was more cautious, and carried a cricket bat around with him on the estate in case of ursine aggression. But the bear seemed to be settling in splendidly: 'It is such fun rolling around the place with him and taking him for walks,' the Baroness enthused. 'Yogi is perfectly sweet, and so huge, with enormous claws that could destroy you.'

Within a month, however, disaster struck. Yogi ran amok throughout the house, and was swiftly despatched to a zoo at Cromer.

 26th

Denis Hills, b. 1913, d. 2004

Denis Hills, who died on Monday aged ninety, lived his life like an old-fashioned *Boys' Own* adventure.

He is probably most widely remembered as the man whom Idi Amin condemned to death by firing squad for describing the Ugandan dictator as a 'black Nero'. The Queen interceded on Hills' behalf, and the then Foreign Secretary, James Callaghan, flew out to Kampala to bring her outspoken subject home.

Hills was teaching at Makerere University in the Ugandan capital, Kampala, when Amin seized power in 1971. He was appalled by Amin's butcheries, and in April 1975 was arrested and incarcerated in a squalid prison where his diet consisted of boiled cabbage leaves, stale porridge and grub-infested beans.

Charged with espionage and sedition, he was tried and condemned to death. While awaiting execution, he was summoned to see Amin, who told Hills that he had been consorting with the wrong sort of people, and was due to be shot the following day; however, Amin went on, since the Queen was a good friend, he was prepared to reconsider. Hills was forced to apologise and retract his remarks, and the following day he was flown back to England with Callaghan – during the flight, Callaghan gave Hills the latest cricket scores.

Denis Hills was born on 8 November 1913 at Moseley, a suburb of Birmingham, where his father managed the local branch of the Midland Bank.

He was, possibly, something of a bully. One of his fellow pupils at King Edward's School, Birmingham, was a pallid, reclusive and scholarly figure named J. Enoch Powell. Years later, at *The Spectator*'s annual summer party, Powell could be seen shrinking back as his former tormentor advanced upon him with a demonic smile, making jerking movements with both hands as if passing an imaginary rugger ball.

In 1932 Hills went up to Lincoln College, Oxford, where he read PPE.

He was sturdily built, with fair hair, blue eyes, a noble head reminiscent of one of the fitter Roman emperors, a teasing smile and the most winning of manners. He liked women, and they liked him. During one vacation in Devon, he was so taken with some German girls whom he encountered that he decided to visit their country at once, so initiating a connection which lasted a lifetime.

In 1935, after leaving Oxford, Hills spent some months travelling rough in Germany. On his return England seemed dull, if homely, by comparison; and after a short spell of tedium with Shell Mex, in 1937 Hills took a job in Poland as the English editor of a cultural magazine published in Gdynia. In 1939 he moved to Warsaw to teach English; it was there that he met and married his first wife, Dunia Lesmian, the daughter of a Polish poet.

The outbreak of war found the newlyweds in south-west Poland, and as the Red Army moved in they slipped across the border into Romania. Hills got a job with the British Council, where his colleagues included Hugh Seton-Watson, Ivor Porter and the exuberant Reggie Smith and his wife Olivia Manning. But watching Reggie Smith's wig fall off during a production of *Othello* was thin gruel for a man of action in time of war, and before long Hills was agitating to join the fray.

Accordingly, he made his way to Cairo, via the Black Sea and the Middle East. For a time he was seconded to General Kopanski's Polish Carpathian Lancers Brigade, and then to the King's Own Royal Regiment.

One of the regiment's jobs was to guard the thousands of Italian soldiers captured during one of Wavell's offensives. The officer in charge set the prisoners to work making colonnades of naked women out of concrete (he liked to tap their bottoms with his cane).

As a Polish-speaker, Hills joined the 5th Kresowa Division, initially in Iraq and Palestine, before being sent to Italy in January 1944. He took part in the Battle of Monte Cassino and the slow advance up the spine of Italy.

With the fighting virtually over, Hills left his beloved Poles to act as an interpreter and liaison officer with the Soviet military mission at Taranto. He enjoyed swimming and the company of buxom Russian girls, and was provided with two German PoWs as batmen. But Hills was to spend the next two years involved in work which he found profoundly distasteful: the return, under the terms of the Yalta Agreement, of Russian nationals who had fought on the wrong side, and who would be condemned to death or the Gulag once they reached their destination.

After accompanying a boatload of credulous Turkomans to Odessa, Hills realised that Stalin's promise of an amnesty was a fraud; and from then on he did everything in his power to thwart the return of all but a bare minimum of the Georgians and Don Cossacks with whom he had to deal.

Hills took a similarly humane and independent line over the question of the *Fede*, a decrepit hulk which was anchored off La Spezia and crammed with 1,200 Polish Jews, survivors of the Holocaust who were determined to make their way to Palestine in the face of a British blockade and quota restrictions on Jewish immigration.

The Jews were already on hunger strike, and their leaders were threatening to blow up the boat if the British refused to allow them to sail. Hills persuaded the authorities to look the other way as the *Fede* raised anchor, an episode immortalised by Leon Uris in his novel *Exodus*.

After his demobilisation Hills taught English and worked as a navvy in Germany. Restless as ever, he bicycled the length of Europe, from the Arctic Circle to Salonika; not surprisingly, perhaps, his marriage came unstitched at about this time.

After a short spell as a prep school master, he moved to Turkey in 1955, initially as a teacher of English in Ankara, and later as an instructor at the Technical University there. He spent a good deal of time climbing among the peaks and remote mountain tarns of Turkish Kurdistan, and swimming in the Black Sea; he marked his farewell to Turkey by scaling the dome of Santa Sofia in Istanbul.

In 1963 Hills moved to Uganda, to teach at Makerere University in Kampala. For a while he found the life idyllic, but everything changed with the advent of Amin.

In 1985 he realised his long-held dream of returning to Poland, only to find himself summarily expelled as a result of a piece in *The Daily Telegraph*'s Peterborough column, in which he was unhelpfully described as travelling through Poland in order to write a 'less than complimentary book about the Communist regime'. With the fall of Communism, Hills became a regular visitor to Poland – as well as to Germany, where his second wife, Ingrid, still lived.

Not a man who had much time for pension schemes or amassing savings, Hills spent most of his last years in the Star and Garter home at Richmond, Surrey, where, ever the loner, he chafed at the restraints of institutional life.

⊰ 27th ⊱

Dominique Aury, b. 1907, d. 1998

Dominique Aury, who has died aged ninety, was long known in Paris as a distinguished literary figure, not least as a translator of Evelyn Waugh; until 1994, however, she remained elusive about being the author of the sado-masochistic bestseller *Histoire d'O* (1954).

The heroine of *Histoire d'O* is chained, whipped, tortured and degraded in the very best French prose: cool, elegant and unemotional. More curiously, though, the book had been written, as Dominique Aury finally admitted in an interview with the *New Yorker*, on that most pressing of Gallic imperatives: to keep a lover.

In the early 1950s Dominique Aury felt she was losing her hold over the seventy-year-old Jean Paulhan, who had been editor of the prestigious *La Nouvelle Revue* between 1925 and 1939 and was still a power in the publishers Gallimard. 'What could I do?' she demanded later. 'I couldn't paint, I couldn't write poetry. How could I make him sit up?'

Then she recalled that Paulhan had insisted that a woman could never write a truly erotic novel. Here was a challenge. Aware of his enthusiasm for the writings of the Marquis de Sade, and drawing on the fantasies of her lonely adolescence in Brittany, she set pencil to paper, and discovered for the first time in her life that composition flowed easily. Better still, Paulhan declared that the result was 'the most ardent love letter that any man had ever received'. Though he was unable to persuade Gallimard to produce it, he found a willing accomplice in Jean-Jacques Pauvert, who had already published the Marquis de Sade.

To emphasise its artistic credentials, *Histoire d'O* was given to the world in a beautifully produced edition. Paulhan himself provided a preface, entitled 'Happiness in Slavery', arousing speculation that he was the author of the whole book. Other possible authors mentioned by the cognoscenti included Andre Malraux and Henry de Montherlant.

Graham Greene was an early admirer of *Histoire d'O*, and his taste proved contagious. The book was eventually rendered into more than twenty languages; in England readers were undiscouraged by an appalling first translation. In fact, the arch-sadist in the book was an Englishman, Sir Stephen. If he were to leave her, O pleads, she would die. 'Sir Stephen gave his consent.'

Histoire d'O became the best-selling contemporary French novel outside France. There was also a film, issued in 1975, though critics doubted whether the subtleties of the original French had been entirely caught.

⊰ **28**th ⊱

Bill Bailey, b. 1933, d. 2009

Bill Bailey, who has died aged seventy-five, was known as 'the father of surfing' in the British Isles, transforming the wave-cresting sport from esoteric pastime of Hawaiians and Australians to a hugely popular pursuit even on these chilly shores.

His breakthrough came in the late 1950s when he was a lifeguard on Newquay beach, posted there to monitor the increasing numbers of holidaymakers taking to the water.

The role drove Bailey to consider using gently hollowed-out lifesaving rafts, much in service in Australia, and normally operated by two guards with paddles. He quickly realised that his life-saving rafts, on which guards sat, could be made smaller and lighter, and used – while standing – for recreation; soon he had embarked on the creation of Britain's first surfboard factory.

Production, with many false starts, got under way in 1963. Early experiments were dogged by somewhat comic misfortune. On one occasion Bailey failed properly to seal his surfboard mould, and was forced to flee the caravan where he was working as it filled with rapidly hardening foam. He said he was still scraping the substance from the ceiling years later.

Such mistakes were rare for Bailey – usually considered a masterly artisan. According to Chris Jones, who joined the surfboard factory two years after it opened its doors, Bailey once broke down on a road near Bristol. Opening the bonnet of his car, he removed the gearbox, hitchhiked with it to his workshop in Newquay, machined the parts he needed, fixed the gearbox and hitchhiked back to repair his stricken vehicle. 'He could do anything with his hands,' said Jones.

John Michael Bailey, always known as Bill, was born on 27 September 1933, growing up at Inglesbatch near Bath, in Somerset. He was a troublemaker at school, and his father removed him from lessons at fourteen and put him in the RAF as a boy entrant.

Bill quickly learned some discipline, and began training as an engineer. He worked on, among other things, Sunderland flying boats, and was deployed several times to warmer climes, including Ceylon, where he developed a love of the sea during service on air-rescue.

Among the interesting characters he met there were the French naturalist Jacques Cousteau, who was pioneering the early aqualung, and Arthur C. Clarke, who was freediving.

Bailey left the RAF at the end of the 1950s, but retained a highly practical mind. As interest in his home-made boards took off in the early 1960s, he found partners to expand his business. Among them was Bob Head, an Australian who (unlike Bailey, only a proficient boarder) was a great surfer. By combining their two names, the pair came up with the moniker Bilbo, derived from Tolkien's hobbit hero, with which to christen their surfboards.

Over the next few years production moved from the garages and Nissen huts which had provided early shelter to a new purpose-built factory, and Bailey and his team began to sell up to sixty boards a week.

Then, the 10ft custom-built surfboards cost about £25. Now, boards whose design has changed little in the intervening years cost about £700.

In the late 1960s Bilbo opened a shop outside the station in Newquay, which was rapidly becoming Britain's surfing capital. With the business well established, Bailey left to pursue other interests in the early 1970s. He briefly returned to the RAF as an engineering consultant.

During postings to Saudi Arabia and Oman he delighted in capturing local creepy-crawlies, later showing off scorpions encased in resin to bemused visitors. He even sold some of these exhibits to oil executives stationed in the kingdom, becoming known as Scorpion Bill.

For much of the 1970s, however, he enjoyed spending time on his farm, Pensilva, outside Goonhavern, just south of Newquay, bringing up his two young sons.

In the 1980s he left for France, where he used his skill with foam to set up a factory making windsurfing boards. There he met two brothers who were working on exotic carbon-fibre boat designs in Corsica. Bailey travelled to the island in the mid-1980s and his technical skills were prized as he successfully adapted Formula One offshore powerboats by incorporating cockpit canopies from F-16 fighters, an important safety advance.

It was in Corsica that he acquired a boat of his own, the ketch *Punch Coco*, and he and his family proceeded to spend much of the next eight years cruising the Mediterranean. Bailey, who had a long-standing interest in firearms, ensured that the boat had more than enough firepower to ward off potential pirates. From little more than a tube of metal, he once created and rifled his own elephant gun, which he attached to a hand-carved stock and filled with bullets of his own manufacture.

Bill Bailey maintained a pioneering spirit all his life. Two years before his death he left on a trip to Canada, assuring incredulous friends that he would come back heavy with gold. After a panning expedition of three months, he returned, pockets bulging, true to his word.

⇥ **29**th ⇤

Albert Hofmann, b. 1906, d. 2008

Albert Hofmann, who has died aged 102, synthesised lysergic acid diethylamide (LSD) in 1938 and became the first person in the world to experience a full-blown 'acid trip'.

That was on 19 April 1943 – a day which became known among aficionados as 'Bicycle Day', as it was while cycling home from his laboratory that Hofmann experienced the most intense symptoms.

The first effects, which he experienced forty minutes after swallowing 0.25 of a milligram, and which he noted down in his laboratory journal, included 'dizziness, feeling of anxiety, visual distortions, symptoms of paralysis, desire to laugh'. But then, unable to write any more, he asked his assistant to take him home by bicycle.

'On the way home, my condition began to assume threatening forms. Everything in my field of vision wavered and was distorted as if seen in a curved mirror. I also had the sensation of being unable to move from the spot. Nevertheless, my assistant later told me that we had travelled very rapidly.'

Back home, when a friendly neighbour brought round some milk, he perceived her as a 'malevolent, insidious witch' wearing 'a lurid mask'. After six hours of highs and lows, the effects subsided.

The drug company Sandoz, where Hofmann worked, gave his new substance the trade name Delysid and began sending samples to psychiatric researchers. By 1965 more than 2,000 papers had been published offering hope for a range of conditions from drug and alcohol addiction to mental illnesses of various kinds. But the fact that the chemical was cheap and easy to make left it open to abuse, and from the late 1950s onwards, promoted by Dr Timothy Leary and others, LSD became the recreational drug of choice for Western youth.

An outbreak of moral panic, combined with a number of accidents involving people jumping to their deaths off high buildings in the belief that they could fly, led governments around the world to ban LSD.

Hofmann was disappointed. He remained convinced that the drug had the potential to counter the psychological problems induced by 'materialism, alienation from nature through industrialisation and increasing urbanisation, lack of satisfaction in professional employment in a mechanised, lifeless working world, ennui and purposelessness in wealthy, saturated society, and lack of a religious, nurturing, and meaningful philosophical foundation of life'.

Albert Hofmann was born at Baden, Switzerland, on 11 January 1906, the eldest of four children of a factory toolmaker. Having graduated from Zurich University with a degree in Chemistry in 1929, he took a doctorate on the gastro-intestinal juice of the vineyard snail. After leaving university he went to work for Sandoz Pharmaceuticals. His interest in synthesising LSD initially derived from the hope that it might be useful as a circulatory and respiratory stimulant.

In his autobiography Hofmann described meeting Leary in 1971 in the snack bar at Lausanne railway station. Hofmann began by voicing his regret that Leary's experiments had effectively killed off academic research into LSD and took Leary to task for encouraging its recreational use among young people. Leary was unabashed, and maintained that American teenagers were able to make up their own minds.

Hofmann continued to work at Sandoz until 1971, when he retired as director of research for the Department of Natural Products. In addition to his discovery of LSD, he was also the first to synthesise psilocybin (the active constituent of 'magic mushrooms') in 1958; and he discovered the hallucinogenic principles of Ololiuqui (Morning Glory).

In retirement Hofmann served as a member of the Nobel Prize Committee. In 1988 the Albert Hofmann Foundation was established 'to assemble and maintain an international library and archive devoted to the study of human consciousness and related fields'.

⁂ **30**th ⁂

Venetia Phair, b. 1918, d. 2009

Venetia Phair, who has died aged ninety, had the distinction of being the only woman to have named a planet.

On the morning of 14 March 1930 she was having breakfast at the house in Oxford in which she lived with her grandfather, Falconer Madan, the retired librarian at the Bodleian, when he drew her attention to an article in *The Times* which noted that a newly found frozen planet had yet to be named.

Being keen on Greek and Roman myths, eleven-year-old Venetia suggested that Pluto, the Roman god of the underworld who could render himself invisible, would make a good name for the dark and remote world. The idea so impressed her grandfather that he immediately promised to put it to his friend Herbert Hall Turner, Professor of Astronomy at Oxford University.

Turner was in London that day at a meeting of the Royal Astronomical Society, where the question of nomenclature was being anxiously discussed; once Madan had tracked him down, Turner agreed that 'Pluto' was an excellent choice for the ice-covered world and undertook to forward it by telegram to the Lowell Observatory in Arizona.

The astronomers there – including 24-year-old Clyde W. Tombaugh, who had made the actual discovery – were delighted with Venetia's suggestion. For one thing, Pluto was one of the few big names in classical mythology that had not already been used.

Once Turner had cabled her suggestion to the American astronomers, Venetia heard nothing further for more than a month. At last, on 1 May 1930, the name Pluto was formally adopted. As a reward, Madan gave Venetia a white £5 note – a considerable sum at the time. By coincidence, Venetia's great-uncle Henry Madan, a science master at Eton, had, in 1878, successfully suggested the names Phobos and Deimos for the moons of Mars.

Venetia Katharine Douglas Burney was born on 11 July 1918, the daughter of the Reverend Charles Fox Burney. He died when she was six, and she went to live with her maternal grandparents in north Oxford.

She always treasured the press cuttings he had collected about her moment of fame, which proved more enduring than she suspected. In 1987 the asteroid 6235 Burney was named in her honour, as was a student-built instrument on board the *New Horizons* spacecraft during its mission to Pluto in 2006; the American space agency NASA invited her to the launch at Cape Canaveral, but she declined on account of her age.

A highly intelligent, self-effacing girl, Venetia was educated at Downe House, and read Mathematics at Newnham College, Cambridge. During the war she qualified as a chartered accountant, and in the late 1950s switched to teaching economics and maths, first at Gloucester House, Sutton, and later at Wallington county girls' school, Surrey, retiring in the mid-1980s.

MAY

⇒ 1st ⇐

Sir Henry Cooper, b. 1934, d. 2011

Sir Henry Cooper, who has died aged seventy-six, was the most popular and respected British boxer of the post-war era.

Cooper was the only man ever to win three Lonsdale belts, awarded for three successful defences of the British heavyweight title he held for twelve years. His embodiment of the virtues of courage and modesty endeared him to millions of fellow Englishmen as 'Our 'Enery'.

His most celebrated fight took place before a crowd of 35,000 at Wembley in June 1963. Cassius Clay, not yet world champion, had predicted he would win inside five rounds. Cooper had acquired a reputation for cutting easily, and when blood appeared around his eye in the third round, Clay's bragging seemed justified.

But the American had seriously underestimated his opponent. At the end of the next round Cooper caught Clay with his celebrated left hook – ''Enery's 'ammer'. It was the first time Clay had ever been knocked down and he was saved only by the bell, later remarking: 'Cooper hit me so hard my ancestors in Africa felt it.' His canny trainer, Angelo Dundee, made the most of a split in one of Clay's gloves, giving him time to recover. When he emerged he was able to pepper Cooper's eye with the torn glove, and as blood poured down Cooper's face the referee ended the fight.

When Cooper challenged him for the world title three years later, in May 1966, the returning Muhammad Ali paid due respect. In the event his mobility proved too much for Cooper who, cut by the heel of a glove, was again forced to retire, honour intact. Cooper later fought the former heavyweight champion Floyd Patterson, but was knocked out in the fourth round. It was to be his last defeat until 1971, when he retired after losing to Joe Bugner.

Henry Cooper was born in London on 3 May 1934, twenty minutes before his twin brother, George. Their father, a tram driver, was an amateur boxer, while their grandfather had been a bare-knuckle fighter; even their grandmother was said to have boxed like a man.

Henry was brought up at Bellingham, south-east London, and attended Athelney Road school. During the Second World War he and George were evacuated to Sussex. From the age of nine the boys were learning to box, and at fifteen they joined the noted Eltham club.

On leaving school, plastering work developed Henry's physique and he won his first competition at seventeen. Cooper was to win seventy-three of his eighty-four amateur fights, although he lost the first four. Years later he blamed his mother for plying him with bread pudding before those bouts.

He represented Britain at the Helsinki Olympics but lost his first fight. He and George then joined the Royal Army Ordnance Corps for National Service. Both were, unsurprisingly, sent to the so-called Boxers' Battalion, which each year dominated the Army Championships. The Coopers spent rather more time in the gym than on guard duty.

They turned professional in 1954. From the first their manager, Jim Wicks, realised their publicity potential, even televising their signing to him. Wicks was soon content to trust Henry's judgment as to his training regime and ideal fighting weight, for the 6ft tall, 13st 7lb fighter favoured suppleness over bulk.

Cooper had a difficult two years from September 1956, winning only one of seven fights. An open-air challenge for the European heavyweight title was lost to Ingemar Johansson, and Cooper considered quitting boxing. But in 1958 he outpunched Zora Folley, ranked third in the world, to restore his confidence, and in 1959 he won his first British and Empire titles, from Brian London, in fifteen hard rounds.

Cooper's victories were built on technique, aggression and his ferocious left hook, which some observers believe to be the finest of any heavyweight. Although he led with his right, he was naturally left-handed and it was this that lent the blow such power. At its best it travelled only a few inches, yet it landed with a force of four and a half tons. When filmed it proved to be forty times too fast for the eye to see.

The model of gentlemanly courtesy out of the ring, Cooper was streetwise if never dirty within it. He was particularly adept at hitting opponents as they came out of a clinch. He was not a strategic fighter, liking to take a fight as it developed rather than have a set plan.

In 1961 Cooper won the first of his Lonsdale belts, but then lost to Folley. Had he won that fight he would have taken on the waning Floyd Patterson for the world title. He was not at his best against Folley, being hampered by an injury to his left elbow suffered years earlier when he was plastering. It was to trouble him until he retired.

Cooper won his second belt shortly before he fought Clay, and in 1964 claimed the European title for the first time. His elbow injury, however, prevented him from defending it, and the title was stripped from him. The next year he enjoyed knocking out Chip Johnson in their first round – Johnson had effectively ended George Cooper's boxing career the previous year. Then, in 1967, Henry was awarded his unprecedented third belt after defeating Billy Walker.

He regained his European title in 1968 and successfully defended it the next year in the roughest fight of his career. The Italian Piero Tomasoni delivered several blows below the belt, and after the fight Cooper's groin protector resembled a crushed can. The offending Tomasoni was dispatched with a hook that lifted his feet from the canvas.

Cooper had already decided to retire when he lost to Joe Bugner on a controversial points decision in March 1971. He had won forty and lost fourteen of his professional contests, with one drawn.

In retirement Cooper steadily added to the money he had made from his fights. He became a familiar face on television, both as a commentator and as a promoter of everything from cereal to paint. For one brand of cologne he famously urged the nation to 'splash it all over'.

He was a keen advocate of boxing for boys as a means of acquiring self-discipline. Baroness Summerskill once pointed to his battered nose when arguing against the sport. 'Boxing's my excuse,' countered Cooper, 'What's yours?'

A staunch monarchist, Cooper's dignity and charm made him a great favourite with the Royal Family. He was appointed OBE in 1969 and knighted in 2000. He was much loved by the British public, and was twice voted BBC Sports Personality of the Year, in 1967 and 1970.

Henry Cooper married, in 1960, Albina Genepri, an Italian waitress at his favourite restaurant; they had two sons. He adopted her Catholic faith and it was an extremely happy marriage, though she could never bring herself to watch him fight.

⇜ 2nd ⇝

Osama bin Laden, b. 1957, d. 2011

Osama bin Laden, who has been killed by American forces aged fifty-four, was the world's most wanted international terrorist and the presumed architect of the shocking events of 11 September 2001, when hijacked jets ploughed into the twin towers of the World Trade Center in New York and the Pentagon in Washington, killing thousands of people.

Bin Laden became the poster boy for Islamist anti-Western militancy. Yet he had not always been seen as an enemy of the West. During the war in the 1980s to drive the Soviet Union out of Afghanistan, he and his mujahideen allies were feted as freedom fighters against communist repression. His organisation, al-Qaeda, a loose coalition founded in the dying days of that conflict, had initially set its sights on fomenting jihad in 'ungodly' Muslim states.

Bin Laden's initial aim was to bring all Muslim lands and holy places into a 'Caliphate' under strict Sharia (Islamic law), and in the 1990s extremists trained in al-Qaeda camps became a destabilising factor throughout the Middle East. Beyond that, they fought in Bosnia, Chechnya, Tajikistan, Kashmir and even the Philippines.

The road to 9/11 began in 1990 when an 800,000-strong American-led force arrived in Saudi Arabia following the invasion of Kuwait by the Iraqi dictator Saddam Hussein. To bin Laden, America's presence represented a violation of Islam's holiest sanctuaries and proof of the irredeemable corruption of the ruling Al Saud dynasty. As a result he vowed to 'liberate the Holy Places' in a jihad against the American superpower and its acolytes in the region.

And yet there was nothing inevitable about 9/11. Before the attacks on America Al-Qaeda had left a trail of clues that could have been followed up – but were not. So the story of Osama bin Laden is also a story of bureaucratic bungling in the American intelligence services, and of tactical miscalculation and political failure at the highest reaches of the American administration.

Osama bin Mohammed bin Laden was born in Riyadh, Saudi Arabia, on 10 March 1957. His father, Mohammed bin Awad bin Laden, had started out as an illiterate dockside labourer in Yemen before buying a place on a camel caravan to the newly created kingdom of Saudi Arabia. There he worked as a porter, saved money, and founded a construction company. During the 1950s he underbid other contractors to work on the palaces of King Abdel-Aziz al Saud.

He became close to the king, and he and his family grew extremely rich even by Saudi standards. Osama (which means 'young lion' in Arabic) was the seventeenth of Mohammed's fifty-two (or fifty-three) children. His Syrian-born mother, Alia Ghanem, was Mohammed's tenth wife.

When he was four or five his father divorced his mother and awarded her to one of his company executives, Mohammad al-Attas, by whom she had several more children. Soon afterwards Mohammed bin Laden died in a plane crash on his way to marry his twenty-third wife. His estate passed to his children in the form of shares in the family company. Estimates of Osama's share range from $35 million (the figure given by sources close to the family) to $250 million, as cited by American officials in 1991.

While most of Osama's siblings were sent to Lebanon to be educated, Osama remained in Jeddah and enrolled at al-Thager, Jeddah's best school. He was shy, immature and not particularly bright, but at the age of fourteen seems to have experienced some sort of religious awakening, possibly influenced by a charismatic Syrian gym teacher who belonged to the Muslim Brotherhood. As a result he stopped watching the Western films he loved and refused to wear Western dress.

His religious views hardened at King Abdel Aziz University in Jeddah, where he studied Economics and Public Administration during the late 1970s. There he was inspired by the writings of Sayyid Qutb, a major figure in the Muslim Brotherhood and in radical Islam. Qutb, who was executed by the Egyptian authorities in 1966, argued that modern societies, including most Muslim ones, are in 'Jahiliyyah', the state of ignorance that existed in pre-Islamic Arabia before the perfect revelations of the Koran. True Muslims, Qutb said, must free themselves from the 'clutches of jahili society' by jihad.

Bin Laden dropped out of university early to work for the family company, but in 1979 he found the cause that was to change his life when the Soviet Union launched an invasion of Afghanistan. 'I was enraged and went there at once,' he claimed, though some accounts suggest that he did not go until 1984.

In 1984, with Abdullah Azzam, a charismatic Palestinian theologian, he established the Maktab al-Khadamat (Services Office) to organise paramilitary training camps in Afghanistan for international recruits for the Afghan war. Osama bin Laden emerged as a talented fundraiser, persuading wealthy individuals, including members of the Saudi royal family, to contribute to the cause. He brought in equipment from his family's firm to build tunnels, camps and hideaways in the mountains. In 1986 he established his own training camp for Persian Gulf Arabs called al-Masadah, or the Lion's Den.

Arab mythology holds that the 'Arab Afghans' played a decisive role in the struggle against the Soviet Union. In fact there were never more than about 2,000 Arabs fighting at any one time – compared with about 250,000 Afghan fighters and 125,000 Soviet troops. They were a ragbag, ranging from disaffected radicals and suicidal zealots to rich kids looking for adventure. Journalists covering the conflict saw them as a curious sideshow, set apart from the other players in the conflict by their obsession with martyrdom and their indiscipline. Many Afghan fighters regarded them with barely concealed contempt (during one fracas in 1986, they asked bin Laden to withdraw because his forces were more of a hindrance than a help).

By the end of the war bin Laden's politics had moved in a more radical direction. In around 1986 he had met Ayman al-Zawahiri, a member of Egyptian Islamic Jihad. Zawahiri had moved to Peshawar after spending several years in a Cairo jail, from which he had emerged embittered, determined and short of cash. Bin Laden was exactly what he had been looking for.

Under Zawahiri's influence bin Laden envisioned an all-Arab legion which would eventually wage jihad in Saudi Arabia and Egypt; Azzam strongly opposed making war against fellow-Muslims, limiting his ambitions to ousting the Soviets from Afghanistan. When, on 24 November 1989, Azzam and two of his sons were killed in a car bomb as they were driving to a mosque in Peshawar, there were suspicions that either bin Laden or Zawahiri had ordered the attack, though there was never any definite proof.

In 1988, with the Soviets in full retreat, a meeting took place in the Afghan town of Khost at which it was agreed to establish a new organisation that would wage jihad beyond the borders of Afghanistan. The organisation came to be called al-Qaeda ('the Base') and was conceived as a loose affiliation among individual mujahideen and jihadist groups dominated by Zawahiri's Islamic Jihad. The ultimate leader, however, was Osama bin Laden, who held the purse strings.

When bin Laden returned to Jeddah and to the family business in autumn 1989, he was hailed as the conquering hero who had humbled a mighty superpower. Hoping to build on his celebrity, he approached Prince Turki Al Faisal, then head of Saudi Intelligence, with a plan to overthrow the Marxist regime in Yemen. The Saudi government refused and was worried enough to withdraw bin Laden's passport.

But it was America's involvement in the Gulf War that turned bin Laden into an implacable opponent of the Saudi royal family. The Saudis were not disposed to tolerate his calls to insurrection, and quickly acted against him. In 1991 he was expelled from the country, and in 1994 his citizenship was revoked for 'irresponsible behaviour'. Together with his family and a large band of followers, bin Laden moved to Khartoum in Sudan, where he was joined by Zawahiri and his followers in Islamic Jihad.

In the early 1990s al-Qaeda-trained fighters were involved in a number of attacks around the world, including the 1993 World Trade Center bombing. But by the mid-1990s very little had come of them; there had been a series of high-profile defections and, as most of his business ventures lost money, for the first time in his life bin Laden found himself short of cash. Though his hatred for America remained undiminished, he reportedly told friends that he was thinking of quitting al-Qaeda to become a farmer.

In May 1996 bin Laden chartered a private jet and returned to Afghanistan, where he was greeted by a delegation sent by the Taliban's leader Mullah Omar. The Taliban gave bin Laden a house in Kandahar, a force of bodyguards and the title 'Sheikh', though he was not a cleric.

From then on, bin Laden began to lay out his case against America in a series of fatwas faxed to the outside world. These began in August 1996 with 'The Declaration of Jihad on the Americans Occupying the Country of the Two Sacred Places' and culminated in 1998 with 'World Islamic Front Against Jews and Crusaders', which ordered Muslims to kill American civilians anywhere in the world.

The fatwa received little attention until August 1998, when hundreds of people were killed in simultaneous car bomb explosions at the American embassies in Dar es Salaam and Nairobi. The attacks resulted in the FBI placing bin Laden on its '10 Most Wanted' list.

The Taliban refused to hand bin Laden over to the Americans despite punitive sanctions imposed by the UN; but with a $5 million reward on his head, bin Laden could not afford to take chances. He led a peripatetic life, moving frequently between several bases in Afghanistan. Three attempts on his life were reportedly made, but all ended with the deaths of his would-be assassins.

Bin Laden's goal in striking the American embassies was to lure the Americans into that same trap the Soviets had fallen into: Afghanistan. When the attacks failed to provoke the massive retaliation he craved, he set to work to create an outrage that no one could ignore.

The three years between the embassy attacks and 9/11 were notable for a series of bureaucratic and diplomatic blunders by those whose business it was to prevent another attack. From phone-tapping activities, the CIA knew that high-level al-Qaeda operatives had held a meeting in Malaysia in January 2000, and, later, that two of them had entered the United States. Both men turned out to be part of the team that hijacked the planes on 9/11, yet the CIA failed to inform the FBI, which might have been able to locate the men and break up the plot, until it was too late.

A month after 9/11, the United States and its allies launched an invasion of Afghanistan with the stated purpose of capturing bin Laden, destroying al-Qaeda and removing the Taliban regime which had given them sanctuary.

The initial attack removed the Taliban from power, but was less successful in locating bin Laden. In December, anti-Taliban tribal militia, backed by American and British air power, launched an attack on caves in the mountain region of Tora Bora, where bin Laden was thought to be hiding. When US ground troops arrived fourteen days later they discovered more than a hundred bodies, and they were able to identify eighteen of them as top al-Qaeda lieutenants. But of Zawahiri and bin Laden there was no sign.

Over the next few years various claims were made as to his location, though none was definitely proved. The consensus was that he and his followers had slipped away into the tribal areas along the rugged border between Afghanistan and Pakistan. And it was here that they began to regroup as the US-led coalition became bogged down in a war against a resurgent Taliban and in Iraq. The 7 July bomb attacks in London in 2005 and the discovery of a plot in August 2006 to blow up ten aircraft en route from Britain to the US provided incontrovertible evidence that al-Qaeda was back, and that it was prepared to go after hard targets.

Zawahiri was the mastermind behind this process, and by 2006 he was reported to have taken over operational command of al-Qaeda, leaving bin Laden as the organisation's charismatic figurehead. Zawahiri reformed the group around a core of some one hundred Arab trainers – experts in explosives, finances, communications, military training, urban warfare and propaganda. In 2006 Afghanistan saw 139 suicide bombings, compared with twenty-seven in 2005.

There were several rumours of bin Laden's death. Some had him among the 73,000 victims of the Pakistan earthquake in 2005. There were suggestions at various times that he might have died of kidney failure (Western intelligence reports claimed that he was on a dialysis machine after suffering kidney damage, possibly as the result of an attempt to poison him).

But when George W. Bush left office in 2009, bin Laden was still at large and still dangerous. In the end it was Bush's successor Barack Obama who, in the early hours of 2 May 2011, announced bin Laden's death at the hands of US forces in a targeted attack on a compound just thirty-five miles from the Pakistani capital Islamabad.

⊰ **3rd** ⊱

Christine Jorgensen, b. 1926, d. 1989

Christine Jorgensen, who has died at San Clemente, California, aged sixty-two, became a woman in 1952 as a result of the world's first legal sex-change operation.

She was born George Jorgensen in the Bronx, New York, in 1926. George's childhood was troubled by envy of his elder sister's pursuits and by his male peers shouting such epithets as 'sissy' at him.

Acting on a tip-off, Jorgensen left for Denmark in 1950 'when life as George was no longer tolerable'. He interrupted the pioneering Professor Christian Hamburger at his country retreat outside Copenhagen, and the professor agreed to treat him free of charge.

Christine never married, despite 'dozens of offers'. She confessed: 'Men are wary of me – and I'm wary of the ones who aren't.'

Sir John Junor, b. 1919, d. 1997

Sir John Junor, who has died aged seventy-eight, was editor of the *Sunday Express* for the thirty-two years to 1986, and as a columnist won a keen following for the blunt manner in which he wrote.

His pieces, and especially the abusive passages, profited from being read out aloud in Junor's rich Scottish tones. He dismissed homosexuals as 'poofs', 'powderpuffs' and 'pansies', and expressed the view that Aids was the punishment ordained by God for sodomy. Other categories which aroused his wrath included Anglican bishops – 'trendy old women'; the Irish – 'wouldn't you rather,' he demanded after the Brighton bombing, 'admit to being a pig than to being Irish?'; the Press Council – 'po-faced, pompous, pin-striped, humourless twits'; and the Greenham Common women – 'sluts'.

Taxed with racism, Junor would point out that the President of Gambia was a friend. But he did not disdain general principles: 'Never trust a bearded man,' he would tell subordinates, or 'Only poofs drink white wine'. Concerned by the rising crime statistics, he wanted to hear more of 'the whack of birch on bare backsides'.

Particular *betes noires* were Lord Denning – an 'unctuous old humbug'; Lord Attenborough – 'ancient, affected, side-whiskered trendy'; the Archbishop of Canterbury Dr Runcie – 'a pathetic old man' who deserved 'a kick up the backside'; and the Bishop of Durham – 'a really nasty piece of work, an evil man', whose ordination had provoked the Almighty into hurling a thunderbolt at York Minster.

Viscount Whitelaw 'would not be two-faced if there were a third one available'; Neil Kinnock was 'a weak, wet Welsh windbag'; and President Bush appeared as 'a neutered old tabby'.

'Pass the sick bag, Alice' was the stock conclusion to his reflections on the passing scene. Alternatively, 'aren't there times when you truly feel like pulling the duvet over your head and turning your face towards the wall?'

On the positive side, Junor believed that Britain was 'the greatest nation in the world', though he also nursed a surprising weakness for the French. Mrs Thatcher, the Princess of Wales and Selina Scott all aroused his passionate enthusiasm.

But Junor's greatest strength as a columnist was that his contempt for the chattering classes was even more intense than theirs for him, so that he never cared a scrap about provoking their disdain. Nor did he make cowardly calculations of self-interest. No good journalist, he used to say, should ever go anywhere without his resignation in his pocket.

For it was rage that drove him. Aware of this, he always carried a tape recorder so that he could catch his fury on the wing. The style that resulted was once described as that of a Rotarian on Ecstasy.

John Donald Brown Junor was born in a Glasgow tenement on 15 January 1919. His father was foreman in a steel roofing works, but it was his mother, a fanatical whist player, who was the dynamo of the family. She pushed her three sons to work hard, so that John and his brothers (one became a schoolmaster, the other a doctor) all went from state school to university.

Junor read English Literature at Glasgow University, then joined the Navy as a midshipman (RNR), serving in the armed merchant cruiser *Canton*, a converted P&O liner. Later he transferred to the Fleet Air Arm.

His training revealed that he was by no means a natural pilot. Yet he survived a critical moment when his plane's directional instruments failed in pitch darkness. There was nothing to do but to pray, 'my mouth quite dry'. Salvation duly arrived in the shape of another plane, which guided him in to land. 'I came to the conclusion,' Junor said, 'that someone up there had decided I had some purpose still to serve in life.'

In 1945 Junor was demobbed as a lieutenant and in 1947 joined the *Daily Express* as a reporter under Arthur Christiansen. He was Crossbencher on the *Sunday Express*, and then assistant editor of the *Daily Express*. In 1953 he moved to the *Evening Standard* as deputy editor, and the next year became editor of the *Sunday Express*.

Under his leadership the paper notably failed to move with the times. Well into the 1980s there were contemptuous references to artists and 'long-haired' pop stars, and advertisements that seemed to concentrate heavily on garden sheds.

᙭ 4th ᙭

Brigadier the Reverend Charles 'John' Harris,
b. 1896, d. 1996

Brigadier the Reverend Charles 'John' Harris, who has died aged ninety-nine, fought in both World Wars and took part in the cavalry charge on horses at the Battle of Cambrai in November 1917.

Although the British achieved a breakthrough with tanks at the start of the Battle of Cambrai, the Germans successfully counter-attacked and drove them back. Haig had kept a large force of cavalry in reserve to exploit the expected success of the tanks; and even though the initial advantage was lost, Harris's regiment, the 2nd Lancers (Gardner's Horse, Indian Army) was ordered nonetheless to charge the German position. As the Lancers advanced on a shallow valley, they came under German machine-gun fire from right and left. They suffered 100 casualties, including their Colonel who was killed early, and came to a halt after 3,000 yards, in a wired sunken road.

In June 1941, then aged forty-five, Harris took command of the 2nd Lancers with orders to reconstitute it as an Indian Armoured Car Regiment. It was very badly cut up at Bir Hacheim when the British armour proved no match for the Germans.

Towards the end of the war he joined General Slim's 14th Army HQ in Western Bengal, but after contracting pneumonia and malaria simultaneously, he was evacuated to England on a cargo ship carrying onions.

Harris left the Army in 1946, entered Ridley Hall, Cambridge, and after eighteen months was ordained. His clerical duties began with a curacy at Dorchester, where he was chaplain to the prison.

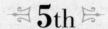

5th

Major John Howard, b. 1912, d. 1999

Major John Howard, who has died aged eighty-six, was awarded a DSO in June 1944 for leading the successful glider-born assault which captured the bridges over the Caen Canal (Pegasus Bridge) and the River Orne (Horsa Bridge) at Bénouville.

Possession of the bridges was vital to the second phase of General Montgomery's plan, not only to protect the left flank of the Normandy bridgehead and enable reinforcements to reach the main airborne forces, but also to provide an exit route when the moment for an armoured break-out past Caen should arrive. But the Germans had already wired the bridges for demolition as part of their defensive plan, so it was essential to seize them before the charges could be blown.

Shortly before 11 p.m. on D-Day minus One, 5 June 1944, Howard and four platoons of the Oxfordshire and Buckinghamshire Light Infantry, part of 6th Airborne Division, packed themselves into six Horsa gliders ready to be towed across the Channel by Halifax bombers.

The operation went almost faultlessly. At six minutes past midnight, Howard and his men landed silently fifty yards away from the canal bridge just outside the small hamlet of Bénouville near Caen. On arriving at the bridge they took a German pillbox by surprise; the two sentries later told him they had been paralysed with fear when they saw the blackened faces and guns of the assault force. Within ten minutes both bridges had been captured.

They then held the bridges, until joined by men from the 7th Battalion of the 5th Parachute Regiment. They were relieved at 1.30 p.m. on 6 June by Commandos led by Lord Lovat, who apologised for being two and a half minutes late.

Howard then moved his men on to take part in the fighting around Escoville, where a sniper's bullet went through his helmet but only grazed his skull. Later he was wounded by shrapnel in his back, although he was not aware of it at the time. Covered in blood, he was thought by his comrades to be dead. Told by a doctor he must be evacuated, he lay on a stretcher, but became so bored (the medics being extremely busy) that he got up, recovered his shirt and went back to his unit, which had now lost nearly half its men.

John Howard was born in Camden Town on 8 December 1912, the eldest of nine children. His father was a cooper. Although he won a scholarship which would have taken him on to further education, he had to leave school at fourteen to work as a stockbroker's runner, though he continued his education by attending evening classes until the firm collapsed in 1931.

As jobs were hard to find, he then enlisted in the King's Shropshire Light Infantry, where he rose to the rank of sergeant. At the end of his military engagement in 1938 he joined the City of Oxford police, but in 1939 he was recalled to the KSLI, was promoted rapidly and became Acting Regimental Sergeant Major.

He was then selected for officer training, and after the Officer Cadet Training Unit (OCTU), was commissioned into the Oxford and Buckinghamshire Light Infantry.

Two months after the mission to capture the Bénouville bridges, when on leave in England, Howard was badly injured when the jeep he was driving was hit by a queue-jumping truck approaching an American convoy. His right hip and both his legs were smashed, and he was invalided out of the Army.

After the war, he worked briefly with National Savings, and then for the Ministry of Agriculture. In 1962, Howard's role in the war was made famous in the film *The Longest Day*, in which he was portrayed by the actor Richard Todd.

He returned regularly to Bénouville on the anniversary of D-Day to lay a wreath at the site where the gliders landed and to host a dinner for his men. He was present in 1995 when a bust representing him was unveiled there.

Reflecting in old age on the events of 1944, Howard remarked: 'We were given a job to do on the day and we did it. We were very proud to do that job and if I held that bridge as long as I did, well, I bloody well did it because it was my job.'

❧ 6th ❧

Marlene Dietrich, b. 1901, d. 1992

Marlene Dietrich, the sensational German-born film star and singer who has died aged ninety, was one of the great names of twentieth-century entertainment.

Husky-voiced and fair-haired, with heavily lidded eyes, she displayed a cool 'don't care' expression of world-weary disillusion. In an age when stardom is transitory, she proved enduring. Blonde, Teutonic, with high-chiselled cheekbones, she mesmerised her audiences by innuendo, letting her vacant eyes drift over the room, pulling in her heavily magenta-ed lower lip, displaying all the artifice of languor.

As a singer she was a polished performer, alternatively lazy in mood and powerfully aggressive, almost paramilitary. Her delivery was both breathy and erotic and she manipulated the microphone in a manner nothing less than sexual.

No one who saw her spectacular entrance down the winding staircase of London's Cafe de Paris in the 1950s is ever likely to forget it. Sparkling from head to foot with no shortage of white mink, she did not so much descend as glide down like a serpent, disdainful, glamorous, a little threatening.

Marlene Dietrich was born in Berlin on 27 December 1901, the younger daughter of a Prussian officer, Louis Dietrich, and his wife, Josephine Felsing. She was keenly musical and learned the violin. From 1906 to 1918, she attended the Auguste Viktoria School for Girls in Berlin. At the end of the First World War, she was enrolled in the Berlin Hochschule fur Musik but stayed only for a few months.

In 1919 she entered the Weimar Konservatorium to study the violin. She hoped to become a professional violinist but a damaged wrist destroyed this hope. In

1920, Marlene was back in Berlin. The next year she auditioned for the Max Reinhardt Drama School and played the widow in *The Taming of the Shrew*. A string of minor parts followed. She lived in virtual penury, worked in a glove factory and acted and danced. It was a depressing way of life.

But in 1930 she was discovered by the Viennese director, Josef von Sternberg, who detected in her the raw sexuality of a seductive vamp and brought her to fame in his film *The Blue Angel*. Von Sternberg transformed her from a rather brawny girl with the slight air of a female impersonator into a creature of glamour.

Originally Dietrich had been rejected for the part as 'not at all bad from the rear but do we not also need a face?' But then von Sternberg saw her by chance in the Georg Kaiser play *ZweiKrawatten*. She was gazing bored at the action on stage and he was drawn to her disdain and poise.

Despite her success, her contract was not renewed so she signed with Paramount and emigrated to Hollywood. There she made several memorable films, again for von Sternberg.

Morocco, in which she played a cabaret star in love with a French legionnaire (Gary Cooper), included a scene in which Dietrich, dressed as a man, plants an unchaste kiss on a girl's mouth in a cafe. *Dishonored* followed, in which she played an Austrian spy, who fixed her make-up in the reflection of an officer's sabre and applied her lipstick while a German officer ranted at her. The firing squad then shot her dead.

In 1939 came her energetic portrayal of Frenchy, the Wild West saloon keeper in *Destry Rides Again*. This classic included Dietrich's spirited wrestling with James Stewart, and she gave tongue to the evocative song 'The Boys in the Back Room', while bestriding the bar.

In the early years of the Second World War, Hitler went to great lengths to try to lure Dietrich to his cause. But in 1943 she assumed the honorary rank of Colonel in the American Army and made radio broadcasts and personal appearances on behalf of the American war effort. In 1944 she joined the United States Overseas Tour and paid extensive visits to the Allied troops in Europe.

Dressed in an elegant version of military uniform, her mission was to boost morale, to entertain and to encourage Allied victory. There is film footage of Dietrich greeting the Fifth Army with a jaunty 'Hello, Boys'. She described her war-work as 'the only important work I've ever done'.

After the conflict she made many further films, including Billy Wilder's *A Foreign Affair*, and Hitchcock's *Stage Fright*. She also appeared in *Touch of Evil* for Orson Welles and Stanley Kramer's *Judgment at Nuremberg* opposite Spencer Tracy. In 1956 she contributed a memorable cameo to Mike Todd's *Around the World in 80 Days*, perched on a stool, Destry-style.

Dietrich also ran her own radio spy series, *Cafe Istanbul*, on America's ABC Network. But it was as a singer that her later career blossomed. By now in her fifties, she began by compering a Madison Square benefit arranged by her daughter. Out of a wish not to sit on an elephant, she took the role of ringmaster in top hat, tailcoat and tights. This white-tie look was to be a lasting trademark.

Dietrich made her debut at the Sahara, Las Vegas, in 1953 and the next year took

London by storm at the Café de Paris. Thereafter she made long tours all over the world, invariably accompanied by Burt Bacharach.

In 1967 she made her debut on Broadway. Dietrich's one-woman show carried on until the late 1970s when accidents recurred with startling frequency. She broke so many bones that comedians used to mimic her, singing 'Falling off stage again ...' Finally, she broke her thigh in Sydney in 1976 and gave up.

It was Kenneth Tynan who best summed up her appeal: 'She has sex but no particular gender. Her ways are mannish: the characters she played loved power and wore slacks and they never had headaches or hysterics. They were also quite undomesticated. Dietrich's masculinity appeals to women and her sexuality to men.'

⚜ 7th ⚜

Gunter Sachs, b. 1932, d. 2011

Gunter Sachs, who has died aged seventy-eight, was a multi-millionaire German playboy, scion of the Opel motor dynasty, European bobsleigh champion of 1958 and the third husband of Brigitte Bardot.

Having achieved celebrity status after a relationship with Soraya Esfandiary, the former Queen consort of the Shah of Iran, Sachs first met Brigitte Bardot at San Tropez in May 1966. She was drinking champagne with friends in a bar when she spotted the handsome German with striking blue eyes: 'I thought he was magnificent,' she recalled. 'I was hypnotised ... he had the same Rolls as me! The same model, the same colour. In fact, the same everything!' The next day Sachs paid for a helicopter to fly over her Côte d'Azur home, La Madrague, and shower it with thousands of red roses. 'It's not every day that a man drops a tonne of roses in your garden,' she later wrote.

Domenico Chioccetti, b. 1910, d. 1999

Domenico Chioccetti, who has died aged eighty-eight, was one of the band of Italian prisoners-of-war that during the Second World War turned two Nissen huts into a remarkable chapel on the isle of Lamb Holm, in the Orkneys.

Chioccetti, a painter and decorator by trade, was captured by the Eighth Army in North Africa and with several hundred of his compatriots was despatched to the Orkneys. In late 1943, the prisoners of Camp 60, housed on the bleak and windswept island of Lamb Holm, approached the commandant to ask if they might build a chapel such as might be seen in any Italian hill village.

They were given two huts which they joined end to end, adding a portico with concrete pillars, a pediment, and a decorated gable with belfry, white-painted finials and a head of Christ stained red to resemble terracotta.

Inside, they pierced the end wall with lancet windows and then covered the tin of the hut with plasterboard, which Chioccetti painted to look like brick and carved stone, adding for good measure a dado of trompe l'oeil marble. An altar and altar rail were constructed of cement, while wood from a shipwreck and scrap iron were used to make candelabra and an elaborate rood screen. The prisoners paid for altar cloths out of their cigarette money.

The paintings in the chapel were Chioccetti's particular contribution. The low vault he frescoed with portraits of the four evangelists as well as seraphim and cherubim. Behind the altar he painted a picture of the Virgin and Child based on Nicolo Barabino's *Madonna of the Olives*, a postcard of which Chioccetti carried with him throughout the war.

The Christ Child holds an olive branch, while a cherub carries the badge of Moena (Chioccetti's birthplace) which depicts Christ guiding a boat through a storm. Outside the chapel, the prisoners built a statue of St George slaying the Dragon, constructed from barbed wire and concrete. All of it was done as a labour of love after their working day had ended. So committed was Chioccetti to the venture that when, in 1945, the prisoners were released from Camp 60, he stayed on for several weeks to complete his work.

The chapel is now a listed building and Mass is celebrated there during the summer; last year [1998] the Italian chapel was seen by more than 75,000 visitors.

Domenico Chioccetti was born in Moena, near Bolzano, northern Italy, on 15 May 1910. After the war, he returned to his home town, where he worked as an artist.

In the years after the Italians left Lamb Holm, the elements took a steady toll of the fabric of the chapel. But so firm a hold had the place taken on the Orcadian imagination that in 1958 a preservation committee was formed, and in 1960 Chioccetti was persuaded to return to Lamb Holm. There he spent three weeks restoring his handiwork.

Four years later he returned again, bringing with him fourteen Stations of the Cross, hand-carved in wood, and a Calvary for which an Orcadian joiner made a canopy. Chioccetti also brought with him a gift from the people of Moena, a crucifix and altar fittings fashioned from Venetian glass.

In 1996, Chioccetti was given the freedom of Moena; the ceremony was witnessed by three guests from the Orkneys.

8th

Luis Miguel Dominguin, b. 1926, d. 1996

Luis Miguel Dominguin, who has died aged sixty-nine, was the pre-eminent Spanish matador from the death of Manolete in 1947 until the rise of El Cordobes in the 1960s, and was arguably the greatest bull-fighter of the century.

Celebrated in print by Ernest Hemingway, adored in the flesh by a host of beautiful and famous women, and dressed in costumes designed by his good friend, Pablo Picasso, Dominguin was surely among the most glamorous of his kind. Dynamic and charming in social situations, he was thought an ice-cold, analytical genius in the bullring. His cool, elegant flourishes – kneeling before the bull, walking disdainfully away, kissing the head of the wounded animal before dispatching it with a sword – led to accusations of arrogance and disrespect, but brought him a huge following.

Having slain his first bull aged fourteen, by 1955 he was a 29-year-old millionaire with 2,300 kills to his credit. He then decided to retire, declaring, 'I have lost the feeling and when one loses the feeling one cannot play with one's life.' Considered impossibly handsome, Dominguin was also influenced in his decision to quit by the chance of a Hollywood film career. But four years later, in 1959, he was back, in a series of *mano a mano* fights with Antonio Ordonez, an equally arrogant matador who was married to Dominguin's sister.

Their rivalry was written up in a series of articles by Hemingway for *Life* magazine, which became the posthumously published book *The Dangerous Summer* (1985). Dominguin thought that Hemingway overstated the matadors' mutual antipathy and anyway knew nothing about bulls; but the summer was indeed dangerous.

In the first fight at Valencia, Dominguin swiftly dispatched two bulls but, when a gust of wind tore his red cape to one side, he was gored in the stomach by the third. Three weeks later he was back on the sand. Fighting in Bilbao, with his admirer Lauren Bacall watching, he was again gored, the eleventh goring of his career.

Luis Miguel Gonzalez Lucas was born in Madrid on 9 December 1926. His father was a celebrated bull-fighter of the 1930s whose fighting name, Dominguin, young Luis adopted. He flourished his first cape at the age of five. Commanding intense devotion in his heyday, Dominguin caused a stir in 1949 by courting Angelita, the eighteen-year-old daughter of the Duke of Pinohermoso.

The Duke looked with less favour on the young blade than did his daughter, whom he locked in her room. Using the traditional method of knotted sheets she escaped through a window and was rescued by her matador. Their subsequent engagement was not fulfilled, and by 1954 Dominguin's friendship with Ava Gardner was being widely reported.

He considered her the most beautiful woman he had ever seen, but liked her more, he said, for her humour and understanding; he confessed himself unsure what he looked for in women. 'Men fall in love with a woman's faults rather than her qualities,' he mused. By the time Dominguin married, in March 1955, the Italian actress Lucia Bose, he felt more confident on the subject: 'She speaks Italian. I speak Spanish. We do not know what the other one says and we get mad. It is perfect. But what is speaking? If you say nothing you are always right.'

The following year, the Czech film actress Miroslava Sternova was found dead from an overdose, clutching a photograph of Dominguin. His name was further linked with Brigitte Bardot, Rita Hayworth, Lana Turner and Olivia de Havilland.

He retired for a second time in 1962, but returned to the ring in 1971, aged forty-five, when he attempted to fathom the sport's continuing allure. 'How to describe it?' he wondered, 'It is like being with the woman who pleases you most in the world when her husband comes in with a pistol. The bull is the woman, the husband and the pistol, all in one. No other life I know can give you all that.'

≋ 9th ≋

Jeff Kitcher, b. 1943, d. 2011

Jeff Kitcher, who has died aged sixty-eight, was a member of the Verderer's Court, an ancient body which preserves the natural beauty and traditional character of the New Forest; he earned his living from timber and had roots in the forest as deep and fixed as the trees with which he worked.

As one of about 500 commoners – farmers and smallholders – who maintain the New Forest's character and ecology, Kitcher took a major role in ensuring that their animals, mainly ponies and their foals, continue to graze wild in the forest. The Verderer's Court, which he joined in 1988, regulates and protects the commoners' interests; he brought to it his knowledge of how wild livestock is cared for and managed.

As a verderer Kitcher also took control of and responsibility for the activities of the agisters (the five men who ride the forest ensuring the welfare of commoners' ponies, cattle, donkeys and pigs). He also established the New Forest Stallion Syndicate, a group set up to help ensure that there are enough quality stallions available to run on the forest.

Surprisingly perhaps, he was an outspoken critic of moves to turn the New Forest into a national park. 'I can't see the necessity,' he said. 'The forest is well protected now. We've got all sorts of bodies here looking after it and it works all right. I liken it to going into the euro. You don't know what it's like until you're in it. Then it's too bloody late to change.'

Jeffrey Frank Kitcher was born on 3 January 1943 in his family's cottage at Furzey Lodge, Beaulieu; he lived there all his life. After school he worked on the Beaulieu estate. In the early 1960s he joined the Forestry Commission, working with his father, a contractor to the commission, pulling out timber with heavy horses; as a young man he was probably the last person to use horses in this work.

But he also trained to operate the various new machines that were phased in to modernise forestry operations, and continued to drive them for the Forestry Commission until 1983 when he decided to start his own forestry contracting business.

Kitcher saw no good reason to go away on holiday; he believed that nowhere else could match the New Forest, an area of outstanding natural beauty and Britain's richest nature reserve.

≋ 10th ≋

Lieutenant-Colonel T.A. Robertson, b. 1909, d. 1994

Lieutenant-Colonel T.A. Robertson, who has died aged eighty-four, was the architect of the 'double cross' system, one of the most successful intelligence operations of the century.

Known to his friends as 'Tommy' and within the Secret Service as 'Tar' (from the initials he attached to memoranda), Robertson laid the foundations of his coup when he gained the trust of Arthur Owens, a notoriously slippery Welshman. For some years before the Second World War Owens had been supplying information to Naval Intelligence while working as an electrical engineer in the shipyards of northern Germany.

Robertson discovered, through the scouting of Owens' mail, that the Welshman and his mistress, a Mrs Funnell, were also in contact with the German Abwehr. When he was arrested on the outbreak of war, Owens (codenamed Snow, a partial anagram of his name) agreed to develop this association with the enemy for Robertson.

As the deception gained momentum, and more double agents were recruited, MI5 created a special unit, known as the Wireless Board, to supervise the supply of information to the Abwehr. In January 1941 a specialist sub-committee chaired by J.C. Masterman, one of Robertson's subordinates, was set up to co-ordinate the activities. By the end of the war the double cross organisation, masterminded by Robertson as head of the 1(a) section of MI5's B Division, ran to more than forty agents.

By far the most successful agent was the Spaniard 'Garbo', who helped to persuade the Wehrmacht that the D-Day invasion would occur in the Pas-de-Calais. Robertson's section played a key role in mounting the deception which suggested to the Abwehr that the Normandy landings in June 1944 were a diversionary feint intended to draw German troops away from the real target area. German documents captured after the Second World War showed that the bluff had been effective.

Always self-effacing, Robertson was admired both by his agents and by the very talented case officers he gathered around him. His humour relieved the tension; and agent 'Tate', for one, felt that he owed his life to him. After the war Robertson was appointed OBE.

A banker's son, Thomas Argyll Robertson was born on 27 October 1909 at Medam in Sumatra, and educated at Charterhouse. He went on to Sandhurst before being commissioned into the Seaforth Highlanders.

One of his close friends was John Kell, son of Sir Vernon Kell, the Director-General of MI5; Robertson was accepted as one of the two dozen officers on Kell's staff. His first brief was to make an extended tour of public houses at Invergordon to report on the disaffection within the Royal Navy after the mutiny of September 1931.

After the war Robertson disliked the atmosphere at Leconfield House, and was transferred to GCHQ to head its internal security branch. Upon his retirement he took up farming.

In 1972 he was publicly identified as the man who had created and managed MI5's outstanding wartime success, but in 1981 the Security Service refused him permission to publish a short account of his role in double cross. Nevertheless at the fortieth anniversary of the D-Day landings official consent was given to his participation in the celebrations, which included an emotional reunion with Garbo, previously believed to be dead.

In 1990 he accompanied Tate back to the field near Cambridge where local police had intercepted the Nazi spy.

⊰ 11th ⊱

Elisabeth Svendsen, b. 1930, d. 2011

Elisabeth Svendsen, who has died aged eighty-one, founded the Donkey Sanctuary, a charity that has rescued thousands of neglected, mistreated and overworked beasts of burden in Britain and around the world.

Her mission began in 1969, when she decided to breed donkeys at the country house hotel at Ottery St Mary, Devon, that she ran with her husband Niels. Visiting a livestock auction in Exeter she saw seven donkeys corralled in a cramped, lice-infested pen and, horrified, resolved to help.

She began collecting neglected donkeys but by 1973, when she had thirty-eight of them, the cost of their continued upkeep alongside running the hotel was becoming prohibitive. Then Violet Pippin, the elderly proprietor of a small donkey sanctuary near Reading, bequeathed her another 204 animals, so Elisabeth Svendsen and her husband decided to sell the hotel and go into donkey protection full-time.

Since then the Donkey Sanctuary has taken in more than 15,000 needy donkeys and now employs more than 500 people around the world. Sixty of them travel around Britain investigating complaints of abuse, also checking up on the 1,000 donkeys for hire at British beaches that children traditionally ride on holiday.

Some donkeys arrive at the sanctuary's headquarters on a farm at Sidmouth with mutilated ears and festering sores. Others have simply been abandoned at the end of long working lives hauling carts and carrying heavy loads. Once at the sanctuary, however, injuries are treated at a modern veterinary hospital, and once back to full fitness each animal is given its own specially made jacket.

In 1976 Elisabeth Svendsen launched the International Donkey Trust to tackle the care and welfare problems facing millions of donkeys and mules worldwide. By 2010 it had rescued more than 400,000 donkeys in twenty-nine countries.

But for some, the charity has become almost too successful. Tapping into Britain's natural reservoir of affection for animals, the sanctuary admits 200,000 visitors a year, and in 2009 had an income of £22 million. In the past it has received more in donations than such charities as Age Concern, Mencap and the Samaritans. Fundraisers are often exasperated by the priorities of the giving public, which often ranks animal charities ahead of children's charities. For that reason the Donkey Sanctuary is sometimes cited as an example of what the Charities Aid Foundation calls 'the eccentric nature of British philanthropy'.

Elisabeth Doreen Knowles was born on 23 January 1930 in Elland, West Yorkshire. Educated at St Mary's High School, Halifax, and Brighouse Grammar School, she loved donkeys even as a girl. 'They had such soft, warm muzzles, such beautiful, trusting eyes,' she said.

For two years she worked as a primary teacher at West Vale School, Halifax, before joining her father's pipeworks business as company secretary. In March 1954, when her car caught fire, she met Niels Svendsen, who put out the blaze with an extinguisher. They married later that year.

Some 5,000 donkeys and mules live on the Donkey Sanctuary's farms in Britain and abroad, a total which includes 1,500 in donkey fostering schemes, living with families who meet the sanctuary's rigorous requirements.

In 1976 she founded the Elisabeth Svendsen Trust for Children and Donkeys, a charity giving children with disabilities the opportunity to have contact with and ride donkeys. She retired in 2007. A son, Paul, succeeded as the Donkey Sanctuary's director of care and welfare.

❧ 12th ❧

Simon Raven, b. 1927, d. 2001

Simon Raven, who has died aged seventy-three, set himself up, convincingly, as a bounder; yet retained the discipline, wit and intelligence to become the author of thirty-six books and several television scripts.

Raven the cad attained his finest hour when his wife sent the telegram: 'Wife and baby starving send money soonest'. He replied: 'Sorry no money suggest eat baby'.

Raven the writer produced his best work in the ten novels – from *Fielding Gray* (1959) to *The Survivors* (1976) – which make up the *Alms for Oblivion* sequence. The series follows the fortunes of a group of public schoolboys in the post-war years; and has been described by the critic A.N. Wilson as 'the jolliest *roman-fleuve* ever written'.

Fielding Gray is based on Raven himself, while other characters are derived from the author's friends: Peter Morrison MP from James (later Lord) Prior; Somerset Lloyd Jones from William (later Lord) Rees Mogg; Sir Gregory Stern from the publisher Anthony Blond and Max de Freville from John Aspinall.

All the characters in Raven's novels can be guaranteed to behave badly under pressure; most of them are vile without any pressure at all. They are also afflicted by sexual kinks which are described in gloating detail.

For himself, Raven played under all rules. 'I like all four types,' he once said, 'amateur and professional men and amateur and professional women.' His one caveat was never to become involved.

Yet Raven loved institutions. Though extruded in turn from Charterhouse, Cambridge and the Army, he retained a deep affection for them all. To the end of his life he remained captivated by his schooldays. 'There were sports which I enjoyed; there was homosexuality which I enjoyed; there was intrigue for power which I enjoyed.'

There was something of Lord Byron about Raven: if not the same genius, at least the same energy, contempt for cant, unshocked eighteenth-century acceptance of human folly, urge towards sexual experiment and – underlying the hedonistic philosophy – the same desire to court retribution.

Writing of gambling, Raven observed that 'there is nothing arid in the deep, the almost sexual satisfaction, which comes from an evening of steady and disastrous losses'. If he rejected the Christian God, he believed most passionately in the Furies, forever on hand to cut down human presumption. Raven also held that life is too short and too insignificant to get worked up about. Behind his characters' twisted strivings lies the bleak realisation that they have lost touch with what they are competing for. 'The answer,' Raven knew, 'is six feet of earth, and that pretty quickly.'

Simon Arthur Noel Raven was born on 28 December 1927, the eldest of three children. 'My background,' he later explained, 'was middle-class, for which read respectable, prying, puritanical, penny-pinching, joyless.'

His grandfather William, born in 1832, had begun his career at Leicester as a knitting frame operator, and built up one of the largest hosiery works in the country, employing over a thousand hands.

The boy was brought up in commodious houses in the Surrey stockbroker belt, at Virginia Water and on the Wentworth estate. At Cordwalles School, near Camberley, he was, aged nine, 'deftly and very agreeably' seduced by the games master. The episode, he considered, taught him 'several valuable and lasting lessons. Firstly that sex (of whatever kind), although matchless as an occasional diversion, is too ridiculous to be taken seriously; secondly, that it is too trivial to be allowed to interfere with more stable and satisfying preoccupations, such as cricket and the flicks or (later) horse racing and books; and thirdly, that sex is best spiced with a degree of shamelessness which love or serious affection would probably inhibit.'

He won a scholarship to Charterhouse, where he won his cricket colours in a side which included Peter May, the future captain of England. But in 1945 his school career ended in expulsion – 'for the usual reasons'.

Raven did his National Service in the Parachute Regiment, where he found ample opportunity for cricket and lechery before being sent as an officer cadet to Bangalore, where he received his commission in May 1947. Back in England he joined the Oxford and Buckinghamshire Light Infantry.

Going up to Cambridge in 1948, he found the somewhat louche atmosphere of King's – 'nobody minded what you did in bed or what you said about God' – entirely to his taste. He honed his snobbery, kept up his dissolute life ('the only true aphrodisiac is variety') and ran up debts. Even so, he won two English essay prizes, and King's awarded him a Studentship for a thesis on the influence of the Classics on Victorian public schools.

Raven began to dabble in journalism. 'I promoted myself "Man of Letters",' he remembered, 'when in fact I was just a tiresome and impecunious research student, neglecting his research.'

In 1952 King's declined to continue supporting this way of life. In May 1953, after nearly a year in London – 'a wild, Cattulan' period – Raven joined the King's Own Shropshire Light Infantry. Over the next four years he served in Germany and saw action against the Mau Mau in Kenya.

Gambling eventually ended Raven's military career. Though he had one great win in October 1956, when a four-horse accumulator brought him £5,000 (he bought a Bentley to celebrate), the money soon disappeared, and gave way to new debts. In 1957, as local tradesmen and bookmakers began to close in, the Army sportingly allowed him to resign rather than making him face a court martial.

Raven now settled down 'to write my way back into a decent and solvent existence'.

In the next decade he was a regular contributor to *The Spectator*. His first published novel was *The Feathers of Death* (1959), the story of a homosexual romance in the Army. It was well received, but Raven could never make ends meet while living among the fleshpots of London. At this point his publisher, Anthony Blond, rescued him by proposing a bargain which would condition his life for the next thirty years.

In return for Raven agreeing to live at least fifty miles from London, Blond undertook to pay him £15 a week in cash against royalties, to settle various bills (including, up to a point, the wine merchant's) and to stand the cost of his evening meal at a local hostelry. Raven went to live at Deal, near his brother Myles, a prep school master. In the next five years he wrote five novels, two non-fiction books, six television plays, eight radio plays, a stage play and a host of articles and reviews.

Raven remained in Deal or nearby Walmer until 1995. Then, after a prostate operation, he found a place at Sutton's Hospital, an almshouse for indigent old gentlemen that occupies the remains of the London Hospital in Charterhouse Square.

The hospital's constitution gave preference to 'souldiers maymed or ympotent'. By that time there was general agreement that Raven qualified.

❧ 13th ❧

Frank Shackleton-Fergus, b. 1911, d. 2000

Frank Shackleton-Fergus, who has died aged eighty-nine, was the first man to X-ray a live duck-billed platypus.

In July 1936 Shackleton-Fergus, an Australian radiographer, received a message that a platypus had been found on the banks of a creek. 'The specimen used was brought to Melbourne,' he wrote, 'and returned to its haunts on the following day. The behaviour of the animal was good; it seemed to like the cold aluminium surface of the film holder, and remained still while successful exposures were made. A view from the side was taken by placing the platypus on a slightly inclined piece of wood. When the subject walked into a suitable position, the exposure was made.'

When news of the platypus reached Europe for the first time in the late eighteenth century, the animal was considered by many to be a hoax, so unusual did it appear. One hundred and fifty years later Shackleton-Fergus's series of X-ray photographs, widely publicised, proved a sensation, and were displayed in several exhibitions.

Some animals he found easier to photograph than others. The easiest were the lizards; these remained still for relatively long exposures, making it possible to obtain better details.

The tortoise too was a good subject 'when it can be persuaded to extend its head from underneath its carapace, otherwise it is hard to distinguish the bones of the head and neck from the shell.' More difficult were birds, which moved the whole time and so required short exposures – a quarter of a second for a magpie and half a second for a kookaburra.

⚞ 14th ⚟

Ronald Bailey, b. 1917, d. 2010

Ronald Bailey, who has died aged ninety-two, enjoyed a wide variety of postings during his 35-year diplomatic career, of which the most striking was Taiz in the Yemeni Highlands, once described as 'hastening at full speed into the fourteenth century'.

As minister and chargé d'affaires, he received only three visitors from abroad in two years. His residence was a tall stone building, guarded by five askaris, with slits for firing rifles and a fine view of a boarding school for chiefs' sons known as 'Hostage Castle'.

There was no bank and no hotel. Telephone bills had to be paid in Maria Theresa silver thalers (dated 1780). Nevertheless, Taiz was an important market for many British imports, including fur coats which were not required for the tropical climate but for Russians to buy in local currency and take home. Even more curious, the local market sold lots of bikinis.

Bailey had such difficulties obtaining a visa for his wife that an official eventually gave him a note for the immigration officer at the frontier declaring: 'When the British chargé d'affaires arrives, accompanied by a lady, you are not to see her.'

At first he was not allowed to venture beyond the town. But the Imam, a Liverpool fan who liked to watch films of his favourite team in his private cinema, agreed that Bailey could go outside the town if he carried an open umbrella — so that the locals would know who he was and show him appropriate respect.

On the night of 14 January 1962 Bailey sleepily answered the door of the legation in the belief that a telegram was being delivered — only to be stabbed in the chest by a man with blazing eyes. The would-be assassin also attacked the night watchman and was continuing to stab Bailey with a long knife as the diplomat retreated upstairs.

At this point Bailey's wife emerged from their bedroom. The villain saw her but turned back to finish off his victim, at which the former Wren gave him a powerful push, propelling him back down the stairs. She then helped the two wounded men to stagger into the flat and slammed the door.

The intruder escaped over a garden wall.

An Italian doctor gave the still-conscious Bailey seventy-four stitches without an anaesthetic, and warned that the patient was not fit enough to be moved. His redoubtable wife decided to accept an RAF offer to fly him to hospital in Aden, and as Bailey was driven to the plane all the shopkeepers closed their premises and lined the street.

Although revolution was in the air the attacker — a well-known criminal known as 'The Bomb' — seemed to know nothing of his victim. He was apprehended and identified as the intruder on the evidence of two bruises that exactly matched the horns of the family's pet gazelle, which must have butted him, but complained bitterly about Mrs Bailey 'behaving in an unladylike manner, coming downstairs like that in her nightdress'.

Bailey pleaded for the fellow to be jailed rather than executed; and later the attacker was freed in an amnesty and became a state executioner before himself being murdered.

Joan Bailey was praised in Parliament for her pluck. The Imam wanted Bailey (who took a year to recover) to return, but the Foreign and Commonwealth Office appointed him Consul-General in Gothenburg.

Ronald William Bailey was born on 14 June 1917 and went to King Edward VI School, Southampton, and Trinity Hall, Cambridge.

His first posting was Beirut, where he dealt in the mornings with visas for British subjects going to Palestine and studied Arabic at the American University in the afternoons.

After the fall of France in 1940 he arrived in Alexandria as vice-consul to receive a telegram announcing the arrival next day of 2,000 refugees from Greece. Two thousand mattresses were found; local ladies made corned beef soup; and ambulances were summoned after one of the ships was bombed. Among the refugees were the novelist Lawrence Durrell, King George II of the Hellenes (who shared Bailey's office) and a Greek priest with the name Jesus Christ on his passport – the man said God had called him to Jerusalem, but he was not entitled to a visa.

After marrying Joan Gray in 1945, Bailey remained in Egypt. Another spell in Beirut was followed by a posting to Washington, replacing the Soviet spy Donald Maclean.

In 1967 Bailey was appointed ambassador to Bolivia, where his cocker spaniel, Sally, once suddenly froze in the garden. Bailey's bodyguard fired towards a bush, and an armed man was dragged out, claiming that he wanted to see how a British ambassador lived.

Bailey arrived in Morocco for his last posting just after an attack had been made on the royal aeroplane, during which the king, Hassan II, had been forced to take the controls. But Bailey found it a tranquil appointment, not least because he could speak to the sovereign in Arabic, Spanish and French.

15th

Dennis Heymer, b. 1929, d. 2009

Dennis Heymer, who has died aged seventy-nine, was the long-time companion and manager of the comedian Frankie Howerd.

As Howerd's partner for more than thirty years, he shared houses in London and Somerset with him until Howerd's death in 1992. Described as Howerd's biggest secret, he was obliged to disguise the true nature of their relationship – Howerd was paranoid that being unmasked as a homosexual would lead to blackmail threats.

A dapper figure, Heymer was working as a wine waiter at the Dorchester on Park Lane when he met Howerd, who was having dinner there with Sir John and Lady Mills; it was 1958, homosexuality was still illegal, and Howerd was beginning to despair about his career and his physical attractiveness. Over the following weeks, Howerd regularly reappeared at the hotel on his own.

At the star's home, Heymer took charge of the cooking, cleaning, chauffeuring and (after Howerd's death at the age of seventy-five) curating the comedian's collection of memorabilia.

This included his dentures, hernia belt, hundreds of photographs, and a teapot from the actress Bette Davis, who jokingly suggested it be used to gently steam Howerd's toupées 'to give them a little lift'.

⊰ 16th ⊱

Frank Dye, b. 1928, d. 2010

Frank Dye, who has died aged eighty-two, was a cult figure among small-boat sailors for undertaking numerous voyages in his open 15ft 10in wooden Wayfarer dinghy *Wanderer*; these trips featured mountainous seas, gales up to Force 11 and numerous capsizes and broken masts.

Dye made his most famous voyages in the early 1960s. During his 11-day, 650-mile North Atlantic crossing from Scotland to Iceland, armed with just a compass and sextant for navigation and with a makeshift cockpit tent for shelter, he and his one-man crew, Russell Brockbank, endured seasickness, sodden clothing, freezing temperatures and broken rigging.

On his second major sea passage, a Norwegian Sea crossing from Scotland to Aalesund, Norway, Dye and his crew, Bill Brockbank (no relation to Russell), narrowly survived four capsizes and a broken mast during a Force 9 storm. In *Ocean-Crossing Wayfarer* (1977), written with his wife Margaret, Dye recalled the scene: 'It was impossible to look into the wind. It was screaming and the tops of the waves were blown completely away, feeling like hail. Within our limited vision the whole sea seemed to be smoking. Just to see such seas break away on the beam was frightening – 25ft of solid water, with another 12ft of overhanging crest above it. It was only a matter of time before we got one aboard.'

When the inevitable happened, both men hauled on the warps, frantically trying to pull *Wanderer* through the crest: 'She rose gallantly, but it was an impossible position: she seemed to be rising at 60 degrees and there was still a 15ft crest curling above us. Down it came and we were driven bodily under. With ears roaring under immense pressure, and swallowing water, I fought back to the surface, only to find *Wanderer* was lying bottom up.'

After three more capsizes, Dye reflected: 'Possibly we were the only people alive to have taken an open dinghy through a Force 9 gale, but we felt no elation, just a reaction of wetness, coldness and extreme tiredness.' The pair recovered the mast from the sea, made a jury rig and went on to make landfall in Norway without further incident.

Dye's Norfolk-built *Wayfarer* logged tens of thousands of miles and took him across the North Atlantic and further afield. In 1988, sailing single-handedly, he survived a hurricane off the United States as Force 11 seas battered his tiny craft. In *Sailing to the Edge of Fear* (1999) he recalled his near-death experience as the genoa sheet jammed and the boat hurtled down cresting seas at 20 knots (the theoretical hull speed of a 16ft dinghy is about 5.5 knots), while he struggled to free the sheet and lower the sail.

'Offshore cruising in an open boat can be hard, cold, wet, lonely and occasionally miserable,' Dye reflected, 'but it is exhilarating too. To see the beauty of dawn creep across the ever restless and dangerous ocean; to make a safe landfall – is wonderful and all of these things develop a self-reliance that is missing from the modern, mechanical, safety-conscious civilised world.'

Frank Charles Dye was born at Watton, Norfolk, on 23 April 1928 and educated at Hamond's Grammar School, Swaffham, before joining a Ford car dealership founded by his father. He took up sailing in his early thirties and in 1958 bought his first of what became half a dozen Wayfarers.

By 1963 he was sufficiently well known to be a feature at the Earl's Court Boat Show, and it was there that he met his wife Margaret. After a year of suffering discomfort in damp sleeping bags, she decided to marry him in 1964, even though she had been warned not to sail with 'that man; he'll kill you'.

Their honeymoon was spent voyaging to the remote uninhabited Hebridean island of St Kilda; their wedding breakfast consisted of 'green pea soup and scrambled eggs' served in an insulated mug. Margaret Dye recalled that, despite wearing many layers of clothing, 'never before had I known what it was like to be so cold'. She confessed that the experience had been 'quite a shock', though she went on to sail with her husband for thirty years.

In 1974 Dye started a marina in Cheshire, where he spent eight years working hard until the business was successfully established. Then he returned to the ocean again – and to Norfolk, settling at Wells.

His exploits earned him a place in the National Maritime Museum at Falmouth, in a display entitled 'Endurance and Survival', which featured the Dyes alongside Sir Ernest Shackleton. *Wanderer* is now on permanent display at the museum.

≈ 17th ≈

The Reverend Bill Shergold, b. 1919, d. 2009

The Reverend Bill Shergold, who has died aged eighty-nine, enjoyed unusual celebrity in the 1960s when he was known as the 'ton-up vicar' or the 'biker priest'; decked out in black leathers astride his trusty Triumph motorcycle, Shergold ministered to the rocker fraternity in east London as leader of the 59 Club.

In 1959 Shergold had been appointed vicar of St Mary at Eton, Hackney Wick. By the time he arrived one of the curates, the Rev. John Oates, had started a youth group called the 59 Club which had been opened in a blaze of publicity by Cliff Richard – then the hottest pop singer in Britain – in the presence of Princess Margaret and the Bishop of Bath and Wells.

Shergold, however, had visions of something that would be 'a breakaway from all those other fuddy-duddy youth clubs' and attract the disaffected young, of whom the rockers were one of the most high-profile examples.

At the time the Ace Café on the North Circular was where many of the bikers congregated to drink coffee and listen to the jukebox, and one day in 1962 Shergold rode there on his Triumph dressed in his leathers and with his dog collar disguised beneath a scarf. 'I was convinced that I was at least going to lose my trousers or have my bike heaved into the canal,' he later confessed.

He summoned up his courage, handed out church leaflets in the café and invited the bikers to come to the Eton Mission on Saturday nights. This was the beginning of the biking section of the 59 Club, which soon had more than 4,000 members who came weekly from as far afield as Oxford and Kent. The attractions at the church hall included a jukebox, espresso machine and table tennis.

Shergold – known to his new flock as 'Father Bill' or 'Farv' – held services for the bikers, whom he compared to the 'knights of old', suggesting that they should uphold the same ideals of courage, courtesy and chivalry. He addressed them from the pulpit and blessed their machines, parked neatly in the aisles.

William Frank Shergold was born in London on 17 October 1919. After reading History at Durham University he trained for the priesthood at St Chad's College, Durham, and at the College of the Resurrection, Mirfield, in West Yorkshire.

His initial intention was to become a monk, but after being ordained in 1942 he began his ministry as curate of All Saints with St Frideswide, Poplar, in the East End before being appointed vicar of All Saints, Hanworth, west London, where he served for ten years.

Shergold remained at Hackney Wick until 1964, when he became vicar of Paddington St Mary's, where he continued to minister to bikers. Five years later he was appointed vicar of St Bartholomew's, Charlton-by-Dover, where he established, with local motorcyclists, the 69 Club. He went on to hold three more livings until he retired in 1984, after which he carried out unpaid duties at his old parish in Poplar.

Shergold was elected life president of both the 59 and 69 Clubs, both of which continue to this day. In 1991, when he was over seventy, Wrangler jeans invited Shergold to spearhead a new advertising campaign, for which he was photographed under Southend Pier astride a 1960s motorbike.

When he was approached by Wrangler, Shergold sought the advice of his rector, who told him: 'Of course you must do it. Good for the Church to be seen doing ordinary, rather silly things.'

⊰ 18th ⊱

The 8th Earl of Clancarty, b. 1911, d. 1995

The 8th Earl Of Clancarty, who has died aged eighty-three, devoted his life to propagating belief in flying saucers.

Brinsley Clancarty, a tall, amiable figure with a rather haunted expression and elegant braces, claimed that he could trace his descent from 63,000BC, when beings from other planets had landed on Earth in spaceships. Most humans, he said, were descended from these aliens: 'This accounts for all the different colour skins we've got here,' he said in 1981.

A few of these early aliens did not come from space, he explained, but emerged through tunnels from a civilisation which still existed beneath the Earth's crust. There were seven or eight of these tunnels altogether, one at the North Pole, another at the South Pole, and others in such places as Tibet. 'I haven't been down there myself,' Clancarty said, 'but from what I gather [these beings] are very advanced.'

He once produced a satellite photograph showing a large circular blob in the North Polar ice which, he said, was the entrance to one of the tunnels. He remained adamant even when it was pointed out to him that he was looking at part of the camera.

Clancarty said that most of the aliens who were still arriving from space (and from the centre of the Earth) were friendly. But then he pointed to the sky and added: 'I'm told there is one hostile lot.'

For years he was frustrated in his desire to see a flying saucer. He installed a UFO detector in the bedroom wall at his flat in South Kensington, but with disappointing results. 'It did buzz one Saturday afternoon,' he said, 'but when I rushed out I found that the sky was cloudy and completely overcast. Presumably it was above the cloud.'

At last he spotted his first (and last) UFO: 'It was an eerie white light zigzagging over South Kensington,' he recalled. 'I had to climb into the kitchen sink to get a good look at it through the window.'

The fifth son of the 5th Earl of Clancarty, William Francis Brinsley Le Poer Trench was born on 18 September 1911 and educated at the Nautical College, Pangbourne.

In the 1950s he edited the *Flying Saucer Review* and founded the International Unidentified Object Observer Corps. He also found employment selling advertising space for a gardening magazine housed opposite Waterloo Station.

When he succeeded to the Earldom (created in 1803) on the death of his half-brother in 1975, the new Lord Clancarty founded a UFO Study Group at the House of Lords, and introduced *Flying Saucer Review* to its library.

Four years later he organised a celebrated debate on UFOs which attracted many speeches on both sides of the question. Lord Strabolgi, speaking on behalf of the government, declared that there was nothing to convince him that any alien spacecraft had ever visited the Earth.

Lord Clancarty's books, written under the name Brinsley Le Poer Trench, included *The Sky People*; *Men Among Mankind*; *Forgotten Heritage*; *The Flying Saucer Story*; *Operation Earth*; *The Eternal Subject*; and *Secret of the Ages*.

⤝ 19th ⤞

Cyril Freezer, b. 1924, d. 2009

Cyril Freezer, who has died aged eighty-four, inspired generations of schoolboys to move on from simple train sets to more sophisticated and intricate model railways with sidings, points, branch lines, signals, tunnels, fiddle yards and miniature landscapes; his contribution to his hobby, particularly to small layout design, would be hard to exaggerate.

As editor for more than thirty years, first of *Railway Modeller* magazine, then of *Model Railways*, 'CJF' as he was affectionately known, did much to encourage the idea that railway modelling should be about the realistic operation of railways as well as the building of models.

Few model railway enthusiasts are without copies of his *60 Plans for Small Layouts* or his *Model Railway Manual* on their bookshelves. Taking account of family budgets, he gave advice on how to 'scratch-build' (use raw materials) or 'kit-bash' (cannibalise pieces from commercial model railway sets).

He was particularly celebrated for three pioneering designs: the 'Fiddle Yard to Terminus', featuring a terminus with a track leading into a tunnel containing an extensive traverser; the 'Rabbit Layout', designed to exploit the sharp radii possible with narrow gauge to 'allow trains to pop out of tunnels all over the place'; and the classic Minories layout, consisting of a three-platform city terminus set in a cutting with retaining walls, built on a pair of folding baseboards and featuring a neat arrangement of crossovers which ensured that any movement only involved one reverse curve. The idea for the Minories came to Freezer on a visit to the old Metropolitan Station at Liverpool Street and is probably his best-known and most popular design.

Cyril John Freezer was born in Poplar, east London, on 27 June 1924 and went to Barking Abbey School where he developed a fascination with the local railway lines. After the outbreak of war in 1939, he was evacuated to Weston-super-Mare, but returned to London after the Blitz. He worked as a shipyard apprentice on the Isle of Dogs and qualified as an engineer in 1945.

After the war Freezer worked in a newspaper print room on Fleet Street and developed his interest in model railways by joining the Model Railway Club, which then held twice-weekly meetings in a side arch at Waterloo Station. At the time the club was roughly organised into four groups, LMS, LNER, GWR and Southern, and the groups took turns to organise weekly 'track nights' when members would bring in their models to run on test tracks.

In 1950 his love of railways won Freezer the job of editor of a new magazine, *Railway Modeller*. Over the next twenty-seven years, Freezer turned the magazine into the leading publication for model railway enthusiasts before moving on to edit a rival publication, *Model Railways*.

His editorship of these magazines was not without controversy. When real steam trains were in decline, there was resistance to his argument that enthusiasts should move with the times and adopt model diesel locomotives. As Continental kit became more widely available, there were frequent divisions over model rail gauges and scales.

Sir Larry Lamb, b. 1929, d. 2000

Sir Larry Lamb, the newspaper editor who has died aged seventy, created the tabloid version of the *Sun*, the greatest commercial success in modern British journalism. Lamb believed that the most important thing in his readers' lives, with one exception, was television and so determined to give it extensive coverage. The exception, of course, was what subsequently came to be known as 'bonking'.

From these principles the *Sun* began to take shape. In the first issue under Lamb's editorship, on 7 November 1969, there was a centre spread featuring a naked blonde at the feet of the Rolling Stones.

It was not until the first birthday of the revamped newspaper that the unclothed Page Three Girl began to appear as a regular feature. Lamb insisted that the models should be 'nice girls' – 'Big-breasted girls look like tarts,' he used to say – and ordered that the women's editor, Joyce Hopkirk, should have an absolute right of veto over the daily offering.

⊰ **20**th ⊱

Stephen Jay Gould, b. 1941, d. 2002

Stephen Jay Gould, who has died aged sixty, was one of the world's best-known scientists, a prolific author and a controversial thinker on evolution.

Gould took issue with the Darwinian view of evolution as based on the mechanisms of long-term adaptation over relatively long periods of time; instead, he suggested, evolutionary change came by fits and starts.

He first expounded this theory, known as 'punctuated equilibrium', with his colleague Niles Eldredge in 1972. Most important change, they contended, takes place in the geological 'instant' when a new species is born, lasting perhaps 5,000 to 50,000 years – virtually no time at all compared with the millions of years most species survive.

Furthermore, they argued, some features of organisms exist not because of evolution but simply as the result of how an organism is built, and do not necessarily have any adaptive purpose.

'Humans are not the end result of predictable evolutionary progress,' he maintained in a characteristically purple passage of *Wonderful Life: The Burgess Shale and the Nature of History* (1989), 'but rather a fortuitous cosmic afterthought, a tiny little twig on the enormously arborescent bush of life which, if replanted from seed, would almost surely not grow this twig again.'

Gould achieved a public profile unprecedented among modern evolutionary biologists. In countless essays and articles, he expounded on topics from religion to the evolution of typewriters, and from Gilbert and Sullivan to space travel. He wrote with authority and wit, and for Americans, Gould's heavy-lidded eyes and bushy moustache represented the public face of science; he was even depicted in cartoon form on *The Simpsons*.

But the public acclaim did not spill over into university laboratories and the backrooms of museums. In a famous put-down, John Maynard Smith, Professor of Biology at the University of Sussex, wrote in the *New York Review of Books* in 1995 that 'evolutionary biologists tend to see [Gould] as a man whose ideas are so confused as to be hardly worth bothering with'. Indeed, Gould achieved the notable distinction of making enemies both of creationists and neo-Darwinian theorists such as the zoologist Richard Dawkins.

Stephen Jay Gould was born on 10 September 1941 in Manhattan, and grew up at Forest Hills in Queens, New York. His father was a court stenographer and a left-wing activist, his mother an artist and entrepreneur.

He claimed to have decided to become a palaeontologist at the age of five when his father took him to see a Tyrannosaurus Rex at the American Museum of Natural History; until then he had planned on a career as a garbage collector. By the age of eleven he had read *The Origin of Species* and Charles Darwin had assumed hero status, alongside Joe DiMaggio.

From Jamaica High School, Gould enrolled at Antioch College, Ohio, where he studied Geology. He went on to study at Columbia, where he earned a doctorate in 1967 on the fossil land snails of Bermuda. He joined Harvard as an assistant professor of geology, eventually becoming Professor of Geology in 1973. He was one of the university's star performers, running hugely popular undergraduate courses in geology, biology and the history of science.

He was the author of twenty-two books, his last being what he described as his magnum opus, *The Structure of Evolutionary Theory*, a 1,433-page tome that took twenty years to write and in which he sought to reformulate Darwin's theory of evolution by synthesising it with his own.

It was while he was working on this project that, in 1982, he was diagnosed with an abdominal mesothelioma, a cancer linked to exposure to asbestos. In a well-known essay entitled 'The Median Is Not the Message', he described being told that the median survival time after diagnosis was a mere eight months. Rather than giving up hope, he used statistics to demonstrate that half those in whom the disease was diagnosed survived longer than eight months. This realisation gave him the strength to carry on.

⊱ 21st ⊰

Dame Barbara Cartland, b. 1901, d. 2000

Dame Barbara Cartland, who has died aged ninety-eight, was a confection entirely of her own making: a romantic novelist of unrivalled output, a doughty champion of unlikely causes, the most reliable sound-bite artiste of her times, and step-grandmother of Diana, Princess of Wales.

In her later years, she cut an unmistakeable figure in a froth of pink ball gown with extravagant, almost clown-like, make-up – her cheeks pulled back with sadly visible bits of sticking plaster.

This facade of pancake and tulle, however, concealed an iron constitution, a steely determination, and a mind which, though often contrary and in an eccentric orbit of its own, was seldom less than razor sharp. She was a formidable fairy queen.

Although there was once public embarrassment when it was discovered that an inaccurate birth-date appeared in *Who's Who* (secretarial error, claimed the Dame) she was actually born Barbara Hamilton Cartland on 9 July 1901, at her grandparents' house at Edgbaston.

Although Dame Barbara was always at pains to stress her aristocratic ancestry the truth of the matter is that her antecedents were solidly middle class. Barbara herself was educated at Worcester High School and Malvern, which she hated. She boarded with families in and around Bath before going to a finishing school on the Solent called Netley Abbey.

For most of her life she was fascinated, professionally and personally, by the relationship between the sexes. In private she would discuss sexual matters with an explicitness verging on the bawdy (she was fascinating on the subject of the Duke and Duchess of Windsor's private parts); but in public she proclaimed a virginal romanticism verging on the prudish.

Her first brush with men came in the Bath period, when a libidinous major invited her to his bedroom in order to show her 'how his revolver worked'. But in 1919, on holiday, she first discovered the thrill of male company. She claimed to have received three proposals of marriage that fortnight alone. In time this rose to around fifty.

There was even an engagement to one of the many young men who proposed. He was an officer in the Life Guards. However, when her mother warned her about the 'facts of life' Barbara was so disgusted that she broke it all off.

One evening at a cocktail party she bumped into a man from the *Daily Express* who suggested she might supply paragraphs for his gossip column at five shillings a time. Before long, she had graduated to writing feature articles. Soon she attracted the attention of the *Express*'s proprietor, Lord Beaverbrook, and became a regular luncheon guest at his house in Hurlingham, where she met such cronies as F.E. Smith, Winston Churchill and Sir James Dunn.

Beaverbrook seems almost certainly to have made some sort of pass at his young protégée, but she resisted. However, she always said that it was Beaverbrook who taught her most about writing. Certainly the short sentences, short paragraphs and short words that characterised her work are very much the style of *Express* editorials of the day. Beaverbrook also inculcated the notion that name-dropping was a useful device, especially when the names had titles attached to them.

She had begun her first novel before meeting him and in 1923, *Jigsaw*, a thinly disguised autobiography of a young society girl, was published by Duckworth. The reviews were mixed.

She remained hard up and, as with others of her sex and generation, the obvious solution was marriage. In 1927 she became engaged to Alexander 'Sachie' McCorquodale, son of the chairman of the country's largest printing company.

It did not last. She bore him a daughter, Raine; he gave her a house in Mayfair and a Rolls-Royce, but he had a serious drink problem and before long was conducting an affair with a major's wife.

The resulting divorce case was spectacular. It was alleged that she had been conducting an affair with her husband's cousin Hugh. He had a key to her house and used to go to her bedroom, kiss her on both cheeks and she would mix him cocktails and address him as 'Darling'. Cutting a demure figure in the witness box, Barbara protested that all her friends – of both sexes – were treated in similar fashion.

She was believed. Nevertheless, in 1936 she married Hugh and the couple lived happily until Hugh's death many years later.

Satisfactory though this second marriage was, it was her brother Ronald who loomed largest in her life. Very early in married life, Hugh was going off on Scottish fishing holidays while his wife and Ronald went on reading and walking holidays to Switzerland. She once said that she and her brother had everything together with the single exception of sex.

Apart from her journalism, she continued to write novels, though before the war they were not on the whole the sort of books that came to be associated with her when she blossomed as the world's most prolific romantic novelist. She tended to write about contemporary life, though at 'a safe distance from everyday life'.

The greatest tragedy of her life occurred in 1940: both her brothers were killed at Dunkirk. Tony, the younger, was much loved but not in the same almost obsessive way as Ronald. For the next fifty years and more she used to say that Ronald frequently appeared in her dreams and even – she being susceptible to the preternatural – in visions.

During the war she became a welfare officer with the Women's Voluntary Services. Her most impressive coup was to organise a wardrobe of white wedding dresses so that girls serving with the forces did not have to get married in uniform. Many of these wartime brides were to write to her on their golden wedding anniversaries to thank her for giving them the chance to wed in white.

By the end of the war, smarting at not having been awarded even a 'measly MBE', she was forty-four and, despite her happy home life, felt that her whole world was 'smashed in ruins'.

Some of her energies were channelled into launching Raine on the world, and it was due to Barbara as much as her daughter that Raine became 'Deb of the Year' in 1947. A year later, Raine married Gerald Legge, heir to the Earldom of Dartmouth.

A woman's magazine, spurred by this romantic event, asked Barbara to write a historical romance. This was *Hazard of Hearts*, the first of her novels which belongs decisively in the genre which the world has now come to recognise as Barbara Cartland's own.

From then on she wrote historical Cinderella stories with heroic heroes and heroines, villainous bad guys of both sexes who always got their come-uppance, and happy endings with definite, though understated, sexual connotations. At her most productive, dictating from the depths of her chaise-longue she 'wrote' them at the rate of about one every fortnight.

In 1991, thanks (she liked to intimate) to the personal intervention of the Queen Mother, she was appointed Dame of the British Empire.

Outliving her few rivals as the 'Queen of Romantic Fiction', she became almost a self-parody, and yet was saved by herself from becoming as absurd as her detractors might have liked. She had a wry self-awareness, never more so than when she declined to appear on stage with Danny la Rue, on the grounds that no one in the audience would know who was who.

Despite failing eyesight, she continued to produce novels until almost the very end and became an aged pin-up, widely loved. In 1991 she circulated to newspaper editors a folder tied with pink ribbon, labelled in blue felt-tip: 'The History of Barbara Cartland' and 'How I Want to be Remembered'. It was wholly positive in approach. 'In 1981, I was chosen,' she told the world, 'as Achiever of the Year by the National Home Furnishing Association of Colorado Springs.'

⇥ 22nd ⇤

Keith Jessop, b. 1933, d. 2010

Keith Jessop, who has died aged seventy-seven, was an expert deep-sea diver and treasure hunter responsible for retrieving hundreds of gold bars from the British warship *Edinburgh*, lying in the depths of the Barents Sea.

Born at Keighley, West Yorkshire, on 10 May 1933, Keith Jessop was the illegitimate son of a seventeen-year-old mill-girl. He never knew the identity of his father and grew up in poverty, leaving Eastwood School at fourteen without any qualifications.

Taking a dead-end job in a textile mill, he lived for the weekends, excelling at outdoor pursuits. Such was his skill at rock-climbing and general level of fitness that he completed his National Service with the Royal Marines.

Afterwards a friend who was a keen diver offered to lend Jessop his scuba equipment, and he took his first dive in the River Lune beneath the Devil's Bridge in Kirkby Lonsdale. There he came face to face with a shoal of salmon and was hooked.

Jessop also discovered that there was money to be made beneath the waves. One weekend, diving on the Mull of Galloway, he retrieved hundreds of brass and copper fittings from a wreck lying on the seabed. The money he made from the scrap metal convinced him that he could make a living as a recovery diver, and he immediately quit his job.

With two partners from Keighley, Jessop began work as an underwater rag-and-bone man. At first it was a hand-to-mouth existence: he dived in a second-hand, ex-Royal Navy dry suit; his first air compressor was home-made from parts of a washing machine and a vacuum cleaner; and his first recovery vessel was the inner tube of an old tractor tyre fitted with a wire-mesh basket.

If a piece of metal was too big or too heavy to raise to the surface, he and his partners would simply hoist it on to their shoulders and walk it across the seabed to the shore.

Very little was then known about the perils of 'the bends' or 'the narcs' (nitrogen narcosis) and it was perhaps extraordinary that Jessop survived; he was largely self-taught and absolutely fearless, even learning to use explosives by trial and error. Later he acknowledged that he was 'lucky not to blow myself into oblivion in the process'.

After earning sufficient money to buy a redundant Fleetwood trawler – renamed *Black Pig* in tribute to Captain Pugwash and because it was smothered from stem to stern in oil – he began working on ever bigger and more valuable wrecks.

When his business partnership dissolved, amid some acrimony, he carried on alone. Jessop had a real gift for research, burrowing in files and archives and gleaning information from trawler skippers and lobstermen. He could also tell when official documents were hiding more than they revealed.

As his experience and expertise grew, Jessop began pestering the Salvage Association (which was set up to act on behalf of underwriters in obtaining a return on cargoes lost at sea) for recovery rights to some of the wrecks it administered. Eventually, perhaps more in the hope of some peace than in expectation that Jessop would succeed, the clerk to the association wrote three words on a piece of paper, '*Johanna Thorden*, Swona,' and told him: 'Find it or don't come back.'

Laden with copper, the *Johanna Thorden* had sunk in the treacherous tidal waters of the Pentland Firth, off the island of Swona. No other salvage team would go near the area, but Jessop succeeded in recovering the cargo in 1969, in the process establishing a formidable reputation for recovering goods from 'impossible' wrecks.

Jessop was the first man to realise that the new saturation diving techniques (allowing exposure to great depths) were bringing previously inaccessible wrecks within reach. He took a job in the oilfields to gain experience and then began deep-water recoveries in the frigid waters of the Arctic. But his eyes were firmly fixed on one prize in particular: the ten tons of 'Stalin's Gold' on the British light cruiser *Edinburgh*, sunk after being attacked by a U-boat in 1942. She was lying 800ft down in the Barents Sea.

The gold – 465 ingots – had been payment for supplies which the Allies were shipping to the Soviet Union. In the quest for salvage rights, Jessop had one crucial advantage over his far larger competitors: *Edinburgh* was a designated War Grave for British seamen, and his proposal to deploy saturation divers on the site – rather than rely on the explosives and crude mechanical grabs favoured by his rivals – proved decisive.

At the time Jessop was so short of money that he even took out a second mortgage on his home to help finance the project; had the *Edinburgh* recovery failed, he would have lost everything. In addition his team faced enormous technical difficulties in locating the wreck and operating at unprecedented depths, in freezing waters and surrounded by unexploded ordnance. Yet in the autumn of 1981 Jessop and his divers succeeded in raising tens of millions of pounds' worth of gold bars.

The British and Soviet governments took the lion's share, but Jessop's personal cut came to about £2 million. His moment of triumph, however, was soon soured. In a newspaper article, and then in a book, a writer who had accompanied the *Edinburgh* recovery claimed that the divers had desecrated the War Grave – a charge that, as a proud ex-Royal Marine, Jessop found particularly offensive – and that an official of the Salvage Association had been bribed to secure the contract.

Jessop sued for libel; the book was pulped, he accepted an out-of-court settlement and was awarded costs.

The police investigated the allegations and concluded that there was no case to answer. But the DPP overruled them, and in 1984 Jessop went on trial at the Old Bailey charged with conspiring to contravene Section Two of the Official Secrets Act and with conspiracy to defraud the unsuccessful bidders for the Edinburgh contract. The prosecution case collapsed and Jessop was acquitted on all charges, but his reputation had been tarnished.

He believed to his dying day that he had been the victim of a conspiracy and, bitter at his treatment, left Britain to live abroad. The stress of those years also contributed to the end of his marriage.

Although the recovery of the gold from *Edinburgh* remained his crowning achievement, Jessop's subsequent life was also highly adventurous. He searched, unsuccessfully, for the lost treasure of the pirate Henry Morgan and also for the wreck of Christopher Columbus's flagship *Santa Maria*. By the end of his life he had been wreck-hunting in every ocean of the world.

⇝ 23rd ⇜

Sam Snead, b. 1912, d. 2002

Sam Snead, who has died at Hot Springs, Virginia, aged eighty-nine, was one of the greatest players in the history of golf, and with Ben Hogan and Byron Nelson part of the triumvirate that dominated the game from the late 1930s through to the era of Arnold Palmer and Jack Nicklaus.

Snead won both the US Masters and the US Professional Golfers' Association championship three times, and won the Open in 1946. Just as impressive as his record, however, was the peerless beauty of his swing. Commentators vied with each other to do justice to Snead's action. It was 'like a Faulkner sentence,' wrote one, 'long, laced with the perfect pause and blessed with a powerful ending.'

'Anyone who would pass up an opportunity to see Sam Snead swing a golf club at a golf ball,' enthused another, 'would pull down the shades when driving past the Taj Mahal.'

Snead himself, a countryman who did not go in for flowery prose, took a practical view: 'Ah jes' takes tha club back nice and lazy and then ah try to whop it down on the barrelhead.' It did not look like that. Yet his rhythmical acceleration into the ball made him the first player regularly to drive 270 yards, and earned him the nickname 'Slammin' Sammy'.

Between 1937 and 1965 (when, at nearly fifty-three, he became the oldest man ever to win a professional golf tournament, the Greater Greensboro Open), Snead scored eighty-four victories on the US PGA tour – a record which not even Jack Nicklaus matched.

Yet Snead was just as exceptional for the tournaments he let slip through inconsistent putting. 'One has to be very good,' observed the *New York Herald Tribune*, 'to toss away as many Open titles as Snead has done through the years.'

At the US Open of 1939, held on the Spring-Mill course in Philadelphia, Snead threw away his lead when he took an eight on the last hole. In the play-off for the US Open of 1947, at St Louis, he led by two strokes with three holes to play, only to condemn himself to a second play-off (which he lost) when he missed a thirty-inch putt at the last hole. He never won the US Open, though he finished second four times.

Samuel Jackson Snead was born on 27 May 1912 at Ashwood, near Hot Springs in the foothills of West Virginia. Less than seven months separated Sam's birthday from those of his rivals Ben Hogan and Byron Nelson.

The boy's father, Harry Snead, who was of Dutch and German extraction, maintained the boilers at a local hotel, and supplemented his income with chickens and cows. Sam grew up wild, sharpening the accuracy of his eye by shooting squirrels, and developing the rhythm of his swing by practising with a crooked stick and a stone.

A superb all-round athlete at school, Snead began to devote his energies to golf after a back injury ended his ambitions in American Football. He would hit the ball along a fence, measuring distance by the number of posts his ball passed. Since his precious golf ball would be lost if he sliced it over the fence, he early learned to hit the ball with draw.

Soon Snead was caddying on his local course, barefoot as becomes the legend. His break came when the manager of a hotel in White Sulphur Springs gave him a living wage as an assistant professional.

His game developed rapidly – though for some time he was still dependent on nine unmatched clubs that had cost him $9. In 1936 he won the West Virginia championship. One of his rounds was a 61; twenty-three years later he would break his own record with a 59 on the same course, a round which he described as 'the highlight of my golfing career'.

In 1937 he won his first PGA Tour event at Oakland, California, and was a member of America's victorious Ryder Cup team. In 1938, having carried off $19,534 in prize money, he won the Vardon Memorial Trophy for the best golfer of the year.

Crowds flocked to see the new star, hailed as 'the next Bobby Jones'. Snead was amazed to see a picture of himself in a New York paper. 'Gee, Fred,' he asked his manager Fred Corcoran, 'how could they get a picture of me in New York? I ain't ever been there.'

Snead won his first major, the US PGA, in 1942 (a victory repeated in 1949 and 1951), and carried off the Masters in 1949, 1952 and 1954 – on the last occasion after an eighteen-hole play-off against Ben Hogan. He featured in seven Ryder Cups, twice as captain, and won ten of his thirteen matches.

Having come second in the Open of 1939 at St Andrews, Snead carried off the claret jug by four strokes when the championship resumed at that course in 1946. He was impressed neither by St Andrews ('the sort of real estate you couldn't give away'), nor by the drabness of post-war Britain, nor by the fact that the prize money failed to cover his expenses. He did not return next year to defend his title.

In 1947 Snead developed a twitch with his putting (always dangerously wristy in style), but found a cure in 1949 when he began to use a centre-shafted putter. The 1950s were golden years for him, but in the mid-1960s he was once more afflicted by nerves on the green. 'Sometimes when I putted,' he said, 'I looked like a monkey trying to wrestle a football.'

Eventually deteriorating eyesight took its toll. But he continued to appear annually at Augusta as the official honorary starter of the Masters, sending the ball 230 yards down the middle of the fairway even in his eighties. And in 2000 he returned to St

Andrews to take part in a four-hole tournament for former winners of the Open, and showed that there was still rhythm in his swing. In acknowledgment of the applause he executed a shoe-shuffle on the Swilcan Bridge of the eighteenth.

As a teacher he had little patience or understanding with the problems of the ordinary golfer. 'Lay off for three weeks,' he told one pupil, 'and then quit for good.'

⊰ 24th ⊱

Captain Piers St Aubyn, b. 1920, d. 2006

Captain Piers St Aubyn, who has died aged eighty-five, was one of only three officers of 156 Parachute Battalion to emerge unscathed from the battle of Arnhem.

A modest aristocrat with a languid, deprecating manner of speech and a reputation for leading from the front, he was one of thirty-four officers and more than 500 men dropped, as part of 4th Parachute Brigade, near the Dutch town of Arnhem on 18 September 1944. They were charged with reinforcing the party ordered to capture the bridge over the Rhine; but the operation was sixty miles behind enemy lines, and the Germans proved to be in far greater strength than expected.

Although he had been appointed battalion intelligence officer, St Aubyn was leading thirty tired and hungry men two days later when they came across the enemy firing down into the brigade headquarters established in a hollow by Brigadier 'Shan' Hackett.

Being low on ammunition, St Aubyn told the Germans with a mixture of hand signals and choice Anglo-Saxon to put down their arms and 'f*** off''; which, to his relief, they did. Hackett then called together all those who could walk and led them in a wild dash through the astonished German lines to his division's defensive position several hundred yards away.

After resisting two fierce attacks, in which he lost eight more men, St Aubyn joined the rest of the battalion holed up in three nearby houses. By now his men had only boiled sweets to eat. On visiting brigade HQ to obtain rations he found no food, but happily fell into conversation with his cousin, Lord Buckhurst, until Hackett told them sharply to get into a trench before they were killed.

Back in his house, St Aubyn dispatched a foraging party, then settled down to read *Barchester Towers*, reasoning that if he seemed relaxed it would have the same effect on his men. When a private started to run from window to window, shouting 'I'll get you, you bastard' at a German sniper, St Aubyn told him to be quiet, and returned to the reassuring story of Victorian clerical squabbles.

The following day, as his men were digging trenches, the enemy tried a new tack, using a loudspeaker to play the 'Teddy Bears' Picnic' and to relay a female voice telling them to surrender if they wanted to see their wives and sweethearts again.

When the withdrawal was ordered on the eighth day the men shaved and wrapped their boots in carpet and curtain material to deaden the noise. At nightfall they proceeded through the woods, each man holding the unfastened smock of the soldier in front, as if they were children playing a game. When they reached the riverbank a

Canadian engineer called from a boat: 'Room for one more.' As St Aubyn held back to offer another man the place, a fresh machine-gun burst decided the issue, and the passengers pulled him aboard.

⚔ 25th ⚔

The Reverend Antonio Ferrua, b. 1900, d. 2003

The Reverend Antonio Ferrua, who has died aged 102, was the Jesuit archaeologist responsible for uncovering what is believed to be the tomb of St Peter in the grottoes under St Peter's Basilica in Rome.

The venerable tradition which links the leader of the Apostles with Rome began in the earliest days of the Christian Church. At the end of his first epistle Peter writes from 'your sister church in Babylon' ('Babylon' being, according to many theologians, a Christian code for Rome); he is also believed to have been crucified upside down in the city, possibly on the orders of the Emperor Nero in AD64.

By the end of the first century AD it was assumed that Peter's body had been rescued by fellow Christians and laid to rest in the pagan cemetery on Vatican Hill. The burial place was thought to have been marked by the basilica built in AD325 on the instructions of Constantine, the first Christian emperor. This building was replaced in 1570 by the Renaissance cathedral which stands there today.

Ferrua's discovery came quite by chance. In 1939 Pope Pius XI died and plans were made to bury him beside Pius X in the crypt below the basilica. But when workmen began to dig under St Peter's they came upon a street of Roman tombs dating from the second century AD.

Under the supervision of Monsignor Ludwig Kaas, the Administrator of St Peter's, the Vatican appointed four archaeologists, including Ferrua, to investigate the tombs. Their appetites were whetted when the epigraphist Professor Margherita Guarducci discovered a Latin graffito on a tomb wall which read: *Petrus roga Christus Iesus pro sanctis hominibus Chrestianis ad corpus tuum sepultis*. ('Peter, pray Christ Jesus for the holy Christian men buried near your body.')

The excavators were still more excited when they came upon an aedicula, an altar-like structure dating from around AD160, which was positioned immediately below the high altar of St Peter's. Behind this was a thick red-plastered wall, beneath which they discovered a small pile of bones. Initially these seemed to belong to a powerfully built man of sixty-five or seventy (Peter's age when he died) but they were later proved to be the remains of two middle-aged men and an elderly woman.

Beyond the red wall, however, the excavators found an empty marble-lined repository, although there appeared to be no more bones. In 1950, while examining the interior of this repository, Ferrua discovered that a piece of plaster from one of its walls had fallen off. Scratched on to the plaster were fragments of Greek letters which read: *Petros eni* ('Peter is within here'). This fragment became one of the most important pieces of evidence that the saint had indeed been buried beneath the basilica and, on 23 December 1950, Pope Pius XII announced in his Christmas radio message that 'the tomb of the Prince of the Apostles has been found'.

Antonio Ferrua was born in 1900 in the northern Piedmont region of Italy and joined the Society of Jesus in 1918, studying epigraphy, Latin literature and archaeology.

In 1947 he became secretary of the Pontifical Commission for Sacred Archaeology, a position he held for twenty-four years, during which time he explored numerous ancient cemeteries and catacombs. A man of deep faith, Ferrua was a rigorous scholar, much admired for his refusal to allow his beliefs to compromise his work. His discovery was shrouded in controversy and, while Pope Paul VI announced on 26 June 1968 that 'the relics of St Peter have been identified in a manner which we believe convincing', Ferrua was more circumspect. Aware of the scepticism that surrounded even the analysis of the Greek fragment – which others had read as *Petros endei* or 'Peter is not here' – he told the Italian Catholic newspaper *L'Avvenire* that he was 'not convinced' that the saint's bones had been found.

⚜ 26th ⚜

The 4th Earl of Kimberley, b. 1924, d. 2002

The 4th Earl of Kimberley, who has died aged seventy-eight, achieved a measure of fame as the most-married man in the peerage; once known as 'the brightest blade in Burke's', he worked his way through five wives in twenty-five years before settling down contentedly with a former masseuse he had met on a beach in Jamaica.

Johnny Kimberley was a jovial extrovert whose interests included shark fishing, UFOs and winter sports – for much of the 1950s he was a member of Britain's international bobsleigh team. There was a serious side to him too: he played championship tiddlywinks, bred prize pigs, and as a Liberal spokesman in the Lords advised the electorate to vote Conservative, whereupon David (now Lord) Steel sacked him. Once on the Tory benches, he took a keen interest in defence and foreign policy, although not in social reform. 'Queers,' he declared, 'have been the downfall of all the great empires.'

However, it was his frequent trips to the altar, and those shortly thereafter to the divorce courts, that most naturally caught the eye of the public. His first marriage, in 1945, was to Diana, daughter of Sir Piers Legh, Master of the King's Household and a former equerry to Edward VIII; Kimberley had met her on a blind date at the Ritz. The wedding took place at St George's Chapel, Windsor, and was attended by the Queen, Princesses Elizabeth and Margaret, and King George VI, who proposed the toast to the bride and her groom, then a Guards officer.

Kimberley already knew that he had made a mistake. 'I couldn't stop it,' he said later, 'because the King and Queen were there, and I was in my best uniform.' Within a year the marriage was all but over and Kimberley was a free-spending, hard-driving member of London's *beau monde*. One night, he was caught naked by an irate husband in a hotel cupboard.

His second marriage, in 1949, was to Carmel Dunnett, one of the five daughters of Mickey Maguire, sometime welterweight champion of Australia; number three was Cynthia Westendarp, a Suffolk farmer's wife whom the Earl met at Newmarket. After she contracted polio, he invited her to recuperate at Kimberley, his seat near Wymondham, Norfolk, 'and she never moved out'. Five years after they were married in 1953, he had sold Kimberley, a Queen Anne brick mansion built on land held by his forebears for five centuries – 'it was the easiest way to get rid of Cynthia. All I could think about was buying a new Aston Martin.'

Next up was Maggie Simons, a 23-year-old fashion model and the daughter of a café owner. She refused to sleep with him until he proposed marriage, which he did within a week. They were married in 1961 but 'we both drank a fair amount and had fearful fights'. Kimberley's fourth divorce came through in 1965. He was thirty-nine.

His fifth marriage, in 1970, was to Gillian Raw (nee Ireland-Smith), 'and that was a disaster from the word go'. He had met Janey Consett, a soldier's daughter, in the Caribbean some years before, and now decided to 'sugar off' with her instead. Once more divorced, he married her in 1982, and happily it proved to be sixth time lucky.

No other peer had ever had so many wives. Ready as he was with explanations as to the failure of his marriages, the simpler truth was that Kimberley was for much of his life a charming but egotistical, idle and rather weak man who craved attention and sought only pleasure. He was also, as he admitted in 1980 in a debate in the Lords, an alcoholic.

'Helping to liberate Brussels in 1944 was the beginning of my downfall,' he wrote. After capturing an almost inexhaustible supply of Champagne, he kept a crate in his tank, regularly refreshing himself from it with a tin mug. 'I spent much of the war tight and when it was over I couldn't stop.' By the 1970s, it had begun to affect his health, and he joined Alcoholics Anonymous. He later became vice-president of the World Council on Alcoholism and a member of the National Council on Alcoholism.

As it was, this did not prevent him in his later years from consuming a bottle of white wine each day, although, as he pointed out, this was an improvement on the years when he counted himself 'insane'. 'After all,' he reasoned, 'no normal person would try to drive a car up the steps of the Grand Hotel in Brighton.'

⇥ 27th ⇤

Henry Johns, b. 1910, d. 1996

Henry Johns, who has died aged eighty-five, was the world's senior real tennis professional, and a veteran of the Golden Age of tennis – the age of the leisured patron, the elegant amateur and, above all, the cultivation of style.

As head professional at Lord's for twenty-one years, Johns coached several generations of top players. He was the archetypal professional of the old school: deferential, but never subservient, he demanded from his pupils exemplary manners both on and off the court.

His own skill at the game was consummate. His service showed effortless skill, subtle change of pace and great variety; his anticipation of return was faultless; and his strokes were smooth and accurate, using the minimum force required for each type of shot. All these qualities are reflected in the play of the past and present champions he taught.

Before going to Lord's, Johns worked at the old Prince's Club, in Knightsbridge, where he played real tennis against Sir Edwin Lutyens, whose reflexes, he recalled, were 'nearly non-existent'; and against the Maharajah of Alwar, whose service, he was instructed, was not to be returned.

Tumultuous applause from the Maharajah's retinue in the dedans greeted every winning point. Before he played, the court was always searched by one of his servants, because a soothsayer had predicted that he would die by the bite of a mad dog. But it was tennis that got the Maharajah in the end: he fell down the steps of a French court and broke his neck.

Henry Johns was born in Fulham on 21 July 1910, and grew up close to Queen's Club, where he occasionally earned sixpence an evening as a ball-boy. He was offered a job in the tennis professional's shop just before his fourteenth birthday, working a six-and-a-half day week for four shillings, sewing balls and stringing racquets.

During August, when the clubs closed, young Henry would be taken by Lord Revelstoke on a 'poor boy's holiday' to stay in his Lutyens castle on Lambay Island. There he played on the eccentric, roofless Irish court, where the main hazards were rainwater in wet weather and seagull droppings in dry.

He first joined Lord's in 1936 and in August 1939 enlisted in the Army, and went on to serve throughout the Second World War, attaining the rank of sergeant.

After the war he returned to Lord's, taking over from Jack Groom as head professional in 1954. He remained there until 1975, when he went into semi-retirement and was accorded honorary full membership of MCC, only the third employee of the Club to receive this accolade.

No expert was more modest than Johns, and no professional better loved. His eightieth birthday luncheon at Queen's Club attracted elderly and middle-aged players from every corner of Britain. It is a great tribute to the younger generations – the fit, fiercely competitive (and often Australian) athletes who have developed real tennis skills to a level never before seen – that they are seen to practise the true courtesies with Club members and among themselves which came so naturally to Johns.

⊰ 28th ⊱

Sydney Guilaroff, b. 1906, d. 1997

Sydney Guilaroff, who has died aged ninety, was chief hair stylist at Metro-Goldwyn-Mayer from 1934 to the later 1970s, and responsible for the hairstyles of virtually every MGM actress from Greta Garbo to Elizabeth Taylor.

Guilaroff was the first of his craft to receive screen credits. He worked on more than a thousand films, and his glamorous and devoted charges would not have dreamed of making a movie – or even a move – without his expertise.

He gave Claudette Colbert her bang, Louise Brooks her bob, and Judy Garland her *Wizard of Oz* braids. He created Vivien Leigh's hairdo for *Gone with the Wind* (1939), and Marlene Dietrich's extraordinarily elaborate curls for *Kismet* (1944), as well as her dark gypsy looks in Orson Welles's *Touch of Evil* (1958). Guilaroff did Ava Gardner's hair for *Pandora and the Flying Dutchman* (1950) and for *Showboat* (1951). He worked for Marilyn Monroe when she first appeared on the screen and maintained the connection to her last film, *The Misfits* (1961).

Guilaroff's instinct was unfailing. He had the knack of looking at a face and seeing instantly how it might be transformed with a clip of the scissors, or by a curl, a flip, a wave or a dash of colour.

His greatest challenge, he reckoned, was the production of *Marie Antoinette* in 1938. He travelled to Paris to do his research before constructing 2,000 court wigs (some with live birds in cages), lesser wigs for 3,000 extras, and the monumental bejewelled and feathered creation which Norma Shearer wore as the doomed queen.

Naturally, Guilaroff was a trusted confidant as well as a hairdresser. He was summoned to Monaco by Grace Kelly to style her hair for her marriage to Prince Rainier; he sat with the bedridden Joan Crawford the night she won an Oscar for *Mildred Pierce* (1945); and was the man to whom Elizabeth Taylor turned when her husband Mike Todd was killed in a plane crash.

But Guilaroff was not simply an elegant and witty courtier; he was also, if his own account is to be believed, a lover. In his autobiography, *Crowning Glories* (1996), he told of affairs with Greta Garbo and Ava Gardner – and hinted that there was a great deal more about the private lives of his devoted clients that he knew but chose not to divulge. For all his talent and celebrity, however, he had become a hairdresser by accident.

Of Russian extraction, Sydney Guilaroff was born in London on 2 November 1906, the sixth of seven children. He grew up in Canada, first in Winnipeg, and later in Montreal, displaying a flair for the piano and painting. At first he dreamed of becoming an architect – but the family's slender means forced him to leave home at thirteen.

He sought employment in New York where he was initially so poor that he sometimes slept on park benches. He held a series of menial jobs before landing a position as handyman in the hair salon at the McAlpin Hotel. He picked up his trade by instinct, proving so adept that by the time he was sixteen he was already much in demand in the theatre and society.

The first star for whom he worked was Claudette Colbert, but it was Louise Brooks who truly launched 'Mr Sydney's' career. He created the 'shingle' for her, a boyish style that set off a fashion across America. In fact, Guilaroff did not recognise his client until, a few months later, he saw his handiwork on the silver screen.

Within a few years, he had his own salon called Antoine's, but it was not until Louis B. Mayer discovered why Joan Crawford insisted on travelling to New York before a film that he was summoned to a new career in Hollywood.

The regard and trust in which he was held was vividly demonstrated when Elizabeth Taylor threatened to pull out of *Cleopatra* (1963) after union officials had refused to allow him to work. Eventually it was agreed that he could style her hair at her hotel but never at the studio.

His last job was a television film, *The Two Mrs Grenvilles* (1987). This reunited him with his first star client, Claudette Colbert.

'She was the first star I styled and the last,' he recalled. 'I originally styled her at Antoine's when she was filming in New York. I studied her lovely face and cut her hair very short, then gave her a bang. She kept that hairdo for the rest of her life.'

﹌ 29th ﹌

Coral Browne, b. 1913, d. 1991

Coral Browne, the actress who has died aged seventy-seven, was one of the most elegant and sophisticated players of her time – notable almost as much for her waspish wit and sexual candour off-stage as for her allure on it.

Her off-stage persona, her irreverent witticisms, real and apocryphal, became legendary. She had a deep, throaty voice and impeccable timing. It is not difficult to imagine the effect of her whispered but reverberating aside as a giant golden phallus was unveiled at the end of Peter Brook's production of *Oedipus*: 'Nobody we know, darling.'

Another story has her casting a lubricious eye over a young actor, only to be assured by a friend, David Dodimead, that the cause was hopeless. Undaunted, Coral Browne bet Dodimead £1 that she could gain her end that very night. Her friends waited anxiously for the outcome. 'Dodders,' the actress drawled when she saw him across a crowded room the next morning, 'I owe you twelve and sixpence.'

Browne was a Catholic convert. She was once standing on the steps of Brompton Oratory after mass when a theatrical queen bustled up with the latest gossip. She stopped him with: 'I don't want to hear such filth, not with me standing here in a state of f****** grace.'

David Jefferies, b. 1972, d. 2003

David Jefferies, who has been killed in a motorcycle crash aged thirty, was the pre-eminent Isle of Man TT racer of his generation.

The sheer speed with which Jefferies could wrestle a 190mph racing motorcycle around the 37-mile TT course put him in a different league from other competitors. His record lap in 2002, 127.29mph, was nothing less than astonishing.

After setting that record, he remarked, 'I learn tracks pretty quick, and really enjoy riding ordinary road bikes on public roads, so this place really suits me ... The buzz you get round here is mega – the buzz of getting it right is just so good.'

It was, perhaps, inevitable that Allan David Jefferies (known as 'DJ' to his fans) would grow up to participate in some form of competitive motorcycle sport. His grandfather, Allan, was the pre-eminent British trials rider of the late 1930s, and founded the famous Scott Trial; and during the 1970s his father, Tony, won two TT races, while his Uncle Nick won the Formula One TT in 1993 and was a top-class trials rider.

Indeed, David's arrival was precipitated when his mother, Pauline, went into labour after watching her husband crash at Mallory Park race track. In case their first-born proved to have a talent for cricket, the family hurried back to Bradford, in Yorkshire, where he was born the following morning, 18 September 1972.

He first competed in motorcycle trials at the age of seven, on an 80cc Yamaha, a Christmas present from his parents. At fourteen he began racing in motocross events, but knee ligament damage cut short his off-road career. Instead, he began Tarmac racing on a 600cc Yamaha in 1990.

In 1998 Jefferies entered his first TT meeting, claiming the best newcomers' award with a lap at more than 115mph. The following year he missed the Manx races through injury, but returned in 1999 to win three TT races, a remarkable achievement in only his second year. Over the next two TTs, 2000 and 2002 (the 2001 races were cancelled due to the foot-and-mouth epidemic), he scored two further triples, a feat unique in the races' long history.

David Jefferies was killed when he lost control of his 1,000cc Suzuki at Crosby while practising for the TT races.

⊰ 30th ⊱

Lorenzo Odone, b. 1978, d. 2008

Lorenzo Odone, who died the day after his thirtieth birthday, became famous throughout the world with the release, in 1992, of the film *Lorenzo's Oil*, starring Susan Sarandon and Nick Nolte.

At the time that the film was made, Lorenzo was fourteen and had been suffering for eight years from adrenoleukodystrophy (ALD) a genetic disease, affecting mainly boys, which usually results in brain failure and, ultimately, death.

The film dramatised the attempts by his parents, Augusto and Michaela Odone (played by Nolte and Sarandon), to find an effective treatment, a quest which culminated in the invention of 'Lorenzo's oil', a derivative of olive and rapeseed oils and the first agent to have demonstrated a therapeutic effect by halting the destruction by the disease of the myelin sheathing of the nervous system.

The treatment was patented by Augusto Odone, and a study published in 2005, based on research with eighty-four boys, demonstrated its efficacy in preventing the onset of the disease's symptoms for a majority of boys diagnosed early with ALD. This discovery came too late for Lorenzo Odone, who was already suffering from the irreversible neurological effects of the disease.

Augusto Odone and his wife went further, however, founding a charity called the Myelin Project, an international scientific body which seeks to promote research into those diseases which destroy myelin, the white matter of the central nervous system without which the brain cannot transmit messages to other parts of the body. The goal is to bring hope to those suffering from conditions such as multiple sclerosis and the leukodystrophies (of which ALD is one).

Lorenzo Michael Murphy Odone was born on 29 May 1978 in Washington DC, the son of Augusto Odone, an Italian-born economist with the World Bank, and his second wife, Michaela, a linguist. It was clear from his earliest years that Lorenzo was a precocious, bright child, and one who was hungry for knowledge. By the age of five he was fluent in English, French and Italian, and his parents hoped that he was destined for Harvard.

At kindergarten in Washington he seemed normal and talkative, and it was only when his father was posted abroad, and Lorenzo began classes at a French school on the Comoros Islands in the Indian Ocean, that his teachers reported problems with his behaviour and a deterioration in his attention span.

By 1984, when he was six, Lorenzo's behavioural problems had worsened and he began to suffer from blackouts and memory lapses, symptoms akin to those of stroke victims. At first, Augusto and Michaela Odone believed that their son might have contracted a tropical disease in the Comoros Islands, but a brain scan finally confirmed that Lorenzo was suffering from ALD.

The prevailing medical wisdom decreed that children with ALD typically lived for only a few years beyond diagnosis. But Augusto and Michaela Odone refused to accept this, and began an exhaustive quest for an effective treatment. Despite having no medical training, they contacted specialists and combed the scientific journals.

Lorenzo's father was granted leave by the World Bank to work from the family home outside Washington so that he could help to care for his son. Then, in 1987, having taken early retirement, he invented a treatment, in the form of a vegetable oil, that appeared to arrest the progress of ALD.

To help with the oil's development, the Odones enlisted a British scientist, Don Suddaby, who had worked at the Croda Universal chemical company in Hull. He came out of retirement to help produce an edible mixture of olive and rapeseed oil extract, finally sending the Odones a bottle of what would become known as 'Lorenzo's oil'.

Although the Odones were told that the oil might have a deleterious effect, they decided, in view of the rapid deterioration in their son's condition, to risk administering it. Augusto Odone believes that the treatment was responsible for giving Lorenzo many extra years of life.

By now, however, Lorenzo had become bedridden; he was blind, deaf and almost completely disabled physically. He could signal 'yes' and 'no' by blinking or moving his fingers.

Occasionally it was possible to discern a nuance in Lorenzo's largely unchanging expression that seemed to signal a response to what was going on around him – for example, he appeared to be able to tell if someone walked into the room – but for the most part he remained inert, a gentle dreaminess about the face disturbed only by the occasional spasm.

His condition required round-the-clock medical care. He was nursed in the family home outside Washington, attended by five nurses working in shifts, as well as by his parents – his mother would spend up to sixteen hours at a stretch at her son's bedside. Because he was unable to swallow saliva, he had to be suctioned, sometimes every few minutes. Every bodily function had to be monitored, and he had to be fed five times a day through a tube.

Throughout the years of his illness Lorenzo displayed exemplary courage. He had lain paralysed in a darkened room, unable to see or speak, while his body developed normally through childhood and adolescence.

He remained completely unaware of the global celebrity conferred on him by the Hollywood film that told his story. 'Michaela once said that the real Lorenzo was locked in his ALD body,' Augusto Odone told a British journalist in 2001, 'and I believe that is true.'

After Michaela Odone's death, in 2000, Augusto played his son tapes of her voice which she had recorded for him, and Lorenzo appeared to respond to these with conscious and voluntary sounds.

⇥ 31st ⇤

Peter Kershaw, b. 1915, d. 2000

Peter Kershaw, who has died aged eighty-five, was for more than thirty years chairman of Joseph Holt's brewery in Manchester.

His working methods were far removed from the ideals of business schools. In his prime at Holt's there were no financial advisers, management strategists, or monthly balance sheets. The chairman held all the facts in his head, and proceeded entirely on his own judgment.

He had no time for executive trappings, positively relishing the Dickensian office conditions at the brewery. He wrote all his letters longhand and, in his early days, passed them to office boys for typing – women secretaries being unknown at Holt's before the 1970s. He was once informed that the sunshine roof of his company car was leaking.

'That may be so,' he returned, 'but not on my side.'

JUNE

⚜ 1st ⚜

Vincent O'Brien, b. 1917, d. 2009

Vincent O'Brien, who has died aged ninety-two, was arguably the greatest racehorse trainer in the history of the sport.

Nor is it easy to imagine anyone surpassing his achievements under the two codes of racing: in National Hunt, O'Brien won four Cheltenham Gold Cups, three Champion Hurdles and three consecutive Grand Nationals; when he turned his attention to the Flat, at the age of forty-one, he went on to take twenty-seven Irish Classics, three Prix de l'Arc de Triomphes and sixteen English Classics, including six Epsom Derbies.

When his former stable jockey, Lester Piggott, was invited to locate O'Brien in racing's pantheon, he replied simply: 'Of course Vincent was the greatest – look at the figures.'

O'Brien's career spanned an era in which racing changed from being merely a sporting pastime to a multi-million-pound industry, and it was a change in which this Irish trainer played no small part through his association, in the late 1970s and early 1980s, with Robert Sangster and John Magnier. Their syndicate enjoyed ten extraordinary years, thanks to O'Brien's skill and eye for a horse, Magnier's acumen and Sangster's money, with which they bought the finest yearling colts (usually by Northern Dancer).

Trained at Ballydoyle, O'Brien's stable, to win Classic and other major races, the successful horses would then stand at the partnership's Coolmore Stud to be syndicated as stallions for millions of pounds. O'Brien's role in this was crucial. There was no better judge of a yearling, and he had an unrivalled knowledge of pedigrees.

Michael Vincent O'Brien was born at Churchtown, Co. Cork, on 9 April 1917. He left school at fifteen to work with his father, but also had a sideline breeding and selling greyhounds to England, a trade that was ended by the outbreak of the Second World War.

Having resolved to become a trainer, O'Brien visited England for the first time in December 1943 and, at Newmarket sales, paid just 130 guineas for Drybob, a three-year-old of little visible merit. At the same time Sidney McGregor, breeder of both a Derby and a Grand National winner, asked him to train a moderate four-year-old, Good Days. In 1944, his very first year as a trainer, O'Brien pulled off the Irish Autumn Double at the Curragh; Good Days won the Cesarewitch and Drybob dead-heated for the Cambridgeshire – O'Brien had £2 each way on the double at 800–1.

The horse that put O'Brien on the map, however, was Cottage Rake. The young trainer was in the lavatory of a Dublin hotel when he overheard two vets discussing this fine horse, whose sale had twice fallen through because it suffered from a respiratory problem. 'But at his age, I don't think it will ever affect him,' O'Brien heard one vet say to the other.

The young trainer rushed to a telephone: 'I immediately called Mr [Frank] Vickerman, the only man I knew with any money, and told him to buy the horse.' Cottage Rake duly arrived at Churchtown, and in the autumn of 1947 won the Irish Cesarewitch. The following year he won the Cheltenham Gold Cup; on Easter Monday, at a party in Dublin, horse and trainer were toasted with pre-war vintage champagne.

In 1948 O'Brien bought an insignificant-looking eight-year-old called Hatton's Grace. On his second visit to Cheltenham's National Hunt Festival, in 1949, O'Brien achieved a remarkable double: the Champion Hurdle with Hatton's Grace, and a second consecutive Gold Cup with Cottage Rake. He completed a Gold Cup hat-trick with 'The Rake' in 1950, also taking three consecutive Champion Hurdles with Hatton's Grace (1949–51). His fourth Gold Cup winner was Knock Hard, in 1953. O'Brien also won the Grand National in three successive years (1953–55) with Early Mist, Royal Tan and Quare Times.

In his early days as a National Hunt trainer, O'Brien needed to gamble simply to make the money to keep going; later, successful coups helped to finance expansion. His gambling successes helped him, in 1951, to set up at Ballydoyle, near Cashel in Co. Tipperary. This was a Georgian house set in 320 acres of parkland which he gradually turned into a top-class training establishment.

Having conquered the jumping scene, O'Brien decided to concentrate on the Flat. He won the 1953 Irish Derby with Chamier; then, at Doncaster Sales, he met an American owner, John McShain, for whom he bought five yearlings. Among them was Ballymoss which, in 1957–58, came second in the English Derby and won the Irish Derby, the St Leger, Eclipse, Coronation Cup, King George VI and Queen Elizabeth Stakes and the Arc de Triomphe.

But these early triumphs were short-lived.

Early in 1960 the Turf Club (the Irish equivalent of the Jockey Club) concluded that Chamier's son, Chamour, had been doped after winning a minor race at the Curragh, despite the fact that no solid scientific evidence could be produced to support the accusation. O'Brien, who claimed he was the victim of small-mindedness and jealousy, had his licence withdrawn for eighteen months.

Later, however, the Turf Club backed down, and O'Brien was exonerated. Thirty years later, at the Curragh, one of the stewards who had warned off O'Brien approached him and extended his hand with the words: 'O'Brien, I'll forgive you if you forgive me.' The trainer turned his back and left the room.

In 1962 O'Brien won the first of his six Epsom Derbies, with Larkspur. He won the Irish Oaks in 1964, and the following year the Oaks at Epsom with Long Look, and the Irish Oaks with Aurabella. In 1966 he took the 1,000 Guineas at Newmarket with Glad Rags.

O'Brien was now deciding to book Lester Piggott as his jockey whenever possible, leading to an inevitable showdown with Piggott's retaining trainer, Sir Noel Murless. There was a sensation before the 1966 Oaks when the jockey insisted on riding O'Brien's Valoris instead of Murless's Varinia; when Valoris won (Varinia finished third), Piggott announced that he was now a freelance jockey. O'Brien merely remarked: 'He is the best jockey. It's as simple as that.'

In 1968 O'Brien was asked by the platinum magnate, Charles Engelhard, to go to Canada to inspect a colt by Ribot. Having seen the horse, O'Brien advised against a purchase – but recommended that Engelhard instead buy a son of the then untried stallion, Northern Dancer.

This was Nijinsky, who went on to make history in 1970, winning under Lester Piggott the Triple Crown (2,000 Guineas, Derby and St Leger); the horse also won the Irish Derby and the King George VI and Queen Elizabeth Diamond Stakes.

Among O'Brien's owners was the Irish-American Jack Mulcahy; and it was he who told the trainer to 'get a piece of the action' — that is, to become a part-owner in the horses he trained, thereby profiting from their prize money and, more importantly, their value at stud. O'Brien was to call this 'the best advice I ever got', and he became a very rich man.

O'Brien trained his sixth and final Epsom Derby winner, Golden Fleece, in 1982. By now, though, Arab owners – and particularly the Maktoum family from Dubai – were beginning to dominate the Flat racing scene; the ascendancy of Ballydoyle was over. In 1987 O'Brien, Magnier, Sangster, Michael Smurfit and John Horgan launched Classic Thoroughbreds; but in 1991 the Ballydoyle-based racing company was wound up, and O'Brien cut back his string of horses. In 1994 he retired.

O'Brien had, in his native country, won 1,529 races to the value of £5,789,460, and been champion Irish trainer thirteen times. He had twice been British champion trainer on the Flat, and twice over obstacles.

⚜ 2nd ⚜

Brian Booth, b. 1927, d. 2008

B rian Booth, who has died aged eighty, was an explorer and naturalist in the tradition of a vanished golden age of discovery.

He was almost certainly one of the last British Army officers to be given unpaid leave to undertake extended expeditions, and in the Sahara in the 1950s led a scientific journey to look for evidence of Neolithic remains which he believed offered clues to the origins of ancient Egyptian civilisation.

He remained in the Army until 1963, reaching the rank of major. In his autobiography Ranulph Fiennes, who served under him, described Booth's leaving party at the Vier Jahrezeiten Hotel in Hamburg as including 'a great deal of alcohol and operatic performance by officers on the table top. Baron Franckenstein sang *Figaro* to the music of the Four Seasons orchestra.'

Brian Derek MacDonald Booth was born on 20 July 1927 at Arkley, Hertfordshire.

At Oundle he was inspired by the ornithologist James Fisher, who encouraged him to take an interest in natural history. After his parents divorced, Brian spent lonely summer holidays on the island of Coll, an experience that fostered his love of flora and fauna.

At the age of eighteen, in 1945 Brian Booth joined the Royal Scots Greys and was sent to Germany as a lieutenant in the army of occupation. As the junior officer in charge of field sports he was responsible for 96,000 acres of what had previously been Goering's personal hunting ground. Booth's finest sporting accomplishment with a double-barrelled shotgun was a right-and-left, when he shot a snipe with the right barrel and a wild boar that leapt out of a ditch at his feet with the left.

In 1957 he led the British Berkou-Ennedi expedition, which involved a journey of some 5,500 miles, including a 1,600-mile desert crossing. In Chad, Booth was arrested at an oasis by the Foreign Legion for shooting what he later described as 'the wrong sort of crocodile' – which he knew to be a rarity and which he had planned to bring back to the Natural History Museum in London for its collection.

Fined for not having the right permit, Booth persuaded his captors to take a cheque; but the indignant French ambassador in London later wrote to Booth at the Cavalry Club demanding more in the way of reparation.

In 1956 and 1959 Booth made ornithological trips to Iceland, in particular to study the snowy owl breeding in lava fields in the interior; and in 1960 he found himself at the River Hofsa in remote north-east Iceland. He spent the savage winter of 1962–63 in a hut he had built on the riverside, studying bird life of the Arctic winter and meeting local farmers when he was not snowed in. In 1967 he helped these farmers form their own fishing club and agreed to lease the river from them, setting in motion the restoration of the salmon runs in one of the world's great salmon rivers.

He remained fit even into old age. In his sixties he was climbing forty feet up oak trees in search of butterflies, and at the age of seventy-five fell eighteen feet out of a tree when a branch he was leaning on gave way while he was trying to shoot a roebuck – he walked away. In his late seventies he was still travelling, shooting ptarmigan in the winter in Sweden and dog sledding (and camping out in the snow) in Swedish Lapland.

 3rd

Jack Kevorkian, b. 1928, d. 2011

Jack Kevorkian, the American pathologist who has died aged eighty-three, attracted considerable notoriety through his strenuous efforts to assist the terminally ill to commit suicide.

A macabre embodiment of society's moral confusion over the issue of voluntary euthanasia, Kevorkian, a gaunt, white-haired figure who favoured sensible cardigans and clip-on ties, was dubbed 'Dr Death'.

Since law forbade him to kill the terminally ill at their request, he provided the facilities, demonstrated the apparatus of self-destruction, and then watched.

Kevorkian claimed to have helped some 130 people to commit suicide. In 1999, after the television show *60 Minutes* broadcast a videotape he had made of the assisted suicide of a 52-year-old man, he was convicted of second-degree murder. He served eight years in a prison in Michigan.

Renowned for his good humour, Kevorkian termed himself an 'obituarist' – the first of a new variety of medical specialist who would assist the terminally ill to kill themselves under strictly controlled guidelines.

For his first deaths, in 1990, he used a complicated suicide machine he called a 'mercitron', an apparatus which pumped saline into the 'client', switching to a lethal solution when the client pressed a button; in 1991 he switched to the simpler, and less expensive, process of gassing by carbon monoxide.

His supporters pointed to the ageing population and the ability of modern medicine to prolong life almost indefinitely, at astonishing cost; and even his detractors admitted that his activities ensured that the issue of euthanasia remained in the public conscience.

The son of comfortably off Albanian immigrants, Jacob Kevorkian was born in Detroit on 26 May 1928. One of his two sisters, Margo, later helped in his 'medicide' practice, often videoing the patients as evidence that the procedure was carried out at their explicit request.

He trained in Pathology at Michigan University, where he was considered an exceptional student; but during the 1950s Kevorkian became somewhat isolated from his colleagues, and began to advocate increasingly controversial measures such as the use of the organs of condemned prisoners for experimentation. He went to practise in California, attempting to make a film about organ harvesting, but finally drifted back to Michigan, where he found himself unemployed.

In 1989 he demonstrated his 'suicide machine' on television and had business cards printed advertising his services – though he never accepted payment.

His first client was Janet Adkins, a 53-year-old sufferer from Alzheimer's, who died in a Michigan forest in the back of a Volkswagen camper van in 1990. Over the following years Kevorkian continued to practise exclusively in Michigan, where he assisted sufferers from cancer, Alzheimer's, arthritis, heart disease, emphysema and multiple sclerosis through the final exit. Among them were a disproportionate number of women.

The more the authorities attempted to restrain him, the more publicity he garnered – and the more requests for assistance he received. By November 1993, despite the introduction of laws in his home state of Michigan banning citizens from assisting in a suicide, Kevorkian had helped nineteen people take their own lives. He was unsuccessfully tried by prosecutors four times before finally being imprisoned in 1999.

But there was little prospect of him turning his hand to a production line of death, as he claimed that he found his work exhausting: 'You really couldn't do one a day of these. It just takes too much work.'

❧ 4th ☙

Ernest Borneman, b. 1915, d. 1995

Ernest Borneman, who has died aged eighty, was known in German-speaking countries as the 'Pope of Sex' on account of the authority with which he addressed that subject in his frequent television appearances.

A lifelong obsession with sex crystallised during the 1960s into an academic calling. Borneman carried out a study of 5,000 children which, he explained, yielded 'relatively little evidence of penis envy, but a lot of evidence of bosom envy'. In consequence he predicted the extinction of the patriarchal system, and elaborated this conclusion in a 1,000-page tome entitled *Patriarchy*.

❧ 5th ☙

Viola Keats, b. 1911, d. 1998

Viola Keats, who has died aged eighty-seven, had good looks and vitality which made her a heart-throb of the London stage in the 1930s.

Her stage and screen career lasted for five decades, and was not without incident. In 1958 she played the murder victim, Anja Hendryk, in the short-lived first run of Agatha Christie's *Verdict at the Strand*.

On the first night, the final curtain came down forty seconds too soon, cutting out the surprise ending of the play. 'There was no dextrous twist at the end,' wrote one critic, unaware of the disaster in the flies. 'Instead there was a great scene of renunciation and parting which rang false and fell flat.'

On the second night, everything went smoothly, and the booing was replaced by six enthusiastic curtain calls.

George Chatham, b. 1912, d. 1997

George Chatham, who has died aged eighty-five, was acknowledged by his fellow rogues as the finest cat burglar of the century.

His most publicised theft took place in April 1948, when he stole from the Victoria and Albert Museum two jewelled swords that had belonged to the 1st Duke of Wellington.

Chatham had gained access to the building in, by his standards, rather mundane fashion, lashing two ladders together and entering through a rear window forty feet up. Having escaped the police's search of the area by crouching in a telephone box in Exhibition Road, he swiftly frittered away the proceeds on girlfriends and gambling.

More than thirty years later, Chatham, aged seventy-two, made a renewed assault on the museum. His attempt to break into the Jewel House from the roof one November night was foiled only by a blizzard, which made his footing too precarious and forced a retreat.

George Henry Chatham was born in Fulham, west London, on 3 April 1912. His first conviction for theft came in 1931, aged nineteen. He was to spend a total of thirty-five years in prison.

From early in his career, Chatham concentrated on stealing wealth in its most portable forms. He had a particular penchant for the furriers and galleries of Mayfair, as well as for jewellery, whose location he gleaned from dishonest servants, corrupt insurance clerks and the records he stole from underwriting firms. He assiduously studied the gossip columns and *Country Life* and liked to work when dinner parties were in progress, so that alarms would be off.

His exploits and preferred targets were first recorded by the press in the late 1930s, when he took advantage of an impenetrable pea-souper to burgle several houses around Hyde Park, leaping unobserved from balcony to balcony. The newspapers said he had 'made hay while the sun wasn't shining'. Later prominent victims included the Duke of Windsor's confidant 'Fruity' Metcalfe, the hairdresser 'Teasy Weasy' Raymond and the Maharajah of Jaipur, whose safe he opened with a custom-made foot-long key.

Chatham also stole a fur coat and an eternity ring from Lady Rothermere. He readily returned the items when approached by one of Associated Newspapers' editors – the coat, he complained, was far too poor in quality to be given to one of his girlfriends.

His trade was not without peril. When about to burgle Raine de Chambrun, then Countess of Dartmouth, he accidentally stepped off the roof and dropped four floors. Within six weeks, swathed in bandages, he was back at work, terrifying a maid who thought she had discovered a mummy lumbering through her employer's residence.

Chatham did not confine himself to burglary. In 1952 he participated in the largest armed robbery to that date, the hijacking of a mail van carrying £287,000. The raid was meticulously rehearsed on suburban roads under the pretence of making a film. It was Chatham who sauntered into the Post Office depot by St Paul's Cathedral to disconnect the van's alarm. It was such nerveless cool that brought him the nickname 'Taters', derived from the rhyming slang for cold, 'Taters-in-the-mould'.

Chatham's share from the robbery was £15,000, but he quickly lost it at the rigged gaming tables of Billy Hill, leader of the robbers and self-proclaimed 'boss of the underworld'. Hill spared Chatham when he was caught trying to steal back the money from his safe, knowing that he would soon return to lose more.

For Chatham was a compulsive gambler, an unhappy trait in someone who was not a good judge of horses and a bad card player. It was this weakness, together with a flashy lifestyle, that drove his career. He was in constant need of cash, once hawking a stolen Renoir for only £5,000.

There were many tales of his leaving a casino after an expensive night, only to return a few minutes later with fresh collateral acquired from a trip to Belgravia in his twelve-cylinder Lagonda.

He continued to burgle well into old age, sometimes accompanied by his friend Peter Scott. In 1985 Chatham was arrested after a rooftop chase, having scaled a 50ft building and burrowed through a wall into a London dress shop. He was seventy-three, and a bad fall through a roof thereafter limited his activity to shoplifting. He had saved none of the several million pounds that he had stolen, and died penniless in a nursing home in Battersea.

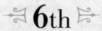 6th

Anne Haddy, b. 1927, d. 1999

Anne Haddy, who has died aged seventy-one, played Helen Daniels in the remarkably popular Australian television soap opera *Neighbours*, of which she was the longest-serving cast member.

Neighbours, set on Ramsay Street in the fictional Melbourne suburb of Erinsborough, was created in 1985 by Reg Watson, the original producer of *Crossroads*. In the 1970s he had returned to his native Australia to devise such pearls of Antipodean television as *Prisoner: Cell Block H*, *Sons and Daughters* and *The Young Doctors*.

The first series of *Neighbours*, however, was not well received by the Australian public. It was judged to be too serious, and to have too many middle-aged characters, among them Helen Daniels, a mother-in-law and grandmother.

The programme was taken off the air, and when it returned the next year it began to make more play of the Australian appetite for good, clean fun, and of the wholesome charms of two teenage characters, Scott Robinson (Jason Donovan) and Charlene Mitchell (Kylie Minogue).

The show's breakthrough came in the autumn of 1986, when the BBC was looking for cheap material to fill its new daytime schedules. It began showing *Neighbours* twice a day, five days a week, originally at 10 a.m. and 1.30 p.m. Within a year it had attracted a devoted following (comprised principally of students, mothers and schoolchildren), and within two years it was being watched by more viewers than *Coronation Street*.

When Michael Grade's teenage daughter complained that because she was at school she could not watch *Neighbours*, the then director of BBC programmes astutely moved the repeat to 5.30 p.m., which furthered increased its daily audience to eight million people. *Neighbours'* success would subsequently enable Minogue and Donovan to enjoy lucrative musical careers in Britain itself.

The source of the programme's appeal eluded even the most learned cultural commentators. They speculated that viewers were attracted by the Australian sunshine, by the show's relative classlessness, by the good looks of the cast, even by its perky theme tune ('Neigh-bours, everybody needs good neigh-bours'). In truth, perhaps any of the above were welcome novelties for an audience reared on the homespun delights of *Take the High Road*.

Chic, calm and reasonable, Helen Daniels was the one to whom the neighbourhood turned in moments of crisis, for instance when Scott's marriage to Charlene was failing, or when the Ramsay Street dog, Bouncer, went missing.

Helen's own life had not been without its trials. After the death of her husband in the 1970s, she discovered that he had been having an affair with her sister. A few years later her daughter died in childbirth; to console herself, Helen took in a homeless orphan. Shortly afterwards, her trusting nature was exploited by a suave con-man, who persuaded her to hand over her life savings to him. Having survived blackmail and a coma, romance arrived in the shape of her husband's cousin. The pair were married, but sadly he turned out to be a bigamist.

Helen then accidentally revealed to Julie Martin that the latter was not, as she believed, the daughter of Jim Robinson, but had been conceived when her mother was raped. Later Helen turned for consolation to Len Mangel, the ex-husband of Erinsborough's resident busybody, but luckily she discovered that he had another girlfriend and was just after her for her pension.

Helen's passion was her art, and although the results ('painted,' Anne Haddy revealed, 'by someone in scenery') were uniformly terrible, some viewers were deceived; Anne Haddy said that the lowest point of her twelve years in the series came when a boy wrote to ask her to paint a picture of his dead cat, and she had to explain that she was not really an artist.

Anne Haddy was born on 5 October 1927 at Quorn, South Australia. An only child, she would invent playmates for herself and spent much of her time dressing up.

In 1948 she made her debut on ABC Radio, and pursued an interest in drama while working as a librarian at Adelaide University. She came to England in 1950, intending to study further rather than to act. Consequently, she refused an offer from a friend, the budding cartoonist Rolf Harris, to send her picture to his agent. Instead she wound up at Kellogg's as a secretary.

Having married her first husband, Max Dimmit, Anne Haddy returned to Australia, where she eventually landed the job of presenting the Australian version of *Playschool*. Later she appeared in such staples of Australian broadcasting as *Skippy the Bush Kangaroo*.

Throughout much of her adult life, Anne Haddy suffered from ill health, and she survived three heart operations and a fight with stomach cancer before kidney failure following a hip replacement finally compelled her to leave *Neighbours* in 1997. Her character departed the programme by dying while watching a video recording of Scott's wedding.

⊰ 7th ⊱

Kenneth (b. 1911) and Audrey (b. 1917) Austin, d. 1999

The Grimaldis, the clowns Kenneth and Audrey Austin, who have been killed in a motor accident in Florida aged eighty-seven and eighty-one respectively, were veterans of the heyday of the British circus and variety theatre in the 1930s and 40s.

They first teamed up as a musical double act in February 1939, shortly before their marriage, and soon became familiar figures on the variety circuit. Between them they could play fifteen instruments proficiently.

By the late 1960s, however, the Grimaldis discovered that the fairs on which they relied for their livelihood were more interested in booking country and western stars than old-fashioned British variety acts. They therefore developed a circus act with a clever poodle, the success of which allowed them to continue performing even as octogenarians.

The Grimaldis were killed instantly in a collision with a lorry a few days before they were due to receive American citizenship; their toy poodle, Lucky, was rescued from the ensuing conflagration only lightly singed.

Victor Sassie, b. 1915, d. 1999

Victor Sassie, the restaurateur who has died aged eighty-four, founded and ran the Gay Hussar, the Hungarian restaurant in Greek Street, Soho, which was for more than thirty years one of the most distinctive places to eat in London.

Only authentic Hungarian dishes created between 1850 and 1938 were admitted, and the menu barely changed from the opening in 1953. Customers were greatly surprised when they discovered that Sassie, for all his Hungarian style, was born in Barrow-in-Furness.

In the late 1950s and throughout the 60s the Gay Hussar was a favourite haunt for leading Labour lights of the day, for Sassie was a romantic socialist. But the odd bold Tory and plenty of publishers also made themselves regulars on Sassie's red-plush banquettes arranged around the small ground floor that seated thirty-six.

Tom Driberg, chairman of the Labour Party and an astonishingly promiscuous homosexual, was a cherished customer, and was responsible for introducing the loud and gluttonous Hugh Dalton to the restaurant. It is said that Aneurin Bevin would pause momentarily on the pavement before entering and, if he heard Dalton's unmistakable boom within, do an abrupt about-face.

Sassie always believed that 'indiscretion is the better part', and the restaurant became a hotbed of gossip and intrigue. It was strange, then, that politicians should meet journalists to share secrets that were only too audible to fellow lunchers.

Victor Sassie was born in 1915, the son of a Barrow ship's joiner. As a teenager Victor joined the British Hotel and Restaurant Association, which sent him to Budapest in 1932. Here he 'became Hungarian', under the tutelage of a famous restaurateur, Karoly Gundel, who died while Sassie was working for him. He returned to England in 1939, to open his first restaurant, Budapest, in Dean Street, with goulash at 1s 9d.

During the Second World War he served with British Intelligence, later joining the military mission in Budapest, where he met and married his wife Elizabeth.

In the late 1960s he installed an aquarium in the restaurant, in which he was able to keep live carp to be cooked to order for his clients. 'In Hungary,' he liked to say, 'nobody ever buys dead fish.'

≋ 8th ≋

Omar Bongo, b. 1935, d. 2009

Omar Bongo, who has died aged seventy-three, was the longest serving president in African history, leading Gabon for forty-one years and shamelessly looting the country's oil wealth.

A diminutive, dapper figure, who conversed in flawless French and alternated between pomposity, courtesy and cruelty as required, Bongo treated Gabon as a self-obsessed landlord treats his private estate. He considered everything inside its borders to be his personal property and elevated corruption to a method of government.

Bongo amassed enough wealth to become one of the world's richest men. He carefully allowed just enough oil money to trickle down to the general population of 1.4 million, thus avoiding any serious unrest. Meanwhile, he offered his domestic critics a bargain they could not refuse: drop your opposition in return for a modest but glittering slice of the nation's wealth.

The largest share of the oil money was, of course, reserved for Bongo himself – and slavish glorification of the leader became de rigueur. Thus Gabon acquired Bongo University, Bongo Airport, numerous Bongo Hospitals, Bongo Stadium and Bongo Gymnasium. The president's home town, Lewai was, inevitably, renamed Bongoville.

Occasionally, Bongo would boast of his great benevolence. One American ambassador was summoned to the presidential palace in the capital, Libreville, to hear the president proclaim that he intended to make a multi-million-dollar donation to charity. 'And will this sum come from your personal funds or from state funds?' asked the diplomat. Bongo was genuinely bewildered by the question. The two men quickly agreed that such fine distinctions were meaningless in Gabon.

Omar Albert Bernard Bongo was born on 30 December 1935 in the town of Lewai near Gabon's eastern border, into one of France's smallest and most placid African colonies.

The youngest of twelve children, he was an intelligent and ambitious young man and chose the only career open to young blacks under French rule: a junior clerical job in the colonial administration followed by a place in the armed forces. Bongo was a lieutenant in the air force when Gabon won independence in 1960.

He was fortunate to receive the patronage of the country's first president, Leon M'Ba, who gave him a series of junior cabinet posts. In 1966, M'Ba promoted Bongo to become vice-president, probably judging that the young man, who was barely thirty, posed no political threat. But M'Ba became gravely ill and died the following year, allowing Bongo to succeed him as president on 2 December 1967.

This was an era when France made no effort to disguise its direct influence in former colonies and, by the same token, African leaders did not pretend to conform to democratic norms. Bongo, an ardent Francophile, was happy to strike a favourable bargain with the old colonial power.

He gave the French oil company Elf-Aquitaine privileged rights to exploit Gabon's oil reserves, while Paris returned the favour by guaranteeing the young president's grip on power for the indefinite future.

France kept its military bases in the country and a contingent of paratroopers underwrote Bongo's rule. The president trusted no one but the French and his own family. Bongo duly made his son, Ali-Ben, defence minister and his daughter, Pascaline, foreign minister and then chef de cabinet.

He spent as much time as he could in Paris, revelling in his friendship with a succession of French presidents, particularly Valéry Giscard d'Estaing and Jacques Chirac.

Bongo behaved like an ageing sybarite during these long sojourns. An Italian fashion designer has testified that he kept Bongo supplied with prostitutes. When an international beauty contest was held in Libreville, Bongo took a shine to Miss Peru, who found herself ushered into the presidential bedroom. The terrified young woman managed to flee.

When the Cold War ended, the old bargain between Bongo and Paris required modest adaptation. The president legalised opposition parties in 1993 and allowed a series of supposedly fair elections. In fact, all his opponents had been bribed and suborned.

Even in death it seemed Omar Bongo had only a modest acquaintance with the truth. He died in Barcelona, despite officials in his government insisting that he was 'alive and well'.

≈ 9th ≈

Lawrence Isherwood, b. 1917, d. 1989

Lawrence Isherwood, the artist who has died aged seventy-two, was driven by his muse to abandon a career as a cobbler. To begin with he painted the women of his native Wigan but he later found a more lucrative market with imaginary nude studies of such public figures as Barbara Castle, Field-Marshal Viscount Montgomery of Alamein and Mary Whitehouse.

Isherwood's first major celebrity nude was of the singer Dusty Springfield (1966), which infuriated her but was sold to a Hampshire pig farmer for 75 guineas. Inspired by his frequent difficulties with traffic wardens, he went on to paint a nude of Mrs Castle, who was then Minister of Transport, with her body decorated by such signs as 'NO ENTRY', 'NO WAITING' and 'NO THROUGH ROAD'.

A later portrait of Mrs Whitehouse showed her with five breasts; it was bought by Sir Hugh Carleton Greene, a former Director-General of the BBC.

The son of a cobbler, James Lawrence Isherwood was born at Wigan on 7 April 1917 and studied Art at Wigan Technical College from 1934 to 1953. To make ends meet he followed his father's trade.

In 1956 he exhibited at Wigan, to a mixed reception from the locals. Several exhibits were damaged; the titles under portraits of a Nigerian nurse and a coalminer were switched; and a miniature sculpture in wire and plaster, entitled *Wigan's Wire Women*, was entirely crushed. 'Must have been somebody who didn't like modern art,' Isherwood said.

His output was prolific and eventually he was able to give up cobbling, though his finances remained precarious. He often paid hotel and garage bills with his work and once offered a watercolour of Wigan jetty in payment of a court fine for speeding, though the magistrate declined the barter. In the early 1960s he was asking an average price of eight guineas for his works, though he admitted: 'If anyone offers me four I snatch their hand off – it's a couple of beers and bed and breakfast, isn't it?'

Isherwood would paint until he had enough pictures to fill a van and would then set off on a sales tour with his mother, Lily, who frequently sat for him. He had innumerable one-man exhibitions, often at unusual sites – beneath Boadicea's statue at Westminster, for example, or in a lay-by on the East Lancashire Road. He regularly exhibited at Oxford and Cambridge, and when the Prince of Wales was an undergraduate at Trinity he bought a seascape by Isherwood.

The standard critical response to his work was epitomised by the opinion of Lt-Col A.D. Wintle, who championed the artist at an exhibition in a Trafalgar Square coffee house in 1959. 'What I like about Isherwood's paintings,' announced the monocled colonel, 'is that there is no doubt about which way they hang.'

Lady Jeanne Campbell, b. 1928, d. 2007

Lady Jeanne Campbell, who has died aged seventy-eight, was the former wife of Norman Mailer, the daughter of the reprobate 11th Duke of Argyll and the favourite granddaughter of Lord Beaverbrook.

So numerous were her love affairs that James C. Humes (a speechwriter for many American presidents) claimed in his memoirs, *Confessions of a White House Ghostwriter*, that she was the only woman to have known 'Biblically' Presidents Khrushchev, Kennedy and Castro – and all, he claimed, within the space of a year.

⪦ 10th ⪧

Sir Patrick Leigh Fermor, b. 1915, d. 2011

Sir Patrick Leigh Fermor, who has died aged ninety-six, was one of the few genuine Renaissance figures produced by Britain in the twentieth century, a man both of action and learning, a modern Philip Sidney or Lord Byron.

Leigh Fermor was the architect of one of the most daring feats of the Second World War, the kidnapping of the commander of the German garrison on Crete, and also the author of some of the finest works in the canon of English travel writing.

His most celebrated book (*A Time of Gifts*, 1977) told the story of his year-long walk across Europe from Rotterdam to Istanbul in 1934, when he was eighteen and the Continent was on the verge of cataclysmic change. The journey was a cultural awakening for Leigh Fermor that bred in him a love of language and of remote places and set the pattern for his future life. The exuberant personality revealed in his writing won him many admirers, who also revelled in the remarkable range of his learning and the irresistible flow of his descriptive prose.

Though he at first kept to his aim of travelling 'like a tramp or pilgrim', sleeping in police cells and beer halls, by the time he reached Central Europe his charm led to his being passed from schloss to schloss by a network of margraves and voivodes. The architecture, ritual and genealogy of each halt were later recalled with a loving eye.

Leigh Fermor completed his journey on New Year's Day 1935, albeit by train rather than on foot, having been compelled to travel thus across the militarised zone that then constituted the Turkish frontier. He next visited the country with which he would become most associated, Greece, spending his twentieth birthday at St Panteleimon, the Russian monastery on Mount Athos. Later he attached himself to some friends fighting on the royalist side of the Venizelist revolution and took part in a cavalry charge with drawn sabres at Orliako Bridge, in Macedonia.

Following a spell in Athens, he moved to Romania to live with his first love, the painter Balasha Cantacuzene, at her country house in Moldavia. There he passed most of the three years before the outbreak of the Second World War, at which point he joined the Intelligence Corps due to his knowledge of the Balkans. He was initially attached as a liaison officer to the Greek forces fighting the Italians in Albania, then – having survived the fall of Crete in 1941 – was sent back to the island by SOE to command extremely hazardous guerrilla operations against the occupying Nazis.

For a year and a half Leigh Fermor, disguised as a Cretan shepherd (albeit one with a taste for waistcoats embroidered with black arabesques and scarlet silk linings) endured a perilous existence, living in freezing mountain caves while harassing German troops. His occasional bouts of leave were spent in Cairo, at Tara, the rowdy household presided over by a Polish countess, Sophie Tarnowska. It was on a steamy bathroom window in the house that Leigh Fermor and another of Tara's residents, Bill Stanley Moss, conceived a remarkable operation that they subsequently executed with great dash on Crete in April 1944.

Dressed as German police corporals, the pair stopped the car belonging to General Karl Kreipe, the island's commander, while he was returning one evening to his villa near Knossos. The chauffeur disposed of, Leigh Fermor donned the general's hat and, with Moss driving the car, they bluffed their way through the centre of Heraklion and a further twenty-two checkpoints. Kreipe, meanwhile, was hidden under the back seat and sat on by three hefty Cretan partisans.

For three weeks the group evaded German search parties, finally marching the general over the top of Mount Ida, the mythical birthplace of Zeus. It was here that occurred one of the most celebrated incidents in the Leigh Fermor legend.

Gazing up at the snowy peak, Kreipe recited the first line of Horace's ode *Ad Thaliarchum* — *'Vides ut alta stet nive candidum Soracte'* (See how Soracte stands white with snow on high). Leigh Fermor immediately continued the poem to its end. The two men realised that they had 'drunk at the same fountains' before the war, as Leigh

Fermor put it, and things between them were very different from then on.

Kreipe was eventually taken off Crete by motorboat to Cairo. The exploit was later filmed (in the Alps) as *Ill Met by Moonlight* (1956), with Dirk Bogarde implausibly cast as Leigh Fermor, who was awarded the DSO for his part in the mission. Such was his standing thereafter on Crete that in local tellings of the deed Kreipe was heard to mutter while being abducted: 'I am starting to wonder who is occupying this island – us or the British.'

Patrick Michael Leigh Fermor was born in London on 11 February 1915. He was of Anglo-Irish stock and the son of Sir Lewis Leigh Fermor, director of the Geological Survey of India and a naturalist after whom the mineral fermorite was named.

His parents divorced and his mother, a glamorous red-headed playwright, set up home in Primrose Hill, and persuaded a neighbour, Arthur Rackham, to decorate Paddy's room with drawings of hobgoblins.

Formal education was thereafter sporadic. It was decided that he should be sent to Sandhurst, but while up in London studying for the necessary exams he drifted into the fringes of the bohemian set and lodgings in Shepherd's Market, Piccadilly, with Beatrice Stewart, once the model for the figure of Peace in the quadriga atop Constitution Arch at Hyde Park Corner. In her rooms Leigh Fermor began (unsuccessfully) to write verse and then, in the winter of 1933, to plan his walk across Europe.

After the war, which ended while he was preparing for a potentially suicidal mission to penetrate Colditz, Leigh Fermor first worked for the British Institute in Athens. Then in the late 1940s he was commissioned to write the text to a book of photographs of the Caribbean.

It was this trip that gave direction to his later career. From the captions he wrote for the pictures sprang two of his first three books, *The Traveller's Tree* (1950) and his only novel, *The Violins of Saint Jacques*, based on an incident in which a ball on Martinique was abruptly ended by the eruption of a volcano. These two titles were separated by a short meditation on monasticism, *A Time to Keep Silence* (1953).

But after this flurry of activity, the rest of his slender literary output appeared at intervals of a decade or more. In general he much preferred research to the business of writing; it could take him half a dozen drafts before he would be satisfied with a sentence.

Then there were friends to entertain, among them Cyril Connolly, the present Duke of Devonshire and Bruce Chatwin, who chose to be buried near Leigh Fermor's home in Greece. This was a house at Kardamyli, deep in the Peloponnese and overlooking the sea, which he and his wife designed themselves. Leigh Fermor liked to bathe, and at the age of seventy swam the four miles across the Hellespont.

Into his mid-eighties, he retained the handsome looks of a man twenty years younger, and remained amused, energetic and excellent company. His mild manner concealed a sharper mind, and broader tastes, than might have been expected. High on his left shoulder rode a large tattoo of a full-breasted, two-tailed Greek mermaid.

⊰ 11th ⊱

DeForest Kelley, b. 1920, d. 1999

DeForest Kelley, who has died aged seventy-nine, became entirely identified in the public mind with the character of Dr Leonard 'Bones' McCoy in the original *Star Trek* television series.

Such is the power of *Star Trek* fanaticism that McCoy has, without irony, been called 'the most famous doctor in the universe'. Though Kelley did have a pre-*Star Trek* career in Hollywood, he found – as did William Shatner, Leonard Nimoy and others – that *Star Trek* celebrity became a comfortable prison from which there was no escape.

Star Trek drew a following more intense than many another so-called television 'cult'. Trekkies shared favourite moments, exchanged dialogue learned by heart, swapped fantasy experiences on the internet and bought *Star Trek* books and memorabilia.

Kelley brought considerable added value to the role of Dr McCoy. On paper McCoy was very much the cantankerous, old-fashioned country doctor of Hollywood tradition, but DeForest Kelley helped to make the doctor into a person rather than a cliché.

In many ways he was the most human and likable of the original *Enterprise* crew. He was not an unruly egotist like Captain Kirk, a lonely misfit like Mr Spock, or an anxiety case like the engineer Scott. But he did have a famous distrust of machines, especially the transporters which 'beamed' people from the *Enterprise* down to the planetary surface: 'I am a doctor not a radio message,' he would say.

He was born Jackson DeForest Kelley on 20 January 1920, in Atlanta, Georgia, the son of a Baptist minister. He wanted to become a doctor, but his family did not have the money to send him to medical school.

In his teens he went off to California and worked for a time as a lift operator. Fortunately he showed some aptitude for acting and singing and landed a part in a US Navy training film where he was spotted by a talent scout from the Paramount studio, who gave him a contract as a bit player.

After small parts he was given more of a showing in 1965 in the film *Apache Uprising*, produced by A.C. Lyles. 'I always used him as a heavy, a mean man,' Lyles said, 'and he was marvellous at that.'

But he was not a star when he landed his role as McCoy. Nor was *Star Trek* any great success when it was first shown between 1966 and 1969. At that time the Apollo moon programme provided far more compelling space adventures. It was in the 1970s, when the original seventy-eight episodes started to be shown in syndication that the *Star Trek* cult grew.

All over America *Star Trek* fan clubs were started, and they were soon holding vast conventions. DeForest Kelley, Leonard Nimoy (Mr Spock) and William Shatner (Captain Kirk) found to their surprise that they were stars after all. By the time of the first *Star Trek* feature film in 1979 the show had become part of the popular cultural furniture of the West. The expression 'Beam me up, Scotty' (which was never actually used in the series), became universally understood.

⊰ 12th ⊱

Charles Benson, b. 1935, d. 2002

C harles Benson, who has died aged sixty-six, was a racing tipster, socialite and incorrigible gambler.

He had tremendous charm and charisma, and an uncanny ability to make himself indispensable to the rich and famous. In particular, he had known Lord Lucan since Eton and as a fellow member of the 'Clermont set' (centred on John Aspinall's Clermont Club). In his autobiography, Benson gave a vivid account of Lucan's life and of the events leading up to 7 November 1974, when the Lucans' nanny was murdered.

Lucan had booked a table at the Clermont for 10.30 p.m., but when his guests arrived he was not there, and they started without him. The next day, after Sandra Rivett's murder, Lucan's car was found parked at Newhaven, with a piece of lead piping, similar to the murder weapon, wrapped in tape in the boot. That same morning, John Aspinall summoned those closest to Lucan to his house in Lyall Street to discuss what should be done. Those present included Benson, Dominic Elwes and Bill Shand-Kydd. The luncheon would later become the subject of interminable speculation in the press, fanned by the refusal of those present to talk to journalists about Lucan.

In his book, Benson expressed no doubts about the fate of the notorious peer. His chapter ends: 'I believe he planned it, did it, and killed himself. I don't know where or how he hid his body, but I believe he did to himself what he intended to do to the body of the victim.'

Charles Edward Riou Benson was born on 23 October 1935. His addiction to backing racehorses started at Eton, where one of his friends was the son of the Royal National Hunt trainer, Peter Cazalet. This addiction was the one serious flaw in an otherwise strong and determined character. When he was having serious losses he became a changed person. His problem was that, although he received excellent information from his owner and trainer friends, he was unable to stop backing all the mundane tips that abound in the racing world. He would bet on every race at the many meetings he attended, and at many 'away' meetings as well. Inevitably, there were serious losses; and although he was often bailed out, there were some very low periods.

Benson's lifestyle, meanwhile, was breathtaking. Jeffrey Bernard once wrote in a newspaper column about Benson having had a free holiday every calendar month of the previous year. Three trips he would never miss were a lengthy stay in Barbados with Robert Sangster after Christmas; a few weeks' sojourn on the Aga Khan's yacht in midsummer; and a further period taking in the Melbourne Cup with Sangster in Australia after the close of the English Flat season.

In later life Benson managed to find two or three mature, very rich ladies who enjoyed his company and were prepared to fund holidays in Florida or the Bahamas. He always demanded a first-class ticket, and at one time got so many that he was known as '1A' after the seat he preferred.

⊰ 13th ⊱

Flossie Lane, b. 1914, d. 2009

Flossie Lane, who has died aged ninety-four, was reputedly the oldest publican in Britain, and ran one of the last genuine country inns.

For seventy-four years she had kept the tiny Sun Inn in the pre-Roman village of Leintwardine on the Shropshire- Herefordshire border. As the area's last remaining parlour pub, and one of only a handful left in Britain, the Sun is as resolutely old-fashioned and unreconstructed today as it was in the mid-1930s when she and her brother took it over.

According to beer connoisseurs, Flossie Lane's parlour pub is one of the last five remaining 'Classic Pubs' in England, and is listed by English Heritage for its historical interest. She held a licence to sell only beer – there was no hard liquor – and was only recently persuaded to serve wine as a gesture towards modern drinking habits.

Although acclaimed as 'a proper pub', the Sun is actually Flossie Lane's eighteenth-century vernacular stone cottage, tucked away in a side road opposite the village fire station. There is no conventional bar, and no counter. Customers sit on hard wooden benches in her unadorned quarry-tiled front room. Beer – formerly Ansell's, latterly Hobson's Best at £2 a pint – is served from barrels on Flossie Lane's kitchen floor.

After she began to ail following a fall in 2006, her customers helped themselves. There is no till. People put the money in a row of jam jars, one for each denomination of note and coin; although she was never observed to be watching, from her command-post in her favourite armchair she could distinguish between the different clinking sounds they made.

The broadcaster Jeremy Paxman once described the pub as his discovery of the year. 'Flossie, the landlady, sits in the middle of the room, wearing a pair of surgical stockings. The only food is a pot of eggs, which Flossie pickled several moons ago.' Her regulars have formed themselves into a Flossie Lane Society, run as a kind of guild, and are known as Aldermen of the Red-Brick Bar. Every year they appoint a mayor, nominated by the outgoing one, who wears a squirrel-skin cape made by a local butcher.

The mayoral handover involves the eating of squirrel pie and a parade through the village, led by the new mayor wearing the honorary mayoral chain, hat and staff which bears a symbolic sun in homage to the pub. When Hobson, the Rhodesian ridgeback belonging to the owner of the fish-and-chip shop next door, was appointed mayor, the dog was quickly found to be not up to the job and in turn appointed a successor.

Florence Emily Lane was born at the Sun Inn, Leintwardine, on 10 July 1914, the only girl in a family of five. Her father had been a policeman at Ross-on-Wye and her mother was the first member of the family to hold the licence.

Educated at the village school, as a teenager Flossie waited on the customers and helped out in the kitchen by washing bottles and glasses. After the death of her parents, her brother Charlie took over the licence in 1935 – the year of George V's Silver Jubilee – and held it jointly with Flossie until his death half a century later. Flossie Lane ran the pub single-handedly after that.

Both she and her brother were particular about who drank there; sons of the tillage were preferred, although some approved non-rustics were tolerated. The pub is still the base and meeting point for the local cricket club, bell ringers and fly fishermen drawn to the River Teme which runs through the village.

During her infirmity Flossie Lane's regulars rallied round to keep the Sun going, manning it on a rota basis. The owner of the chip shop ordered the beer from the brewery, served the customers, and delivered chip suppers which were washed down with pints of Flossie Lane's ale. The accounts, the washing-up, the laying of the fire and even the sweeping-up were undertaken by volunteers.

Flossie Lane was proud of not having kept up with the times, and did not hold with modernisation. In an age of lager louts and binge drinkers, no one at the Sun Inn can ever recall the slightest hint of trouble there.

'The pub hasn't changed in all the years, and they are all good people here – I won't have no rough,' she insisted. A chronic agoraphobic, Flossie Lane was never known, within living memory, to have ventured outside her pub (other than to take the air in the rear garden). She never learned to drive and took her holidays at home. She enjoyed a reputation as the best-informed person in the village, and every evening cheerfully dispensed local gossip to her customers.

In her advanced old age, Flossie Lane's regulars converted a downstairs room into a bedroom to spare her the stairs, but for the last ten years at least she had slept every night in her customary armchair.

The last person out tucked her up. Her secret recipe for a long life was simple. 'I'm teetotal,' she said. 'I leave the drink to the others.'

⚜ 14th ⚜

Elsie Widdowson, b. 1906, d. 2000

Elsie Widdowson, who has died aged ninety-three, was one half of the scientific partnership, with Professor Robert McCance, whose work on the chemical composition of foods formed the basis for the austerity diet promoted by Lord Woolton, Minister of Food during the Second World War.

The diet, which included such ingredients as dried eggs and 'Woolton Pie' (made from vegetables and breadcrumbs), has since been acknowledged as the healthiest diet the British population has ever had.

Using themselves and fellow scientists as guinea pigs, Widdowson and McCance lived on the diet for three months, at the end of which they decamped to the Lake District for some vigorous fell walking to test their physical fitness. The experiment was pronounced a resounding success and the diet was subsequently promoted by the Ministry of Food. Further research on the importance of calcium in preventing rickets even led to the statutory inclusion of chalk in bread-making flour.

⇥ 15th ⇤

Sir Fitzroy Maclean, b. 1911, d. 1996

Sir Fitzroy Maclean, 1st Bt and 15th Captain and Hereditary Keeper of Dunconnel in the Isles of the Sea, who has died aged eighty-five, led an extraordinarily glamorous career as diplomat, soldier, politician, writer and traveller.

The most crucial period of his life began in July 1943, when Winston Churchill chose him for a secret mission to Tito, leader of the Partisans in Yugoslavia. What was required, Churchill had informed General Alexander, was 'a daring ambassador-leader with these hardy and hunted guerrillas'.

At that time there was already fierce rivalry between Mihailovic's Royalist Cetniks and Tito's Communist Partisans for the leadership of the resistance to the German occupation forces. Tito accused the Cetniks of attacking Partisans instead of Germans, and of co-operating with the Germans instead of fighting them.

The Foreign Office, anxious to prevent the emergence of a Communist regime after the war, was wary of the Partisans. At the same time the Special Operations Executive wanted to bring all resistance operations under its own control. When Maclean was finally able to read the SOE files, he discovered that the enemy was referred to by the initials PX. He assumed, at first, that this was code for the Abwehr. But he was corrected: 'PX? Oh, that's the Foreign Office.'

Fortunately, Churchill, at least, had a single, clear aim in view. 'My task,' wrote Maclean after seeking the Prime Minister's instructions, 'was simply to find out who was killing the most Germans and suggest means by which we could help them to kill more.'

Ella Fitzgerald, b. 1917, d. 1996

Ella Fitzgerald, who has died aged seventy-nine, had a voice capable of astonishing stylistic variety; she could sing scat jazz or interpretations of popular songs with equal genius.

'Man, woman or child,' Bing Crosby once remarked, 'the greatest singer of them all is Ella Fitzgerald.' Blessed with a range of more than two octaves and an infallible ear, she could analyse and interpret the most recondite harmonic sequences, despite her lack of formal training as a musician.

She once said: 'I've always felt that where I got my education was with the musicians.' Their opinion of her was reflected in the joke: 'Poor Ella, she can't play piano. All she can do is sing everything right on the first take.'

She was born at Newport News, Virginia, on 25 April 1917, but was brought up at Yonkers, New York, by her mother, a cook and manager of a laundry, and her stepfather. She never knew her real father.

As a child she would sometimes play truant to listen to Dolly Dawn, the forceful soloist with George Hall's band; and her schooldays ended at just the right moment for her to be swept up into the era of the Big Bands, when the American popular song was enjoying a golden age.

But things did not go right all at once. After her mother's death in 1932, Ella Fitzgerald was reduced almost to beggary. There was an aunt with whom she did not hit it off; at one stage she became a police lookout in a brothel.

Her break came in 1934, when, with dreams of becoming a dancer, she went in for an amateur talent contest at the Apollo Theatre in Harlem, as the result of a dare among friends. She had intended to dance, but once on stage she lost her nerve, and on impulse decided to sing 'The Object of My Affection', a number made famous by Connee Boswell. She won first prize.

Encouraged by her colleagues – and with the support of a talent scout who saw her 'standing in the wings with some boy's shoes on, eating a hot dog' – she auditioned successfully for Chick Webb. Webb was a hunch-backed drummer of tremendous verve, and the leader of one of the most exciting bands of the era. It was based at the Savoy Ballroom in Harlem and toured frequently.

Webb took charge of her career, though he did not, as later stories went, become her legal guardian. Live radio broadcasts from the Savoy Ballroom led to recordings with Webb's band on the Decca label; her first, 'Love and Kisses', was recorded in 1935. In 1938, her 'swing' variation of an old nursery rhyme, 'A-Tisket, A-Tasket', shot her to national stardom.

When Webb died in 1939, Ella Fitzgerald carried on as the leader of his band until 1942. During the Second World War, she toured with a series of road-shows, appearing at nightspots and jazz clubs all over the United States.

It was at this period that she introduced scat – wordless improvisations – into her songs, in emulation of the harmonic and rhythmic intricacies of Dizzy Gillespie's trumpet technique. She thus won a new following from lovers of be-bop with such recordings as 'Lady Be Good' in 1947.

In that year Ella Fitzgerald signed on with the Jazz at the Philharmonic troupe, led by the impresario Norman Granz. As a member of the troupe, she began to tour internationally. Between 1948 and 1952 she also sang in a jazz combo led by her husband, the double bass player Ray Brown.

But it was her association with Granz which determined the direction of her career. He recognised that in the traditional setting of a jazz jam session Ella Fitzgerald was freer to improvise in the same way as instrumentalists. At the same time he knew that her remarkable vocal range, now enhanced by a rich contralto tone, was ideally suited to mainstream popular music.

After Granz acquired her recording contract from Decca in 1955, Ella Fitzgerald, accompanied by large, lushly scored orchestras, recorded on his Verve label the

Songbook albums, devoted to a series of composers. *The Cole Porter Songbook* (1956) came out on two LPs; five were devoted to the Gershwins. Others contained the music of Harold Arlen, Irving Berlin, Duke Ellington, Jerome Kern, Frank Loesser, Johnny Mercer and Rodgers and Hart. The series won lasting popularity and high praise from the critics.

Ella Fitzgerald continued to tour throughout the 1970s and 1980s, despite failing health. In 1984 and 1990 she was treated in hospital for exhaustion. In 1986 she underwent heart bypass surgery. In 1993 both her legs were amputated below the knee because of diabetic complications. Thereafter she became increasingly reclusive in her house at Beverly Hills.

In addition to her undeniable talents as a vocalist, Ella Fitzgerald had an attractive manner. A large woman, she had laughing eyes and a round face usually creased with a wide smile. But she shrank from giving interviews and always gave an impression of inner insecurity. She once described singing a song in these terms: 'You tell it like a beautiful story, and it's always a story that happened to somebody else.'

⚞ **16**th ⚟

Amedeo Guillet, b. 1909, d. 2010

Amedeo Guillet, who has died aged 101, was the Italian officer who led the last cavalry charge faced by the British Army.

Early in 1941, following outstanding successes in the Western Desert, the British invasion of Mussolini's East African empire seemed to be going like clockwork. But at daybreak on 21 January, 250 horsemen erupted through the morning mist at Keru, cut through the 4/11th Sikhs, flanked the armoured cars of Skinner's Horse and then galloped straight towards British brigade headquarters and the 25-pound artillery of the Surrey and Sussex Yeomanry.

Red Italian grenades – 'like cricket balls' – exploded among the defenders, several of whom were cut down by swords. There were frantic cries of 'Tank alert!' and guns that had been pointing towards Italian fortifications were swivelled to face the new enemy.

At a distance of twenty-five yards the British fired, cutting swathes through the galloping horses but also causing mayhem as the shells exploded amid their own positions. After a few more seconds the horsemen disappeared into the network of wadis that criss-crossed the Sudan-Eritrean lowlands.

It was not quite the last cavalry charge in history – the unmechanised Savoia Cavalry regiment charged the Soviets at Izbushensky on the Don in August 1942. But it was the last faced by the British Army, with many soldiers declaring it the most frightening and extraordinary episode of the Second World War.

Amedeo Guillet was born in Piacenza on 7 February 1909 to a Savoyard-Piedmontese family of the minor aristocracy which for generations had served the Dukes of Savoy, who later became the Kings of Italy.

He spent most of his childhood in the south – he remembered the Austrian biplane bombing of Bari during the First World War – then followed family tradition and joined the army.

Guillet excelled as a horseman and was selected for the Italian eventing team to go to the Berlin Olympics in 1936. But Mussolini's invasion of Ethiopia in 1935 interrupted his career as a competition rider. Instead, using family connections, he had himself transferred to the Spahys di Libya cavalry with which he fought repeated actions.

Before the outbreak of the Second World War he asked for a posting to Italian East Africa, where his intention was to make a life for himself and his beautiful Neapolitan cousin Beatrice Gandolfo in Italy's new empire. Mussolini's decision to enter the war on the side of Germany in May 1940 ended these dreams, cutting off Italian East Africa, which was surrounded by the territories of its enemies, and separating Amedeo from his fiancée, who remained in Italy.

Guillet was given command of the locally recruited Amhara Cavalry Bande, as well as 500 Yemeni infantry – approximately 2,500 men. With almost no armour, the Italians used Guillet's horsemen to delay the advance of the British 4th and 5th Indian Divisions when they crossed the Eritrean frontier in January 1941.

Guillet's actions at Keru, and subsequent hand-to-hand fighting at Agordat, helped allow the Italian Army to regroup at the mountain fortress of Keren, where it mounted its best actions in the entire war. After nearly two months, however, the British broke through, and the road to Eritrea's capital, Asmara, lay clear.

Most of the Italian army surrendered, but Guillet refused to do so. For nine months he launched a series of guerrilla actions against British troops, plundering convoys and shooting up guard posts. At his side was his mistress, Khadija, an Ethiopian Muslim, for he never believed he would ever see Italy or Beatrice again. Two curious British intelligence officers pursued him: Major Max Harrari, later an urbane art dealer who would become Guillet's close friend, and the driven intellectual Captain Sigismund Reich, of the Jewish Brigade, who was eager to get on with the task of killing Germans.

Despite their attentions, Guillet managed to escape across the Red Sea to neutral Yemen, where he became an intimate friend of the ruler, Imam Ahmed. He sneaked back to Eritrea in 1943 in disguise, and returned to Italy on the Red Cross ship *Giulio Cesare*, where he was reunited with Beatrice.

The couple married in April 1944 and he spent the rest of the war as an intelligence officer, befriending many of his former British enemies from East Africa.

In the post-war world, Guillet joined the diplomatic service and, as his Arabic was fluent, served in the Middle East. In 1950s Yemen, he and Beatrice were the only non-Muslims permitted to live within the walls of Sana'a and Taiz. British visitors were struck by his easy friendship with his neighbours in the souk, as well as the incongruity of foxhunting prints decorating his walls.

Guillet later served as ambassador in Jordan and Morocco, and finally India. In 1975 he retired to Ireland, where he had bought a house fifteen years earlier for the peace and quiet.

Barbara Goalen, b. 1921, d. 2002

Barbara Goalen, who has died aged eighty-one, was a mannequin of exceptional beauty and elegance; her haughty demeanour, delicate bone-structure and wasp waist came to represent the height of glamour in the late 1940s and 1950s.

She had not intended to take up modelling, and was happily devoting herself to life as a housewife and mother when her first husband was killed in a plane crash. Finding herself a widow at twenty-five, she decided to look for a job. 'I had to do something and friends suggested I tried modelling,' she recalled. 'I happened to be the right shape at the time. I was seven and a half stone and my measurements were: charlies 33, waist 18 – yes really – and hips 31.'

≋ 17th ≋

Michael Martin, b. 1958, d. 2009

Michael Martin, who has died aged fifty, was better known as the graffiti artist Iz the Wiz, decorated – some would say vandalised – dozens of trains on the New York subway system during a career which occupied him from his early teens.

Modern graffiti was born in New York, where it was associated with the emergence of hip-hop culture. Iz the Wiz was among its most prolific practitioners, making his name among the 'writers' (as graffiti artists call themselves) during the 1970s and 1980s. He began his career – or, as he called it, 'street-taggin'' – in 1972, when he was only fourteen.

Born on 30 November 1958, Michael Martin grew up in the Queens district of New York. He later recalled: 'I wanted to do something with myself and be a part of something. The neighbourhood I was in – it was either become a gangster, a drug addict, a musician or – here's something new. It was creative, it was secretive, it was a secret society.' Line by line, Iz took over the city's subway system, sometimes executing a hundred 'throw-ups' (one-colour outlines with one-colour fill-ins) in a single night. He was also known for his larger, much more elaborate pieces (or 'burners').

The New York 'writers' devised an entire lexicon to describe their art. A 'whole car', for example, was a work that covered the entire visible surface of a subway car. When Iz was asked how many whole cars he had produced, he replied: 'You mean, like, burner top-to-bottom jammies? Oh I don't know, I never counted but I know in the years 81–82 I did no less than twenty-five.' They also created alter egos. Among Iz's writing partners were Epic 1 and 2; FI 1; Vinny; Evil 13; and Jester.

'We were the diehards,' Iz declared. 'We kept on bombing [painting multiple surfaces] till there was no more paint.' Iz the Wiz's style was wild, psychedelic and always idiosyncratic. At one stage he was president of the graffiti group (or 'crew') the Master Blasters and of the Queens division of Prisoners Of Graffiti. He also painted for The Odd Partners, The Crew and The Three Yard Boys.

One of the attractions for the subway writer was that his creations moved constantly around the city, thus reaching a wide audience – 'a way of getting your name from Point A to Point B', as Iz put it. A fellow graffiti artist, Asis, said: 'I remember riding the trains and walking the tunnels through Queens when I was a kid. All I saw was Iz everywhere I turned. He had tags [signatures] and throw-ups in the wildest places in every tunnel through Queens and Brooklyn.'

By the mid-1980s the authorities in New York were beginning to eliminate graffiti from the city's subway system, thanks principally to the introduction of much improved security. Iz diversified, painting freight trains and walls in Queens, and in the 1990s was instrumental in the development of the Phun factory as a place where writers could paint legally, allowing many writers to emerge from retirement.

For the past decade Michael Martin had suffered from kidney problems, and many believed that his illness derived from his years inhaling toxic paint fumes and dust from the subway tunnels.

Iz the Wiz appeared in a documentary film, *Style Wars*, and in the early hip-hop film *Wild Style*, and his work has been displayed in galleries throughout the world.

Cyd Charisse, b. 1922, d. 2008

Cyd Charisse, who has died aged eighty-six, was one of the leading dancers at MGM in the heyday of the Hollywood musical; she regularly partnered Gene Kelly and Fred Astaire on screen and was famous for the length and shapeliness of her legs, which were insured in her prime for $10 million.

They were so long and lissom that they gave the impression of a woman over 6ft tall, though in fact she was a surprisingly petite 5ft 6in. Astaire, with whom she starred in *The Band Wagon* (1953) and *Silk Stockings* (1957), paid her perhaps the ultimate, if grammatically suspect, compliment: 'That Cyd! When you've danced with her you stay danced with.'

Tom Corbett, b. 1917, d. 1999

Tom Corbett, who has died aged eighty-one, was a clairvoyant consulted by a numerous and diverse array of private clients.

His sessions included Tarot readings, though he would knock off at 6.30 p.m. sharp – often to play orthodox card games with friends. 'I do not use my powers to anticipate my opponent's hand,' he declared. 'That would be caddish.' By the same token, he once ran through the card at the White City greyhound stadium – but, he said, 'I don't approve of doing that in general.'

⇥ 18th ⇤

Ronald Allen, b. 1934, d. 1991

Ronald Allen, the actor who has died aged fifty-six, spent sixteen years in the role of David Hunter, the debonair motel manager in the legendary television soap opera *Crossroads*.

Before it folded in 1988 – after disastrous attempts to rejuvenate both its script and cast – the twice-weekly series, which recounted the ups and downs of life in a motel somewhere outside Birmingham, enjoyed a faithful following of about 26 million viewers.

Even in its heyday, though, *Crossroads* was not distinguished by polished performance – for years it was made on such a punitively low budget that it was shot virtually 'live', and ham acting was par for the course.

Characters supposed to be away on business would reappear inexplicably in crowd scenes; and almost invariably the person on the other end of Meg Richardson's telephone could quite clearly be heard talking from the other side of a thin partition wall.

But 'Ronnie' Allen, with his male-model good looks, his transatlantic smile, his wide 1970s suits and his perfectly coiffed hair – just a hint of grey at the temples – was in his element amid all the bland roadside sophistication.

He first joined the motel staff in 1969, and was promoted manager in 1981, when Noele Gordon's part – as the tight-lipped manageress Meg Richardson – was written out. From then, until Hunter was himself written out in 1985, Allen glided gracefully through a welter of farcical tragedies – fires, blackmailings, murders, kidnaps, armed robberies, frauds, threats and inter-staff tiffs – without having so much as to straighten his tie.

As Hilary Kingsley put it, in her seminal study *Soap Box*: 'David was the most famously dull character in the history of soap operas ... with the charisma of an ashtray and all the life of Sooty without Matthew Corbett's hand ... To describe him as wooden would bring a libel suit from the Forestry Commission.'

Ronald Allen was born at Reading, Berks, in 1934, and trained at the Royal Academy of Dramatic Art, where he won the John Gielgud Scholarship.

He worked in repertory before joining the Old Vic company, where he played

Benvolio in *Romeo and Juliet*, Mountjoy in *Henry VI* and Paris in *Troilus and Cressida*, which went to Broadway. Back home, Allen appeared in a number of television plays and made a notable impression as the honeymooning husband in *A Night to Remember*, a poignant film about the *Titanic*.

Allen was highly regarded by his fellow actors, who thought it a pity that for much of his career he never quite fulfilled the promise of his early classical roles. Only last year he returned to the London stage and showed theatre-goers what a fine and under-rated player he was, with a bravura performance as the leading man in Tom Stoppard's sunny play, *Rough Crossing*.

Brian Haw, b. 1949, d. 2011

B rian Haw, who has died aged sixty-two, became famous when he set up home in a tent in Parliament Square in a quixotic peace vigil and, despite (or because of) heavy-handed efforts by the authorities to silence him, acquired the status of a folk hero and thorn in the side of an unpopular government.

Brian William Haw was born on 7 January 1949, the eldest of five children. He found his faith aged eleven and, apprenticed to a boat builder at sixteen, he joined the Merchant Navy, sending home £4 a week before embarking on a freelance mission to bring peace to the world.

Northern Ireland during the Troubles was his first port of call. At Christmas 1970 he took himself and his guitar to Belfast, singing carols in the streets round the Shanklin and Falls Roads and handing out white peace balloons in Republican pubs.

Having, by some miracle, survived this adventure, he moved to Essex where he started a removals business, also working part-time as a carpenter.

In 1989, powerfully affected by the films of John Pilger, he set off for the killing fields of Cambodia. He stayed there for three months, but when he returned he found that people did not want to hear about it.

On 2 June 2001 he set up a makeshift camp on the grass in Parliament Square. Subsisting on tobacco and food brought by well-wishers, Haw stuck it out through wind, hail, sleet, baking sun and torrential rain, haranguing the passing world through a megaphone while fielding the verbal bouquets and brickbats of passers-by. Meanwhile a rickety 40-metre-long wall of banners, placards, knocked-together information boards, handmade signs, peace flags, photographs (Tony Blair with a Hitler moustache), slogans ('murderer Bush', 'You Lie Kids Die BLIAR', 'Christ Is Risen Indeed!' etc.), mushroomed around him and the local mice established new colonies amid the detritus.

Although at first Tony Blair had cited Haw as a symbol of Britain's love of free speech, come 2005 he was desperate to get rid of him. In May 2006, seventy-eight police arrived and removed all but one of his placards. In January 2007, however, charges against him were dropped.

Meanwhile Haw had become an internationally recognised figure. He appeared on CNN and for a while had his own daily 45-minute slot on Mexican radio. In Britain, tour guides included him in their itineraries.

Although rumours that Haw would stand as a candidate in the 2008 mayoral elections proved unfounded, he remained determined to soldier on: 'On 2 June 2001, the police came along and said, "How long you going to be here, Brian?" I said: "As long as it takes."'

⊰ **19**th ⊱

Sir William Golding, b. 1911, d. 1993

Sir William Golding, the novelist who has died aged eighty-one, was the only British writer born in this century to win the Nobel Prize for Literature.

There has never been a novelist quite like William Golding and there is never likely to be anyone like him. His was an entirely individual voice, yet, paradoxically, there was no such thing as a Golding novel. Even admirers of his work tend to choose different titles as their favourite. To his widest audience, he was best known as the author of *Lord of the Flies* (1954). Its radical re-working of the century-old boys' book, *Coral Island*, drew an immediate response from an audience reacting against the stiff-upper-lip attitude that had won the war.

Abandoned on a desert island after a plane crash, a group of choirboys lose their prep-school veneer to become savages. The writing is vivid; the symbolism clear. It is not surprising that it should have been seized upon by schoolmasters seeking a new 'text' suitable for discussion. But, in a way, this was a pity.

Much of Golding's later work was more subtle, particularly the three best novels of his first period of fluency, *The Inheritors* (1955), *Pincher Martin* (1956) and *The Spire* (1964). These, in their various ways, explore man's nature – and the capability that he has for his own destruction – to far more pertinent effect.

Golding's more personal books – the over-heavily-laden-with-symbols *Free Fall* (1959) and the almost incomprehensible *Darkness Visible* (1979) – did not endear him to the passionate admirers of his previous work. But the arrival of his Booker Prize-winner, *Rites of Passage* (1980) and its two sequels, with their brilliant descriptions of the terrors of a long voyage under sail to the newly founded colony of New South Wales, restored a great part of his audience. The symbolism of the vessel as the ship of life made the understanding easier, and the extraordinary mixture of characters among the passengers and crew made the novel more accessible than some of his more austere creations.

The sea was always of importance to Golding. His family came from Cornwall, where nowhere is far from the coast.

William Gerald Golding was born on 19 September 1911. His father, Alec Golding, a schoolmaster, taught science at Marlborough Grammar School, where young William was educated.

He went up to Oxford to read science at Brasenose College, but soon changed to English. After coming down he published two volumes of poetry, but they have been lost. After a short period touring with small theatre companies, he turned, in 1939, to schoolmastering at Bishop Wordsworth's School, Salisbury, returning there after naval service during the Second World War, when he commanded a rocket ship operating close to the beaches on D-Day.

As so often happens, *Lord of the Flies* (then with the rather unattractive title of *Strangers from Within* and concentrating at the beginning on an atomic war), did the rounds of publishers. Eventually it was spotted by Charles Monteith of Faber who insisted on a substantial re-write which produced the final book. In a way that is now rare, Golding remained faithful to his first publisher for all the rest of his work.

Golding was someone who never sought publicity but never made a fetish of shunning it. He allowed two television programmes to be made in which he appeared, and happily submitted to interviews when he won the Booker Prize.

His long though somehow insubstantial beard gave a piratical look to his face, but the expression was serene with something of the look of a medieval saint about it. His father had been an insistent atheist while Golding himself was a Christian, though a member of no established church.

He once told an interviewer that he did not believe in the afterlife and had no desire to live with himself for a thousand years. This is strange when *Pincher Martin* is re-read. The most logical interpretation of the narrative is that the agonies of the book are in fact those of a soul in purgatory. Certainly, Golding was a moralist – undoubtedly the novelist of his generation most interested in morality.

One of his passions in life was the Classics, particularly Greek. He once told Prof. Frank Kermode that he did not think that life would be worth living if he could not at regular intervals re-read Homer.

This confession is a clue to Golding's achievement: he was the great mythologist of his age. It could be said that *Lord of the Flies* was his *Iliad* and *Rites of Passage* his *Odyssey*.

⊰ 20th ⊱

The 2nd Lord Tweedsmuir, b. 1911, d. 1996

The 2nd Lord Tweedsmuir, who has died aged eighty-four, was dedicated to public service, and, as became a son of the novelist John Buchan, relished field sports and adventure.

John Norman Stuart Buchan was born on 25 November 1911, the second of four children, and the eldest son. His mother, the former Susan Grosvenor, was a kinswoman of the Dukes of Westminster and Wellington.

After Eton, Johnnie Buchan drifted into Brasenose, Oxford, scraped a Fourth in History, and passed into the Colonial Service. He acquired a pet cheetah called Sally, whose loud purring about the house reminded him of 'a tea-kettle on the boil'. Sally would cause acute discomfort by licking his hand; 'her tongue was as rough as a nutmeg-grater'. There was a less friendly encounter with a python, which chased him around a room before he managed to spear it through the back of the neck.

At the end of 1935 Buchan was struck down with amoebic dysentery, and heard the natives making his coffin. Invalided back to England, he found the medical experts in London could do nothing for him. When he joined his parents in Canada in the spring of 1936 he was so ill that his mother failed to recognise him.

A 'strong animal instinct' told him that the amoebae could only be eradicated by the rigours of an open-air life in the sub-zero world. A winter in north Saskatchewan, in eighty-two degrees of frost, proved his theory correct. It was so cold that he had to be careful, when feeding the dogs, not to leave out the axe with which he had cut up the meat, for when the dogs licked it, their tongues froze to the blade, and were torn away in efforts to break free.

On the outbreak of the Second World War Johnnie Buchan joined the Governor-General's (his father's) Foot Guards and in June 1940 he crossed to Brest, only to retreat to England within a few days in the wake of the French surrender.

Back in Britain, Tweedsmuir was called upon to investigate the appearance of 'Dieppe' as a *Telegraph* crossword clue on 17 August 1942. The answer was published on 18 August; and the raid on Dieppe took place on 19 August. He decided that the clue was mere coincidence. But two years later, Leonard Dawe, the crossword's compiler, would be interviewed in connection with the appearance of the code-words Utah, Omaha, Mulberry, Neptune and Overlord in crosswords before D-Day. Again, nothing was proved.

⇜ 21st ⇝

Ezequiel Gamonal, b. 1918, d. 2000

Ezequiel Gamonal, who has died aged eighty-two, was a Peruvian prophet regarded by tens of thousands of followers as the Messiah.

A diminutive, rather bad-tempered figure who suffered from arthritis, Gamonal was worshipped by his sect, the Israelites of the New Universal Covenant. Its members were mainly Andean peasants who wore Old Testament costumes modelled on the Hollywood epics of Cecil B. De Mille.

Gamonal, a former village shoemaker, taught that he had been chosen by God to inaugurate the new Israel, which had been transferred from the Middle East to Peru as a punishment for the original Israelites' loss of faith. The new kingdom would extend far into the Amazon, where it was believed the last Inca emperor had been sleeping since the Spanish invasion in the sixteenth century.

Belief in the sacredness of the jungle led the Israelites to found a number of 'colonies' deep in the rainforest, where they sang psalms in wooden temples and farmed. However, Peru's media insisted that they were, in fact, a 'diabolical cult' which murdered its own members. No evidence of this ever came to light, but unsubstantiated rumours continued to circulate of brethren killed because they had displeased the Messiah.

In fact, most Israelite brothers and sisters seemed utterly devoted to their grumpy prophet. At his month-long birthday celebrations in 1999, 1,000 of the faithful crowded into the courtyard of his desert headquarters outside Lima and serenaded him for hours.

The music swelled imposingly as an Indian dressed as Atahualpa, the last Inca emperor, handed over a golden sceptre to Gamonal, signifying that he was destined to bring the fabled empire back to life.

Ezequiel Ataucusi Gamonal was born in 1918 to a peasant family in southern Peru.

It was while working as a shoemaker in the 1950s that he converted from Roman Catholicism to Seventh-day Adventism, though he was quickly expelled from the latter denomination after dressing as a Hebrew prophet and claiming to receive divine revelations.

Chief among these was a visit to what Gamonal called the 'third heaven', in which he met the Father, Son and Holy Ghost and was ordered to copy the Ten Commandments on to a blackboard. From then on, observance of the Commandments became the first duty of the Israelites. In 1969, the new religion was recognised by the Peruvian state, and by the 1990s estimates of its strength ranged from 60,000 to 200,000.

Gamonal's cosmology was a complex and often confusing mixture of Seventh-day Adventism, Judaism and Inca legend. From the 1960s until his death, he taught that various apocalyptic disasters were about to befall the world, although on several occasions he was able to delay their arrival by petitioning God for more time. As a result, the deadline for the end of the world was regularly pushed back.

Gamonal, who was married several times and renowned for his voracious sexual appetite, nurtured political ambitions, twice running for President of Peru. He himself never wore the priestly robes of the Levites, explaining that he would only do so when it was time to announce the apocalypse.

He died during the Israelites' Pentecost celebrations, and disappointed many of his followers by failing to fulfil his promise that he would rise again after three days.

⁂ 22nd ⁂

William Donaldson, b. 1935, d. 2005

William Donaldson, who has died aged seventy, was described by Kenneth Tynan as 'an old Wykehamist who ended up as a moderately successful Chelsea pimp', which was true, though he was also a failed theatrical impresario, a crack-smoking serial adulterer and a writer of autobiographical novels; but it was under the nom de plume Henry Root that he became best known.

Willie Donaldson's alter ego was a right-wing nutcase and wet-fish merchant from Elm Park Mansions, SW10, who specialised in writing brash, outrageous and frequently abusive letters to eminent public figures, enclosing a one-pound note. Donaldson's genius was to write letters that appeared absurd to the public but not to those to whom they were addressed. The recipients duly replied, often unaware that the joke was on them.

Root chastised the Archbishop of Canterbury for failing to thank him for the five pounds he had donated towards roof repairs; suggested to Margaret Thatcher (who kept the enclosed one pound) that Mary Whitehouse should be made Home Secretary; sympathised with the Queen about the 'problems' she was having with Princess Anne ('My Doreen, nineteen, is completely off the rails too, so I know what it's like'); and told the Thorpe trial judge, Sir Joseph Cantley: 'You tipped the jury the right way and some of your jokes were first class! Well done! You never looked to me like the sort of man who'd send an old Etonian to the pokey,' a communication which brought a visit from the police, investigating allegations of attempted bribery.

He volunteered to run sundry failing football clubs; to visit the Chief Constable of Manchester with his newly formed group The Ordinary Folk Against The Rising Tide of Filth in Our Society Situation; asked Angela Rippon to send him a photograph of Anna Ford and enquired of the Tory Party director of finance the going rate for a peerage. He wrote to the late Sir James Goldsmith urging the elimination of 'scroungers, perverts, Dutch pessary salesmen and Polly Toynbee'. 'Dear Mr Root,' Goldsmith replied, 'Thank you for your letter which I appreciated enormously.'

Some recipients were puzzled, some furious, and some swallowed the hoax, hook, line and sinker. Nicholas Scott MP answered Root's letters about his love life, claiming that all was well between himself and his wife. The Foreign Office replied to Root's enquiries as to whether Mrs Root might be assaulted by 'local Pedros' on holiday in Ibiza, informing him that 'the activities to which you refer are indeed apt to occur in most popular tourist centres'. When he told Sir David McNee, then Police Commissioner at Scotland Yard, that it was 'better that ten innocent men be convicted than that one guilty man goes free', he was told: 'Your kind comments are appreciated.'

He had an unerring eye for the approach which would rankle most with his recipients. Writing to Harriet Harman, then of 'The National Council for so-called Civil Liberties', he began: 'I saw you on television the other night ... Why should an attractive lass like you want to confuse her pretty little head with complicated matters of politics, jurisprudence, sociology and the so-called rights of man? Leave such considerations to us men, that's my advice to you. A pretty girl like you should have settled down by now with a husband and a couple of kiddies.' If she must work, he continued, she should consider a career such as 'that of model, actress, ballroom dancing instructor or newsreader', before enclosing a pound for her to buy a pretty dress and urging the future MP to get in touch with 'my friend Lord Delfont'.

Compiled and published in 1980, *The Henry Root Letters* became the number one bestseller that year.

Donaldson readily accepted there was something unpleasant and dishonourable about the whole operation. But one of his more redeeming features was that while he hated pomposity and hypocrisy in others, he disliked himself even more.

This might have been so, had he not enjoyed hating himself so much: 'The salient features about me are laziness, self-indulgence and sex addiction,' he confessed, in his characteristic melancholy drawl. 'I'm genuinely shocked by my own behaviour.'

Charles William Donaldson, the son of a Scottish-born shipping magnate, was born on 4 January 1935 at Sunningdale, Berkshire, where he grew up, surrounded by servants, in a thirty-room mansion. He was fond of his father, but disliked his snobbish, bullying mother and never forgave her for firing the family's faithful chauffeur after she discovered that he voted Socialist.

Donaldson was educated at Winchester, where he discovered that he had lost the contest for the title of stupidest boy in the school when his competitor, an Earl, was advised to 'try Eton' after just one term. When he was called up for National Service in the Navy, his mother rang up the First Sea Lord and told him that her son was about to do the season – 'affianced to Isabelle Giscard d'Estaing, the future President of France's sister' – and was not ready. 'The First Sea Lord realised that he had met his match and suggested that I pitched up when it suited,' Donaldson recalled. He served as an officer in submarines then went up to Magdalene College, Cambridge, to read English.

On graduation, Donaldson joined Ogilvie and Mather, but resigned two days later after being asked to write a commercial for Ovaltine. After leaving advertising, he bought a theatrical company – 'in order to audition actresses' – and became an impresario.

He first came to prominence in 1961 as the London producer of *Beyond the Fringe*, which brought together Peter Cook, Alan Bennett and Jonathan Miller. Other successes included *The Bedsitting Room* and *An Evening of British Rubbish*. But four years of success were followed by a string of failures, beginning with the aptly named *Knights of Catastrophe* (1965), a doomed attempt to revive British music hall. From then on it was all downhill.

By the late 1960s, Donaldson was losing so much money he had to sell the family house in Berkshire; in 1970 he went into voluntary liquidation. He did not, though, divide up his life by reference to his fluctuating fortunes, but rather to his wives and lovers; and more often than not, it was his personal life that won him headlines.

His first marriage, in 1957, was to Sonia Avory, the daughter of tennis champion Ted Avory. But Donaldson had never been attracted to the 'squashy, pink-faced tennis type', and he regretted the marriage even before he had walked down the aisle. On honeymoon he read pornography wrapped in the cover of Kingsley Amis's *Lucky Jim*.

By the time his only son was born in 1959, he had begun an affair with Jeffrey Bernard's actress wife, Jackie. When, two years later, they agreed to elope, Donaldson hurried home to tell his wife and left with his pyjamas in a suitcase. Three days later Jackie rang to tell him that they were 'ships that pass in the night' and that the deal was off.

After a six-month affair with a dancer who had appeared in *Summer Holiday*, he spent two years with the actress Sarah Miles. He moved into her flat but when she went off to make a film in Ireland, he invited a 'page three model' round, who left her shoes behind. When Sarah Miles found them, she kicked Donaldson out. Later, she wrote a memoir in which she described Donaldson 'adjusting his cufflinks' as he seduced her.

The following years were a blur of starlets and minor celebrities, including the American singer Carly Simon, whom Donaldson jilted when she was preparing to come to Britain to marry him.

In 1968 he married another actress, Claire Gordon, whom he had auditioned for Lady de Winter, a nude role in his production of *The Three Musketeers*. She introduced him to cannabis and they held orgies, with call girls, naked DJs and two-way mirrors. In 1970 a headline read 'Cannabis case impresario fined. When cautioned the accused asked the arresting officer: "Haven't I seen you at one of my pot parties?"'

In 1971 Donaldson fled wife and creditors and left for Ibiza, where he spent his last £2,000 on a glass-bottomed boat, hoping to make money out of tourists. By the end of the season, he had no money left and had to sell the boat for £250. He returned to London when he heard that a former girlfriend had gone on the game, moved in to her Chelsea brothel as a 'ponce' and used his experiences as the basis for his first book, *Both the Ladies and the Gentlemen* (1975).

The book prospered modestly and Donaldson was astonished to find himself being taken seriously as a writer. Kenneth Tynan compared Donaldson's prose to P.G. Wodehouse and bought the rights to the book, hoping (in vain) to turn it into a musical. One day, a friend in America sent Donaldson a book called *The Lazlo Letters*, the published correspondence between a character calling himself 'Lazlo Toth' and the likes of L.B. Johnson and Richard Nixon.

By the time Henry Root put pen to paper, Donaldson was living with his former secretary, Cherry Hatrick. They married after she told him that he had behaved so badly that they would have to get married if he wanted to continue living with her. The marriage lasted six months before she walked out.

Donaldson made a good deal of money from Henry Root, and there were Root sequels (including *Root into Europe* (1992) and Henry Root's *World of Knowledge* (1982), a television series and a column in the *Independent*, in which Donaldson chronicled the bad behaviour of his friends.

In the mid-1980s, Donaldson moved back to Ibiza where he became infatuated with Melanie Soszynski, who in 1986 was charged, along with the Marquess of Blandford and others, with supplying cocaine. After the trial (at which she was acquitted) Donaldson sent her to a clinic in Weston-super-Mare, where the doctor told her: 'I can help you, but I don't think I can help Mr Donaldson.'

When Melanie Soszynski dumped him, Donaldson wrote *Is This Allowed?* (1987), inspired by their life together. In 1986 there was a stint as Talbot Church, friend of the royals and the author of a book about Prince Andrew and Sarah Ferguson entitled *101 Things You Didn't Know about the Royal Lovebirds*.

In 1994 Donaldson went bankrupt for a second or possibly third time, after failing to open several years' worth of tax demands. When rung by *The Daily Telegraph*'s Peterborough column to ask how he had managed to run through the Root takings in such a short period, he candidly admitted that he had been an idiot. (Though he put it more bluntly: 'I've been a complete c***.')

Donaldson pitched proposals for television shows to Dawn Airey at Channel 5, including such gems as Topless Gladiators, with the former Judge Pickles acting as arbitrator; succeeded in involving the Dean of St Paul's in a Princess Diana 'Compassion video' (featuring Esther Rantzen and a group of grieving mothers reciting prayers over footage of catastrophes), and offered James Boyle at Radio 4 a game show with 'in the hot seat a celeb, who in spite of mega achievements, is thought by everyone to be a total pillock. Jeffrey Archer, Andrew Lloyd Webber, Janet Street-Porter ...'

Donaldson painted himself as a sordid sexual obsessive indifferent to the misery he heaped upon others: 'My life is f***ed up – I've used people, and on the whole I haven't had a good time. I say to young people, "steady on, or you'll end up like me".' In his sixties he claimed to have been in thrall to a prostitute, used crack, and taken the date-rape drug Rohypnol recreationally: 'The trouble is, it wipes your memory. You have to video yourself to appreciate just what a good time you had.'

⊰ 23rd ⊱

Doris Thompson, b. 1903, d. 2004

Doris Thompson, who has died aged 101, was popularly known as the Queen Mother of Blackpool, reigning over an amusement park covering more than forty acres, and visited by more than seven million people a year, making it Europe's most popular tourist site after EuroDisney and the Vatican.

The Pleasure Beach was founded by her father, Alderman William Bean, in 1896, and she pre-dated its oldest surviving ride by one year and continued to go on all the rides well into her nineties. From the charming Edwardian River Caves to the wooden dippers and roller coasters of the 1920s and 1930s and the high-tech rides of the 1980s and 1990s, she had tried them all: 'My last trip was on the Avalanche with the Bishop of Blackburn. I don't think we've seen him here since,' she reported blithely, in her early nineties.

As the rides became faster and roller coasters were introduced in the 1920s, it was not always easy to maintain due decorum. When, in 1994, the lake through which the Log Flume runs underneath the Big Dipper was drained, among all the purses, wallets and jewellery that had been shaken out of passengers on the ride, there was found a large collection of dentures, toupees and glass eyes.

She was born Lilian Doris Bean at Great Yarmouth on 12 January 1903, the daughter of William Bean, a businessman, and Lilian Crossland, who came from a Yorkshire family living in the town. It was there that Bean first set up his Patent Bicycle Railways, based on a contraption which he had seen while visiting Coney Island, New York, to transport the staff of an armaments factory across a river. It did not do as well as he had hoped, however, so he transferred it to Blackpool and thus laid the foundations of the Pleasure Beach, established, as he claimed, to 'make adults feel like children again and to inspire gaiety of a primarily innocent character'.

Doris Bean was educated at Malvern Ladies' College and was never expected to work. However, when her father died suddenly, at the age of sixty, in 1929, he left her his entire estate, including all the holdings in the Pleasure Beach companies. For the best part of fifty years Doris Bean's husband continued the work of her father, and it was not until he died in 1976, that, at the age of seventy-three, she became a force in the Pleasure Beach in her own right.

She proved particularly adept at PR, and a bright-eyed photograph of her with a queasy-looking celebrity by her side, and a ready quip, could be guaranteed at the opening of each new ride.

When the 235ft Pepsi Max Big One opened in 1994, at the time the world's tallest and fastest roller coaster, she was ninety-one and admitted that her family were worried it might give her a heart attack, although she gamely declared: 'I've been riding these things all my life, it doesn't worry me in the slightest.' Three years later she went up with the pop group Boyzone for the official opening of 'PlayStation: The Ride'. She was catapulted up a 210ft tower at 80mph and back. As she got off, she was heard to say: 'That's the closest I've been to heaven so far.'

⤞ **24**th ⤝

The 5th Lord Vivian, b. 1906, d. 1991

The 5th Lord Vivian, who has died aged eighty-five, became a national celebrity in 1954, when he was shot by Mavis Wheeler, the former wife of Sir Mortimer Wheeler and the former mistress of Augustus John.

At the trial, the principal problem, for both the defence and the prosecution, was that Vivian himself did not seem to be clear about what had happened. He admitted to the court that during the time between his arrival at the cottage that day and the shooting that night he had drunk a quarter bottle of wine, three liqueurs, seven to eight glasses of sherry, three to four bottles of stout and 'possibly two other drinks'.

Vivian insisted that 'some sort of accident must have occurred', and made no secret of his wretchedness at Mrs Wheeler being 'pilloried' by everyone; he said it was quite untrue that she had broken up his marriage.

Mrs Wheeler was found guilty of maliciously wounding Vivian and sentenced to six months' imprisonment. Ten minutes after the sentence the couple were to be found, locked in the most unmurderous of embraces, in a cell beneath the courtroom.

Anthony Crespigny Claude Vivian was born on 4 March 1906 into a long-established Cornish family. After being invalided out of the war in 1940 he served as a special constable and as a war correspondent before becoming a theatrical impresario.

His first venture, *Bless the Bride* (1947), ran for two and a half years at the Adelphi. But *Tough at the Top*, which replaced it, was a failure, and in 1954, after a production of J.B. Priestley's *The White Countess* made a loss of £8,000, he closed it down.

All in all 1954 was a bad year for Vivian. Not long before being shot by Mrs Wheeler he had been arrested for being 'drunk and indecent' at South Eaton Place. At Marlborough Street magistrates' court afterwards – where the charge was proved against him but he received an absolute discharge – Vivian caused some amusement by saying that his occupation was 'a peer of the realm'.

'That is a description,' replied the magistrate, 'but it is not an occupation, is it?'

'I beg your pardon, sir,' said Vivian, 'I thought it was.'

⇜ 25th ⇝

Michael Jackson, b. 1958, d. 2009

Michael Jackson, who has died aged fifty, was a precociously talented performer and songwriter whose childhood was blighted by the pressures of stardom, and who was in later life better known for his bizarre behaviour and allegations of sexual abuse against children.

For legions of fans around the world, such grave suspicions meant little. Jackson styled himself 'The King of Pop' and for them he was just that. An unrivalled catalogue of dance-floor-filling hits – from the joyous 'ABC' to the infectiously bass-lined 'Billy Jean' and the pastiche-horror anthem 'Thriller' – seems certain to ensure that his musical legacy survives and thrives well beyond the memory of the legal proceedings that tainted his reputation and his life during its last years.

That his recorded and onstage achievements have been able to overwhelm the seriousness of the charges laid against him is possibly the greatest testimony to his talent.

Few could generate the hysteria that Jackson could. Whether propelled into a stadium arena from a trapdoor or exiting it via jetpack, screams of adulation – sometimes lasting minutes – were guaranteed. And that was without his even opening his mouth, or gyrating the hips and ankles that could propel him backwards (while apparently walking forwards) in a dance move with which he will ever be associated: the Moonwalk.

When the vocals did come, however, they hinted at the bizarre personal life that lay behind Jackson's musical career. Neither manly bass, hot funk nor steamy soul, his timbre was set apart from the vocal traditions of America's greatest black singers, from Marvin Gaye to James Brown. His boyhood treble endured, it seemed, well into adulthood. For much of his career that did not matter. The falsetto cries that greeted each new crotch-grabbing dance move seemingly referred to the classic eroticism that infused so much of that black music.

But as the years passed, the enduringly whispery, high-pitched voice carried with it the sombre suggestion that Jackson had failed to move on from his childhood years – and, indeed, was determined to remain rooted in a reassuringly prepubescent world.

Whatever his musical reputation, it was clear that he sought the company of children in ways that most adults found, at best, distasteful and ill-advised, and at worst illegal and depraved.

Michael Joseph Jackson was born on 29 August 1958 at Gary, Indiana. His father Joseph, a steelworker, had pursued a less than brilliant career as a musician and was determined that his children would succeed where he had failed. The young Michael showed amazing early promise, and from the age of four he would stand in front of his four older brothers as the lead singer of the family group, The Jackson 5.

After winning talent contests and becoming local celebrities, they were discovered by Gladys Knight, and were signed to Berry Gordy's Motown label. The subsequent move to Los Angeles meant separation from Jackson's beloved mother Katherine, a devout Jehovah's Witness, but Michael soon found a surrogate mother in Motown's biggest act, Diana Ross.

After a year of recording and grooming for stardom, The Jackson 5 released their first single, 'I Want You Back', in November 1969, which became a US chart-topper. Over the next seven years, The Jackson 5 released thirteen albums and became huge stars, even having a cartoon series based on them. 'Baby' Michael, the focal point of the band, endured a whirlwind of recording, touring, television appearances and media attention.

The demands on him were not eased by Joseph, who took his role as manager to the band more seriously than that of father. Years later, Jackson was still tormented by the fact that Joseph 'never told me he loved me'. Always softly spoken, polite and reserved, he withdrew further into himself, only really coming to life when performing.

In 1977, as part of his bid to escape the confining clutches of his family, Jackson, now twenty-one, moved to New York to appear as the scarecrow in *The Wiz*, an all-black film version of *The Wizard of Oz*, starring Diana Ross. He formed a bond with the film's musical director, Quincy Jones, and later that year the pair worked together on Jackson's hugely successful *Off The Wall* (1979).

It was on this album that Jackson's adult solo sound came to fruition, and he began to eclipse his work with the Jacksons. He also found his form as a songwriter with the hit single 'Don't Stop (Til You get Enough)'. After another tour and album with his brothers, Jackson started work on what was to become *Thriller* (1982). The album spent thirty-seven weeks at the top of the US charts, spawned four US number one singles – including the self-penned 'Billy Jean', 'Gotta Be Startin' Somethin'', and 'Beat It' – and went on to sell 46 million copies, making it the most successful album of all time. The video for the album's title song, directed by Hollywood director Jon Landis, was half an hour long and cost $10 million.

Infused with a simple but driving bass line, it also featured a Hammer House of Horror-style voice-over from Vincent Price. It was the dance routines, however, expertly choreographed and performed, that set Jackson apart from other performers.

Dressed and made-up as zombies, the dancers shuffled, stamped, clapped and boogied as the undead never had before. At the head of the file was Jackson himself, transformed in the song from dream date to nightmare stalker, enthralling viewers around the world.

Thriller's enormous success made Jackson an international media icon, his single sequinned glove, his unlaced sneakers and his Moonwalk instantly recognisable the world over. But it also made him the target of unwanted attention.

He then bought a Californian ranch. Having always identified strongly with Peter Pan, he called his new home Neverland. Here he started building up his collections of amusement park rides, mannequins and animals (among them the infamous Bubbles, the chimpanzee). Jackson also embarked on a course of plastic surgery.

Nicknamed 'Big Nose' by his brothers as a child, and repeatedly described as 'ugly' by his father, he had never been happy with his appearance. His increasingly strange transformation prompted a media frenzy, with allegations that he was trying to look like his friend Elizabeth Taylor (among others).

There was also his ever-whiter skin, a result, said his publicists, of the skin condition vitiligo, but deemed by critics as a deliberate effort to escape his blackness.

The more famous Jackson became, the more he retreated into his own world, and the more rumours of his increasingly odd behaviour titillated the public. 'Wacko Jacko', as he was now called in the British tabloids, allegedly had an eating disorder, slept in an oxygen tent, tried to buy the remains of the Elephant Man, and wore a surgical mask on his rare public outings.

In 1987 Jackson released *Bad*, which once again was a huge worldwide hit, but inevitably failed to match the success of *Thriller* despite Jackson's gruelling world tour. For the first time, his music took second place to his lifestyle in the public's attentions. *Dangerous* (1991) was not exceptional, and it seemed that Jackson's detachment from reality meant that he was no longer in tune with his audience. But the gradual decline in record sales was as nothing compared to the scandal which broke in 1993, from which his career was never fully to recover.

There had always been doubts about Jackson's sexuality; a claimed teenage liaison with Diana Ross was hotly denied by her, a brief relationship with Tatum O'Neal following a first date at Hugh Hefner's Playboy Mansion came to nothing. Over the years, Jackson's image was repeatedly tarnished by rumours.

The father of Jordan Chandler, one of Jackson's young 'friends', took accusations of molestation to the police. They were unable to press charges after the thirteen-year-old boy declined to testify, having received an undisclosed settlement (believed to be $26 million) from Jackson. This payment damned Jackson as guilty in the eyes of many, despite his emphatic denials. Pepsi dropped his sponsorship deal, and the following year he was admitted to a British drug rehabilitation clinic for treatment for addiction to the painkillers morphine and Demerol.

Many of Jackson's subsequent acts seemed like stunningly ill-advised and cynical attempts to rehabilitate his image.

Neither of his two marriages, firstly to Elvis Presley's daughter, Lisa-Marie, in 1994, and secondly to his dermatologist's assistant, Debbie Rowe, in 1996, lasted more than two years. The fact that he had two children with Rowe (allegedly by artificial insemination) – Prince Michael, born in 1997, and Paris Michael, born in 1998 – made the liaison seem only more grotesque.

Rowe later complained that she had hardly seen her children since their birth. According to the tabloids, they were brought up in a fittingly freakish manner, with six nannies and six nurses, and toys and cutlery discarded after a single use.

Jackson's next three albums, *HIStory, Past Present and Future Part 1* (1995), *Blood On the Dancefloor* (1997) and, in 2001, *Invincible* (said to be the most expensive ever recorded), all performed underwhelmingly, despite enormous promotional budgets.

For the British public, Jackson's image as a slightly sinister figure of fun was cemented by his friendships with the celebrity spoon-bender Uri Geller (at whose wedding he was best man), and the Harrods owner Mohamed Fayed, whom he accompanied to a Fulham versus Wigan football game at which the away supporters chanted 'I'm Forever Blowing Bubbles'.

For many, Jackson calling for a 'greater understanding between children and adults' in a lecture at the Oxford Union to publicise his Heal The Kids 'initiative' was deeply offensive, as was his being made UN Special Ambassador for Children in 2001. But there seems little doubt that Jackson's love of children, however misguided, was genuine. Michael Jackson was as much a victim as he was an offender, a victim of his upbringing, and of the modern obsession with celebrity.

In 2003 he was charged with seven counts of sexually abusing another young boy, Gavin Anzio, whom he had entertained at 'sleepovers' at Neverland. When the case came to court two years later Jackson claimed that he and Gavin had merely watched television together in bed, a claim supported by his friend Elizabeth Taylor. He spent much of the trial in a wheelchair, explaining that he was in serious pain owing to a broken vertebra.

The trial was the centre of an extraordinary media circus reminiscent of the O.J. Simpson case and lasted five months, ending in the singer's acquittal on all counts. But the sordid details that had emerged during the proceedings had done nothing for his reputation, and the verdict could hardly be deemed a triumph.

Jackson remained beleaguered, and he went to live in Bahrain at the invitation of Sheikh Abdullah. It was now rumoured that Jackson was in severe financial difficulties: he was said to have borrowed more than $250 million against his music publishing interests; Neverland was closed down to save money; he became bogged down in protracted lawsuits.

In recent months there had been much fanfare about a projected comeback tour. The singer had been due to launch a series of concerts in London. The dates had sold out within five hours of the tickets going on sale. According to the promoters of the shows, Jackson had been subjected to, and passed, an intensive medical examination before the tour was announced.

He made a brief, and typically mysterious, appearance at the O2 to publicise the events, punching the air and announcing: 'This is it!' in a voice a full octave lower than his customary girlish whisper; some observers even began to wonder whether they were not being addressed by a look-alike.

In 1982 he narrated the storybook album of *ET: The Extra-Terrestrial*, an outsider from children's fiction he identified with. He said: 'ET's story is the story of my life in so many ways.' Unlike ET, Jackson never found a home except on stage, which was, he said in 1979, 'where I'm supposed to be, where God meant me to be'.

◄ 26th ►

Ian Board, b. 1929, d. 1994

Ian Board, who has died aged sixty-four, was the proprietor of the Colony Room, a Soho drinking club favoured by bohemians, artists, homosexuals and assorted loafers. He inherited the club in 1979 from his patroness, the legendary Muriel Belcher, on whose birthday he died.

Perched on a stool by the door, clad in tasteless leisurewear, his eyes protected by sunglasses, 'Ida' (as he was known to his closest friends) would trade coarse badinage with his regulars. He had a kind side, though, and could be extremely courteous to visiting mothers, whom he immediately enlisted as allies against everyone else.

Board was an heroic smoker and drinker – until recently he would breakfast on brandy, and he once consumed a bottle of crème de menthe at a sitting – and if his drinking destroyed his youthful good looks it also shaped and nourished his magnificent nose.

A labourer's son, Ian David Archibald Board was born in Devon on 16 December 1929. His mother died when he was four, and he was brought up by a woman who, as he recalled, had 'been bunged in the pudding club' by his father.

'Boards are very randy,' he declared. 'They all have strings of children. I think I'm the only poof in the family.' There were seven full Boards and one half Board.

Young Ian ran away to London at sixteen and returned to Devon only twice in later life. He managed to avoid National Service because he was a bed-wetter ('an hereditary affliction,' he explained, 'which runs in cycles of seven years'), as well as a conscientious objector and a homosexual.

He became a commis-waiter at Le Jardin des Gourmets in Dean Street, and it was there that he met Muriel Belcher, who had run away with her mother from Birmingham at sixteen, after being slapped by her father for wearing lipstick.

Muriel fulfilled the role of 'a queens' moll' at Le Jardin, which was frequented by the likes of Noel Coward. She took a liking to Ian, calling him 'gel' from the start, and when she opened the Colony Room Club – so called because her lifelong companion Carmel came from the colonies – he joined her as barman.

At first the Colony clientele were stockbrokers and City types, mostly 'rich queens', but Muriel disapproved of any hanky-panky. Couples of either sex holding hands were told to 'save it for the bedroom, dear'.

One day Francis Bacon arrived, and he and Muriel immediately became friends. Bacon was on his uppers, and she gave him £10 per week to act as a 'hostess', bringing people into the club.

By the 1950s the Colony had become the haunt of artists, writers and actors. The only unforgivable sin was to be boring. Some, like Dylan Thomas and Brendan Behan, failed the test. Tom Driberg, Johnny Minton, Terence Rattigan, the Hermiones Baddeley and Gingold, Frank Norman, James Robertson Justice, Lucian Freud, Joan Littlewood, George Melly and Craigie Aitchison were among the regulars.

In August, Muriel, Bacon and Board used to holiday in the casino towns of the south of France. Bacon shunned the sun because it made his hair dye run. In the evenings, Ian and Muriel would watch him play roulette. It was in the days of currency restrictions, and they once found themselves stranded.

They decided to rob a rich acquaintance who was staying nearby. Board stood lookout while Bacon shinned up a lamppost. Then they went to the casino where Bacon gambled the loot. He began to win at the tables, but as he did so his face slowly turned a frightening black (he had run out of hair dye and had used boot polish instead). Having won their fares and more besides, Bacon shinned up the lamppost and replaced the stolen money.

Beneath its tough exterior the Colony had a heart of gold, and every year the club gave a party for disabled children.

Now that Board has fallen off his perch by the door, regulars must look to its next occupant, Michael Wojas. As Board noted, 'People say Soho isn't what it was. But Soho never was what it was.'

Sir Denis Thatcher, b. 1915, d. 2003

Sir Denis Thatcher, 1st Bt, who has died aged eighty-eight, carved himself a notable place in history as the first man to be the consort of a British Prime Minister.

His popularity was fuelled by the Dear Bill letters in the magazine *Private Eye*. Purporting to be his correspondence with a friend, popularly assumed to be Lord Deedes, the former Cabinet minister and editor of *The Daily Telegraph*, they caricatured him as a golf-addicted, drink-loving, hen-pecked husband who stole furtive moments of relaxation with elderly cronies, in between the demands placed upon him by 'the Boss'.

The satire was successful because it contained elements of truth, notably about Denis Thatcher's love of golf (he played off a handicap of twenty in later years) and his mode of expression. His blimpish views, so often parodied in the letters, were also true to life. In private, he would castigate 'pinkos' who stood in the way of the reforms his wife planned for Britain, and he believed that the Labour Party and its members were, broadly speaking, Communists (unlike his wife, however, he did not support the death penalty, viewing it as 'absolutely barbaric').

He met the future prime minister after the war when he became active in the local Conservative Party, standing unsuccessfully for Kent County Council. His involvement led to his being co-opted to the selection committee, in 1949, of the Dartford constituency, when it chose Margaret Roberts to fight the 1950 general election.

They began a discreet courtship. Asked later whether it had been love at first sight, his wife replied: 'Certainly not.' Years later, when Denis Thatcher was asked what had first attracted him to his future second wife, he replied: 'Several things. She's got a good pair of legs.'

He decided to propose while on a motoring holiday (in his 'tart-trap' sports car): 'I suddenly thought to myself, "That's the girl".' Having been accepted, Thatcher went to the Roberts's house in Grantham to meet the future in-laws: 'Margaret made the introductions and said, "Denis likes a drink", and I swear her father had to blow the dust off the sherry bottle.'

Thatcher was a man of simple tastes who favoured soups, smoked salmon, tinned tongue, corned beef, and baked beans on toast. Meat had to be cooked almost to a crisp; in a London restaurant, he once sent back his poussin with the instruction: 'I want you to take it away, kill it and cook it.' He hated the smell of fried onions, and detested garlic. As for drink, he refused ice because it 'diluted the alcohol'.

⊰ 27th ⊱

The Very Reverend Lord MacLeod of Fuinary,
b. 1895, d. 1991

The Very Reverend Lord MacLeod of Fuinary, who has died aged ninety-six, a former Moderator of the Church of Scotland, was a preacher given to burning jeremiads in the manner of an Old Testament prophet; the central achievement of his life was the creation of a community on Iona to be a spiritual forcing-house amid the religious indifference of the modern world.

A preacher in the great Scottish tradition, whose impassioned eloquence swept through the congregation like a rushing mighty wind, MacLeod never hesitated to denounce the evils of this world. His later utterances were haunted by the apocalyptic nightmare of racial war; and he feared that the time might come when one would pray to be delivered from being born white.

As for the power of international finance: 'This new Moloch devours our young,' he thundered. And MacLeod was sure that God would regard the Common Market beef and butter mountain as 'sin'.

Another target was 'the gross impurities of secular science', a phrase which chiefly related to research on chemical warfare. Notably valiant as a soldier in the First World War, MacLeod afterwards became a dedicated pacifist, in contrast to the vast majority of Christians, whom he dubbed 'passivist: they have neither the gumption to be pacifist nor the guts to be participant'.

By the 1950s MacLeod believed that the British people had learned that Christian Socialism would alone save humanity. The coming of Mrs Thatcher, far from undermining this faith, left him all the more convinced that it was securely founded.

George Fielden MacLeod was born on 17 June 1895 into a family which had already given notable service to the Church of Scotland – both his great-grandfather and grandfather had been Moderators of the General Assembly.

He was educated at Winchester and Oriel College, Oxford. In the First World War he served in Salonica and France, mostly with the Argyll and Sutherland Highlanders, of which he was adjutant for three years; his gallantry was recognised by the award of an MC and the Croix de Guerre with palms.

Upon his return from the war he took his degree at Oxford, and passed through the Divinity Hall at Edinburgh. In 1921 he obtained the Scottish nomination to the Union Theological Seminary in New York, and then undertook missionary work at the Arrow Lakes Lumber Camps in British Columbia.

Those who take to the straight and narrow path in adulthood are inclined to dwell somewhat exaggeratedly upon the sins of their youth; before he 'surrendered his life to Christ' MacLeod had been given to drinking and gambling and had smoked fifty cigarettes a day.

In the early days of ministry, when he was an assistant at St Giles's, Edinburgh, he would arrive dashingly at the cathedral door in an open-topped sports car, before proceeding to stir the consciences of the rich and the hearts of the women in the congregation. The genteel church-goers of Edinburgh decided that here, indeed, was a preacher for the Jazz Age.

Already, though, a transformation was bubbling up through the yeast of his spirit – born partly, perhaps, of his experiences in the trenches, and partly of a steadily growing rage for social justice.

From 1926 to 1930 MacLeod was Collegiate Minister at St Cuthbert's in Edinburgh, where he won golden opinions for his work among the young, 'for whom he seemed to have a magnetic attraction'; and then from 1930 to 1938 he was minister of Govan Parish Church in the depressed shipyards of Glasgow.

In the Second World War MacLeod appeared on Hitler's list for liquidation – the Nazi 'roll of honour' as Humphrey Bogart described it in *Casablanca*. At the same time, thanks to his pacifism, the British would not allow him to broadcast.

He was certainly a fine speaker. 'We have had enough books to declare the superiority of the Kingdom of God over Fascism and Communism,' he declared. 'What men begin to want is a little more evidence that we believe in the efficacy of that Kingdom with something of the forthright intensity that these lesser creeds might seem able to command.'

⇥ 28th ⇤

Sergeant Jack Hinton, b. 1909, d. 1997

Sergeant Jack Hinton, who has died at Christchurch, New Zealand, aged eighty-seven, was awarded a Victoria Cross for his actions in the battle at the port of Kalamata in the Peloponnese in 1941.

On 6 April the Germans, with overwhelming tank and air superiority, had invaded Yugoslavia and Greece simultaneously. Yugoslavia collapsed within ten days; the Greeks held out for a few days longer.

On the night of 28 April Hinton was among troops in the port of Kalamata when an armoured German reconnaissance column reached the outskirts. The order to retreat closer to the port was given.

When he heard the order, Hinton shouted: 'To hell with this, who will come with me?' – though using slightly stronger language. He then rushed forward to attack the nearest gun in the German column. The gunners fired a shell at him but missed; Hinton threw two grenades which killed them.

The Germans on the following six-inch self-propelled gun took fright as they saw the party of New Zealanders, including Hinton, racing towards them. They abandoned their guns and took refuge in two nearby houses. Hinton rushed into the nearest house, killing the Germans with his bayonet. Turning into the second house, he finished off the occupants there.

Meanwhile, the rest of his party captured a six-inch German gun which they could turn on the rest of the enemy column. However, the main German force was now reaching the area, and after further desperate fighting overwhelmed the defenders and captured the port.

Hinton fought to the end, but was captured after being badly wounded in the stomach. His spirited counter-attack had delayed the German advance, and enabled more of the Allied force to be evacuated.

John Daniel Hinton, whose father had served as a sergeant in the New Zealand forces in the South African war of 1899–1902, was born in New Zealand on 17 September 1909.

Aged twelve Jack ran away from home to work for a grocer, later becoming a farm worker, travelling salesman, swagman (tramp), gold prospector, and galley-hand on a whaler which spent many months in the Antarctic.

On the outbreak of the Second World War, Hinton was a foreman-driver with a public works department on South Island. He enlisted and, though thirty years old and with no military experience, was soon promoted sergeant.

After being wounded in Greece, Hinton spent months in hospital near Athens, and then in the hospital of a prisoner of war camp in Germany. When the notice of his VC award came through the Germans paraded a special guard of honour for him.

The next year, when he was in solitary confinement for an attempt to escape from Bad Suiza, he was taken out and paraded in front of a German general. To Hinton's surprise, the general put a VC ribbon on his shirt and offered him some champagne. Hinton, suspecting this was a propaganda ploy, brusquely refused the champagne and was promptly put back into solitary.

A later attempt to escape was also short-lived, but when the camp was liberated by the Americans, Hinton borrowed an American uniform and fought briefly as a GI – until an officer learned that he was a New Zealander and sent him to the rear.

The VC was presented to Hinton by King George VI at Buckingham Palace in 1945.

After the war, Hinton returned to New Zealand and entered the hotel business, managing, leasing and finally owning his own hotel. He was very much at home in the horse world, being an expert in trotting races.

Kind and with a great sense of fun, Hinton was also a man of innate wisdom and great courtesy, even to people he did not particularly like.

⇛ 29th ⇚

Russell 'Big Russ' Hinze, b. 1919, d. 1991

Russell 'Big Russ' Hinze, the Queensland politician, who has died aged seventy-two, became known as 'the minister for everything' during the free-booting reign of Sir Joh Bjelke-Petersen.

Big Russ was a kind of natural wonder: built on the scale of Ayers Rock, he possessed a hide seemingly impervious to considerations of public propriety. From the time he became a cabinet minister in Bjelke-Petersen's National Government in 1974 until he resigned from politics in 1988, he was continually the target of corruption allegations

– although in the tradition of Queensland politics, he laughed them off.

Hinze once described himself as 'the roughest, toughest bloody politician you could come across'. He gained nationwide notoriety for his keenness to enter beer-belly competitions, his habit of stirring his tea with his finger, and his regular nomination as one of Australia's worst-dressed men.

A large, rumbustious man, grossly overweight in his later years, Hinze pulled no punches. He called for rapists to be castrated, murderers to be executed by firing squad, and 'dole bludgers' to wear dog tags.

He was, in fact, the consummate populist, whose larrikin style and amiable nature earned him genuine affection among many of his political foes.

Cabinet colleagues respected him not only as an able administrator, but also because he was one of the few figures in the National Party prepared to stand up to Bjelke-Petersen. Indeed, he spoke openly of his ambitions to become premier.

Hinze could have flourished nowhere but in Bjelke-Petersen's Queensland, where the dreams of entrepreneurs were endlessly indulged, corruption was a way of life, and civil liberties and social justice received short shrift.

As Minister for Police, Hinze was asked what special qualities he brought to the post. 'I've got big feet,' he volunteered, 'no brains, and I'm twenty-one stone.' Pulled over once by a young traffic constable, he allegedly opened up a map of Queensland and said, 'Right, son, where would you prefer to go, Birdsville or Bedourie?' – referring to two remote townships in the far outback.

As Minister for Local Government, Hinze was also a land developer; as Minister for Main Roads – known as the 'Colossus of Roads' – he was a major supplier of gravel for road works; and as Minister for Racing, the proud owner of more than 100 racehorses. Questioned about conflicts of interest, he would insist that his public and private lives were entirely separate. 'Say what you like,' he would laugh, 'I'm a good bloke.'

Russell James Hinze was born in Brisbane in 1919, and left school at the age of twelve to help his father run cows and haul logs behind what is now the surfers' paradise – the Gold Coast strip of southern Queensland.

He milked cows seven days a week for fifteen years, but managed in the interim to educate himself in his spare time, and also acted as secretary of the local cricket club.

By 1952 he was a member of the local shire council, and subsequently served for nine years as chairman. He was elected to the Queensland parliament in 1966.

Even in those early years Hinze's frankness disarmed his enemies. Soon after being appointed a cabinet minister he said, with apparent seriousness, 'I told the Premier, "If you want the boundaries rigged, let me do it and we'll stay in office forever. If you don't, people will say you are stupid."'

As it was, the Nationals stayed in power for thirty-two years, mostly in coalition with the Liberal Party. Hinze's downfall, and that of the National Party government, came after the 1987 Fitzgerald Report into corruption in the Queensland police force. Hinze was charged with having accepted $520,000 in bribes from three property developers and an accountant. He was one of seven Queensland cabinet ministers, including Bjelke-Petersen himself, to be charged with a whole range of crimes.

Hinze brought a rare light moment to the Fitzgerald inquiry when, during eight days in the witness box, he was asked about allegations that as a minister he had been seen in a brothel. This was impossible, he replied, since his knees had been giving him trouble at that time; he had been on crutches and could not have got up the stairs.

❧ 30th ☙

Shi Pei Pu, b. 1938, d. 2009

Shi Pei Pu, who has died in Paris aged seventy, was a Chinese opera singer whose name would have remained obscure to the world were it not for his starring role in one of the most bizarre espionage cases of the last century.

In the 1960s Shi (pronounced 'Shuh') embarked on a prolonged affair with Bernard Boursicot, a junior French diplomat posted to Beijing. Shi was a man, and lived as such, but told Boursicot that he had been born female and brought up by his mother as a boy.

The credulous (and sexually uninquisitive) diplomat swallowed this story – even when Shi announced that he had given birth to their son; in 1986, when the two men were convicted in Paris of passing French documents to the Chinese and sent to jail, Boursicot became a national laughing stock.

The whole sorry rigmarole inspired a Broadway play, *M. Butterfly*, in 1988 and, five years later, David Cronenberg's film of the same name, which featured Jeremy Irons as Boursicot.

Shi Pei Pu was born in the eastern Chinese province of Shandong on 21 December 1938, and by the age of seventeen had found some success as an actor and as a singer in Beijing opera. He met Boursicot in 1964 at a diplomatic party in Beijing.

The Frenchman, then only twenty, had failed to distinguish himself at school but had managed to secure a job as an accountant at his country's embassy. Shi, who spoke fluent French and taught Chinese to the diplomatic community, claimed to be a member of the Beijing Writers' Association and the author of several operas and plays.

A few days later, when the two men met for dinner at a restaurant, Shi announced that his late father had been a university professor, and that one of his two sisters was a champion ping-pong player while the other was the wife of a famous artist. He also claimed to have a degree in Literature from the University of Kunming. Boursicot was dazzled.

Then, one evening, Shi told his new friend about *The Story of the Butterfly*, the opera in which he claimed to have performed one of his most famous roles. It concerns a beautiful girl who is unable to attend one of the imperial schools because of her sex; so she swaps clothes with her brother, and goes to school in his place.

Shi then claimed that he had in fact been born a girl, but his mother had passed him off as a boy because her husband had only two daughters and wished for a son; he had lived a masculine life ever since.

Boursicot was plainly ingenuous when it came to sex; his experience had been limited to a few fumbles with male schoolfriends, and he recorded in his diary that he was determined to have a physical relationship with a woman. His first such encounter with Shi, however, was not promising: the opera singer was wearing a leather jacket over a Mao suit, and in order to explain certain anomalies he said that he had been taking hormones to reinforce his male credentials.

In December 1965, shortly before the diplomat was due to leave China, Shi revealed that 'she' was pregnant. It was four years before Boursicot returned to Beijing, this time as an archivist at the embassy. China had been in the grip of the Cultural Revolution, and Shi told him that their son, who had been born in August 1966, had been sent to a remote location near the Russian border for his safety. Boursicot was consoled with a photograph of the boy, who was called Shi Du Du.

It was during this posting that Boursicot met, at Shi's house, two Chinese men to whom he confided that he had access to the contents of the French diplomatic pouch and other documents, including regular reports from French diplomats in Moscow, as well as from the embassy in Washington. He proceeded to bring them examples, which the men copied, until the end of his tour of duty in 1972.

In 1977 Boursicot managed to get himself posted to Ulan Bator, the capital of Mongolia. This was France's smallest and most miserable diplomatic posting – but there was an opening for a typist and archivist, and Beijing was only a 36-hour rail journey away.

Meanwhile, security at the mission was almost non-existent, and he continued to pass information to the Chinese. Every six weeks he visited Beijing, where Shi now had 'their' son living with him. Boursicot had developed into a practising bisexual, and no longer had any romantic interest in Shi; but he wished to maintain a relationship with Shi Du Du, whom he called 'Bertrand'.

In October 1982, by which time Boursicot had returned to Paris, Shi Pei Pu and Shi Du Du arrived in the French capital on a three-month cultural visa. 'Monsieur Shi', as the Parisians called him, was briefly lionised as he performed traditional Beijing opera and appeared in two television shows. He was granted a one-year extension of his visa.

Almost immediately, however, agents of the Direction de la Surveillance du Territoire discovered that Boursicot and Shi were living together, and in the summer of 1983 they questioned both men.

Unimpressed by Shi's insistence that he was in fact a woman, a French judge ordered a thorough medical examination, and sent him to Fresnes, a men's prison. Boursicot was listening to the radio in his remand cell when he heard a newsreader's laconic announcement: 'The Chinese Mata Hari, who was accused of spying, is a man.' Boursicot responded by attempting to cut his throat with a razor blade.

The trial of the two men took place in Paris in May 1986. The defence made much of the fact that the information to which Boursicot had had access was very low-grade – requests, for example, from the mission in Ulan Bator for humidifiers and a cheese tray, and a note that the Mongolians were planning a production of *Carmen* for which they required photographs of scenery and costumes. 'This case is absolutely at the bottom of the ladder in the spying world,' said the diplomat's counsel.

It was to no avail. Shi and Boursicot were found guilty and sentenced to six years in prison, although they served only a fraction of that; the following year they were pardoned by President Mitterrand.

After his release Shi remained in Paris, where he enjoyed his notoriety and performed as an opera singer. He and Boursicot spoke occasionally, but were no longer friends. 'I never told Bernard I was a woman,' Shi later claimed. 'I only let it be understood that I could be a woman.'

JULY

⛤ 1st ⛤

Fred Trueman, b. 1931, d. 2006

Fred Trueman, the Yorkshire and England cricketer who has died aged seventy-five, was one of the greatest fast bowlers, all the more renowned for his ripe and stormy personality.

Above all, he never failed in immodesty. But then who could argue with his record? Not only was he the first player to take 300 wickets in Tests; in a first-class career lasting from 1949 to 1969, an extraordinarily long span for a fast bowler, he claimed 2,304 wickets at only 18.29 apiece. Among genuinely fast bowlers, only Brian Statham (2,260 wickets at 16.37) approached this total. Clearly Trueman's strength and stamina were as exceptional as his speed and his skill.

The young tearaway of the early 1950s matured into the master craftsman, still a fearsome proposition for batsmen, yet now as vain of his guile as of his pace. This batsman, Trueman would explain, had been bowled by an inswinging yorker; that one deceived by a slower ball; another caught at slip off a late outswinger.

'Did you ever bowl a plain straight ball?' a sceptical team-mate once enquired.

'Aye, I did – and it went straight through like a stream of piss and flattened all three.'

The outswinger, in particular, really was a formidable weapon. But there was never anything subtle about Trueman's temperament; he always remained a fast bowler pure and simple in his hostility towards batsmen. Many an old foe smiled wryly when, in retirement, he said that he had hardly ever deliberately tried to hit batsmen.

His bowling action was instinct with beauty, violence and menace. At 5ft 10in, 46in around chest and hips, and weighing over 13 stone, he could seem heavy and muscle-bound as, muttering dark imprecations, he made his way back to his mark. With his run-in, however, the sense of constriction dropped away.

John Arlott wrote that he approached the wicket 'with the majestic rhythm that emerges as a surprise in the Spanish fighting bull'. Beginning at a steady pad, he gradually accelerated, hair flopping, until he completed his charge in an explosion of malevolent power. Trueman rounded off this spectacle with histrionic gestures of despair, rage or triumph.

Frederick Sewards Trueman was born on 6 February 1931 at Seven Springs, a row of terraced houses (now lost under colliery waste) near Stainton, some seven miles east of Rotherham in South Yorkshire. The first notable statistic he registered was his weight at birth, 14lb 1oz.

At fourteen he left school and took a variety of jobs: newspaper boy, bricklayer, factory hand in both a Sheffield wire works and a Rotherham glass works. He never, though, abandoned his cricketing ambitions, and by seventeen had shown sufficient talent to play for Sheffield United CC. He obtained a job in the tally office at Maltby Main colliery. Contrary to the legend, however, he never worked underground.

Trueman's reputation reached Yorkshire's committee, who paid for him to be coached at Leeds during the winter. Though still wild, and over-enamoured of the bouncer, he showed sufficient promise to be invited in May 1949 to play for Yorkshire against Cambridge University. On his debut at Lord's in June 1949 he took eight for seventy in the Minor Counties second innings.

By the beginning of 1952 it was evident that he had become one of the world's fastest bowlers. With thirty-two wickets from four county championship games, he was picked to play for England in the first Test against India at Headingley.

It proved a sensational debut: after fourteen balls of India's second innings the score stood at four wickets (three to Trueman) for no runs. Several Indian batsmen made no effort to conceal their apprehension. When Trueman went on to take twenty-nine wickets in that summer's four Tests, excitement grew to fever pitch, all the more so because the Australians were due next year.

Yet with the RAF, where he was doing his National Service, granting him only spasmodic leave in 1953, Trueman was unable to find his form, and was not chosen for England until the decisive final Test, when he took four wickets in Australia's first innings. England won the Ashes for the first time since 1932–33, and Trueman departed with MCC for the West Indies with high expectations.

But the tour turned out to be the worst disaster of his career. It was bad enough that he rarely bowled at his best in the Tests; worse, that his crude language and unruly behaviour sharply antagonised West Indian players and crowds. He hit a popular tail-ender in the face with a bumper, and while the other fielders went to the stricken man's assistance, returned bristling to his mark before following up next ball with a lightning full toss.

By 1964 there were at last signs that Trueman's powers might be on the wane. In the third Test at Headingley, England had Australia on the defensive at seven for 178, but Trueman, called back to finish off the tail, bowled a series of medium-paced long-hops which were dispatched with relish by Peter Burge. Australia reached 389, and England lost. Dropped from the next Test, Trueman was still three wickets short of 300 Test victims when was recalled for the final game at the Oval.

At first he made no impression, bowling twenty-six overs for eighty runs and no wickets; then he snapped up two victims in two balls. His 300th Test wicket came shortly afterwards, when Neil Hawke was caught by Cowdrey at slip. For good measure Trueman then removed the Australian No. 11. He had taken the last four wickets for seven runs.

Soon after retiring, Trueman set up as a purveyor of blue humour in northern clubs, and became involved in a number of unsuccessful business ventures. When

Brian Statham fell on hard times, Trueman laboured hard and long to make his last years more comfortable.

By far the most successful of his jobs was his place, from 1974, as a regular member of the *Test Match Special* commentary team. The former rebel now showed himself shocked by the undisciplined ways of the younger generation, and by the technical incompetence of the play he beheld. Many felt he was at his best when rain stopped play.

The events of 1984, when Trueman was voted out of the Yorkshire committee by the supporters of Geoffrey Boycott, whom he loathed, left Trueman lastingly embittered. He was never the type to forget and forgive.

Ganju Lama, b. 1924, d. 2000

Ganju Lama, who has died aged seventy-five, was awarded a Victoria Cross in Burma for his action on 12 June 1944 when B Company, 7th Gurkha Rifles, were checking a Japanese tank attack, in the Imphal and Kohima area.

In spite of a broken left wrist and two other wounds, one in his right hand and one in his leg, caused by withering cross-fire concentrated on him, he succeeded in bringing his anti-tank gun into action within thirty yards of the enemy tanks. He knocked out first one, and then another.

Despite his serious wounds, he then moved forwards and engaged with grenades the tank crews who were now attempting to escape. Not until he had killed or wounded them all, thus enabling his company to push forward, did he allow himself to be taken back to the Regimental Aid Post to have his wounds dressed.

Ganju Lama was born in India at Sangmo, southern Sikkim, on 22 July 1924 and, although neither an ethnic Gurkha nor a Nepalese subject, enlisted in the 7th Gurkhas in 1942. His real name was Gyantso, but a clerk in the recruiting office wrote it down as Ganju, and Ganju he remained.

In 1965 he was appointed ADC to the President of India. The year before, a large boil had developed on his leg; when it burst, a Japanese bullet came out.

⊰ 2nd ⊱

Jean Mostyn-Owen, b. 1908, d. 1999

Jean Mostyn-Owen, who has died aged ninety-one, was one of the greatest goat breeders of recent times.

Her Mostyn herd won fifty-four championships as 'Best Goat in Show' at the Great Yorkshire, thirty-six titles at the Royal Highland Show, and forty-two at the Royal Show. Mostyn goats have been exported all over the world; the Mostyn prefix is as well known in Australia and New Zealand as it is in Britain, and one goat, Mostyn Majolica, was even used to improve native stock on the Caribbean island of St Kitts.

Jean Marguerite Mostyn-Owen was born on 23 March 1908. Her father was an

Army officer; her maternal grandfather, Sir Robert Gunter, 1st Bt, served in the Crimean War, was MP for Knaresborough and was a noted Dairy Shorthorn breeder in Yorkshire.

A country child, Jean Mostyn-Owen grew up with a love of livestock, and in the late 1920s began to establish a stud of exhibition-quality goats. Her favoured breed was the Saanen, a large, white, hornless goat which comes from the north-west of Switzerland and is the basis of several European breeds. The breed gives vast quantities of milk from a frame which is small when compared to a cow's.

The Mostyn herd was kept comparatively small and very select. No more than twelve to fifteen goats were kept on six acres at Jean Mostyn-Owen's house at Minskip, North Yorkshire, where sufficient hay and green crop was grown for the herd's year-round needs. Jean Mostyn-Owen was as happy hoeing kale as she was showing at the Royal.

The shows were her holidays, and she slept in the livestock van until she was eighty. A great hoarder, she kept every rosette and silver spoon won since her earliest days. As a judge, she was decisive yet patient. If an animal was misbehaving, she would go to the other end of the line and give it time to settle down.

She judged at the Royal Show and all the other important exhibitions, except the Great Yorkshire, where she said she knew too many of those showing. Goats are judged at competition on milk yield and by a visual inspection. The goats are milked under supervision at 6.30 p.m., and again twelve hours later. The yield, including butterfat percentage, is then assessed.

Jean Mostyn-Owen was appointed MBE in 1985. She was only the second goat breeder to receive the honour, and was delighted with her trip to London.

Mario Puzo, b. 1920, d. 1999

Mario Puzo, who has died aged seventy-eight, was the author of *The Godfather*, the hugely successful story of a Mafia family that was made into an even more successful film.

By the mid-1960s, Puzo had written two well-received but poor-selling novels and was $20,000 in debt. Furious at the failure of his books, he deliberately set out to write a blockbuster and chose a hitherto neglected subject, the Italian-American underworld. His publisher rejected Puzo's outline of the book and he was forced to take it elsewhere; after *The Godfather* was published in 1969, it would sell more than 20 million copies.

Puzo cheerfully admitted to knowing very little about the underworld, but he remained unabashed about his success. 'I am terribly, terribly grateful that I have stopped writing small classics,' he said. 'It's a mug's game. If you're a guy who has a wife and children and you continue to write small classics, you're committing murder. You're murdering your family for the sake of your ego.'

Count Gottfried von Bismarck, b. 1962, d. 2007

Count Gottfried von Bismarck, who has died aged forty-four, was a louche German aristocrat with a multi-faceted history as a pleasure-seeking heroin addict, hell-raising alcoholic, flamboyant waster and a reckless and extravagant host of homosexual orgies.

The great-great-grandson of Prince Otto, Germany's Iron Chancellor and architect of the modern German state, the young von Bismarck showed early promise as a brilliant scholar, but led an exotic life of gilded aimlessness that attracted the attention of the gossip columns from the moment he arrived in Oxford in 1983 and hosted a dinner at which the severed heads of two pigs were placed at either end of the table.

When not clad in the lederhosen of his homeland, he cultivated an air of sophisticated complexity by appearing in women's clothes, set off by lipstick and fishnet stockings. He became an enthusiastic, rubber-clad member of the Bullingdon Club.

Von Bismarck's university career ended in catastrophe in June 1986, when his friend Olivia Channon was found dead on his bed, the victim of a drink and drugs overdose. Von Bismarck admitted that his role in the affair had brought disgrace on the family name; five years later there were still people who would not speak to his parents on account of it.

Back in the reunified Germany, he managed several telecoms businesses and, armed with a doctoral thesis on the East German telephone system, oversaw the sale to the private sector of companies formerly owned by Communist East Germany. He eventually returned to London, where he became chairman of the investment company AIM Partners, dabbled in film production and promoted holidays to Uzbekistan.

Never concealing his homosexuality, he continued to appear in public in various eccentric items of attire, including tall hats atop his bald, Mekon-like head. Although described personally as quiet and impeccably mannered, von Bismarck continued to live high on the hog, hosting riotous all-night parties for his (chiefly gay) friends at his £5 million flat off Sloane Square.

It was at one such event, in August 2006, that von Bismarck encountered tragedy for a second time when one of his male guests fell 60ft to his death from the roof garden. While von Bismarck was not arrested, he was questioned as a witness and there were those who wondered – not, perhaps, without cause – whether he might be the victim of a family curse.

Gottfried Alexander Leopold Graf von Bismarck-Schonhausen was born on 19 September 1962 in Brussels, the second son of Ferdinand, the 4th Prince Bismarck, whose own father had served in the German embassy in pre-war London until a feud with the ambassador, von Ribbentrop, ended his career.

As a talented young scholar, Gottfried had studied at what he described as 'an aristocratic Borstal' in Switzerland and worked at the New York stock exchange before going up to Christ Church, Oxford.

Von Bismarck never fully recovered from the death of Olivia Channon, the striking

22-year-old daughter of Paul Channon (later Lord Kelvedon), then one of Margaret Thatcher's cabinet ministers. Following her funeral, at which he was said to have 'wept like a child', he was ordered home to the family castle near Hamburg by his father.

His removal from Oxford was so abrupt that he was not given time to settle his bills; Prince Ferdinand sent a servant bearing a chequebook who did the rounds of von Bismarck's favoured watering-holes, restaurants and his tailor.

He returned briefly to Oxford, where local magistrates fined him £80 for drug possession; he wiped away tears as his lawyer offered mitigation. Olivia Channon's death, his barrister said, would prove to be a shadow over von Bismarck's head 'probably for the rest of his life'. So it proved.

He never married.

3rd

Emma Blair, b. 1942, d. 2011

Emma Blair, the romantic novelist who has died aged sixty-nine, was, in reality, Iain Blair, a burly 6ft 3in Glaswegian actor with a sixty-a-day habit and a fondness for a good pint.

As Emma Blair he became one of Scotland's most popular romantic writers, the author of twenty-nine bodice-rippers with such titles as *Arrows of Desire*, *This Side of Heaven* and *Passionate Times*, many of which sold more than 100,000 copies. The devotion of his fans put him in the top-twenty list of libraries' most borrowed authors.

His literary sex change came about when, after writing four thrillers which sank without trace, he tried his hand at his first romantic novel, *Where No Man Cries*. His agent rang to say that she had found a publisher, but there was a snag. As women tend to buy romantic novels written by women, Iain would have to become Emma.

For years Blair maintained the fiction and even developed a personality for his alter ego. Emma, he explained was a 'feisty lady, not a drum-banging feminist', who had experienced personal tragedy: 'I see her as being in her late fifties and probably alone, still quietly grieving for her childhood sweetheart who was killed in the Second World War. I dare say she enjoys a small sherry now and again, and always bakes cakes for the church fete.'

Emma Blair's true identity was revealed in 1998 when 'her' novel *Flower of Scotland* was nominated for the Romantic Novel of the Year award. 'I was left with the choice of coming out, sending someone from the publishers or doing a Tootsie,' Iain Blair recalled.

He was born in Glasgow on 12 August 1942. His father died when he was six weeks old, followed, five years later, by his mother. He and his grandmother then emigrated to America to live with an aunt in Milwaukee. But he missed Scotland so badly that, by the age of fifteen, he had found a part-time job after school and saved up for his fare home.

A career in journalism was interrupted after a visit to the cinema to see Burt Lancaster in *The Flame and the Arrow*. Transfixed by his performance, Blair resolved to become an actor and won a place at the Royal Scottish Academy of Music and Dramatic Art. After graduation, he took small roles with the Royal Shakespeare Company, in repertory and West End plays, did commercials and voice-over work.

He survived twenty years as an actor, 'with a few highs and a lot of lows', but soon realised that he was never going to be a star. The turning point was when he turned up to audition for a small part in *Raiders of the Lost Ark*.

The journey to the studio had taken hours and, as Blair himself described, he was then kept waiting for several more: 'Eventually a rather small man came into the room. "I'm Steven Spielberg. Can you come back tomorrow?" he announced, not expecting a negative. "No, I f****** can't," I replied in traditional Glasgow fashion. And that was the end of my acting career.'

⇜ 4th ⇝

Eva Gabor, b. 1921, d. 1995

Eva Gabor, who has died in Los Angeles aged seventy-four, was the youngest of three Hungarian-born sisters, all actresses by profession and celebrities by instinct.

Magda, Sari (Zsa Zsa) and Eva Gabor shared a predilection for jewellery, mink and matrimony, notching up nineteen husbands between them. Five of these husbands belonged to the petite (5ft 2in) Eva, who was given to addressing all and sundry as 'dahlink'. 'Hello, Mr President, dahlink,' she greeted Lyndon Johnson.

But she never appreciated being mistaken for her sister Zsa Zsa. 'I'm much tinier,' she would say, 'and thinner.' She also took pride in having worked for her living: 'Unlike my sister, I have never accepted alimony.'

No less beautiful that Zsa Zsa, Eva often appeared the lighter spirit. She revelled in the role of exotic emigrée, and insisted that her mink should be the same colour as her hair and her pets.

On one occasion she tried to smuggle one of her Yorkshire terriers through Customs by hiding it under her jacket. 'It was ridiculous, really,' she recalled. 'I was staring deep into the eyes of the official and trying to distract him but he just said, "Miss Gabor, your mink is staring at me too."'

Eva Gabor was born in Budapest on 11 February 1921. Her father was a former cavalry major who owned a jewellery business; her mother, who believed she had come down in the world, planned brilliant marriages for her daughters. 'I promise that you will all be rich and famous,' she told them, 'and you will all marry kings.'

To that end, she urged her girls to acquire every accomplishment. 'When will you be able to do that?' she demanded when they saw a fire-eater at a circus.

By the age of four Eva was set on Hollywood. In the late 1930s, accompanied by her first husband, she arrived in the United States; almost immediately – on the recommendation of a dentist who had been struck by her potential when extracting a tooth – she gained a contract with Paramount.

Eva learned English by attending the local cinema twice a day for eight months – though few were convinced by her claim that thenceforward she had to assume a

Hungarian accent. She also divested herself of her first husband, who disapproved of Hollywood.

Her first film was *Forced Landing* (1941), which she described as 'a B-picture only to those too lazy to go down the alphabet'. Subsequently she had parts in *The Wife of Monte Cristo* (1946); *Song of Surrender* (1949); *The Mad Magician* (1954) and many others.

As her vision of Hollywood stardom faded, so Eva Gabor began to diversify into television and repertory theatre. She gave up acting in the 1970s. A student of the *Wall Street Journal*, she successfully formed a wig company, Eva Gabor International. She took a keen interest in horticulture, and became one of the biggest non-commercial orchid growers in the United States.

In 1988 she came out of retirement to record the voice of an aristocratic mouse in the cartoon *The Rescuers*. She had also been heard in *The Aristocats* (1970).

Eva Gabor married first, in 1939 (dissolved 1942), Dr Eric Drimmer; secondly, in 1943 (dissolved 1950), Charles Isaacs, a property tycoon; thirdly, in 1956 (dissolved 1957), Dr John Williams, a surgeon; fourthly, in 1959 (dissolved 1973), Richard Brown, a former stockbroker; and fifthly, in 1973 (dissolved 1986), Frank Jameson, a businessman.

Men, she concluded in 1986, were a necessary evil, whatever the perils of matrimony. 'I could not possibly live without them, nor do I intend to. Sex is very good for pimples.'

⁘ 5th ⁘

Ernie James, b. 1906, d. 2005

Ernie James, who has died aged ninety-nine, was said to be the last of the 'Fen Tigers' – men who scratched a seasonal living on the East Anglian fens.

The term 'Fen Tiger' was originally coined by the Dutch engineers who came to England in the early seventeenth century to help Cornelius Vermuyden in the drainage and reclamation of the fens. It referred to the local inhabitants who fought to protect their traditional livelihood, gained from fishing, wildfowling and reed and turf-cutting, by vandalising the drainage works, and by occasional violent attacks on the 'strangers' in their midst.

The forces of progress prevailed, and most of the natural fen was turned into farmland; but pockets of fenland remained which, together with drainage ditches, newly cut rivers and washes (flood plains), continued to support the traditional way of life for some local families.

Ernie James was born on 8 January 1906 in the small village of Welney, near Downham Market in south-west Norfolk. His parents' cottage stood on a high bank between two rivers, the Delph and the Old Bedford, and had been in his family for generations. It was known as the 'Ferry House' because James's father operated a ferry across the washes during the winter when the main Wisbech to Ely road was flooded. He also ran a basket-making business near Welney Bridge, growing his own willows in osier beds by the side of the Delph, out of which he made 'grigs', a sort of elongated, waisted basket into which eels swim and get trapped because they cannot turn round and swim out.

James recalled the pleasures of fenland winters when the rivers and washes became huge ice rinks, and he and his friends would skate for miles on wooden 'fen runners'. He remembered the day in 1912 when a 34lb sturgeon was found stranded near Wellmore Sluice: 'The fish was sent to a fish merchant in London who gave such a good price that the men of the village stayed away from work for a week and went on the booze with the money.'

James spent the rest of his life at Welney, and never had a regular job. He lived by the seasons, and chiefly earned his living out of perhaps a square mile of land: 'In the springtime there was willow-cutting and eel-catching. This was followed in summertime by ditching in the washes and harvest work. Autumn saw the start of plover-catching which continued until the frost came, when we would be punt-gunning for wildfowl until spring.'

When he was sixteen, James's father handed the ferry over to him, and he continued to run it throughout the Second World War, in which he also served as a fireman.

At the age of twenty-one he married Doris, a Welney girl whose father was employed as a mole-catcher by the local drainage authority. Soon after their marriage, James's father-in-law became ill and asked James to take on the job.

The secret of setting mole traps, he explained, is to ignore the molehills, which merely indicate where the moles have been digging for worms, and look instead for small depressions in the ground indicating a mole run underneath. To tell whether a run is still in use, he advised pressing a heel into the ground, then looking at the indentation the following day; if the heel mark shows any signs of disturbance, the moles are still using the run.

He continued to trap eels into his nineties.

Ely Callaway, b. 1919, d. 2001

Ely Callaway, who has died aged eighty-two, owned the world's leading manufacturer of golf equipment; its development of clubs with outsized heads revolutionised the sport for many recreational players.

Callaway had already been president of the largest textile firm in the world, Burlington, when in 1982 he bought a struggling maker of golf clubs, Hickory Shafts, for $364,000. The firm had three employees. By the early 1990s, the company was valued at $1 billion.

The designer Richard Helmstetter first developed for Callaway a club in which mass was moved from the shaft into the club head without increasing the weight. Named Big Bertha, after the First World War siege gun, it was launched in 1991 and, since it made it far easier to hit a good shot, was soon being used by weekend golfers everywhere. 'We turned the driver,' said Callaway, 'from being the hardest club in the bag to use into one of the easiest.'

⚜ **6**th ⚜

West de Wend-Fenton, b. 1927, d. 2002

West de Wend-Fenton, who has died aged seventy-five, was the bohemian squire of Ebberston Hall in the North Riding of Yorkshire.

A wildly romantic figure, he was passionate and impulsive, with an insatiable thirst for adventure and no comprehension of convention. As a young man he often proposed marriage to Margaret Lygon; after her nth rejection, and three days' drinking, he flew to Paris and joined the Foreign Legion.

Fenton saw action against the Fellagha in the mountains of Tunisia; he deserted, was captured, imprisoned, made to dig his own grave, and finally rescued by Michael Alexander, who wrote a book about the 'escapade': *The Reluctant Legionnaire* (1956).

The adventure earned Fenton the nickname 'Beau West', as well as the hand of Margaret Lygon (they married soon after his return to London), and was the most public event of a largely private existence. But the rest of his life was lived in the same spirit. Breakfast was an adventure in his company, dinner much more so.

Adventures of another kind were to be had in Greece, where Fenton built a house on a plot of land bought in exchange for a .410 shotgun; and in the Soviet Union, where he ran anarchic charabanc tours. There were gaudy nights in London and Paris ('West the enemy of sleep!' a friend recalled, 'West the scourge of night clubs!'). But his greatest adventure was in the Vale of Pickering, at Ebberston.

Like its late squire, the house is charming and eccentric. Variously described as a lodge, a folly, a shooting box, and 'England's smallest stately home', it was built in 1718 for William Thompson, MP for Scarborough and Warden of the Mint.

Over the years the hall degenerated into a farmhouse, and when West inherited it (his father, Major William de Wend-Fenton, had bought the estate in 1941 for £5,000), Ebberston was in a sorry state. With the help of various grants, his children and the paying visitors, he spent the rest of his life putting it right.

The family lived in a relaxed style that was truer, perhaps, to the eighteenth-century spirit than the conventions of costume drama would allow, in a jumble of chamber pots, gnawed bones and empty bottles, and on an equal footing with a menagerie of goats, chickens, pot-bellied pigs, deer, llamas, peacocks, and a baleful turkey called Henry. Some of the paying visitors were shocked.

Fenton farmed his fifty acres on loosely organic principles ('It's just easier, you don't have to buy fertiliser'), grew his own vegetables, made his own wine, and shot his own rooks, which he would throw into the freezer with their feathers on.

He did not like to wait for drinks, and once at the Ritz summoned a tardy waiter by throwing his dentures at him. At a London party this year, old and blind and ill with cancer, his excuse for leaving at 3 a.m. was that he had been out until 5 a.m. the night before.

Michael Richard West de Wend-Fenton was born on 2 February 1927. His singular character was evident from an early age. He was educated at a number of schools (including Eton) and served in a number of regiments (including the Scots Guards).

In his twenties Fenton cut a dash among the Bright Young Things of the day, but on a fateful visit to London in 1954 ('I've just sold a pig, that ought to keep me going for a few days') friends remembered him as gloomy and restless. It was reported that, in a Kensington pub, he had taken exception to a gang of noisy lesbians sitting in a row, lifted one end of their bench and tipped them in a heap on the floor. At a party he announced that he was off to join the Foreign Legion.

It was not until his passport was confiscated by a German sergeant ('You vill not need this any longer') at the Legion's headquarters in Paris that he realised his folly in enlisting as 'a stepson of France'. Still, he found the Troisieme Bataillon du March no tougher than the Guards, and enjoyed his time in military prison. His only complaints were of boredom and the wine ration. His memories of his service were mainly ornithological, of goldfinches, larks, and rare tits.

At a London party Michael Alexander heard some friends bemoaning West's fate ('Only one bottle of wine a day!'). Alexander had fought in Libya during the war, and been a PoW, and written a book about Colditz. With the support of Jock Murray and the *Daily Mirror*, and accompanied by Lady Marye Rous (daughter of the Earl of Stradbroke) and Nick Mosley (son of Sir Oswald), he set about the rescue of 'Beau West'.

Gavin Maxwell suggested hiring the Sicilian Mafia to ship Fenton to Malta; Xan Fielding, wary of the 'imponderables of land-sea operations', suggested a dash to Libya. After a wild goose chase, from Carthage to Sidi Bel-Abbes, dogged by the Deuxieme Bureau, Alexander finally met a couple of English legionnaires who knew West: 'Fellow always seems to be short of cash! He once tried to sell me one of his cows for 5,000 francs. Said it was worth at least eighty quid in England!'

When Alexander found Legionnaire Michael Fenton, he took him to lunch, and after a couple of bottles they made a run for it. If Fenton were caught he would have spent at least a year at Colomb-Bechar, the dreaded Saharan penal unit, but they made it to London.

Roy Rogers, b. 1911, d. 1998

Roy Rogers, who has died aged eighty-six, appeared with his horse Trigger in more than eighty Westerns, all featuring, as he put it, 'a little song, a little riding, a little shooting and a girl to be saved from hazard'.

Slim and lithe, in tight breeches and rose-embroidered shirts, Rogers possessed what one Beverly Hills hostess remarked was 'the pruttiest backside in Hollywood'; critics commented on his 'good, rolling gait'. But he was nothing without his hoss.

'Often I wonder if I could have made it in Hollywood without Trigger,' mused Rogers. He paid $2,500 for Trigger in 1938, and the horse remained Roger's totem for almost three decades; it eventually had fifty-two tricks in its repertoire and was as great an attraction as his owner.

In fact, when Trigger died, aged thirty-three, in 1965, Rogers had the horse stuffed and put on display in a rearing posture in his personal museum. 'When my time comes,' he said, 'just skin me and put me right up there on Trigger as if nothing had ever changed.'

Roy Rogers was born Leonard Franklin Slye on 5 November 1911 at Cincinnati, Ohio. His family was poor, and Slye headed west to California as a migrant worker, drove a truck, picked peaches and poked cows.

According to legend, he was loitering in a cowboy outfitter's when a man rushed in and bought a Stetson to audition for a Western; Slye followed him to the studio, and landed his first big role, in *Under Western Stars* (1938), for which he changed his name to Roy Rogers.

⊰ 7th ⊱

Syd Barrett, b. 1946, d. 2006

Syd Barrett, the founder of Pink Floyd who has died aged sixty, provided one of rock music's most enduring and confounding legends; some critics thought him a modern-day Rimbaud, others dismissed him as a deranged under-achiever.

His entire recorded output amounted to little more than three albums, and having severed his links with the music industry by 1974 he steadfastly resisted all attempts to entice him back. Widely believed to have suffered psychosis, exacerbated by prolific use of hallucinogenic drugs in the 1960s, he retreated to the cellar of his childhood home in Cambridge where he shunned all contact with the outside world.

The Barrett legend was fired by half-truths and apocrypha which blended in a spiral of exaggeration until his name became synonymous with drug-induced madness. Fanzines acclaimed his work, and Pink Floyd's own 1975 tribute 'Shine On You Crazy Diamond' fanned the flames still further. Barrett became the most celebrated acid casualty in rock.

What is beyond dispute is that Barrett's influence on the early Pink Floyd after their formation in 1965 was immeasurable. He was their singer, lead guitarist and principal songwriter, composing ten of the eleven songs on their 1967 debut album *The Piper at the Gates of Dawn*, which cemented the group's reputation as the darlings of London's psychedelic scene; he also gave the group its name.

Roger Keith Barrett was born in Cambridge on 6 January 1946, the fourth of five children of Dr Arthur Max Barrett and his wife Winifred. His musical nature was encouraged from an early age. Inspired by the skiffle craze of the mid-1950s, he took up the ukulele and by the age of fourteen had graduated to the guitar, playing with several local groups before gaining a place at London's Camberwell Art College in 1964 to study Fine Art.

It was during this period that Barrett formed Pink Floyd with his former schoolmate Roger Waters, who was studying Architecture with the organist Rick Wright and the drummer Nick Mason. The group's name was an amalgamation of two bluesmen Barrett admired – Pink Anderson and Floyd Council – although he told interviewers that the name was transmitted to him by a flying saucer.

The Floyd's debut at London's Marquee Club in February 1966, in which the group played layer upon layer of howling feedback, was well received. They became the house band at the UFO club in Tottenham Court Road, where their crazed performances and primitive light show became the focus of the underground.

Yet by the summer of 1967 Barrett's friends and associates noticed a change. His LSD consumption was now fearsome and his behaviour became erratic. Sometimes he would strum the same note throughout a performance, or fail to turn up altogether. Although *The Piper at the Gates of Dawn* was well received, a series of walkouts and temperamental fits, coupled with the fact that the Floyd's third single 'Apples and Oranges' failed to make an impact on the charts, served to hasten Barrett's departure.

Following a disastrous tour of America, by which time Barrett's on-stage demeanour bordered on the catatonic, plans were made to replace him with an old Cambridge friend, Dave Gilmour. The Floyd briefly struggled on as a five-piece, before Barrett's break with the band became final.

By 1972, as Pink Floyd continued to cement their reputation as one of the world's premier rock bands, their erstwhile leader was back in Cambridge, living in the cellar of his mother's home. Barrett told a reporter who tracked him down that he was 'full of dust and guitars'.

Ironically, during this period of inactivity, Barrett's personal income began to grow, along with his waistline. Fat royalty cheques from various Floyd compilation albums enabled him to stay at swish London hotels, where he spent his time watching television. When he unexpectedly turned up during the recording of *Wish You Were Here* – a belated tribute – in 1975, his shaven-headed, bloated appearance meant that his former bandmates failed to recognise him.

In 1992 Atlantic Records offered Barrett $500,000 for new material; the offer went unheeded. He apparently spent his time painting and writing; in 2002 his sister, who had kept an eye on him since their mother's death in 1991, gave him a stereo, but he expressed little interest in *Echoes*, a compilation of Pink Floyd's recordings. He had written nearly a fifth of the tracks on it, though he had worked with the group for less than a thirtieth of its existence. He deigned to watch an *Omnibus* documentary about himself, but found it 'a bit noisy'.

⚜ 8th ⚜

Air Commodore 'Freddie' West, b. 1896, d. 1988

Air Commodore 'Freddie' West, who has died aged ninety-two, was the last surviving British VC of the First World War.

When war broke out West was eighteen, employed as a clerk in the foreign correspondence department of a Zurich bank. Deciding that fist-fights with the German clerk on the next stool were an inadequate response to the Kaiser, he returned home to London to enlist.

By May 1915 he had been commissioned in the Royal Munster Fusiliers, and in November he arrived in France in charge of twenty men. In 1917, convinced that 'trench warfare was for rats, not men', he joined the Royal Flying Corps.

He trained as a pilot and joined No. 8 Squadron at Amiens, where his commanding officer, Major Trafford Leigh-Mallory, greeted his new recruits with the words: 'You gentlemen are just the chickens the red German eagles are looking for.'

Leigh-Mallory's warning referred to the famous ace Manfred von Richthofen, the 'Red Baron', and his 'circus' of red-painted Fokkers, whom West was soon to encounter. One Sunday in April 1918 he was patrolling the area of St Quentin-Amiens when his observer spotted three red Fokkers.

To his astonishment, West saw one fall to the ground. He landed near the crashed enemy machine and was greeted by a jubilant Australian artillery officer who said: 'We've had a bit of luck. Guess who we've shot down?' West inspected the dead pilot and found himself looking at the Red Baron, 'quite calm in death – he might have died in bed'.

On 10 August of that year, flying a two-seater Armstrong F8 reconnaissance machine in the recently formed RAF, West was attacked by seven enemy aeroplanes while on hedge-hopping reconnaissance far over enemy lines. Early in the engagement one of his legs was partially severed by an explosive bullet; it fell powerless into the controls and rendered the machine unmanageable.

West managed to extricate his disabled leg, regained control and, although wounded in the other leg, manoeuvred his aircraft so skilfully that his observer, Alec Haslam, was able to open fire on the enemy machines and drive them off.

In the words of the citation: 'Captain West then, with rare courage and determination, brought his machine over our lines and landed safely. Exhausted by his exertions, he fainted, but on regaining consciousness insisted on writing his report.'

Ferdinand 'Freddie' West was born in London in 1896. After the death of his father in the Boer War, his mother, Countess Clemence de la Garde de Saignes, took him to Italy, where he became trilingual in English, French and Italian – an asset in later postings as a diplomat.

After the action for which he was awarded the VC, West was treated at the London Hospital and fitted with an artificial leg at Roehampton. Awarded £250 compensation for loss of a limb, he invested £200 in war bonds and went off to Paris, where he paid

£20 for a superior wooden leg. Later he was made an even better one by the Swiss tool manufacturer de Soutter, who had also lost a leg.

In June 1940, when Italy came into the Second World War, West was ordered to Switzerland as air attaché — though he was effectively head of British air intelligence.

Freddie West soon became a familiar figure there, limping through the streets of Berne, followed by his White Russian bodyguard. He engaged in a range of covert activities, his most notable coup being the retrieval from a crashed German aircraft of a tin box containing an extensive card index of Luftwaffe dispositions in Italy, which was rapturously received by the Air Ministry.

It was not until 1971 that West acknowledged his disability by selling his house at Sunningdale and moving into a nearby bungalow — and he was still playing golf at eighty.

❧ 9th ❧

Barbara Woodhouse, b. 1910, d. 1988

Barbara Woodhouse, who has died aged seventy-eight, became famous with the BBC series, *Training Dogs the Woodhouse Way*, in the 1970s, sweeping the nation with her ringing catchphrase: 'Walkies!'

A real life Dr Dolittle in a tweed skirt, Woodhouse enjoyed a magical ability to communicate with animals, using love, enthusiasm, will-power and 'the telepathic communication without which I could never talk to animals at all'.

Woodhouse had such rapport with animals that when she kept a boarding school for dogs her charges kept running away from their owners and coming back to her. Altogether she trained more than 17,000 dogs – a world record.

The daughter of a clerical headmaster, Barbara Blackburn was born near Dublin in 1910. She once overheard her mother say: 'Why can't Barbara be beautiful, like the other children?' From that moment she decided that she preferred animals, because they did not care what she looked like.

After school at Headington and in Switzerland, she boldly went to Harper Adams Agricultural College in Newport, Shropshire, where she was the only woman among sixty men. She studied Veterinary Science, Building Construction and Engineering, and gained the second highest marks in the college: she became an expert motor mechanic, and could lay bricks as fast as a professional.

After a time running a riding school, the redoubtable Miss Blackburn set off, aged twenty-four, on a cargo boat to seek adventure in Argentina. During her time there she contracted foot-and-mouth disease, and suffered from diabetes. She spent four years on great estates on the pampas, and earned a wide reputation for her skill in breaking wild horses, which was considered an exclusively masculine occupation.

Back in England in 1940, she married Dr Michael Woodhouse, and during the Second World War kept cows, discovering that milk production improved if the animals wore rugs in winter.

In 1954 she published her enduring bestseller, *Talking to Animals*, which she had dashed off in only five days. She later wrote more than twenty books, including an autobiography, *Just Barbara* (1981).

Her television career began in the early 1950s, when she demonstrated her animal-training skills on Scottish television. After appearances on *Pebble Mill at One*, she was finally given the series which made her a celebrity.

***

Melvin Belli, b. 1907, d. 1996

Melvin Belli, who has died aged eighty-eight, was one of America's most flamboyant lawyers.

If there was publicity, or even notoriety, to be gained, Belli (pronounced Bell-Eye) was up for the job. It was typical of him to volunteer, live on television on 24 November 1963, to defend Jack Ruby, who had shot Lee Harvey Oswald (under arrest for the murder of President Kennedy).

Dubbed 'the King of Torts', Belli specialised in gaining his clients huge sums in damages from actions arising out of professional malpractice or negligence. He had no qualms about 'putting the fear of God into some of the unqualified men in medicine'. In pursuit of these 'bums' Belli developed what he rather grandly characterised as the use of

'demonstrative evidence'. Translated, this simply meant letting the court see for itself.

Thus, when in 1949 he represented a woman who had been disfigured by breast surgery, he made his client take off her upper garments in front of the judge and jury.

'What were you thinking,' a reporter asked him afterwards, 'when she had her head bowed and the tears dropped out of her eyes and fell upon the scars of her breast?'

'I could hear the angels sing and the cash register ring,' Belli replied.

❧ 10th ❧

Albert Pierrepoint, b. 1905, d. 1992

Albert Pierrepoint, who has died aged eighty-seven, was Britain's leading executioner for twenty-five years, but later campaigned for the abolition of the death penalty. Short and dapper, with mild blue eyes, a pleasant singing voice and a fondness for cigars and beautiful women, Pierrepoint was fascinated by bar tricks with coins and matchboxes – which were in plentiful supply at the oddly named Help the Poor Struggler, a pub he kept in Lancashire.

While employed as a hangman he never spoke of 't'other job', and he hated the thought of any impropriety, unseemliness or vulgarity connected with his craft, which he viewed as sacred. After his retirement, however, he spoke of it freely – notably in his autobiography *Executioner: Pierrepoint* (1974).

'Hanging must run in the blood,' he explained (his father and an uncle were both hangmen). 'It requires a natural flair. The judgment and timing of a first-rate hangman cannot be acquired.'

Pierrepoint was undoubtedly a first-rate hangman: 'I hanged John Reginald Christie, the Monster of Rillington Place,' he wrote, 'in less time than it took the ash to fall off a cigar I had left half-smoked in my room at Pentonville.'

During his career he hanged more than 400 people – his record was seventeen in a day ('Was my arm stiff'). In 1946 he went to Vienna, where he ran 'a school for executioners'; the British authorities had sentenced eight Polish youths, but refused to hand them over to Austrian hangmen, whose methods were brutally unscientific. Pierrepoint hanged the youths at the rate of two a day, and stayed on for a fortnight to give further instruction.

He recalled only one awkward moment in his career. 'It was unfortunate. He was not an Englishman. He was a spy and kicked up rough.'

In 1956 Pierrepoint resigned, incensed at the meanness of the Home Office, which had granted him only £1 in expenses, and began his campaign against capital punishment.

'If death were a deterrent,' he wrote, 'I might be expected to know. It is I who have faced them at the last, young lads and girls, working men, grandmothers. I have been amazed to see the courage with which they take that walk into the unknown.

'It did not deter them then, and it had not deterred them when they committed what they were convicted for. All the men and women whom I have faced at that final moment convince me that in what I have done I have not prevented a single murder.'

Albert Pierrepoint was born on 30 March 1905 at Clayton, a district of Bradford in the West Riding of Yorkshire, and brought up in Huddersfield and Manchester. His father, Harry, had been an executioner for ten years, and his uncle for forty-two. Young Albert was nine when he first conceived the ambition to become an executioner.

He wrote his first application to the Home Office to be included in the list of official executioners in 1930, but there were no vacancies. A year later Pierrepoint was invited to an interview at Strangeways Prison, and accepted. His first execution as principal hangman was that of a gangland murderer at Pentonville in London, and further engagements soon followed.

In 1943 he was sent to Gibraltar to execute two saboteurs. During the Second World War there were sixteen spies convicted in Britain, and Pierrepoint hanged fifteen of them (the sixteenth was reprieved).

He always maintained that there was no glamour in taking the lives of others, and he abhorred all publicity, so he was displeased when General Sir Bernard Montgomery announced from his headquarters in Germany that Pierrepoint was to hang the convicted staff of Belsen.

Appointed an honorary lieutenant-colonel for the purpose, he duly travelled to Hameln in Germany, where, on Friday 13 December 1945 he hanged thirteen people before lunch. There was a strange sequel to these executions: every Christmas thereafter, for a number of years, Pierrepoint received a £5 note in an envelope, with a slip of paper reading simply 'Belsen'.

Rocky Aoki, b. 1938, d. 2008

Rocky Aoki, who has died aged sixty-nine, was selected to compete as a wrestler in the Olympics, launched a porn magazine, became a record-breaking balloonist and powerboat champion and was credited with introducing the West to Japanese cuisine.

Aoki arrived in New York from Japan in 1960 with little money but a determination to succeed. In 1964 he opened a four-table restaurant, Benihana, on West 56th Street. He built it into a multi-million-dollar international corporation that, at its peak, had a hundred restaurants around the world, three of them in London.

Aoki then set about making himself a minor celebrity, defying the stoic, conformist Japanese stereotype. He posed for photographs in a hot tub in his stretch Rolls-Royce; competed in a cross-country race in a stretch Volkswagen Beetle; had a walk-on part in *Hawaii Five-O*; won a national backgammon championship; set a world record in 1981 by becoming the first person to cross the Pacific in a hot-air balloon; won the 1987 inaugural Milan-to-Moscow road rally; nearly killed himself powerboat racing; and launched a soft-porn magazine, *Genesis*, with 'two centrefolds for the price of one'.

In 1979 he featured on the cover of *Newsweek* under the headline 'Making it in America – an embodiment of the American Dream'.

'I was like Trump,' he recalled. 'Anything to promote my company, I did it. Richard Branson? He copy me.'

11th

Arturo Gatti, b. 1972, d. 2009

Arturo Gatti, who has been murdered aged thirty-seven, may not have been the most talented boxer in the world, but few others have captured the hearts and admiration of so many fans of the sport.

The Italian-born Canadian's all-action style and indomitable spirit made him hugely popular; he will forever be remembered for his epic trilogy of fights with the American 'Irish' Micky Ward. These rip-roaring encounters – spread over a thirteen-month period in 2002–03 – provided thirty rounds of some of the most compelling and savage ring action in recent years.

Ward won their first encounter at Uncasville, Connecticut, on a majority decision after a point deducted from Gatti for a low blow proved crucial. 'The guy must be made of granite,' a battered Ward said afterwards. 'What's he got in his head? My hands are killing me.'

Gatti gained his revenge when the pair met again six months later. Although his points triumph in Atlantic City in November 2002 lacked the intensity of their first meeting, Gatti showed that he was no mere slugger as, boxing superbly behind his jab and showing sound defence, he seized the initiative and maintained control of the fight. Moreover, he won despite a broken right hand sustained when Ward was floored heavily in the third.

Their final fight – again at Atlantic City's Boardwalk Hall, in June 2003 – saw Gatti conclusively prove his superiority with a unanimous decision, following another no-holds-barred encounter in which both men suffered broken right hands and the Canadian was forced to overcome a sixth-round knockdown. The 37-year-old Ward left the ring on a stretcher and never fought again.

Arturo Gatti was born in Calabria, Italy, on 15 April 1972, later emigrating to Montreal with his family.

Having taken up boxing at the age of eight, he elected to turn professional at the age of nineteen. His progress through the paid ranks was swift.

He was found dead at a hotel in the Brazilian resort of Porto de Galinhas, where he had gone for a 'second honeymoon' with his wife, Amanda Rodrigues, twenty-three. Rodrigues – who has been charged with his murder – and the couple's one-year-old son survive him.

❦ 12th ❦

John Boon, b. 1916, d. 1996

John Boon, who has died aged seventy-nine, was chairman of the publishers Mills & Boon, and an architect of its modern success.

The romantic formula that the firm developed has been much mocked, not least by feminists. But though many have felt themselves called to write novels for Mills & Boon, relatively few have succeeded in mastering the art. To write a good Mills & Boon novel, John Boon insisted, it was necessary to believe. 'It is exceptionally difficult,' he added. 'You can't do it if you have your tongue in your cheek.' But, for those writers who made the grade, the rewards were generous. No other publishing house has made so many novelists so rich.

Mills & Boon was the first British publisher to take market research seriously. It discovered that its readers were represented in all income groups and classes, both in Britain and overseas. The firm publishes nearly 700 titles a year and sells in 23 languages in more than 100 countries.

'I'd like the company to continue,' Boon observed in 1989. 'I think it will, provided someone doesn't do anything silly. Someone might suddenly decide they want to educate the public. Bloody disaster. The public don't want to be educated by us. They want to be amused. We really think we serve a most valuable function. We ought to be prescribed by the NHS. We're much better than Valium.'

Lieutenant-Colonel Cecil Merritt, b. 1908, d. 2000

Lieutenant-Colonel Cecil Merritt, who has died aged ninety-one, won the VC for gallantry during the disastrous raid on Dieppe in 1942.

He landed with the South Saskatchewan Regiment at Pourville, west of the main port, in the half-light of early morning on 19 August 1942. Their objective was to seize a beachhead and capture the high ground between Pourville and Dieppe. Landing in one wave, they were at first virtually unopposed, but heavy firing broke out as they scaled the sea wall and advanced into Pourville by a bridge which was soon carpeted with dead.

Seeing the situation, Merritt took off his helmet, walked on to the bridge and shouted: 'Come on, these Germans can't hit a thing.' Apparently oblivious to the enemy fire, he strolled across waving his helmet to encourage his men forward. But without artillery the heavily fortified main positions could not be breached.

Shortly after 9 a.m., orders for withdrawal were received from the Force Commander. Casualties were heavy as they pulled back to the beach, where Merritt organised a rearguard to cover the evacuation of the Canadian 6th Brigade. His group could not be brought off. At 1.30 p.m., disdaining to raise a white flag, Merritt sent a German prisoner to invite the enemy to come forward and take the surrender.

He did not prove a tractable prisoner.

⚜ 13th ⚜

Dr Cicely Williams, b. 1893, d. 1992

Dr Cicely Williams, the doyenne of paediatrics and child nutrition, who has died aged ninety-eight, survived harrowing experiences as a prisoner of the Japanese during the Second World War.

In 1942 she was conducting a survey in the remote Trengganu Sultanate, in north-east Malaya, when the invading Japanese armies arrived. She managed to escape through uncharted jungle-clad mountains to reach Singapore, but there she was incarcerated in the notorious Changi Jail, interrogated by the Kempe Tai, the Japanese secret police, and locked in a fetid, overcrowded cage.

During her period in the cage Williams lost a third of her body weight and developed beriberi, which left her with permanent numbness of the feet.

Cicely Delphine Williams was born on 2 December 1893 in Jamaica, where her father was director of education. She was educated at Bath High School for Girls and Somerville College, Oxford, and proceeded to King's College Hospital Medical School.

After junior hospital posts in the East End of London she spent a year as a medical officer in the malarial swamps of Greece, before joining the Colonial Medical Service in 1929. Her first appointment was on the Gold Coast, to work in preventive medicine.

In 1933 in the *Archives of Diseases in Childhood* she published an article, 'A Nutritional Disease of Childhood', which has proved of paramount importance in the field. The paper described a condition known as 'Kwashiorkor', a Ga word meaning 'the deposed one'.

This syndrome afflicted children who had been abruptly banished from the maternal breast by the arrival of a new baby. Although first diagnosed among African children, it also occurs in many other parts of the world, especially the tropics.

A number of authorities attributed kwashiorkor to a lack of calories, but Williams persisted with her view that the disease was caused by protein deficiency. It took a long time for her opinion to be accepted by the male-dominated medical establishment, but eventually it prevailed.

After six years on the Gold Coast Williams returned to England to write her dissertation on child health in Africa. In 1936 she moved to Malaya, where she staged a determined campaign to persuade mothers to breast-feed their babies.

At that time baby-food firms were vigorously promoting artificial feeding in the back streets of Singapore, and so began Williams' campaign against the marketing activities of the manufacturers of infant foods. At the Singapore Rotary Club she delivered an uncompromising lecture entitled 'Milk and Murder'.

At the end of the war she was repatriated to Britain and, in 1946, after a brief period of rehabilitation, returned to duty in Malaya. In 1948 she was appointed head of Maternal and Child Health of the World Health Organisation and five years later she was given the job of senior lecturer in nutrition at London University.

Between 1955 and 1959 she visited various countries as a consultant, and from then until 1964 she was a visiting professor at the American University in Beirut. In the late 1960s she was overseas training adviser to the Family Planning Association. Latterly she described herself in *Who's Who* as 'retired (except on demand)'.

Unworldly, she could survive on very little; the only possessions she kept throughout her life were the tin mug and plate which had seen her through her internment in Changi Jail.

≋ 14th ≋

Dame Cicely Saunders, b. 1918, d. 2005

Dame Cicely Saunders, who has died aged eighty-seven, was regarded as the mother of the modern hospice movement; at St Christopher's Hospice, Sydenham, south London, founded in 1967, she charted new approaches in techniques for treatment of the terminally ill, based on her Christian belief that no human life, no matter how wretched, should be denied dignity and love.

Before St Christopher's opened its doors, there had been hospices, mostly run by nuns, which provided comfort for the dying; but they were backward in their understanding of medical techniques. Even on busy hospital wards where many people spent their final hours, very little was known about the management of pain. With a few exceptions, medical and surgical textbooks disregarded the problems of pain control; and chronic pain in the dying was usually either ignored or treated too late.

Cicely Saunders first had the idea of creating a modern hospice in 1948, when she was working as a lady almoner at St Thomas's Hospital in London. There she met David Tasma, a young Polish waiter who, having escaped from the Warsaw ghetto, was dying of cancer, in great pain, on a ward she was visiting. Though he had little English, they spent their time together talking about death and the care of the dying.

Cicely Saunders fell deeply in love and, when Tasma died, he left her all he had – £500 – and told her: 'I'll be a window in your home.'

'It was as though God was tapping me on the shoulder and telling me, "You've got to get on with it",' she recalled.

Carrying Tasma's memory with her, Cicely Saunders became a physician and went on to found St Christopher's Hospice, where she hoped to 'help the dying to live until they die and their families to live on'. She had no new drugs, but showed how, by using them earlier in anticipation of, rather than in response to, the onset of pain, terminally ill patients could be kept comfortable until the end.

As a Christian, she saw dying not as something to be feared, but as a spiritual event which can bring meaning to life and provide an opportunity for reconciliation. In *Living with Dying* (1983), she explained that hospice care involves not only the alleviation of pain, but addresses patients' 'mental, social and spiritual pain'. St Christopher's boasts, among other things, a hairdressing salon, and lays on activities such as creative writing, discussion groups and indoor gardening, reflecting its founder's belief that the last months of life can be lived happily and creatively.

In her campaign to establish a hospice, Cicely Saunders encountered apathy, even outright hostility, from the medical profession. Though she was widely revered as a sort of secular saint, it was only through being tough and authoritative, and often downright difficult, that she succeeded in forcing the medical profession to acknowledge what medicine can do for the dying.

The movement she began changed the face of death for millions of people, not only the dying, but also those around them. By 1993 there were 173 hospices in Britain adhering to her philosophy.

Cicely Mary Strode Saunders was born on 22 June 1918 at Barnet, north London, the eldest child and only daughter of an estate agent. Her parents' marriage was a catastrophe that ended with the whole family turning against their mother. It was Cicely herself who was sent by her father to tell her mother that their marriage was over: an action for which she later suffered terrible pangs of guilt.

Cicely went up in 1939 to St Anne's, Oxford, to read PPE, but when war began she abandoned her studies and trained to be a nurse, qualifying in 1944. A severe back problem forced her to give up shortly after qualifying and, after returning to complete her degree, she became a lady almoner.

While training for this role, she went on holiday with some evangelical Christians and underwent a dramatic conversion. 'It was as though I suddenly felt the wind behind me rather than in my face,' she recalled. 'I thought to myself: "Please let this be real." I prayed to know how best to serve God. Then I met my Pole.'

She began to learn about the needs of dying people by spending an evening a week as a ward sister at St Luke's in Bayswater, studying ways to reduce pain and offer comfort. But she soon came to realise that, in order to make real changes, she would need to become a doctor and study pharmacology. She started training at St Thomas's at thirty-three and qualified in 1957.

For seven years she did research into pain control at St Joseph's, Hackney, a hospice run by the Roman Catholic Sisters of Charity, but soon decided that she wanted to found her own hospice as a centre for research and medical education. It was while she was acquiring funds that she fell in love with another Pole, dying on her ward at St Joseph's.

Again there was a short, passionate relationship restricted to brief meetings in the ward and ending with his death: 'I loved him very much,' she recalled. 'He taught me what it was like to be dying and to be bereaved; he showed me the achievement of a good death, that as the body becomes weaker, so the spirit becomes stronger.'

By this time, plans for her hospice were slowly coming to fruition. Her brother found her a site in Lawrie Park Road, Sydenham, and in 1963 the King Edward Hospital Fund gave her £63,000. Through a series of introductions, she went round charitable foundations and lured as many as possible to St Joseph's to see what could be done.

Though the philosophy underlying St Christopher's was Christian, it welcomed patients of any persuasion or none. Cicely Saunders noticed that those who coped best always had a shining faith, but that atheists often died as peacefully as Christians. The people with the most problems were those who had not sorted out their ideas. Clergymen, oddly, and the affluent, often turned out to have the most difficulty.

By 1980 the principles of pain relief which she had set out had become standard practice in the health service. In 1987 palliative medicine was recognised as a speciality in its own right.

Cicely Saunders had learned, from watching patients at St Joseph's, the importance of symbols to the dying. She was wondering what she could put on the walls of the hospice when she was driving past a gallery in Connaught Square and saw a picture of a crucifixion. Deciding it was exactly what she wanted, she bought it. Afterwards she wrote a letter to the artist, her 'third Pole', Marian Bohusz-Szyszko. Though he was eighteen years older than she, and in poor health, she married him in 1980. He gave her immense joy in the later years of her life, but needed her constant nursing care. He died in 1995.

⚜ 15th ⚜

Gianni Versace, b. 1946, d. 1997

Gianni Versace, who has been shot in Miami aged fifty, established a huge fashion empire by following Oscar Wilde's dictum that nothing succeeds like excess.

To some he seemed obsessed by *nostalgie de la boue*, ambitious chiefly to turn men into studs and women into wholly unobscure objects of desire. Uncompromisingly glitzy, he developed a style that was typified by the dress which Elizabeth Hurley wore to the premiere of *Four Weddings and a Funeral*, a covering that revealed a great deal more than it concealed.

Versace's designs were the antithesis of those of Giorgio Armani, who deals in discretion and understatement, and who once accused him of turning fashion into a porno show. ('Armani is a bore,' returned Versace.) Whereas there was never any shortage of stars – Elton John, Joan Collins, Ivana Trump, Madonna, Bruce Springsteen, Prince, Elizabeth Taylor – ready to wear Versace's creations, it remains a mystery how a business which has so little affinity with the needs of ordinary men and women could flourish on such a scale.

It was not as though Versace's prices were designed to entice. In his 1993 collection, for instance, there was a $1,750 silk shirt, a $6,000 evening gown and an $800 gold-studded belt.

Versace insisted that the cost of his clothes was immaterial, for their fashion spread way beyond the elite. Yet perhaps the real secret of his success was that he had discovered that there is no better way of seducing the bourgeoisie than by insulting it.

To that end Versace masterminded a great soufflé of froth and hype. Where Chanel might take three pages in *Vogue* and Yves Saint Laurent five, Versace would buy a run of twenty. He created the impression that to wear his clothes was to declare oneself (whether male or female) free-thinking, fearless, unconventional. He mouthed cant about liberating the modern woman, and discovered there was no shortage of people with money eager to lap up his propaganda. 'Shorter! Tighter! Higher!' the maestro cried at his atelier in Milan.

On the shores of Lake Como he restored the Villa Fontanelle, an eighteenth-century palace that doubled as his design studio. And in America he could seek refuge from the press of the world at his mansion on Ocean Drive, Miami.

He had come a long way from Reggio, in Calabria, where he was born on 2 December 1946, the son of a coal merchant who later opened a shop selling electrical goods. Versace did not care to dwell upon his father, preferring to remember that his mother was a dressmaker who owned a boutique.

'I was born and raised amidst dresses,' he said, 'and everything I know about fashion I owe to my mother.' Even his love of erotic clothes, he claimed, derived from the walks he took with her as a child. As they passed the local brothel she would shield his eyes – 'But I looked. Those brothel girls were magical, beautiful.'

By twenty-two he was producing his own designs, which caught the attention of a clothing manufacturer in Milan. For a while he worked freelance for the Complice, Callaghan and Genny labels; then in 1978 he brought out a collection of women's ready-to-wear clothes under his own name. He opened a boutique, and later in the year showed his first collection for men, on the theme of 'disciplined masculine negligence'.

At this period Versace was influenced by the clean lines of military uniforms, right down to the jaunty epaulettes and the raised piping on the trousers. Then in 1982, inspired by the punks he had seen in London, he took the military theme into another dimension by creating a woven metal mesh dress.

It took some time to convince the wider world of his genius. But by sheer persistence and personality Versace prevailed. He made himself increasingly respectable by creating costumes for operas and ballets in Milan, Leningrad, Brussels and other cities. In the mid-1980s he explored daring contrasts: black leather appliquéd with velvet; grey flannel doubled with shiny silk. Purists dismissed his creations as vulgar, but the beau monde flocked to buy. 'People love me,' he explained.

By the end of 1993 Versace was selling clothes, jewellery and accessories in 345 outlets, including 138 Versace stores, from Tokyo to the Caribbean. Only a few critics dared to resist the trend. 'I have to say I hated it,' declared Holly Brubach of the *New Yorker*. 'Versace's designs, more than anyone else's, suggest specific sexual practices. They strike me as needing equipment.'

Versace never married. 'As a person, he is not very sexual,' a woman colleague explained, 'but there is plenty of suggestion.'

⇒ 16th ⇐

Beate Uhse, b. 1919, d. 2001

B eate Uhse, who has died aged eighty-one, became the doyenne of the German sex industry, and thereby one of the most famous women in Germany, after wartime service as a Luftwaffe pilot.

Although she was at one point blackballed from her local tennis club, respectability of a sort was conferred on her by the successful flotation of her business in 1999 on the Frankfurt stock exchange. Uhse saw nothing embarrassing in her chosen trade and placed her own name and face on her products even in the 1950s. In her sensible clothes, she looked towards the end of her life more like an elderly but sprightly GP than a remorselessly energetic pornographer.

She was born Beate Kostlin on 25 October 1919. Her father farmed an estate near Konigsberg in East Prussia, the German territory on the south-east corner of the Baltic. He was shot dead when he walked out to meet the advancing Russian soldiers in the winter of 1944–45.

Her mother was a qualified paediatrician and wanted Beate to be a doctor too, but the girl had a passionate desire to fly. Thinking it would be a good idea to learn English first, she went to Britain for a year as an au pair. In August 1937, she took her first flying lessons at Rangsdorf near Berlin, and after qualifying as a pilot she got a job with an aircraft manufacturer running in new aircraft.

She was nineteen when war broke out. She and her boyfriend of two years, Hans-Jurgen Uhse, her former flying instructor, married in haste in September 1939 before he was posted to his unit. She herself delivered aircraft to the Luftwaffe and gave birth to a son, Klaus. On the night of 30 May 1944 she went to sleep after her husband, now flying night fighters, had telephoned to say he would not be in action that night. An hour later, he was ordered to intercept British planes heading for Berlin and was killed as he was taking off when another German plane taxied into his path.

At the age of twenty-four, Beate Uhse joined the Luftwaffe, still as a delivery pilot, flying low to try to escape attack by enemy aircraft. In April 1945, as the Russians closed in, she flew herself out at the last moment with her baby, the baby's nurse, a mechanic and two wounded men, landing at Leck near the Danish border and becoming a British prisoner of war. On visiting the Russian zone of occupation, where she hoped to retrieve some of her belongings, she was imprisoned in a cellar and raped.

It was while making a precarious living as a small-time black marketeer in Schleswig-Holstein, trading in butter, coffee and other goods, that she made the discovery which was to change her life. Woman after woman in the village where she was living asked her advice about how to avoid getting pregnant. Beate Uhse remembered her own mother telling her about the rhythm method of birth control, refreshed her memory with a book by a Swiss doctor, wrote a short account of it which she called 'Schrift X' and had 2,000 copies printed in return for five pounds of butter.

The pamphlet sold like hot cakes. Customers started writing to her, asking if she could supply them with condoms, sex education books and sexual stimulants. By the end of 1953 she had fourteen employees, by 1961 over a hundred, and today the firm employs 1,000 people. Her second husband, Ernst-Walter Rotermund, felt she devoted too much time to the business, which he helped to run. Announcing that he did not intend to work himself to death and would retire on his fortieth birthday, he gave up cigarettes, turned vegetarian, betrayed her with Helga, the couple's 21-year-old housemaid, and went off to meditate.

Beate Uhse said that the business ran even better without him, but admitted she 'suffered like a dog' from his infidelity.

She met her last great love when she was fifty-two. He was a black 27-year-old teacher from New York called John Holland, with whom she lived for nine years, although she remained married to Rotermund until 1972, when the marriage was dissolved.

⊰ 17th ⊱

Shoe Taylor, b. 1944, d. 2003

Shoe Taylor, who has died aged fifty-eight, became the long-standing mistress of the eccentric politician, businessman and writer Jonathan Guinness (now Lord Moyne) after an eventful decade during which she pursued the life of a wandering hippy.

Her story was told in 1989, when Guinness (best known for his vigorously right-wing views) published an account of her life in a doomed attempt to forestall tabloid gossip about his polygamous relationship with Shoe, with whom he had three children, and his second wife Suzanne, with whom he had two.

Susan Mary Taylor (known as 'Shoe') was born over her father's butcher's shop at Oldham, Lancashire, on 26 July 1944. As a child, she helped out in the slaughterhouse.

After leaving school aged fourteen, she drifted from job to job, working as a nursing cadet, delivery van driver for her father and eventually setting up in business as a hairdresser. But she longed to escape. After seeing *The Sound of Music*, it 'became obvious' that her destiny lay in Austria, even though she knew nobody there and had not a word of German.

Accordingly, aged twenty-one, she hitchhiked across Europe hoping to meet a version of the von Trapp family, thus becoming perhaps the only person in the world to have been inspired to adopt an alternative lifestyle by Julie Andrews.

Instead, she charred for a princess and became a hippy, embarking on a vagabond life of hitching and busking her way round squats and communes in Europe, north Africa and Asia, risking her health with drugs while trying to improve it with macrobiotics, Eastern mysticism, alchemy and magic.

In Britain, she joined 'love-ins' and Legalise Pot rallies and associated with Alan Ginsberg, Felix Topolski and Venetia Stanley Smith; in Beirut, she became a circus performer, riding a hermaphrodite elephant called Sally; in Munich, she danced in the chorus of *Hair*. She also worked as a tea lady for the Beatles at Apple Studios and performed topless as 'the world's strongest woman' with a burlesque circus act from Paris.

She sat at the feet of a guru in India; worked as a geisha in Japan (where her form was used as a mould to make dummy Western women for shop windows), and spent a summer on the Spanish island of Formentera where she got high and learned to play the tom-toms.

Shoe Taylor survived several brushes with the law – and with death. In Tunis she was jailed, then deported, for taking cannabis through Customs; she did two stints in Holloway for the same offence. Following the hippy trail to Marrakesh, she met Jean François, a young Frenchman who 'was on a serious spiritual search'. Looking for the best hash cakes in Morocco, he took her to Rabat, where they were kidnapped – and she gang-raped – by five Arab men.

By the time she met Jonathan Guinness in 1978, Shoe Taylor had become a bulimic recluse living in a stone hut in the foothills of the Pyrenees.

She turned up at a St Sebastian's Day party which Guinness was giving at his house in the Costa Brava village of Cadaques; they met again at a local art exhibition and struck up a conversation. Although Jonathan Guinness was twice married and had several children, he and Shoe began an affair. She bore him three more children and eventually moved to Cornwall as his mistress. Guinness paid for her upkeep while remaining married to Suzanne, his wife since 1964.

Shoe's affair with the Guinness heir was a society rumour for years before he published her biography, *Shoe: an Odyssey of a Sixties Survivor*, in 1989. The experience would have been humiliating for most women, but not for Shoe, who gamely undertook publicity photographs with her children, as well as with Jonathan (both standing on their heads).

She drew strength from her lover's devotion, shaking off her addiction to drugs and her bulimia, though not her enthusiasm for New Age therapies. In 2000, after Lord Moyne was declared bankrupt, he and Shoe helped to make ends meet by selling magnetised wristbands as a treatment for arthritis. They remained devoted to each other.

⚔ 18th ⚔

Bertie Blount, b. 1907, d. 1999

Bertie Blount, who has died aged ninety-two, spent the Second World War inventing ingenious methods of assassination for the Special Operations Executive; his ideas included a plan to kill Hitler using anthrax.

Operation Foxley, which aimed at the assassination of Hitler, was raised with Blount in December 1944, when he was told that any plan he devised could employ chemical or bacteriological agents. Blount warned that 'the difficulty lies not in finding the toxic substance but in getting it to the spot where it can do its work'.

One of the methods was inhalation. 'This is a fruitful method,' Blount wrote in a report, 'if access can be gained to living quarters or to clothing. N [the codename for anthrax], a bacterial substance, is lethal by this route in a minute dose.'

Looking for ways of hiding the lethal agent, Blount asked if the assassin could wear glasses or false teeth, and if he might have 'any physical peculiarity such as wearing a truss or a false limb'.

The German section's response was that, while the possibility of 'physical peculiarity' was unlikely, the assassin could wear glasses and 'we can give him false teeth even if he does not want them'.

Pressed, as ever, on the possibility of 'a number of alternative gadgets', Blount remained sceptical. 'Guns and hypodermic syringes disguised as fountain pens are usually not a bit convincing and are likely to lead to the death of the operator before he has had any opportunity of making his attack.'

Although none of the plans devised to kill Hitler ever left the drawing board, the possible use of anthrax, and a suggestion during the discussions that 'a study of the Heydrich operation will be profitable', remain intriguing. Operation Anthropoid, the SOE assassination of Reinhard Heydrich, the Nazi Governor of Bohemia and Moravia, by Czech agents in 1942, has been persistently surrounded by unproven claims that anthrax was used.

Bertie Kennedy Blount was born at Shoeburyness on 1 April 1907. His father was an artillery colonel who won the DSO in the First World War, his mother the daughter of a major-general.

He was educated at Malvern College and Trinity College, Oxford, where he took a first in Chemistry. He then studied for a doctorate in Natural Sciences at Frankfurt University. Here he befriended Alex (later Lord) Todd, who went on to carry out pioneering research on DNA.

Blount returned to Oxford, where he became Dean of St Peter's Hall (now St Peter's College). Two years before the outbreak of the Second World War he joined Glaxo as its head of chemical research, and in 1939 was commissioned into the Intelligence Corps.

He was soon transferred to the SOE, where his scientific expertise was put to full use. For secret assignments he was parachuted into Greece behind enemy lines and served in the Far East with the Chindits.

After the war Blount was appointed director of scientific intelligence at the Ministry of Defence with a seat on the Joint Intelligence Committee. Two years later, he was persuaded to move to the Department of Scientific and Industrial Research, which was subsumed into Harold Wilson's flagship Ministry of Technology in 1964.

Blount retired in 1966 but was far from inactive. He lived the latter part of his life at the family home in the Dorset village of Tarrant Rushton, where he was known as 'the Colonel', his eccentricities being regarded with affection. Though he was president of the International Institute of Refrigeration, he spent many years without a refrigerator, until it was pointed out to him that this was why his milk went off. He immediately drove into nearby Blandford Forum and bought a large refrigerator.

⊰ 19th ⊱

Paolo Borsellino, b. 1940, d. 1992

Paolo Borsellino, the Italian judge who was blasted to death in a motor-car bomb attack in Palermo, aged fifty-two, seemed to foresee his future just two months before his own death, at the funeral of his fellow judge and anti-Mafia crusader, Giovanni Falcone.

With his hands on Falcone's coffin, he said to the other judges present: 'Who wants to leave Palermo should do so – here, this is our future.' But despite his sombre words Borsellino stayed at his post, although he admitted to periods of pessimism and frustration.

A pharmacist's son, Paolo Borsellino was born in Palermo on 19 January 1940 and went to school with young Giovanni Falcone. He was more impressed, however, by another schoolmate, the son of the local Mafia boss.

But Borsellino put away his adolescent envy and went on to study law at Palermo University. His first important investigation as a magistrate was for the killing of an anti-Mafia *carabiniere* in 1980. His big break followed shortly after, when he was invited to join the anti-Mafia pool formed by Judge Chinnici in the late 1970s.

Borsellino was Falcone's right-hand man in the investigation which led to the 'maxi-trial' of 1987, when nearly 400 members of the Mafia were sent to jail. Chinnici was murdered in the course of the investigation, and after the trial a number of relations of *pentiti* (Mafiosi-turned-informers) were also liquidated.

Borsellino was forced to live a life of virtual imprisonment. Bullet-proof police cars always stood outside his apartment, while at work he used to play 'the obits game' with his colleagues.

They all had to learn to live with the thought of death – Borsellino even took the precaution of asking Falcone to give him the combination for his office safe, so that he could open it when his friend was killed. The atmosphere at the Palermo Law Courts was, in short, deeply gloomy and the moustached Borsellino had a melancholy air.

The Mafia menace restricted even his simple pleasures, which included throwing barbecues for friends at his seaside villa, and he constantly feared for his family's safety. In 1985 both Borsellino and Falcone, for security reasons, took their families to spend their summer vacation at the prison in Asinara, Sardinia.

His reputation for integrity won the confidence of ex-Mafia members who turned State's evidence. On one occasion a killer was advised to stand by for the order to kill Borsellino, but, believing himself in danger of his own life, confessed all to his intended victim.

⤛ 20th ⤜

Tammy Faye Messner, b. 1942, d. 2007

Tammy Faye Messner, who has died aged sixty-five, was better known as Tammy Faye Bakker, the former wife of the American televangelist Jim Bakker; together they collaborated in a ministry of spectacular vulgarity until he was defrocked for adultery and financial mismanagement and jailed on twenty-four counts of fraud and conspiracy.

The Bakkers founded their Praise the Lord ministry (PTL) in 1972. At the height of their popularity in the 1980s they had forty-seven bank accounts, six well-appointed houses, three Cadillacs and a Rolls-Royce; they were said to have $60,000-worth of gold plate in their bathrooms and an air-conditioned dog kennel.

Between 1984 and mid-1987 the Bakkers received annual salaries of $200,000 each, and Jim Bakker awarded himself more than $4 million in bonuses. On one occasion PTL spent more than $100,000 for a private jet to fly their wardrobes across America. Material wealth, the Bakkers argued, was a sign of God's grace.

All this was financed by an estimated $1 million a day in donations from the faithful, for at its peak PTL broadcasts were beamed into 13.5 million American homes. The Bakkers hobnobbed with tycoons and presidents – in 1980 Jimmy Carter invited Jim Bakker aboard Air Force One to pray for American hostages in Iran.

Tammy Faye's self-confidence was unassailable. 'Television,' she once remarked, 'likes people like me who dare to look straight into the camera and will hold nothing back. When I cry, people believe in the reality of it and tell me, "I cry with you".'

She was born Tamara Faye LaValley on 7 March 1942 at International Falls, Minnesota. Both her parents were Pentecostal preachers, but they divorced when she was a young child; her mother went on to marry a paper-mill worker.

At the age of ten Tammy Faye was taken to the Assemblies of God church, where, she said, she experienced the glow of God's love. As a pupil at Falls High School she sang in the choir and spent the summers at Bible camp. She was forbidden to attend school dances or to go to the cinema.

It was at North Central Bible College that she met Jim Bakker, a fellow student and former high school disc jockey. They married in 1961 and moved to North Carolina.

Three years later they began working with Pat Robertson on the Christian Broadcasting Network (CBN), developing their own daily children's show, *Come On*

Over, which was an immediate hit. Within a few years they were among the most popular religious broadcasters in America.

But their success and their closeness to Robertson aroused jealousies, and in 1972 the Bakkers decided to found their own ministry, PTL.

Jim Bakker was defrocked by the Assemblies of God after his affair with a 24-year-old church secretary, Jessica Hahn, became public. 'Oh, my heavens, it was a nightmare,' Tammy Faye later recalled. 'I had no idea that Jim had been unfaithful, and I cried for three days after he confessed to me. Our lives fell to pieces almost overnight.'

There were also allegations about the Bakkers' finances, and in 1989 a no-nonsense district judge known as 'Maximum Bob' sentenced Bakker to forty-five years (in the event he served only four and a half) after he was found guilty of stealing $3.7 million from his flock. PTL was taken over by the Baptist televangelist Jerry Falwell in 1988, but soon went bankrupt.

The Bakkers, who had a son and a daughter, were divorced in 1992. Tammy Faye abandoned televangelism, acquired a new pair of tattooed eyebrows and, in 1996, began to appear on a syndicated television talk show, *The Jim J and Tammy Faye Show*. Her co-host was Jim J. Bullock, a gay, HIV-positive actor.

Ron Taylor, b. 1910, d. 2006

Ron Taylor, who has died aged ninety-five, was the owner of Britain's last fairground boxing booth.

A showman for more than sixty years, Taylor travelled the country with his Excelsior booth every summer, offering contenders the opportunity to step into the ring and take their chances with his team of boxers and wrestlers.

Diminutive, and always immaculately dressed in a dinner-jacket, he would work the crowd from the front of the booth with a practised spiel. 'Sportsmen, please, we accept Army, Navy, Air Force or civilian, all respective weights,' he would begin, before slipping in the obligatory disclaimer of responsibility for broken noses, backs, torn limbs, ruptured spleens or fatalities. 'Don't be afraid to put your hands up ...' he would go on, as he offered the winner £5 and the loser 'a bloody good hiding'.

Over the years, Taylor became an astute cartographer of the violent disposition. 'Colliers and farmers,' he once explained, were the most likely to step into the ring. The Nottingham Goose Fair, where the Excelsior pitched each year, was a particularly fruitful locale, and so was Llanybydder in South Wales: 'There's some real tough ones around there. I remember when the farm boys were wading through the mud and climbing in the ring in their Wellington boots.'

Rhys Rowland Taylor was born at Cardiff on 31 December 1910 into a family which had run the Excelsior booth since his great-grandfather, a bare-knuckle fighter, had founded it in 1861. Taylor's grandfather did not box, though his grandmother did, wearing breast-protectors. 'But she was so fast,' Taylor remembered, 'that no one could hit her anyway.' The booth, containing a 40ft by 60ft ring in a tent that could seat some 250 people, passed to Taylor's father, who taught his sons that the easiest way to get a broken nose was to stand still for ten seconds.

Taylor was a boxing champion in the Army and, like his four brothers, fought in the Excelsior ring. In 1936 he took over the booth following the retirement of his father.

At the peak of the fairground business there were more than fifty boxing booths travelling Britain, though by the time Taylor retired in 2002, the Excelsior was the only one still in business. He would defend it on the ground that it was 'much better for people to take out their aggressions by fighting in a ring, with rules, than brawling outside. If people have an argument they can come and settle it in the ring where all is fair.'

At its height, the booth employed six full-time boxers, mostly from Gloucestershire, where Taylor had his winter quarters. He claimed that the Excelsior was 'a training ground for champions', and over the years such well-known boxers as Hal Bagwell, Johnny Melfah and Terry Thompson, along with the champions Randolph Turpin and Tommy Farr, took on all-comers.

The most famous fighter to step into the Excelsior ring was Muhammad Ali, who gave an impromptu exhibition when he visited the north of England in 1977. Taylor befriended the champion and he and his wife Lily were guests at the blessing of Ali's wedding to Veronica Porche at the Azhar Mosque in South Shields. 'Lily and I both held his daughter, Hana, as the couple were blessed,' Taylor recalled, 'and then we went on to have a big party with him and his friends.'

⚜ 21st ⚜

David Ogilvy, b. 1911, d. 1999

David Ogilvy, who has died aged eighty-eight, was by any standards – and certainly by his own – one of the most influential people in the history of advertising. 'Modesty forbids,' he once replied to a questioner who asked from where New York's Madison Avenue agencies derived their inspiration.

It was, above all, the creative side of the business which appealed to Ogilvy. Yet he was never a man to tolerate self-indulgent frippery. Throughout his career he remained crystal clear that the object of advertising was not to divert or amuse (though it might well do both) but to sell.

'People don't buy a new detergent because the manufacturer told a joke on television last night,' he told a conference in 1992. 'They buy it because it promises a benefit.' He had nothing but contempt for 'these little pipsqueaks with Thirds from Oxford', or the 'pseuds, and frustrated artists and writers', who followed their own agenda without careful reference to market research and the requirements of the client. A campaign such as the multicoloured Benetton babies left him incoherent with rage.

He insisted that potential customers must be neither underrated nor shocked. 'The consumer is not a moron,' he once pronounced, 'she is your wife.'

David Mackenzie Ogilvy was born at West Horsley in Surrey on 23 June 1911.

Educated at Fettes, he won a scholarship to read History at Christ Church, Oxford, only to suffer the humiliation of being thrown out: 'I couldn't pass the exams.'

From 1932 Ogilvy worked as a door-to-door salesman for Aga Cookers. An important breakthrough came when he sold an Aga to the Roman Catholic Archbishop of St Andrews and Edinburgh, who gave him introductions to every convent in the archdiocese. In the end, Ogilvy was so successful that the company commissioned him to write a handbook for other salesmen. *Fortune* described it as 'the best sales manual ever written'.

In 1935 Ogilvy joined the advertising agency Mather & Crowther, where his brother Francis had already been working for several years. David immediately realised he had found his metier, and in 1938 went to the United States – 'the most wonderful, delightful, marvellous country on earth', he thought – to study American advertising techniques.

He worked for Dr George Gallup, who gave him a lasting appreciation of the necessity for carefully investigating public taste. He worked on 439 nationwide surveys for Gallup, discovering, among much else, that the public was four times more likely to go to a film which starred Clark Gable than to one which featured Ronald Reagan.

During the Second World War, Ogilvy worked for British Intelligence in America, and later as Second Secretary at the British Embassy in Washington. In 1946 he bought a farm among the Amish community in Lancaster County, Pennsylvania, and devoted himself to growing tobacco.

In 1948, having organised financial backing from Mather & Crowther and S.H. Benson, and having persuaded Anderson Hewitt, a J. Walter Thompson executive, to serve as president, Ogilvy opened an agency in New York. There were four names in the new firm's title – Hewitt, Ogilvy, Benson and Mather – but only two members of staff.

The venture was an immediate success. Ogilvy worked every minute of every day, and for much of the night too.

At first he had meant to keep the office small; by 1964, however, Ogilvy, Benson and Mather (as it was then called) had become the twentieth largest agency in America. In that year Ogilvy formed an equal partnership with Mather & Crowther (in Britain) to create Ogilvy & Mather; he himself was chairman of the new company. In 1965 it became one of the first advertising firms to go public, much to Ogilvy's subsequent regret.

Greed, he confessed, had been his principal motive; he wanted to buy a sixty-bedroom chateau at Touffou, 100 miles south-west of Paris. In 1973 he stepped down as chairman of his ever-expanding empire, and went to live – and more particularly to garden – at Touffou.

In 1990 the financier Martin Sorrel's company WPP bought Ogilvy & Mather for $862 million. Ogilvy, appointed non-executive chairman of WPP, publicly acquiesced in the takeover; in private, his sentiments were very different. 'God,' he exclaimed, 'the idea of being taken over by that odious little s**t gives me the creeps.'

The episode left him thoroughly depressed, to the extent of going to see an

American psychoanalyst. The shrink wrote him out a prescription that made him feel wonderful – 'sweet-natured, optimistic, gay and kind to my dear wife. Unfortunately, I couldn't pee. You can't live very long with a full bladder, so I had to give up the pills.'

⚜ **22**nd ⚜

Sacha Distel, b. 1933, d. 2004

Sacha Distel, who has died aged seventy-one, only had one hit single in Britain, but for many Englishwomen he epitomised French charm, sophistication and tanned good looks; for their husbands he embodied all they feared about the Gallic race.

The tune that brought him to public attention in Britain was 'Raindrops Keep Falling on My Head', written by Bacharach & David for *Butch Cassidy and the Sundance Kid*. As sung by B.J. Thomas, it reached No. 1 in America in 1970, but in Britain it was Distel's version that prevailed, climbing to No. 10 and spending almost seven months in the charts.

Its popularity led in the early 1970s to Distel becoming a fixture on television shows such as *Morecambe and Wise*, where his accent, teeth and green eyes were all displayed to advantage. Yet while in Britain he was dismissed as a crooner, he had in fact made his reputation as a well-respected jazz guitarist and, though content to play along with his image as a Lothario for English audiences, in France he was regarded as a family man, albeit one who had almost married Brigitte Bardot.

Sacha Distel was born in Paris on 29 January 1933. His father had fled Russia during the Revolution and after walking, it was said, from Odessa to France, settled in Paris. There he built a prosperous electrical goods business and married the daughter of a jeweller.

Sacha was their only child, and from an early age showed musical promise. His mother was a talented pianist, while her brother, Ray Ventura, led a band, Les Collegiens. However, the Nazi occupation cast a shadow over Sacha's life, for his mother and her family were Sephardic Jews.

Sacha's father placed him in a Roman Catholic boarding school, then went into hiding. It was two years before the boy saw his parents again.

After the war, Sacha studied the piano, but at fourteen he had also started to learn the jazz guitar, being particularly influenced by flamenco and the gipsy-style of musicians such as Django Reinhardt. His uncle, who by now had diversified into music publishing, then sent him to New York to learn the rudiments of the business.

There Distel met Stan Getz, who let him copy his arrangements, and when he returned to Paris he found himself much in demand as an accompanist. He regularly jammed with the American stars who were then influencing French bebop, notably Dizzy Gillespie and Miles Davis. Among others, he recorded albums with the Modern Jazz Quartet.

By the mid-1950s, Distel, still in his early twenties, was recognised as the leading jazz guitarist in France, as well as a songwriter of some talent. He had begun, however, to discover two important new influences in his life, the beatniks and beautiful women, and he first came to wider attention in France by combining the two things as the lover of and guitarist for the singer Juliette Greco.

It was also the beginning of the era of St Tropez, and in 1958 Distel met its guiding lights, Roger Vadim and Brigitte Bardot, when he offered to publish the soundtrack to Vadim's cinematic celebration of his former wife, *And God Created Woman*.

Bardot was smitten with the exquisite young guitarist, and they became engaged. But after eight months Distel broke off the relationship after catching her in flagrante. Essentially a conservative, home-loving man, he longed to have the kind of stable family life of which the war had deprived him and had come to realise that (at that stage at least) Bardot did not want children. Worse, he recalled later, 'there was never anything to eat in the house'.

In 1963, he married Francine Breaud, a member of the French Olympic ski team, with whom he had two sons. Their marriage was regularly extolled as exemplary in the press, even if Distel occasionally admitted that he was still fond of the company of pretty girls. 'Just because you are on a diet,' he once said, 'it doesn't mean you can't look at the menu.'

Jessica Mitford, b. 1917, d. 1996

Jessica Mitford, who has died in California aged seventy-eight, was the most rebellious of the celebrated Mitford sisterhood, to the extent of embracing Communism and marrying an American.

As a writer and journalist 'Decca' Mitford gloried in the sobriquet 'Queen of the Muckrakers'. But she showed in her autobiography *Hons and Rebels* (1960) that she had inherited her full measure of the family's ruthless wit.

In addition she sparked lively controversy with her investigations of American consumerism. In *The American Way of Death* (1963), she laid bare the gruesome and exploitative antics of the self-designated 'grief-therapists', who bled the bereaved of their last cent. The book became a bestseller. The author basked in her macabre celebrity, and was especially proud when a company produced a simple, cheap coffin which was called the 'Jessica Mitford Casket'.

Jessica Lucy Freeman-Mitford was born on 11 September 1917, the fifth daughter of the 2nd Lord Redesdale and his wife, Sydney, the models for Uncle Matthew and Aunt Sadie in Nancy Mitford's *Love in a Cold Climate*.

By her own account Jessica had 'a perfectly horrid childhood'. She was brought up in the hideous barracks of a house built by her father at Swinbrook, near Burford, Oxfordshire, almost entirely cut off from everyone save her own family. Her father would foam at the mere mention of outsiders.

This category, as Jessica explained, 'included not only Huns, Frogs, Americans, blacks and all other foreigners, but also other people's children, the majority of my older sisters' acquaintances, almost all young men – in fact the whole teeming population of the earth's surface, except for some, though not all, of our relations and a very few tweeded, red-faced country neighbours'. Anything, or anybody, that smacked of the literary or artistic was dismissed as 'Damn sewer! Stinks to merry hell.'

Mitford turned to Communism in her teens, partly in reaction to the burgeoning fascist sympathies of her sister Unity. The two sisters took turns with a diamond ring to carve their appropriate political insignia on the windowpane of their shared sitting-room.

Marxism appeared to help Decca make sense of her mad beginnings. 'Farve,' she would announce at the breakfast table, 'd'you realise that as well as being a Sub-Human you're a Feudal Remnant?' In the circumstances it was not surprising that she did not enjoy being a debutante.

The longed-for release came in 1937 when Decca, at nineteen, met her second cousin Esmond Romilly, a nephew of Winston Churchill and a born anarchist. He too was nineteen, and had already founded a subversive magazine and been invalided home after fighting for the Republicans in the Spanish Civil War. Jessica found him irresistible.

They fell in love and ran away to Bilbao. When her sister Unity relayed the terrible news to Hitler, the Führer sank his head in his hands and sighed '*Armes Kind*' ('Poor child').

'Find Jessica Mitford and persuade her to return,' telegrammed the Foreign Secretary, Anthony Eden. 'Have found Jessica Mitford, impossible to persuade her to return,' replied the British Consul. Even the arrival of a destroyer, the captain of which attempted to lure her aboard with promises of chicken and chocolate cake, left her unmoved.

In 1939, having married, Decca and Romilly emigrated to the United States. They worked as bartenders and sold silk stockings door to door. In 1940 Romilly left America to join the Royal Canadian Air Force, glumly observing to his wife: 'I'll probably find myself being commanded by one of your ghastly relations.' He was killed in action in November 1941.

Between 1941 and 1943 Jessica Mitford worked as an investigator in the Office of Price Administration, first in Washington and then in San Francisco. In 1943 she married an American Jewish lawyer, Robert Treuhaft, and together they joined the Communist Party.

In her second volume of autobiography, *A Fine Old Conflict* (1977), she described how she ducked subpoenas in the McCarthy witch-hunts. The Treuhafts left the Communist Party in 1958, not in a fanfare of disillusion, but to concentrate their energies on the civil rights movement.

In 1955 Jessica Mitford brought her husband and children to England, her first visit for eighteen years. Though she kept a distance between herself and her sisters, her childhood favourite, Diana, married to the fascist leader Sir Oswald Mosley, was the only one from whom she remained estranged.

When the Mosleys were released from prison in 1943 Jessica Mitford wrote to Winston Churchill: 'They should be kept in jail, where they belong.' Nancy Mitford reprimanded Jessica for this 'not very sisterly' approach.

⚔ 23rd ⚔

Iain West, b. 1944, d. 2001

Iain West, who has died aged fifty-seven, was the foremost forensic pathologist in Britain; his casebook was a portfolio of the disasters, terrorist outrages, gangland atrocities and famous murders of recent years.

It was West who demonstrated that WPC Yvonne Fletcher had been shot from the window of the Libyan Embassy. His interpretation of the injuries received by the victims of the Brighton bombing helped to locate where the bomb had been hidden. He also conducted the second post-mortem on Robert Maxwell and showed from torn muscles in his back – overlooked in the first post-mortem – that suicide was a real possibility.

More recently, he combed through the wreckage of the Paddington rail disaster, and demonstrated that a single shot to the head had killed the television presenter Jill Dando.

In 1996, in collaboration with the journalist Chester Stern, West published accounts of some of his best-known investigations under the heading *Dr Iain West's Casebook* (1996). The book was characteristically low-key. West vetoed the use of many photographs and cut prose he thought might offend. But, though lacking the Jacobean relish of the memoir published by Professor Keith Simpson, his illustrious predecessor at Guy's, his book nevertheless made fascinating reading.

Iain Eric West was born on 25 April 1944, the son of a squadron leader in the RAF. After Carrs Grammar School at Sleaford, Lincolnshire, he read Medicine at Edinburgh University, then became a trainee pathologist at Addenbrooke's Hospital, Cambridge, where he learned the techniques of post-mortem under Professor Austin Gresham.

West was regarded by the judiciary and Bar as a formidable witness, but was always scrupulously honest, and would never alter his evidence to fit a particular scenario. His skills were much sought to help solve cases abroad, including an investigation of Saddam Hussein's genocide of the Kurds.

⚔ 24th ⚔

Alex 'Hurricane' Higgins, b. 1949, d. 2010

Alex 'Hurricane' Higgins, the snooker player who has died aged sixty-one, was once described by his bugbear Steve Davis as 'the only true genius I have encountered in the game'; his talents, however, were at the mercy of a seriously deranged, even psychotic personality.

He was at once the George Best and John McEnroe of snooker, with crowd-pulling powers enhanced by his haunted personality and little-boy-lost appeal. During matches he would fidget impatiently on the bench, chain-smoking and often the worse for drink, until his chance arrived. Then he would move jerkily around the table, radiating tension and nervous energy, in search of that elusive moment when touch, instinct and will would come together in perfect, irresistible alliance.

To his fans, who were legion, he was simply the most exciting player of all time. For years, moreover, he was a potential winner. In 1972, when he was still twenty-two, he became the youngest ever world champion, winning the title at his first attempt.

In 1978 and 1981, he carried off the Benson and Hedges Masters; in 1982, he regained the world championship; and, in 1983, he achieved the most dramatic of all his victories, coming from 0–7 down to beat Steve Davis 16–15 in the final of the Coral UK Snooker Championship.

But there was something more alarming than the light of battle in Higgins' eyes. Though he exhibited no prejudice against drugs, Higgins' principal hobby was alcohol. When Oliver Reed offered him some Giorgio Armani scent, he drank half a pint of it straight off. As for women, his habit of alternating violent rows with lachrymose apology afforded unending fodder for the tabloids.

Every year, every tournament almost, brought its crop of outrages. The most sensational, perhaps, was in 1986, when Higgins head-butted an official at the UK Open at Preston, after being asked to take a drugs test. Fined £12,000 by the World Professional Billiards and Snooker Association, and banned for ten months, he was asked whether he could live without snooker. 'Can snooker live without me?' he returned.

If he lost, there was always an excuse. The cloth was the wrong pace; his cue was badly balanced; the temperature was too cold; the walls were painted the wrong colour; the referee was standing too close, or perhaps wearing an off-putting bow tie. It hardly mattered what was amiss, so long as Alex Higgins was not at fault.

Nor did he feel that he had achieved adequate financial award. His prize for winning the world championship in 1972 had been a measly £480. The young players who followed him, he said, did not know how lucky they were. In truth, he was beyond satisfaction. 'Do you know what really gets me?' he asked when his career was already in sharp decline. 'I've never played my best in front of the TV cameras. People just don't know how good I am.'

Alex Gordon Higgins was born on 18 March 1949 into a Protestant family in the Shankill area of Belfast; he had three sisters. His father, who had been struck by a lorry as a boy and was unable to read or write, worked as a wheel tapper. His mother brought in extra money from her job as a cleaner. It was a secure and loving background, and Higgins would later look back on his childhood as 'the good old days, when there was real camaraderie'.

At school Alex fidgeted and could not sit still. The turning point of his life came when, aged eleven, he happened to wander into the Jampot Snooker Club in Donegal Road. He then spent four hours there every day after school.

At fifteen, hoping to become a jockey, Higgins moved to Berkshire to work for the trainer Eddie Reavey. But he soon abandoned this ambition, and drifted around England and Ireland in a number of jobs, playing snooker in his spare time. At Accrington, he challenged the world champion, John Spencer, to play him for £100 and won.

He turned professional, and immediately triumphed in the world championship of 1972, beating Spencer 37–31 in the final, held at the British Legion Club, Selly Park, Birmingham. He celebrated this achievement by travelling to Australia, where he was thrown out of a club for insulting a senior player, and out of a hotel for demolishing his room. On the way back he ran into trouble in India after getting drunk, stripping off and putting his hand up an old man's *dhoti*.

When a system of world rankings was introduced in 1976, Higgins took second place, but even in his palmy years his general tendency was downward, apart from 1982 when he returned to second place after beating Ray Reardon 18–15 in the final with a spectacular last clearance break of 135. This time he won £25,000, though £1,000 was surrendered in fines.

In 1982 Higgins recorded a song, '147, That's My Idea of Heaven', but it failed to reach the charts. He was rather more successful with the purchase of two plots of land in the Highlands in 1983, and two years later he bought a house in Cheshire's stockbroker belt.

This period was punctuated by spectacular rows with his second wife, Lynn. There was an almost successful suicide attempt in Spain in 1983, and in 1985 Higgins was handcuffed by police after throwing a television out of the window of the matrimonial home. It was better than hitting his wife, he explained.

Yet he was still playing snooker well enough to score two rare victories over Steve Davis: the stunning comeback at the UK Championship in 1983, and two years later a 5–4 triumph in the first round of the Benson and Hedges Masters at Wembley, after which he was fined £1,500 for swearing.

By 1987 Higgins had acquired a new girlfriend called Siobhan Kidd, an art restorer and psychology graduate, who described him in 1988 as 'the gentlest man I have ever met'. Three years later she was telling police how he had held her down and broken her cheekbone by striking her with a hairdryer.

The previous year, 1989, he had ejected himself from the first-floor window of their flat, gashing his head and breaking his ankle. Yet a month later, still hobbling, he pulled off the last great victory of his career, when he beat Stephen Hendry 9–8 to win the Irish Open at Goffs, Co. Kildare.

By 1995 he was obliged to qualify for the world championships, losing to Tai Pichit, a former Buddhist monk. Yet for a moment in the twelfth frame he was suddenly brilliant again.

Having reached 103 in a break, he asked the referee, John Williams, to move. Williams refused to do so, pointing out that he was not in the line of sight. 'You're in my line of thought, though,' protested Higgins, who proceeded nevertheless to clear the colours for a break of 137, sobbing loudly as he did so.

In 1996, he was accused of attacking a fourteen-year-old boy who had interrupted a conversation with his former wife; after admitting the charge, Higgins was conditionally discharged and ordered to pay costs. That year he had a growth removed from his palate.

Matters did not improve in 1997. Higgins attacked a photographer with a luggage trolley, and was stabbed by a former girlfriend. He could not stop himself getting into fights, and at 10 stone and 5ft 9in he invariably lost them.

In 1998 Higgins attended the twenty-first anniversary of the Benson and Hedges Masters in Dublin, and celebrated by punching a guest and pouring red wine into the pocket of the tournament director. By the beginning of 1999, with no money, no fixed abode, and nowhere to practise, he was ranked 387 in the world. And by this stage he had been diagnosed with throat cancer.

At the end of his life he was more or less destitute; he had lost his home in Cheshire and was living in sheltered accommodation in Belfast. He continued, however, to play the game he loved, appearing at the Irish Professional Championship in 2005 and 2006. In 2007, he published an autobiography, *From the Eye of the Hurricane: My Story*.

Alex Higgins was twice married, first to an Australian called Cara. 'She was the daughter of a racehorse trainer, so she had lots of money,' he explained. 'I'm sure she would say our five-year spell together was very pleasant.' What Cara actually said was: 'That lunatic has beaten me up.'

Henry Metelmann, b. 1922, d. 2011

Henry Metelmann, who has died aged eighty-eight, was a dedicated Nazi and fought and killed on the Eastern Front; after the war, however, he settled in England, joined the Communist Party and CND, and worked as a groundsman at Charterhouse, the public school at Godalming, Surrey.

An only child, Heinrich Friedrich Carl Metelmann was born on Christmas Day 1922 into a working-class family in Altona, an industrial town near Hamburg. As soon as he was eighteen, he joined the Army and was sent to the Eastern Front as a driver in the 22nd Panzer Division. 'I was so excited,' he recalled. 'I thought: "Now I can show the Führer what I'm made of."'

Nine out of ten German soldiers who died in the war were killed in Russia – including half of Metelmann's own class at school. His lowest point came when one of his closest friends was wounded in the snow by fire from a Russian plane. 'There was nothing we could do with him. So I held his head in one hand and with the other I took out my pistol ...'

In 1945 he was captured by American soldiers in Germany, and was later transferred to England, where he remained a PoW until 1948, working as a farm labourer in Hampshire. By the time he returned to Germany, his parents were dead (his mother from Allied bombing). After just four weeks he returned to the farm in Hampshire, where he was given his old job back.

In 1952 he married Monika, the farmer's Swiss au pair. Later he took a job as a railway signalman and in 1987, Charterhouse offered him a job as groundsman.

While several of Metelmann's old army comrades committed suicide, Metelmann joined the Communist Party and CND and became a committed peace activist. In the 1960s he protested against the Vietnam War. In recent years he attended all the Stop the War marches against the invasion of Iraq and protested against the American bombing of Afghanistan.

A history master at Charterhouse asked Metelmann to give a talk to his students about his experiences in the war. More invitations followed from schools and colleges. At Eton, his audience included Princes William and Harry.

⚔ 25th ⚔

Margaret, Duchess of Argyll, b. 1912, d. 1993

Margaret Duchess of Argyll, who has died aged eighty, was one of the most photographed and publicised beauties of the twentieth century and a seemingly indomitable social figure.

But between 1959 and 1963 she was involved in a sensational and sordid divorce case, when her second husband, the 11th Duke of Argyll, Chief of the Clan Campbell and Hereditary Master of the Royal Household in Scotland, sued her for divorce on grounds of adultery.

The court case lasted eleven days, and its piquant details included the theft of a racy diary, in which the Duchess listed the accoutrements of a number of lovers as though she was running them at Newmarket. The 50,000-word judgment, in which the Duke was granted a decree, was one of the longest in the history of the Edinburgh court.

The Duchess was found to have committed adultery with three men named in her husband's petition and with a fourth, unidentified figure. A pair of photographs was produced in court showing the Duchess, naked save for three strings of pearls, engaged in a sexual act with a man whose face was not shown and who passed into folklore as 'the Headless Man'.

Lord Wheatley, who tried the case, described the Duchess as 'a completely promiscuous woman. Her attitude towards marriage was what moderns would call enlightened, but which in plain language was wholly immoral.'

Margaret Argyll continued to be a favourite subject of gossip columnists long after the furore about her divorce had died down. Her feuds with her family, her landlords, her bankers and her biographers were all lovingly documented, usually with her own connivance.

In her later years the Duchess fell on hard times, although she still retained the shadow of her remarkable beauty – melting green eyes and pale magnolia skin.

At one point her debts were gallantly paid off by her first husband, the American golfer Charles Sweeny. She reserved her virulence for her second husband. 'Ian Argyll,' she would announce at regular intervals, 'was a fiend and a sadist.'

The daughter of George Whigham, a self-made businessman from Glasgow, she was born on 1 December 1912 and christened Ethel Margaret. She was educated at Miss Hewitt's Classes in New York, at Miss Wolff's in London, at Heathfield and with Mlle Ozanne in Paris. Miss Whigham was launched as a debutante in London with an extravagant coming-out ball in 1931. Her striking looks and perfectly formed figure immediately made her the toast of numberless hopeful swains.

After her marriage, in 1933, to Charles Sweeny, a tall, dashing American, Margaret Sweeny appeared to carry all before her. Cole Porter immortalised her in his hit song 'You're The Top', from the musical *Anything Goes*: 'You're the nimble tread of the feet of Fred Astaire, You're Mussolini, You're Mrs Sweeny, You're Camembert ...'

But the Sweenys were divorced in 1947, and four years later she became the third and penultimate wife of the 11th Duke of Argyll.

Her memoirs, *Forget Not* (1975), were generally judged a disappointment. No clues were offered as to the identity of the 'Headless Man'. Reviewing the book, Alastair Forbes observed: 'Her father may have been able to give her some fine ear-rings – but nothing to put between them.'

Private Harry Patch, b. 1898, d. 2009

Private Harry Patch, who has died aged 111, was believed to be the last surviving British soldier to have gone into action on the Western Front, an experience about which he retained bitter memories.

Of his four months in the trenches at Ypres, Patch vividly remembered the fear and bewilderment of going 'over the top', crawling because to stand up meant the certainty of being mown down by German machine guns.

As his battalion advanced from Pilckem Ridge, near Ypres, in the summer rain of 1917, the mud was crusted with blood and the wounded were crying out for help. 'But we weren't like the Good Samaritan in the Bible, we were the robbers who passed them by and left,' said Patch.

At Passchendaele his unit came across a member of the regiment lying in a pool of blood, ripped open from shoulder to waist. The man was pleading to be shot. But before anyone could draw a revolver, the man died with the word 'Mother' on his lips. 'It was a cry of surprise and joy,' recalled Patch, 'and I'll always remember that death is not the end.'

⊰ 26th ⊱

Andras Kalman, b. 1919, d. 2007

Andras Kalman, who has died aged eighty-eight, was among the luminaries of the Hitler-enforced diaspora which has transformed modern British life.

He was born at Mateszalka, Hungary, on 24 May 1919, into a prosperous middle-class family. His father was a pharmacist and inventor ('Kalman's ointment against smelly feet'); his mother taught him tennis, saying it would stand him in good stead wherever he went.

In January 1939, he arrived in England to study Chemistry at Leeds University. He had little interest in the subject and less English, but soon made friends playing for the university's football and tennis teams.

After the war, during which he was spared internment and volunteered for SOE, Kalman went back to Hungary, where he learned the horrific fate of his family: his parents had died in the camps; one brother was beaten to death in the town square, and the other survived Auschwitz only to succumb immediately to typhoid.

In 1949 he opened Manchester's first contemporary art gallery. One day a big man came in and 'zoomed around like a huge bluebottle'. It was L.S. Lowry, marking the start of Kalman's most fruitful artistic association. Kalman was known as an astute judge of character, so it was surprising when he insisted on treating the modest Lowry to lunch at the Ritz. 'D'you think they'd do me egg and chips?' asked the artist.

❧ 27th ❧

Oscar Beuselinck, b. 1919, d. 1997

Oscar Beuselinck, who has died aged seventy-seven, was a celebrated show-business solicitor, known for his fierce negotiating skill and his boisterous and often unprintable bravado.

His advice to his clients was nothing if not straightforward. 'If you must see her,' he would tell male divorce clients, 'keep your thing in your trousers.' Or, as he asked Kathleen Tynan when she went to see him for a divorce: 'Now, who have you been having it off with?'

His instinct for settling other people's lives did not carry over into his own, which was colourful and at times chaotic. He listed his recreations in *Who's Who* as 'getting married and Mozart', and he was notoriously boastful about his sexual exploits.

While Beuselinck was explaining the playwright John Osborne's poor chances for a divorce, the telephone rang. Cupping his hands over the receiver, Beuselinck whispered: 'This is my bank manager. I'm screwing his cashier only he doesn't know that.' Then after he put the phone down: 'No, Johnco, if I don't get it three times a day I feel physically ill, I really do.' His closing remark, as he saw Osborne out, was: 'Have you ever had it on the kitchen table?'

'You couldn't help liking him,' Osborne wrote. 'Like Max Miller. No inner life to hinder.'

❧ 28th ❧

Francis Crick, b. 1916, d. 2004

Francis Crick, who has died aged eighty-eight, was the most important biologist of the twentieth century; with his younger colleague Jim Watson, he revealed the double helix structure of DNA, the chemical of which genes are made; the achievement won both men the Nobel Prize for Medicine in 1962.

Later, with Sydney Brenner, Crick unravelled the genetic code, the biological rulebook used by all living cells to translate the information contained in the double helix into specific proteins. Among other things, this paved the way for the modern industries of biotechnology, genetic fingerprinting and screening for inherited diseases.

There had, however, been little in Crick's early life to suggest that such greatness lay ahead.

Francis Harry Compton Crick was born on 8 June 1916 at Northampton, where his father and uncle ran a family firm which produced boots and shoes. Neither of his parents was scientifically inclined but by the time he was ten, Francis was conducting chemical experiments at home, blowing up empty bottles with explosive mixtures, a practice soon banned by his parents.

From Northampton Grammar School he won a scholarship to Mill Hill, though he was not exceptionally precocious. Crick went on to University College, London, and during the war joined the Admiralty's Research Laboratory at Teddington, working on the development of magnetic and acoustic mines.

In 1949, having refocused on molecular biology, he went to join a team under Max Perutz at the Cavendish Laboratory, studying the structure of proteins using X-ray diffraction.

Crick's colleagues at the Cavendish found him direct, tactless, arrogant and noisy. In 1951, however, he met his match in Jim Watson, a 23-year-old American scientist who had come to Cambridge hoping to discover what genes were, and thinking that solving the structure of DNA might help.

Perutz said of the pair: 'They shared the sublime arrogance of men who had never met their intellectual equals. Crick was vicious at pouncing on non sequiturs and Watson would demonstratively unfold his newspaper at lectures which bored him.'

Before Crick and Watson joined forces, it had already been established that DNA carries genetic information from one generation to the next, but the structure of DNA and the mechanism by which genetic information is passed on remained the single greatest unanswered question in biology.

Crick and Watson concluded that the way to solve the structure was not by experimentation but by building models and attempting to assemble the information like pieces of a jigsaw puzzle. At first the pair floundered but, in 1953, they succeeded in constructing a three-dimensional model consistent with the evidence. The model consisted of two chains of DNA coiled around the same axis to form a right-handed double helix.

That evening, according to Watson's account, Crick strode into The Eagle, a pub in the centre of the city, and announced to the assembled crowd that he had 'discovered the secret of life'.

DNA, they revealed, consists of a double helix of sugar-phosphate molecules cross-linked by nucleic acids. If the two spirals were separated, each would serve as a template for the formation of a sister strand identical to its former partner, which provided a neat explanation for what happens in cell division. Throughout the 1960s and into the 1970s, Crick remained a colourful and noisy figure on the British academic scene. At his Cambridge home, the Golden Helix, he and his wife Odile threw wild fancy-dress parties.

In 1977, then aged sixty-one, he shocked the scientific establishment by announcing his decision to leave Britain for the Salk Institute in San Diego, and his intention to abandon the field of molecular biology for the dark and confusing waters of neurobiology, the study of the brain.

His work over the next decade on the mystery of consciousness culminated in the publication in 1991 of *The Astonishing Hypothesis*, a heroic – though ultimately inconclusive – attempt to wrest consciousness from philosophers and place it in the hands of scientists.

Crick argued that everything that goes on in our heads can be explained by the behaviour of billions of nerve cells; most controversially he deduced (from evidence of people whose brains had been damaged) that free will comprises a bundle of cells on the inside top surface at the front of the brain. This discovery, he believed, provided a scientific refutation of the Roman Catholic definition of the soul as a living being without a body, having reason and free will.

The Right Reverend Dr Frederick J. Eikerenkoetter II,
b. 1935, d. 2009

The Right Reverend Dr Frederick J. Eikerenkoetter II, who has died aged seventy-four, was a pioneer preacher of what has become known as the 'Prosperity Gospel'; this is based on the claim that the root of all evil is not the love of money, but the lack of it.

The Reverend Ike, as he was known to his followers, offered to open people's hearts to the love of God: 'But it won't be the God you learned about in Sunday School. It won't be that stingy, hard-hearted, hard-of-hearing God-in-the-Sky.' Instead it would be a God who teaches that salvation lies in being rich.

'Close your eyes and see green,' he exhorted his followers. 'Money up to your armpits, a roomful of money and there you are, just tossing around in it like a swimming pool.'

The main beneficiary of this approach was the Reverend Ike himself. As well as founding no fewer than three churches, he was one of the first evangelists to exploit the power of television. At the height of his success, in the 1970s, he reached an audience estimated at 2.5 million.

In return for spiritual guidance, he requested cash donations – notes, preferably, rather than coins ('Change makes your minister nervous,' he claimed). The Reverend Ike had no qualms about flaunting it with luxurious homes in New York and Hollywood, a huge rhinestone-encrusted wardrobe, drawers full of flashy jewellery and a fleet of Cadillacs, Bentleys and Rolls-Royces. 'My garages runneth over,' as he put it.

⊰ 29th ⊱

Rajmata Gayatri Devi, b. 1919, d. 2009

Rajmata Gayatri Devi, who has died aged ninety, was an Indian princess of renowned beauty whose life encapsulated the glamour and romance of the Raj.

Known to her friends as 'Ayesha', she caused a minor sensation in India when, in 1940, she married for love rather than by parental decree, to become the third wife of the dashing Maharajah of Jaipur.

Princess Gayatri Devi was born in London on 23 May 1919, the fourth child of the ruler of Cooch Behar State in eastern India.

When Gayatri Devi was twelve she fell for the most glamorous young man in India, the Maharajah of Jaipur, then twenty-one years old. He was not only exceedingly rich and handsome but also a nine handicap polo player, leading his Jaipur polo team to victory in every tournament they entered.

Maharajah Man Singh already had two wives, both married for reasons of state, but this did not prevent him from becoming captivated by this beautiful and spirited tomboy princess who was quite unlike the more orthodox Rajput ladies whom he knew.

When Gayatri Devi was sent to the Monkey Club finishing school in Knightsbridge, they met secretly and became unofficially engaged. Their romance aroused opposition on all sides, and when in 1939 they let it be known that they intended to marry, there was consternation in princely circles.

In the event the marriage was a great success. The third Maharani of Jaipur accepted her role as the Maharajah's favourite but junior wife with good grace. She adjusted to the formality and restrictions of life in a Rajput royal zenana, but at the same time used her authority to bring the palace women forward into the twentieth century.

Despite the wealth of the Jaipur royal house, however, both Gayatri Devi and her husband were renowned for their parsimoniousness. Nonetheless, when her autobiography, *A Princess Remembers*, was published in paperback in England in the 1980s she asked her publishers if she might have a chauffeur-driven car for a morning's shopping; the chauffeur later reported that the 'shopping' constituted a drive out to Surrey and the purchase of a large house.

Gayatri Devi had a natural beauty that achieved international recognition after Cecil Beaton photographed her in Jaipur in 1943; and she retained that beauty into old age.

⊰ 30th ⊱

Robin Cook, b. 1931, d. 1994

Robin Cook, the novelist, who has died aged sixty-three, was a devotee of the low life and wrote chiefly about the milieu in which the upper and criminal classes meet.

An Old Etonian, employed at various times as a pornographer, organiser of illegal gambling, money-launderer, roofer, pig-slaughterer, minicab driver and agricultural labourer, Cook spent much of his early career among criminals.

'My involvement,' he explained, 'was largely a protest against society. But in fact I was indirectly working for the Kray brothers. You see, I've always been ready to do anything – a weak character who'll always say yes. Because it's much easier to say yes than to say no.'

Cook was jailed only once – in Spain, for voicing anti-fascist opinions in a bar in the late 1950s.

'I have wandered between two very different worlds,' he once said, 'and I am a contradiction in terms. This is a very useful thing for a writer, because it means you can hold as many opinions as possible, all of them opposite.'

Robert William Arthur Cook was born in Baker Street, London, in 1931. His father was chairman of a City textile firm and a director of the Royal Exchange insurance company.

He was educated at Eton, which he left after three years. 'An absolute hot-bed of buggery,' he recalled. 'Terrible bloody place. They were trying to make you into a good all-rounder: a future banker; a cabinet minister, a bastard.'

Having completed his National Service, he went to Spain, where he was involved in smuggling tape recorders and cars. After a period in North America he returned to England, broke, in 1960.

As a result of a chance encounter in Soho he began 'fronting' for property companies run by Charles de Silva ('The Colonel'). 'The villains needed people like me,' Cook recalled, 'because we were plausible and didn't have any form.'

In the days before the 1961 Gaming Act he helped to run illegal gambling tables in Chelsea, and at one stage peddled pornography in Soho. 'We had to pay protection to the police,' he recalled. 'Prominent public figures used to come in, trying to get something for nothing. Eventually we put a sign up saying: "The following MPs will not be served".'

In the 1960s Cook published a number of novels based on his experience of Soho and Chelsea. *The Crust on Its Uppers*, his debut, lovingly chronicled the slang and mores of the London underworld. Like its successors it attracted a cult following but earned him little money.

In 1966 Cook moved to Italy, where he struggled to combine a literary career with wine-making. By the time he settled in France, in 1973, his muse seemed to have deserted him, and he earned his living as a farm labourer, living in a fifteenth-century tower in Aveyron in the Gorges du Tarn. Cook was taken much more seriously as a writer in France than he ever was in Britain, and in 1991 he was made a Chevalier des Arts et des Lettres.

In the 1980s, still based in Aveyron, he began turning out such thrillers as *How the Dead Live* and *He Died with His Eyes Open*, which concerned the exploits of a maverick detective working for a unit called 'Unexplained Deaths', who quotes liberally from *The Faerie Queen*.

The instability of his professional life was reflected in his marital career. He married five times: Dora ('a terrible sixty-three days ... I knew things were going wrong by day twenty, when I put the shopping on the table and the table coughed'); Eugenie ('Fourteen months. A nice girl from Clerkenwell; I took a powder there'); Rose ('nine years with a year's sabbatical'); Fiona ('twelve months'); and Agnes ('French. Fourteen months').

⇜ **31**st ⇝

Vice-Admiral Sir Ian McIntosh, b. 1919, d. 2003

Vice-Admiral Sir Ian McIntosh, who has died aged eighty-three, was a submarine ace in Norwegian waters and the Bay of Biscay as well as the co-leader on an epic lifeboat voyage during the Second World War.

Ian Stewart McIntosh was born in Melbourne on 11 October 1919, and educated at Geelong Grammar School before joining the Royal Navy in 1938. On joining his first submarine, *Porpoise*, in 1941, he was reticent about where he had been since completing his submarine training six months previously.

In fact, McIntosh had been a passenger on the Anchor Line steamer *Britannia* when she was sunk by a German raider some 600 miles off the West Africa coast. He found himself with eighty-two fellow passengers and crew in a lifeboat designed for fifty-six, awash to the gunwales. After they had all baled furiously, he was held over the side by his legs while he stuffed the larger shrapnel holes with torn blankets and covered them with sheets of tin. With just sixteen gallons of fresh water, forty-eight tins of condensed milk and two bags of hard biscuits, but no oars, they were forced to sail westwards across the Atlantic.

McIntosh sketched a chart from memory and with the *Britannia*'s Third Officer, Bill McVicar, who 'became like a twin brother' to him, the lifeboat was steered by the sun and stars. Their navigation was only a few miles in error when they smelled land twenty-three days later. Just thirty-six survivors staggered ashore at Sao Luis, Brazil – emaciated, burned by the sun and covered in sores and boils – after a voyage of 1,500 miles.

AUGUST

⊰ 1st ⊱

Pola Negri, b. 1894, d. 1987

Pola Negri, who has died aged ninety-two, was the legendary silent-screen siren whose career ranged from the 1914 Polish film *Love and Passion* to Walt Disney's *The Moonspinners*, made in England in 1964.

Essentially an actress of strong personality, she exuded an aura of slink and mink, of vamping heroes that stayed vamped. Although her three husbands were styled baron, count and prince, she was more famous for her liaisons with Rudolph Valentino and Charlie Chaplin as well as a bitter row with her rival Gloria Swanson.

As an actress she had distinct limitations, being almost devoid of humour and incapable of suggesting light and shade. After being smitten with her blonde hair, smouldering eyes and usually black clothes, American audiences began to go off her offbeat pseudo-culture and, with the advent of sound, found her thick Polish accent almost incomprehensible.

Yet she was Queen of Hollywood in the transition period between the decline of the earlier vamps such as Theda Bara, and the great stars of the 1930s, Greta Garbo and Marlene Dietrich.

Born Barbara Apollonia Chalupiec in 1894 at Janowa, Poland, she was supposedly the child of a gypsy violinist who died in exile in Siberia. His daughter, who abbreviated her second forename to Pola and took a surname from the Italian poet Ada Negri, worked as a dancer and violinist before making her stage debut in Warsaw in 1913.

Negri made three films with Aleksandr Hertz before being brought to Berlin for a play by Max Reinhardt. She rapidly became a star of the German cinema, but it was the series of costume films she made with the young director Ernst Lubitsch, particularly *Carmen* (1918) and *Madame du Barry* (1919), that led Paramount to invite her to the United States in 1922.

Her first American films fell far short of her German work until she made *Forbidden Passion* with Lubitsch in 1924. Raoul Walsh's *East of Suez* (1925) and Malcolm St Clair's *Good and Naughty* were among her other films, but while her star began to dim Negri started to attract widespread attention with her private life.

She had married first Baron Popper, a Polish Army officer; then, in Berlin, the Polish Count Eugene Domski after a tempestuous affair which involved an escape from his castle. He was granted a divorce, but when she told the world of her devotion to Charlie Chaplin the Count turned up to challenge the comedian to a duel. Later, there were several well-publicised engagements until she met Rudolph Valentino.

'Our souls', she proclaimed, 'met upon our lips, and we were one. Two aching hearts, tired of the battle.'

A year later Valentino died, and Negri made a dramatic appearance at his funeral, clad all in black, with a doctor and a nurse, dressed entirely in white, supporting her on either side. 'All joy has fled from my life for ever,' she cried, fainting over his coffin.

Six months afterwards, she married the *soi-disant* Prince Serge Mdivani, a Georgian. 'I did love my husband; I adored Valentino; and I grew very fond of Charlie Chaplin,' she said. 'But Serge means more to me than them all.'

'I have no doubt that at the time she was sincere,' observed Campbell Dixon, *The Daily Telegraph* film critic. But soon she was announcing that yet another romance was broken.

Negri left Hollywood to make a film in England, *The Woman He Scorned*, which was not a success, and began to make another in Paris – only to tear up her contract because there was no bathroom in the studio. It was later claimed that she sacrificed the £1,000-a-week contract because the script required her to strip to the waist and undergo ordeal by fire.

Her name continued to be linked with supposed fiancés, including an unnamed former British MP and Adolf Hitler. There were even stories that the dictator had sent special agents to Poland to check her Aryan blood.

By the time Miss Negri returned to America in 1941, she wanted to forget her romantic past. For her last thirty years she settled in Texas, attracting brief attention in London when she appeared, dressed in black as always, with a cheetah which went with her cameo part in *The Moonspinners*.

Only an autobiography, *Memoirs of a Star*, describing her love affairs with Chaplin and Valentino, brought her to any public notice again in America. But she never forgot her past glory. Even when in hospital during her last illness she continued to put on her false eyelashes, and she rose in her bed to tell a young doctor who did not know who she was: 'I was the greatest film actress in the world.'

⊰ 2nd ⊱

Trevor Pryce Leggett, b. 1914, d. 2000

Trevor Pryce Leggett, who has died aged eighty-five, was a renowned judo trainer at the Budokwai in London – the oldest judo club outside Japan – where he influenced a generation of British judoka.

Once a year he held a *katsu* (resuscitation) class. Leggett would make the announcement: 'All black belts downstairs to the lower dojo!' In the lower dojo (judo hall) each member of the class would pair up and take it in turns to strangle his partner until unconscious, and then revive him.

A Japanese friend once described Leggett as 'more Japanese than the Japanese'. Such was his love of Japan custom that he even wore a *fundoshi*, the loin cloth worn only by the most traditional Japanese man.

Fela Kuti, b. 1938, d. 1997

Fela Kuti, who has died aged fifty-eight, was known internationally for his Afro-Beat music, his twenty-eight wives, his astonishing stage performances and his implacable opposition to the Nigerian government.

A late-night drive from the West End of London in a maverick mini-cab is likely these days to be accompanied by a soundtrack of Fela Kuti's music. His reputation as Nigeria's most successful musician was built on his formidable talents as a saxophonist, keyboard-player, singer and songwriter.

The twenty-eight wives, all groomed and dressed like Parisian catwalk models, travelled as singers and dancers and his personal attendants. Off-stage, Fela Kuti was famous for lying around in his underwear – even during press interviews – while his wives flitted about.

On stage, he performed bare-chested, swapping instruments, dancing, smoking and frequently stopping to harangue the audience with political diatribes, while the band played on.

During one visit to London, he brought his latest mentor, a Professor Hindi, who professed magical powers. Hindi sliced victims' tongues and sealed them together, and on one unforgettable night, slit the throat of a volunteer, buried him outside the club (in Hampstead), and returned next night to exhume him – alive again. Hindi's connections with Fela Kuti were never very clear.

Kuti never reached the political goal he aspired to – the Presidency of Nigeria. For most of his career, he was the scourge of the Nigerian establishment, and his frequent clashes with the authorities and periods in prison only enhanced his reputation among his followers.

His experiences were instantly translated into songs which detailed his mistreatment. He was one of the few to speak out against the country's corruption and its treatment of the poor.

Fela Ransome-Kuti was born on 15 October 1938 into a prominent Yoruba family in Abeokuta, north of Lagos. His parents were both musicians. His father, the Rev. Israel Ransome-Kuti, was headmaster of the local grammar school.

In 1958 Fela's parents sent him to London to study medicine. Instead, he enrolled at Trinity College of Music, to study trumpet and theory. He also formed his first band, the Koola Lobitos, which played a mixture of American jazz, rhythm and blues, and West African Highlife music. They performed regularly on the growing R&B club scene in London and also on the Nigerian ex-pat Saturday-night dance circuit.

In 1961, Kuti married Remi Taylor. The next year he returned to Lagos, where his music developed to include the influences of American soul and Nigerian traditional rhythms; he called it Afro-Beat. Although he preached the rejection of American music, in favour of home-grown styles, his songs have always been scattered with familiar riffs from James Brown's most famous songs.

In 1968, Fela Kuti went to America, where he met members of the Black Panthers. He returned to Nigeria fired with new political ideas, just as the country was sinking into decline after the Biafran war. The next year he had his first hit song, and a succession of hits followed. Kuti sang in pidgin English, which made his songs comprehensible across the country's ethnic divides. His witty and caustic lyrics dealt with political corruption, skin-bleaching or traffic problems, and always included references to drugs and sex.

He also established a large complex for his family, which he called the Kalakuta Republic and surrounded with an electrified fence.

In 1974 the police raided the Kalakuta Republic, and attacked its inhabitants. Fela reacted by dropping the so-called 'slave name' Ransome. He became Fela Anikulapo-Kuti – 'He who emanates greatness, Having control over death'.

In February 1977 came the most brutal of the police raids on the family compound. More than 1,000 police and armed soldiers smashed up the place and beat those they found there. Fela Kuti suffered a broken skull; his mother was thrown from an upstairs window, and died a year later of her injuries. His instruments, studio, and master tapes were all destroyed, as was the clinic run by his brother.

Kuti moved briefly to Ghana, but was deported for political reasons and returned to Lagos. Then, in a magnificent gesture of defiance of modernity, he married twenty-seven women in a traditional ceremony.

In 1979 he founded his own party, Movement for the People, and stood for President, without success.

Meanwhile, his records continued to carry stinging messages and he enlarged his touring band to eighty people, including hangers-on, and renamed it Egypt 80. It had become one of the most exhilarating and unpredictable stage acts in the world.

On returning to Nigeria from a tour of Britain, Fela Kuti was arrested for currency smuggling and given a five-year sentence. There were protests from around the world; a campaign by Amnesty International secured his release after twenty months.

In 1988 he divorced all his wives, saying he no longer believed in marriage. Many had already run away.

At the end of his life, sick with Aids-related diseases, he refused medicine and food, and accepted only fruit juices and treatment from a traditional healer.

⇌ 3rd ⇌

Alexander Solzhenitsyn, b. 1918, d. 2008

Alexander Solzhenitsyn, who has died aged eighty-nine, was not only a great writer but also one who was passionately committed, believing it to be his moral duty, in the face of systematic totalitarian obfuscation, to record Russia's twentieth-century experience for posterity.

In a country where autocratic leadership had long obliged the populace to seek more inspiring government, Solzhenitsyn – like Tolstoy or Dostoevsky before him – became a vital source of spiritual succour to his huge circle of readers.

Despite the ban imposed on all his works after the publication of *One Day in the Life of Ivan Denisovich* (1962), he was very widely read – in photocopied *samizdat* form – in his native Russia. He was also the only Russian writer to achieve the bestseller lists in the West, and sold more than 30 million books in more than thirty languages.

Not that fame or fortune held much temptation for Solzhenitsyn. A big, loose-limbed figure with a booming voice and a face like an Old Testament prophet's, he was a fundamentally serious, ascetic individual – even something of a masochist, who distinguished himself, even among his long-suffering compatriots, with his capacity for enduring emotional and physical pain.

After being expelled from Russia, where he survived for nearly a decade in Stalin's gulag archipelago, he emigrated to America – only to shut himself away behind barbed-wire-topped walls at a remote mountain village in Vermont, the better to maintain his punishing working regimen. Each year on 9 February he commemorated the day of his first arrest in 1945 by having a 'convict's day', rationing himself to the diet he had eaten in the camps: twenty-three ounces of bread, a bowl of broth and a ladle of oats.

Alexander Isayevich Solzhenitsyn was born at Kislovodsk, in the Caucasus in southern Russia, on 11 December 1918 in the thick of the post-revolutionary civil war. His father, an artillery officer who fought throughout the First World War in the imperial Russian Army, was killed in a hunting accident six months before his son was born, and Alexander was brought up in a ramshackle cabin behind the city jail, at Rostov-on-Don, where his mother eked out a living as a stenographer.

Even as a schoolboy he knew that he would be a writer. According to his own account, he read *War and Peace* in its entirety at the age of ten. But it was Mathematics, rather than Literature, that he went on to study at Rostov University.

At university Solzhenitsyn was awarded a Stalinist scholarship for his keen work in the Communist youth league; and, before long, political and academic commitments so consumed him that during his courtship of his future wife, Natalya Reshetovskaya, he could spare only an hour late at night, after the libraries had closed at 10 p.m., for their trysts. Even during those precious rendezvous he would bludgeon his sweetheart into testing him on his history dates; and on their brief honeymoon in 1939 he was reported to have attended more to his copy of *Das Kapital* than to his young bride.

When war broke out between the Soviet Union and Germany in 1941, Solzhenitsyn immediately volunteered for the Red Army. He fought, first as a second lieutenant and subsequently as a captain in the artillery, across the Ukraine, Byelorussia, Poland and into East Prussia. He was twice decorated for gallantry, and it came as a terrible shock when he was arrested, in January 1945, by Smersh.

The astonished young Marxist was shipped back to Moscow, where he was sentenced without trial to eight years in labour camps and exile in perpetuity – apparently for having criticised Stalin's policies in a letter to a friend on another part of the front. So began his fierce struggle against the Soviet system.

In 1947 he was transferred to Marfino prison, a penal scientific research institute in Moscow, on which he would later model the 'Mavrina' prison of his novel *The First Circle* (1968).

His refusal to co-operate with the institute's research projects probably accounted for his relocation, in 1950, to a hard-labour camp at Ekibastuz, Kazakhstan, in Central Asia. There Solzhenitsyn worked as a bricklayer and smelter in some of the harshest conditions that the inclement Soviet climate could provide. Nonetheless, he managed to write, using tiny scraps of paper which he destroyed after committing their contents to memory. These tracts would eventually make up his first 'camp' novel, *One Day in the Life of Ivan Denisovich* (1962).

On the day of Stalin's death on 5 March 1953, Solzhenitsyn was released from prison having served his eight-year term. Subsequently, in exile at Kok Terek in southern Kazakhstan, he was allowed to teach Mathematics and Physics at a rural school.

In retrospect, this was one of the most tranquil and productive, if not exactly happy, periods of Solzhenitsyn's life, during which he wrote voraciously in secret in his spare time. Besides creating new works, he transcribed many of the plays and poems that he had composed and memorised while in the camps.

Until the 22nd Congress of the Communist Party in 1961 heralded a cultural thaw, Solzhenitsyn had worked under the assumption that none of his works would ever be published. He nevertheless felt compelled to keep writing, if only because, as he later put it: 'When you've been pitched headfirst into hell you just write about it.'

Now, finally, it all seemed worthwhile. When he submitted the manuscript of *Ivan Denisovich* to the literary monthly, *Novy Mir*, it was accepted enthusiastically by the editor, who arranged for it to be submitted to the Kremlin for approval. Its publication in 1962 was a major event in the Soviet Union, and made its writer famous overnight. He was admitted to the Union of Soviet Writers and feted in *Pravda*. Within a year the book was translated into all the major European languages, and met with almost universal praise.

At the centre of the story was Ivan Denisovich Shukhov, who, like his creator, served in the Red Army in the war only to be interned in a labour camp on suspicion of being a spy. The book described one day in Ivan's life, which began in the bitter cold of a Siberian winter at 5 a.m., when every man rose and had to submit to a body search in the freezing wind, before going out to work on nothing more than a bowl of fish broth.

Solzhenitsyn did not succumb to the temptation of wallowing in details of torture and abuse. He made his point by concentrating on the relentless minutiae of everyday life. If Ivan did not watch his food bowl, someone would steal it; informers were quickly knifed, as were attempted escapees, for if one man defected the rest were punished. In the camps there was one law: dog eat dog.

Meanwhile, Solzhenitsyn's marriage faltered. For when he was not demanding absolute submission from his wife, the moral disciplinarian was said to be occupied in affairs with other women. And the connubial split only widened as the political climate took another turn for the worse. Khrushchev was ousted, de-Stalinisation was curtailed, and Solzhenitsyn came under suspicion. In 1965, before it could be published, the manuscript of *The First Circle* as well as Solzhenitsyn's archives were confiscated by police in what the writer later referred to as 'the greatest misfortune' of his life so far.

Solzhenitsyn, by now a seasoned self-publicist, set about countering the state's smear campaign with angry letters to Brezhnev. In 1967 he addressed a moving appeal to the Writers' Union to defend literary freedom. But he was soon beaten into silence, and, removing to a small cabin at Obninsk, outside Moscow, withdrew completely into himself and his next work, *The Gulag Archipelago*. This, his first non-fiction work, confirmed that he was not so much a lyrical narrator as a brilliant chronicler of historical detail. In contrast to his novels, which focused on the Stalinist terror, *Gulag* struck at the still officially idolised figure of Lenin. Rejecting the Kremlin's thesis that Stalin alone was responsible for the 'excesses' of his time, Solzhenitsyn devastatingly demonstrated that the imprisonment of millions under Stalin was made possible only by Lenin's establishment of a ruthless police state.

By the early 1970s Solzhenitsyn's status as an internationally celebrated symbol of resistance inhibited the Soviet authorities from taking the fatal action which befell many lesser-known citizens at the time.

But, with the publication of *The Gulag* in the West in 1973, the Soviet authorities resolved to take action. Fearing that a trial and another prison sentence would serve only to provoke worldwide protest and damage East–West détente, the Kremlin decided to expel him from the country, in the hope that, once abroad, his voice would begin to pall and his authority decline.

But time, seclusion and the advent of the democracy movement in Russia, far from tempering Solzhenitsyn's ferocious Slavic conservatism, seemed only to fuel his zeal. In 1990 he published a 16,000-word manifesto, entitled *Rebuilding Russia*, in which he advocated a return to a monarchic nation, 'one and indivisible', with the emphasis on stern local government. With the 'alien' Central Asian Muslim states cast off, there was to be a central role for the Orthodox Church. A democratically elected leadership, maintained the dissident, was not really desirable. After his return home President Vladimir Putin – whom he admired – presented him with the State Prize of the Russian Federation for humanitarian achievement.

⇥ 4th ⇤

Victor Mature, b. 1916, d. 1999

Victor Mature, the American film actor who has died aged eighty-three, was best known as the beefcake hero of epics derived from the Old Testament or ancient Rome.

Where some performers were criticised for acting only from the neck up, Mature, to widespread feminine satisfaction, worked chiefly from the neck down. His films evoked much mockery, for Mature's torso was often more in evidence than his acting ability. But having assiduously promoted himself as 'Mr Beautiful' and 'the irresistible male', he could scarcely complain if people laughed. He therefore took to sending himself up.

'I'm no actor,' he would say, 'and I've taken sixty-four films to prove it'.

⇜ 5th ⇝

Flotillenadmiral Otto Kretschmer, b. 1912, d. 1998

Flotillenadmiral Otto Kretschmer, who has died aged eighty-six, was the highest-scoring U-boat 'ace' of the Second World War – the Wolf of the Atlantic as the German press called him.

His record of more than 1,000 tons of shipping sunk for every day spent at sea was never equalled during the war and he was one of only five U-boat commanders to be awarded the Knight's Cross with Swords and Oak Leaves (presented to Kretschmer by Hitler himself in November 1940).

U-boat captains were instructed that 3,000 yards was the best range for torpedoes, which should be fired in salvoes of four or six, so as to make certain of a hit. But Kretschmer evolved his own tactics. His motto was 'one torpedo – one ship'. He stayed on the surface while attacking a convoy, making deadly diagonal strokes through the convoy's ranks, picking off individual ships from close range with a sniper's skill. Trimmed down at night, with only the conning tower showing above water, *U-99* was almost impossible to detect by escorts which still lacked radar, and with a surface speed of seventeen knots *U-99* was faster than a corvette.

U-99 sailed from Lorient for its eighth patrol on 22 February 1941. On 16 March, Kretschmer penetrated the columns of the homeward-bound convoy HX112 to make one of the most accomplished surface attacks of his career, in which he sank five ships in an hour.

U-99 was clearly illuminated in the flames from burning tankers – Kretschmer said later he felt 'as exposed as a man sunbathing on a beach'. He was retiring, having expended all his torpedoes, when *U-99* was detected by the escort in the early hours of 17 March.

Diving, *U-99* was immediately detected by radio and attacked by the destroyer *Walker*. In what Kretschmer realised was the worst attack he had ever suffered, six depth charges burst around *U-99*, which plunged to 700ft below the designed crushing depth before pulling out of the dive.

U-99 rose uncontrollably to the surface, where the destroyer *Vanoc* illuminated the U-boat with a searchlight and *Walker* opened fire with main and secondary armament. Kretschmer ordered 'Abandon ship'.

He then had the message flashed to *Walker*: 'Captain to Captain: Please save my men drifting in your direction. I am sinking.' *U-99* sank but Walker picked up Kretschmer and all but three of the ship's company of forty-three. Kretschmer became a PoW.

Otto Wilhelm August Kretschmer was born on 1 May 1912, the son of a schoolmaster. He did his basic naval training at Stralsund on the Baltic coast and was rated sea cadet in October 1930, before joining the sail training ship *Niobe*. Rated petty officer in January 1932, he served in the pocket battleship *Deutschland* and the cruiser *Emden*.

He was commissioned Leutnant in October 1934 and joined the U-boat Command in May 1936, being appointed to the 2nd U-boat Flotilla. From 1935 to 1936 he was a Watch Officer in *U-35*, serving in Spanish waters during the Spanish Civil War.

After the sinking of *U-99*, Kretschmer was a prisoner for the rest of the Second World War, in Bowmanville Camp, Ontario, where he devised a system, circumventing camp censorship, of transmitting intelligence back to Germany.

It was so refined that he was able to arrange for a U-boat to rendezvous at the mouth of the St Lawrence River to pick up escaped prisoners. The prisoners were recaptured before they could be picked up, but the U-boat did appear punctually at the right place.

Released in 1947, Kretschmer married Dr Luise-Charlotte Mohnsen-Hinrichs, nee Bruns, in 1948.

He was the first President of the newly formed German Marine-Bund (Navy Federation) and joined the Bundesmarine in 1955. Promoted to Kapitan zur See, he served in the United States, France, Belgium, Britain, Denmark, Norway, Greece, Portugal, the Netherlands and Turkey. Frau Dr Kretschmer launched *U-1*, the Bundesmarine's first U-boat, in 1962.

Kretschmer was promoted to flotilla admiral in 1965 and was Chief of Staff, Allied Naval Forces Nato Baltic Approaches, until his retirement in 1970.

Perhaps the most telling appraisal of Kretschmer came from an opponent. In 1941, Captain George Creasy, Director of the Anti-Submarine Division at the Admiralty, especially asked to meet him.

'I was anxious,' Creasy recalled, 'to judge for myself what manner of man a successful U-boat captain might be. I saw a young and obviously self-confident naval commander who bore himself with self-respect, modesty and courtesy.

'His record stamped him as brave and quick-witted; his appearance and manners were those of an officer and a gentleman. When he left me, I sincerely hoped that there were not too many like him.'

⊰ 6th ⊱

Larry Adler, b. 1914, d. 2001

Larry Adler, who has died aged eighty-seven, was the world's best-known exponent of the mouth organ, a self-confessed name-dropper who couldn't tell the time without dragging in Sammy Davis Jnr, and an inveterate writer of letters and articles.

Adler liked to give the impression that he had known every celebrity of the last century – with some justification. He played alongside Duke Ellington, Benny Goodman and George Gershwin; had pieces composed for him by Vaughan Williams and Sir Malcolm Arnold; appeared on stage with Marilyn Monroe and Fred Astaire, and – by his own account – conducted a two-year affair with Ingrid Bergman (about which he refused to give any further details).

Those he counted friends included the Duke and Duchess of Windsor, the King of Sweden, Marlene Dietrich, James Cagney, Billie Holliday, Prince Philip, Cary Grant,

Virginia Wade, Martin Amis and Bertrand Russell; of more casual connections, it would be easier to list those with whom he did not claim to be acquainted.

Lawrence Cecil Adler was born in Baltimore, Maryland, on 10 February 1914. His parents, who had both been born in Russia, were fluent in Yiddish. The family name had been Zelakovitch, but Adler's grandfather Zadie, fed up with always being at the end of immigration queues, opted to change it to one beginning with 'A'.

Larry attended Baltimore City College and the Peabody Conservatory of Music, and after winning the Maryland Harmonica Championship of 1927, he never looked back.

He quickly learned the value of self-promotion. Called upon to perform with Guy Lombardo's Orchestra for the film *Happy Returns*, with George Burns, Gracie Allen and Ray Milland, Adler declared he would rather play with Duke Ellington. Ellington was persuaded, and after performing 'Sophisticated Lady', Adler was offered the chance to record with the bandleader. Having read that Bing Crosby received 5 per cent of royalties, Adler asked Joe Glasier, Ellington's manager, for the same. Glasier told him – with gestures – what he could do with his mouth organ.

His first solo appearance with an orchestra was with the Sydney Symphony Orchestra in 1939. During the war, Adler made several tours for Allied troops; he was later to do the same during the Korean, Six Day and Yom Kippur wars. In the early 1950s, he became involved in the defence of those suspected of Communist sympathies by Senator Joseph McCarthy and his supporters. Although never called before the House Un-American Activities Committee himself, Adler left for Britain.

Here he became an obsessive writer of letters to *Private Eye*, and a regular contributor to *The Spectator*, the *New Statesman* and – in later years – the *Oldie*, for which he reviewed videos. He was also a keen cyclist and tennis player – once playing a doubles match with Salvador Dali, Charlie Chaplin and Greta Garbo (he and Chaplin won).

⊰ 7th ⊱

Nancy Wake, b. 1912, d. 2011

Nancy Wake, who has died aged ninety-eight, was 'White Mouse', and among the most decorated secret agents of the Second World War.

When fighting broke out, however, she seemed nothing more than the frivolous young fiancée of a wealthy Marseilles industrialist. But by war's end in Europe she had become famed as a resourceful, dauntless Resistance leader, who topped the Gestapo's most-wanted list and had saved hundreds of Allied lives.

Nancy Grace Augusta Wake was born in Wellington, New Zealand, on 30 August

1912, the youngest in a family of six. She grew up at Neutral Bay, Sydney, where the family had settled. A good-looking girl with a streak of rebelliousness, she set out alone in December 1932 to explore Europe, living by freelance journalism.

In the summer of 1936 she met a 'charming, sexy and amusing' man in Juan-les-Pins named Henri Fiocca. By the time France was overrun in 1940 they had married and, though initially squeamish, she was driving an ambulance. Then, in Marseilles, she embarked on an exhausting double life.

She had acquired perfect French, and a chance meeting in a bar led to her employment as a courier for Captain Ian Garrow, a Scot who had helped create an escape route for officers and airmen from Vichy France across the mountains into Spain. Henri Fiocca contributed money freely to this enterprise.

Nancy Wake made frequent train journeys escorting escapers towards the Pyrenees; as a courier for a French Resistance group based in Toulon, she also provided the Fioccas' chalet at Nevache, in the Alps, as a safe house. When Garrow was captured and imprisoned in Mauzac concentration camp, she contrived his escape by bribing a guard.

In the autumn of 1942 the Germans occupied Vichy France, and the Gestapo became aware of a troublesome agent whom they called White Mouse. But White Mouse proved elusive. Finally, when it seemed that the net was closing, Nancy Wake was advised by her husband to flee to England, where he hoped to join her.

In Toulouse, while she waited for the escape circuit to extricate her, she was arrested in a random round-up and accused (falsely) of blowing up a cinema. Bruised and weary after four days of interrogation, she was astonished when her group leader, Patrick O'Leary, appeared. O'Leary, who had succeeded Garrow in the role, was a Belgian army doctor (real name Albert Guerisse) and his exploits would also become famous.

He told the French police chief that he was a friend of Pierre Laval, the Vichy premier, that Mme Fiocca was his (O'Leary's) mistress, and that the story she had told was a cover to deceive her husband. The police chief felt he understood this intimate dilemma and set her free.

Nancy Wake made several attempts to reach Spain, but was thwarted each time by arrests that broke up the circuit. On her final attempt she had to leap from a train window and run for it with several companions, dodging bullets before escaping through a vineyard. She concluded that a German counteragent had penetrated the circuit; when O'Leary was arrested back in Toulouse, she knew she was right.

Eventually she found guides who buried her in the back of a coal truck with a New Zealander and two Americans, then led her by rocky Pyrenean tracks into Spain. She reached England in a convoy from Gibraltar in June 1943.

Within eight months Nancy Wake had become a fully trained agent of the Special Operations Executive, and had been commissioned in the First Aid Nursing Yeomanry. The official history SOE in France records: '[Nancy Wake's] irrepressible, infectious high spirits were a joy to everyone who worked with her.' She and Violette Szabo once debagged an SOE instructor in London, hoisting his trousers up a flagpole.

Her training complete, she was parachuted into central France in April 1944, landing near Montluçon. As she came down her parachute became tangled in a tree. 'I hope,' said Henri Tardivat, the Resistance fighter who greeted her, 'that all the trees in France bear such beautiful fruit this year.'

Nancy Wake's role was as assistant to J.H. Farmer in running the circuit known as Freelance, part of SOE's 'F' section, the 'Independent French' section headed by Maurice Buckmaster in London. She threw herself into building up various maquis groups into a formidable force 7,500-strong, controlling communications with London, allocating arms and equipment that were parachuted in, and holding the purse strings.

To coincide with the Normandy landings, the Auvergne maquis launched a furious assault on factories and communications. A powerful German counter-attack, with aerial support, failed to stop them, but had the effect of cutting Nancy Wake's lines of communication with London when her wireless operator, Denis Rake, expecting capture, burned the code books.

To re-establish contact, essential before D-Day, she rode a bicycle from Auvergne to Châteauroux – 250 miles in 72 hours on a round trip through German-held territory. Rejected by one Resistance wireless operator because she had no password, by good fortune she found another, who informed London of the situation. 'When I got off that damned bike I felt as if I had a fire between my legs,' Nancy Wake recalled later. 'I couldn't stand up. I couldn't sit down, I couldn't walk. When I'm asked what I'm most proud of doing during the war, I say: "The bike ride".'

For the remainder of the war she was involved in ambushing German convoys and destroying bridges and railway lines. When ten men in her camp refused to perform their water-carrying duties she persuaded them by emptying a bucket over each. She interrogated a woman spy and ordered her execution, but saved two girls she considered innocent.

She was also on a raid that destroyed the Gestapo's headquarters in Montluçon, leaving thirty-eight Germans dead. It was, she wrote later, 'the most exciting sortie I ever made. I entered the building by the back door, raced up the stairs, opened the first door along the passage way, threw in my grenades and ran like hell.'

On her thirty-second birthday – shortly after the liberation of Paris – her maquis comrades paraded in her honour at the chateau they had appropriated for their headquarters. 'When we were fighting we were fighting,' she said. 'When we weren't we were having a jolly good time. I never was scared.'

With victory came the bitter news that Henri Fiocca had been tortured and then executed by the Germans. Nancy Wake was not only a widow, but also without means.

She duly continued in intelligence, attached to British embassies in Paris and

Prague, where she developed a loathing of communism to rival her enduring hatred of Nazis. Then, in 1949, she returned to Sydney. There she stood for the Federal Parliament in the Liberal cause against Labor's deputy leader, Dr H.V. Evatt; at the second attempt, in 1951, she got to within a few hundred votes of him.

After the 1951 election Nancy Wake returned to England, spending five happy years as an intelligence officer in the department of the Assistant Chief of Air Staff at the Air Ministry in Whitehall. In 1957, however, she married John Forward, an officer in the RAF, and resigned her post. Three years later they returned to Australia.

In the 1966 Australian elections she once again tried unsuccessfully to enter the Federal Parliament, running for the Sydney constituency of Kingsford Smith. Her profile gradually lowered until 1985, when she published an autobiography, *The White Mouse*.

She settled in Port Macquarie, on the north coast of New South Wales. After her husband died in 1997 she lived there for four further years until, in 2001, she decided to return to England for good.

Initially she became a resident at the Stafford Hotel in St James's Place, off Piccadilly, which had been a British and American forces club during the war. Nancy Wake had ordered her first 'bloody good drink' there in 1946, lured to the bar, like many former secret agents, by the hotel's then general manager, Louis Burdet, who had himself also worked for the Resistance in and around Marseilles.

In old age Nancy Wake was to be found on a leather stool in the hotel bar most mornings, nursing the first of the day's five or six gin and tonics. Though she celebrated her ninetieth birthday there, and the hotel's owners welcomed her, they were obliged to absorb most of the costs of her stay, helped occasionally by anonymous donors – thought to include the Prince of Wales.

The hotel said it was looking forward to planning her hundredth birthday, but in 2003 Nancy Wake moved to the Star and Garter forces retirement home just outside Richmond Park, where she remained until her death.

8th

The 4th Lord Oranmore and Browne, b. 1901, d. 2002

The 4th Lord Oranmore and Browne, who has died aged one hundred, is believed to hold the record as the longest-serving member of the House of Lords, having taken his seat in 1927 and been evicted under the government's reforms of 1999.

He earned the unspoken admiration of many by never speaking in the chamber, and was better known for his three marriages, particularly to the heiress Oonagh Guinness and to the actress Sally Gray.

It was also his misfortune to be associated in the public memory with the tragic deaths in traffic accidents of first his parents in 1927, and then of his son Tara Browne, an icon of the Swinging Sixties, almost forty years later.

When his parents were involved in their accident at Southborough, Kent, in 1927, Dominick knew that peers were supposed to be buried in lead coffins. He therefore ordered one from a local undertaker, whose men managed to get it upstairs to receive the body. Unfortunately, they found it too heavy to carry downstairs and put it into a service lift; the ropes broke, sending the casket crashing through the basement. On the death of his mother two days later, the hearse with her coffin caught fire, and another vehicle had to be ordered.

Oranmore and Browne married three times, first Mildred Helen, daughter of Thomas Egerton, a cousin of the Duke of Sutherland; they had two sons and three daughters (one of whom died aged thirteen). They divorced in 1936, so he could marry Oonagh Guinness, one of the 'Golden Guinness girls'; she was a considerable heiress in her own right and the owner of Luggala, a fairytale Gothic lodge in the Wicklow mountains.

They had three sons, the eldest of whom is Garech Browne, the pony-tailed squire of Luggala, a guardian of Irish lore and founder of The Chieftains. The second son died after a week. The third was Tara Browne, a friend of John Lennon who drove his Lotus Elan into a lamppost in Redcliffe Square, London, in 1966. Tara was the subject of the Beatles' song 'A Day in the Life', which contained the verse:

> He blew his mind out in a car
> He didn't notice that the lights had changed
> A crowd of people stood and stared
> They'd seen his face before,
> Nobody was really sure if he was from the House of Lords.

After divorcing Oonagh in 1950, Oranmore and Browne married Constance Vera Stevens, the actress Sally Gray who had been trained as a dancer by Fred Astaire and starred in the films *Dangerous Moonlight* (1940) and *Green for Danger* (1946). The marriage remained a secret until the couple attended the Coronation in 1953.

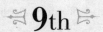

9th

Harold Edwards, b. 1896, d. 1998

Harold Edwards, who has died in Brisbane aged 102, was the last known survivor of the Australian Flying Corps, precursor of the Royal Australian Air Force.

Having stood guard over the corpse of Manfred von Richthofen, the 'Red Baron', after the German air ace was shot down over the Somme River in northern France on 21 April 1918, Edwards was frequently called on for his memory of that celebrated affair.

'The baron's face was typical of the Huns,' he wrote in a letter home at the time, 'but the shabby clothes he had on were a surprise to me. Just a day or two before his death his 79th and 80th planes [victims] had been recorded.

'He was recognised as a great airman and a clean fighter and he was buried with full military honours. A coffin was supplied, four large wreaths were brought from various squadrons and a number of our boys went as a firing party.'

An apprentice watchmaker, Edwards also had the task of engraving a plate for von Richthofen's coffin, the top half in English and the bottom in German, and another plate for the cross, which was fashioned from a propeller.

His time in uniform, when not spent on repairing altimeters, inclinometers, rev-counters and other instruments, was largely given to tending the watches of officers and their friends.

Some 2,000 francs had been discovered on von Richthofen's body, and the man who alternated on guard duty told Edwards that if he had known it was there he would have helped himself.

Edwards thereupon told the man what he thought of him, and a fist-fight ensued. Edwards was hardly more than five feet tall but drew blood with his long reach, ending the fight. It was, he used to say, his only fighting of the war.

In the argument as to who shot von Richthofen down – Canadian airmen, who received the official credit, or an Australian machine gunner on the ground – Edwards backed the Australian. He saw the fatal wound, and said that the angle suggested a ground shot.

⚜ 10th ⚜

Jennifer Paterson, b. 1928, d. 1999

Jennifer Paterson, who has died aged seventy-one, was a fat, loud, outspoken, laughing cook much loved in society despite her eccentricities, but known to the nation only in her last years as one of the *Two Fat Ladies* in the television series of that name.

Under the direction of Patricia Llewellyn, the show was immensely successful, as the Fat Ladies jumped through ever more unlikely hoops – performing aerobatics in a light aircraft for example – and presented stewed brains or puddings like volcanoes of cream to surprised communities of nuns in Irish castles or boy scouts at midge-infested lakesides.

While the other Fat Lady, Clarissa Dickson Wright, would reminisce in a collected manner about her drunk relations and men's legs, on screen Jennifer Paterson was always an actor.

Scripts were abandoned because neither Lady could keep a straight face, but Jennifer Paterson could always produce a good line. In a memorable sequence in which both extracted meat from a lobster with the help of violently wielded choppers, Jennifer Paterson demonstrated the best way of killing the crustacean in the first place, reserving for the faint-hearted the remark: 'If you don't want to know the score, look away now.'

Jennifer Mary Paterson was born on 3 April 1928 at Redcliffe Gardens, Kensington, though she was proud to point out that she had been conceived in China.

Her father, a 6ft 3in officer of the Seaforth Highlanders, had been posted there by his civilian employers, the Asiatic Petroleum Company, and it was there she spent most of her first five years, with an amah to look after her and unclean water to drink, which, she liked to think, made her immune from food-poisoning for the rest of her life.

She was naughty at school – the convent of the Assumption at Ramsgate – where she developed her talent for showing off. Some of the nuns were French and worked culinary wonders despite the war with home-grown vegetables.

Her first job was as an assistant stage manager at the Windsor Rep. Then in 1946 she went to live in Berlin, where her father had been posted. Always fond of music, he had requisitioned a grand piano; with the help of cheap spirits and cigarettes, it was easy to create a party atmosphere.

She next took a job looking after some children in Portugal where she discovered the Mediterranean preference for food that tastes. Bacalao, garlic, anchovies, olives, shellfish and robust red wine were unfamiliar to most British people of the time. Her next stop was Sicily, where (from her love of swimming) she became known to the diet guru Gayelord Hauser as the 'Mermaid of Taormina'.

Next came Benghazi, where she contrived to cook large meals on a Baby Belling stove, with saucepans balanced on one another. She learned too that freshly slaughtered meat is too tough to eat, but that, treated correctly, almost every part of a beast may be devoured.

Back in London in the year of the Coronation, she found a job working on magazines from an office in Trafalgar Square. Then, after a few months as an unlikely matron at Padworth School, where she dosed the girls with gin, she found a billet as cook-housekeeper at the Ugandan Legation in London. This ended when she berated diplomats for bringing back tarts at night. In 1978 she began a more congenial decade-long spell as cook at *The Spectator*'s weekly lunches, though drunken finishes at 5 p.m. tried her patience.

It was Charles Moore's idea to get her to write as well as cook for *The Spectator*. Her prose style was chiefly exclamatory, but in addition to recondite details of saints' lives, she provided recipes that were usually cookable.

She sometimes washed her hands, but hygiene was not her first anxiety. Once she was found tossing the salad for a *Private Eye* lunch in the washbasin of the gents at the Coach and Horses, Soho.

Her daily routine at her flat behind Westminster Cathedral when she was seventy would be to get up at 6.45 (awoken by her uncle on his way to daily Mass), drink tea and read the paper, ride her motorcycle to the swimming pool and swim thirty-two lengths, shop in the open market at Tachbrook Street, write an article for *The Spectator* or *Oldie* on a manual typewriter, drink vodka, lunch late on pasta and red wine, take a two-hour siesta, go to a party or watch rather loud television, sitting on an upright chair with a whisky until 11 p.m.

She always rode home from boozy lunches fantastically over the limit; her only precaution was to suck a creosote cough lozenge, lest she meet a policeman. Once, puzzled by the big roundabout at Shepherd's Bush, she rode up on to the grass for a better view. Luckily she never killed anyone.

Matt Lethbridge, b. 1924, d. 2010

Matt Lethbridge, who has died aged eighty-six, was coxswain of the St Mary's lifeboat on the Isles of Scilly for nearly thirty years, and one of the most highly decorated lifeboatmen in Britain.

In all Lethbridge was skipper on 151 'shouts', many of them hazardous, and some of which were the subject of national attention. In 1983 the helicopter transporting passengers from Penzance crashed in thick fog into the sea four miles off St Mary's. Twenty people died, but the six who survived were rescued by Lethbridge's lifeboat.

Among the survivors was Lucille Langley-Williams, a resident of the Isles of Scilly. When she heard the explosion of the maroons (the fireworks that summon the lifeboat crew on St Mary's) she told her fellow survivors in the water: 'We'll be all right, because Matt will come.'

⊰ 11th ⊱

Professor E.T. 'Teddy' Hall, b. 1924, d. 2001

Professor E.T. 'Teddy' Hall, who has died aged seventy-seven, was a gentleman scientist and leading expert in 'archaeometry', the development of scientific techniques to examine archaeological discoveries; among his successes was the carbon-dating test for the Turin Shroud in 1988, but he first came to prominence in the 1950s when he analysed the remains of Piltdown Man, one of the most notorious frauds of the century.

In 1912, a workman in a gravel pit on Piltdown Common, near Uckfield, East Sussex, had found a buried skull and jawbone, which he accidentally shattered with his pickaxe. Charles Dawson, an amateur palaeontologist, collected the fragments, and with Sir Arthur Smith Woodward of the British Museum, reconstructed a head which seemed to indicate a new type of hominid, with the jaw of an ape but the cranium of a man – the missing link, it was presumed, in human evolution.

The discovery of *Eoanthropus dawsoni* caused great excitement in Britain, but foreign scientists were sceptical. When more fossils of Neanderthal man were found, Piltdown Man was left wholly isolated in the evolutionary sequence.

In 1953, Teddy Hall used X-ray fluorescence to show that the bones had been stained with potassium dichromate to make them look fossilised; the jawbone was later proved to be that of an orang-utan, and Hall found iron filings, indicating that someone had filed down the teeth to make them look more human. Various theories were put forward about Piltdown Man, with at least ten men – including Sir Arthur Conan Doyle – accused as the forger. Hall was always of the view that Dawson, a proven fraudster in other fields, was the villain.

Hall's success with Piltdown Man persuaded Oxford University to let him establish the Research Laboratory for Archaeology and History of Art to further his work. In the 1970s, he was quick to latch on to the possibilities of radiocarbon dating.

In 1988 he and his colleagues dated the Shroud of Turin (said to have wrapped the body of Christ after the Crucifixion) to between 1260 and 1390. 'Some people may continue to fight for the authenticity of the shroud,' said Hall, 'but this settles it once and for all as far as we are concerned.'

Lady Mosley, b. 1910, d. 2003

Lady Mosley, who has died aged ninety-three, was a friend of both Winston Churchill and Adolf Hitler, and decidedly more fascinated by the Führer.

The third and the most beautiful of the six Mitford sisters (daughters of the 3rd Lord Redesdale), she left her first husband Bryan Guinness to unite her destiny with Sir Oswald Mosley, founder of the British Union of Fascists. The uncompromising temperament of the Mitfords, combined with Mosley's rebarbative politics, involved renouncing the social life of which she had previously been a leading ornament.

In Diana Mosley's memory, Sir Oswald was a figure of unequalled glamour. 'He had every gift, being handsome, generous, intelligent, and full of wonderful gaiety and *joie de vivre*. Of course I fell in love with him ... and I have never regretted the step I took then.'

She left Bryan Guinness in 1932, just as Mosley was forming the British Union of Fascists. To the horror of her family and friends – her father forbade her younger sisters to see her again – she set up house with her two small sons in Eaton Square, and placed herself at the Leader's disposal.

At first, it seemed that she might keep him within the bounds of respectability. 'The Leader is so clever and in his way so civilised and English,' she explained to Roy Harrod in 1933, 'that [his Blackshirts] could not be comparable to the German movement.'

But that same year, on the invitation of Hitler's stooge Putzi Hanfstaengl, Diana Guinness visited Nazi Germany. For her sister Unity, who accompanied her, the holiday was the beginning of an obsession that would destroy her life. Diana was also deeply impressed, and ever afterwards disposed to ignore what she heard of anti-Semitism and concentration camps.

Unity Mitford finally succeeded in making Hitler's acquaintance in January 1935, and in March proudly introduced him to her sister. Diana Guinness, in the full flower of her beauty, made a considerable impression; she herself was dazzled. 'His eyes were dark blue,' Diana rhapsodised about Hitler, 'his skin was fair and his brown hair exceptionally fine. In certain moods he could be very funny. He was extremely polite towards women. He was the most unselfconscious politician I have ever come across. He never sought to impress, he never bothered to act a part. If he felt morose, he was morose. If he was in high spirits he talked brilliantly.'

On 6 October 1936, two days after the Blackshirts' humiliating withdrawal from Cable Street, Diana secretly married Mosley in Berlin – a wedding arranged under the auspices of Dr Goebbels, whose wife Magda was a friend of Diana's. Hitler came to dinner after the wedding, presenting a picture of himself in an eagle-topped silver frame.

Diana Mosley continued to visit Germany frequently, being involved in negotiations to set up an independent radio station to broadcast to Britain from Heligoland; Mosley hoped that this scheme would finance his movement. She had several private late-night meetings with Hitler in the Chancellery, and he invited her to Bayreuth.

Mosley, meanwhile, took the line that Britain should stay out of any conflict with Germany, in order to preserve the Empire by leaving Hitler a free hand in Europe. As Hitler swept through France in May 1940 Mosley was arrested and imprisoned in Brixton under Defence Regulation 18b, which empowered the Home Secretary to detain in prison 'any particular person if satisfied that it is necessary to do so'.

The Mitfords were cousins of Clementine Churchill, the Prime Minister's wife, and as a girl Diana Mosley used to stay with the Churchills at Chartwell. This did not prevent her own imprisonment, in Holloway, at the end of June 1940.

The conditions under which Diana was imprisoned were ghastly, but she was never one to sue for mercy. Interviewed by a Home Office Advisory Committee under Lord Birkett in 1940, she put her worst foot forward. She admitted that she would like to replace the British political system with the German one 'because we think it has done well for that country'. Did she approve of the Nazi policies against Jews? 'Up to a point,' she declared. 'I am not fond of Jews.'

When her lawyer asked if she knew anyone in the government who might help, she gave further hostages to fortune. 'Know anyone in the government?' she cried. 'I know all the Tories beginning with Churchill. The whole lot deserve to be shot.' This was reported to Churchill, who was not amused.

Not until December 1941, after the intervention of Diana's brother Tom with the Prime Minister, was Mosley allowed to join her in married quarters at Holloway. After two more years, in November 1943, they were both released on grounds of Mosley's health, and placed under house arrest until the end of the war. Evelyn Waugh, who encountered Diana Mosley when she was just out of prison, told his daughter that he was shocked to observe that his friend was wearing a swastika diamond brooch. But then the Mitfords had been brought up to pay scant attention to the opinion of others.

Diana Freeman-Mitford was born on 17 June 1910 into a family which her sister Nancy would immortalise in *Love in a Cold Climate*. Their parents, Lord and Lady Redesdale, featured as Uncle Matthew and Aunt Sadie.

Diana remembered her father with a great deal more affection than Nancy or Jessica did. 'Not only did he make us scream with laughter at his lovely jokes,' she wrote, 'but he was very affectionate. Certainly he had a quick temper, and would often rage, but we were never punished.'

In 1919 Lord Redesdale sold the house his father had built at Batsford, Gloucestershire, and moved to Astall Manor in Oxfordshire. The children loved it, and a succession of governesses – Diana thought fifteen – abandoned the attempt to instil some education.

The idyll did not last; after six years Lord Redesdale decided to build a new house on the hill above Swinbrook. It turned out to be a monstrosity, but for the children there was the compensation that he also bought a large house in London, at 26 Rutland Gate. In 1926 Diana was sent to stay in Paris, where she attended a day school and in six months learned more than she had during six years in England.

Evelyn Waugh thought that her beauty 'ran through the room like a peal of bells'. Jim Lees-Milne, who was a friend of Tom Mitford's at Eton, remembered her as 'the most divine adolescent I ever beheld: a goddess, more immaculate, more perfect, more celestial than Botticelli's sea-borne Venus'. In 1928 this vision came to the attention of Bryan Guinness, and within weeks they were engaged.

Lady Redesdale objected strenuously to her prospective son-in-law on the grounds that he was 'so frightfully rich'. Eventually, though, consent was granted, and the wedding took place on 30 January 1929.

At Biddesdon, their country house near Andover, Diana was able for the first time to employ her talent for interior decoration. At the end of her life she expressed gratitude for having lived in three beautiful houses: Biddesdon, Wootton and, from 1950, the pretentiously entitled (though not by the Mosleys) Temple de la Gloire on the outskirts of Paris; the house was known to their foes as 'The Concentration of Camp'.

In France, Diana Mosley edited *The European*, a magazine that boasted contributions from Ezra Pound, Henry Williamson and Roy Campbell. Her loyalty to Mosley remained absolute.

He died in 1980, and a year later Diana Mosley suffered from a brain tumour. It turned out to be benign and was operated upon successfully. While convalescing she was visited by Lord Longford. 'Of course, he thinks I'm Myra Hindley,' Diana remarked.

Although her book of memoirs, *A Life of Contrasts* (1977), was deliberately provocative, most of those who met her found her a delightful companion, while to her sisters' children she was Aunt Honks. On one subject, however, she remained incorrigible.

'They will go on persecuting me until I say Hitler was ghastly,' she acknowledged. 'Well, what's the point in saying that? I was very fond of him. Very, very fond.'

⚜ 12th ⚜

Konrad Kujau, b. 1938, d. 2000

Konrad Kujau, who has died aged sixty-two, admitted in 1983 to forging the 'Hitler Diaries' in one of the most audacious journalistic hoaxes ever attempted; the sixty-two volumes of diaries, purporting to chronicle Hitler's years of power between 1933 and 1945, were bought by the German magazine *Stern* for £2.5 million.

Stern announced the acquisition in April 1983 under the headline 'Scoop of the Century'. Publishing rights were sold to *Times* newspapers after the historian Professor Hugh Trevor-Roper authorised them as an archive of 'great historical significance'.

But the scoop aroused as much controversy as astonishment. Within days Trevor-Roper was having second thoughts, and two weeks later the West German Federal

Archives announced that tests had proved that the paper and ink used were of post-war manufacture and that the diaries were 'blatant forgeries'.

For the *Sunday Times*, which had broken the news in Britain, it was a severe embarrassment; for *Stern* it was a disaster. Not only had the magazine lost a lot of money, it had also apparently been deceived by one of its own journalists.

The diaries had been bought by an investigative reporter named Gerd Heidemann from a dealer in Nazi memorabilia known as Konrad Fischer. Fischer, Heidemann claimed, had obtained the diaries from a general in the East German Army who had pulled them from a burning Nazi aeroplane that crashed at Bornersdorf on 21 April 1945 and had kept them hidden in a hay loft ever since.

The story soon unravelled. 'Fischer', it turned out, was Konrad Kujau, the manager of a rather unsuccessful cleaning company in Stuttgart who carried on a discreet business buying and selling Nazi memorabilia. He was also known to police as a small-time forger of luncheon vouchers.

An emigrant from East Germany, Kujau had established himself as a dealer in Nazi mementoes during the 1970s and had begun to supplement genuine artefacts with fakes, often supplying his own authentications. Kujau had all the qualities of the successful conman – a complete disregard for the truth, a remarkable ability to make up stories as he went along and undoubted skills as an imitator of other people's handwriting.

He soon established a group of collectors who met at his offices in Stuttgart. One of his best customers was Fritz Steiffel, the owner of an engineering works who possessed a large collection of Kujau's fakes. In the late 1970s Kujau had offered to supply Steiffel with a diary by Hitler, rumours of which reached the ears of Gerd Heidemann.

Heidemann was in deep financial trouble at the time and felt that here at last was the scoop that would make his name. Having confirmed through his own researches that an aircraft reportedly carrying trunks of Nazi documents had indeed crashed in 1945, he had no difficulty in believing Kujau's story that more volumes existed.

Kujau set to work forging volume after volume of the diaries using an old steel pen and staining the pages with tea to give them a faded appearance.

It was by any standards an extraordinary achievement. Week after week, year after year of bureaucratic and personal minutiae were recorded in a spidery antique script which fooled three handwriting experts. 'Originally I copied Hitler's life out of books,' Kujau confessed afterwards, 'but later I began to feel I was Hitler. As I wrote about Stalingrad, my hand began to shake.'

Over a period of two years, Heidemann would at intervals collect suitcases of cash from *Stern*'s offices, returning with volumes of the 'diaries'.

After the hoax was discovered, Heidemann claimed he had been the victim of a swindle, though it later emerged that he had kept much of the money for himself. Kujau owned up after police searching his home had found forgeries of works by Durer, Rembrandt and Goya. In 1985 both Heidemann and Kujau were convicted of fraud and given four-and-a-half-year jail sentences.

Konrad Kujau was born in 1938, the youngest of five children, in the small town of Lobau, about forty miles from Dresden in what was to become East Germany. In 1957 he was 'allotted' a job as a manager in the clubhouse of the Free German Youth at Lobau. After three weeks, however, he made up his mind to escape to the West to avoid conscription.

Kujau returned to Lobau in 1970, laden with gifts and stories of his success in the West. With the help of friends, he began a trade in military relics which he smuggled out of East Germany on annual visits.

In 1980 friends noticed that he was spending a great deal of his time on a project which required him to work alone, day and night. Then towards the end of 1980, he began to acquire a reputation as a big spender; in the nightclubs of Stuttgart he would appear with a bodyguard and spread tips of £250 around the hostesses.

After his release from prison, he opened a gallery in Stuttgart specialising in fakes of works by famous artists. He became popular with the German media and made dozens of appearances on the country's most popular TV chat shows.

Julian Anthoine, b. 1939, d. 1989

Julian Anthoine, who has died aged fifty, was one of the best-loved characters in modern British mountaineering; his Rabelaisian approach to life sometimes disconcerted even hardened fellow climbers.

He began climbing in the 1950s with a select group of friends known as the Wallasey Mountaineering Club whose bacchanals soon became legendary. 'Mo' Anthoine was himself the inaugurator of their regular concluding ritual, the so-called 'dance of the flaming arsehole' – an exhibition which impressed itself forcibly on anyone who witnessed it.

13th

Jack Ryan, b. 1926, d. 1991

Jack Ryan, who has died aged sixty-five, was an inventor and designer of astonishing breadth – his creations ranged from the Sparrow and Hawk missiles to the once ubiquitous Barbie doll.

When she first hit the market in 1957, Barbie marked a radical new departure from the dolls of the past – she had the anatomy of a young woman rather than that of a new-born babe.

The body, as Ryan had cunningly surmised, had to be dressed, and clothes were duly designed for every conceivable occasion – for the beach and the disco, for riding and playing tennis. She also needed a boyfriend, and so Ryan created Ken. More dolls followed: White Barbie, Black Barbie, and even a sun-kissed Malibu version.

And then Ryan let loose his darkest fetish: hair. He designed creatures with magically manipulative nylon tresses which could be made to curl or straighten according to their owners' whim.

Jack Ryan was born in 1926 and early manifested individual tastes. He was dubbed 'The Professor' by the other children in his neighbourhood, for whom he built an entire telephone system using one uninsulated wire.

He was educated privately and at Yale University. He then worked at Raytheon for some years, designing anti-aircraft missiles for the American Government, brooding on his Barbie doll the while.

Ryan visited toymaker after toymaker with his brainchild before he found a home for Barbie with Mattel. He went on to design some thirty-five of America's best-selling toys, including the Chatty Cathy talking doll, Hot Wheels and various bits of electronic nonsense. By the time he was appointed vice-president of research and design for Mattel, Ryan held more than 1,000 patents around the world.

In the 1970s he built himself a replica of a medieval fortress in Bel-Air, arranging for much of the architectural planning and engineering work to be done cost-free through his unusual, personally designed scholarship programme for students from California University – ten strong young men were selected and provided with food and board in exchange for twelve hours' work a week.

The finished building had a vast entrance hall, banqueting rooms, ballrooms, dungeons and a heated moat. It also contained more than 300 telephones, programmed by Ryan to deliver all sorts of tricks.

Ryan was married five times. In 1975 he became the sixth husband of Zsa Zsa Gabor – though the union was of brief duration.

❧ 14th ❧

The 3rd Lord Kilbracken, b. 1920, d. 2006

The 3rd Lord Kilbracken, who has died aged eighty-five, hit the headlines in 1957 when he succeeded in gate-crashing the Great Red Square Parade in Moscow on the fortieth anniversary of the October uprising, wearing a pink Leander tie and with his trousers turned inside out.

John Raymond Godley was born in Chester Street, Belgravia, on 17 October 1920, the son of Hugh Godley, later the 2nd Lord Kilbracken.

When war broke out, he joined the Royal Navy Fleet Air Arm and for the first two years flew at every opportunity, 'perfectly convinced of my own immortality, despite a number of exciting prangs, a ditching in the Firth of Forth and quite a bit of tracer'.

In 1943–44 he served on convoy escort duty on merchant aircraft carriers in the North Atlantic, flying single-engined Fairey Swordfish biplanes, machines which 'seemed to have been left in the war by mistake'. Later, posted lieutenant-commander in charge of 835 Squadron (then equipped with Wildcat fighters), he conducted night strikes on enemy shipping off the Norwegian coast. He was awarded his DSC for one of these attacks, on the night of 29 January 1945.

By this time, though, he had begun to have serious doubts about his immortality. Just before VJ Day a fault developed in the hydraulic system of his Fairey Barracuda, and he found himself being liberally sprayed with highly anaesthetic hydraulic fluid.

Fortunately, he was almost directly over an airfield, and he managed to land the aircraft before passing out.

After the war Godley joined the *Daily Mirror* and wrote human interest stories. After joining the *Sunday Express* in 1949, he embarked on an overland trip to New Zealand to join the celebrations marking the centenary of the founding of Christchurch by an ancestor, John Robert Godley. While he was there his father died, and the new Lord Kilbracken made his way back to England by sea.

The family house in Ireland was damp and dilapidated and the estate neglected, its sole stock consisting of one aged cow. He launched himself into a range of unsuccessful enterprises: growing Christmas trees, making cream cheese and selling square yards of Irish bog to Americans for a nickel apiece. He failed to make any money out of this last venture, since the cost of sending a receipt for each nickel was two nickels.

One day in 1957 the telephone rang and a suave American voice asked whether Kilbracken would like to spend the next four days in London with the Hollywood film actress Jayne Mansfield, who was there to attend the premiere of her new film *Oh for a Man!* The fee would be 100 guineas – enough to buy him 'a couple of cows'. He knew little about Jayne Mansfield, other than that 'her dimensions were apparently very unusual', and found to his relief that his duties were mainly formal.

The *Daily Express* invited him to write on 'My Four Days with Jayne Mansfield', for a fee of 'two more cows'. A few weeks later, hoping to add to his herd, Kilbracken suggested to Charles Wintour, the *Express*'s editor, that he might go to Moscow to cover the fortieth anniversary celebrations of the October 1917 revolution.

Travelling on a tourist visa, since it was not possible to gain a visa as a journalist, Kilbracken set himself two goals: to see the Great Red Square Parade and to interview Khrushchev. Unfortunately, though, there were no seats left for the parade, and as a 'tourist' it would be impossible to arrange an interview with Khrushchev through official channels. Subterfuge was the only solution.

On the day of the parade Kilbracken rose early and dressed with particular care, hoping to slip out of the hotel and avoid his official minder, and then to pass himself off as a member of the Russian proletariat. With his trousers on inside out under his overcoat, wearing a pink Leander tie and a fur hat pulled down over his ears, he launched himself on to the Moscow streets.

By degrees he managed to work his way to the steps of the Moscow Hotel on Red Square, where he had a front-row view of the military parade; later he insinuated himself into the civilian parade, marching past the rostrum with the other 'comrades'.

That evening he received a telegram from Wintour which read: 'Hail Hail Hail Ace Newsman stop Congratulations on wonderful story leading *Daily Express* tonight'.

Kilbracken achieved his second goal by posing as a photographer and gate-crashing a reception at the Egyptian embassy which Khrushchev was attending. He managed to engage Khrushchev in conversation for nearly half an hour, and the crowd around them became so great at one point that they ended up crushed together, belly to belly.

With the money from Jayne Mansfield and Moscow, Kilbracken was able to buy several more cows. The best milker he christened Jayne.

Kilbracken continued to work as a freelance journalist, and, during the 1980s, wrote a series of guides to identifying plant and animal species. His first such guide, *The Easy Way to Bird Recognition* (1982) won the *Times Educational Supplement* book award and sold out at its first printing.

~ **15**th ~

Idi Amin, b. c. 1925, d. 2003

Idi Amin, the former dictator of Uganda and self-styled 'Conqueror of the British Empire' who has died aged around seventy-eight, was one of the most reviled individuals in recent history.

Six foot four and, at his peak, twenty stone, the former heavyweight boxing champion of Uganda appeared to relish his monstrous reputation. Subject to 'visitations from God', and reputedly boasting a collection of human heads extensive enough to require its own deep-freeze, Amin was popularly considered to be deranged.

This impression was reinforced by claims from one of his surviving physicians that he had at various times administered treatment for hypomania, schizophrenia, tertiary syphilis and general paralysis of the insane. Amin, however, survived too long, exhibiting too shrewd an instinct for manipulation and too ruthless a capacity for cruelty to be dismissed as a mere madman.

As many as half a million Ugandans died under his regime, in well-documented ways ranging from mass executions to enforced self-cannibalism.

In one of the ugliest incidents in post-war history, the majority of Uganda's Asian population was expelled. Uganda, the 'Pearl of Africa', a 'fairytale world' in the eyes of the young Winston Churchill, was pillaged and bankrupted. Amin's famous summation of his attitude towards opponents – 'I ate them before they ate me' – was later given an unholy twist. His exiled Health Minister, Henry Kyemba, confessed that 'on several occasions he told me quite proudly that he had eaten the organs or flesh of his human victims'.

Idi Amin Dada Oumee was born around 1925 at Koboko, in the impoverished north-western part of Uganda, into a poor farming family of the small Kakwa tribe. A large child with a reputation as a playground bully, Amin received little formal education and, attracted by the mystique and power of the British military, joined the King's African Rifles aged eighteen.

He was attached first to the 11th East Africa Division, in which he fought as a rifleman in Burma during the closing days of the Second World War, and then to the 4th Uganda Battalion, in which he was dispatched to quell tribal marauders in northern Uganda. Subsequently, he was involved in operations against the Mau Mau in Kenya.

Amin was a sergeant-major by 1957. He was popular with his English officers, who appreciated his skill on the rugby field, unquestioning obedience and touching devotion to all things British. Despite failing to complete courses of training in both England and Israel, he was a major by 1963, and by 1964 a colonel and deputy-commander of Uganda's Army and Air Force.

Amin's rise was greatly assisted by the patronage of Dr Milton Obote, a leader in the struggle for independence who became Prime Minister in 1962. In 1966, Obote sought to secure his authority by abolishing the old tribal kingdoms. The Baganda rebelled, and Amin, by then in charge of the Ugandan Armed Forces, proved his loyalty by brutally curtailing the uprising.

On 25 January 1971, when Obote was absent attending a Commonwealth conference, key units of the army and police loyal to Amin staged a traditional coup, with Amin presiding over affairs from his heavily fortified residence on Prince Charles Drive, overlooking Kampala.

In the aftermath, Amin declared himself a populist devoid of personal ambition. He would provide free and fair elections and then return the army to barracks. Crowds chanting their approval of Amin thronged Kampala.

Upon reflection, however, Amin added that it would be at least five years before the population were ready for free elections. In the meantime, a military government would be necessary. He promptly abolished parliament and announced he would rule by decree. Britain recognised Amin's government, though several African nations, including neighbouring Tanzania, were openly critical or hostile.

In secrecy, large-scale purges began. The initial targets were members of the Acholi and Langi tribes, from which Obote and other potential rivals sprang. Killer squads and a range of security departments with names of a chilling ambiguity sprang up: 'The Public Safety Unit'; 'The State Research Bureau'.

When in doubt of whom to arrest, Amin's supporters simply picked up those whose names began with 'O', a common feature of Acholi and Langi surnames.

Thousands were massacred. The rivers, lakes and forest around Kampala overflowed with human debris. From time to time the Owen Falls hydro-electric dam on Lake Victoria became clogged with bodies, precipitating power cuts in Kampala. The killing, for tribal, political and financial reasons, continued unabated throughout Amin's reign.

This did not prevent Amin launching himself upon the international circuit with the charming naivety of a debutante. In Britain, he was received by Edward Heath and the Queen. He made a visit to Scotland which had a lasting impression on him. Some years later, he was to declare that he would be happy to accept the Scots' secret wish to have him as a monarch.

In 1975 he had himself inaugurated as President-for-Life, and was borne aloft by fourteen indigent whites, to symbolise the 'white man's burden'. The cabinet was subject to violent fluctuations in its size, presaged by radio announcements publicising the latest 'unfortunate motor accident' to involve a civil servant. Such frantic activity led to the occasional hiccup. One former Amin employee, Frank Kalimazo, was attending his daughter's wedding when he was informed that his demise had been announced on the radio. He was part of an administrative backlog.

The country's predicament was not assisted by Amin's revelation that he was taking his economic advice from God, who appeared to Amin on 5 August 1972, and ordered him to expel the Asians. There were some 80,000 Asians in Uganda, who were responsible for up to 90 per cent of commerce and 50 per cent of industry.

By the late 1970s Amin had outlived his novelty value. The event he intended as the re-launching of his international career ended in humiliation. In 1977, an Air France flight carrying 300 passengers from Tel Aviv to Paris was hijacked by Palestinian terrorists.

Amin colluded with the PLO and allowed the aircraft to land at Entebbe, from where the hijackers demanded the release of fifty-three imprisoned terrorists.

All non-Jewish passengers were released, and the remaining hostages taken to the airport terminal, where Amin mingled benignly with them while Ugandan troops stood guard. Dora Bloch, an elderly woman of joint British and Israeli nationality, fell ill and had to be taken to hospital. While she was away, Israeli commandos landed at the airport, routed Amin's troops, destroyed a flight of MiG aircraft, and flew out again one hour and sixteen minutes later, taking all the hostages, with the exception of Dora Bloch. All seven hijackers were killed.

Amin was furious. Dora Bloch's body turned up on waste ground outside Kampala. It became a capital offence to joke about the affair.

In October 1978, Amin sent an invading force of 3,000 troops into Tanzania. They raped and massacred their way through the border countryside. Amin promptly announced he had conquered his neighbour. However, by the spring of 1979, the retaliating Tanzanian forces were in Kampala, Obote was back in power and Amin found himself hiding in Libya.

From Libya he went to Saudi Arabia, which became his principal home. He was often to be seen in Safeway or Pizza Hut in Jeddah. Twice he applied for an American visa, first to visit Disneyland, and subsequently to enable him to pursue a new career as a professional ten-pin bowler. He was refused on both occasions.

Lancelot Ware, b. 1915, d. 2000

Lancelot Ware, who has died aged eighty-five, co-founded Mensa, the society for people with high IQs.

On 1 October 1946, Ware and a wealthy Australian eccentric, Roland Berrill, set up the organisation in Oxford. The original intention was that Mensa should become a panel of the intellectually gifted which could be consulted by governments. However, as governments showed no enthusiasm for consulting Mensa (whose members' opinions, when voiced, tended to come from the far right), the organisation became better known as a social forum for people who scored more than 148 points in IQ tests. Its convocations became known as 'the place where eggheads go to get laid'.

⊰ 16th ⊱

Captain George Hunt, b. 1916, d. 2011

Captain George Hunt, who has died aged ninety-five, sank more enemy ships than any other British submariner of the war, commanding patrols that were considered of 'unsurpassed' daring and brilliance.

His successes were based on a technical mastery that was allied to steely courage, and for these qualities he was awarded a DSC and Bar and a DSO and Bar as well as being twice mentioned in despatches – making him one of the nation's most highly decorated naval officers.

Perhaps his greatest feat came on 27 June 1944, when he detected the 3,317-ton cargo ship *Cap Blanc* close to Cap Antibes; despite her four escorts he managed to sink her with four torpedoes. He was hunted for an hour, but eluded the depth charges and, as he slowly drew away, spotted the 5,260-ton tanker *Pallas* under tow of two tugs, with five more escorts and four aircraft circling overhead.

Though conditions were good for an anti-submarine chase, Hunt succeeded in penetrating the strong escort 'screen', and at 08:31 fired his last two torpedoes from 1,500 yards: both hit.

He dived to 300ft, near to maximum safe diving depth, to endure what he knew would be a heavy counter-attack; he stopped counting the depth charges after the first hundred. The detonations started several leaks but none proved catastrophic and Hunt crept away until, at about noon, he came to periscope depth and saw his enemy hull down on the horizon.

By the end of the war he held the title of deadliest submarine captain: of the sixty-eight torpedoes he fired, 47 per cent were hits. While Lt-Cdr David Wanklyn, VC, sank most tonnage, Hunt, who attributed his success to his 'marvellous team on-board', sank most ships.

Shirley Eskapa, b. 1934, d. 2011

Shirley Eskapa, who has died aged seventy-seven, was a novelist who also wrote the non-fiction work *Woman Versus Woman* (1984), in which she noted that a husband's extra-marital affair need not be a reason for divorce.

For years, she argued, family therapists had encouraged the wronged wife to blame herself with the belief that men stray only when they are trapped in unhappy marriages. This, Shirley Eskapa maintained, was nonsense. Men have a built-in predisposition to wander, and a happy marriage is no guarantee that they will not succumb to erotic stimuli. Whether this ends in the breakdown of a marriage, she believed, depends to a great extent on the cheated wife.

Some wives, she found, became so stricken by anger, jealousy or guilt that they unwittingly helped their rivals. Many women, however, managed to manipulate the situation to win back the errant spouse, either by pretending not to notice and waiting for the 'crisis of ecstasy' to burn itself out, or by mounting a subtle campaign of calculated revenge, with the aim of 'diminishing the Other Woman without diminishing the man'.

In one case a wife arrived at her husband's love-nest, where she left their four young children and badly behaved cross-bred Alsatian, along with a note containing elaborate instructions for their care and the declaration: 'I'm going to Los Angeles.

Like you, I am following a thing bigger than me.' After three weeks, the husband returned to the marital home, not merely repentant, but supremely grateful.

Another wife lent her rival a strapless dress which displayed to particular disadvantage her large, masculine shoulders.

The daughter of a businessman, Shirley Joan Barnett was born in Johannesburg, South Africa, on 30 July 1934. A bright child, she secured the top grades in the country at school and had her first short story accepted for publication aged sixteen.

She first met her husband Raymond Eskapa when she was fourteen and he eighteen. They married when Shirley was nineteen.

While she was still living in South Africa, Shirley Eskapa became active behind the scenes in the anti-apartheid movement. As a member of the non-violent white women's resistance organisation, Black Sash, she often found herself being followed around by South Africa's secret police. Eventually her husband persuaded her that they should leave South Africa, and in 1969 he sold his business. The family moved to Geneva then, in the early 1980s, to London.

A warm and generous woman, Shirley Eskapa enjoyed bringing writers together at her flat in Chelsea. Though she wrote about marital discord, her own marriage was both happy and secure.

ᗌ 17th ᗍ

Piper Bill Millin, b. 1922, d. 2010

Piper Bill Millin, who has died aged eighty-eight, was personal piper to Lord Lovat on D-Day and piped the invasion forces on to the shores of France; unarmed apart from the ceremonial dagger in his stocking, he played unflinchingly as men fell all around him.

Millin began his apparently suicidal serenade immediately upon jumping from the ramp of the landing craft into the icy water. As the Cameron tartan of his kilt floated to the surface he struck up with 'Hieland Laddie'. He continued even as the man behind him was hit, dropped into the sea and sank.

Once ashore Millin did not run, but walked up and down the beach, blasting out a series of tunes. After 'Hieland Laddie', Lovat, the commander of 1st Special Service Brigade (1 SSB), raised his voice above the crackle of gunfire and the crump of mortar, and asked for another. Millin strode up and down the water's edge playing 'The Road to the Isles'.

For many, the piper provided a unique boost to morale. 'I shall never forget hearing the skirl of Bill Millin's pipes,' said one soldier, Tom Duncan, decades later. 'It is hard to describe the impact it had. It gave us a great lift and increased our determination. As well as the pride we felt, it reminded us of home and why we were there fighting for our lives and those of our loved ones.'

Gilyan Francesco, b. 1919, d. 2001

Gilyan Francesco, who has died aged eighty-two, was known as South Africa's 'National Clown' but was a performer of volatile temperament.

On one occasion, while he was working with a small circus in Mauritius, two of the show's performing monkeys escaped. They found Francesco's make-up kit, daubed themselves like clowns and ran into a dressing tent, destroying all the costumes before being caught. Francesco insisted either the monkeys went or he did; so they were given away to a local Mauritian.

A few weeks later Francesco asked how the monkeys were. 'They were delicious,' the man replied.

≈ 18th ≈

Burnum Burnum, b. 1936, d. 1997

Burnum Burnum, who has died in Sydney aged sixty-one, had the audacity to raise the black, red and yellow Australian Aboriginal flag below the White Cliffs of Dover on 26 January 1988, and claim England for his people.

As a publicity stunt it drew enormous attention, but its serious message may not have always been understood. The date marked the 200th anniversary of the day on which Captain Arthur Phillip, a Londoner, hoisted the British flag in Australia and formally took possession of the eastern part, territory that had been Aboriginal since time immemorial.

At Dover, Burnum Burnum, tall, dignified and massively white-bearded, read a proclamation declaring himself a nobleman of ancient Australia, who wished no harm to the European natives, but wanted to bring them good manners, refinement and an opportunity to make a 'koompatoo' – a fresh start.

He was showing present generations the other side of the coin, and asking the international community to understand that Australian Aborigines had suffered an overwhelming invasion, with disastrous consequences to this day.

To his sorrow, he was never fully accepted by his own people, a burden he carried from his upbringing as one of those Aborigines known as the 'stolen children'. They were Aboriginal children taken from their parents and raised in white institutions, a now discredited policy.

Burnum was born in January 1936 at Wallaga Lake, New South Wales. His mother died when he was three months old, and under his original name of Harry Penrith he began life in institutions. He found some kindness, but later endured physical and psychological abuse.

He changed his name to Burnum Burnum when he was forty, trying to find the sense of Aboriginal belonging that he had never known. It was his great-grandfather's name, and meant 'Great Warrior'.

He took the Aboriginal case to white audiences, and encouraged each side to see acceptable things in the other. Accredited as a story-teller by the State Education

Department, he spread the Aboriginal word among children.

A gentle soul, he was gratified that 26 January, Australia Day, with its unhappy meaning for Aborigines, was followed immediately by the birthday of his idol, Mozart. 'When I go to the desert,' he told a journalist, 'my emotions are in harmony with Mozart. I play him in my head, especially the slow second movements, which are in perfect harmony with my footsteps.'

Burnum's magnificent appearance won him film roles and the hearts of ladies. He was married three times. His last wedding, to the very attractive Marelle Dickson, was celebrated in a Sydney park, with the groom wearing a cloak of kangaroo skin.

⚛ 19th ⚛

The 6th Marquess of Aberdeen and Temair, b. 1920, d. 2002

The 6th Marquess of Aberdeen and Temair, who has died aged eighty-two, was known to connoisseurs of botanical art as Alastair Gordon, a painter of flowers and plants; at the age of eighty he became better known to a wider public when he gave a frank account of his youthful exploits among the bordellos of Beirut, London and Paris.

At Mme Jannette's in Beirut, Lord Aberdeen recorded, an afternoon's pleasure with Olga, a refugee from Yugoslavia – 'the sort of attractive girl you could meet at a point-to-point in Gloucestershire' – could be bought for as little as five pounds.

At Mrs Fetherstonehaugh's in Knightsbridge, the girls were so high-class, Lord Aberdeen recalled, that, rumour had it, one Coldstream Guards officer discovered to his horror that 'the girl assigned to him was his own sister'.

In Paris, at the Viscomtesse de Brissac's house in the XVI arrondissement, Lord Aberdeen's favourite, a 'chestnut-haired beauty', was so used to entertaining Germans that she would cry out in her ecstasy: '*Ach! Mein Gott.*'

'Tactfully I didn't remind her that the Germans had left, defeated,' Aberdeen recalled. 'You English,' his companion informed him, 'are happily different to French men, who are all played out by their mid-twenties'.

As he moved about from country to country, Lord Aberdeen described how he had discovered the location of the best bordellos by a sort of bush telegraph, though it was not always straightforward: 'In Paris you had to be proposed and seconded by Frenchmen of some standing to be admitted at all.' Nevertheless, 'my experiences of the oldest profession,' he concluded, 'give me almost entirely pleasant memories.'

The 6th Marquess was born Alastair Ninian John Gordon on 20 July 1920, the youngest of five children and the fourth son of Lord Dudley Gordon, who would become the 3rd Marquess of Aberdeen and Temair on the death of his brother George in 1965.

Alastair was brought up at Haddo House and sent to Harrow, where his fagmaster was Keith (later Lord) Joseph. After leaving school, he trained at Gray School of Art, Aberdeen.

On the outbreak of war in 1939 he was commissioned into the Scots Guards and sent to the Middle East, then to North Africa, where he was accidentally shot in the shoulder by an Irish Guardsman and sent to Syria to recuperate. It was at this time, while on leave with fellow officers in cosmopolitan Beirut, that his sexual adventures began.

After the war, Gordon resumed his art studies for two years at Camberwell School of Art, then spent several months painting in Kenya, a trip that yielded a short book, *A Slight Touch of Safari*.

He became a member of the International Association of Art Critics and, during the 1960s, was modern art correspondent for *Connoisseur* magazine.

In spite of his colourful younger days, his marriage was a very happy one; his wife always regarded his interest in matters sexual with tolerant amusement.

❦ 20th ❦

Professor Sir Fred Hoyle, b. 1915, d. 2001

Professor Sir Fred Hoyle, who has died aged eighty-six, was Britain's best-known astronomer; he was also an outrageous mischief-maker who took a delight in enraging his academic colleagues.

He and his close associate, Prof. Chandra Wickramasinghe, head of Mathematics at University College, Wales, used to make other scientists so angry that some even wrote a special sub-program for their word processors which, by pressing a single key, caused the words 'Contrary to the views of Hoyle and Wickramasinghe ...' to appear on the screen.

The keyboard combination was pressed liberally in January 1990, when the two men published an article in the journal *Nature* claiming that sunspots caused flu epidemics. Their conclusion, which infuriated medical scientists, was based on their rigidly held belief that space is full of viruses that cause not only flu but Aids and legionnaire's disease as well. Storms on the sun's surface (indicated by sunspots) were supposed to drive these viruses into the Earth's atmosphere, whereupon diseases spread.

Still greater fury arose from their claim that Darwin's theory of evolution by natural selection was wrong, and that evolution occurred because mutating life forms continually fall from space. Nor, Hoyle thought, was this an accident. It was deliberately arranged long ago by a super-intelligent civilisation who wished to 'seed' our planet.

The most puzzling aspect of these disputes was that Hoyle made many genuine and significant contributions to physics and astronomy. The most important was his discovery in 1958, with the American physicist William Fowler, of the way that the heavy chemical elements that fill our bodies, such as oxygen, carbon and iron, were forged in the nuclear furnaces of giant stars which later exploded and from whose relics the solar system was born.

In short, we are literally made of stardust. But this epochal discovery was strangely rewarded. Fowler won a Nobel prize for it, but Hoyle, to his justifiable annoyance, did not.

Fred Hoyle was born on 24 June 1915, at Bingley in the West Riding of Yorkshire. He was educated at Bingley Grammar School and Emmanuel College, Cambridge, where he studied Mathematics. In 1939 he was elected a fellow of St John's College, Cambridge. He conducted research for the Admiralty during the Second World War.

Until the end of his life, Hoyle championed the 'steady state' theory of the universe which maintained that the cosmos had no beginning. This was despite increasing evidence, amounting in the view of many to proof, that the cosmos began in a Big Bang some 12,000 million years ago. (It was Hoyle himself who, mockingly, coined the term 'Big Bang'. But the phrase stuck.)

He challenged the evidence of the radio astronomer Sir Martin Ryle, who in the 1960s had found evidence of cosmic origins. Barbara Gamow, the wife of the pro-Big Bang astronomer George Gamow, was inspired to describe their dispute in verse:

> 'Your years of toil,'
> Said Ryle to Hoyle,
> 'Are wasted years, believe me.
> The steady state
> Is out of date
> Unless my eyes deceive me.
> My telescope
> Has dashed your hope;
> Your tenets are refuted.
> Let me be terse:
> Our universe
> Grows daily more diluted!'

⇥ 21st ⇤

Leo Castelli, b. 1907, d. 1999

Leo Castelli, who has died aged ninety-one, was the most influential American art dealer of the twentieth century.

Impeccably dressed and possessed of exquisite manners, Castelli was the master of the charming and highly effective soft-sell. 'You could give that son of a bitch two beer cans and he could sell them,' went the painter Willem de Kooning's famous remark. Jasper Johns responded by making a bronze painted sculpture of two Ballantine Ale cans, which Castelli promptly sold.

The son of a successful Hungarian banker, he was born Leo Krauss on 4 September 1907 at Trieste. There his father married into the Castelli family, and when Italy annexed the city in 1919 Castelli was adopted as the family name.

In 1924 he took a job in a large insurance firm in Trieste. Transferred in 1932 to Romania, he fell in love there with Ileana Schapira, daughter of one of the country's wealthiest industrialists, and the couple were married the following year. In 1937 they moved to Paris, where Castelli secured a job with the Banca d'Italia. They met many of the leading surrealist painters, and in 1939 Castelli and the architect Rene Drouin opened a gallery on the Place Vendome.

Their first exhibition, a group show of surrealists, was a spectacular social success; but that year France declared war on Germany. In 1941 the Castellis moved to New York to join Ileana's father. Castelli joined the US Army, and in 1944 went to Bucharest with Military Intelligence to work with the anti-Nazi underground. After accomplishing this mission Castelli was granted US citizenship.

Their first post-war shows were of work by such established names as Leger and Pollock, but Castelli, realising that abstract expressionism had run its course, started looking for new work in a different vein.

Seeing a painting titled *Green Target* by an unknown named Jasper Johns, he had what he called his 'first great epiphany'. Castelli described first entering Johns' studio as 'seeing the treasures of Tutankhamen'. He gave him a show in January 1958 and three months later exhibited Robert Rauschenberg.

The effect on the New York art world was instantaneous. Johns and Rauschenberg became overnight stars, credited as the first artists to break with abstract expressionism, and Castelli became the man who could spot new talent.

Other discoveries followed. Roy Lichtenstein, James Rosenquist and Andy Warhol all joined the Castelli stable. Warhol's Campbell's soup tins and Coca-Cola bottles became the defining images of pop, and their creator the biggest art superstar since Dali.

Castelli himself acquired the aura of a Svengali and star-maker. The man now seen as responsible for the eclipse of abstract expressionism was held all the more in awe because of that movement's own claims to greatness and 'objective' truth.

Accused of promoting in pop art 'an episode in the history of taste' rather than of art, Castelli remained unrepentant. 'There are those unsuccessful abstract expressionists who accuse me of killing them,' he said. 'They blame me for their funerals. But they were dead already. I just helped remove the bodies.'

≈ 22nd ≈

Hope Bourne, b. 1918, d. 2010

Hope Bourne, who has died aged ninety-one, was an author who celebrated life on Exmoor, where she lived for more than sixty years; her knowledge of its flora and fauna and its traditional communities was encyclopaedic, and was gained by submission to a lifestyle which few in the twentieth century would have dared even to contemplate.

For more than two decades – between 1970 and the early 1990s – Hope Bourne lived in isolation in an old, leaking caravan in the ruins of a farm at Ferny Ball above Sherdon Water, about four miles from Withypool. To her, untamed nature was not just something she desired, it was also a means of testing human resilience and ingenuity.

At Ferny Ball she kept bantams. A small but wiry figure, she was often seen in pursuit of wood pigeon, deer, rabbit or hare, wielding her American-made .22 rifle or 12-bore shotgun – 'What one didn't get, t'other did,' she would say. To feed herself, as well as shooting for the pot, she fished and grew vegetables. She ate a pound of meat a day (some of which was none too fresh) and drank from a stream.

Her caravan was 14ft long by 6ft wide, providing only one room which was festooned with the skins, antlers and hooves of animals she had slaughtered and gutted herself. At the centre was a wood-burning stove. She converted two of the three bunks into bookshelves and slept in the third.

Hope Bourne's eating equipment was equally rudimentary. She had three mugs (one for tea, one for coffee, one for water or lemonade), and ate her enormous breakfast of meat and vegetables straight from the frying pan. There was thus no need to wash up.

Throughout her life she earned a small amount of money by helping farming friends, tending their stock and helping out during the lambing season. Her income was usually about £100 a year, of which she saved nearly half, claiming to live on £5 a month, most of which went on cartridges.

Hope Lilian Bourne was born in Oxford on 26 August 1918 (she claimed not to know her age, having lost her birth certificate), but in childhood was taken to Devon, where her widowed mother became headmistress of the village school at Elmscott, near Hartland.

Hope herself left school aged fourteen, and as an asthmatic remained at home with her mother, who in 1939 moved to the Cotswolds; there Hope worked on the land, but she missed the wildness of Devon. She was in her thirties when her mother died, and their house had to be sold to pay off debts. Hope was therefore left with no home, little money and no income, and no qualifications on which to build a normal life. She decided to become as self-sufficient as possible, in the area of England that she loved. Knowing the countryside intimately, she carried no map; if she found herself lost, she put her trust in her inner compass.

In 1979 Daniel Farson interviewed her for *The Sunday Telegraph Magazine*. She told him: 'I have never taken a penny from public money. Friends tell me I could live better on National Assistance, or whatever they call it now. Over my dead body!

'It's a good life but it's a tough life. You've got to be 100 per cent physically fit to live as I do. You've got to be tough, body and soul. Whatever happens at Ferny Ball, I've got to cope with it alone.'

She eschewed the companionship of a dog, explaining that 'my meat supply is so irregular that it couldn't feed a dog. I can pull in my belt and live on potatoes when things get bad, but I couldn't expect that of a dog.'

In the late 1980s she was eventually persuaded to install a telephone in case of emergencies. But as her asthma worsened, concerned friends persuaded her to move to a new house at a community housing scheme in Withypool.

Although the house was fully equipped, she rarely used the electricity and never the central heating, sleeping on the living room floor in front of the open fire. The rest of the house she left to her bantams.

❧ 23rd ❧

R.D. Laing, b. 1927, d. 1989

R.D. Laing, the psychiatrist and author who has died at St Tropez aged sixty-one, was an exponent of new and unorthodox views on the causes of mental illness, and a guru to the disaffected youth of the 1960s.

'Ronnie' Laing was convinced that many delusive actions were a form of defence or protest against an unacceptable external world. He saw 'normal' life and social behaviour as shrivelled, inhuman and corrupt: 'We are all fallen Sons of Prophecy,' he wrote in one of his more oracular flights, 'who have learned to die in the Spirit and be reborn in the Flesh.'

It was this poetic and iconoclastic approach – together with his enthusiastic endorsement of such psychotropic drugs as marijuana and LSD – that earned Laing a wide following in the 'counterculture' of the hippies: his first book, *The Divided Self: An Existential Study in Sanity and Madness* (1960), sold 400,000 paperback copies in Britain alone.

Laing helped to change ideas but encountered heated professional opposition – and at times disbelief. He could be outré, too, in his own behaviour. It was his habit, for example, to howl at the moon. In 1984 he was in a bar in California when other drinkers took exception to his howling. Matters came to a head when he decided to exorcise a neighbouring drinker, who hit him over the head with a shovel, shouting: 'I'll knock the Devil out of you!'

Laing's reaction to the incident was typical: 'I don't blame the man who did it to me. I'm sure deep down he's really a gentle loving creature. I only hope I can still play the piano.'

The son of working-class Presbyterians, Ronald David Laing was born on 7 October 1927 in Glasgow. His childhood was unhappy – he was frequently beaten and his stern mother kept him apart from other children – and this helped shape his adult thought. After attending a local grammar school – where he read widely, particularly in the classics – he studied Medicine at Glasgow University and Psychiatry at the West of Scotland Neurological Unit.

Having made his name with his first and most influential book Laing went on to write a dozen more; in later years these became more speculative and metaphysical, and as he made wide changes in his earlier thinking he fell out of favour with his readers.

In 1964 Laing published *Reason and Violence* (with David Cooper), to which Jean-Paul Sartre contributed an introduction: 'Like you,' wrote the Frenchman, 'I regard mental illness as "the way out" that the free organism invents in order to be able to live through an intolerable situation.'

⚔ **24**th ⚔

Sir Wilfred Thesiger, b. 1910, d. 2003

Sir Wilfred Thesiger, who has died aged ninety-three, was the quintessential English explorer, and the last and greatest of that small band of travellers who sought out the secrets of the desert in the years before Arabia was transformed forever by the oil beneath her sands.

Thesiger's reputation was established by two epic journeys he made in the 1940s across the Rub al Khali, or Empty Quarter, the most forbidding, least known and least penetrated region of Arabia.

His motive for crossing it was not primarily to reap glory for himself, but to share the hardship of the life of the Bedu and to earn their comradeship. He was not in thrall to the desert itself but, like T.E. Lawrence, to his admiration of those who lived there: 'The harder the life,' ran his credo, 'the finer the person.'

The Empty Quarter is the largest sand desert in the world. It covers 250,000 square miles and contains ranges of dunes 100 miles long and 1,000ft high. At noon, the temperature of the surface of the sand reaches 80C.

The first European to traverse this fearsome waste had been Bertram Thomas in 1932, later followed by St John Philby, the father of Kim. But both these had travelled as well-supplied Westerners; Philby had even carried with him a wireless to listen to Test matches. Thesiger's achievement was to make longer journeys than either, dressed like the Arab tribesmen with whom he rode and rationed to their daily pint of water and handful of dates.

It was a spare, almost monastic way of life, and one in which Thesiger found a near-spiritual contentment. 'In the desert,' he wrote, 'I found a freedom unattainable in civilisation; a life unhampered by possessions.'

Ostensibly in Arabia to search for the breeding grounds of locusts, Thesiger made his first crossing of the Empty Quarter – a circular journey by camel of some 1,500 miles – in 1946, becoming in the process the first European to see the fabled quicksands of Umm al Samim. His second expedition, two years later, took him even further through the desert and, in constant peril from hostile Bedu, was still more dangerous.

It was also the most fulfilling experience of Thesiger's life, albeit a humbling one; for though he withstood the physical hardship, he felt that he rarely matched the standards of behaviour the Bedu expected of themselves.

In the 1950s, as Arabia began to change, he took to the mountains, travelling in remote parts of Kurdistan, the Karakoram and later Afghanistan. There, on the banks of the Panjshir, he and Eric Newby had the most celebrated meeting between travellers since that of Livingstone and Stanley, with Thesiger (presented in Newby's account as the hardened professional to his own inept amateur) deriding the attempts of Newby and his companion to blow up their rubber mattress: 'God,' he scoffed, 'you must be a couple of pansies.'

Thesiger made a new base in the marshes of Iraq, where he lived for eight years in the 1950s, travelling by canoe and giving basic medical assistance to its inhabitants; he also became expert at circumcision.

Paradoxically, one modern invention gave Thesiger an edge over predecessors such as Wilfrid Scawen Blunt – the camera. Thesiger taught himself to become an excellent photographer and perhaps his most enduring legacy will prove to be his vast photographic record (willed to the Pitt-Rivers Museum in Oxford) of ancient races and ways of life since extinguished within a generation.

His great fortune was to see them just before they were lost from sight; his tragedy that the ones he cared for most have vanished forever.

Wilfred Patrick Thesiger was born on 3 June 1910 within the mud walls of the British Legation in Addis Ababa, Abyssinia. His father, a younger son of the 2nd Lord Chelmsford – commander of the force destroyed by the Zulus at Isandhlwana – was Consul-General and Minister at the court of Emperor Menelik.

After Eton, Thesiger went up in 1929 to Magdalen College, Oxford, to read History. He spent his summer vacations working on tramp steamers and fishing trawlers, but the high point of his time at Oxford came in the winter of 1930 when he was invited to Addis Ababa to attend the coronation of Haile Selassie (the former Ras Tafari), who remembered the help afforded by Thesiger's father during the civil war.

While in Ethiopia, Thesiger took the opportunity to plan his first expedition, a journey north into the Danakil country to search for the destination of the Awash River. This he carried out in 1933, although the Danakil had a murderous reputation and accounted a warrior's standing by the number of men he had killed and castrated. The success of Thesiger's enterprise began, at the age of twenty-three, to make his reputation as an explorer and helped win him a place in the Sudan Political Service.

He served in the Sudan from 1935 to 1940, although he was too unconventional to make a success of it as a career and spent his last years there as a freelance District Officer. He used much of his time to travel as far afield as Chad, and relished the opportunities for hunting lion, which preyed on village cattle. He bagged more than seventy, and raised two cubs himself. Thesiger, though, was not a sentimental man, and subsequently shot both the cubs. He did this in the belief that, having been tame, they would grow up to become man-eaters.

On the outbreak of war Thesiger was assigned to the Sudan Defence Force, and later, under the command of Orde Wingate, helped organise the Abyssinian resistance to the occupying Italians. In May 1941 Thesiger led a flying column which marched fifty miles in a day through sweltering heat to harry a much larger retreating force at Wagidi. Having accomplished this, Thesiger went on to force the surrender of 2,000 Italian troops and the fort at Agibar. His leadership in this action was recognised by the award of the DSO.

Having been recruited by David Stirling, Thesiger later served briefly in the Western Desert with the SAS, but then saw out the rest of the war in some frustration as political adviser to the Abyssinian Crown Prince.

In March 1945 he resigned this post, and while waiting for an aeroplane back to London, was invited to dinner with O.B. Lean, head of the Middle East Anti-Locust Unit. Lean was looking to employ somebody to investigate locust sites in the Arabian desert; Thesiger had accepted the job before the meal was over.

After leaving Iraq, from 1968 onwards Thesiger lived for much of the year in northern Kenya, with the pastoral Samburu and Turkana peoples, although he dwelt apart from them and, unlike in Arabia, retained his English identity. In reference to this, and to his outsized ears and jutting nose, the tribes called him *sangalai*, 'The Old Bull Elephant Who Walks By Himself'.

Occasionally, Thesiger returned to the flat he kept in Chelsea; but England was an unfamiliar country to him, and he hoped to see out his years in Kenya, with his corpse being left on the hill for the jackals. But after the death of the two Kenyan men whom he had treated as sons, he reluctantly returned to England for good in the mid-1990s, living out his days at a retirement home in Surrey, where he coped valiantly with the effects of Parkinson's Disease.

≼ 25th ≽

Lord Kadoorie, b. 1899, d.1993

Lord Kadoorie, who has died in Hong Kong aged ninety-four, was the last of the colony's old-style 'taipans'.

His life spanned almost the entire modern history of Hong Kong – from shortly after the granting of the New Territories lease, to the debates on the return to Chinese rule; he believed with Deng Xiaoping that 'in time the threads in the cloth will be so closely woven that capitalism and socialism will be as one'.

Kadoorie's experience gave him a philosophical view of Hong Kong's notoriously volatile economy and stock market. His father had told him not to worry about the colony 'as long as people keep digging holes', and there was rarely a time when the panorama from his office did not include massive construction works along the harbour front.

During the Communist riots of 1967, he ordered welders to keep working on his own sites so that sparks in the night would show people he had confidence in the future. Kadoorie was saddened, however, by the fever for short-term speculative gains among the colony's younger businessmen; such dealing, he held, 'destroys the past'.

≼ 26th ≽

Francesco Crucitti, b. 1931, d. 1998

Francesco Crucitti, who has died aged sixty-seven, was credited by Pope John Paul II with having saved his life by carrying out an emergency operation after the assassination attempt in 1981.

On 13 May 1981, Mehmet Ali Agca fired three shots from a 9mm Browning automatic at Pope John Paul in St Peter's Square. Two bullets hit him and he fell back into the arms of his chamberlain. (Alois Estermann, a Swiss Guard, jumped on to the Popemobile to shelter him from possible further attack; Estermann was shot dead in 1998 in his Vatican apartment.)

The Popemobile carried the Pope, gravely wounded in the abdomen, to the nearest ambulance, which took him to the Gemelli hospital in Rome. It took eight minutes for the sixty-year-old to reach its doors.

Meanwhile Crucitti was driving in his own car in Rome when he heard on the radio that the Pope had been shot. He stopped a police officer and asked for an emergency escort through the traffic, saying: 'I am the surgeon who will operate on the Pope.'

He found the Pope at the Gemelli hospital with blood pressure that had fallen alarmingly. He was given the last rites before Crucitti spent five hours and twenty minutes at the head of a team operating on him.

The bullets had missed his spine and one had come within a few millimetres of his aorta, which, had it been punctured, would have led to his immediate death. Crucitti had to remove twenty-two inches of the Pope's intestine and do much other repair work. The Pope had also lost part of the index finger of his left hand, which was later put into a metal splint, and had his elbow grazed.

'I cannot hide from you that the situation is serious,' Crucitti, still in his surgeon's gown, told waiting pressmen after the surgery. Just when the Pope seemed to be rallying, he fell into a high fever. There was speculation that blood used for a transfusion had been infected with a virus. Finally, however, the Pope made a full recovery.

Francesco Crucitti was born in the southern city of Reggio Calabria in 1931. He qualified as a doctor at the age of twenty-two, and then specialised in general surgery. He then undertook research in cancers of the breast, pancreas and stomach.

In 1967 Crucitti was appointed director of the Institute of General Surgery at the Catholic University in Rome, to which the Gemelli hospital is attached.

During the period when he acted as a consultant surgeon to the Pope, Crucitti frequently appealed to him to rest and reduce his exhausting schedule. After hearing of Crucitti's death, the Pope went straight from his audience in St Peter's Square to visit his widow, Allessandra. 'I came here expressly to show you in some way my appreciation of this man who saved my life,' he said.

⊰ 27th ⊱

Anne Cumming, b. 1917, d. 1993

Anne Cumming, who has died in London aged seventy-five, was a sexual adventuress who wrote two erotic travelogues and last year appeared topless in the *Sunday Sport* newspaper under the headline 'Stunnagran'.

Cumming dressed conservatively and with style. But her conversation and behaviour were shocking. A fellow guest at a dinner party fainted when Cumming described to him in detail a sex-change operation she had attended in Casablanca.

Her candour was usually laced with wit. Asked why she had written her memoirs, she replied: 'What can an old pensioner do to get by? Either take in the laundry – or do your dirty washing in public.'

Cumming said that she had slept with several hundred men. Her first memoir, *The Love Habit* (1977), detailed her exploits in the late 1960s and 1970s, which included a string of affairs with teenaged boys in New York. The *News of the World* bought the rights and dubbed Cumming the 'Randy Granny'.

The Love Quest (1991), which chronicled Cumming's life from 1950 to 1965, was if anything more explicit. Cumming told how she blazed a trail through Europe and North Africa, and had one sexual encounter on horseback while galloping round the Sphinx.

She spent her first night in Rabat with a professional cyclist: 'All I can remember about him,' she wrote, 'was his remarkable muscle tone and his beautiful strong thighs. I like a man from the waist down.'

Feeding such an appetite was hard work. Cumming recalled a night in Paris when she stood on the street dressed only in a mink coat and fluffy slippers, baring her body to passing men. No one stopped.

A grand-daughter of Sir Grimble Groves, a Conservative MP and brewery-owner, Felicity Anne Cumming was born on 14 December 1917 at Walton-on-Thames, Surrey. She spent much of her childhood on a farm in South Africa, but was educated at Horsely Towers, Kent, and at finishing schools in Germany and Switzerland.

She studied drama at the Old Vic and at Dartington Hall, where she met her first husband, Henry Lyon Young. The marriage was dissolved in 1948, and the same year she married and divorced the novelist Richard Mason.

After ten years' travel Cumming settled in Rome, where she lived for five years with the set designer Beni Montressor before deciding to devote herself to casual love affairs. She also became a respected publicist and dialogue coach in the burgeoning Italian film industry, working on films by Dino de Laurentiis and Federico Fellini, in whose *Roma* and *8½* she also appeared.

In 1979 she moved to New York, where she taught at the Michael Chekhov drama studio.

When Cumming was diagnosed HIV positive seven years ago she stopped sleeping with men, but continued to travel. In her last two years she visited Brazil, Oman, India and Russia.

Her final public appearance, earlier this year, was on a Channel 4 nude chat show, for which she wore only a pearl necklace and drop-earrings.

⊰ 28th ⊱

Wing Commander John Freeborn, b. 1919, d. 2010

Wing Commander John Freeborn, who has died aged ninety, was one of the RAF's leading fighter 'aces' in the Battle of Britain, during which he flew more operational hours than any other pilot.

Freeborn had already seen much action before the battle. Flying Spitfires with 74

(Tiger) Squadron, he was heavily engaged in the air fighting during the retreat of the British Expeditionary Force to Dunkirk in May 1940.

Over a six-day period, the squadron accounted for nineteen enemy aircraft, two shot down by Freeborn. On one occasion his Spitfire was badly damaged and crash-landed on the beach near Calais; he managed to get a lift home in a returning aircraft.

On 10 July, the opening day of the battle, Freeborn shot down a Messerschmitt Bf 109 over Deal. For the next few weeks he flew continuously and his successes mounted. On 11 August he flew four missions in eight hours and was credited with shooting down three fighters and probably a fourth. Two days later he shot down a Dornier bomber, and later in the day learned that he had been awarded the DFC for his 'high courage and exceptional abilities as a leader'.

He was appointed a flight commander and by the end of the battle on 31 October had been credited with shooting down at least seven aircraft in addition to his earlier successes over Dunkirk.

No. 74 Squadron remained in the front line, and by the end of November Freeborn had been with the squadron longer than any other Battle of Britain pilot. In December he shot down two more Bf 109s and damaged others.

Then, in early 1941, Fighter Command went on the offensive, with Freeborn flying sweeps over northern France. At the end of February he was awarded a Bar to his DFC, the citation confirming that he had destroyed twelve enemy aircraft and damaged others. He was rested in June, having served on No. 74 Squadron for almost three years.

John Connell Freeborn was born at Middleton, Yorkshire, on 1 December 1919, and educated at Leeds Grammar School. He joined the RAF in March 1938 and, after training as a pilot, joined No. 74 Squadron to fly Gauntlet biplane fighters before the squadron was re-equipped with the Spitfire.

On 6 September 1939 Freeborn was at the centre of a tragic 'friendly fire' incident when ground controllers plotting incoming aircraft scrambled the Spitfires of No. 74 Squadron from Hornchurch in Essex. Due to a series of misunderstandings, the squadron commander ordered his pilots to attack. In fact the detected aircraft were returning Hurricanes that had been scrambled against a 'phantom raid'. Freeborn shot down the Hurricane of Pilot Officer Montague Hulton-Harrop, who was killed. A second Hurricane was shot down by another pilot of No. 74 Squadron.

The two pilots were court-martialled but acquitted of any liability or blame, despite their squadron commander testifying against them. The 'Battle of Barking Creek', as this incident was later to become known, led to a complete review of Fighter Command's plotting system.

He returned to operational flying in 1943, when he flew Spitfires with No. 602 Squadron, providing fighter escort to RAF bombers attacking shipping and port installations. On 1 June he was given command of No. 118 Squadron, flying in a similar role.

Freeborn was promoted to become one of the RAF's youngest wing commanders and spent the first six months of 1944 commanding 286 Wing, flying operations from southern Italy in support of the Allied armies. This was a period of intense activity, as the RAF attacked German installations and convoys in the Balkans and provided defence for Allied convoys in Italian waters. He returned to Britain in late 1944 and left the RAF in 1946.

After qualifying as a driving instructor, Freeborn was invited to join Tetley Walker as regional director for their Minster soft drinks brand. He took early retirement, and in the early 1980s moved to Spain. In 2000 he came back to Britain, settling in North Wales.

Self-confident to the point of bloody-mindedness, Freeborn was always happy to express his opinions. As an eighteen-year old he had once informed his CO that he could outfly him, and his brushes with authority made for a colourful life both in the RAF and elsewhere. He never lost his affection for his native Yorkshire, nor for a pint of Tadcaster ale.

Although he had been cleared of any blame for the death of Montague Hulton-Harrop in 1939, the death of his fellow fighter pilot was always in his thoughts. Shortly before his death Freeborn admitted: 'I think about him nearly every day. I always have done. I've had a good life – and he should have had a good life, too.'

⚜ 29th ⚜

Mike Terry, b. 1925, d. 2011

Mike Terry, who has died aged eighty-six, was a journalist of the sort that has now all but disappeared from Fleet Street; many of the tales told about him involved his glass eye – a legacy of the war – staring up from the bottom of someone else's pint glass.

His career inside the office reached its peak in the 1960s, when he was one of the gifted young editorial figures on Hugh Cudlipp's *Daily Mirror* who took tabloid newspapers into the hitherto uncharted territory of in-depth news and features. Terry did so as the *Mirror*'s features editor, a pivotal post in the paper's campaign to show its new ambition.

His career beyond the office – usually in the *Mirror* pub known as The Stab in the Back – was just as celebrated. One colleague recalled being joined by Terry at The Stab. Asked what he wanted to drink, Terry replied: 'I'll have a double brandy and a vodka and Scotch with some ginger ale, and not too much ginger ale.' Having explained that he wanted this concoction in one glass, Terry then added: 'When I drink this I may go a bit of a funny colour. I'm taking these tablets to stop me drinking. Take no notice.'

During such hard-drinking sessions Terry would frequently remove his glass eye and drop it into a pint of beer. Occasionally he would forget it in the gents. Either way, it provoked shouts of anguish from whichever unlucky soul discovered it leering up at him.

Such excesses took their toll, and Terry was fired from the *Mirror* in 1970. He then found a sub-editing berth on the *Sun*, gave up the drink, and passed on the fruits of his undoubted charm, talent and experience with unfailing good humour. He did, however, make one notorious cock-up.

This occurred due to an uncharacteristic failure to check the paper's bingo numbers. The subsequent misprint, on 19 May 1984, left 3,000 *Sun* readers under the impression that they had scooped the top prize of £40,000. One hired a Rolls-Royce to arrive at the paper's office and claim his 'prize'. It was typical of Terry's good grace that, to assuage readers' ire, he agreed to appear in an apology wearing a dunce's cap, under the headline 'I'm the Bingo bungler'.

Michael Dungate Terry was born on 15 February 1925 in Findon Valley, at the foot of the South Downs. He attended Worthing Grammar School, but left when his father's business went bankrupt to start his career in journalism on the *Worthing Herald*.

Aged eighteen he joined the Wiltshire Regiment, where he served as a lieutenant. After D–Day he was involved in fierce fighting around the village of Tilly-Sur-Seulles. After one patrol was cut down by a booby trap, Terry led a platoon to see if there were any survivors, only to trigger a landmine; he lost his right eye in the blast and sustained shrapnel injuries so severe that doctors thought he would not walk again. Despite his wounds he managed to drag one injured soldier back behind the lines, but the rest of his platoon was killed in the explosion.

After rejoining the *Worthing Herald*, he moved to London, working at the *South London Chronicle*, the *Evening News* and the *News Chronicle*. There was more to him than drinking and bungled bingo: Terry had a love of poetry and lone country hikes. One such ramble almost ended in disaster when he fell while descending Great Gable, in the Lake District, after nightfall. Coming to in the dark, bleeding from a cut head and not knowing if he had landed on a precipice, he decided that the safest course of action was to stay awake until daybreak. To keep himself going he set about reciting every piece of Shakespeare he knew. Several hours later he still had not reached the end of his repertoire when dawn enabled him to complete the descent in safety.

⊰ 30th ⊱

Jose Luis de Vilallonga, b. 1920, d. 2007

Jose Luis de Vilallonga, who has died aged eighty-seven, was a Spanish nobleman, playboy, wastrel, author, fortune-hunter and bit-part actor who appeared briefly with Audrey Hepburn in *Breakfast at Tiffany's*.

A self-proclaimed seducer and cad, the tall and elegant Vilallonga flaunted conquests ranging from Magda Gabor, the sister of Zsa Zsa, to the wife of a British admiral. In his vainglorious and – in the opinion of some – highly unreliable memoirs, he described himself as 'a hardened alcoholic who, without ever taking precautions of any kind, has slept with more whores than a porcupine has quills'. He claimed that when his first wife had fallen asleep on their wedding night, he had slipped out to spend the rest of the night in a brothel with French prostitutes.

His unfortunate first wife was Priscilla Scott-Ellis, a daughter of the 8th Lord Howard de Walden, one of Britain's richest peers; she and Vilallonga had met early in 1944. A former debutante known as 'Pip', she had joined Franco's forces as a field nurse during the Spanish Civil War, one of only two British women volunteers to serve with the Nationalists. Before Vilallonga came along, she had been in love with

Prince Ataulfo de Orléans, a cousin of King Alfonso XIII.

Described by Pip's biographer, the historian Paul Preston, as 'handsome and dissolute', Vilallonga seemed to Pip's parents to be a most unpromising match; such were their misgivings that they did not attend their daughter's wedding in Cadiz in September 1945. Nor was Vilallonga's own father too pleased, fulminating how he had heard that during the civil war his son's bride had slept with half the Spanish Army, if not the entire Nationalist forces – suggestions that prompted Lord Howard de Walden to challenge him (without success) to a duel.

Cut off without a penny, Vilallonga looked to his young wife and her family as a potential source of funds, and so was dismayed to learn that most of the Howard de Walden fortune (deriving from family ownership of a large patch of London) would pass to Pip's brother. When the couple arrived in England in the spring of 1946, Lord Howard de Walden – scenting Vilallonga's predatory motives – changed his will in what proved to be a fruitless effort to protect his daughter's financial interests.

While Vilallonga continued to accept large sums of money from his wife, he treated her abominably, confessing in his memoirs to having humiliated her and made her miserable. 'I regret infinitely,' he wrote, 'that I made a good and loyal woman suffer so much for the dreadful error of falling in love with me.'

By the time Lord Howard de Walden died in November 1946, Vilallonga and his wife were living in Argentina, allegedly for the sake of Pip's health. Returning alone to London, Vilallonga moved into a property in Cadogan Lane that Lord Howard de Walden had bequeathed to Pip – and proceeded to sell off the contents, including a valuable collection of modern art, to finance a spending spree.

Although his wife returned to Europe and helped to establish Vilallonga as a full-time writer in France, there was no hope for their marriage and the couple separated in 1958; the flow of novels from Vilallonga's pen soon came to an end as well. Instead he landed small roles in more than sixty films; a high point in Vilallonga's acting career came when he was cast as José da Silva Pereira, the dashing Brazilian multi-millionaire whom Holly Golightly plans to marry in Blake Edwards' film *Breakfast at Tiffany's* (1961).

José Luis de Vilallonga y Cabeza de Vaca was born in Madrid on 9 January 1920, the eldest son of the Marqués de Castellvell, a cavalry officer. Unloved by his mother, the boy had a bleak childhood. 'I would have given anything,' he wrote later, 'for my mother to take me in her arms and kiss me.'

Vilallonga lived in exile in France between 1950 and 1976. A series of anti-Franco novels saw him sentenced in absentia to imprisonment for sedition – and every three months he was retried and had his sentence increased. In time his sentence was said to have amounted to more than 300 years.

He returned to Spain following Franco's death and the restoration of the monarchy in 1975 to work for various media outlets, including the Spanish version of *Playboy* magazine.

⇥ 31st ⇤

Sid Rawle, b. 1945, d. 2010

Sid Rawle, who has died aged sixty-four, was the so-called King of the Hippies, a veteran of the New Age movement of the 1970s and a fervent follower of the alternative lifestyle.

He was also a serial squatter, having occupied flats, houses, common land, forests, an entire village in Wales, boats, an Irish island, an Army camp and – incurring royal displeasure – Windsor Great Park. His argument was that since young men and women could be called upon to die for their country in time of war, it was only fair that each should have a right to a few square yards of meadow or mountain for themselves. 'In the end,' he declared, 'it all gets back to land.'

Rawle believed that it was becoming harder for ordinary people to get access to land, and his efforts to ensure it made him something of a folk hero. 'Shared out equally,' he noted, 'there would be a couple of acres for every adult living in Britain. That would mean each family or group could have a reasonably sized smallholding of ten or twenty acres and learn once again to become self-sufficient.'

Sidney William Rawle was born (he believed reincarnated) on 1 October 1945 at Bridgwater, Somerset, the son of a sheep farmer on Exmoor who was forced to sell up and become a labourer. As a teenager in the late 1950s he became a beatnik, drifting to the artists' colony at St Ives in Cornwall, living on the beach and sleeping on the sea wall.

When he was sixteen he traced his mother, who had left home when he was six, to Slough, and moved to live with her there. Having worked variously as a cowman, wine waiter, cellarman and gravedigger, Rawle became a militant shop steward for the Amalgamated Engineering Union, in which role he organised a strike by Asian workers at a local factory and, in his free time, a love-in at the town's municipal gardens.

Rawle resented being described as a layabout, but would earn the ire of his young wife who complained that 'Sid seemed to think people who worked were out of their minds'. When he heard of a small village on the North Wales coast that had been abandoned after the war, he and twenty or so followers occupied it for several weeks before being evicted.

In 1971 Rawle helped Michael Eavis organise the first Glastonbury Festival, and was the only person to make a profit from it by cooking up a huge cauldron of fruit and vegetables discarded from Bristol market. The same year he started a commune on Dorinish, an island off the coast of Co. Mayo in Ireland, which the Beatle John Lennon bought as a hideaway in 1967. Rawle lived there until 1973.

His biggest battle involved Crown land at Windsor Great Park, where Rawle had helped establish a free (but illegal) Festival of the People on the royal meadows in 1972. Efforts by the Crown Estate to ban it proved unavailing (reportedly inducing fury in the festival's neighbour, the Duke of Edinburgh, as he balefully surveyed the scene from Windsor Castle), and in 1974 the festival was broken up by police, who made 200 arrests for drugs and violence.

The following year Rawle was jailed for three months for promoting a similar event in the *International Times*, the underground paper of which he had by then become editor. Freed after four weeks, he set about organising an alternative festival on a site at a derelict paratroopers' base at Watchfield, Oxfordshire, which went ahead in August 1975.

As Rawle, walkie-talkie in hand, took up position in his command post in the old control tower, uniformed police and drug squad officers moved in on some 3,000 flute-toting, sandal-shod hippies, some of whom were to be seen openly having sex. 'No one knows what's going on,' he confessed, 'and nobody cares.'

Rawle was a burly red-bearded six-footer with a mane of ginger hair, invariably clad in boiler suit, brightly coloured shawls and tapestry hat, with strings of beads and animal teeth rattling at his throat.

In 1997 the Halifax Building Society used a picture of him without his permission in an advertising campaign. The photograph dated from 1982 when Rawle was presiding at a baby-naming ceremony at the Stonehenge Free Festival. Above his image was a speech bubble with the slogan: 'Be Part Of Something Big, Man'. Rawle unsuccessfully tried to sue the company.

Ken Campbell, b. 1941, d. 2008

Ken Campbell, who has died aged sixty-six, was an actor, writer and director of wilful eccentricity, whose work in experimental theatre embraced such diverse projects as hammering a nail into his nose, a twelve-hour ('with intervals – they loved the intervals') adaptation of Robert Anton Wilson's conspiracy theory novel *Illuminatus!* and a translation of *Macbeth* into the pidgin English of Vanuatu, the South Seas island whose inhabitants worship the Duke of Edinburgh.

Perhaps his finest hour came when he issued a spoof press release in the aftermath of the Royal Shakespeare Company's success with Trevor Nunn's adaptation of *Nicholas Nickleby*, declaring that the company would henceforth be known as the Royal Dickens Company. This missive (signed 'love, Trev') convinced a surprising number of journalists, and enraged Nunn so much that he brought in the police to investigate.

SEPTEMBER

❧ 1st ❧

Doreen Valiente, b. 1922, d. 1999

Doreen Valiente, who has died aged seventy-seven, was one of Britain's most influential witches; hailed by many practising pagans as the mother of modern witchcraft, or 'Wicca', she herself declined any such title, describing herself as a practitioner of the Old Religion.

Her contribution to the body of Wiccan ritual cannot be overstated. She established the tone of modern witch rites. It amused her when she met people claiming to be 'hereditary witches' who quoted, as proof of their ancient lineage, rituals which she herself had written up in the 1950s.

She was born Doreen Dominy in 1922 in London. Her father's family came from Cerne Abbas in Dorset, home of the Giant, a priapic chalk man of enormous proportions. As a young child, Valiente claimed that she began to experience psychic episodes. By her late teens she was a practising clairvoyant.

She worked as a secretary by day, and spent her evenings immersed in the esoteric works of ritual magicians such as Aleister Crowley and theosophists such as Madame Blavatsky.

In 1944 Doreen married Casimiro Valiente, a refugee from the Spanish Civil War. The couple settled in Bournemouth, but the marriage was not a happy one. Casimiro was less enthused by the 'craft of the wise' than his spouse.

At the age of thirty, Doreen Valiente contacted Cecil Williamson, then owner of the Witches' Mill Museum, for information on witchcraft. Williamson passed her letter to Gerald Gardner who, after the repeal of the Witchcraft Act in 1951, proclaimed himself to be the museum's 'resident witch'.

She and Gardner met in 1952 in the New Forest home of the witch Dorothy Clutterbuck. Doreen Valiente recalled that she had misgivings about initiation, fearing she would be required to sell her soul to the Devil, but decided to go ahead anyway. 'To be willing to sell one's soul to the Devil,' she said, 'was a state of mind that living in Bournemouth readily induced.'

On being reassured that the 'Old Religion' admitted no devil-worship, Valiente joined Gardner's New Forest coven in 1953, eventually becoming High Priestess. It was then that she reworked and created a large body of ritual material for his *Book of Shadows*, a hotchpotch of ancient ritual on which he based his new Wiccan cult in the 1950s.

Though she and Gardner were only intermittently on speaking terms, Doreen

Valiente remained staunchly loyal to her initiator. She was never under any illusions about his sexual preferences, for example, describing him on more than one occasion as 'a thoroughly kinky old goat who was into flagellation'. At the same time she defended Gardner, and pointed out that the lash was an integral part of many ancient mystery religions.

In 1957, after falling out over the issue of secrecy, Doreen Valiente left Gardner's coven. In 1964 she began working with the hereditary witch Robert Cochrane. Valiente approved of Cochrane's use of rhythmic poetry, dance and chanting, but had little time for his fondness for sexual liaisons with coven members. She later left and in 1966 Cochrane committed suicide by taking an overdose of belladonna juice.

After the death of her husband in 1972, Doreen Valiente devoted herself full-time to writing about witchcraft. At the age of seventy-five, she developed a penchant for 'skunk', a strong variety of cannabis, which she smoked in a newly acquired 'bong', a kind of hubble-bubble. She also indulged more freely her interest in tantric sex, with an emerging passion for black leather. But to the last, Doreen Valiente maintained she was nothing more than 'an old-fashioned witch'.

⊰ 2nd ⊱

Christiaan Barnard, b. 1922, d. 2001

Christiaan Barnard, who has died aged seventy-eight, performed the world's first successful heart transplant, an achievement that brought him fame and fortune; he used his new-found celebrity to transform himself into an international playboy.

On 3 December 1967, in the operating theatre of the Groote Schuur Hospital in Cape Town, South Africa, Barnard transplanted the heart of Denise Darvall, a 25-year-old who had died in a car accident, into the chest of Louis Washkansky, a 55-year-old grocer. Washkansky lived for eighteen days before dying of pneumonia. Many more transplants followed, despite early complaints from some doctors that they achieved little other than feeding the vanity of surgeons.

Barnard himself was not averse to the acclaim he received and responded with boyish enthusiasm to his star status. He had an affair with Gina Lollobrigida, the Italian film star. At the age of sixty-three his girlfriend was a 22-year-old South African model, Karin Stezkorn; she became his third wife, but that marriage also ended in divorce, when, aged seventy-seven, he set out on a Viagra-fuelled affair with another, even younger, girlfriend. 'Anyone who dislikes publicity must be mad,' he said.

Christiaan Neethling Barnard was born on 8 November 1922 in the village of Beaufort West in South Africa, the son of a Dutch Reformed Church minister. He was educated at Beaufort West High School and then at Cape Town University medical school, from which he qualified in 1946 and where he took his MD degree in 1953. He entered general practice briefly before re-joining the university medical school's research staff.

His research interests were wide-ranging, if seldom attentive to questions of ethics. In 1960 he transplanted a second head on to a dog, having travelled to the Soviet

Union to discuss the process with surgeons who had already carried out the operation there.

In 1974 he was the first to demonstrate a technique to give heart disease victims a 'piggy back' second heart, and in June 1977 became the first surgeon to transplant a live animal heart – a baboon's – into a patient.

She was a woman aged twenty-five who died shortly after the operation. The woman's husband claimed that if the operation had not been carried out she would have lived. Barnard retorted that he performed the operation as a doctor – to save a life. But of heart transplants in general, he said: 'For me, the goal of medicine is not the prolongation of life; it is improvement in the quality of life that is important.' He was an enthusiastic supporter of euthanasia.

Barnard regarded his South African background as a positive advantage in his work. 'We didn't have the legal restraints that exist in America,' he said in 1996. 'I didn't even ask the hospital authorities if I could do that first transplant – I just told them after I'd done it. Can you imagine that happening anywhere else in the world?'

On 2 January 1968, less than a month after his first success, Barnard performed his second heart transplant. The recipient was Philip Blaiberg, a retired dentist aged fifty-eight, and the donor Clive Haupt, a 24-year-old coloured man who had died from a stroke. The transplant of the heart of a coloured man to a white in South Africa aroused racial controversy. Blaiberg left hospital seventy-four days after the operation and lived for nineteen months.

After divorcing in 1970 the first Mrs Barnard claimed that her husband had reacted to sudden fame by spending most of his time gazing in a mirror. He told her: 'You must stay in the shadow – everyone is interested solely in me.' Within a year he had married Barbara Zoeller, then nineteen. Barnard's private life, and public announcements, continued to raise eyebrows, even after arthritis – from which he had suffered since his thirties – caused him to give up surgery in 1983.

As he grew older, he became obsessed with the idea of prolonging youthful activities. He described ageing as 'abnormal' and conducted research into injecting animal embryo cells into older people to restore their fading body functions. Barnard admitted to having several injections himself: 'I have had heart, lung, testes, brain. I don't know what they're doing to me but it's worth a try.'

Barnard made no great intellectual claims, maintaining that 'stupid doctors become surgeons – all we have to do is cut things out, put things in and sew things up'.

His favourite book was *Gone with the Wind*, and he was also fond of women, wine, birdwatching and the Greek islands. He died in Cyprus; the cause of death was thought to be a heart attack.

⊰ **3rd** ⊱

Diana Lady Delamere, b. 1913, d. 1987

Diana Lady Delamere, who has died aged seventy-four, became the central figure in what has popularly been portrayed as one of the *crimes passionnel* of the century when her elderly second husband Sir 'Jock' Delves Broughton, 11th Bt, was tried in Kenya for the murder of her lover, the 22nd Earl of Erroll, in 1941.

Broughton was acquitted at the trial, which caused a major sensation even though it took place in the middle of the Second World War, but committed suicide the following year. His widow, who subsequently married twice more, took to her grave the full story of who was responsible for the body in the Buick on the Nairobi Road.

The case inspired James Fox's book *White Mischief* (adapted as a feature film), and also the television play *The Happy Valley*. Fox's fellow sleuth into the mystery, Cyril Connolly, who had been at Eton with the dashing Joss Erroll, described Lady Delamere as 'one of those creamy ash blondes of the period with a passion for clothes and jewels, both worn to perfection, and for enjoying herself and bringing out enjoyment in others'.

Quite apart from her familiar role as the femme fatale of the Erroll case, Diana Delamere was a woman of considerable fascination. She rode fearlessly to hounds, flew with Amy Johnson, fished the sea for marlin, owned a string of racehorses, shrewdly managed vast estates and eventually became the doyenne of white Kenyan society.

Born in 1913, she was the daughter of Seymour Caldwell, an Old Etonian gambler of The Red House, Hove.

In November 1940, in South Africa, she married Sir Henry John ('Jock') Delves Broughton, a Cheshire baronet thirty years her senior with whom she had emigrated from England. Immediately afterwards they settled in the so-called 'White Highlands' of Kenya, where she soon met the 22nd Earl of Erroll, hereditary Lord High Constable of Scotland, Chief of the Hays, Military Secretary of the East Africa Command and a philanderer notorious even by the louche standards of the 'Happy Valley'.

By Christmas Lord Erroll and Lady Broughton were embroiled in a passionate love affair. On 18 January, Lady Broughton's lover and husband confronted one another. 'Diana tells me she is in love with you,' was the Baronet's opening gambit according to the evidence of Lord Erroll's garden boy. 'Well, she has never told me that but I am frightfully in love with her,' replied the Earl.

On 23 January Broughton dined with his wife and Erroll at the Muthaiga Club, and, in the course of a bizarre evening, proposed a toast: 'I wish them every happiness and may their union be blessed with an heir. To Diana and Joss.'

In the early hours of the following morning two milk boys discovered Erroll's corpse. The following month Lady Broughton and her husband went off on a shooting safari into the Southern Masai Reserve.

On the first day of Broughton's trial for murder in May 1941, his wife made a memorable entrance into the court attired in an elegant widow's ensemble of black hat, veil and a profusion of diamonds. She left the court only once in the three-week trial, when Erroll's ear, preserved in a jar, was handed round as a exhibit.

Following Broughton's acquittal and suicide, she married Gilbert Colvile, an extensive cattle-rancher at Naivasha, Kenya. They were divorced in 1955 and later that year she married the 4th Lord Delamere, who died in 1979.

Lady Delamere continued to live in semi-regal state at Soysambu, Elmenteita, where her father-in-law, the 3rd Lord Delamere, had pioneered the gilded exodus to the heady freedom of the White Highlands.

✠ 4th ✠

Jeffrey Bernard, b. 1932, d. 1997

Jeffrey Bernard, the laureate of Soho who has died aged sixty-five, won a devoted following for his 'Low Life' column in *The Spectator*, and a wider band of admirers when Keith Waterhouse brilliantly adapted that mournfully funny epic of self-destruction for the stage.

Jeffrey Bernard is Unwell opened in 1989, with Peter O'Toole as Bernard, and enjoyed a triumphant year-long run (with Tom Conti and then James Bolam taking over the lead).

It might seem strange that a column which presented a catalogue of alcoholic and sexual disaster should have so delighted the bourgeoisie. Bernard himself attributed his success to his readers' *Schadenfreude*. 'If you're living where the grass is greener,' he explained, 'it must be reassuring to glance occasionally at the rubbish dump.'

For years he had consecrated his days to the Coach and Horses in Greek Street, where he would drink vodka, lime and soda. (After he developed diabetes he cut out the lime.) The most promising time for conversation was between 11.30 a.m. and 1.00 p.m. – after two double vodkas, but before the sixth.

'I absolutely loathe getting drunk,' Bernard would say. 'It's an inevitable accident that happens every day.' The same *faux-naiveté* appeared in his relations with women. Somehow – he couldn't really explain why – he seemed to make the silly creatures unhappy.

His wives and mistresses were more forthright: 'You make me sick,' was their refrain in *Jeffrey Bernard Is Unwell*. Bernard could only wonder at their failure to heed the warning signs – 'I mean,' he said, 'you can see a train when it's coming.'

The fourth of five children, he was born Jerry Joseph Bernard at Hampstead on 27 May 1932. Jerry, as he still was, was only seven when his father died, leaving debts. His mother gamely struggled to keep up a stylish front. 'My mother looked like Ava Gardner,' Bernard would remember. 'I actually fancied her when I was sixteen.'

He attended a number of prep schools where his first name provoked mockery, being associated with the dreaded Germans; so Jerry became Jeffrey.

Soho, to which his brothers introduced him at the age of fourteen, 'was magic, like walking out of Belsen into Disneyland'. Soon Bernard had begun his career as a full-time truant from life. He revelled in the cast-list of Bohemia: 'Francis Bacon, Lucian Freud, Colquhoun and McBryde, Sid the Swimmer, Ironfoot Jack, Nina Hamnett,

Muriel Belcher, Gaston Berlemont, Frank Norman, and a hundred more.'

To survive he offered limited favours to the homosexual artist John Minton. There was never much doubt, however, of his own sexual orientation, or of his powerful appeal to women. 'He was stunning, and surly – James Dean before James Dean,' one of his early girlfriends remembered.

National Service intervened in 1950. A trooper with the 14/20 King's Hussars, he tried to sell his tank's petrol before going AWOL for four months. Through the intercession of one of his brothers his punishment was light and he was discharged.

Bernard celebrated his freedom by marrying, though it lasted only four months. He kept himself in drink through jobs as a dishwasher, a fairground boxer, a navvy and a miner.

As the years passed it was increasingly as an alcoholic blur, so that when Bernard was commissioned to write an autobiography, he had to place an advertisement asking if anyone could tell him what he had been doing between 1960 and 1974.

Undoubtedly the most significant event of that period was in 1964, when the poet Elizabeth Smart secured him a racing column in *Queen*. Bernard immediately found his style with a mixture of tips, anecdotes and chit-chat. He worked at his journalism with more dedication than he cared to admit and he soon found slots – usually short-lived – in the *Daily Mirror* and *Town*.

In 1970 he began a column in *Sporting Life*. Professionally, it was a brilliant success; as one appreciative reader wrote, he was 'the first journalist to understand the average punter – self-destructive, paranoiac, a loser, yet richly human'. But to Bernard a racecourse was 'simply an alfresco piss-up'. Eventually the paper sacked him for what the editor described as an 'unpardonable exhibition at the point-to-point dinner'.

There was another professional breakthrough in 1972, when Bernard began to write for the *New Statesman*, for which he produced some of his best work. After three years he was lured away by *The Spectator*, which set him up as its television critic. It was soon necessary to find a replacement – Bernard was far too drunk to watch television regularly – but Alexander Chancellor, the editor, determined to keep him in another role. The 'Low Life' column began in August 1978.

Bernard's finances improved – without, however, impairing his facility for cadging on friends. He also attracted the unwelcome attentions of the dreaded 'Taxwoman'. And in 1986 no fewer than nine policemen and three Customs men descended on the Coach and Horses to arrest him for making a book without a licence. He was fined £200 and ordered to pay £75 costs.

By the end of the 1960s he was six-to-four favourite for the next Soho death, but the opposition constantly made it to the finishing post before him. For long the doctors remained confounded. 'This, gentlemen,' the specialist at the Middlesex Hospital would say, 'is Mr Jeffrey Bernard, who closes his veins each day with sixty cigarettes and then opens them again with a bottle of vodka.'

A message was planned for his memorial service: 'I'm sorry I cannot be with you today due to foreseen circumstances.'

⊰ 5th ⊱

Jean Rook, b. 1931, d. 1991

Jean Rook, the journalist, who has died aged fifty-nine, revelled in being 'Britain's bitchiest, best-known, loved and loathed woman journalist'; she also owned up to having been the model for *Private Eye*'s female columnist, Glenda Slagg.

In her weekly column in the *Daily Express*, crammed with superfluous punctuation and an excruciatingly alliterative mixture of mangled metaphors, she wrote exactly what she thought of those in public life. She was nothing if not inconsistent, and her never less than outrageous column became the vehicle for wild swings of opinion – a vacillation she considered necessary to reflect the public mood.

Thus, one week Rook would hold Prince Philip in favour; the next she would think nothing of describing him as 'a snappish OAP, with a temper like an arthritic corgi'.

The Duchess of York was treated with similar schizophrenic hyperbole. 'Sarah Ferguson looks like an unbrushed red setter struggling to get out of a hand-knitted potato sack,' wrote the rancorous Rook – only to temper her description with the revelation that she was also 'great fun, powerfully sexy, tremendously boisterous and thrilling to men'. As for the Duke of York his taste, 'let's face it, is about as subtle as a sat-on whoopee cushion'.

Alan Clark, b. 1928, d. 1999

Alan Clark, who has died aged seventy-one, was an irrepressible free spirit on the Conservative benches with a habit for outspokenness that ensured he never gained high office.

Clark was renowned not only for frequent public rows, but also for the candid and outrageous content of his very readable diaries. He said things of a kind many readers kept to themselves.

The *Diaries* gave a surprisingly open account of his own vanity, hopes, lusts, political ambitions and amused contempt for his fellow politicians and constituents. He also revealed an anxiety about becoming unattractive to women in old age and a fear of sickness. ('I am now convinced I have got cancer of the jaw,' he wrote erroneously in 1987, after looking in the shaving mirror.) His jaundiced attitude and cynical laughter were reminiscent of Philip Larkin.

There were endless surprises in Clark's character. He was a country landowner but was repelled by hunting, a loving husband yet a flagrant womaniser, an admirer of the martial qualities of the SS but a stout defender of Britain's capacity to defend her liberties.

Much of Clark's character was to be explained by his similarity to his father, the art historian Kenneth Clark. To him he owed his money, sharp intellect and breeding.

Alan Kenneth McKenzie Clark was born on 13 April 1928. The family's roots were bourgeois – Clark's grandfather had made his fortune from cotton. Saltwood, the boyhood home of *The Daily Telegraph* journalist W.F. Deedes, was bought 'for a song' in 1953. Alan spent his childhood miserably 'behind the green baize door' from his father. He hated Eton, receiving 'an early introduction to human cruelty, treachery and extreme physical hardship'.

During 185 days' National Service in the Household Cavalry, Clark acquired a third share in his first Jaguar and a taste for strong language. In 1948 he went up to Christ Church, Oxford, to read History. After taking his degree, he combined dinners at the Inner Temple with a colourful career as a 'runner' for a used-car dealer in Warren Street.

When unemployed he would 'nip round to Annabel's where the barman would cash a cheque for £50'. He was called to the Bar in 1955, but never practised. Instead, the super-fit Clark became involved with the Festival Ballet, and in 1957 passed himself off as a wrestler to gain experience of Russia.

In July 1958, now thirty, he caused a stir by marrying sixteen-year-old Jane Beuttler, whom he had courted for two years, collecting her from convent school in a Cadillac. His bride declared: 'I am not even nervous. I intend to have a lot of fun in my married life.' So did her husband. A former girlfriend turned up on the honeymoon in Positano.

In 1961 Clark published his first book of military history, *The Donkeys, A History of the BEF in 1915*. It heaped obloquy on British generals – particularly Haig – for their readiness to sacrifice lives to an unimaginative strategy and provided much material for Joan Littlewood's musical *Oh! What a Lovely War*. Clark enhanced his reputation as a military historian with *The Fall of Crete*. In 1965 he published *Barbarossa: The Russo–German Conflict 1941–45* and in 1973 *Aces High: The war in the air over the Western Front*.

But he was never far from controversy. In 1984, in *The Daily Telegraph*, he contrasted the 'inefficiency' of Eisenhower's army in Normandy with the 'physical splendour' of the SS infantry who resisted it. In 1993 he outraged many by claiming that Churchill lost the Empire through not making peace with Hitler in 1941.

Politically, Clark yearned to be in the Cabinet. In the late 1960s, armed with £30,000 in royalties from *Barbarossa* and convinced that Labour was ruining the country, he sought a seat, despite his father's view of politics as 'degrading'.

He spurned Swindon in 1969, considering it unwinnable. Edward Heath then reputedly barred him from the candidates' list as a reactionary. It was 1972 before Clark was chosen to fight Plymouth, Sutton. Elected in February 1974, he held the seat for eighteen years, developing little affection for the constituency or most of the worthies he had to humour.

Singled out by whips as 'the most dangerous man in the Commons', Clark was an early supporter of Mrs Thatcher, not just because he thought her the most sexually attractive woman in politics ('Eyes, wrists ... ankles!'). He always took his own line. He voted against reforms to the Anglican liturgy, and spoke strongly against abortion.

Convinced he had no prospect of office, he launched an unsuccessful bid for the ownership of *The Spectator*. But after the 1983 election, Mrs Thatcher, admiring his stand on the Falklands and his rakish demeanour, took a risk and made him junior employment minister.

Already fifty-five, he was not cut out for Whitehall and by the end of his first day was convinced that his private secretary Jenny Easterbrook, 'her sexuality tightly controlled', thought him 'an uncouth chauvinist lout' likely to last weeks rather than months.

In 1985 Clark – motto 'only servants apologise' – outraged the Foreign Office by describing sub-Saharan Africa as 'Bongo-Bongo Land'; the remark was made in private, but leaked.

The previous October, Clark had what he took as a providential escape from death. He and his wife decided on a whim to leave the party conference in Brighton a day early. That night the IRA bombed the Grand Hotel. Clark noted apocalyptically: 'What a coup for the Paddys. The whole thing has a smell of the Tet Offensive.'

In January 1986 Mrs Thatcher made him Minister of State for Trade. Douglas Hurd advised the Prime Minister not to appoint Clark because of 'Bongo-Bongo Land'. (His own characterisation of Hurd was: 'Might as well have a corncob up his arse.') President Bongo of Gabon jokingly sent Clark a poster reading: '*Gagnez avec Bongo!*' which he displayed at his 1987 adoption meeting.

The 1987 campaign gave Clark new scope to break ranks. Mrs Thatcher moved him sideways to become Defence Procurement Minister and he devoted his energies to undermining Tom King, his former boss at Employment, whom he described as 'indecisive, blustering, bullying, stupid and cunningly cautious even when he didn't need to be'.

Clark was an outspoken supporter of Mrs Thatcher when Sir Geoffrey Howe dramatically resigned and Heseltine challenged for the leadership. After her resignation, Clark was keen to write her official biography, but she preferred first to publish her own memoirs.

Clark had expected to 'go out' with Mrs Thatcher, but John Major reappointed him with a Privy Counsellorship. Hoping for a peerage, Clark decided not to stand for the Commons again. Yet after becoming embroiled in the arms-to-Iraq 'Matrix-Churchill' affair (when he conceded he had been 'economical with the actualité') Clark tried to revive his parliamentary career, applying for the Newbury nomination as a Eurosceptic Major supporter. He was blackballed by Sir Norman Fowler, the party chairman, amid nervousness about the impending publication of his *Diaries*, for which Weidenfeld had bid £150,000.

On publication, colleagues were devastated to find that Clark regarded them – after his publisher had toned down the language – as 'spastics' or 'creeps'. Kenneth Clarke was dismissed as a 'pudgy puffball', Heseltine as 'jerky, wild-eyed, zombie' and a 'charlatan' and Sir Peter Morrison, Mrs Thatcher's hapless PPS, as 'sozzled'.

He also discussed frankly his sexual experiences before and outside marriage. He recalled the halcyon summer of 1955 when he was 'running' three girls within half a mile, one of whom – a nurse named Marye – gave him 'the ultimate sexual experience' while her matron banged on the door.

He fantasised about his female civil servants and girls on the Folkestone train, confessed himself 'in love' with his 1983 Labour opponent and hinted at a spectacular range of sexual escapades. Yet he confided that his wife was his personal rock. 'I could not, never would wound her, the best human being in the entire world,' he wrote.

Clark's most scandalous revelation concerned a 'coven' of three women, Valerie, Alison and Josephine; he disclosed the temptation, at least, to bed all three at the Ritz after dinner at Brooks' the day he was made a minister in 1983. What he omitted was that Valerie was the wife of a judge who had emigrated to South Africa, and the two girls her daughters. In 1994 she went public in the *News of the World*, stating that her affair with Clark lasted fourteen years, even though she knew well before the end that he had slept with her daughters. The judge, his wife and Josephine flew to London to confront Clark, hiring the publicist Max Clifford on Lady (Benvenida) Buck's recommendation. Clark eventually conceded: 'I deserve horsewhipping.'

In 1995, even to his own surprise, he decided to try Parliament once more, securing the candidature at Kensington and Chelsea only after the deselection of Sir Nicholas Scott. In May 1997 he returned to the Commons, aged sixty-nine.

Clark was constantly aware of mortality. 'A hesitation in the tail rotor and the frail little machine would have crashed,' he wrote in 1990 after a helicopter flight. 'I draw strength from reflections such as this. Because if God wants to plunge in the knife, then He can do so – at any time.'

⊰ 6th ⊱

Luciano Pavarotti, b. 1935, d. 2007

Luciano Pavarotti, who has died aged seventy-one, can safely be called the best-known tenor of all time, acclaimed by a public far beyond the select circle of operagoers.

Indeed those who promoted Pavarotti realised very quickly that, with his appealing voice and larger-than-life personality, he could become the darling of millions. Already widely known and admired by 1990, the selection of his disc of 'Nessun Dorma', from Puccini's *Turandot* as the theme song of that year's football World Cup brought him new legions of fans. People who had never thought to hear a note of opera were suddenly humming the tune and adoring Pavarotti.

The 'Three Tenors' concerts he performed with Carreras and Domingo, the last of which took place in Bath in 2003, reinforced Pavarotti's appeal, as did his appearances with artists from the world of pop. Yet although these arena and open-air concerts gained him the acclaim of the masses, he never prostituted his art or lost sight of a career in serious opera.

Pavarotti – known affectionately to his fans as 'Big Lucy' – was still adventurous enough in 1991 to lay his career on the line by climbing that Everest for the operatic tenor, the title role in Verdi's *Otello*, albeit only in concert form, and proved in his performance that he had the innate ability to fulfil its extraordinary demands.

Pavarotti's immense size – he was constantly dieting, but never to any lasting effect – did not give much credence to his acting, but that larger-than-life form was just what appealed to the general public. As his huge frame stood on the platform, with the familiar white handkerchief held out in one hand, and as the golden tenor poured forth its caressing sound, audiences willingly capitulated.

Luciano Pavarotti was born on 12 October 1935 at Modena. His exact contemporary in the same town was the future soprano Mirella Freni (with whom Pavarotti often appeared). They shared the same wet nurse, and Freni used to joke: 'You can see who got most of the milk!' At the age of twelve Luciano contracted tetanus. He was in a coma for two weeks, and was twice given the last rites. 'When you come through something like that,' he remarked later, 'you are definitely a survivor. That is why I think you see me optimistic all the time.'

Luciano's father, who worked in a bakery, was an accomplished tenor and encouraged his son to become a singer.

He studied with Arrigo Pola and Ettore Campogalliani over a period of six years, then won an international competition at Reggio Emilia, which gave him the opportunity to make his stage debut there as Rodolfo in *La Bohème* in 1961. Two years later he appeared for the first time at Covent Garden in the same role, taking over from an indisposed Giuseppe di Stefano.

In 1965 he toured Australia as partner to Joan Sutherland with the Sutherland-Williamson company. It was at about this time that he signed as an exclusive Decca artist, and began his long and lucrative partnership in the studios with Sutherland. They appeared together in numerous operas, most notably *Rigoletto; La Traviata; Lucia di Lammermoor; L'elisir d'amore; La Fille du Régiment* (in which Pavarotti's successive high Cs in the tenor aria was a singular and exciting feat) and *Norma*.

Pavarotti made his La Scala debut in 1965, and sang there in the Verdi *Requiem* in 1967 to mark the centenary of Toscanini's birth. Karajan was the conductor and a film was made, showing the young tenor looking almost shy, a marked difference from his later persona.

His first appearance at the Metropolitan, New York, was in 1968. Although never attached to this house or to La Scala, he appeared at both with reasonable frequency. He also became a regular – though increasingly infrequent – visitor to Covent Garden. He appeared in the house as an endearing Nemorino in *L'elisir d'amore* in 1990. Although by then his stage movement was somewhat restricted by his bulk, Pavarotti made an appealing character out of the lovelorn youth.

It had been his New York agent and publicist, Herbert Breslin, who had seen the potential of Pavarotti as a popular star and who had diligently promoted a new image for the singer throughout the 1980s. This project led to an appearance in a somewhat ludicrous film, *Yes, Giorgio* (1981).

But Pavarotti soon became the highest-paid singer in the history of opera. In 2001 he appeared in court in Italy charged with evading tax to the tune of £14 million between 1989 and 1995, but was later acquitted.

In 1981 Pavarotti published an autobiography, *My Own Story*. The book included frank cameos of the singer by some of his notable contemporaries. It also recalled the occasion, in 1975, when an aeroplane bringing him back to Italy from New York crashed on landing at Milan airport. Before this incident, the singer had been suffering from mild depression, and he wrote in his book: 'It was as though God had grabbed me by the neck and said, "You are so indifferent about life? Here, take a look at death and tell me how you like that!" If that was His plan, it worked.'

***

Professor Michael Argyle, b. 1925, d. 2002

Professor Michael Argyle, who has died aged seventy-seven, was a social psychologist noted for his studies of what makes for happiness.

In 1996 he published *The Social Psychology of Leisure*, a book in which he put forward the view that the best guarantee of long-term happiness was 'serious leisure'; that is, a hobby or activity that involves the 'whole being'.

Himself an enthusiastic Scottish country dancer, he ranked dancing top of the list of activities most likely to elicit happiness. Watching television was, he said, because of its essential passivity, one of the activities least likely to bring it about; on the other hand he pointed out that it was often the focus for family gatherings and that soap operas could produce a 'sort of fantasy social life'. In 1998, after more research, he went further: soap fans, he had found, were quantifiably happier than the rest of the population.

≼ 7th ≽

Mobutu Sese Seko, b. 1930, d. 1997

Mobutu Sese Seko, who has died aged sixty-six, ruled Zaire for thirty-two years, amassing a colossal private fortune as his country drifted into chaos and despair.

Yet when Mobutu came to power in 1965, Zaire (or the Congo, as it was known until 1971) appeared as a particularly promising model of development. Bigger than the United Kingdom, France, Germany, Italy, Spain and Poland combined, the Congo was endowed with rich resources of cobalt and copper, as well as with its own gold, diamonds, bauxite and zinc. In 1965 the country's foreign reserves stood at £90 million, and in the late 1960s the value of copper soared.

But when copper prices began to fall in the early 1970s, the financial reserves were soon exhausted. After that estimates of Mobutu's private fortune tended to coincide with the figure given for the country's foreign debt. By the 1990s both statistics exceeded £3.3 billion.

Mobutu acquired houses in Belgium, Italy, Spain, France, the Ivory Coast and the Central African Republic. In Zaire, he built a pink marble palace at Gbadolite, his ancestral village deep in the equatorial rainforests 600 miles north of Kinshasa.

Known as 'Versailles in the jungle', it boasted an airport capable of taking the biggest jets. Whenever the President left, the generators at Gbadolite were switched off, and the wilderness resumed its sway.

Mobutu would cruise down the Congo in a decaying Belgian steamer, occasionally embarking to bestow gifts on bemused villagers along the bank. A French journalist who witnessed the scene was reminded of Kurtz in Conrad's *Heart of Darkness*: 'His intelligence was perfectly lucid, but his soul was mad.'

Meanwhile Zaire was tumbling into ruin. Copper prices collapsed further in 1975, and within two years the country held the world's highest per capita debt. For a time the IMF provided support, but in the 1980s the currency went into free fall. Roughly at par with the dollar in 1982, the zaire was valued ten years later at 7,500 to the dollar, and by 1993 at 2.6 million.

When it was suggested to Mobutu that he should use his own fortune to relieve his people's sufferings, he observed, justly enough, that they could never afford to repay him. Not for nothing did he keep Machiavelli's *The Prince* beside his bed.

If 200-odd ethnic groups made Zaire difficult to govern, it also ensured that the opposition was disunited. And Mobutu was always careful to retain control of the treasury, the media and the security services.

Mobutu was shrewd, too, in playing the anti-Communist card. He endeared himself to the Americans especially, by allowing Zaire to be used as a base for CIA-sponsored raids against Angola. Neither the United States nor Zaire's European allies ventured on the one step that might really have embarrassed Mobutu – freezing his assets abroad. In consequence Mobutu survived three decades without proper elections.

Joseph-Desire Mobutu was born on 30 October 1930 at Lisala in the north of the Belgian Congo, the son of a hotel cook. Educated at mission schools, at eighteen he was selected to attend the Institut d'Etudes Sociales de l'Etat in Brussels.

After a year he returned to the Congo to join the colonial army, the Force Publique, as a clerk in its finance department. He rose to the rank of sergeant-major – the highest attainable for a native.

In 1958 he joined the Mouvement National Congolais as a supporter of Patrice Lumumba, who ran its militant wing. When Lumumba was imprisoned, Mobutu was sent to represent him at a Brussels conference on the Congo's future. Mobutu's proposals for a strongly centralised state were adopted, and after the Congo became independent in 1960 President Kasavubu made him Defence Secretary in Lumumba's government.

This meant Mobutu was a key figure in the power struggle between Kasavubu and Lumumba. When the president dismissed the prime minister, Lumumba refused to budge. Mobutu, who had contacts with the CIA, removed both Kasavubu and Lumumba from office. The army, he announced, would rule for the rest of the year.

When Lumumba attempted to get away to his supporters in the north, he was seized by Mobutu's men, trussed up like a chicken, and taken to a military camp. In February 1961 he was killed, 'trying to escape'. Mobutu restored Kasavubu as president before, in 1965, assuming control himself.

Having instituted a civilian government, Mobutu systematically undermined its powers, placing his own decrees outside the jurisdiction of Parliament. 'All rights guaranteed by the constitution will be respected,' he promised – and then ordered the public hanging of four Cabinet ministers.

For years Mobutu succeeded in putting down internal unrest – though in 1977 he had to be saved by the French, who provided aircraft which flew in Moroccan troops to repel an Angolan-backed invasion of the breakaway province of Katanga.

It was not until the end of the Cold War, in the early 1990s, that Mobutu's position came under serious threat. America, France and Belgium withdrew aid, and President Bush wrote three times asking him to step down. At home inflation and riots forced Mobutu to talk of establishing a multi-party system. He called a national conference on democracy, which in August 1992 imposed Etienne Tshisekedi as prime minister.

The conference gave way to the High Council of the Republic. In December 1992 it produced a constitution which reduced the president to a figurehead. Mobutu responded by sending his guard to surround the prime minister's office, sacking Tshisekedi's Cabinet, and refusing to authorise the new constitution. Zaire was left with two governments.

In January 1993 the High Court judged Mobutu guilty of treason, and spoke of locking him up. The president, still in command of his forces, sneered at the opposition, but it was becoming harder to enforce his will. In 1994 eastern Zaire was destabilised when a million Hutu refugees fled into the country from Rwanda to escape the genocidal attacks of the Tutsi.

In 1996 the situation further deteriorated when the Tutsis swept into the east of Zaire. The Zairian army proved incapable of stopping them; 'The only thing worse than being attacked by the Tutsis,' remarked one victim, 'is being defended by the Zairian army.'

With Mobutu away in Switzerland being treated for cancer, the Presidential Guard remained hors de combat. By October 1996 the Tutsi rising had turned into a full-blown political rebellion against the dictator, led by Laurent Kabila.

Mobutu returned in an attempt to muster his forces, but this time the game was up. In May 1997 he was forced to flee to Morocco.

8th

Leni Riefenstahl, b. 1902, d. 2003

Leni Riefenstahl, who has died aged 101, was perhaps the most talented female cinema director of the twentieth century; her celebration of Nazi Germany in film ensured that she was certainly the most infamous.

The last surviving member of the cultural elite of the Third Reich, Leni Riefenstahl was for fifty years vilified by successive generations as Hitler's film-maker, a propagandist whose images – notably her films of the Nuremberg rallies – exulted in German strength and glorified the Nazi creed of racial purity.

Her films were the more dangerous, it was held, because of their dazzling beauty. They were films that radiated such love of the subject matter that many felt they could have been made only by someone who shared Hitler's goals.

Leni Riefenstahl spent half of a very long life trying to counter these charges.

It was in the mid-1930s, before the outbreak of war or the revelation of the Holocaust, that she made the two films on which her moral and artistic reputation rests. She was then principally known as a film actress, and Hitler was an ardent admirer. He and Goebbels had grasped the importance of film to their plans for 'public enlightenment', and invited Leni Riefenstahl to record a Nazi Party rally at Nuremberg.

Her first attempt, *Victory of Faith* (1933), was never released, for several of the leading players were purged by Hitler shortly after the rally. Undaunted, she recorded the next one. The result, *Triumph of the Will* (1935), stands with *Battleship Potemkin* (1925) as the most masterly propaganda film ever made.

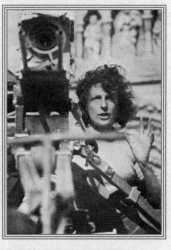

Leni Riefenstahl orchestrated a crew of 120 and more than thirty cameras (many of which were mounted on special tracks) to overcome brilliantly the static, repetitive nature of the rally. She flooded the screen with contrast and movement.

Among the film's enduring images is that of the Messianic descent, through clouds, of the Führer's Junkers, the shadows of the aircraft passing over the crowd below. Memorable, too, are shots of the massed banners and torches in the narrow streets, the image of the sun resting in Hitler's palm, and the long walk through the ranks of the SS by the trinity of Himmler, the SA leader Lutze and the Führer himself. Above all, there was the sense of the imposition of the will of one man on a million spectators.

A year later she began to make her second remarkable film, a record of the 1936 Olympic Games, held in Berlin. The result, *Olympia*, was even more technically dazzling (if more stylised and less powerful) than *Triumph of the Will*. Cameras were mounted beneath balloons, on rafts, in trenches and under saddles to try to capture the effort of performance.

On the outbreak of war, Leni Riefenstahl enlisted as a reporter; but after witnessing a massacre of Polish civilians, she refused to make propaganda films, and spun out the war in abortive projects, notably a version of D'Albert's opera *Tiefland*. By 1944 her stock with her admirer Hitler had so diminished that she could not stop her brother being sent to die on the Russian Front.

After the war, Leni Riefenstahl was kept under arrest for four years by the Allies, but she was then twice cleared by special courts of having been a Nazi. Controversy clung to her, although none of the more sensational charges (that she had knowingly used concentration camp inmates as film extras; had encouraged the Polish massacre she had witnessed; that she had been Hitler's lover) was substantiated. Her reputation, however, meant that she could never make another film.

Helene Bertha Amelie Riefenstahl was born in Berlin on 22 August 1902. While studying painting at Berlin's Kunstakademie she took lessons in acting and dancing.

She gave her first recital in 1923, and soon came to the notice of the producer Max Reinhardt. With his patronage, she made a highly successful tour of Europe, but while on stage in Prague she suffered damage to her knee, abruptly ending her dancing career.

A despondent Leni Riefenstahl then happened to see one of the alpine dramas filmed by Arnold Fanck. He was pioneering a genre that was to become extremely popular in Germany, tales of courage, set against mountain scenery. She engineered a meeting with Fanck, who was much taken with her beauty. He wrote a film especially for her, *The Holy Mountain* (1926), about a dancer turned mountain climber. It made her a star in Germany.

Films such as *The White Hell of Piz Palu* (1929) and *SOS Iceberg* (1933), made under highly dangerous circumstances on location rather than in a studio, maintained her popularity. Yet she might have been a still bigger star, had she not lost the role of a cabaret singer to the unknown actress who lived in the flat next to hers. The film was *The Blue Angel*; the actress Marlene Dietrich.

In 1932 Leni Riefenstahl turned to directing. Her first film, *The Blue Light*, a fantasy in which urban rationalism indirectly kills an untamed spirit of the mountains, won the Silver Medal at the Venice Biennale.

It was to an African example of this uncontaminated spirit that Leni Riefenstahl was drawn during the years after the Second World War. On reading Hemingway's *The Green Hills of Africa*, she found herself enamoured of the image of the continent presented by him, and in 1956 went to Kenya, intending to make a film about the modern slave trade.

The project collapsed, and she was also badly injured in a car accident, but in the meantime she had found a new passion: the Nuba tribesmen of Sudan. Leni Riefenstahl made a number of lengthy visits to a people comparatively untouched by the modern world. Knowing nothing of her past, they accepted her as a friend. The result was several fine books of photographs.

Leni Riefenstahl remained vital, active and unrepentant into extreme old age. At seventy she learnt to scuba-dive. Accompanied by her lover, Horst Kettner, a man forty years her junior, she continued to travel (usually clad in Versace leggings) into her late nineties.

⇥ 9th ⇤

Edward Teller, b. 1908, d. 2003

Edward Teller, who has died aged ninety-five, was the Hungarian-born physicist commonly called the 'father of the hydrogen bomb'.

A man of enormous intellect, and one of the most controversial scientific figures of the twentieth century, Teller made important contributions to the field of quantum mechanics as well as nuclear physics; but it was as an ardent 'Cold War Warrior' that he entered the popular mind.

Teller's short stature, artificial foot, thick European accent, glowering beetle-browed features, intense grey eyes and combative pronouncements led to a perception of him as the quintessentially sinister and fatalistic scientist. The malevolent Dr Strangelove of Stanley Kubrick's apocalyptic 1963 film was a conscious amalgamation of Teller and the German rocket scientist Wernher von Braun.

Teller himself was consistently content to embrace the possibility of nuclear destruction rather than Communism, which he preached against with evangelical fervour. After the atomic detonations at Hiroshima and Nagasaki, few scientists were as eager as he to pursue the goal of thermo-nuclear weapons. With the research guided by Teller, the first American hydrogen bomb was successfully exploded on Eniwetok in 1952.

Edward Teller was born on 15 January 1908 in Budapest, the son of a prosperous lawyer. After studying Chemical Engineering at the Technische Hochschule in Karlsruhe, Germany, his interest was aroused by quantum mechanics, and he continued his studies at the University of Munich and afterwards in Leipzig, obtaining a doctorate in Theoretical Physics in 1930. While in Munich, Teller lost his right foot in a tram accident and thereafter walked with an artificial prosthesis.

Still apolitical when Hitler came to power, Teller quickly recognised that it would be impossible for a Jew to pursue an academic career in Germany. He emigrated to America, where he became increasingly involved with nuclear physics, contributing significantly to the understanding of radioactive decay.

By 1939 scientists had become aware that the enforced disintegration of uranium isotopes could produce a chain reaction of potentially vast proportions. When the Second World War broke out the military applications of this discovery assumed terrifying significance; the race to build the atomic bomb began.

The Americans formulated two main paths to the atomic bomb, one using plutonium and one using enriched uranium. Teller was to work on both. His work made the hitherto fantastic notion of an implosion bomb – in which plutonium would be forced into itself by a surrounding ring of explosives – a possibility. The bomb dropped on Nagasaki was of such a design. Teller was also responsible for the calculations which discounted the likelihood of an atomic explosion setting fire to the oceans and atmosphere.

To emphasise his belief in the safety of the weapon's after-effects, he turned up at the site of the first atomic test in New Mexico clutching a bottle of sun-tan lotion.

Teller, a household name in America after the war, had dropped from public prominence by the 1970s. But in 1980 Ronald Reagan was elected President, which Teller regarded as a 'miracle' for Western civilisation. He had, as ever, schemes to expound, and found Reagan a willing audience.

In September 1982, Teller visited the White House for a meeting with Reagan's science adviser, at which they discussed the feasibility of establishing an anti-ballistic missile system based in space. Thus was born the Strategic Defence Initiative (SDI), popularly known as 'Star Wars'.

Initially conceived as a grandiose system in which heat-seeking lasers or ray-guns would shoot down incoming missiles, the project was reviewed and scaled down in 1989 under President Bush; the rise of Gorbachev had brought a thaw in international relations, and the swollen American budget deficit demanded stringent cuts. In 1993, Star Wars was axed by the Clinton administration.

A consummate chess player, Teller remained active despite his disability until a stroke a few days before his death; swimming and ping-pong were favoured pursuits.

❧ **10th** ☙

Lieutenant-Colonel Uziel Gal, b. 1923, d. 2002

Lieutenant-Colonel Uziel Gal, who has died aged seventy-eight, gave his name to the Uzi, the sub-machine-gun favoured by the American Secret Service and street gangsters alike, and used in numerous wars, commando missions and action films.

The weapon was commissioned by the Israeli army in 1951 and named after its inventor, the young Lieutenant 'Uzi' Gal. A compact 9mm gun, the Uzi was simple, robust and inexpensive to make. It also tolerated dust and grit, making it more suitable for desert operations.

The son of a Jewish artist, Uziel Gal was born Guthardt Glass on 15 December 1923 in Weimar, Germany, where he went to Jewish schools. When Hitler came to power, the ten-year-old Guthardt moved with the entire school to England. Three years later, he went to live in Palestine, then under British Mandate, joining his parents at Kibbutz Yagur, northern Palestine (when the family changed its name to the Hebrew, Gal). He was educated at Nesher, near Haifa, and then at the vocational school of the kibbutz, where he showed a precocious interest in weapons.

Aged fifteen, Gal designed a makeshift automatic gun which fired arrows. He later joined the Haganah, the Jewish clandestine militia in Palestine, and headed its armaments department.

During Israel's 1948 war of independence, Gal took part in battles in Galilee, northern Israel. In the summer of 1949 he underwent an officers' course before joining the ordnance manufacturers (later known as TAAS), where he remained until his retirement twenty-seven years later.

As time went on, there was demand for an even more compact model, and in 1980 the Mini-Uzi was produced. With all the power of the original, the rugged Mini was used mainly by covert special forces. A further development was the Micro-Uzi, a pistol-sized version which could fire its entire twenty-bullet magazine in a mere 0.95 seconds.

In the attempted assassination of President Reagan in 1981, Secret Service agents were seen using the Uzi to subdue the would-be assassin, John Hinckley Jr. Meanwhile, Hollywood cast the gun in dozens of action films, and 'Uzi does it' is still a popular T-shirt slogan. The designer himself was a modest man. When visiting weapons exhibitions, he would introduce himself simply as 'Gal'.

❧ **11th** ☙

Pamela Schwerdt, b. 1931, d. 2009

Pamela Schwerdt, who has died aged seventy-eight, was one of the pair of head gardeners at Sissinghurst Castle in Kent who began work under Vita Sackville-West and stayed after her death to make it the most admired garden in England; few people in the country knew as much about hardy flowers as she did.

Pamela Helen Schwerdt was born on 5 April 1931 in Surrey. She came from a family of keen amateur botanists: her maternal grandmother, Edith Vere Annesley, had founded the Wild Flower Society in 1886. It is said that, while still in her pram, Pamela was told the Latin name for the daisy, *Bellis perennis.*

At the age of eighteen she was faced with a choice between studying at Wye College or Waterperry School of Horticulture. She discovered that at Wye she would need a cap and gown, while the clothes list for Waterperry included two pairs of gumboots and a mackintosh. Pam remembered saying: 'I think I'm the gumboot and mackintosh type.'

She stayed on to teach at the school for eight years, but in 1959 decided to start a small plant nursery with a student contemporary, Sibylle Kreutzberger. Looking for land, they put an advertisement in *The Times* and received a letter from Vita Sackville-West. Vita wrote that she could not help with the nursery, but did require one – and only one – head gardener.

Sibylle accompanied Pam to the interview and, by the end of the afternoon, they had been offered the jobs of joint head gardeners, which they eventually accepted. Sibylle became the propagator, while Pam took on the duties of a conventional head gardener. It was a fruitful collaboration, which lasted her lifetime.

Although their personalities were different, the 'Waterperry girls' were universally referred to as 'PamandSibylle' since they were rarely seen on their own when away from Sissinghurst. Pam had the higher public profile, while Sibylle preferred working in the background. 'Women were rare in horticulture in those days,' recalled Sibylle in an interview in *The Garden* in 2006. 'When we first went to Sissinghurst, people used to point at us as though we were baboons at the zoo.'

Things were not easy at first, since there were four male under-gardeners below them; but Pam was a good manager of people, and they were brought round by her kindly encouragement, high standards, and appetite for hard work.

In summer they worked in the garden for fourteen hours a day, until it was dark. For the first fifteen years they also worked every weekend, never taking a holiday. Vita Sackville-West died in 1962 but, even before that, they had a free hand in the garden, renovating much that had become overgrown.

The 'Sissinghurst look', so widely copied, owed as much, if not more, to Pam and Sibylle as to Vita Sackville-West. The structure and ideas (Purple Border, White Garden, Lime Walk and so on) were there, but the head gardeners were free to plant them as they liked. Pam confessed that 'playing around with colour is great fun'.

After Vita's death they carried on, although it was five years before the National Trust finally took over the running of the garden, at which point the numbers of visitors began to climb dramatically – so much so that, eventually, a system of timed tickets had to be instituted.

In 1991 the two women retired and bought a house near Stow-on-the-Wold, where they made a garden that was much admired by plantsmen and gardeners.

⚛ 12th ⚛

Charles Horace Jones, b. 1906, d. 1998

Charles Horace Jones, the South Wales street-corner poet who has died aged ninety-two, stood beside a lamppost in the High Street at Merthyr Tydfil, Glamorgan, for forty-five years with a knuckleduster in his pocket as protection against the Welsh – whom his poems attacked.

In 1950 Horace the Poet, as he was known, earned as much as £138 a week running a crafts business, but he gave it up to write poetry after waking in the middle of the night and feeling compelled by the Muse to scribble down his first verses on the back of a cigarette packet.

In the years that followed, his wife, Delia, became the breadwinner, taking a part-time job in a baker's shop. Her husband would meanwhile spend the entire day at the lamppost, with only an hour's break for lunch. He denounced with increasing violence the Welsh Establishment, such as BBC Wales and the Church, as well as local politicians.

His passion to discredit the corrupt at first endeared him to passers-by. But over the years even old friends disappeared, for eventually ordinary people too were castigated in his sour poetry. In time all came to tire of Horace the Poet and avoid the lamppost where he stood.

He was short and chubby with bushy, crescent-shaped eyebrows. A pencil-line moustache failed to strap down an upper lip that, even when he smiled, would curl towards hairy nostrils in a sneer. His demeanour was suggestive of a paradise lost, perhaps his own, and implied that a tail might fall unnoticed from behind his Chesterfield overcoat. If Satan had been a spiv he would have looked like Jones.

Charles Horace Jones was born on 6 February 1906 and educated at Abermorlais school. When he was twelve his father was killed in a mining accident, and Charles left school two years later to work in the pits, at his mother's insistence.

In adulthood Jones paid the price of his lamppost lampoonery. He was beaten up in the high street, strangled in cafés, knocked unconscious and even set on fire. Asked once why he stood next to the lamppost, he said it was because it left one less side from which he could be attacked.

A poem of his about Welsh rugby that appeared on the sports pages of a national tabloid before an international game in 1956 did little for his reputation in the Valleys. It read:

> 'Ich Dien! I serve.'
> The motto of a nation
> That has lost its nerve.
> Lost its nerve and found it all,
> In the blown-up bladder
> Of an elongated ball.

After those verses appeared, a gang of thugs closed in on him outside a butcher's shop. He escaped into the shop and got out through a side door without their knowing. An hour later they were still gathered outside the crowded shop waiting for him to come out. 'After that,' Jones explained, 'I carried a knuckleduster wherever I went.'

Sir Ewan Forbes, b. 1912, d. 1991

Sir Ewan Forbes of Craigievar, 11th Bt, doctor, landowner and farmer, who has died aged seventy-nine, was registered as a girl at his birth and went by the name of Elizabeth Forbes-Sempill until 1952, when he re-registered his birth and changed his name to Ewan Forbes-Sempill; he later became embroiled in a three-year dispute to establish his claim to the baronetcy.

He was born on 6 September 1912 and baptised Elizabeth as the third and youngest daughter of the 18th Lord Sempill. Young 'Betty' endured a girlhood that was dominated by general gender insecurity. Sir Ewan later remarked that 'everyone realised my difficulties but it was hard in those days for anyone to know what to do'.

During the Second World War she went to Aberdeen University to study Medicine, and, after graduating in 1944, worked for a year as a senior casualty officer at the Aberdeen Royal Infirmary. In 1945 she took up practice in the Alford district and it was from this point onward that Elizabeth Forbes-Sempill looked and behaved like the man she knew she really was.

Then, on 12 September 1952, there appeared a notice in the advertisement columns of *The Press and Journal*, Aberdeen, which stated that henceforth Dr Forbes-Sempill wished to be known as Dr Ewan Forbes-Sempill. Some three weeks later the doctor announced that he was to wed Isabella ('Pat') Mitchell, his housekeeper. It was a quiet ceremony.

On the death of his brother, the 19th Lord Sempill, in 1965, the barony passed in the female line to the 19th Lord's eldest daughter. It was assumed that the baronetcy would pass to Ewan Forbes-Sempill, but his cousin, John Forbes-Sempill (only son of the 18th Lord Sempill's youngest brother, Rear-Admiral Arthur Forbes-Sempill), challenged the succession.

The dispute was taken to the Home Secretary, in whose office the Roll of Baronets is kept by Royal Warrant.

The Lord Advocate was consulted by the Home Secretary, James Callaghan, and eventually, in December 1968, Mr Callaghan directed that the name of Sir Ewan Forbes of Craigievar (he had dropped the name of Sempill) should be entered in the Roll of Baronets.

☙ 13th ☙

Sir Francis Renouf, b. 1918, d. 1998

Sir Francis Renouf, who has died aged eighty, was a flamboyant New Zealand financier nicknamed 'Frank the Bank'.

He was a glamorous and commanding figure, with the physique of the tennis champion he had been in his youth, and maintained large houses in London and Australia as well as a fleet of Rolls-Royces – he once complained about an oil leak in one of them at Rolls's annual general meeting.

But the world stock market crash of October 1987 caused a dramatic reversal in his fortunes. Having already resigned as chairman of Renouf Corporation, he watched its shares lose 90 per cent of their value.

His second wife, the former Susan Sangster, then launched a legal battle to recoup £1.2 million which she claimed he had lost on her account. 'Everything has collapsed around me,' he said. 'A life's work has vanished.'

Renouf's finances were in due course partially restored – he was said to be 'down to his last £15 million' – but his domestic life was not. His marriage to Susan ended in one of the Southern Hemisphere's most acrimonious divorces, and was followed by a third marriage, to a former model and self-styled countess, which lasted a matter of weeks.

Francis Henry Renouf was born on 31 July 1918 and educated in his native city of Wellington. During the Second World War he served as a captain in the New Zealand Expeditionary Force and was taken prisoner, spending four years in a German PoW camp – after which, he said: 'I never want to sit down again.'

Returning from the war, he qualified as an accountant and studied Economics at Oxford, where he twice won a Blue for tennis.

After the end of his first marriage Renouf married, in 1985, the 42-year-old Susan Sangster, daughter of an Australian diplomat and ex-wife of the pools heir and racehorse owner Robert Sangster.

Known to the press as 'The Sheila', the new Mrs Renouf denied that she was marrying for money. Shortly after the wedding, Renouf bought Robert Sangster's £4 million waterfront mansion at Point Piper near Sydney – the most expensive house in Australia at the time – and renamed it, perhaps ill-advisedly, Paradis-sur-Mer.

The couple duly separated, and after two months of legal wrangling she returned to Paradis-sur-Mer to claim possession, provoking a two-week stand-off, dubbed by the local press 'the Siege of Point Piper', which involved rival teams of hired security guards.

Renouf sought unsuccessfully to have Susan removed by the police, while she shouted to reporters over the fence that he was trying to starve her out of the house. They were divorced in 1989, and Paradis was sold for £8 million.

His third marriage, to Michele Ivan-Zadeh-Griaznoff at Chelsea register office in 1991, was, if anything, even more disastrous. She was twenty-eight years his junior and styled herself Countess – the title apparently descended from her ex-husband's

Russian great-aunt – and said she was the daughter of a deceased hotelier.

This claim came as a shock to a retired Australian cab-driver Arthur Mainwaring, her real father, when he read about the wedding in a newspaper. He had never been a hotelier, he told reporters, though he might have played the piano in one. The couple parted after six weeks.

⊰ 14th ⊱

Keith Floyd, b. 1943, d. 2009

Keith Floyd, who has died aged sixty-five, was a flamboyant TV chef who tore up the old formalities of television cookery and spawned a generation of imitators; hugely popular during the 1980s and 1990s both for his programmes and his cookbooks, he was relentlessly unsuccessful in his numerous restaurant ventures.

Combining raffish charm and contagious enthusiasm on screen, Floyd's programmes dispensed with the static formality that had defined the television cookery of his forerunners, such as Fanny Cradock. Indeed they rarely took place in anything that could be defined as a studio. Instead he was likely to be found braced over a camping stove on the heaving deck of a North Sea trawler, rhapsodising over a sea bass. At the time it was revolutionary.

So too was his penchant for ad-libbing jocular instructions to his film crew. A generation of viewers became familiar with Clive and various other long-suffering cameramen, who were forever being ordered to get in close for a look at a fish gill or the marbling on a steak. 'Back to me, Clive,' was a familiar refrain.

Most popular with his viewers was Floyd's habit of never cooking without a glass of some local vintage to hand. This he owed to his long-standing BBC producer David Pritchard, who advised him to fill in the boring bits with 'a quick slurp'. Retakes required refills. A committed drinker, Floyd slurped more than any television chef before or since.

With craggy good looks, slightly askew bow tie and upper-class tones gravelled by a prodigious smoking habit, Floyd had something of the roguish charm of a 1950s chancer about him. This was not an altogether misleading image – as his four wives, most several decades his junior, might attest.

Keith Floyd was born on 28 December 1943 and grew up in Somerset, the son of a meter repairman for the electricity board. It was, he recorded, a very happy rural childhood during which he learned his mother's great love of cookery. By diligent saving, his parents managed to pay for him to attend the local public school – Wellington College, though it had no connection with its more famous Berkshire namesake. His head boy was Jeffrey Archer. Floyd was both popular and a good rugby player, but a lack of money forced him to leave at sixteen. He was mortified by this abrupt curtailment of his youth.

Thereafter he worked first as a clerk, then as a cub reporter for the *Bristol Evening Post* alongside Tom Stoppard. Determined to make it as a hack, he also worked nights on the *Western Morning News* before a showing of the Michael Caine epic *Zulu* convinced him that his future in fact lay with the armed forces.

He turned down the 11th Hussars to take a commission in the less snooty 3rd Royal Tank Regiment, but found the stirring cinematic vision of Rorke's Drift bore little resemblance to his dreary Cold War billet in Germany.

In 1971 he left the Army and set up his first restaurant, in Bristol. The eponymous Floyd's Bistro proved popular, and his empire expanded to three restaurants. However, in what was to prove a perennial feature of his career, popularity stubbornly failed to translate into profitability. Faced with a looming financial crisis, he sold up, divorced his first wife, and bought a yacht called *Flirty*.

For the next five years he pursued a peripatetic existence in France and Spain, indulging a passion for the local cuisine that he had learned from Elizabeth David's *French Provincial Cooking*. As he ran out of money he sold pieces of the yacht until, without a compass or an outboard motor, he settled in Provence and opened a restaurant in Isle-sur-la-Sorgue near Avignon, where he also played for the local rugby club.

In 1979 he returned to England and set up a new fish restaurant in Bristol with money borrowed from friends. It was here, with the bailiffs already circling the struggling venture, that he had his fateful meeting with David Pritchard, a 'large, balding, red moon-faced' producer at BBC Plymouth with whom Floyd developed the style of cookery programme that made him a celebrity at forty-two.

The off-the-cuff style pioneered by his programmes involved tremendously hard work for both crew and presenter, usually in primitive conditions. There was little in the way of script; Floyd and his producer simply made it up as they went along. Cooking equipment was often borrowed from local hotels.

On one occasion Floyd was nearly drowned filming a sequence on the Great Barrier Reef. On another he ran into trouble with the Norwegian Government for flambéing two protected puffins. On a third, a cooking escapade in a hot-air balloon nearly ended in disaster when butane gas was used for cooling a bottle of champagne rather than propelling the aircraft. As the balloon headed for a motorway Floyd reflected that at least 'a juggernaut would squash us instantly and we'd feel no pain'. In the event, traffic stopped and 'we remained alive'.

Despite his charisma, wit, charm and frequent generosity, Floyd was also known for his temper tantrums, towering immodesty and bouts of maudlin despair. He railed constantly against his image as a heavy drinker, and particularly at one critic's suggestion that he was the 'Ollie Reed of TV chefs', claiming that he had been properly drunk on television only once. This was an occasion when, during an interview on an Australian chat show, he objected to the quality of the studio coffee and poured his cupful over the carpet.

In 1989 Floyd put some of his television millions into buying the Maltster's Arms at Tuckenhay, Devon. He aimed to turn it into a gastropub that would serve the sort of unpretentious fare he had learned at his mother's knee. Renamed Floyd's Inn (Sometimes), the pub was enthusiastically received, not least because of Floyd's astute judgment in hiring a soon-to-be famous chef, Jean-Christophe Novelli.

But he grew to regard his diners with ill-disguised contempt, dismissing them as celebrity-obsessed and snobbish. On one occasion he gleefully recalled serving a serially ungrateful diner a carefully cooked beer mat disguised as a breaded escalope of veal. The man ate it without comment but criticised the topping on his *crème brûlée*.

Floyd was diagnosed with cancer in 2009, but had visited his doctor and been told his treatment was going well on the day he died. The news provided all the more reason to celebrate, as it was also the birthday of his last companion, Celia Martin. The couple toasted the good news with a long, well-oiled lunch, at which Floyd declared: 'I haven't felt this well for ages.'

⇒ 15th ⇐

Oriana Fallaci, b. 1929, d. 2006

Oriana Fallaci, who has died aged seventy-seven, was a combative Italian author and journalist whose last public battle was against the Western world's appeasement of Islam.

After the Twin Towers attack, she broke years of silence to write a series of best-selling books, claiming that the West and the Roman Catholic Church were selling the pass. In *The Rage and the Pride*, which sold a million copies when it came out within weeks of the tragedy, she denounced Muslims for multiplying 'like rats' and said that 'the children of Allah spend their time with their bottoms in the air, praying five times a day'.

The Strength of Reason, her next book, led to a prosecution being taken out against her, though she never appeared in court. One group in France tried to stop it being distributed while two others asked for it to carry a warning notice. All this was meat and drink for Oriana Fallaci, who professed to love life so much that she could not compromise, be submissive or take orders.

She first attracted international attention by interviewing such figures as Henry Kissinger and Yasser Arafat, whom she cajoled, bullied and charmed into making revelations – though the results revealed that she was every bit as egotistical as any of her subjects.

She wore a chador to meet Ayatollah Khomeini. But when he told her she did not have to wear it, she removed it, saying that it was 'a stupid, medieval rag'. She walked out on 'Papa Doc' Duvalier in Haiti because he had changed her questions. She threw her tape recorder at Cassius Clay, and complained to Fidel Castro about his body odour. As she told the Shah of Iran in her husky voice, 'I'm on everyone's blacklist, thank God!'

The daughter of a Communist cabinet-worker, Oriana Fallaci was born in Florence on 26 June 1929. During the war she helped Allied prisoners on the run to escape, learning to speak English in the process. Afterwards she began to study Medicine at the University of Florence. But on obtaining work with a local paper in order to make ends meet, she discovered her true vocation.

In the mid-1950s she joined the staff of the weekly *L'Europeo*, and started writing profiles of outstanding women. These made up her book, *The Useless Sex*. To escape from the straitjacket of 'female topics' she tackled the space race, visiting NASA and Cape Canaveral.

Her next significant assignment was the Vietnam War, when she felt sick under constant fire, admitting that she had been 'a champion at running for shelter'. The resulting book, *Nothing, Or So Be It* (1972), took its name from a prayer she had composed after watching a bombing raid on the outskirts of Saigon from a cocktail party on the roof of a hotel. It began: 'Our father, who art in heaven, give us this day our daily massacre ...'

Oriana Fallaci's first book to become a major international success was *Letter to a Child Never Born* (1975), which stated that life was 'a great gift even in the worst circumstances', and irritated and interested both supporters and opponents of abortion.

Although she had started out hailing feminism as the most important contemporary revolution, Oriana Fallaci came to deplore the way it had gradually become a 'sort of political party'. In the first Gulf War she was voluble and so scathing about the constraints imposed on journalists who were trying to reach the front that she became known as 'a tiny journalistic Cruise missile'.

About a decade ago she announced that she had cancer but was too busy with her writing to have it treated, and continued to smoke.

In her last years Oriana Fallaci returned home to her native Tuscany. She had a private audience with Pope Benedict XVI shortly before her death, on the understanding that she would never disclose its contents.

≋ 16th ≋

Helen O'Brien, b. 1925, d. 2005

Helen O'Brien, who has died aged seventy-nine, co-founded, with her husband Jimmy, the legendary Eve nightclub, which opened in an alley off Regent Street in 1953 and ran for thirty-nine years; in its Cold War heyday the Eve was the most discreetly daring establishment in London.

It counted among its habitués Errol Flynn, Judy Garland, Aristotle Onassis and the Dukes of Devonshire and Norfolk. In a setting of plush opulence, maharajahs, business tycoons, diplomats, and politicians drank vintage champagne with scantily clad showgirls, who performed risqué floorshows.

The club was celebrated for its discretion – journalists and photographers were banned – and the beauty of its girls. The O'Briens operated a fierce staff selection policy, interviewing a hundred hopefuls to find one who was 'just perfect'. Christine Keeler failed the test: 'She wasn't suitable,' explained Helen O'Brien. 'I felt she was an easily led girl – and I was proved right.' Norma Levy, the prostitute who became embroiled with Lord Lambton and Earl Jellicoe, also fell at the first hurdle. 'I was impressed by her body, but I had a sixth sense that she might bring trouble,' Helen O'Brien recalled. 'She really didn't have the requisite breeding.'

The club's 1962 brochure, when membership was a guinea a year, said of one of its star performers: 'Her attractions are stunning, her talent is extraordinary and her telephone number, sir, is none of your business.'

Among the Eve's more unusual members was the Bishop of Southall, who ran away with and eventually married a club hostess called Joy. 'One of his favourite sermons before he was found out was the giving and receiving of joy,' Helen O'Brien recalled.

The club's clientele was so international that in a court case in which the O'Briens were prosecuted for some liquor licence irregularity, the judge described it as 'a subdivision of the Foreign Office'. Watched by MI5 and KGB agents, sitting at their favourite tables with their backs to the wall, the hostesses would chat up the Eastern-bloc spies and diplomats who frequented the club, gleaning information which they would then pass on, sometimes unwittingly.

This arrangement was initiated by Helen O'Brien, a fluent Russian speaker and fervent anti-Communist who had fled her native Romania after the war. She had been approached by a Romanian secret agent who wanted to recruit her as a spy in exchange for letting her parents join her in London. She resisted, but her frequent meetings with Romanian diplomats brought her to the attention of the British Secret Service and she soon struck a deal with an MI5 officer. At the height of the Cold War it was said that the 'Nightclub Mata Hari' was so useful that she had not one but a team of handlers from MI5 and MI6.

She was born Elena Constantinescu on 14 December 1925 into a family of Romanian land-owners; her mother was the daughter of an exiled Russian duchess.

Elena spent her early years in the Romanian village of Barcanesti, where she learned riding tricks from Cossack prisoners-of-war in the early 1940s. She remained in Romania until 1947, when she made her way to London, finding work as a dancer at Murray's Cabaret Club in Beak Street. It was here that she met Jimmy O'Brien, a former cloakroom attendant who had been promoted to general manager of the club. They were married in 1955.

O'Brien had thought for some time about opening his own club. Hearing that there were premises available in a large basement off Regent Street, modelled on the first-class passenger deck of an ocean liner, he secured a bank loan as down payment and the Eve club opened on St Valentine's Night 1953.

It enjoyed great success until the permissive society rendered its floorshows rather tame and the O'Briens replaced their thirty-girl extravaganzas with guest acts. The end of the Cold War dealt the club a further blow and it eventually closed in 1992.

Olga Spessivtseva, b. 1895, d. 1991

Olga Spessivtseva, the Russian ballerina who has died aged ninety-six, was generally reckoned the equal of the legendary Pavlova until her obsessive pursuit of artistic perfection drove her out of her mind.

Her interpretation of Giselle, the village girl whose mind gives way because of her lover's duplicity, was unrivalled. Many dancers regard the part as unbearably demanding and avoid it. Spessivtseva, though, felt a tragic affinity with Giselle. Before performing in the role in Leningrad in 1919, she visited an asylum several times to observe patients.

Twenty-three years later, in New York, she herself completely broke down. A rich 'protector' arranged for her to enter a private sanatorium, where she could make a slow but comfortable recovery.

But the protector died, and his executors disclaimed responsibility for the beautiful, brilliant, but broken dancer. Spessivtseva, whose English was poor, was transferred to a state hospital for the insane. The staff there knew nothing of the new inmate's history and took her references to Giselle as *folie de grandeur*. When she berated them for their ignorance she was strapped to her bed and given electric shocks to her skull.

This treatment did not help and she languished in the asylum for more than twenty years before a new drug and the intervention of an old friend secured her release in 1963.

After her return to the world Spessivtseva went to live at the Tolstoy foundation farm in New York State, which had been founded by Countess Alexandra Tolstoy, daughter of the novelist, as a rest home for Russians. The following year the BBC broadcast a short film about her life. Its title was *The Sleeping Ballerina*.

⁓ 17th ⁓

Adrian Nicholas, b. 1962, d. 2005

Adrian Nicholas, who has died in a skydiving accident aged forty-three, was not a man to let the trifling matter of his own mortality get in the way of a good time; known as 'the man who can fly', he pushed the boundaries of 'extreme' sports, pioneering new types of skydiving.

With curly fair hair and dashing good looks, Nicholas was an adventurer in the best British tradition of derring-do. He seemed to spend almost as much time in the air as on the ground, making more than 6,500 jumps in five years in thirty different countries. He baled out of a Russian jumbo jet on to the North Pole; jumped into a Dolgan Eskimo village in Siberia; and made the first free-fall flights through the Grand

Canyon and over the Great Wall of China.

In 1998, wearing a webbed 'Wingsuit', he set world records for the furthest unassisted human flight and for the longest free fall. Two years later he decided to test the theory that Leonardo da Vinci had designed the world's first working parachute.

In 1485 Leonardo had scribbled a simple sketch of a four-sided pyramid covered in linen. Alongside, he had written: 'If a man is provided with a length of gummed linen cloth with a length of twelve yards on each side and twelve yards high, he can jump from any great height whatsoever without injury.'

Defying expert predictions that it would not work, Nicholas and his Swedish girlfriend, Katarina Ollikainen, constructed a parachute according to Leonardo's design; and on 25 June 2000, he launched himself from a hot-air balloon 10,000 feet over South Africa. He parachuted for five minutes as a black box recorder measured his descent, before cutting himself free of the contraption and releasing a conventional parachute.

Although aeronautical experts had predicted that it would tip over, fall apart or spin uncontrollably, Leonardo's parachute made a smooth and slow descent. 'It took one of the greatest minds who ever lived to design it,' Nicholas observed, 'but it took 500 years to find a man with a brain small enough to actually go and fly it.'

The son of a property developer, Adrian Nicholas was born on 4 March 1962. As a boy he was always getting into scrapes, loved every kind of sport and was an avid reader of adventure stories in *Boys' Own* comics.

Nicholas was educated at Aldenham School, Elstree, and at a local sixth-form college. He made his first parachute jump aged seventeen and went on to become a cave diver (a cave in Florida was named after him), skydiver, snowboarder, wrestler, jet pilot and rally driver before joining Capital Radio as the station's 'Eye in the Sky' traffic and travel correspondent, working alongside Chris Tarrant.

He succeeded in raising what was once a prosaic element of Capital Radio's drive-time programming into an essential ingredient of its output. He even had his own fan club. 'He's a madman,' Chris Tarrant observed affectionately, 'absolutely barking. He gave me a lift once from Charing Cross Road. I am never, ever getting into a car with that person again.'

After ten years with Capital Radio, in 1994 Nicholas decided to concentrate on skydiving full time after meeting Patrick de Gayardon, a pioneer of sky surfing. They became friends and dived together everywhere, Nicholas supporting his adventures by working as a photographer, selling television footage and lecturing company employees about how to overcome fears and phobias.

But in 1998 Nicholas watched in horror as de Gayardon plunged to his death when a technical malfunction prevented him from opening either of his two parachutes towards the end of a jump.

Instead of giving up, Nicholas determined to carry on where his friend had left off, and on 12 March 1999 he attempted to break two world records for time and distance. He jumped over California from 35,850 feet, wearing an oxygen mask. Despite nearly choking to death, Nicholas flew for four minutes fifty-five seconds and covered ten miles, establishing new world records for the longest skydive and the furthest human flight. 'I don't think of myself as a nutter but I believe I can fly,' he said afterwards. 'I'm a real life Peter Pan.'

In 2000 BBC1 screened a fifty-minute documentary about his life, as part of its *Extreme Lives* series, called 'Lord of the Skies'. 'I'll die skydiving,' Nicholas predicted. 'It will happen. We all die skydiving, eventually. But it will be worth it.'

⊰ **18**th ⊱

Jill Johnston, b. 1929, d. 2010

Jill Johnston, who has died aged eighty-one, gained notoriety as the first mainstream journalist to 'come out' as a lesbian in print; her book, *Lesbian Nation: The Feminist Solution* (1973), has been described as a 'founding document' of lesbian feminist separatism.

In her book, Jill Johnston declared that it would take a radical 'lesbian nation' to undermine the 'Patriarchy' – the male-dominated system that oppressed all women. All women are born lesbians, she maintained, and those who slept with men were collaborating with the enemy.

She came out a few months before the Stonewall riots in 1969 and lost no opportunity to flaunt her new sexual identity. In 1971 she caused a scandal at a public debate on feminism with Germaine Greer and Norman Mailer, when, after announcing that 'all women are lesbians except those that don't know it yet', she was joined on stage by two women friends with whom she was soon to be seen rolling around the floor in simulated flagrante delicto. An appalled Mailer was reduced to begging impotently: 'Come on, Jill, be a lady.'

⊰ **19**th ⊱

Diana, Duchess of Newcastle, b. 1920, d. 1997

Diana, Duchess of Newcastle, who has died aged seventy-seven, made a significant contribution to horse racing, both as a competitor and as a campaigner for the rights of women jockeys.

Beautiful, courageous and unconventional, with a fondness for 'getting going', Diana Newcastle's interest in speed was not confined to riding. During the Second World War, she served as a motor-cycle dispatch rider for the Motorised Transport Corps (MTC), and in 1954 she entered her Sunbeam Talbot for the Monte Carlo Rally.

Fiercely competitive, in the late 1950s she began promoting the cause of women jockeys, who were then forbidden to race on the flat in mainland Britain. From 1960 she began expressing her views in lively articles for *Horse and Hound*, sparking a vigorous debate with more conservative-minded readers.

There were calls for 'Rossetti-ish dream maidens to stay at home with their knitting'. One correspondent demanded that women be banned from riding point-to-point altogether because of the number of accidents to 'the fair sex'. Diana replied with demands for more women's races, not fewer, arguing that the fault lay with inexperienced riders, unschooled horses, bad tack and worse stewarding. It was to be another eleven years before the rules were changed.

Meanwhile, she rode against men in flat races at Longue, Aix-les-Bains, La Roche-Posay, Vichy, Dieppe and Chantilly. The French were not alone in their admiration for the flying duchess and she eventually held a jockey's licence in four countries, even qualifying as a 'Gentleman Rider of the Fegentri Club'.

She was never put off by her injuries. In 1960 she persuaded Vincent O'Brien to procure her a ride in the amateur Grand National at Merano, Italy. Halfway round, she came off at the timber jump and ended up in hospital. The committee, distressed that a visiting 'Amazone' had come to grief, had the obstacle removed. Three months later, Diana Newcastle was back in the saddle at Larkhill, the first point-to-point of the season. 'I had a collarbone which dislocated from time to time,' she recalled, 'but a horse jumped on me that day and I never had any trouble again.'

Mary Diana Montagu-Stuart-Wortley-Mackenzie was born on 2 June 1920, the second daughter of Viscount Carlton, who succeeded his father as the 3rd Earl of Wharncliffe in 1935.

Diana was brought up at the family seat at Wortley Hall, near Sheffield, where she was educated by governesses. Dark-haired, with piercing blue eyes, a quick smile and an uninhibited laugh, she grew up as free a spirit as her huntress namesake. She liked people with dash and style, and was a friend of such air aces as Hugh Dundas and Johnnie Johnson.

In 1939 she joined the MTC. Three years later she was posted to Cambridge, making the 120-mile round trip to London several times each week. Mud-spattered, with her crash helmet under her arm, she would break her journey by joining her father for lunch at the Ritz. The speed at which these trips were accomplished earned her the nickname 'Hurtle Wortle'.

In 1946 she married, as his second wife, the 9th Duke of Newcastle. The marriage was happy until Pelham Newcastle decided to move home to Rhodesia in 1948. Diana did not like Africa. By 1950 she was back in England. Her marriage withered into estrangement and was dissolved in 1959.

In Wiltshire, where she was to remain the rest of her life, Diana Newcastle found accommodation for herself and her two daughters in a house beside the kennels of the Wylye Hunt. In 1972 the rules were at last changed to permit women to race on the flat. Diana Newcastle was by then fifty-two. She refused to be cheated of an opportunity for which she had fought so long. In six weeks of rigorous dieting, she lowered her weight to nine stone and entered races at Folkestone, Doncaster and Salisbury.

❧ **20th** ❧

Brian Clough, b. 1935, d. 2004

Brian Clough, who has died aged sixty-nine, was one of Britain's most effective, charismatic and idiosyncratic football managers; he was often called 'the greatest manager England never had'.

On two occasions, with Derby County and then with Nottingham Forest, Clough took charge of a down-at-heel Second Division outfit and within a few years had made them League Champions. This achievement, unlikely ever to be matched, was made even more remarkable when he went on to lead Nottingham Forest to successive victories in the European Cup, in 1979 and 1980. The club's record of forty-two league games without a loss was beaten only in the summer of 2004, by Arsenal. Clough generously conceded: 'Arsenal are nothing short of incredible ... they could have been nearly as good as us.'

Clough's successes were said to have been fuelled by the disappointment of a playing career cruelly curtailed by a serious knee injury. Peter Taylor, his assistant in all his greatest managerial triumphs, reckoned that 'mental pain' was Clough's 'driving force'.

Brian Howard Clough was born at Middlesbrough on 21 March 1935, the sixth of nine children. He was educated at Marton Grove Secondary School and joined his local football team as an amateur in 1951. He signed professional forms in 1952, aged seventeen, and then went on to do his National Service in the RAF.

Clough returned to Middlesbrough but took some time to break into the first team. He felt that he only got the recognition he deserved when Taylor, then a goalkeeper, was transferred from Coventry. Taylor ensured that Clough's self-belief burned brightly and they spent all available time together discussing football. Clough eventually made his first-team debut in 1955. But just seven years later, having been transferred to Sunderland in 1961 for £45,000, his playing career effectively came to an end after a collision with the Bury goalkeeper. He had scored 251 league goals in only 274 appearances.

Following his retirement as a player, and a period of desperation, Clough became the youth coach at Sunderland, a role he found surprisingly fulfilling. The job was short-lived but in 1965 Clough was offered the managership of Hartlepools United in the Fourth Division. At the age of thirty he became the youngest manager in the Football League.

His first move was to go behind the chairman's back and enlist Peter Taylor, who had been managing non-league Burton Albion, as his assistant. Clough's managerial style had been learned from his Sunderland manager, Alan Brown, who, Clough said, 'detested shabby appearance, unkempt hair. I always insisted that my players looked smart. Most of all he taught me that a football club manager is boss.'

Clough and Taylor took Hartlepools to eighth in the Fourth Division but soon determined to try for better things. They took over at Derby County, which had just finished seventeenth in the Second Division, in June 1967.

They disbanded the demoralised team and rebuilt the squad by signing such players as the centre-half Roy McFarland from Tranmere and bringing John McGovern down from Hartlepools. In their first season Derby finished eighteenth but the next year, after daringly securing the signature from Spurs of Dave McKay, whose confidence spread to all members of the side, they were champions. Promoted, Derby finished fourth in their first season in the top flight and, having signed Archie Gemmill and Colin Todd, were champions the following year.

Clough was becoming increasingly well known, making numerous television appearances as a soccer pundit. His high profile began to create unease among the Derby board of directors. Questions began to be asked about the role of Taylor; it was largely unspecified but, as far as Clough was concerned, absolutely crucial: 'I'm not equipped to manage successfully without Peter Taylor,' he said. 'I am the shop window and he is the goods in the back.'

Piqued, Clough and Taylor resigned. After an unhappy eight months at Third Division Brighton, Clough was surprised, in the summer of 1974, to be offered the manager's job at Leeds United, whose style of play and previous manager, Don Revie, he had often criticised.

Clough's opening speech to his new squad of players, champions the previous season, was: 'Gentlemen, the first thing you can do for me is throw your medals and your pots and pans in the dustbin because you've never won anything fairly. You've done it by cheating.' The relationship never recovered and, after forty-four days, Clough was sacked for reasons of 'player unrest'. He was handsomely compensated, so that when he returned to management in January 1975, with Nottingham Forest, he felt even more confident about his style; financially secure, he had no more fear of the sack.

Clough immediately recruited Taylor from Brighton. At Forest they inherited a lacklustre squad, resigned to mediocrity. Their subsequent achievements were all the more remarkable considering that the backbone of that triumphant team comprised players already at Forest when they arrived. Probably Clough's greatest asset as a manager was his ability to coax players, sure of their own mediocrity, to greatness.

Humour and imaginative motivational ploys were typical of the Clough/Taylor management style. The week before the 1980 European Cup Final, when Forest defeated Kevin Keegan's Hamburg with a John Robertson goal, Clough and Taylor took the squad to Majorca and told them to concentrate on the sunshine and the beer. This unusual concentration on creating a relaxed mood paid frequent dividends.

Forest were promoted in 1977 and were League Champions the next season playing a simple, quick-passing game which was a joy to watch. With European football came a more defensive approach but a Clough team was never boring; he eschewed the long-ball game because, 'If the game was meant to be played in the air, He would have put grass in the sky'.

The celebrated partnership with Taylor came to an end in 1982 when Taylor apparently retired. But eighteen months later Taylor became the manager of Derby and then, according to Clough, behaved in an underhand fashion over the transfer of a player. The relationship became terminally acrimonious and they were still not on speaking terms when Taylor died in 1990.

Clough was never so successful without Taylor, although his Forest team did win the League Cup in 1989 and 1990. The latter victory was slightly overshadowed by the £5,000 fine Clough received for having punched some rowdy supporters after the quarter-final. The blows were witnessed by television, as were the kisses Clough subsequently planted on the cheeks of his victims. He was a noted kisser.

In 1991 Forest reached the FA Cup final against Spurs when Paul Gascoigne's knee injury (the same sort as suffered by the young Clough) seemed to galvanise his team-mates to greater efforts. Forest lost in extra-time.

It was Clough's greatest regret in his later years that he did not retire on the day of that defeat. He retired two years later when Forest were already condemned to relegation and his eccentric ways had come to seem more of a liability than an inspiration.

The challenge of his retirement Clough considered to be the controlling of his drinking habits. He acknowledged his alcoholism after collapsing and being taken to a clinic at the end of 1996. In January 2003 he had a liver transplant.

He was appointed OBE in 1991. He said that the letters must stand for 'Old Big 'Ead'.

⤙ **21**st ⤚

John Manners, b. 1926, d. 2009

John Manners, who has died aged eighty-three, was one of the great characters of the Turf; universally known as 'Mad Manners', he was a pillar of the point-to-point circuit and also saw success as an owner and trainer at jump racing's most hallowed venues.

A farmer by profession, Manners twice won the Foxhunter Chase at Aintree, with Killeshin (1994) and his homebred Cavalero (1998); while the latter horse also took the Foxhunter at the Cheltenham Festival in 2000. Manners once observed of his triumph at Cheltenham: 'I'm a hunting man. Winning the Foxhunter was my dream. Have you seen the Cup [a vast silver vessel]? It's the most disgusting thing.'

Whatever qualities Manners might have lacked, enthusiasm wasn't one of them. In 1982 he was fined £50 by the Cheltenham stewards after he jumped over the rails and tossed his trilby into the air as he pursued his winning horse Knight of Love up the run-in to the finishing line. He called one horse Biganard. This failed the Jockey Club's decency test until he insisted (untruthfully) that it was the Austrian village at which he had met his wife.

At his farm in Wiltshire, Manners was a night owl, rarely rising before 10 a.m. even on a hunting morning (he was invariably late for the meet). His horses' meal times were set accordingly: breakfast at lunchtime, lunchtime at teatime and a final feed between midnight and 1 a.m. He was in the habit of mowing the lawn in the middle of the night, wearing only long johns or even – in clement weather – nothing at all, guided by the light of a torch fixed to the front of the mower.

His second wife, Audrey, had a hard job getting him to the register office in Swindon when they eventually decided to get married in 1982. Under his suit he was in full hunting kit, and the new Mrs Manners's first job was to drop her husband off at a nearby pub where the Vale of the White Horse Hunt was meeting. His hunting cap was full of confetti – and when he doffed it to the Master everyone knew that he and Audrey had finally tied the knot.

⁂ 22nd ⁂

Brigadier Dennis Rendell, b. 1920, d. 2010

Brigadier Dennis Rendell, who has died aged eighty-nine, had an adventurous career in the Parachute Regiment.

Dennis Bossey Rendell was born in London on 2 October 1920 and educated at St Alban's School. He enlisted in the Army in 1939 and joined the Middlesex Regiment in 1940. The following year he was commissioned.

Dropped into Tunisia in 1942, his platoon engaged in four days and nights of fierce fighting, for which he was awarded an MC. Eventually Rendell was captured, after which he made two unsuccessful attempts to escape. On being moved to Italy he failed twice more but, in September 1943, eventually got away from a camp at Sulmona.

Dodging German patrols, he went south and met other escaped PoWs in the Abruzzi Mountains, where there was already deep snow. He formed an escape organisation and enlisted the help of the local peasants to obtain food and warm clothing. He spoke the most rudimentary Italian and contacted the British Embassy in Vatican City, where he received help from Sir D'Arcy Osborne, the minister,  and Mgr Hugh O'Flaherty. With the assistance of couriers, he obtained money and clothing for the escapees and the intrepid Italians who sheltered them.

With the onset of winter, travel in the mountains became too hazardous, and he returned to Sulmona to hide out and wait for the spring.

One day in November, a travelling fair set up in the main square of the town. Among the sideshows was a short shooting range where customers could try their luck with an air rifle at hitting a plate twenty yards away. If they succeeded, the impact of the slug 'triggered' an automatic flashlight photograph of the marksman.

Rendell and six of his fellow escapees could not resist visiting the fair. Wehrmacht and Luftwaffe servicemen were at the range, but their shooting was poor and the camera seldom flashed.

Two Luftwaffe men put up such an abysmal performance that Rendell, exasperated beyond endurance, could stand no more. He grabbed the rifle, rammed a slug up the breach, aimed and fired. A satisfying clang followed by a large flash signalled a bullseye. The fugitives, rather shaken by attracting so much attention, collected the film and slipped away quickly – leaving the Germans to pay.

Soon after this adventure the organisation was betrayed, and Rendell decided to move his team to Rome. The city was liberated in June 1944 and Rendell was appointed MBE for his work with the escape organisations.

He retired from the Army in 1977 and settled at Selsey, Sussex. He rode his 1911 P&M motorcycle in eight London-to-Brighton Pioneer Runs and many other vintage and veteran events. Aged seventy-five, he still had sixteen vintage motorcycles, twenty-two ancient motor lawnmowers and four stationary engines, all runners that had been renovated by himself.

On 8 August 1990 Rendell, with thirteen other retired officers of the Parachute Regiment, parachuted into Poole harbour. Their ages ranged from seventy to eighty-one years.

⊰ **23rd** ⊱

Colonel Fred Tilston, b. 1906, d. 1992

Colonel Fred Tilston, who has died aged eighty-six, won the VC in March 1945 for his part in an epic battle with German paratroops in the Rhineland.

For two days, the 2nd Canadian Corps had been battling to break through a gap near the southern end of the Hochwald Forest to launch their armour towards the last bridge over the Rhine. Lt-Gen Guy Simonds, determined to outflank the Germans, ordered his 2nd Division to clear the enemy from their immensely strong defences in the northern half of the forest.

In the misty sunshine of early morning, Tilston, with his company of the Essex Scottish Regiment, led the attack. Advancing across 500 yards of open country towards the wood, he kept dangerously close to the bursting shells of his supporting artillery to gain the maximum cover from its barrage.

By the time he reached the enemy's dense belt of barbed wire, he had been wounded in the head. Having forced his way through in front of his men, he silenced a machine gun, which was holding up his left platoon, and was the first into the German position and the first to take a prisoner.

He then ordered his reserve platoon to mop up, and advanced with the remainder of his company towards the enemy's main defences, which lined the western edge of the Hochwald.

As he approached, he was severely wounded in the hip, and fell. Shouting to his men to keep going, he struggled to his feet and rejoined them as they reached their objective. Despite his wounds, Tilston then led an assault on an elaborate trench system, and succeeded in clearing out the near-fanatical paratroops who defended it.

The enemy put up a savage resistance and the company was reduced to only twenty-six men, a quarter of its original strength. Before Tilston could organise a defence, the German counter-attacked repeatedly, supported by a hail of mortar and machine-gun fire from the flank. Moving in the open from platoon to platoon, Tilston positioned his men and directed fire against the attackers, who penetrated close enough to throw grenades into the trenches, now held by the Canadians.

Soon ammunition began to run low; the only source was the company on their right. Six times Tilston crossed the open, bullet-swept ground which separated the two companies to fetch bandoliers and grenades to his troops and to replace a damaged radio, essential to communications with battalion headquarters.

On his last trip, he was hit again, so badly that he could not move. He was found in a shell crater. Although in great pain, he refused a morphine injection until he had given orders for the defence of the position to his one surviving officer and had made sure that the need to hold it was clearly understood.

For his gallantry in securing a base from which to clear the Hochwald, Tilston was awarded the Victoria Cross, but the action cost him the loss of his legs.

Frederick Albert Tilston was born in Toronto on 11 June 1906, and educated at the De La Salle College and Toronto University, where he studied Pharmacy.

During his childhood he conceived a passion for music and his first purchase, after joining Sterling Drug, a Canadian pharmaceutical company, was a piano. He covered Alberta and British Columbia for the firm before being promoted sales manager at Windsor, Ontario. On the outbreak of war, Tilston was commissioned into the Essex Scottish, the local regiment, and joined his battalion in England in 1941.

Within a month of arrival his military career, and his life, nearly ended when a bullet pierced his lung and lodged near his heart. During the bitter fighting in Normandy in 1944, Tilston was wounded a second time when his jeep struck a mine. Tilston had just been promoted to the rank of major, and was commanding a rifle company for the first time when he led the attack on the Hochwald.

After the war he refused to allow the loss of his legs to interfere with his work or his enjoyment of life. One year to the day after being wounded in the Hochwald, he returned to Sterling Drug as vice-president in charge of sales. He subsequently became its chief executive and chairman.

⊰ 24th ⊱

Cyril Ray, b. 1908, d. 1991

Cyril Ray, the journalist who has died aged eighty-three, was a celebrated wine writer and the archetypal Bollinger Bolshevik.

Though he worked for the *Guardian*, he also had a spell on *The Spectator* (which he eventually left for being 'too Tory'). This did not stop him living in a manor house in Kent, owning a double-set in Albany, riding daily in Rotten Row, sending his son to Eton and smoking large Cuban cigars long before Castro came to power. As he puffed, he declared: 'The English class system is death and damnation to English life. It is the curse of England.'

His shoes, like his suitings, were hand-made and always shined to excessive brilliance, which was much remarked upon. There was a man at New & Lingwood who shined them for him. For a long time he would send out for an electrician whenever a light bulb need replacing. 'I always try to give employment to craftsmen.'

Jure Robic, b. 1965, d. 2010

Jure Robic, who has died aged forty-five, was a Slovenian soldier turned extreme cyclist whose extraordinary feats of endurance earned him a place in *The Guinness Book of Records*.

Robic won the Race Across America, a gruelling 3,000-mile coast-to-coast sprint, a record five times. The race is unusual in that there are no stages. Once the riders begin, there are no scheduled breaks until they reach the finishing line – so an ability to go without sleep is the main determinant of who wins. During the 2004 race Robic cycled an average of 350 miles a day to complete the race in just eight days, claiming only eight hours' sleep, and pedalled into the record books by covering 518 miles in 24 hours.

Towards the end of the race, he was known to weep uncontrollably and was sometimes to be seen hopping off his bike to fight imaginary assailants – bears, wolves or aliens – which turned out to be mailboxes. He imagined that cracks in the road were coded messages, and on one occasion became convinced he was being pursued by the Mujahedeen on horseback; his support team encouraged him to ride faster, pretending that they could see them too. 'Sometimes during races he gets off his bike and walks towards us in the follow car, very angry,' recalled a team member in 2006. 'We lock the doors.'

Judith Exner, b. 1934, d. 1999

Judith Exner, who has died in California aged sixty-five, scandalised America in 1975 by claiming to be the former mistress of President John F. Kennedy; the details she gave of their affair were among the first blows to tarnish Kennedy's golden image and, over time, lent credibility to allegations that he had collaborated with the Mafia to buy votes and to plot the assassination of Fidel Castro.

It was Frank Sinatra, with whom she had a brief affair, who introduced her to Kennedy in 1960. He invited her to lunch and thereafter repeatedly telephoned Judith Campbell (as she was then), who bore a marked resemblance to his wife, Jackie. As they began a sexual affair, Kennedy played a recording of the musical *Camelot*.

Two weeks later, at a party in Miami, Sinatra introduced Judith Campbell to a friend of his he called 'Sam Flood'. She soon took Flood as her second lover, and discovered that he was in fact Sam Giancana, boss of Chicago's underworld.

A former chauffeur to 'Machine Gun' McGurn, a prime suspect in the St Valentine's Day massacre of 1929, Giancana had risen to control illegal activities that stretched from Cleveland to New Orleans and which, in 1960, were increasing his personal fortune by an estimated $1 million a week. Some of this he spent on wooing Judith Campbell with yellow roses; simultaneously, Kennedy was sending her red ones.

It was, she said, after she had begun seeing Giancana that he started to put his weight behind Kennedy's candidacy for the White House. On more than a dozen occasions, she claimed, she had given Giancana heavy briefcases entrusted to her by Kennedy.

For those determined to damn Kennedy, this was proof of the suspicion that he had used the Mafia to distribute money to buy him votes, first in the vital West Virginia primary, and then at the election itself in November 1960. Kennedy's winning margin was the narrowest in seventy-six years, and had largely been secured by votes in Cook County, the area around Giancana's stronghold, Chicago.

Furthermore, said Judith Exner, she had used her connections with the two men to arrange a number of meetings between them once Kennedy was President. She had also carried envelopes to Giancana from the White House which the President had told her contained 'intelligence material'.

Many came to believe that this was evidence of co-operation between two organisations which had cause to want Castro dead – the American government, which had been humiliated at the Bay of Pigs, and the Mafia, which had lost control of Havana's casinos.

When her story came to light in 1975, White House staff loyal to Kennedy's memory initially denied that she had had such ready access to the President, but it soon emerged from the White House's log of visitors that she had seen him there more than twenty times. She had made her last telephone call to him the day after Marilyn Monroe's death.

⁓ 25th ⁓

Nicholas Colchester, b. 1946, d. 1996

Nicholas Colchester, the editorial director of the Economist Intelligence Unit, who has died aged forty-nine, was one of the most brilliant journalists of his generation.

He coined the concept of 'slippery-slopemanship', and in an unsigned *Economist* leader in 1988 identified the political distinction between 'Crunchiness', the capacity to take hard decisions, and 'Sogginess', the tendency to go for the soft option.

'Crunchiness,' he explained, 'brings wealth. Wealth leads to sogginess. Sogginess brings poverty. Poverty creates crunchiness. From this immutable cycle we know that to hang on to wealth you must keep things crunchy.'

⊰ 26th ⊱

Paul Newman, b. 1925, d. 2008

Paul Newman, who has died aged eighty-three, was a Hollywood actor of true star quality, who remained at the top of his profession for more than forty years.

He was in the tradition of such players as Clark Gable and Gregory Peck, who achieved fame and favour through ploughing a single furrow. Their range was limited but they were consummate technicians, with an ability to mould any part to the contours of their own personality.

Newman's on-screen persona was essentially roguish – a man to whom audiences could not help warming however huge his faults. He could play this part for laughs, as in *Butch Cassidy and the Sundance Kid* (1969), for sex appeal, as in *The Long Hot Summer* (1958), or for disreputable swagger, as in *Hud* (1963). Yet he never forfeited sympathy.

As an actor he had a commanding presence, dominating the screen by force of personality. It earned him a stream of Oscar nominations but it was not until 1986 that he was finally named best actor at the seventh attempt in *The Color of Money* – a sequel to *The Hustler*, for which many felt that he should have won twenty-five years earlier. Asked how he felt about the award, Newman said, 'A long time ago winning was pretty important. But it's like chasing a beautiful girl. You hang in there for years; then she finally relents and you say "I'm too tired".'

He made his screen debut in 1954 in *The Silver Chalice* – a Biblical epic that proved a commercial disaster. That Warner Bros, to whom he was under contract at the time, did not ditch him was probably due to his striking physical resemblance to Marlon Brando, then at the peak of his powers. As both actors aged, the similarity became less marked, but in the mid-1950s they could have been taken for cousins. It was a comparison Newman resented. 'I wonder,' he said, 'if anyone ever mistakes him for Paul Newman. I'd like that.'

Of German and Hungarian descent, Paul Leonard Newman was born on 26 January 1925 in Cleveland, Ohio, where his father owned a sports shop. He attended local schools in the affluent suburb of Shaker Heights and was encouraged to pursue his interest in the arts by his mother and his Uncle Joe, a journalist and poet.

After graduating from senior high school, he enlisted in the Navy in 1943 but failed to qualify for pilot training because those dazzling blue eyes that were to become his defining feature were actually colour-blind. He served out the war as a radio operator on torpedo bombers in the Pacific and then enrolled at Kenyon College, Ohio, under the GI bill.

Kicked off the football team after a bar-room brawl and a night in jail, he began instead to dabble in college theatricals, to which he took a shine. After graduating (in English) in 1949, he moved to Woodstock, Illinois, where he signed on with a local repertory company and appeared in some sixteen plays during the 1949–50 season.

When his father died in 1950, he was forced at first to shelve his theatrical career to manage the family store in Cleveland. In 1951 he sold out his interest to his brother and enrolled for a year at the Yale School of Drama, after which he headed for New York, where he soon found work in television.

He also studied at the Actors Studio, home of Method acting and the stable from which Marlon Brando emerged. He made his Broadway debut in 1953 in the Pulitzer Prize-winning play *Picnic*. Warner Bros saw him and signed him to a long contract.

By the early 1960s, dissatisfied with the way Warner Bros was handling his career, he asked to buy out his contract. It cost him $500,000 but led to some of his greatest roles, notably in *The Hustler* (1961), as a pool shark, and *Hud* (1963), both of which tapped the macho vein in his screen image.

Highlights of the middle section of Newman's career were the two tongue-in-cheek pictures he made with Robert Redford under director George Roy Hill, *Butch Cassidy and the Sundance Kid* (1969) and the Oscar-winning *The Sting* (1973). Both sophisticated entertainments, they were not among his most demanding work, but were undeniably crowd-pleasers.

After winning an Oscar, Newman was able to be selective about the scripts that came his way. Sometimes he chose badly. But *Blaze*, Ron Shelton's 1989 biopic of the Louisiana governor Earl Long, and *The Hudsucker Proxy* (1994), a black comedy by the Coen brothers, in which Newman played one of his rare villainous roles (albeit with a twinkle in his eye) rapidly acquired a cult following.

Newman was an inveterate prankster. He once sawed George Roy Hill's desk in half and paid back Robert Altman for exploding a mound of popcorn in his dressing room by breading and deep-frying the director's favourite deerskin gloves and serving them for supper. The victims' reactions are not recorded.

In addition to his acting career, Newman had a thriving sideline in the manufacture of food and salad dressings, marketed under the name Newman's Own. The business began in 1962, when he and his neighbour, the writer A.E. Hotchner, set up a company 'as a joke' to sell Newman's original oil and vinegar dressing. Within two years, it had become a multi-million-dollar enterprise, revenues from which were funnelled into charities and social welfare organisations.

⊰ 27th ⊱

Kurt Albert, b. 1954, d. 2010

Kurt Albert, who has died aged fifty-six, invented the 'redpoint' or free style of climbing – in which the ascent is performed without pitons or ropes.

He developed the idea in the early 1970s on expeditions to the Franconian Jura mountains, when he would paint a red 'x' on each piton he could avoid using for a foot- or hand-hold. Once he was able to complete a route avoiding all of them, he would paint a red dot at the base of the climb so that others could have a go. Albert's 'redpoints' sparked the development of the sport climbing movement and the term 'redpoint' is used as a measure of performance.

Albert marked new redpoint routes from Patagonia to the Karakoram and from Greenland to Venezuela. His more audacious feats include the first ascent of 'Eternal

Flame' on Trango Tower (6,239m) in Pakistan's Karakoram Range – one of the finest big-wall rock routes in the world.

His other pioneering climbs included the first ascent of the aptly named 'El Purgatorio' up the North Pillar of the Acopan Tepui in Venezuela (2006), and the 'Royal Flush' on Mount Fitz Roy in Patagonia (with Bernd Arnold, 1995). The latter route is one of the most difficult in the world – and Albert always considered the climb to be his most important.

Kurt Albert was born on 18 January 1954 in Nuremberg and started climbing, at the age of fourteen, with a Catholic youth group in his local Frankenjura mountains. He soon progressed to more challenging climbs, such as the Walker Spur on the Grandes Jorasses and the North Face of the Eiger, which he climbed aged eighteen.

A turning point in his life came in 1973 during a trip to the Elbsandstein in Saxony, where he met climbers who were more interested in pushing the physical limits of rock climbing than in conquering peaks. From then on the ascent became the main challenge, and the more craggy and vertiginous the route the better.

Albert was not a typical fitness fanatic. He liked strong coffee and cigarettes, and confessed to being 'lazy' at home. His commitment to redpointing, however, extended to his mode of travel to and from base camp. He considered it a point of honour to get to the rock face which he intended to climb using 'natural', non-mechanical means of transport and using no advance supplies or porters. On one occasion he undertook the journey from South America to Antarctica in a sailing boat.

Though Albert claimed to have strong feelings about climbing safety, one famous photograph showed him, clad in lederhosen, dangling from a precipice by one hand, while brandishing a stein of beer in the other.

He died from injuries sustained after falling eighteen metres from the Höhenglücksteig via ferrata in Bavaria.

David Croft, b. 1922, d. 2011

David Croft, who has died aged eighty-nine, was the joint creator of some of BBC Television's best-loved and most enduring situation comedies.

With his writing partner Jimmy Perry, Croft devised and wrote *Dad's Army* (1968–77), the whimsical, affectionate lampoon of the wartime Home Guard which, thanks to unceasing repeats, continues to draw viewers, old and new, a decade into the twenty-first century.

After *Dad's Army* ended its original run, two more of Croft and Perry's classic series – *It Ain't Half Hot, Mum* (1974–81) and *Hi-de-Hi!* (1980–88), with Croft producing – enjoyed huge success.

With a new writing partner, Jeremy Lloyd, Croft created and scripted *Are You Being Served?* (1972–85), *'Allo 'Allo* (1982–92) and *You Rang, M'Lord?* (1988–93).

A nostalgic preoccupation with class ran throughout Croft's work, intertwined with repeated references to campness, an echo of his early theatrical background. His characterisations of gay people often proved controversial; one BBC eminence took one look at Mr Humphries, the mincing menswear assistant portrayed by John Inman in *Are You Being Served?* and declared: 'The poof will have to go.'

Inman, stoutly supported by Croft ('If the poof goes, I go'), quickly achieved stardom and weathered the long-running controversy fomented by gay lobbyists who complained that Croft and Lloyd had portrayed the character in a stereotypical and offensive way.

Croft's work frequently placed him at odds with his masters at the BBC. Paul Fox, as controller of BBC1, objected vehemently to the basic premise of *Dad's Army*. 'You cannot,' he told Croft, 'take the mickey out of Britain's finest hour.'

One of Croft's biggest rows within the BBC was over *'Allo 'Allo*, the outrageous farce which poked fun at the French Resistance, the German occupiers of wartime France and the airmen of the RAF, investing everyone with appalling cod accents. Asked how he could countenance equating the heroic French with the evil Gestapo, Croft would patiently explain that *'Allo 'Allo* was not intended as a comment on either.

'What we are sending up,' he told an interviewer, 'is a whole genre of stiff upper-lip films and TV series like *Colditz* and *Secret Army* in which people actually did utter, in deadly earnest, lines like "Listen vairy carefully, I will say thees only once".' Despite frequent complaints about its political incorrectness, *'Allo 'Allo* found favour with many heavyweight fans, among them Lord Rees-Mogg and (it was rumoured) the Queen Mother. Even more remarkably, the BBC succeeded in selling the series to more than forty countries, eventually including France and Germany.

⊰ 28th ⊱

Miles Davis, b. 1926, d. 1991

Miles Davis, the American trumpeter, bandleader and composer who has died aged sixty-five, was probably the most influential and financially successful of all jazz musicians – as well as the most controversial.

Davis was the innovator of more distinct styles than any other jazz musician: he pioneered 'cool jazz', hard bop, modal playing, free-form explorations and the use of electronics. But as he admitted in his autobiography, *Miles* (1989) he was also a drug-addict and wife-beater. He revelled in having played the pimp in order to feed his drug habit and justified every action with reference to the 'racist, white motherf*****' – an omnipresent ogre. Not for nothing was Davis dubbed the 'Prince of Darkness'.

The son of a prosperous dentist, Miles Dewey III Davis was born at Alton, Illinois, on 25 May 1926. A year later his family moved to East St Louis, a small town on the Mississippi River.

Young Miles's mother was deeply conscious of her family's middle-class status and cherished hopes of her boy becoming a violinist. Davis later refused to attend her funeral. His father had a different outlook, and gave the boy a trumpet on his thirteenth birthday.

In 1944 Miles left St Louis for New York after a visit to his home town by Charlie Parker and Dizzy Gillespie, two of the first and foremost exponents of the new bebop jazz. New York was the crucible of jazz, and Davis eagerly wanted to be involved. He played and recorded with Parker, but by the late 1940s had eschewed the brassy stridencies of bop trumpet, electing for a 'cool' approach and keeping within the soft middle-range of his instrument.

Davis's association with a white, one-time dance band pianist, Gil Evans, cemented this transformation. The partnership led to Davis making records with an unorthodox instrumentation that included the French horn and tuba. Nonet recordings of 1949 and 1950, (issued in 1957 on an LP under the title of *Birth of the Cool*), inspired a host of imitators, principally on the West Coast.

In 1955 Davis made a memorable appearance at the Newport Jazz Festival. His sensational improvisations, which were lyrical and tonally pure, created excitement without screaming and made him the hit of the show.

He then teamed up again with Gil Evans to produce three more classic albums – *Miles Ahead* (1957), *Porgy and Bess* (1958) and *Sketches of Spain* (1959). Using an orchestra of more than thirty pieces, the albums produced an unambiguously new sound and sold in their thousands. The crowning achievement of his move from bop to modal music came in 1959 with *Kind Of Blue*, an album now often cited as the greatest (and best-selling) jazz record of all time.

But Davis was totally uncompromising, refusing to bend to public opinion; throughout his career he was insistent that he be accepted solely on the intrinsic value of his music.

Despite his famous hatred of whites – he used to make such absurd statements as 'The blues is a white man's invention' – Davis was frequently seen in the company of Caucasian girls and often used white musicians, incurring the wrath of black players.

He also delighted in the luxuries of the materialistic white society he so roundly condemned. Davis owned a lavish house on West 77th Street in Manhattan, a house in Hollywood and a vast wardrobe of flamboyant clothes and accessories that included diamond-studded wristbands. He was constantly demanding advances from his record company, Columbia.

Moreover, Davis renounced showbiz conventions on the stage: he never smiled; turned his back on audiences; left the stage without acknowledging applause; and frequently played for only a few minutes before leaving. 'People come to see me because they've heard I'm so bad,' he used to say. 'Ain't that a bitch?'

He had a whispery, raspy voice that was caused by his yelling at somebody in 1956 after surgery to remove polyps on his vocal cords. Indeed he was plagued by illness much of his life, at various times battling with diabetes, pneumonia, a stroke, and hip-joint problems caused by sickle-cell anaemia. He broke both legs in a car accident in 1972. Although he overcame heroin addiction in the early 1950s, he continued to use cocaine until 1981.

In the end 'The Prince of Darkness' was a supremely talented, but somewhat bizarre figure. He was perhaps best summed up by the critic Leonard Feather, who wrote: 'Miles Davis – black, volatile, rebellious and resilient as jazz itself.'

'My thing,' Davis was fond of saying 'is time.' He was alluding both to his conviction that correct tempo is fundamental to any piece of music, as well as to his own spectacular creative longevity.

⊰ 29th ⊱

Charles Addams, b. 1912, d. 1988

Charles Addams, the American cartoonist and demonic doyen of the *New Yorker*, who has died aged seventy-six, gave his name to the ghoulish characters inhabiting a spooky Gothic-suburban pile in the popular 1960s television show, *The Addams Family*.

The amiably macabre Addamses – from Morticia, the black-gowned matriarch with the heart of pure embalming fluid, and the grotesque Uncle Fester to Lurch, the giant butler, and Thing, a hand that popped out of a box – were directly inspired by Addams' cartoons which had been one of the most distinctive features of the *New Yorker* for the previous thirty years.

Addams's most reproduced cartoons included the seasonal scene in which the Family prepare to pour boiling oil from the roof of their creepy, gabled residence on to the carol singers below; and the classic study of the lady skier whose downhill tracks lead to a tree and then, mystifyingly, continue in perfectly parallel lines on either side of it. Addams was pleased to hear that a lunatic asylum in Nebraska used this drawing to test the mental level of its patients.

Edmund Trebus, b. 1918, d. 2002

Edmund Trebus, who has died aged eighty-three, became an unlikely 'docusoap' hero during his battle to preserve his rat-infested, rubbish-strewn home from Haringey Council's environmental health department.

Trebus made his television debut in 1999 on BBC1's fly-on-the-wall series *A Life of Grime*. An octogenarian Polish war veteran, he had spent years cramming his five-bedroom villa and garden in Crouch End, north London, with old fridges, rotting clothes, window panes, boxes of broken biscuits, items he had scavenged from local tips – and far, far worse; his home had no running water, working lavatory or electricity.

After complaints from the neighbours about the Augean filthiness of his property, and specifically about the number of rats living there, the council obtained a court order to have the property cleared. But the old man was having none of it, and a long-running feud developed, with the council demanding the right to remove several tons of festering detritus, and Trebus insisting on his inalienable right as a British citizen to live in squalor.

Trebus seemed to see himself as a David battling Goliath. 'I fought for your freedom!' he protested, as a couple of sheepish-looking policemen turned up to remove him from some scaffolding he had climbed: 'I survived the Germans. Stop doing that!'

As the television cameras recorded every skirmish, the environmental health team got to work. After a titanic battle of wills, they eventually succeeded in clearing Trebus's garden of 515 cubic yards of rubbish; it took six men thirty days using five large trucks and eleven skips, and cost more than £30,000.

In 2001, however, the television cameras returned for a *Life of Grime Special*, to find that not only had Trebus filled his garden up again, but large cracks in his house suggested it was on the verge of collapse.

By this time, the old man had got the measure of his opponents. At the eleventh hour, just before the council took him to court, he announced he had his own programme of repairs: a firm of builders would restore the house and turn it into flats, giving him one and splitting the profits on the rest. This was hailed as the rational solution, but no one was surprised when, the council having backed down, Trebus welshed on the whole deal.

The son of a stationmaster, Edmund Zygfryd Trebus was born on Armistice Day, 11 November 1918, at Ostrowo, near the port of Danzig.

After the German invasion, he was conscripted into the German Army in September 1944 and captured in France on 4 March 1945. On being released, he joined the Polish forces in Italy two months later and completed an officers' course before being discharged in 1948. On coming to Britain, he joined the Polish Resettlement Corps and worked as a labourer at Brentford, Middlesex.

He moved to his house in Crouch End during the 1960s. According to neighbours, the rubbish began to pile up as soon as he moved in: 'He started to bring bits and pieces back to the house, especially at night. They got bigger and bigger,' one recalled.

As time went on, Trebus's behaviour became increasingly eccentric. He claimed to have been attacked and burgled and, to thwart intruders, constructed a series of makeshift 'litter traps' in the house. Local residents made repeated complaints to the council, but no action was taken until 1997, when he seemed to have gone missing. Neighbours alerted police to his disappearance and officers forced their way into his house. They found the old man pinned under an avalanche of debris which had collapsed on top of him after he had inadvertently triggered one of the traps he had primed.

After his rescue, Trebus had to go to hospital to receive treatment for gangrene. When he emerged, he found that Haringey Council had branded his house, and a rat-infested tunnel system which extended 300 feet into his garden, unfit for human habitation.

He was finally persuaded to move into a residential care home, where he was obliged to spend the final year of his life in clean, comfortable surroundings.

⚜ **30**th ⚜

Goran Kropp, b. 1966, d. 2002

Goran Kropp, who has died aged thirty-five from a fall while rock climbing, reached the pinnacle of his career as an adventurer by cycling 7,000 miles from Sweden to Nepal, climbing Everest without porters or bottled oxygen, then cycling back to Sweden.

Kropp set out from Stockholm on 16 October 1995, riding a custom-built, 18lb bicycle and towing 240lb of climbing and camping gear in a trailer. His route took him through eastern Europe, Turkey, Iran, Pakistan, India and finally Nepal. By the time he arrived in Kathmandu, he had been pelted with rocks, assaulted with a baseball bat, run off the road, and offered a madam's daughter – free of charge – in a Hungarian brothel. He had repaired 132 flat tyres.

When he left the staging ground in Kathmandu in April 1996, he became the first climber to carry all his equipment (weighing 143lb) to Everest Base Camp, at 17,100ft. From there he made his way up the South Pillar, doing his best to steer clear of other climbers, doing his own route-finding, eschewing the fixed ropes and carrying all his own food.

His first attempt ended in frustration when he was forced to turn back, having run out of steam 350ft below the summit. Despite this blow to his morale, and in the face of rapidly deteriorating weather that would result in the deadliest season in Everest's history, he steeled himself for another try. That failed too, due to dangerous snow conditions. Then, on 9–10 May, the great storm arrived, the worst in living memory, catching forty climbers from eight expeditions high on the mountain; eight died in the disaster, which was later vividly described in Jon Krakauer's book *Into Thin Air*, published in 1997.

A few days after the storm subsided, Kropp set off for his third and final attempt, still without Sherpas and without bottled oxygen. On reaching the summit he lingered for just four minutes, deeming it prudent to get his blue, oxygen-deprived fingers to a lower altitude as soon as possible.

He spent a few weeks in Kathmandu recuperating before beginning the 7,000-mile ride back home.

Goran Kropp was born on 12 November 1966 at Jonkoping, Sweden, and grew up in Italy, where his father worked for the UN. At the age of six, Goran climbed Norway's tallest peak, Galdhoppigen, with his father. The next year they climbed Sweden's highest mountain, Kebnekaise. At school, Goran disliked team sports but was cross-country running champion.

Kropp made his first successful high-altitude climb in 1988, reaching the summit of Pic Lenin (7,134m) in the Soviet Union. The next year, on a trip to Ecuador and Bolivia, he climbed two mountains above 5,000m and three above 6,000m, including Illamni (6,300m) and Cotopaxi (5,897m). In 1990 he completed the technically very difficult climb of Muztagh Tower (7,273m). In 1993 he became the second person to reach the summit of K2 (8,616m) in Pakistan, the world's second highest mountain, alone and without bottled oxygen. In 2000 Kropp attempted to ski unsupported to the North Pole but he abandoned the expedition halfway, due to frostbite suffered after being stalked by two polar bears, one of which he was forced to shoot dead.

His next big expedition, planned for 2004, was to have been to attempt to sail single-handedly from Seattle through the treacherous waters of the Southern Hemisphere to Antarctica, ski 1,490 miles solo to the South Pole – and make the return trip.

Kropp aimed to tackle each expedition 'in harmony with nature', without support and leaving no trace of his passing. 'It is important for me to leave nothing behind me on a mountain,' he said. He gave freely of his time to benefit the poorer regions he visited, and over the past few years he had built a school, a hospital and a power plant for a small Nepalese village in the Himalayas.

He made his living meanwhile by lecturing – he had delivered more than 1,000 talks since 1996 – and through his company, which runs courses on team building and motivation.

OCTOBER

⚜ 1st ⚜

General Curtis 'Old Ironpants' LeMay, b. 1906, d. 1990

General Curtis 'Old Ironpants' LeMay, who has died aged eighty-three, was celebrated for his line that North Vietnam should be 'bombed back to the Stone Age', though he had earned his sobriquet on account of his exploits during the Second World War.

The cigar-chewing general was considered by many to be the father of strategic bombing – he was also known as America's 'architect of systematic destruction'. He said that the American public had developed an absurd phobia about nuclear weapons and that if he himself had the choice between being killed by a rusty Russian knife or a nuclear weapon, he would lean towards the latter.

J.G. Links, b. 1904, d. 1997

J.G. Links, who has died aged ninety-two, achieved prominence in three quite different fields: as an art historian and author of *Venice for Pleasure* (1966); as co-writer, with Dennis Wheatley, of a series of fictional 'crime dossiers'; and as furrier to the Queen and the Queen Mother.

In 1945 Links married Mary Lutyens, the youngest daughter of Edwin Lutyens, the architect, and already an established writer. It proved a singularly happy union.

Early in their marriage they went to Venice, armed with a copy of Ruskin's *Stones of Venice*. Both of them were instantly captivated, and for the next thirty years visited the city two or three times a year, staying always at the Danieli – cheaper, they persuaded themselves, than owning an apartment.

In *Venice for Pleasure* Links adopted the persona of a knowledgeable, entertaining, but rather sybaritic companion. In his anxiety not to bore his more philistine readers he even included instructions on how to 'do' the first nineteen rooms of the Accademia in half an hour.

But Links was a more serious scholar than he gave out, and Bernard Levin described *Venice for Pleasure* as 'the best guidebook to the city, or indeed to any city, ever written'.

❦ 2nd ❦

Roger Vivier, b. 1907, d. 1998

Roger Vivier, who has died aged ninety, was one of the great shoemakers of the twentieth century, a Parisian craftsman who from the 1930s shod the feet of the world's most glamorous women.

Although perhaps best remembered for his invention of the four-inch stiletto heel in the 1950s, it was for his decorative shoes that Vivier was sought out. Delicate and light, but freely embellished with beading and semi-precious stones, Vivier's shoes earned their maker the sobriquet 'The Fabergé of Footwear'.

Vivier desired, he once said, to merge 'the greatest extravagance with the greatest classicism', and, though the line of his shoes, often inspired by eighteenth-century models, may have been purely classical, their surface was unquestionably extravagant.

The trims he favoured – sequins, ribbons, buckles, feathers and bows – and his bold use of colour and material instantly set fashion trends. And where, in the hands of another designer, this decorative approach might well have strayed into the realms of the vulgar, Vivier's sense of style invariably kept him safely on the right side of good taste.

His shoes, moreover, bejewelled and ornamented though they were, were designed for use, and for comfort. 'What is exquisite about Vivier's shoes,' declared Diana Vreeland, American *Vogue*'s celebrated editor, 'is the mounting of his heels. There is exact balance.'

Over nearly seventy years of work as a shoe designer, Vivier assembled a clientele that boasted Josephine Baker, Jeanne Moreau, Ava Gardner, Elizabeth Taylor, Sophia Loren, Catherine Deneuve and the Beatles. Marlene Dietrich sported a pair of Vivier's shoes in Alfred Hitchcock's film *Stage Fright*, and throughout the 1950s the Empress of Iran ordered a hundred pairs a year.

At the Coronation in London in 1953, the Queen trod the processional carpet of Westminster Abbey in a pair of gold kidskin Vivier's, the heels encrusted with garnets.

Roger Henri Vivier was born in Paris on 13 November 1907. Orphaned as a child, he was brought up by an aunt. On leaving school, he intended to become an artist and commenced his studies at the Ecole des Beaux Arts.

Soon, though, he was drawn into the world of fashion. He began by designing fabrics and scarves, but when shoe-manufacturing friends of his family asked him to do some drawings for them, he discovered his true metier. Aged nineteen, he left the Ecole des Beaux Arts, and by the late 1930s he had become an established name, designing shoes for Pinet, Bally, Rayne, Miller and Delman.

During the Second World War, frustrated by the lack of materials, Vivier left Paris for New York where, with Suzanne Remi, he set up a millinery shop on Madison Avenue called Suzanne and Roger.

After his return to France in 1953, he became shoemaker to Christian Dior, for whom he created two collections a year. His work for Dior in the 1950s marked a high-point of the shoemaker's art: his stilettos, dainty shoes dripping with seed pearls, the backward bent 'comma' heel, the square toe and the choc heel, slanting awry from the arch, were all copied everywhere.

Dior and Vivier worked together for ten years, and during that time Vivier's name became known and influential internationally. The relationship with Yves Saint Laurent, for whom Vivier created the distinctive buckled flats to go with Saint Laurent's revolutionary Mondrian shifts of 1965, and the Cinderella boot, was particularly fertile. 'Monsieur Vivier,' said Yves Saint Laurent, 'is a great artist.'

Never cheap – even in 1961 a pair might cost as much as £120 – his shoes have become collectors' items, fetching thousands of pounds. Examples of his work can now be found in the collections of the Victoria & Albert Museum, and of the Metropolitan Museum, New York.

⊱ 3rd ⊰

Ronnie Barker, b. 1929, d. 2005

Ronnie Barker, who has died aged seventy-six, was a comedian, actor and scriptwriter who earned both fame and public affection for his appearances in television shows such as *The Two Ronnies*, *Open All Hours* and *Porridge*.

Barker did not look like a television comedian – his fifteen and a half stones and conservative taste in dress gave him the appearance of a man doing moderately well in chartered accountancy – but his ample build and ability to project an air of unclouded bonhomie provided the perfect counterpoint in his double act with Ronnie Corbett.

The Two Ronnies, with scripts co-written by Barker himself under the pen-name of Gerald Wiley, became a national institution, especially dear to admirers of the double entendre. Meanwhile the impact of *Porridge* was far greater than the number of episodes filmed (twenty) might suggest, and made many wonder what Barker would have achieved had he directed all his energies into acting; Sir Alec Guinness was one of many classical actors who greatly admired Barker's genius for characterisation.

Sir Peter Hall, who was keen for him to play Falstaff at the National Theatre (Barker refused because he could not face the traffic between Pinner and the South Bank), described him as 'the great actor we lost'.

⊱ 4th ⊰

Generalleutnant Günther Rall, b. 1918, d. 2009

Generalleutnant Günther Rall, who has died aged ninety-one, was one of the few outstanding German fighter leaders to survive the Second World War; by the end of the conflict he was the third-highest scoring fighter ace of all time, with 275 aerial victories.

In post-war years he was one of the founding fathers of the modern German Air Force and rose to become its chief.

In the spring of 1941 Rall was a squadron commander in Jagdgeschwader (fighter wing) JG-52 flying the Messerschmitt Bf 109 based in Romania. After shooting down his thirty-sixth victim, Rall was attacked by an enemy fighter and his aircraft badly damaged. He just managed to cross the German lines before crash-landing in a rock-strewn gully. He was severely wounded and knocked unconscious but German tank crews dragged him clear. He eventually reached a hospital in Vienna where it was found that he had broken his back in three places. Here he was treated by a woman doctor, Hertha, who later became his wife.

Having been paralysed for months Rall returned to operational duty in August 1942. On 3 September he was decorated with the Knight's Cross of the Iron Cross after his sixty-fifth victory. During the following month his score increased beyond one hundred, bringing him the oak leaves for his Knight's Cross, the 134th recipient of the coveted award.

In November they were presented to him personally by Hitler. Afterwards, as they sat together by the fire, Rall asked Hitler: 'Führer, how long will this war take?' Hitler replied: 'My dear Rall, I don't know.' That surprised him. 'I thought our leaders knew everything,' Rall recalled, 'and suddenly I realised they didn't know anything.'

In April 1943 Rall was promoted to command III/JG-52. He was constantly in action for the next eleven months. On 29 August he recorded his 200th victory on his 555th operational flight and on 12 September he was again summoned to Berlin when Hitler awarded him the Swords to his Knight's Cross, the thirty-fourth man to be so honoured. Rall returned to operations and in October accounted for another forty aircraft – more than many of Germany's best pilots achieved throughout the entire war.

The great majority of Rall's successes were in fighter-to-fighter combat. During his time on the Eastern Front, Rall came up against many excellent Soviet pilots and was himself shot down seven times. Finally, in April 1944, he returned to Germany.

The son of a merchant, Günther Rall was born on 10 March 1918 in Gaggenau in the Black Forest. When he was three, his family moved to Stuttgart where he completed his education. On graduation in 1936 he joined the Army to be an infantry officer and while at the Dresden Kriegsschule met an old friend whose tales of flying convinced him that he should apply to be a pilot.

In 1939 Rall trained as a fighter pilot on a base east of Berlin and was transferred to JG-52. Flying a Messerschmitt Bf 109, he saw his first air combat in May 1940 during the Battle of France. On 18 May he shot down a French Air Force Curtis Hawk fighter flown by a Czech sergeant who escaped by parachute. With the fall of France, Rall's unit moved to Calais.

He flew throughout the Battle of Britain, when his unit was assigned to escort Junkers Ju-87 Stukas (dive bombers) – very slow-flying aircraft. The fighters had to stick with them, giving up all of their superiority and speed; the unit suffered heavy losses against the Spitfires and Hurricanes, losing the group commander, the adjutant and all three squadron commanders in a few weeks. Rall found himself rapidly promoted to squadron leader before the unit was finally withdrawn in September to rebuild and train new pilots.

Rall was critical of the tactics used that made his valuable and capable aircraft vulnerable to attack by fighters. He always spoke very highly of the RAF. During a post-war interview he said: 'In my experience, the RAF pilot was the most aggressive and capable fighter pilot during the Second World War.'

Once the squadron had been brought up to strength, it was transferred to Romania to defend the oil refineries and bridges over the Danube during the spring of 1941. After providing support for the German airborne assault on Crete, Rall's unit hurried back to Romania following the outbreak of war with the Soviet Union.

Towards the end of the war, having returned from the Eastern Front, Rall was made Gruppenkommadeur of II/ JG-11, flying Bf 109s on homeland defence duties, primarily against the high-flying daylight bomber forces and their escorting fighters of the USAAF 8th Air Force. On 12 May 1944 he attacked a large formation and shot down two USAAF P-47 Thunderbolts, but was then himself shot down. He was severely wounded in the hand but managed to bail out over Frankfurt. His wound became badly infected and he remained in hospital for six months.

Because he was deemed too precious for the morale of the people, and could not fire his guns because of a missing thumb, he was kept from combat. Rall became an instructor, and studied several American planes that had fallen into the possession of the Luftwaffe to find their strengths and weaknesses and to develop better tactics to teach his students. He flew the P-51 and was amazed at the luxury and quality of the American planes. He once explained that being unable to fly in combat probably saved his life at a time when Germany was totally outnumbered and the chances of staying alive were drastically reduced. But he returned to active duty in November.

Rall's last command was as the leader of JG-300 and on arrival at the unit's airfield he was forced to dive into a ditch as USAAF fighters strafed the line-up of Bf 109s – fifteen were left burning. He flew his 621st and final mission at the end of April 1945. Towards the very end of the war he asked the men in his command to try to stay alive rather than get involved in senseless actions. A few days later he was captured by the Americans.

Returning to post-war Germany, Rall was unable to find work. He started a small wood-cutting business in the forest and eventually joined Siemens as a representative, leaving in 1953. After meeting a wartime friend and Luftwaffe pilot he joined the new Luftwaffe der Bundeswehr after the re-militarisation of West Germany in 1955. He converted to jet fighters before becoming the project officer for the introduction of the Lockheed F-104 Starfighter, which became the German air force's main operational fighter until 1980. Rall became the Chief of Staff of Nato's 4th Allied Tactical Air Force and after serving as the Inspector General of the Luftwaffe he was appointed the Chief of Air Staff, a post he held for three years. For two years he was the German military representative at Nato headquarters before retiring in 1975.

In retirement Rall established firm friendships with his former British and American adversaries and made many visits to each country. By any standard, his achievements during the Second World War were outstanding and attracted great admiration from his former enemies. An American aviation historian of the

Smithsonian Institute commented: 'He occupies a special niche among the celebrated military pilots of the twentieth century.'

Yet Rall never considered himself a hero. 'We fought for our country and to stay alive,' he reflected. 'Of course, I tell myself in quiet moments today: "You have killed in order to protect others and not be killed yourself." But in the end: for what? The Third Reich trained 30,000 pilots. Ten thousand survived the war. One-third. This is the highest loss rate along with the U-boat sailors.'

⊰ 5th ⊱

Steve Jobs, b. 1955, d. 2011

Steve Jobs, who has died aged fifty-six, was the visionary co-founder, and later chief executive, of Apple, makers of the Macintosh computer, the iMac, the iPod, iPad and iPhone, and the man behind the astonishing success of the computer animation firm Pixar, makers of *Toy Story*; in consequence he did more to determine what films we watch, how we listen to music, and how we work and play than any other person on the planet.

Jobs never designed a computer in his life, but it was because of him that Apple products, even when they do largely what other products do, are perceived to be different and infinitely more cool. The Macintosh introduced the world to the computer mouse; the iPod became famous for its click wheel; and the iPhone for its 'user-interface' – a sophisticated touchscreen that responds to the flick of a finger.

Jobs emphasised the difference between Macs and the PCs that ran Microsoft software, managing to preserve Apple's image as a plucky, creative, insurgent against the bland Microsoft behemoth even as Apple itself became the biggest company on the planet. 'I wish Bill Gates well,' he once claimed. 'I only wish that at some time in his life he had dropped acid or spent time at an ashram.'

It was a marketing trick that Jobs worked on consumers too, convincing them that purchasing Apple products somehow conferred membership of an exclusive and pioneering club, even when it was transparently obvious that the company's devices were utterly ubiquitous. This corporate reputation for seer-like trailblazing lay completely with Jobs. 'I skate to where the puck is going to be,' he explained, using an ice hockey metaphor, 'not where it has been.'

This inspired almost evangelical devotion among techno-geeks. Jobs was not just the brains behind Apple, he was high priest of the 'Mac' religion. His eagerly anticipated 'MacWorld' shows were adulatory affairs akin to revivalist rallies, with Jobs, in black turtleneck, jeans and trainers, preaching the message that salvation lay in Apple's latest gadget.

The Jobs story – humble birth, rise and fall, miraculous comeback – was even likened by Apple fanatics to the life of Christ. For the less blasphemously inclined it proved that the American Dream is alive and well.

He was born on 24 February 1955 to a Syrian Arab father and an American mother, who travelled to San Francisco to put him up for adoption. Soon afterwards a blue-collar California couple, Paul and Clara Jobs, claimed him and named him Steven Paul.

After completing high school in Cupertino, northern California, Jobs went north to study at Reed College in Portland, Oregon, but dropped out after a term. Returning to California, he took a job at Atari, the video games manufacturer, in order to save money for a 'spiritual quest' to India. There he was converted to Zen Buddhism and vegetarianism and dabbled in hallucinogenic drugs.

On his return to America Jobs resumed his work with Atari and was given the task of creating a more compact circuit board for the game *Breakout*. He had little interest in the intricacies of circuit board design and persuaded his sixteen-year-old friend, Steve Wozniak, to do the job for him, offering to split any bonus fifty-fifty. Jobs was given $5,000 by a delighted Atari, but Wozniak only got $300, under the impression the payout was $600.

In 1976 Wozniak showed Jobs a computer he had designed for his own use. Jobs was impressed and suggested marketing it. They had no capital, but Jobs had a brilliant idea. By persuading a local store to order fifty of the computers, then asking an electrical store for thirty days' credit on the parts to build them, they set up business without a single investor. They called it Apple Computers (which would lead to protracted legal battles with the company behind the Beatles' record label, Apple Corps) and launched their first product, the Apple 1. A year later the more sophisticated Apple 2 hit the jackpot, and by 1980, when the company went public, the pair were multi-millionaires.

The success of Apple launched Jobs into the celebrity circuit. He dated Joan Baez and became a personal friend of California Governor Jerry Brown. But his ruthless streak became apparent aged twenty-three when his then girlfriend gave birth to his daughter. For two years, though already wealthy, he denied paternity while the baby's mother went on welfare. At one point he even swore an affidavit to the effect that he was 'sterile and infertile', so could not be the father.

The strain of running a successful company soon began to tell. Employees complained of Jobs' 'Management By Walking Around Frightening Everyone' technique and even he realised that more seasoned business experience was required. In 1983 he lured John Sculley, president of PepsiCo, to serve as Apple's chief executive, saying: 'Do you want to spend the rest of your life selling sugared water to children, or do you want a chance to change the world?'

But the clash of business cultures proved irreconcilable, and in 1985 Jobs (whom Sculley likened to Leon Trotsky) was forced out by his own board. It was twelve years before he returned.

During those years Jobs started Next Computing and bought what became Pixar from George Lucas, the director of *Star Wars*. Next was a techie's dream – Tim Berners-Lee wrote the software for the web on a Next computer – but a business failure. Pixar struggled for years until 1995, when it contracted with Disney to produce a number of computer-animated feature films. The first of these, *Toy Story*, broke box-office records and Pixar's flotation in 1996 made Jobs a billionaire. Over the next ten years the studio went on to produce a string of hits including *A Bug's Life* (1998), *Toy Story 2* (1999), *Monsters, Inc.* (2001), *Finding Nemo* (2003) and *The Incredibles* (2004). In 2006

Disney bought the company in a $7.4 billion deal under which Jobs became Disney's largest single shareholder with approximately 7 per cent of the company's stock.

Jobs' triumph at Pixar reminded people of his ability to divine the technological future, and in 1997 he persuaded Apple to buy Next – to acquire its forward-looking operating system Nextstep, and, more importantly, Jobs himself.

In his memoirs, published in 1987, John Sculley dismissed Jobs' vision for Apple to become a hi-tech consumer products company as a 'lunatic plan'. But by rejecting this vision, Apple, by 1997, had become a basket case, losing $736 million in one quarter.

Management by committee had blunted its innovative flair and the corporate atmosphere was more that of a student bar than a thrusting business in a highly competitive market.

Jobs' instinctive feel for the consumer zeitgeist soon turned things around. Within a year the company was once more posting handsome profits. The iMac computer was launched in 1998, followed in 2001 by the iPod, a digital music player of strikingly minimalist design. Then came iTunes digital music software, and the iTunes online digital music store. In 2007, Apple entered the cellular phone business with the iPhone, a clever and expensive product combining mobile phone, iPod, and internet device in one streamlined casing. It was followed by the iPad, a tablet device without a physical keyboard, and it became a bestseller too.

But Jobs was not a universally popular figure. He oozed arrogance, was vicious about business rivals, and in contrast to, say, Bill Gates, refused to have any truck with notions of corporate responsibility. He habitually parked his Mercedes in the disabled parking slot at Apple headquarters and one of his first acts on returning to the company in 1997 was to terminate all of its corporate philanthropy programmes.

Jobs' management style owed less to Zen Buddhism than to George Orwell. He ruled Apple with a combination of foul-mouthed tantrums and charm, withering scorn and carefully judged flattery. People were either geniuses or 'bozos', and those in his regular orbit found that they could flip with no warning from one category to the other, in what became known as the 'hero–shithead roller coaster'. Employees worried about getting trapped with Jobs in a lift, afraid that they might not have a job when the doors opened. One senior executive admitted that before heading into a meeting with Jobs, she embraced the mindset of a bullfighter entering the ring: 'I pretend I'm already dead.'

By 2006 Apple had a market value of $108 billion – more than Goldman Sachs. By August 2011, after it reported yet another quarter of record-breaking profits, it briefly became the biggest company in the world, with a market value of $337 billion.

Within days of reaching that corporate milestone, however, Jobs announced his resignation on health grounds. Few were surprised. In 2004 he disclosed that he had been diagnosed with a rare form of pancreatic cancer that had been 'cured' by surgery. Questions about his health resurfaced in December 2008 when it was announced that, for the first time in twelve years, he was pulling out of delivering his annual address at MacWorld.

Feverish speculation over his wellbeing was only fuelled by Apple's fanatical devotion to secrecy. When Jobs went on medical leave in January 2009, the company would not say why. Inevitably, suspicions arose that the cancer had returned. His devoted fans began to scrutinise every public appearance for clues to Jobs' physical fitness. On the stock markets, which considered his presence vital to Apple's own health, the company's shares fell if he looked particularly gaunt. In the first half of 2011 he was seen only a handful of times. Then, on 24 August, he announced he was stepping down, to be replaced as CEO by Tim Cook, who had run the company during Jobs' previous absences. Apple's shares immediately dropped 5 per cent.

⚜ 6th ⚜

Denholm Elliott, b. 1922, d. 1992

Denholm Elliott, the actor who has died aged seventy, was one of post-war cinema's most subtle exponents of inner turmoil, clenched anguish and well-bred rascality. With his singularly well-mapped face – twitchy, cratered, ringed, robustly veined – he specialised in ageing rakes, sexual eccentrics, self-effacing neurotics, cowardly warriors, wine snobs, seducers, cads and con men.

If he was a better actor than his 'character' casting in films allowed, Elliott brought to every role, big or small, an acute sensitivity, precision of observation and ironical edge. He contrived to make each portrait touching as well as compelling, even when it verged on caricature.

Denholm Mitchell Elliott was born in London on 31 May 1922 into a legal dynasty. He was educated at Malvern, which he loathed. 'I used to nick things,' he recalled.

One of what was to become a series of psychoanalysts suggested that young Denholm should try for the Royal Academy of Dramatic Art, in the cause of self-expression. Although at the time he enjoyed it little more than Malvern, Elliott later recalled that he never considered any career other than acting. It was, he said, like dressing up for Mummy and Daddy.

During the Second World War, Elliott served with the RAF as a radio operator and gunner with Bomber Command. He was shot down over Denmark in 1942. For the next three years, as a prisoner-of-war in Silesia, he developed his passion for acting, forming a drama group called the No Name Players.

Back home Elliott went straight into repertory. The next year he made his mark in the West End in *The Guinea Pig*, a play about the difficulties of a state scholar at a public school.

Soon Elliott came to the attention of Laurence Olivier who cast him as his son in Christopher Fry's *Venus Observed* at the old St James's Theatre. Elliott learned a trick or two from the great actor and went on to enjoy success in New York in Jean Anouilh's *Ring Round the Moon*.

Meanwhile, he was forging a career in the cinema. He had made his debut in *Dear Mr Prohack* (1949) and earned favourable notices for his performances as the nervous young flyer in *The Sound Barrier*. But on-stage the second half of the 1950s proved to be rather a lean period for Elliott. His clean-cut, upper-middle-class persona did not chime in with the era of the 'Kitchen Sink'.

In 1960 a season at Stratford-upon-Avon gave Elliott neither pleasure nor satisfaction, though he subsequently enjoyed playing in Arthur Miller's *The Crucible* in New York. By 1964 his career was distinctly in the doldrums. But that year he scored an unexpected hit in the film *Nothing But the Best*, with a witty script by Frederic Raphael.

Elliott played, with endearing élan, a world-weary man-about-town advising Alan Bates on how to bluff his way in society. At a stroke, Elliott's image as a matinee idol *manqué* was banished forever. From then on he was in constant demand for meaty character roles.

He played a seedy abortionist in *Alfie*, a corrupt PoW in *King Rat*, a Swinging Sixties dad in *Here We Go Round the Mulberry Bush*, a moral zealot who closes the burlesque joint down in *The Night They Raided Minskys*, a platoon leader in *Too Late the Hero*, and a drunken director reduced to filming bar mitzvahs in *The Apprenticeship of Duddy Kravitz*.

By the 1980s, firmly established as a supremely dependable character actor, he found himself more than ever in demand. As he himself put it, the heavy lines now marking his face enabled him to switch from saving many a mediocre film to playing challenging roles in films of real quality.

'I'd rather stay in the second line,' he once said. 'As a character actor you get interesting parts and can be in a good position to steal the film.' Certainly his cameos, however brief, would sometimes stick in the memory long after the stars had been forgotten.

⪦ 7th ⪧

Maureen Muggeridge, b. 1948, d. 2010

Maureen Muggeridge, who has died aged sixty-two, led the team that discovered the largest known diamond deposit – the Argyle in the remote north of Western Australia.

A niece of the writer and broadcaster Malcolm Muggeridge, Maureen Muggeridge arrived in Australia in 1972 armed with nothing more than £10 and a degree in Geology from St Andrews University. She spent her first night sleeping under a palm tree in Perth's Kings Park, but within weeks had landed a job with the mining company Tanganyika Holdings.

By 1979 she had married and was six months pregnant with her first child when, in July that year, she discovered diamond samples in the flood plains surrounding Smoke Creek, a small stream in East Kimberley that drained into Lake Argyle.

In order to deceive rival prospecting teams until it had pegged and claimed the land, Maureen Muggeridge's team put it about that she had gone on maternity leave, when in fact she was busily engaged in tracing the source of the diamonds to the headwaters of Smoke Creek in an ancient volcanic crater, surrounded by tawny and mauve crags.

'It all had to be hush-hush,' she recalled. 'You couldn't say you were looking for diamonds because that would spark too much interest. I felt like a character in a James Bond movie.'

It soon became apparent that she had stumbled on the world's largest known diamond deposit, estimated to contain as many diamonds as were then known to exist in the rest of the world.

Today, Argyle's pink and purple stones are eagerly sought by connoisseurs. The mine produces about one third of global output.

❧ 8th ❧

Captain Kenneth Lockwood, b. 1911, d. 2007

Captain Kenneth Lockwood, who has died aged ninety-five, was one of the first six British Army officers to arrive at Colditz Castle in 1940, and remained there to play a key role in many of the escape attempts made during the next four years and five months.

Known as 'the ear', he was the invaluable right-hand man to Pat Reid, chairman of the escape committee. Whenever escapers needed help Lockwood was on hand, slipping one a fifty-Reichsmark note, finding a pair of rubber-soled shoes for another to climb down a wall, or hiding incriminating evidence from constantly snooping guards.

When a manhole that led down to the drains was discovered in the shop floor, he arranged for the ever-present German sergeant to be distracted while he swiftly removed the shop's key to take an imprint in some soap; this was then used to fashion a replica that enabled prisoners to enter the shop at night to work on a tunnel.

He also pretended to be ill in the sick bay so that those working on another tunnel could hide under his bed before continuing with their digging, and acted as a stagehand for the prisoners' show while helping Airey Neave, the future Tory MP, to make his 'home run' back to England.

As news of Lockwood's role in the camp reached London a stream of parcels from supposedly innocent English friends were sent to him by the escape organisation MI9. One consisted of handkerchiefs containing sugared almonds, which revealed instructions for a detailed code when dropped in water; others included money and maps.

Since these were often discovered by the authorities, Lockwood used a skill he had learned at prep school to make maps from jelly. This involved pressing the tracing of a map of Germany, made with an indelible pencil, on to a melted Chivers yellow jelly. When the paper was drawn off the solidified pudding, there was the map.

'The system was good for about thirty copies, working rather like a printing press,' Lockwood remembered. 'And the jelly was never wasted at the end of it. We ate it.'

The son of a London stock exchange jobber, Kenneth Lockwood was born on 17 December 1911, and went to Whitgift. Kenneth worked for his father's firm, starting as an office boy before becoming a 'blue button' clerk on the floor and a dealer.

In 1933 he joined the 22nd London Regiment (Queen's Royal West Surreys). After mobilisation in August 1939 he did training at Yeovil then was sent abroad to Le Mans, where he took the chance to drive a lorry around the famous racing circuit. Two weeks after the Germans attacked France in May 1940 he was captured during the retreat to Dunkirk.

Lockwood was first sent to Laufen Castle, near the Austrian frontier. He was one of six men who, with the aid of two nails and a stone, spent three weeks digging a tunnel that came out in a wooden shed outside the camp. Dressed as a woman, Reid got out first with two others. The following night three more, including Lockwood, also disguised as a woman, made their way through the tunnel – he found that the biscuits with which he had filled his bra crumbled as he scrambled through.

They split into two groups. Reid's was captured first. Lockwood's took a train, which turned out to be going in the wrong direction; they were arrested on the road to Switzerland when they were mistaken for burglars.

All six men were threatened with execution for stealing bicycles that were the property of the Reich, for possessing a compass and cutting up a German army blanket. But after a week in solitary confinement they were dispatched to Colditz, the sinister medieval fortress on the Mulde River in eastern Germany.

As they were marched into the courtyard the six wondered uneasily if they were about to be shot. But when some Polish prisoners suddenly appeared in their quarters with bottles of beer and news of exploration in the castle's 700 rooms, the 'Laufen Six', as they were called, cheered up. By early the next year they realised that they were in a camp for bad boys – those who had tried to escape from elsewhere – and started to make new plans.

Lockwood was still at Colditz when an American relief force finally arrived – and was deterred from shelling the castle only by signs hung out by the prisoners.

He settled back into his father's firm on the stock exchange before moving to run an office on Jersey for almost ten years.

The importance of his role was shown in the Channel 4 documentary series *Escape from Colditz* (2000), in which survivors returned to the fortress for the cameras. He retraced his first steps through the gate into the castle's courtyard, inspected the spot in the lawn where he and Reid had dug a tunnel, and demonstrated how he had made maps from jelly.

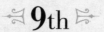 9th

Patric Walker, b. 1931, d. 1995

Patric Walker, who has died aged sixty-four, was the doyen of newspaper astrologers. His column, which appeared in the *Evening Standard* and the *Mail on Sunday*, was syndicated all over the world, and had more than a billion readers. He enjoyed a reputation for unusual accuracy.

People were turning to astrology, Walker said, because they felt they were losing control over their lives; his gentle warnings and measured advice served to restore a sense of structure. 'There are only four problems in the world,' he maintained, 'love, health, work and money – in that order.'

Walker said he was not 'dabbling with entrails' but 'looking at the rhythms, the natural timing of things'. Though a flamboyant figure in London in the 1970s he became reclusive. He said he had grown weary of parties at which people asked him to guess their star sign.

Patric Walker was born at Hackensack, New Jersey, on 25 September 1931. His father was descended from Yorkshire flour millers, and his mother was of Irish gypsy stock. They had moved to the United States in the 1920s, and when young Patric was four they returned to Britain.

After National Service he worked as a waiter, barman and accountant. In the late 1950s one of his aunts gave him her winnings from a sweepstake, and he launched himself as a property developer.

At a dinner party in 1961 Walker found himself next to the American astrologer Helene Hoskins, who was 'Celeste' of *Harpers & Queen*. When she asked him his star sign Walker replied, 'I'm not a sign. I'm Patric Walker.' Hoskins told him not to be fresh, and asked the date of his birth. On learning that he was a Libran born in 1931 she informed him he was 'on a downward spiral to hell'.

A month later Walker telephoned Hoskins to tell her that his life had fallen to pieces. She explained that Librans suffer disasters every twenty-nine years because of the movement of Saturn.

Walker spent the next six years under her instruction. Hoskins was surprised at his talent. 'I knew he would be good,' she told an acquaintance, 'but I didn't think he'd be this good.'

By the early 1970s Walker had his own column in the glossy magazine *Nova*, and in 1974 he took over as Celeste. He entertained on a grand scale at his house in London and indulged his passion for expensive clothes and unusual jewellery. He also started a small theatrical agency.

Before the launch of the *Mail on Sunday* in 1982 Lord Rothermere asked Walker whether the stars augured well for the new project. Though Walker replied that they boded ill, Rothermere went ahead and launched the newspaper. 'And of course,' Walker recalled, 'it failed, and had to be relaunched.'

By the late 1970s, when his columns were syndicated worldwide, Walker began to suffer from stress. He moved to Rhodes, he said, on account of a middle-age panic. 'It's extremely hard to be perceived as someone who is always right,' he explained. 'I was expected to be infallible and it made me start drinking.'

Having become, by his own admission, a 'terrible drunk', Walker decided to give up alcohol in 1986. In 1990 he suffered a heart attack and underwent bypass surgery.

'I never saw Saturn coming round,' he said. 'I'd been ill for two years and nobody knew what was wrong with me. Then I realised that twenty-nine years had gone by and it had got me again.' He fell ill this summer with salmonella poisoning.

⚜ 10th ⚜

John Bindon, b. 1943, d. 1993

John Bindon, who has died aged fifty, was one of the most flamboyant London villains of his day and turned his 'tough guy' persona to legitimate account as an actor in such television programmes as *Hazell*, *The Sweeney* and *Softly, Softly*.

Possessed of a menacing physique and considerable charm, Bindon was a gregarious self-publicist who counted among his friends the Kray twins and Princess Margaret.

Acquaintances were often frightened of him, but recall him as 'screamingly funny'. When the Earl of Longford was engaged in his celebrated investigation into pornography, Bindon 'flashed' at him outside the Chelsea Potter pub. He was justly famed for a party trick which entailed the balancing of as many as six half-pint mugs on one part of his anatomy. He served several prison sentences, and in 1979 was accused of murdering an underworld enforcer in a club brawl.

A taxi driver's son, John Bindon was born in Fulham, London, in October 1943. He recalled his infancy as miserable (his mother used to keep him under the kitchen table) and said: 'I've had this overwhelming urge to smash things up ever since I was a kid.' At the age of eleven, he was charged with malicious damage.

Bindon made a living from such jobs as plucking pheasants and laying asphalt, before progressing to the antiques trade. He was holding court one night in a London pub when Ken Loach, then filming *Poor Cow*, Nell Dunn's gritty story of working-class life, walked in. Noted for his use of amateurs, Loach thought Bindon 'absolutely right' for the film. 'The only thing out of character,' said Bindon of his role, 'is that I have to hit Carol White in one scene – and I never hit women.'

The success of the film launched him on an acting career in which he played criminals. He held his own alongside Mick Jagger and James Fox in *Performance* (1973), and was a drug dealer in *Quadrophenia* (1979). Bindon had no regrets about being typecast, although he expressed a wistful desire 'to play a priest sometime'.

In the early 1970s Bindon dominated many Chelsea and Fulham pubs, where he was rumoured to run protection rackets. He could be gallant, but a close relationship was precarious. On one occasion a young man who offended him was reputedly driven in a car boot to Putney Common where Bindon made him dig his own grave before relenting.

Despite his substantial earnings – not entirely from acting – he was constantly in financial difficulties, and by 1976 he was bankrupt.

Two years later Bindon killed a gangster named John Darke during a struggle outside a pub in Putney. Badly wounded, he fled to Dublin, but returned to England for his trial, where the prosecution alleged he had been paid £10,000 for the killing.

The jury acquitted him after hearing that Bindon had gone to the aid of a man who had been knifed in the face by Darke. The actor Bob Hoskins appeared as a character witness: 'When Bob walked in,' Bindon recalled, 'the jury knew I was OK.'

Lieutenant-Commander Tony Spender, b. 1920, d. 2011

Lieutenant-Commander Tony Spender, who has died aged ninety-one, was a submarine captain during the Second World War whose coolness under pressure enabled him and his crew to emerge intact after their boat, *Sirdar*, had made an involuntary dive and buried its bow in mud during sea trials in 1943.

'She didn't stop until she hit the bottom,' he later wrote. 'By the grace of God there was a bottom there, though we were way beyond the normal diving depth. Almost everything had gone horribly wrong. A torpedo tube reported as dry was in fact flooded, so we were badly out of trim. The forward hydroplanes jammed. The telegraph to the motor room jammed. Then the engine room rating knocked off the telemotor pump as he careered downhill, so the main vents did not shut.'

As the oxygen and the electric power dwindled and the temperature rose, Spender, who was only twenty-three at the time, maintained his composure, attempting various manoeuvres in a bid to break *Sirdar* free of the mud.

He admitted later that it was the first time that he had really had to put his Christian faith to the test. 'I told God what I was planning and just asked Him to let me know if it was the wrong thing to do. I didn't hear from Him so I pushed on.'

He was eventually left with no other option than the unscientific but well-worn trick of 'dancing ship': 'The crew formed a chain and literally climbed up to the stern. They carried what weights they could move and they danced up and down. Suddenly there was a tremendous shudder. The depth gauges spun round and we shot up like an express lift.'

When they surfaced, Spender inspected the forecasing, which he found to be 'covered in thick mud and stones as far as the aft gun'. It had been a narrow escape.

⪻ 11th ⪼

Jörg Haider, b. 1950, d. 2008

Jörg Haider, who has died in a car accident aged 58, was a right-wing Austrian politician whose notoriety far exceeded his influence on national events.

Despite the fact that he never held office in an Austrian government, Haider's gift for self-publicity, and his willingness to venture into territory that others saw as taboo, ensured that he became better known outside his own country than any Austrian politician of his generation.

Precisely what he stood for, however, never became entirely clear. In essence Haider was a populist, appearing to exploit whatever latent passions, fears and insecurities he could detect in his fellow countrymen at any given time. But he did so without much regard for that vital ingredient, judgment.

Thus he was able to describe the Nazi concentration camps as 'penal camps' and SS officers as 'upstanding men of character'. Although he later recanted, it was no wonder that he was vilified as a 'fascist', a 'racist' and a 'neo-Nazi'. He was often accused of anti-Semitism, and he formed a friendship with Saddam Hussein.

That he survived as a political figure was due to his boundless ambition allied to a considerable personal charm. Haider had been a talented actor in his youth, and he developed into a master showman who constantly reinvented himself: the clean-cut young man; the Porsche-driving playboy dressed by Armani; the honest son of the soil. As one of his university friends was to say later: 'Depending on where he went, he was what the people wanted to see and hear. He had a sort of antenna for it.'

Haider was a friend of Arnold Schwarzenegger, and his own public image was relentlessly cultivated to reinforce the perception of a handsome man of action: a permanently suntanned fitness fanatic who was a devil on the ski slopes, he also enjoyed go-karting, roller-blading, bungee-jumping and mountaineering.

For his fiftieth birthday in 2000 Haider commandeered an entire mountain in Carinthia, inviting thousands of supporters to enjoy stunt-flying, traditional Alpine music and a giant apple strudel. The birthday boy was dropped on to the top of the mountain by a helicopter, then skied down to take the plaudits.

Jörg Haider was born on 26 January 1950, in the Upper Austrian town of Bad Goisern. His father, a cobbler by trade, had served as an officer in the Wehrmacht during the Second World War; his mother, a schoolmistress, had joined Hitler's League of German Maidens.

After the war the father was forced for a time to work as a grave-digger, while Frau Haider was sent to perform menial tasks in homes for the elderly. Jörg never forgot these injustices, as he saw them, later complaining that people such as his parents took the rap for the 'really big Nazis', many of whom went unpunished.

Jörg was brought up in the beautiful Salzkammergut area of Austria (immortalised in *The Sound of Music*) and attended school at Bad Ischl, where he shone scholastically, and took up fencing (it was said that on the straw figure he used for practice he pinned the name of the Nazi-hunter Simon Wiesenthal). He went on to study Law at the University of Vienna.

But politics was always Haider's calling. At twenty he had become leader of the right-wing Freedom Party's youth wing in Upper Austria, and he was soon appointed its regional secretary in Carinthia, in the south. In 1979 he was elected to the national parliament – at twenty-nine, he was the country's youngest-ever MP.

At this stage Haider was presenting himself as a Pan-German nationalist, and in 1986 he instituted a daring and successful coup to oust the party leader, Norbert Steger, who was on the liberal wing of the party and at the time Austria's vice-chancellor in a coalition government. One party member enthused: 'With Haider I'd march into Russia again. With Steger I would not even go on holiday.'

The subsequent election, far from consigning Haider's party to oblivion, as had been the hope, saw it double its popular support. The Social Democrats were obliged to enter a coalition with the conservative People's Party. At about this time Haider had an extraordinary stroke of good fortune, unexpectedly inheriting an estate in Carinthia from a great-uncle.

This in itself was to prove controversial, since the estate had been bought for a song from a Jewish professor who fled Austria in the 1930s; but Haider was now a rich man, with all the independence that this status confers. He also now exuded a certain glamour, in sharp contrast to the colourless politicians to whom the Austrian electorate was accustomed.

In 1995, during a national election campaign, Haider was photographed with a group of SS veterans. During the same campaign, however, Haider declared that Pan-Germanism had had its day; instead he argued for what he called 'Austrian patriotism', explaining that this was not 'anti-foreigner' but 'inland-friendly'.

This tactic failed, and the Freedom Party's share of the national vote fell; and for the next election, in 1999, Haider accordingly championed better pensions and the cause of the workers. The party finished in second place, having secured 27 per cent of the vote.

His party subsequently formed Austria's government in coalition with the People's Party, prompting the European Union to impose sanctions on Austria even before the government had announced its programme. Haider observed: 'There is a lot of excitement in the European chicken pen – and the fox hasn't even got in.' Meanwhile, Israel recalled its ambassador from Vienna.

He was not to improve his fortunes on the national stage: in the 2002 national election the Freedom Party lost heavily, a humiliation that led to factional infighting. Finally, in 2005, Haider formed a splinter group, the Alliance for the Future of Austria.

Jörg Haider died in the early hours of Saturday when his Volkswagen Phaeton skidded off a road near Klagenfurt, hitting a concrete traffic barrier. He had been on his way home from a party at which he was guest of honour.

His death came at a time of renewed personal political success and a resurgence of the fortunes of the right. In national elections a month before he died, his Alliance for the Future of Austria polled 11 per cent of the vote; the Freedom Party, from which he had split, took 18 per cent.

⇜ 12th ⇝

Nerina Shute, b. 1908, d. 2004

Nerina Shute, who has died aged ninety-six, wrote acerbic film reviews, risqué novels, histories and memoirs of which none aroused greater interest than *Passionate Friendships* (1992), a 'book of confessions' published when she was in her eighties.

Among other eye-popping revelations, Nerina Shute told how her marriage to Howard Marshall, BBC broadcaster, D-Day hero, Oxford rugby Blue and author of a book about Scott of the Antarctic, hit the rocks after she confessed to having an affair with their French housekeeper. She also chronicled her twenty-two years of 'friendship, happiness and love' with the doyenne of ballroom dancing, Phyllis Haylor.

Nerina Shute was born on 17 July 1908 in North Wales, where her parents had briefly repaired after her father lost all his money on the stock exchange; but she spent her early childhood in a house on Cheyne Walk, Chelsea, her father having inherited money from a relative.

Nerina Shute's mother, Renie, was a novelist and bohemian, and in 1920 abandoned her husband and baby son and took Nerina to Hollywood, having received an offer for one of her books.

There she bought a gold mine in which she lost what remained of the inheritance, created a scandal by embarking on an affair with a married man, then attempted suicide after her lover was killed in a motor accident.

Rapidly recovering from this tragedy, Renie then married a Hollywood actor, despite still being legally married (under English law) to Nerina's father, thus becoming, consciously or unconsciously, a bigamist. It was at this point that the eighteen-year-old Nerina decided to return to London, where her father (now living in Le Zoute, Belgium, a bolt-hole for impoverished gentry) had found her a job as a typist for the *Times* Book Club.

From this small beginning, Nerina Shute became a gossip columnist for *Film Weekly*, writing acerbic pen portraits of film stars and causing offence to a generation of British film personalities. E.A. Dupont, the director of *Piccadilly*, was so annoyed by the comments she made about him that he banned her from the studio floor. She sneaked back disguised as a rabbi.

By now Nerina Shute had become the 1920s equivalent of an 'It Girl', famous for her outspoken opinions, her passion for sexual politics and broad-brimmed black hats. She moved in bohemian circles and attended louche parties at the home of the playwright Aimee Stuart in Carlton House Terrace where 'we talked endlessly about free love and homosexuality'.

At the same time, she embarked on her first novel, *Another Man's Poison*, published in 1930 when she was twenty-two. This was, in effect, an apologia for her mother's life and was thus considered deeply shocking (by this time her mother was on her fourth husband; there would be two more).

Having taken up the cause of free love, Nerina embarked on an affair with 'Charles', a playboy former doctor who had been struck off the medical register for performing an illegal abortion. Their 'trial marriage' soon came to an end. She found consolation in the arms of 'Josephine', a monocle-wearing Roman Catholic who took comfort from the fact that 'there's nothing in the Bible against lesbians'.

Their affair lasted until 1936, when Nerina, in a 'wild attempt to escape the homosexual world', married James Wentworth Day, a prominent High Tory journalist who regarded homosexuals as 'perverts'. Her marriage brought her a brief period of respectability. She went fox-hunting and was photographed at Ascot in a huge hat; but she soon tired of married life and left her husband after a year.

By now Nerina Shute had become an agent for the beauty firm Max Factor in a Bond Street salon. After her marriage ended, she moved in with 'Helen and Andy', a pair of professional women – respectively a dentist and a gynaecologist – who shared a house in Portland Place. Nerina and Helen soon became lovers.

In 1940, by which time she had returned to writing, Nerina Shute was invited to be interviewed on a radio programme by Howard Marshall, a BBC broadcaster and cricket commentator popularly known as the 'Voice of England' for his homely weekly programmes about cricket, fishing, home or family.

Marshall was married with a wife and two sons sitting out the war in America, but he and Nerina began an affair. Marshall became chief war correspondent for the BBC, served in North Africa and accompanied the troops to France on D-Day, filing the first live radio report of the landings before chronicling the campaign in Normandy and the fall of Paris. They married in 1944 when Marshall was home on leave.

Nerina Shute did not tell her husband about her affairs with women, realising instinctively that he would be shocked. But if he was ignorant of this aspect of his wife's past, he could not have harboured any illusions about her morals. In 1945 she published *We Mix Our Drinks*, a selective account of her life in permissive pre-war London. The book (mysteriously dedicated to 'Three I Love') caused a stir in the more puritanical post-war atmosphere. Nerina's mother-in-law never recovered from the shock.

The Marshalls moved to Mayfair, but Nerina again soon found herself becoming bored with the restrictions of married life; her husband did not like parties and she missed her old friends. Her gloom was lifted by the arrival of Renee, a young French housekeeper. The two women became close, and though Nerina regarded their relationship as akin to that between mother and daughter, it soon became obvious that there was more to it. One day, Renee approached her mistress, duster in hand: '"*Madame, j'envie de faire l'amour.*" The next minute she was in my arms.'

But the sudden deepening of their relationship seemed to bring about a crisis in Renee's life. She became emotionally unstable; there were fits of temper, and she began to imagine that Marshall was trying to poison her. After being incarcerated for a time in a mental institution at Epsom, Renee returned to France.

Her lover's departure plunged Nerina into a deep depression from which her husband, ignorant of its cause, was unable to rescue her. It was Nerina who brought matters to a head. On New Year's Eve 1953, in the course of a violent row, she told her husband about her love for Renee. 'You have been unfaithful to me. I can never forgive you,' said Marshall. 'But I haven't been unfaithful,' Nerina protested. 'Loving a woman is quite different from loving a man.' But Marshall could not understand. The marriage was over.

Nerina returned to her mother, by now living in a house near Horsham with her sixth husband, Noel Sparrow. Just before her mother's death in 1958, Nerina decided to take up ballroom dancing and joined a dance club. Before long she had met and fallen in love with Phyllis Haylor, a well-known figure in the ballroom dancing world. After selling the house at Horsham, Nerina moved to live nearer Phyllis in London, where Nerina found work as a secretary at a hostel for unmarried mothers and later as a voluntary social worker with the Samaritans.

In 1967, she and Phyllis bought a cottage together in Hertfordshire and eventually lived together in London. 'I had never been so happy in all my life,' Nerina recalled. Their relationship lasted until Phyllis's death in 1981.

⊰ 13th ⊱

Frank 'Lefty' Rosenthal, b. 1929, d. 2008

Frank 'Lefty' Rosenthal, who has died aged seventy-nine, was a professional gambler and gaming executive in Las Vegas, the city he liked to claim he created, and was the inspiration for the blockbuster film *Casino* (1995).

Throughout the 1970s and into the mid-1980s Rosenthal, who once survived a car bomb, ran the Stardust, Fremont, Hacienda and Marina casinos on behalf of the Chicago Mafia.

Rosenthal enjoyed a reputation as a snappy dresser (owning, it was said, 200 pairs of trousers) and as a mental gymnast (he disdained calculators and could work out complicated odds in his head). At one stage he worked as a part-time gossip columnist on the *Las Vegas Sun* and hosted a late-night talk show on a local television channel, persuading such visiting celebrities as Frank Sinatra and O.J. Simpson to appear as guests.

Frank Lawrence Rosenthal was born in Chicago on 12 June 1929, the son of a produce wholesaler. He learned the gambling trade at baseball stadiums and through illegal bookmaking operations made friends with Chicago mobsters – ties that would last a lifetime.

In 1961 Rosenthal appeared before a Senate hearing on gambling and organised crime during which he invoked Fifth Amendment protection against self-incrimination no fewer than thirty-seven times – even refusing to confirm he was left-handed. He was – hence the nickname.

Rosenthal's Mafia ties may have also taken him beyond the realm of gambling; federal documents claimed that in the 1960s he was associated with a CIA-connected, Cuban-American anti-Castro militant named Luis Posada Carriles. Rosenthal and Carriles denied these claims. Throughout the 1960s Rosenthal was linked to claims that he fixed high-stake sporting events, and in 1967 was implicated in a bombing plot during Miami's so-called 'bookie wars'.

The following year Rosenthal went to Las Vegas, where he ran four casinos, even though he did not have a Nevada gaming licence – the result of a 1971 indictment in California for racketeering. At the Stardust, he became the first casino operator to recruit women as croupiers.

Rosenthal's ties to organised crime, especially with the reputed mobster Anthony ('Tony the Ant') Spilotro, led him into trouble. He fell foul of Nevada's gaming regulators when Spilotro was indicted in a skimming scheme, along with some fourteen others.

Spilotro also had an affair with Rosenthal's estranged wife, Geri, a former topless dancer, one of the many dramatic moments of Rosenthal's life that played out in *Casino*. It featured Robert De Niro as Sam 'Ace' Rothstein, based on Rosenthal, as well as a brutal scene based on the demise of Spilotro and his brother, Michael, who were beaten by mob members and then buried alive in a cornfield.

According to observers Rosenthal was pushed out of the gaming business in the late 1970s and early 1980s, when Las Vegas began transforming itself from a Mafia-infused hotbed of sin into a sanitised, global entertainment Mecca.

That transformation was under way but not complete by 4 October 1982, when Rosenthal turned the key in his parked Cadillac and detonated a huge explosion that wrecked the car but failed to kill him. The case was never solved. Rosenthal left Las Vegas soon afterwards and eventually landed in south Florida, where he served as a consultant for offshore online casinos.

Despite his Mafia ties, shady bookmaking allegations and game-fixing investigations, Rosenthal had few brushes with the law. But he did once reveal his way of dealing with a punter caught cheating at cards. 'He was part of a crew of professional card cheats,' he explained, 'and calling the cops would do nothing to stop them, so we used a rubber mallet – metal hammers leave marks, you know – and he became a lefty.'

Gertrude Shilling, b. 1910, d. 1999

Gertrude Shilling, who has died aged eighty-nine, was known for her annual appearance at Royal Ascot in one of her milliner son David Shilling's extravagant hats; each year the creations she sported grew more theatrical, ranging from one shaped like an apple speared by a crossbow bolt (inspired by the story of William Tell) to a 5ft-high confection from the top of which poked the ears of a rabbit.

She was always admitted to the Royal Enclosure as long as her hats did not block other people's view. In one celebrated incident, in the Jubilee Year of 1977, she was turned away from the enclosure by the Clerk of the Course after her red, white and blue hat proved too large to get through the entrance; indeed, it was so big that it had had to travel to the course in solitary splendour, sitting on the back seat of a Daimler hired especially for the purpose.

❧ 14th ❧

Harold Robbins, b. 1916, d. 1997

Harold Robbins, who has died aged eighty-one, overcame early critical suggestions that he was a writer of some talent, and learned to concentrate exclusively on sex, violence, drugs, perversion and the power struggle; in consequence he earned the sobriquet of 'the world's best-selling novelist', with sales estimated at 750 million books.

It was with *The Carpetbaggers* (1961), apparently inspired by the life of Howard Hughes, that Robbins found his most lucrative vein. Within a few pages the hero,

Jonas Cord, has had sexual intercourse with his recently widowed stepmother. The novel goes on to feature rape, abortion, self-castration, and male and female homosexuality, as well as offering a sexual study of a thirteen-year old girl. 'The Carpetbaggers could have sent any retailer handling it to prison before 1960,' said Professor John Sutherland, Professor of Modern English Literature at University College, London. As it was, the book sold more than six million copies.

Robbins' first three novels had attracted considerable critical esteem. 'But Harold was a smart guy,' reflected Mario Puzo, author of The Godfather. 'He knew he was going to starve to death if he kept writing like that.' Never Leave Me (1953), 79 Park Avenue (1955) and Stiletto (1960) all attested to Robbins' absorption of that lesson.

Yet, though the money poured in, he spent as fast – sometimes even faster – than he earned. His sales pitch came to depend on the illusion – in part the reality – that he was living the same kind of life as the characters in his books. 'My life of sex and riches by the master of steamy epics' ran one tabloid heading.

Robbins wandered between a mansion in Beverly Hills, a hacienda at Acapulco and a house near Cannes, installing gaggles of girls wherever he laid his head. He also treated himself to yachts, taking care that The Joy of Sex was the only publication on board. For driving, he confined himself to nine Rolls-Royces and the odd Maserati.

In Los Angeles Robbins poured out money on a series of parties where decadence was de rigueur – though he himself could not always face them: 'Let's get out of here,' he would urge, 'it's boring.' He seemed better satisfied by drugs: 'Jesus Christ,' he observed in later years, 'I can't believe how good they were. And now they tell you they're not healthy.'

To finance all this he was obliged to keep working, even though at his peak he was selling 40,000 books a day. His publishers would put him up at a hotel in New York, and after eight weeks or so the product would be delivered. Robbins never suffered from writer's block, never produced an outline, and never had any idea how the story would go until he began.

In his prime he would draw the curtains and write for thirty hours at a stretch. The occasional burst of labour was a small price to pay for the escape from his origins.

His story had begun in 1916 when he was presented to a Catholic orphanage in New York. The orphanage gave him the name Francis Kane, which he used for the orphaned hero of his first novel, Never Love a Stranger.

After a childhood being shunted from one foster home to another the boy was adopted at about ten by a Jewish family called Rubin and became known as Harry Rubin. Soon he was running errands for prostitutes and a Jamaican drug dealer: 'I used to deliver cocaine to Cole Porter,' he remembered.

At fifteen Harry Rubin joined the US Navy, only to be thrown out when they rumbled his age. Back in New York during the Depression years he had various jobs – bookie's runner, snow shoveller, ice-cream seller – before becoming an inventory clerk for a chain of grocery stores.

On the side, he began to trade in peas and corn, and soon made his first fortune. No less quickly he lost it by trying to make a killing in the sugar market. Starting again from scratch, he got a job in the New York warehouse of Universal Pictures. He soon worked his way up the organisation and back to prosperity.

The best of the films made from Robbins' books was *The Carpetbaggers* (1964), with George Peppard, Carroll Baker and Alan Ladd. But Robbins did not approve of the cinema's attempt to explore the psychology of his characters. In his books people simply tore off their clothes and got down to it.

Still, the cinema was better than television. 'All the networks can pay a writer is in the low six figures,' Robbins complained. 'I can't do my best work for that kind of money.' Still he was prepared to let others do adaptations for him and collect the proceeds.

He found one admirer in the feminist Camille Paglia, who discovered that he was one of the few post-war figures to have come to terms with 'the huge amoral energies, the tornadoes, that are loose in industrial capitalism.

'Harold Robbins was a prophet of a sensibility that used to be scorned,' she concluded. 'This is America! This is the voice of America!'

ᦂ 15th ᦂ

Ron Cunningham, b. 1915, d. 2007

Ron Cunningham, who has died aged ninety-two, was an escapologist and end-of-the-pier artiste specialising in feats such as eating light bulbs and removing a straitjacket while hanging upside down with his trousers on fire.

The Great Omani, as he was known to his public, began in the 1950s as a regular draw at music halls and piers around the south coast. His career reached a high point in 1977 when, to celebrate the Queen's Silver Jubilee, he performed a handstand on the cliff edge at Beachy Head with a Union flag between his toes; it made the front page of the *People*, and film and television appearances followed.

Other highlights included a journey on the back of a lorry while entombed in a concrete block. It was a slow journey, Cunningham recalled, and his stage partner, Professor Cullen – 'a human reservoir for alcoholic beverage' – stopped the lorry at several pubs along the way. The Great Omani could not hold a glass because he was flat on his back with his hands set in concrete, so the barmaids poured neat rum down his throat. He nearly choked.

In the early days it was difficult to make a living. His long-suffering wife, Eileen (or Marvita, as she was known when she was thrusting swords through him on stage), supported him until her death in 1983. They toured the music halls and expanded his act until he was able to perform daily on Bognor Pier, tied to the pilings in a straitjacket as the tide came in. He also became a regular on Brighton's West Pier, diving into a sea of flames. 'People will always flock to see anyone likely to kill themselves,' he observed.

THINKER, FAILURE, SOLDIER, JAILER

⇥ 16th ⇤

Princess Paul of Yugoslavia, b. 1903, d. 1997

Princess Paul of Yugoslavia, the former Princess Olga of Greece, who has died in Paris aged ninety-four, was the widow of Prince Paul, Regent of Yugoslavia from 1934 to 1941.

'Chips' Channon, admittedly impressionable in the matter of royalty, considered Princess Paul and her sister Princess Marina, Duchess of Kent, 'surely two of the most beautiful princesses, if not women, in the world'. Fate, though, plunged Princess Paul into the quagmire of Balkan politics, from which Machiavelli himself might have been hard put to emerge unscathed.

She was born Princess Olga of Greece at Tatoi, near Athens, on 11 June 1903, the eldest of the three daughters of Prince Nicholas, the artistic second son of King George I of Greece and the Grand Duchess Helen of Russia, a niece of Tsar Alexander III. Princess Olga was therefore the first cousin of the last Tsar, Nicholas II, with whose children she played. Not only was she about as royal as it is possible to be; her otherwise gentle character was shot through with hints of Russian autocracy.

In September 1922, King Constantine was forced to abdicate. Princess Olga's family was condemned to years of poverty and restless travelling, beginning with a dismal sojourn in a hotel at San Remo. But things looked up for Princess Olga herself when the expert eye of the Duke of Connaught, the third son of Queen Victoria, lit upon her.

It was speedily arranged that she should visit London for the season of 1923. Princess Olga was seen at balls, polo matches and on the tennis court; and went more than once to see Fred and Adele Astaire in *Stop Flirting*. And though she failed to fulfil her parents' hope that she might catch the attention of the Prince of Wales, she succeeded in wholly enslaving Prince Paul of Serbia. They were married that October.

On 9 October 1934 King Alexander of Yugoslavia was shot dead by an assassin at Marseilles. Prince Paul became Regent until the majority of King Peter in September 1941. It was a task for which he was – as he himself recognised – wholly unsuited. He detested politics at the best of times; and, in the years leading up to the Second World War, politics in Yugoslavia were more than usually taxing. 'I lead a hard, difficult life with hardly any leisure,' he complained to Mary Berenson. 'I have had to give up all I cared for and must now lead the existence of a galley slave.'

In foreign affairs Prince Paul strove to remain disengaged from the fascist dictatorships which were now dominating central Europe. In April 1939 he and Princess Olga visited Mussolini in Rome, but were careful to avoid making any firm commitments on Yugoslavia's behalf.

Two months later they went to Berlin. Hitler put on a big show for them, spending much time with the Regent, while consigning Princess Olga to the care of Frau Goering. At a parade of German military might Princess Paul was shrewd enough to notice that a seemingly endless line of tanks was in fact the same unit coming round twice. Once again the Prince managed to escape without signing any pacts.

In July 1939 George VI invited them to Buckingham Palace and appointed Prince Paul a Knight of the Garter. Cecil Beaton took some striking pictures of the Princess bedecked in fine jewellery at the Palace.

Her position was difficult on the personal as well as the political level, what with one sister living in England and another – Elizabeth, Countess Toerring-Jettenbach – in Germany. Though Prince Paul's sympathies lay with the British, the shadow of the Axis powers increasingly lay upon Yugoslavia. By the end of 1940 he was contemplating resignation; and he made no secret of his longing to hand over to King Peter in September 1941.

In January of that year Prince Paul was horrified to learn that Winston Churchill intended to send a mechanised force to Greece in order to form a united Balkan front. He saw the plan as doomed from the start; Churchill, for his part, regarded him as 'an unfortunate man in a cage with a tiger, hoping not to provoke him while steadily dinner time approaches'.

In March 1941 Prince Paul had a five-hour meeting with Hitler, from which he returned to Belgrade determined on resistance. But he gave way when his Council voted for Yugoslavia's alignment with the Axis.

The next day there was an uprising in Belgrade. On 27 March 1941 the Regency was overthrown, King Peter (still only seventeen) was proclaimed ruler, and Prince Paul and his family went into exile, leaving the young King to the mercy of the new government. In April the Germans bombed Belgrade, killing 17,000 people, and after twelve days occupied Yugoslavia.

Princess Olga and her husband began a humiliating exile, first in Cairo, and later in Kenya, where they settled at Osserian, near Lake Naivasha, the house of the recently murdered Lord Erroll. Prince Paul was treated as 'a political prisoner allowed the liberty of a normal visitor to the colony'. Their isolation was made harder by lack of funds. 'Olga is wonderful,' Prince Paul reported, 'so brave and so efficient, doing things you wouldn't expect servants to do.'

In August 1942 George VI made it possible for Princess Olga to come to England for a few months to comfort her sister Marina after the death of her husband the Duke of Kent. When she returned to Kenya in January 1943 she found Prince Paul in a state of nervous collapse. 'It would be extremely unfortunate,' reflected Anthony Eden, 'if he became permanently insane while in our custody.' Soon afterwards the Prince and Princess were transferred to South Africa, where the Prince's health improved – notwithstanding fears that he might be tried at Nuremberg.

But they became close to General Smuts, and were comforted when George VI and Queen Elizabeth visited the Dominion in 1947 and extended the hand of friendship.

Later Prince and Princess Paul settled in Paris, where the Prince was able to indulge his artistic bent. They lived there for the rest of their lives, spending summers at Pratolino, near Florence, until 1970. Prince Paul died in 1976.

Princess Paul continued to come to London in her widowhood, staying either at Kensington Palace with Princess Alice, Countess of Athlone (who died in 1981), or at Clarence House with the Queen Mother.

Those who were held in her stern gaze were not always convinced by the suggestion that she might be more frightened of them. Her conversation, too, could be grand. 'Quite nice, my niece-in-law, sometimes,' she remarked of Princess Michael of Kent. 'But I can't bear seeing darling Marina's tiara wrapped up in those dreadful sausage rolls.'

≼ 17th ≽

Sammy Duddy, b. 1945, d. 2007

Sammy Duddy, who has died aged sixty-two, had a rather unusual curriculum vitae for a member of the Loyalist paramilitary Ulster Defence Association in having been a drag artiste who went by the stage name of Samantha.

During the 1970s the self-styled 'Dolly Parton of Belfast' became well known on Belfast's cabaret circuit, presenting a risqué act in Loyalist pubs and clubs, dressed in fishnet tights, wig and heavy make-up. Once he even performed for British troops on tour. 'I wore a miniskirt many a time,' Duddy remembered, 'but it was usually a long dress, a straight black wig, a pair of falsies I bought in Blackpool and loads of make-up to cover my freckles. The darker the mascara the better, and scarlet lipstick, because I was a scarlet woman.'

Duddy was one of the UDA's founding members when it was set up as a Loyalist umbrella group in 1972. From the mid-1970s he became a fixture at the association's headquarters on the Newtownards Road, working by day as the organisation's public relations officer and editing its magazine, *Ulster*, while playing to capacity audiences with his drag act at night. Although he was briefly a suspect in the murder of Pat Finucane, the Catholic lawyer shot dead by the UDA in 1989, he was not charged and he insisted that he never played a 'military' role. Nonetheless, his acceptance within the organisation was probably helped by his reputation for being handy with his fists.

On more than one occasion Duddy's pneumatic alter ego helped him to evade the unwelcome attentions of the authorities and Republican paramilitaries. In the late 1970s he was chatted up by a policeman as he sat in his car, in full drag, at a checkpoint. 'He didn't twig and he asked what time I'd be coming back,' Duddy recalled.

On another evening he had a few heart-stopping moments when his car developed a flat tyre in a staunchly nationalist area of Belfast: 'After ten minutes two guys pulled up and asked for my keys,' he recalled. 'They opened the boot, got the spare wheel out and changed it. I drove off blowing them kisses. I'll never know who they were, but a threat against me was in foot-high writing on a gable wall right by where I broke down.' On another occasion he sparked a fight between two British soldiers who 'just dropped their rifles and started to punch each other, saying, "I saw her first".'

Evan Abbott Samuel Duddy was born on 25 August 1945 and spent much of his life on Belfast's Rathcoole estate.

In 1989–90 he spent eleven months in jail on remand after being arrested during the Stevens Inquiry into collusion between Loyalists and members of the security forces. The charge related to security force documents on Republicans which were leaked to the UDA, and which the organisation attempted, with little success, to use to target IRA members. The charges against him were dropped in October 1990.

Duddy retired from active Loyalism in the 1990s, but later returned to become a member of the 'moderate' UDA advisory body, the Ulster Political Research Group. After the UDA leadership split in a bloody feud, he affiliated himself with John 'Grugg' Gregg and other UDA 'brigadiers' opposed to Johnny 'Mad Dog' Adair.

But in 2002 Duddy paid the price for taking sides in the dispute when two masked gunmen fired shots at his front door. Although he escaped unharmed, his pet Chihuahua, Bambi, was killed by the gunfire.

18th

Ignacio Ponseti, b. 1914, d. 2009

Ignacio Ponseti, who has died aged ninety-five, was the inventor of the Ponseti Method, a cheap yet revolutionary way of treating clubfoot in babies which has become a standard procedure all over the world.

Devised in the 1950s, his method is used to treat some of the tens of thousands of babies worldwide – including some 700 in Britain – who are born each year with a deformity of the foot that causes it to turn inwards.

Discovering that many patients who underwent corrective surgery experienced pain and stiffness later in life, Ponseti devised a treatment for young children and babies that stretches the ligaments rather than cuts them, manipulating the foot into the optimum shape by hand, casts and braces.

Typically, five casts are needed, each of which is changed every few days. When one cast is removed, the doctor bends the foot more, before a new cast is put on to hold the position in place. The treatment works best on those one year old and younger, when the ligaments and muscles in the foot are more flexible.

After about three weeks, the casts are removed and the child is put in a brace that resembles two shoes connected by a metal bar to keep the feet a set distance apart. The brace is worn almost full time for several months and then at night for a further three to five years. The rate of relapse after three years is 10 per cent. After five years, it is almost zero.

Ignasi Ponseti Vives was born on 3 June 1914 on the Spanish island of Minorca. His father was a watchmaker and taught his son the craft. Ponseti would later say that working with the tiny gears of the watches helped prepare him for the delicate work of surgery. He received his medical degree from the University of Barcelona in 1936, a day before the Spanish Civil War broke out.

In 1939, anticipating the start of the Second World War, Ponseti set out for Mexico, where Spanish refugees were being granted citizenship. Ponseti served as the only doctor in Juchitepec, a small town south of Mexico City. There he grappled with an outbreak of typhoid fever and managed to save all sixty of his local patients who came down with the disease.

Ponseti left Mexico in 1941 and travelled to Iowa City by bus to pursue postgraduate studies at the age of twenty-six. In 1944 he became a member of the orthopaedic faculty at the University of Iowa.

There, the softly spoken Ponseti had a difficult time spreading the word about his clubfoot method. But it gained momentum especially after his book, *Congenital Clubfoot: Fundamentals of Treatment*, was published in 1996. It has since become the preferred treatment around the world.

The Reverend Donald Pateman, b. 1915, d. 1998

The Reverend Donald Pateman, who has died aged eighty-three, was perhaps the most 'politically incorrect' clergyman in the Church of England.

He devoted his fifty-year ministry to the East End of London, retiring after forty-two years as vicar of St Mark's, Dalston, only a month before his death.

A man of surprising and strong views, which he was not afraid to voice, he was reported in 1977 to the then Race Relations Board and to the Archbishop of Canterbury for comments on immigrants in the parish magazine.

He described Britain as a scroungers' paradise. 'Money is handed out,' he said, 'on a lavish scale. As soon as you arrive from Zambia or Botswana or Timbuctoo your first question is: "Where's the nearest Social Security Office?" Arrived there, you receive your first handout, the first of many hundred. There are a million abusers in this country, a million cuts waiting to be made, a million scroungers to be given the proverbial kick in the backside.'

No action was taken against Pateman, who in any case had appointed one of his curates to welcome West Indians settling in the parish in large numbers. Pateman not only succeeded in attracting many of them to his church, but also retained their staunch allegiance.

Among others who incurred his wrath were youths who misbehaved, and those whom he believed encouraged them by abandoning corporal punishment. In 1965 he called the Home Secretary, Roy Jenkins, a 'purring old tabby' for closing down Britain's largest approved school and phasing out caning.

Pateman returned to this subject in 1978, when he accused local councillors of wasting ratepayers' money on a 'cosy home for nasty little female muggers'. He wanted the law changed so that those found guilty of mugging, football hooliganism or robbery with violence could be flogged. He conducted a referendum among 5,000 of his parishioners and won overwhelming approval.

The punishment for brides arriving late for their weddings was different. In 1992 he introduced a sliding scale, details of which were handed to couples at wedding rehearsals. Ten minutes late meant the cutting of one of the hymns, twenty minutes the loss of two hymns and the dismissal from church of the photographer, twenty-five minutes to the dropping of all hymns and the dismissal of the choir, and thirty minutes late would cause the wedding to be cancelled.

Twenty years earlier when postmen were on strike, Pateman had announced that any seeking marriage in his church would be given a 'work-to-rule ceremony' – no choir, no bells, no heating, no lighting, no music, no photographs, no confetti. He added: 'Postmen earn the same money as me. I spent three years at university and I am expected to live on £21 a week. Why can't they?'

Donald Herbert Pateman was born at Kirby Muxloe, Leicestershire, on 22 February 1915. He had a strict Victorian upbringing. He worked in commerce and served in the RAF in the Second World War.

At this time he felt drawn to Holy Orders and to the service of the poor. On demobilisation, he went to the London College of Divinity, where the Principal was Donald Coggan, later Archbishop of Canterbury. There Pateman secured a theological diploma.

From 1948 to 1951 he was curate of St James-the-Less, Bethnal Green, and then of All Hallows, Bromley-by-Bow. He also took on the honorary secretaryship of the Society for Relief of Distress – a charity for the East End poor. In 1956 he was appointed vicar of St Mark's.

Over the next forty-two years Pateman never deviated. His sermons were short and down-to-earth; he hated pomposity. The congregation grew, and large sums were raised to maintain the building. He was delighted to be exempt from a regulation requiring clergy to retire at seventy. When, finally, ill health gave him no choice, 1,000 people of all races and faiths attended a service of farewell and thanksgiving for his ministry.

≈ **19**th ≈

Kenneth Wood, b. 1916, d. 1997

Kenneth Wood, who has died aged eighty-one, gave his name in 1950 to the Kenwood Chef, a food mixer which has sold by the million and found a permanent place in the Science Museum for its part in revolutionising work in the kitchen.

Wood became interested in food mixers soon after the Second World War. He bought a Sunbeam mixer, stripped it down, and made a series of design improvements. In 1948 he produced the first British model, the A200.

Wood realised, though, that the A200 was not sophisticated enough to compete with the foreign opposition, and set about designing, in somewhat unscientific fashion, a better model. 'What we did,' he admitted, 'was to take a number of mixer pieces, look at them, and alter this and that.' So the Kenwood Chef was born.

An important reason for the Chef's success was Wood's dynamic approach to the export market. He loved travel, and was determined to enjoy his fortune to the full: 'I don't want to be one of those goons who ends up with £4 million and hasn't lived,' he said.

In the late 1960s Kenwood ran into trouble. Wood placed hopes of recovery in a small dishwasher, but in 1968 Thorn Electrical Group took over the company and ousted its founder. Wood said goodbye to his staff, and then, he remembered, 'went to the lavatory and unashamedly sobbed my heart out'.

⊰ **20**th ⊱

Colonel Muammar Gaddafi, b. 1942, d. 2011

Colonel Muammar Gaddafi, the former Libyan dictator who has been killed aged sixty-nine, liked to promote himself as an instigator of global revolution; for the four decades of his rule, however, this was carried out through the subjugation of his people at home, and the sponsorship of terrorism abroad.

His grip on power always looked solid. But in February 2011, uprisings in North Africa, which had already seen the fall of the governments of Libya's neighbours, Egypt and Tunisia, suddenly put his regime in jeopardy.

After a Nato-backed military campaign, rebels eventually seized Gaddafi, who had been found hiding, like the deposed Iraqi dictator Saddam Hussein before him, in a hole. Mobile telephone pictures of a bloodied figure resembling the dictator began to circulate on the internet. Finally, the news came through that he was dead.

It was a suitably chaotic end for a man who could never be easily pigeonholed. Erratic, vain and utterly unpredictable, he always seemed to be enjoying a joke which no one else could see. His image, plastered on walls all over Libya, seemed a parody of 1960s radical chic – the craggy features, longish hair, the eyes half-hidden behind retro blue-tone shades.

Gaddafi would arrive at summits of Arab leaders in a white limousine surrounded by a bodyguard of nubile Kalashnikov-toting brunettes. At one non-aligned summit in Belgrade, he turned up with two horses and six camels; the Yugoslavs allowed him to graze the camels in front of his hotel but refused to allow him to arrive at the conference on one of his white chargers. Several of the camels ended up in Belgrade Zoo.

At an African Union summit in Durban in 2002, his entourage consisted of a personal jet, two Antonov transport aircraft, a container ship loaded with buses, goat carcases and prayer mats, a mobile hospital, jamming equipment that disrupted local networks, $6 million in petty cash, and 400 security guards with associated rocket launchers, armoured cars and other hardware, who nearly provoked a shoot-out with South Africa's security forces.

Under the banner of pan-Arabism, he offered political unity (under his leadership, inevitably) to Syria, Egypt and Sudan (none of which wanted it), then changed tack to pan-Africanism, calling for a united continent (also to be ruled from Tripoli). As a first step, he threw open Libya's frontiers to all African citizens; the result was that four million, mainly Muslim, Libyans became resentful hosts to at least one and a half million impoverished sub-Saharan migrants.

Yet the self-styled 'Universal Theorist' and 'Guide of the First of September Great Revolution of the Arab Libyan Popular and Socialist Jamahiriya' was no joke. In the 1970s and 1980s, while other tyrants were content to repress their own people, Gaddafi seemed hellbent on bringing murder and mayhem to the whole world.

After Pam Am Flight 103 was blown up over Lockerbie in 1988, leaving 270 dead – the biggest mass murder in British history – a court found two Libyans guilty of planting the bomb on board. In 1984, WPC Yvonne Fletcher was shot dead in London with a machine gun fired from inside the Libyan embassy. Then there was the bombing of a Berlin discotheque, explosions at Rome and Vienna airports and the bombing of a French airliner over Chad.

In addition, Gaddafi sent arms shipments to the IRA, Abu Nidal and numerous other terrorist organisations and set out to export revolution to his neighbours, perpetuating regional conflicts in Sierra Leone, Zimbabwe, Chad and Liberia. Domestic opponents – the 'running dogs' who opposed his dictatorship – were ruthlessly liquidated. In 1984 bomb attacks on seven Libyan exiles living in Britain left twenty-four people injured; one Libyan journalist opposed to Gaddafi's regime was assassinated as he walked past London's Regent's Park mosque.

Indeed, for all his madcap behaviour, Gaddafi was no fool. He survived at least a dozen attempts on his life and remained the longest-ruling revolutionary from the Nasserite 1960s. In the 1970s and 1980s he could defy the might of the United States and laugh off UN resolutions, confident that the Arab world, the Third World and the Soviet bloc would back him. But times changed. By the 1990s the Soviet Union was no more, and Arab leaders had had enough of Gaddafi's troublemaking.

As a result, in the late 1990s he made his most audacious move since coming to power: the reinvention of himself as a peace-loving international statesman. In 1999 Libya finally apologised for the shooting of Yvonne Fletcher, and handed over the men suspected of masterminding the Lockerbie bombing for trial. In 2004, following a British diplomatic initiative, he publicly renounced Libya's weapons of mass destruction programme.

With Libya's proven reserves of 30 billion barrels of oil as bait, it did not take long for Western leaders to bury the past and beat a path to his tent. The British public was treated to the spectacle of Foreign Secretary Jack Straw praising the colonel's 'statesmanlike and courageous' strategy and Prime Minister Tony Blair offering the 'hand of partnership' over a glass of camel's milk.

The reasons for Gaddafi's change of heart aroused much speculation. He had certainly been anxious to end the UN sanctions imposed in 1992, which had crippled his country's economy. But it was the 11 September attacks that appear to have been the catalyst that spurred him on.

Gaddafi was the first Arab leader to condemn the attacks (helpfully suggesting that the United States bomb the safe havens of Islamist militants in London); and the most instantly alert to the implications for his own survival.

For Gaddafi came from a generation of revolutionaries that was motivated by Arab nationalism and the 'anti-imperialist struggle', not by religious extremism. Suddenly he found himself threatened not only by America's assault on the 'Axis of Evil', but also by the underground religious revolutionaries of al-Qaeda. And it was the latter which he saw as the most potent threat.

Muammar Gaddafi was born in a tent near Sirte, Libya, in 1942 (some sources record 7 June as the precise date). He was the youngest child and only son of a nomadic and illiterate Bedouin family of the Gadadfa tribe. It seems to have been the tribal culture and unstructured democracy of Bedouin life that inspired his revolutionary political ideas.

He was sent away to school at nine years old and then went to secondary school at Sebha, where – like many other Arab students at the time – he was inspired by Nasser's call to Arab resurgence through socialism and revolution. Early in his teens he seems to have formed a revolutionary cadre with a group of friends.

Imbibing Greek notions of democracy and Islamic notions of equality while studying History at Tripoli University, he went on to the Benghazi Military Academy. In 1966, having reached the rank of colonel, he did signals training with the British Army at Beaconsfield.

In September 1969 he led a bloodless coup that overthrew the royal regime of the charming but weak British-backed King Idris. Libyans were taught that he led the charge not from the turret of a tank, but at the wheel of a blue Volkswagen Beetle. The battered Revolutionary Vehicle came to occupy pride of place in Tripoli's national museum.

Conventional political institutions, including the government and head of state, were eventually abolished (Gaddafi had no official title), to be replaced by a 'direct democracy' of popular congresses served by people's committees. The result was a system of administrative chaos counterbalanced by a centralised regime of terror and absolute political control.

Opportunistic, idealistic and mercurial, Gaddafi launched a series of attempts to take his revolution forward at home and abroad. While his economic policies – banning wages and private ownership – had disastrous results, he remained genuinely popular because oil revenues enabled him to supply even the poorest peasants with education, health care and imported food.

Meanwhile, state-controlled media elevated him to the status of demigod. 'His teeth are naturally immune to stain, so that when he releases a full-blown smile, the naturally white teeth discharge a radiation pregnant with sweet joy and real happiness for those lucky ones who are fortunate to be around him,' fawned the *Al Zahf Al Akhdar* newspaper.

In Libya much was made of Gaddafi's many cultural achievements. He was the author of a book of allegorical short stories, and the inventor of a car, the Saroukh el–Jamahiriya (Libyan rocket). When Tony Blair paid his visit in 2004, the two leaders apparently swapped ideas about their own versions of the 'third way'. Gaddafi illustrated his version by drawing a circle with a dot in the middle, the dot being himself.

❧ 21st ❧

George Daniels, b. 1926, d. 2011

George Daniels, who has died aged eighty-five, was considered by some to be the greatest watchmaker since Abraham Louis Breguet (1747–1823).

His greatest contribution was to develop a watch mechanism, known as the coaxial escapement, which has helped to revolutionise the performance of high-end mechanical watches and has been described as the most important horological development for 250 years.

Each watch typically involved 2,500 hours of work over a year or more, and Daniels refused to take orders, being particular about his customers: 'I was very selective,' Daniels recalled. 'I never made watches for people if I didn't care for them.'

⊰ 22nd ⊱

Eric Ambler, b. 1909, d. 1998

Eric Ambler, the author who has died aged eighty-nine, changed the rules of one of the most English of literary genres, the thriller.

Before Ambler's novels of the late 1930s, the heroes of such books were square-jawed types, epitomised by Sapper's thuggish Bulldog Drummond and John Buchan's nobler Richard Hannay. The events of the Great War had little altered the style of the thriller, though some serious writers, including Graham Greene, had begun to suggest that Good and Evil were a matter of perspective.

Ambler had no pretensions to serious writing, but his thrillers were the first to have a palpably modern, less naive feel. His heroes were genuinely ordinary people, not ex-soldiers or chaps who had knocked about the veldt, but commercial travellers, engineers and tourists truly out of their depth when caught up in sinister events.

What stimulated Ambler was human character, particularly its performance under stress. 'What I'm really interested in is the endless variety of human behaviour,' he said. 'The framework isn't the important part. It's just a way to get people into certain positions and see what they do when they're frightened.'

Eric Ambler was born in Lewisham, south London, on 28 June 1909. His parents ran a touring marionette theatre.

He was awarded an engineering scholarship to London University in 1927 and began an apprenticeship with an engineering firm. But this bored him, and he took a job as an advertising copy writer. Ambler toiled away at this for six years, using his spare time to write some unsuccessful expressionist plays. Then in 1934 he holidayed in Marseilles, where he was cheated out of all of his money at poker by a bartender.

Waiting hungrily for the boat home, Ambler spent much of the next few days pointing an imaginary rifle from his hotel balcony at the crossroads where the bartender caught his tram. A few weeks later he saw a newsreel showing the murder in Marseilles of King Alexander of Yugoslavia. The place Ambler had chosen for his shot was exactly that picked by the assassin.

'I felt I had found a fresh bit of my character which was an assassin,' Ambler said later. 'I felt there were people all over Europe just like me, just ready for the word to kill.' He set to work, and in the next five years wrote six thrillers that fully exploited the edgy mood of the late 1930s.

During the war, Ambler served initially with an anti-aircraft battery stationed in the grounds of Chequers. Then in 1941 he was posted to the Army Film Unit. There he worked with Peter Ustinov on training films, of which he was to make more than ninety, before being seconded to John Huston's American Army film unit to record at close quarters the Allies' struggle in Italy.

He quickly developed a facility for screenwriting. His first film, a morale-booster derived from one of his Army training films, was *The Way Ahead* (1944), with David Niven and Peter Ustinov. Ambler then moved on to Rank studios, writing scripts for more than a dozen films, including *The Cruel Sea* (1953), for which he was nominated for an Oscar.

In 1957 he went to Hollywood to work for MGM and scripted the first film about the *Titanic, A Night to Remember* (1958). He found the disciplines of screen and novel writing incompatible and for a time believed that he would never write a book again.

But he began to write thrillers again in 1951 and, having returned to London to live in Marylebone, wrote seven days a week. 'Most of it is revision,' he once said. 'The words don't come fluently – if it comes easily I get suspicious.'

⚜ **23rd** ⚜

Commander 'Rags' Butler, b. 1921, d. 1996

Commander 'Rags' Butler, who has died aged seventy-five, won the DSC as a nineteen-year old midshipman in a naval incident that thrilled the free world.

On the afternoon of 5 November 1940 *Jervis Bay*, commanded by Captain Fogarty Fegen, was in mid-Atlantic as sole escort of the 37-ship convoy HX84, homeward bound from Halifax, Nova Scotia, when the smoke and masts of a ship were sighted on the horizon to the north-east.

The stranger proved to be the German commerce-raiding pocket-battleship *Admiral Scheer*, which rapidly closed with the convoy and opened fire. *Jervis Bay* had seven six-inch guns, made in the reign of Queen Victoria, with a range of about 10,000 yards; it was very unlikely that she would ever get within range of the enemy. Nevertheless, Fegen hauled out of line and headed straight for *Scheer*, while the convoy scattered under cover of smoke, as ordered by the Commodore.

One eye-witness said later: 'I can only describe the way the *Jervis Bay* engaged that ship as magnificent. She just turned away as though she was protecting a brood of little chickens from a cat coming over the fence.'

It was not a fight but a massacre. *Scheer*, whose main armament was six eleven-inch guns with a range of over seventeen miles, hit *Jervis Bay* with her third salvo, setting the forward bridge on fire and shattering Fegen's right arm.

Butler's action station was on the after bridge, where he directed the after guns with a Dumaresq, a primitive gunnery instrument. He later gave a vivid account of the moment when the after bridge was hit: 'There was a blinding flash and a ripping rending sound like a thousand gongs. The man beside me literally burst into pieces. I felt my face warm and wet and looking down saw my hands and my coat red with blood, and stuck on it some utterly revolting pieces of flesh and gristle.'

Jervis Bay was hit repeatedly on her superstructure, her hull was holed in several places and major fires started down below. But her guns continued to fire for some time. Her after battle ensign was shot away and, in an episode of pure Elizabethan drama, Butler helped a sailor climb the flagstaff and nail another ensign in place.

Captain Fegen came aft and gave the order 'Abandon ship', telling Butler to make sure that everybody aft heard it. Butler remembered how 'the blood running down the arm glistened, showing red where it ran over the four gold stripes on his sleeve'. Fegen then went back to the remains of the forward bridge. As Butler said: 'We did not see him again.'

Jervis Bay did not sink until almost 8 p.m., nearly three hours after *Scheer* first attacked. This precious delay undoubtedly saved the convoy from annihilation, as *Scheer* could only round up and sink five ships.

One lifeboat and two rafts got away from *Jervis Bay*. Butler swam to a raft and found himself the only officer in it. One ship in the convoy, the Swedish *Stureholm*, returned in the early hours of 6 November to look for survivors, and picked up sixty-eight of *Jervis Bay*'s people, three of them already dead. One hundred and ninety-one officers and men, including Fegen, were lost.

When the survivors reached safety and told their experience, the story of *Jervis Bay*'s self-sacrifice was greeted with awe. King George VI immediately awarded Fegen a posthumous VC.

Ronald Alfred Gardyne Butler, known as 'Rags', was born on 28 June 1921 and went to Pangbourne Nautical College, joining the RNR as a midshipman in 1939.

After *Jervis Bay*, he served in the destroyers *Boadicea* and *Active* and then in 1942 joined the destroyer *Intrepid* as gunnery officer. *Intrepid* took part in Arctic convoys, the Pedestal convoy to Malta in August 1942, and in the Sicily and Salerno landings.

Late in 1943, *Intrepid* took part in a disastrous campaign in the Dodecanese, when the lessons of air power at sea, so painfully taught off Norway and Crete, were ignored; after being bombed by the Luftwaffe in Leros harbour, she capsized on 27 September.

Butler became a prisoner of war, but escaped and stole a motor launch, only to be recaptured when it was sunk. He escaped again, stole another launch and was again recaptured. He succeeded at the third attempt, in another stolen ship, and reached Beirut, where he caught a plane for Cairo which crashed on landing.

Butler accepted a year's accelerated seniority in lieu of a Bar to his DSC, and in 1944 was appointed gunnery officer in the fast minelayer *Apollo*, taking part in the Normandy landings.

After the war Butler accepted a regular commission in the Royal Navy. In his later years, before he retired in 1967, he was an Inspecting Officer in the Naval Ordnance Department.

⋙ **24**th ⋘

Hazel Pelling, b. 1937, d. 2003

Hazel Pelling, who has died aged sixty-six, was the landlady of the Fox and Hounds at Toys Hill, near Westerham in Kent, for thirty-four years.

The Fox became renowned as a last bastion of civilised drinking values when, in

1986, the customers fought a vigorous and successful campaign against the parent brewery, Ind Coope, which proposed to evict the Pellings and redevelop the pub.

Regulars preserved their right to enjoy the ancient sofas and armchairs that gave the bar the appearance of 'your favourite aunt's front room', as well as the large selection of chocolate bars and piles of *Country Life, Private Eye* and *Hello!* magazines that could be perused in front of two blazing log fires.

Mobile phones were forbidden and there was no electronic cash register, just a battered wooden till lodged in the old cast-iron slops sink, and two tankards in which the notes were kept.

Hazel Underwood was born at Otford, Kent, on 11 April 1937, the eldest of three children, and grew up in the village, attending Walthamstow Hall school in Sevenoaks, originally established for the daughters of missionaries. Following several dismal romances in her early twenties, in 1963 she responded on impulse to an advertisement for a secretarial position with the construction company Parkinson Howard, at Tema, Ghana.

It was there that she met her husband Ronald, a quartermaster nearly thirty years her senior with a roguish past (he had been declared *persona non grata* in Iraq in the 1950s), who had spent most of his post-war years in the Middle East and been married twice previously.

Knowing that the company might think the match unsuitable, they went off secretly in their lunch hour and got married. When this came to light, one of her bosses sent a telegram home to the British office announcing: 'That swine Pelling has married Hazel.'

The couple returned to England in 1967 with two small children, but nothing in the bank. With the confidence of the expert drinker, Ron Pelling decided that running a pub would solve the issue of house and job in one. In the spring of 1968, after subtracting ten years from his age, he secured the tenancy of the Fox and Hounds for his ever-expanding family (he impressed locals by fathering his fifth child at the age of seventy). He kept a shotgun behind the bar for repelling undesirables; when his eyesight began to fail, Hazel hid the gun in the airing cupboard, fearing he would shoot one of the family by mistake.

Customers loved the idiosyncrasies of the Fox, but Ind Coope was less keen, arguing when Ron Pelling reached seventy-five that it would be 'kinder' if he retired.

The regulars were outraged, and formed The Friends of the Fox and Hounds to preserve the Pellings' livelihood. The campaign took on aspects of an Ealing comedy. Plots were hatched to install protected species in the pub's attic (bats) and garden (orchids), while espionage missions were conducted on a rival landlord who was tipped to take over the licence.

Ind Coope capitulated. Shortly afterwards, Greene King purchased the pub and proved most sympathetic landlords.

Hazel Pelling was tireless. She worked from dawn to midnight, 364 days a year, and took just one short holiday in thirty-four years. After her husband's death she not only ran the Fox and raised five children alone, she cooked the pub food, did all the cellar work, swept chimneys, chopped wood and unblocked drains.

She thought kindly of everyone except environmental health officers ('the enemy') and ramblers who bought half a pint of orange squash, then tried to eat their packed lunches on her lawn.

⁓ 25th ⁓

Vincent Price, b. 1911, d. 1993

Vincent Price, the actor who has died aged eighty-two, was a Hollywood star in the *Grand Guignol* tradition.

His peculiar achievement was to blend horror with humour, high camp with menace. He enhanced the macabre, particularly the film adaptations of Edgar Allan Poe, with a ghoulish relish all his own.

While he deployed to great effect his expressive eyes, perpetually aghast beneath elegant eyebrows, he relied above all upon his extraordinary voice, which dripped with suave menace. It worked to particular effect for the video of the Michael Jackson hit, *Thriller*.

He described its timbre as the result of a bizarre accident. 'I was doing a one-man show about Oscar Wilde, and I got a recording of him reading *The Ballad of Reading Gaol*. And Wilde had a very high voice, so I pitched my voice higher. And I did the play – about 800 performances – for about five years, and it changed my voice.

'It's very difficult now for me to bring my voice down lower to its natural pitch. I'm stuck with the voice of Oscar Wilde.'

⁓ 26th ⁓

Lieutenant-Colonel Stuart Townend, b. 1909, d. 2002

Lieutenant-Colonel Stuart Townend, who has died aged ninety-three, was the owner and guiding spirit of Hill House, the world's largest private junior school, which he founded in London in 1951.

Townend, who as a young man had enjoyed an outstanding record as an athlete, had originally set up the school in Switzerland in 1949 after leaving the Army. At first he intended to do no more than teach mountain sports to English children in their holidays; but, after he had failed to enter Parliament as the Liberal candidate for Torquay in 1950, his wife suggested that he turn the Swiss venture into a full-time school in London.

'Don't be silly,' he told her, 'I'm not a nanny.' Nevertheless, her counsel eventually prevailed, and he opened his school in Knightsbridge with one table, one chair and a tennis ball. When asked by his first parent where the other children were, he had to pretend that they were late.

The school offered more than thirty sports, with children encouraged to try everything from rifle shooting to abseiling. Townend himself was a man of extraordinarily robust health. He rose at four to take the first of ten cups of tea, with eight lumps of sugar in each. He also drank twelve cups of Ovaltine a day, with five lumps of sugar. He had no teeth of his own, having many years ago told his dentist, 'Knock out the whole shooting match.' He smoked thirty cigars a day.

Townend took full advantage of the independence conferred on him by his owning the school rather than being a mere employee of governors. He hired and fired teachers at will and docked staff £50 a day for sick leave ('The weather is unavoidable; illness is not'); he even fined himself when he broke a leg. Staff meetings were governed by a giant alarm clock placed on the common room table.

Yet, although his outlook was traditional and his vocabulary archaic, Townend was not the peppery colonel portrayed in the newspapers. He was fonder of the company of women than of men, was strongly opposed to corporal punishment (a sacking offence at the school), and believed the Falkland Islands should have been given to Argentina.

He was a meritocrat rather than a snob, and allowed the children of school employees including minibus drivers and lavatory cleaners to attend Hill House for £10 a term. Nor was he above impulsive acts of kindness. When, on his eighty-fifth birthday, he was unexpectedly presented with a giant cake by his staff, he raised everyone's salary by £1,000 on the spot, a gesture which cost him £150,000.

Hill House was certainly not a conventional school (Townend saved the cost of a bursar by doing the accounts himself), but it thrived to the point where, by the 1990s, it had 1,100 pupils (700 boys and 400 girls), half of them from non-English backgrounds; the school was spread over six sites in Chelsea and Knightsbridge.

Stories were rife of overcrowding and of impromptu lessons on the stairs. Long crocodiles of Hill House pupils attired in their distinctive uniform of cinnamon knee-breeches and gold sweaters were a familiar sight on the streets around Sloane Square – the colours were chosen by Townend's wife, who would have none of the prevailing grey, believing 'a grey uniform produces grey minds, grey boys'.

Henry Stuart Townend was born on 24 April 1909, one of four children. His father, the vicar of a parish in Devon, was killed in the First World War in 1915, and at the age of nine young Stuart was sent to St Edmund's, Canterbury, a school for the orphans of clergymen.

It was there that he met the influence that shaped his life, a games master named Powers who discerned in him a talent for athletics and a taste for competition. Largely on the strength of his sporting prowess, in 1928 Townend was offered a place at Brasenose College, Oxford, where he read Mathematics. He reserved most of his effort, however, for the track, and each year from 1929 to 1931 won Blues for the mile and half-mile, becoming President of the University Athletic Club in 1930.

After leaving Oxford in 1931, Townend went to Rosenberg College, Switzerland, where he studied languages, mountaineering and skiing – taking first place in a downhill race held over the border in Austria. He then accepted a commission in the Royal Artillery, and in 1936, as a German-speaking officer attached to the British Olympic team, he met Hitler at the Berlin Games.

During the Second World War, Townend served principally on the staff at the War Office; but after D-Day he commanded a battery in the drive across north-west

Europe. He was mentioned in despatches, and then severely wounded when struck by a mortar shell; he had been shaving outdoors and, characteristically, had refused to interrupt his toilet in order to seek shelter. Having recovered from his wounds, Townend helped to liberate the Buchenwald concentration camp before leaving the Army in 1947.

Townend was no believer in the benefits of retirement, and continued to run Hill House into his nineties. 'Once you retire you absolutely go to pieces,' he pronounced. 'All you do is moan about taxes and young people.'

⊰ 27th ⊱

Andre de Toth, b. 1913, d. 2002

Andre de Toth, the Hungarian-born film director who has died aged eighty-nine, somehow managed to make the cult classic *House of Wax* (1953) in 3-D, despite the fact that he only had one eye.

De Toth's own life was as packed with incident as his films. He related how the piratical black patch he wore over his missing eye (lost as the result of an accident in childhood) once nearly cost him his life.

Scouting for locations in Egypt shortly after the Yom Kippur War, he was mistaken for Moshe Dayan and kidnapped, pistol-whipped and interrogated by a group of youths. He only escaped after a physical examination established the fact that, far from being an Israeli, he was not even Jewish.

His appetite for love was as immense as his appetite for life. In 1934 he followed a girl to Vienna and, blundering into an attempted Nazi coup d'état, was shot and woke up in the city's morgue. Later he fell in love with an anti-Nazi courier carrying jewels across European frontiers, an affair which ended when her counterfeit passport in the name of Mrs de Toth was returned to him covered in blood. He married seven times (Veronica Lake was his first wife) and had nineteen children.

Andre de Toth was born Sasvari Farkasfalvi Tothfalusi-Toth Endre Antai Mihaly at Mako, Hungary, on 15 May 1913. He studied Law at the University of Budapest to please his mother, but spent most of his time writing plays and working as a cameraman for the cinematographer Istvan Eiben.

By the late 1930s, de Toth had fathered a child, qualified as a pilot in the Hungarian air corps (he once performed an emergency landing in a snowstorm with the radio on fire), and had learned to drive a racing car and play polo. He was initiated into the world of international cinema by working for Alexander Korda in London on *The Elephant Boy* (1938).

His first film *Toprini Nasz* ('Wedding in Toprin', 1938) received an award from the Hungarian Ministry of Culture. Then he was tricked into filming second unit work in Poland by a German intelligence unit posing as a film company, only realising part-way through that he was filming the Nazi invasion.

After making four more features in Hungary, in 1940 de Toth sailed for America on a ship which sank on its next voyage. The Kordas too soon crossed the Atlantic and de Toth got work on *The Thief of Baghdad* (1940) and on Rudyard Kipling's *Jungle Book* (1942), during the filming of which he and Korda found themselves trapped in a cage with an ill-tempered tiger called Rajah. *None Shall Escape* (1944) anticipated the Nuremberg Trials by demonstrating how a Nazi war criminal could be brought to justice.

He had many other credits before working as second unit director on David Lean's *Lawrence of Arabia* (1962).

But he remained most celebrated for *3-D House of Wax*, starring Vincent Price as a deranged sculptor badly deformed in a fire, who rebuilds his collection by making wax statues out of his murder victims. The film is still regarded as the best of a dismal genre, despite its gruesome content: 'The possible effect on children of such a picture,' noted *The Daily Telegraph*'s critic enthusiastically, 'is awful to contemplate.'

John Roberts, b. 1945, d. 2001

John Roberts, who has died aged fifty-five, financed and promoted the Woodstock rock music festival in 1969 after he and a friend placed an advertisement in the *New York Times* which read: 'Young men with unlimited capital looking for interesting, legitimate opportunities and business propositions.'

The advertisement was not meant to be taken seriously but was background research for a sitcom about two young venture capitalists with money but no ideas, which Roberts and his friend Joel Rosenman were trying to sell to a television agent.

They received some 5,000 responses, mostly from cranks, but the idea for a rock music festival struck them as interesting and, forgetting television, they decided to go ahead using money Roberts had inherited from his family toothpaste business: 'Somehow, we became the characters in our own show,' Rosenman recalled.

The Woodstock Festival, billed as 'Three Days of Peace and Music', was held in August 1969 on sodden fields near Bethel in upstate New York and was expected to attract an audience of 50,000. In the event, half a million people turned up.

⊰ 28th ⊱

Josef Stawinoga, b. 1920, d. 2007

Josef Stawinoga, who has died aged eighty-six, was a hermit who lived for nearly forty years in a tent on the central reservation of the A4150 Wolverhampton inner ring road – between PC World and a bathroom showroom.

The Polish-born Stawinoga, known locally as Fred, Trampee or Shakespeare, arrived in Britain after the Second World War, settled in Wolverhampton and dropped out of normal society for unknown reasons sometime in the 1960s. By the 1970s he had moved into a makeshift tent of plastic sheeting erected underneath a weeping willow on the ring road, where he was allowed to remain by the local council.

Unkempt and dirty, with long matted hair and a two-foot straggly, yellowish beard, he became a local celebrity. He was revered by local Hindus and Sikhs as a saint who had shunned all worldly possessions; was awarded an honorary degree by Wolverhampton Polytechnic; and even had his own 6,500-strong fan group – 'we love you Wolverhampton ring-road tramp' – on the internet site Facebook.

Local folklore offered several explanations for Stawinoga's chosen way of life. Some claimed he had served as a lance-corporal in the Polish Army Medical Corps and had developed a fear of confined spaces after being detained as a prisoner of war by the Russians. Certainly his well-attested dislike of anyone in uniform seemed to support this theory. Others suggested he chose a solitary life after a failed love affair.

Josef Stawinoga was born on 15 December 1920. Little is known about his early life until he arrived in Britain after the war. He worked briefly as a hospital orderly in Wales before finding a job at the steelworks in Bilston. In 1952 he married an Austrian woman with whom he lived in a single room in a boarding house.

By all accounts it was not a happy relationship: Stawinoga was said to have taken to locking up his wife when he went to work. She would cry and scream until one day, several years later, a neighbour smashed down the door to let her out. She fled.

During the 1960s Stawinoga became increasingly eccentric. Before he moved into his tent he was evicted from nine lodging houses for not paying his rent, and he was often seen pushing a pram containing all his worldly goods. Stawinoga rejected all attempts by the council to rehouse him and eventually the authorities sanctioned his unorthodox living arrangements, arranging for nine replacement tents to be erected over the original plastic sheeting to keep the rain out.

Though he did not have a bath in thirty years he never went short of the essentials. Every day members of the local Asian community would come to pay homage with gifts of blankets, clothing and food – including, on one occasion, a live chicken which took up residence inside the tent until it vanished, probably under the wheels of a passing car.

Sandy Lehmann-Haupt, b. 1942, d. 2001

Sandy Lehmann-Haupt, who has died aged fifty-nine, was one of the 'Merry Pranksters' who accompanied the novelist Ken Kesey on his psychedelic 'magic bus' in the 1960s.

Lehmann-Haupt's experiences formed the basis for Tom Wolfe's book *The Electric Kool-Aid Acid Test* (1968) which portrayed the journey as a metaphor for the transition from the 'Beatnik' to the 'Hippie' generation.

His adventure began in the spring of 1964 when Kesey invested some of the royalties from his first two novels in an old 1939 International Harvester school bus. After equipping it with bunks and a kitchen, installing a sound system (internal and external), and painting it in swirling psychedelic colours, he and some friends, including the 22-year-old Lehmann-Haupt, set off from California. The destination sign on the front of the bus read 'Further' and on the back it said 'Caution – Weird Load'.

The Merry Pranksters, as they called themselves, had stocked up on gallons of orange juice laced with LSD; their plan was to film the tour on the way as an 'acid movie' while promoting their philosophy of 'living now'. A hole in the roof of the bus enabled its occupants to sit outside on a makeshift platform to play music and enjoy trips of various kinds.

Dressed in combinations of fluorescent orange and green, the Pranksters acquired new names as their personalities developed. Female Pranksters included 'The Slime Queen', 'Gretchen Fetchin' and 'Stark Naked'; their male equivalents included 'Mal Function' and 'Hardly Visible'; Kesey was 'Swashbuckler' and Lehmann-Haupt 'Dismounted' on account of his habit of getting off the bus every time it stopped.

The Pranksters struck fear into the hearts of Middle America, staging public 'acid tests', at which people were encouraged to explore the 'far reaches of consciousness' with psychedelic drugs. As LSD was not then illegal, there was little the police could do to stop them.

Lehmann-Haupt lived to regret his involvement. As a result of 'bad trips' and prolonged drug abuse, he became mentally ill and spent many years living on benefits. Later, he described his experiences to Tom Wolfe over long walks in Central Park: 'Sandy had a mad sense of the world torn apart into stained-glass shards behind his eyelids,' Wolfe recalled.

Hellmut Alexander Lehmann-Haupt was born on 22 March 1942 in Manhattan, the youngest of three sons of a writer and bibliographer. His brother Christopher became chief obituary writer on the *New York Times*.

Lehmann-Haupt first met Kesey when the writer visited New York for the stage version of *One Flew Over the Cuckoo's Nest*. He soon moved into Kesey's home in California, where he installed a new sound system and tried LSD.

Lehmann-Haupt had recovered from the bus trip only in the last decade when, inspired by a deepening religious faith, he gave up using drugs, found a job, got married and bought a house.

⊰ 29th ⊱

Jo Jo Laine, b. 1953, d. 2006

Jo Jo Laine, who has died aged fifty-three after falling down a flight of stairs, led a fast-paced life which bore witness to the dangers of too much beauty combined with an almost total lack of self-restraint.

Petite, wide-eyed and with waist-length dark auburn hair, she became famous as a model but notorious as a groupie who numbered among her conquests some of the most glamorous icons of the 1960s and 70s rock scene.

After losing her virginity to Jimi Hendrix, her lovers included Rod Stewart, Jim Morrison and the Wings (and former Moody Blues) guitarist Denny Laine, to whom she was briefly married. After a fling with Randy Rhoads, the Black Sabbath guitarist, she began a relationship with Peter O'Donohue, a builder who was jailed in 1988 for eleven years for his part in a £40 million armed raid on a safety deposit centre in Knightsbridge. Later she became one of the live-in 'wifelets' of the Marquess of Bath, occupying a cottage on the Longleat estate. Cream's drummer Ginger Baker was quoted as saying: 'No sane man would go near her.'

She was born Joanne LaPatrie in Boston, Massachusetts, on 13 July 1953, but gave herself the name Jo Jo in fan letters she wrote as a girl to Paul McCartney. Aged seventeen she moved to Los Angeles to work as a professional fashion model, appearing in television commercials and on the covers of magazines, including *Vogue*.

By this time she had already become a fixture on the rock scene. She met Jimi Hendrix backstage at the Woodstock Festival in 1969. 'Those were wild times,' she recalled. 'Everyone was tripping. I was introduced to him in his dressing room and then he shooed everyone out and locked the door and we started kissing. He started singing "Foxy Lady" and then we made love.'

The perfunctory nature of their courtship established a pattern from which Jo Jo Laine rarely deviated. She spent a 'crazy night' with Jim Morrison (of the Doors) who was, by her account, 'already out of it and on a bottle of whisky a day'. She dated Rod Stewart, 'virtually my first love', on and off for two years, later recalling: 'He may not have been the best lover, but he was the best kisser. He never seemed bothered that I wasn't blonde.'

She met Denny Laine backstage at a gig in 1972, and within two days they were an item. 'It was the ultimate groupie's dream,' she recalled. They had a son and a daughter, and she accompanied Wings on tour, though she recalled that Linda McCartney was not happy with her presence on the tour bus, fearing she was trying to steal her husband. She and Laine married in 1978 and bought Yew Corner in Sussex, the innocent inspiration for A.A. Milne's *House at Pooh Corner*, which subsequently became notorious for Jo Jo Laine's wild parties.

In 1978 Jo Jo Laine's brother, a heavy drug-user and schizophrenic, shot their father at the home they shared in Florida after a row about his drug taking. Her father survived, but remained paralysed for more than a year before dying in 1980.

The tragedy put a strain on Jo Jo Laine's marriage: Denny began having an affair with her best friend, and Jo Jo took to drink and antidepressants, filed for divorce and embarked on an affair with Randy Rhoads which ended with his death in a plane crash six months later.

By now drinking heavily, she began an affair with Peter O'Donohue, with whom she had another child before the relationship broke down amid violent rows. In 1991 she met Alexander Thynn, the Marquess of Bath, at an art exhibition.

Within weeks she and her children had moved into a cottage on his estate. During her Longleat period (which ended in 1996, when she moved back to London), she was photographed in *Playboy* cavorting naked on a tiger skin – at a photo session attended, bizarrely, by the Tory MP Sir Antony Buck and his then wife, Bienvenida.

Her worsening health failed to dampen Jo Jo Laine's enthusiasm for partying. In 2003 she stunned partygoers attending a book launch in the Cabinet War Rooms by embarking on a 'sex romp' with the transsexual performer Sasha de Suinn. Jo Jo was unrepentant about the incident, though she confessed: 'I can't believe he was a she.'

Anton LaVey, b. 1930, d. 1997

Anton LaVey, the founder and high priest of the Church of Satan, who has died aged sixty-seven, had begun his career in the circus, putting his head into the jaws of a lion; when the beast removed a chunk of his neck, however, he decided to look for alternative employment.

In April 1966, on Walpurgisnacht, when evil is supposed to hold sway over the world, he shaved his head, declared himself a prelate in the House of Satan, and established his headquarters in a former brothel in the suburbs of San Francisco. He developed elaborate rituals for black mass, advocating the use of buxom nude girls as servers.

The west coast of America proved fruitful of disciples, some of them celebrities. The cult's most prominent champion was Jayne Mansfield. This alarmed Sam Brody, her lover and lawyer, who vigorously resisted LaVey's influence. When Jayne Mansfield and Brody were killed in a car crash in 1967 – the actress being partially decapitated – LaVey let it be known that at the time of the accident he had been cutting out her photograph and had accidentally snipped off the top of her head.

⚜ 30th ⚜

Craig Russell, b. 1948, d. 1990

Craig Russell, the transvestite comedian who has died aged forty-two, had the unique honour of being judged both Best Actor and Best Actress at the Virgin Islands Film Festival.

He won this distinction with his bravura performance in a low-budget film called *Outrageous* (1978), as a transvestite Canadian hairdresser who throws up his job to become a professional female impersonator in New York, wallowing in the borrowed glamour of Judy Garland and Bette Davis. The role bore striking similarities to Russell's own history, and he approached it with a winning insouciance and a wistful bitchiness which somehow avoided the worst excesses of camp.

'Female impersonation,' he once said, 'is one of the oldest traditions of theatre. I'd like to see it shake off some of the tacky associations it's picked up and recognised as an art in itself.' In *Outrageous* he achieved this ambition.

An insurance salesman's son, Craig Russell was born in Toronto in 1948. At the age of thirteen he fell in love with Mae West, an actress whom many would regard as the ultimate female impersonator – and who was to become the inspiration of his career.

Young Craig wrote to Miss West, claiming to have started a fan club with twenty-five members and enclosing the requisite number of forged signatures as evidence. Racked with adolescent guilt at this deception, he went on to found a genuine fan club which eventually rose to a membership of 2,000.

The actress and the schoolboy entered into correspondence, and then into regular telephone conversations. In due course Russell followed his father into the insurance business, but by 1967 was complaining to Miss West that the office routine was driving him mad.

She invited him to stay at her beach house, where he remained for nine months. 'She taught me everything I know,' he recalled. 'She still had closets full of wonderful dresses, and for some reason they fitted me, so I would dress up for her, just doing routines and songs from her films. She loved it.'

Refreshed by this transvestite idyll, Russell returned to Toronto where, resuming the conventional apparel of his sex, he found employment as a hairdresser. After a few years of this he found himself drunk at a Hallowe'en party dressed as Tallulah Bankhead, and was so gratified at the applause which greeted his impersonation that he resolved to turn professional.

With money borrowed from his parents he set himself up as a solo performer, beginning with a repertoire of six Hollywood *monstres sacrés*, which he gradually built up to twenty-five.

Russell was meticulous in his preparation for each new role, and would immerse himself in old newspaper clippings to find every detail and nuance of his subject's character. His old mentor, Miss West, was greatly flattered by Russell's act, but was much happier when he had worked his way up to 'class joints', as she called them.

'When you were working in those dives,' she said, 'I was afraid that people would get drunk and think it was me on the skids.' Peggy Lee and Carol Channing were also among his admirers.

After his triumph in *Outrageous* Russell continued to tour with his impersonations, impressing audiences with the speed and wit of his delivery; and in 1988 he made a sequel called *Too Outrageous*. But *autres temps, autres moeurs* and in the era of Aids – to which Russell himself succumbed – it did not enjoy a comparable success.

⊰ 31st ⊱

Gaston Berlemont, b. 1914, d. 1999

Gaston Berlemont, who has died aged eighty-five, was the licensee of the remarkable Soho pub where he was born.

For forty years he presided over a daily gathering of bohemian painters, poets, layabouts and eccentrics. In the single small bar of the York Minster, known as the French pub, the usual cast of Soho – Nina Hamnett, Lucian Freud, Bruce Bernard, George Melly, John Davenport, Frank Norman – ebbed and flowed.

The obvious advantage of the French was that it did not have a juke box or a one-armed bandit, so you could hear yourself and, sometimes, even other people speak.

Gaston Berlemont also cashed cheques, even for people who knew in their hearts that they would bounce. He advanced loans and threw people out with his charmingly artificial French manners. 'One of us has to leave,' he might say, 'and it is not going to be me.'

The Reverend Roger Holloway, b. 1933, d. 2010

The Reverend Roger Holloway, who has died aged seventy-six, led a life of rich and unusual variety as a soldier, big-game hunter, international wine and spirit merchant and Anglican priest.

He was born on 24 November 1933, the youngest of six children of a civil servant. The family was a military one, and while a small boy in his high chair he was delighted to discover that every time he hummed the National Anthem at the dinner table, all would rise; in such a fiercely patriotic family this rapidly became very trying.

NOVEMBER

⚞ 1st ⚟

Robert Rines, b. 1922, d. 2009

Robert Rines, who has died aged eighty-seven, was an American lawyer, composer, inventor and physicist but best known in Britain as a cryptozoologist who used some of his inventions to try to prove the existence of the Loch Ness Monster.

Rines invented prototype technology that led to sharper resolution in radar, sonar and the ultrasound imaging of internal organs.

In 1985 researchers used underwater vessels with sonar equipment developed by Rines to find the wreck of the *Titanic*, which sank in waters a mile and a half deep in the North Atlantic in 1912. The systems were also used in 1989 to find the wreck of the German battleship *Bismarck*, which was sunk at the Battle of Denmark Strait off Iceland during the Second World War.

While his inventions had obvious and important military and medical applications, they also led to some remarkable images from the depths of Loch Ness, produced by sonar and underwater cameras. Rines claimed that they showed evidence of the existence of a huge beast, possibly a plesiosaur, an aquatic reptile thought to have died out with the dinosaurs 65 million years ago.

'It's a ridiculous idea,' Rines admitted in 2000. 'If I didn't trust the people I've talked to and our own scientific evidence, I'd say I was crazy. I may not be able to prove it, but I know there was a plesiosaur in Loch Ness because I saw it.'

Rines' epiphany occurred on 23 June 1972, when he apparently sighted the creature while attending a tea party on the banks of the loch near Inverness with his first wife, Carol, and two friends. Spotting an odd shape moving across the water, he grabbed a telescope and through it saw 'a large, darkish hump, covered ... with rough, mottled skin, like the back of an elephant'.

In an attempt to record the beast on film as well as sonar, Rines deployed a series of underwater cameras, suspended from two boats, with strobe lighting to illuminate the loch's murky depths. In August 1972 the cameras captured an image that seemed to show a large flipper, and in June 1974 another apparently showed a close-up of the head and upper neck of an unknown creature. A further shot seemed to show something with a long neck, small head and large body, something resembling a plesiosaur.

The pictures, published in the highly respected *Nature* magazine in December 1975, caused a sensation. Experts including the British television naturalist Sir Peter Scott agreed that they indicated the existence of some sort of large animate object in the waters of the loch. Furthermore, Scott declared that he was convinced that 'this is no hoax', and bestowed the Latin name *Nessiteras rhombopteryx* on Rines's 'monster'.

'I thought that would clinch it,' Rines remarked gloomily, 'but, as you know, it didn't at all.'

In 2008 Rines announced that he was giving up his search for 'Nessie'. His fears that she may have perished, the victim perhaps of global warming, generated the improbable *Daily Star* headline 'LOCH NESS MONSTER DIES AGED 3 MILLION'.

Robert Harvey Rines was born on 20 August 1922 in Boston, the son of a patent lawyer who taught at Harvard. At Massachusetts Institute of Technology, Rines studied Physics and Engineering. As an outstanding student at MIT's new radiation laboratory, he worked on the development of high-resolution image-scanning radar, knowledge that he applied to his wartime service with the US Signal Corps.

Posted to Britain, he trained to operate anti-aircraft radar and carried out crucial research during the establishment of the US Army's top secret microwave early warning system, used to detect aircraft movement in overcast skies at 200 miles range. By the end of the war he was commanding officer of the research group stationed at Fort Drum laboratory in upstate New York.

Returning to civilian life, Rines received a Law degree from Georgetown, and worked for more than fifty years as an attorney specialising in patent law. Rines also taught at MIT, focusing on invention, patents and innovation.

Away from his laboratory bench, he also wrote music for more than ten Broadway and off-Broadway productions, and shared an Emmy for his work on *Hizzoner – The Mayor*, a show about the former New York City Mayor Fiorello LaGuardia. One of his ventures in the entertainment world was a ballet he produced, *Life at MIT*.

⊰ 2nd ⊱

Hal Roach, b. 1892, d. 1992

Hal Roach, who has died aged a hundred, was the last surviving giant of the silent film industry, responsible for the discovery of such legendary figures in screen buffoonery as Harold Lloyd and Laurel and Hardy.

Rotund and dapper, until the end of his long life Roach retained the appearance of a Hollywood mogul of the old school.

He was born at Elmira, New York, on 14 January 1892. His career began in picaresque style when he ran away from home at the age of seventeen. He walked and hitchhiked to Seattle, where he was taken in by a kindly aunt and found a job selling ice cream. His ambitions were modest enough: 'I thought I'd stay out West for a year, hitchhike back to Elmira, become an engineer, marry a local girl, and live there for the rest of my life.'

Before the year was out, however, he had made his way to Alaska, where he spent several months running mule trains and prospecting – unsuccessfully – for gold. He then moved on to California, where he worked first as a truck driver in Los Angeles and then on a construction site in the Mojave Desert before stumbling into the film business.

Roach appeared as a cowboy extra for Bison Films for a dollar a day, and spent the next two years as a bit player in countless one-reelers. In 1914, while working as a stunt man and odd-jobber at Universal Studios, he met Harold Lloyd, another struggling nobody.

Roach decided that he could make Lloyd a great comedian and in 1915, after inheriting $3,000, he formed his own company and hired his friend to play a character called Willie Work in a series of comedy shorts.

Roach and Lloyd enjoyed a remarkably happy partnership, and stumbled on their best ideas accidentally. The classic *Safety Last* (1923), for instance, in which Lloyd performed a number of extraordinary stunts, was conceived by Roach after a film was wrongly developed so that Lloyd appeared to be dangling from a building in Los Angeles.

By the mid-1920s Roach was devoting less of his time to directing and more to the administration of his growing company – although he continued to contribute to the scripts of many of his films. His stable of talent expanded rapidly.

His most inspired move was to bring together an English comedian named Stanley Jefferson (who changed his name to Laurel) with a 'good ole boy' from Georgia named Oliver Hardy. Roach had first come across Jefferson playing the vaudeville circuit in downtown Los Angeles, and immediately signed him up. But after discovering that 'his eyes didn't photograph good' Roach made 'Stan' a writer and forgot about him. When some superior film stock came in the Englishman was photographed again – 'And his eyes looked all right. So we tried him.'

He already had Hardy on contract. 'When we saw the two of them working together – a little Englishman and a real fat Southern heavy – we decided that they just might make a team. It was another one of those lucky hunches that made me a lot of money.'

Richard Waddington, b. 1910, d. 1999

Richard Waddington, who has died aged eighty-eight, was once described as 'the world's greatest salmon fisherman', and was celebrated for inventing the Waddington lure. This consisted of a treble-hooked design, resembling the tail fin of a small fish, attached to a shank of metal wire, up to three inches long. On to this were tied some lengthy heron feather fibres, to make the lure look like a small fish.

Unlike some earlier writers on salmon fishing, Waddington was not concerned about the colour of his flies. 'It is the tone of the fly that is important,' he wrote. 'And for this reason the colour of the wing of the sunk salmon fly is of little importance, save in giving a certain tenuous bulk to the thin body.'

Waddington also spent some of his time on the once-fabled rivers in Norway. One of his great moments came on the mighty Aaro in Songefjord, when he caught a huge salmon of 51lb. 'To me,' he wrote, 'this fish represented the fulfilment of a dream: it was caught on a fly of my own tying, played and tailed entirely alone and in a tremendous river. Such luck occurs but once in a lifetime!'

⇒ 3rd ⇐

Jean Bedel Bokassa, b. 1921, d. 1996

Jean Bedel Bokassa, who has died aged seventy-five, was President of the Central African Republic between 1966 and 1979, and for the last three of those years self-proclaimed Emperor.

One of the monsters of the twentieth century, he was for a long time backed by France, eager to be involved in the Republic's uranium trade. For his part, Bokassa claimed to model himself on Napoleon, and in 1970 was led from de Gaulle's grave crying 'Papa, papa'.

It was not until May 1979, when Amnesty International reported that 200 children had been murdered on Bokassa's orders, that the French organised a coup against the Emperor. Amnesty revealed that the children had been killed after they had refused to buy uniforms from a shop belonging to one of the Emperor's wives. The children were rounded up, herded into prison, and beaten, tortured, suffocated and shot.

It was said that the remains of forty corpses had been found in a crocodile pool beside Bokassa's palace, and that mutilated bodies had been discovered in his cold store. Commentators remembered that he belonged to the M'Baka tribe, once known for cannibalism. The palace cook was supposed to have flambéed human remains for the Emperor and his guests. Such accounts lost nothing in the telling. But the authenticated truth about the Emperor was alarming enough.

One of twelve children, Jean Bedel Bokassa was born on 21 February 1921, the son of a chief in Lobaye Province, in the French colony of Oubangui-Chari. His uncle, Barthelemy Boganda, led the independence movement until his death in 1959; his cousin, David Dacko, became the first president of the Central African Republic in 1960.

Educated at mission schools, Bokassa originally had some idea of becoming a priest, but in 1939 joined the French army. After the fall of France he became a member of the Free French forces, and fought in French Equatorial Africa.

He went on to serve in Indo-China, surviving the rout of the French army at Dien Bien Phu in 1954, and earning his commission in 1956. In 1960 he retired from the army with the rank of captain and a dozen medals.

At home, he accepted an invitation from David Dacko to reorganise the Central African Republic's army. Within four years he was commander-in-chief and head of the general staff.

In 1965 President Dacko, enmeshed in economic crisis, imposed austerity measures and proposed a substantial reduction in the military budget. Bokassa, who had taken over the Ministry of War, launched a coup on New Year's Eve 1965, arresting the police chief and several ministers. The presidential palace was ringed with paratroopers, and Dacko put under house arrest. Early on New Year's Day, he handed over full powers to Bokassa, who appointed himself prime minister, commander-in-chief and leader of the only political party, Mouvement pour l'Evolution Sociale de l'Afrique (MESAN).

His portrait appeared everywhere. Public buildings, streets and squares were named after him. Elections were banned and democracy became an unmentionable word. And in 1976 he decided to make himself Emperor Bokassa I.

Although his country was one of the poorest in the world, with one child in five dying before the age of twelve months, Bokassa ordered a coronation that would cost £10 million.

He ordered his coronation robes from Guiselin, the Paris firm which had embroidered Napoleon's uniforms. A Paris jeweller was charged with making a crown studded with 138 diamonds for £2 million. The throne was also constructed in France, a plush high-backed fauteuil, topped by a huge gilded eagle; it weighed two tons. Eight white horses were flown in from Normandy to pull the imperial coach. Bokassa emulated Napoleon by crowning himself.

The Emperor reigned for less than three years. On 20 September 1979, while he was away seeking aid from President Gaddafi in Libya, French paras dropped into Bangui and restored Dacko to power.

Bokassa found sanctuary in the Ivory Coast for two years, and then went to France, where he lived in one of his four chateaux. In 1986, after five years of increasing depression, he returned to Bangui to face trial.

Though convicted of murder and sentenced to death, Bokassa was acquitted on the cannibalism charges for lack of evidence. Subsequently, President Andre Kolingba commuted his sentence to twenty years in prison; in the event Bokassa was released in 1993.

≋ 4th ≋

Colonel Sir David Stirling, b. 1915, d. 1990

Colonel Sir David Stirling, who has died aged seventy-four, was the creator of the Special Air Service.

Nicknamed the 'Phantom Major' by the Germans for his remarkable exploits far behind their lines in the Western Desert, he and his desert raiders destroyed aircraft, mined roads, derailed trains, fired petrol dumps, blew up ammunition depots, hijacked lorries and killed many times their own number. Rommel admitted that Stirling's men caused more damage than any other British unit of equal strength.

In 1942 the SAS was given the status of a full regiment. Montgomery said of its creator: 'The boy Stirling is quite mad. However, in war there is a place for mad people.' Stirling himself designed the regiment's cap badge, bearing the words 'Who Dares Wins'. The motto summed up his philosophy.

Archibald David Stirling was born on 15 November 1915, the son of Brigadier-General Archibald Stirling of Keir and his wife, Margaret, fourth daughter of the 13th Lord Lovat. David's brother, William Stirling, commanded the 2nd SAS Regiment.

David was educated at Ampleforth and Trinity College, Cambridge, but he was sent down after a year and began to study painting. On the outbreak of the Second World War he was in the Rocky Mountains practising climbing with the ultimate object of attempting Everest.

He served with the Scots Guards (the family regiment) for the first six months of the war, and then transferred to No. 3 Commando and went to the Middle East as a member of Bob Laycock's 'Layforce', which planned to capture Rhodes. When 'Layforce' was disbanded, Stirling and a few of his commando friends decided to teach themselves parachuting with a view to landing behind German lines in the desert and destroying aircraft on the ground.

The first venture by parachute, on 17 November 1941, was a total disaster, because of a sudden sandstorm with winds of 90mph. Of the sixty-six who set out, only twenty-two survived.

Undeterred, Stirling continued with his plans, now using trucks and the expertise of the Long Range Desert Group to navigate in the desert. One of its most spectacular exploits was the raid on Sidi Haneish airfield, when eighteen jeeps, each carrying four Vickers K-machine-guns, drove straight down the central runway, destroying Junkers, Heinkels, Messerschmitts and Stukas. They completed their work by driving around the perimeter, destroying no fewer than forty aircraft.

The vital achievement of the SAS was that it destroyed on the ground the latest German aircraft, such as Messerschmitt 109Fs (armed with cannon), which in the sky totally outclassed the ageing Hurricanes and Gloster Gauntlets of the scanty Desert Air Force.

Soon the SAS was raiding far and wide, taking pressure off Malta by destroying the airfields from which German bombers took off; it also raided Crete several times. But in 1942, while his regiment was operating in northern Tunisia, Stirling was captured as 500 Germans surrounded the cave in which he was sleeping. He soon escaped, but he was recaptured.

After being flown to Italy he escaped four more times, but each time his height – 6ft 5in – gave him away. Eventually the Germans interned him in Colditz.

On his release Stirling went to live in Rhodesia and Kenya, where he founded the Capricorn Africa Society with the objective of promoting racial equality, tolerance and understanding. He was the society's president for twelve years and made more friends among the black than the white community. In 1959, when he returned to England, he became involved with the syndication of television programmes.

Stirling was always careful not to interfere in any way with the SAS which, having been disbanded, was reconstituted to fight in the Malayan emergency. His military expertise, however, and wish to be concerned with projects beneficial to Britain drew him into advising units countering terrorism and subversion in countries where Britain had interests. In 1967 Stirling and his friends created the Watchguard Organisation, which, based in Guernsey, employed ex-SAS soldiers to provide bodyguards for Middle Eastern rulers and others. Occasionally, as in Kenya and Dhofar, he was overruled by Whitehall which sent the SAS, with its larger resources, instead.

Extremely courteous, soft-spoken and self-effacing, David Stirling was worshipped by the men of the unit he had created and many more outside it. He regarded killing as an unfortunate necessity and, for a man of his size, could move extremely swiftly and silently; in his younger days he had been able to stalk a stag and kill it with a knife.

⪦ 5th ⪧

Sir Isaiah Berlin, b. 1909, d. 1997

Sir Isaiah Berlin, who has died aged eighty-eight, was one of the foremost liberal thinkers of the twentieth century.

No one has written more convincingly or lucidly about the world of thought. In the estimation of Lord Annan, Berlin produced 'the truest and most moving of all interpretations of life that my own generation has made'.

Berlin came to prominence at a time when the world was divided by political ideology, and his most important work was in political thought. Perhaps his greatest achievement was to turn the attention of post-war philosophy, which was largely preoccupied with esoteric problems of linguistics and logic, to the consideration of the political issues of the age.

Berlin saw the totalitarian advances of the previous decades in the East, and their intellectual apologists in the West, as an enormous threat to the Anglo-Saxon tradition of liberty and freedom. His passionate defence of J.S. Mill's view of liberty in *Four Essays on Liberty* became the starting point for any modern discussion on freedom, and also helped to revive a subject that had fallen into the doldrums.

Isaiah Berlin was born on 6 June 1909 in Riga, Latvia, then part of the Tsarist empire. His father, Mendel Berlin, was a Jewish timber merchant who supplied sleepers to the Russian railways. In 1915 the family left Riga for Andreapol, and two years later moved to Petrograd, where young Isaiah witnessed both the Liberal and Bolshevik Revolutions of 1917. Isaiah's father was a fervent Anglophile, and in 1919 he brought the family to live in England.

Isaiah was educated as a scholar of St Paul's School and Corpus Christi College, Oxford, where he began to read the great philosophers. He had already been interested in philosophy for some years – aged eight he had impressed a five-year-old friend with some informal lectures on Schopenhauer.

After taking Firsts in Greats and PPE, he moved from one Oxford college to another, briefly teaching philosophy at New College before obtaining, in 1932, a Prize Fellowship of All Souls, where he remained until returning to New College as a Fellow in 1938.

Berlin's first book, published in 1939, was a study of Karl Marx. The result has seldom been out of print.

During the Second World War, Berlin served as a British official in America, first with the Information Service in New York, from 1941 to 1942, and then at the embassy in Washington, from 1942 to 1944.

At the Washington embassy, Berlin assembled all the American political intelligence he could muster, and served it up in highly readable form. His weekly briefings to London commenting on the American scene became celebrated in Whitehall for their wit, insight and lucidity – suggesting to some who saw them that Berlin might have missed his métier as a journalist.

They were read with notable pleasure by Winston Churchill, and when, in 1944, a visitor from America named I. Berlin arrived in London, he was summoned to lunch at Downing Street to be closely questioned by Churchill on Roosevelt's chances of re-election for a fourth term.

After the baffled Irving Berlin had left No. 10, Churchill, wilting from the long and ill-informed discourse on American politics he had just heard, pronounced that Mr Berlin did not seem to talk as well as he wrote.

That was anything but the case with Isaiah Berlin, who in half a dozen languages was one of the most spellbinding, and amusing, talkers of his time. His deep, sonorous voice and high-speed conversational cascade, once likened to a running bath tap – and once clocked at nearly 400 words a minute – never failed to delight any gathering he attended.

In 1950 Berlin went back to All Souls, where he switched from philosophy to the study of intellectual history and political theory and revealed his fascination with the subject of freedom, which he considered best defined in negative terms. 'The fundamental sense of freedom,' he believed, 'is freedom from chains, from imprisonment, from enslavement by others. The rest is an extension of this sense, or else metaphor.'

It was then fashionable to denigrate J.S. Mill's view of liberty and to praise T.H. Green's definition of freedom as the freedom of being one's own master, with all members of society making the best of themselves.

In a lecture Berlin elegantly demolished the latter concept by showing that the formulation could be used by a totalitarian ruler to justify the worst acts of oppression. The lecture, delivered only two years after the Hungarian uprising of 1956, and at a time when Marxism held sway in numerous universities all over the Western world, was a powerful blow for liberalism and helped to revive the fortunes of political philosophy as a subject.

Berlin himself always maintained philosophy to be of vital importance. In the essay 'The Purpose of Philosophy, in Concepts and Categories: Philosophical Essays' (1978), he wrote that 'the goal of philosophy is always the same, to assist men to understand themselves and thus operate in the open, and not wildly, in the dark'.

He was appointed CBE in 1946, and knighted in 1957. He liked to recall his old friend Sir William Hayter's puzzled reaction on hearing the news of the knighthood: 'I wonder why?' In 1971 Berlin was appointed to the Order of Merit (on hearing the news of which Sir William 'almost fainted').

'I have been overestimated all my life,' Berlin reflected. 'I will not pretend that this has been a source of grave distress. As someone once said to me, it is much nicer to receive more than one's due than one's due, and I cannot deny it. All the same, I cannot deceive myself.'

⚞ 6th ⚟

Fred Dibnah, b. 1938, d. 2004

Fred Dibnah, who has died aged sixty-six, was the Bolton steeplejack made famous by television; he set out to preserve the factory chimneys of Lancashire, but ended up demolishing many of them.

In 1979 the BBC showed *Fred Dibnah: Steeplejack*, giving an insight into his trade and allowing him to hold forth on how Britain in that decade was nothing compared with the Victorian age.

Dibnah was a natural broadcaster, no different on or off camera. His unscripted, conversational yarn-telling made the audience feel that he was addressing them personally, and his antics up 200ft chimneys were compelling. 'A man who says he feels no fear is either a fool or a liar,' he said. 'One mistake up here and it's a half-day out with the undertaker.'

The drama in the films came with the demolitions. Dibnah did not bother with dynamite, but drilled out courses of bricks at the foot of the chimney to be felled. He wedged heavy timbers into the gap then lit a fire. When the props burned away, the chimney collapsed into the space cleared for it. Dibnah, hovering nervously nearby, would signal the end with a couple of toots on an old motor horn he carried with him.

At one job in Oldham, the nearest houses were twelve yards from the base of the stack. It was wet and windy and the fire would not take hold properly at first. The chimney refused to budge. Dibnah had once before returned to a stack that would not fall after the timbers had burned, bashing away until the rumble of bricks told him it was time to clear off. It was not a technique he wished to demonstrate again.

At Oldham, the fire was dying down and the chimney remained upright. Dibnah paced about, a cigarette waggling in his mouth. Suddenly, the stack gave way, crumbling on to its base. Everybody nearby ran for it, pursued by flying bricks and clouds of soot and mortar dust. Miraculously, no one was hurt and the houses were undamaged.

Frederick Dibnah was born on 28 April 1938 and named after his Uncle Frederick, who kept a temperance bar in Bolton. His career plans were laid early. He spotted steeplejacks from his pram and later traipsed around the town learning by observation how they laddered chimneys.

At school, Fred always finished near the bottom of the class, though when he was twelve he redeemed himself by making new keys for the school after the only set was stolen.

At the age of sixteen, he put a new chimney on the family home. It was not much compared to a factory chimney, but it towered above those on the surrounding terraces. 'People came for trips on Sundays to see it,' his mother said. 'Everyone said our Fred was a lunatic.'

He started work on his own as a steeplejack in the few months between his National Service medical and basic training at Aldershot, though he made very little money. After the Army he returned to Bolton in 1962, and resumed the trade. One of his first major jobs was to gild the weather vanes on Bolton parish church. He later claimed that he only got it because he turned up to give an estimate on his 1927 AJS motorcycle, to which the vicar took a shine.

When he began to appear on television, Dibnah's views on Britain's glorious industrial past did not always find favour. He said he had been born into a world going downhill fast. The high point of civilisation had already been reached: that was in 1913 when Britain's coal and cotton production achieved a level never to be equalled.

Writing in *The Daily Telegraph* in 1994, Stephen Pile said that Dibnah was 'an insufferable, pompous man, hopelessly stuck in the steam age ... he appears to think the Roman Empire ended because they all became homosexuals with the result that all Italians do today is design racing cars and lampshades'.

Dibnah's treatment of his first wife, Alison, with whom he had eloped to Gretna Green in 1964 while she was a teenager, was another sore point. Viewers found it bad enough watching Alison being carted around in his 1963 ex-Army Land Rover and seeing her helping him put ladders on a chimney in a thunderstorm during a supposed family holiday to Blackpool; but when she had to make do in a leaky caravan at a rain-soaked steam traction rally while her husband swaggered off with his oil-stained cronies, the complaints of chauvinism came thick and fast.

Dibnah, also a steam-engine enthusiast, did not much care for holidays and never wanted to go abroad. Alison, stoic for years, decided that there was more to life than climbing chimneys. She took their children on a package holiday to Greece, and on her return moved out with them.

Dibnah's parting shot was to tell his television audience that not every woman had a steam roller named after her. 'Steam engines don't answer back,' he said. 'You can belt 'em with a hammer and they say nowt.' The marriage was dissolved in 1984.

⋞ 7th ⋟

Alexander Dubcek, b. 1921, d. 1992

Alexander Dubcek, the Czechoslovak leader who has died aged seventy, was the architect of the Prague Spring, the dream of a gentler version of Communism which was smashed by Russian tanks in August 1968.

Dubcek's heroism at that time is imperishable. But his status as a victim of Soviet oppression created in the West a delusion, enhanced by his charm and openness, that he was a liberal – in the tradition, almost, of John Stuart Mill. In truth, he aimed to modify and not to abolish the Communist system. His ideal was the eternally elusive one of Socialism with a human face.

After eight tense months of confrontation, Dubcek was crushed by Brezhnev's decision to snuff out the Czechoslovak experiment. 'They have done this to me, who has devoted his entire life to co-operation with the Soviet Union,' he remarked uncomprehendingly shortly after the tanks rolled in.

The Russians, he believed, originally planned to execute him, and it was only the worldwide protest against the invasion that saved his neck. But whatever his disillusion with Brezhnev, Dubcek never lost his admiration for Marx, Engels and Lenin – who had, he declared in 1988, created a legacy for future generations of revolutionaries.

Alexander Dubcek was born on 27 November 1921 at Uhrovec in Slovakia. His parents had met and married in America, to which they had emigrated in 1909. As a cabinet maker Stephan Dubcek could earn $30 a week in Chicago. Nevertheless he was a dedicated Socialist, who spent more than a year in an internment camp during the First World War because he refused to be conscripted.

Stephan Dubcek returned to Czechoslovakia in 1921, only a few months before Alexander was born. In 1925 he became a founding member of the Czech Communist Party, and later that year took his family to Kirghizia in Soviet Central Asia, where he helped organise an industrial co-operative.

Alexander, after education at Frunze, the regional capital, became a machine locksmith and engine fitter in a motor-car factory at Gorky. But in 1938 Stalinist purges forced the Dubceks to return home, just in time for Germany's invasion of Czechoslovakia.

At the age of eighteen Dubcek joined the outlawed Communist Party, and was soon active in its guerrilla wing. During the bitter winter of 1944–45 he fought in the Slovak national uprising against the Germans in the Tatra Mountains. He was twice wounded, and his elder brother was killed.

After the war Dubcek won swift promotion in local party organisations, and when his country was taken over by the Soviet Union in 1949 he secured his first important position as secretary of the district party committee at Trencin. Two years later he was a member of the National Assembly. In 1955, as a promising young apparatchik, he was sent to Moscow for a three-year course at the Political College of the Central Committee, where he came to the notice of Antonin Novotny, first secretary of the Czechoslovak Party.

Back in Czechoslovakia Dubcek rose swiftly to become the highest-ranking Slovak on the Central Committee. He also built up a power base in the Slovakian Communist Party, of which he became leader in 1963.

He sealed this advance by inveighing against 'bourgeois nationalism'. By 1966, however, he had abandoned this position and began to espouse the cause of the Slovaks, the smaller and poorer half of Czechoslovakia. The next year Dubcek became the first member of the Central Committee to dare to make an open challenge to Novotny, who retaliated by flinging the 'bourgeois nationalist' epithet in his tormentor's face. When Novotny went to Moscow that November the champion of Slovakia launched his campaign for a takeover.

By January 1968 Dubcek had forced Novotny's resignation as First Secretary (although not from the ceremonial post of President), and was unanimously elected in his place. Immediately the repressive atmosphere began to ease.

In March, Dubcek promised 'the widest possible democratisation'. Courts, labour unions and business were all to be less directly controlled by government. He also pledged an independent foreign policy, while assuring other Eastern Bloc leaders that

Czechoslovakia's socialism would not be compromised.

The militant Writers' Union was allowed to publish a remarkably frank literary journal. Demands were made for the release of 30,000 Slovaks imprisoned during the Stalinist era; and there was some devolution of power between Czechs and Slovaks. Dubcek also ordered an inquiry into the mysterious death of Jan Masaryk, the former Foreign Minister who was believed to have been killed on Soviet orders in 1948.

On 22 March 1968, Novotny was removed from the presidency and replaced by General Ludvik Svoboda, a popular moderate. This marked the beginning of the Prague Spring, a period of high hopes that ran on into the summer, underscored by Dubcek's pledge: 'There is only one path and that is forward.'

Basking in his popularity, the new leader felt secure enough to refuse an invitation in July to a meeting of the USSR, East Germany, Poland, Hungary and Bulgaria to debate the new situation in Czechoslovakia.

The five Communist nations condemned the Prague Spring, and railed against the 'counter revolutionaries' who were threatening Socialism there. Dubcek answered by confirming his allegiance to the Warsaw Pact, and won a renewed vote of confidence from his Central Committee.

On 22 July, surprisingly, Brezhnev agreed to talks with Dubcek in Czechoslovakia, and at Cierna there were bitter exchanges over the conference table. Yet some agreement was reached, with Dubcek making few concessions and being allowed the right to chart the future of his country's internal affairs. The Soviet Union even agreed to withdraw its troops from Czechoslovakia.

It seemed that Dubcek had won, and he received support from President Tito of Yugoslavia and President Ceausescu of Rumania.

Suddenly, however, all hopes were dashed. On the night of 21 August the forces of five Warsaw Pact nations, led by Russian tanks, crossed the Czechoslovak border. Moscow assured the world that the invasion was in response to appeals from Czechoslovak leaders – although these petitioners were never identified.

The Russians encountered brave resistance from the Czechoslovak people, who surged on to the streets of Prague shouting their support for Dubcek and facing the Soviet troops with cries of 'Russians go home'. Dubcek and five of his chief lieutenants were seized and flown to Moscow, where they were ordered to rescind their reforms and end the opposition to the Soviet intervention. There was no way out for Dubcek, who returned to Prague a broken man.

Fighting back tears, he broadcast to the nation to announce that there might have to be 'temporary measures' to limit democracy in Czechoslovakia. In the event Dubcek was deposed as First Secretary of the Communist Party, had his party membership rescinded, and was sent to internal exile in Bratislava, where he was given a part-time job as a forestry clerk.

During his exile he was isolated from his friends and unable to make even the most innocent contact with his compatriots, let alone the outside world. No one was allowed to visit him without a rigorous interrogation before and a thorough debriefing afterwards. He was even forbidden to talk to his co-workers in the forestry department.

Throughout this time he relied heavily on the support of his wife and three sons, and spent many hours reflecting, reading, and cultivating his garden.

After eighteen years of internal exile, Dubcek's passport was returned to him, and in 1988 he was allowed to travel to Bologna to accept an honorary doctorate from the University. The ceremony was seen by many Czechs on Hungarian and Austrian television and raised hopes for his rehabilitation.

Yet when the Velvet Revolution came, he never quite shrugged off the demoralising effect of nearly two decades of exile. 'Today I am nowhere,' he reflected. His dream of Communism had been ruined, and he now looked to Sweden rather than to Russia as a model for the future.

Yet no one could deny him the memory of that 'far fierce hour and sweet', when he embodied the hopes of the free world.

⚶ 8th ⚶

Melvin Burkhart, b. 1907, d. 2001

Melvin Burkhart, who has died aged ninety-four, was a fairground sideshow performer known as the Human Blockhead because of his ability to drive a five-inch nail or an ice pick into his head without flinching.

The Human Blockhead worked under a number of alternative titles, depending on which of his extraordinary repertoire of physical contortions he happened to be performing at the time.

As the Anatomical Wonder, he could inflate one lung at a time and dislocate his shoulders; as the Man Without a Stomach, he could suck his stomach back to his spine; as the Two-Faced Man, he could frown with half his face and smile with the other half. Among many other accomplishments, he swallowed swords, threw knives and ate fire.

He was universally admired by his fellow performers, one of whom observed: 'Anyone who has ever hammered a nail into his nose owes a large debt to Melvin Burkhart.'

⚶ 9th ⚶

Charles Fraser-Smith, b. 1904, d. 1992

Charles Fraser-Smith, who has died aged eighty-eight, was the Secret Service's gadgets wizard during the Second World War, a role which made him the model for 'Q' in the James Bond books.

His professional pride, however, was offended by Ian Fleming's amateurism. He had sent golf balls with compasses inside to prisoners in Germany; the tricked-up golf balls in *Diamonds Are Forever*, by contrast, would not even have bounced.

Much of Fraser-Smith's work was directed towards helping prisoners of the Reich, or agents in Nazi Germany. There were metal saws sewn into regulation-issue military shoelaces – sometimes used for cutting off frost-bitten fingers. There was a briar pipe with asbestos lining which allowed maps to be concealed in the bowl. Maps were also hidden in hairbrushes which could be opened by the tugging of particular bristles, or printed on silk in invisible ink, which, Fraser-Smith explained, 'you could develop in your own Jimmy Riddle'. (After the war the silk was sold as scarves to unsuspecting debutantes.)

Agents were given cigarette lighters that contained cameras, and shaving brushes that opened (by unscrewing a special left-hand thread) to provide space for film. It was thus possible to send back ground-level pictures of the damage wrought by Bomber Command, and to pinpoint the V-1 launching pads. Fountain pens, fake cigarettes and even false teeth were all useful receptacles, whether for mini-telescopes, compasses or other miniature tools.

Particularly valuable to agents in the field was a magnet which Fraser-Smith invented to immobilise the house electricity meter during radio transmission, leaving the enemy direction-finding teams with no surge to track down.

In 1943 Fraser-Smith was asked to provide a special watertight container measuring 6ft 3in by 3ft, complete with valve, vacuum pump and a Mae West life jacket. As he later discovered, it was required by that master of deception Lt-Cdr Ewen Montagu for his plan to wash up a corpse carrying documents designed to put the enemy off the scent about the Allies' invasion of Sicily. This exploit was subsequently celebrated in the book and film *The Man Who Never Was*.

Officially, Fraser-Smith was attached to the clothing and textile department of the Ministry of Supply, in a building opposite St James's Park underground station. Neither his colleagues nor even his secretary were *au fait* with the true nature of his work: orders would come over the telephone.

One of four children of a solicitor who owned a wholesale grocery business, Charles Fraser-Smith was born in 1904. Orphaned at the age of seven, he was brought up by a missionary family in Hertfordshire.

After a spell at Watford Grammar School he went to Brighton College where he proved 'scholastically useless except for woodwork and science and making things'. He then became a prep-school master at Portsmouth. Later, drawn to agriculture, he paid £1 a week for the privilege of working from dawn to dusk on a farm.

In the hope of weaning him from this life, his family sent him to France to learn the language. Having mastered French, Fraser-Smith moved on to Morocco, where he bought a farm between Marrakesh and the Atlas Mountains. Here he proved a quick learner and an inspired improviser, introducing new ploughs, irrigation schemes and proper fertilisation. Before long he was running estates for the chief religious judge and the Moroccan royal family.

At the same time, inspired by two aunts who had died of typhoid while working as missionaries in Tangier, Fraser-Smith managed to build up two orphanages, one near Marrakesh, the other near Tangier.

On his return to England in 1939, he could only find a job as a motor-bicycle dispatch rider. Later he worked at the Avro aircraft factory, until the day that he went to deliver a sermon at the Open Brethren Evangelical Church at Leeds.

As luck had it, George Rice, head of the Ministry of Supply in Leeds, was in the congregation with Sir George Oliver, from the same Ministry in Whitehall. Fraser-Smith described his Moroccan experience in some detail, unwittingly giving a compelling picture of his inventiveness and self-reliance. Afterwards the men from the Ministry approached him with the offer of 'a funny job in London'.

When the war was over, he stayed on to discharge more mundane tasks at the Ministry of Supply, until he suffered a breakdown in health, doubtless brought on by his long period of secret work without any break for holidays. Fraser-Smith contemplated a return to Morocco, but settled instead for Devon, where he bought a derelict dairy farm, which he restored to prosperity.

Hugh Paddick, b. 1915, d. 2000

Hugh Paddick, the actor who has died aged eighty-five, was a stalwart of *Round the Horne*, where his most celebrated character was Julian, to Kenneth Williams' Sandy. He began every sketch with the words: 'Hello, I'm Julian and this is my friend Sandy.'

As the outrageously camp proprietors of such enterprises as Bona Productions (film producers), Bona Caterers, Bona Bijou Tourettes (travel agents) and Bona Law (solicitors), 'Jules' and Sandy skilfully avoided the attentions of the censor with double entendres and innuendo.

'Jules had a nasty experience in Malaga,' remarks Sandy in the travel agent episode. 'You see he got badly stung.'

'Portuguese man-of-war?' inquires Horne.

'Oh,' replies Jules, 'I never saw him in uniform.'

10th

Anne Mustoe, b. 1933, d. 2009

Anne Mustoe, who has died in Syria aged seventy-six, gave up her career as headmistress of an independent girls' school to cycle around the world and describe her journeys in a series of lively books.

A widow with three grown-up stepchildren, she was on holiday from Saint Felix School, Suffolk, in 1983 when the glimpse of a European cyclist pedalling through the Great Indian Desert in Rajasthan decided her to do the same. She was over fifty, out of condition and had no interest in bicycles. But, in the tradition of indomitable Englishwomen abroad, she was untroubled by such trifles.

It took some three years to withdraw from her commitments before pupils and staff gave her a green Condor bicycle, specially built with real leather seat, two sets of brakes, ten gears and a speedometer. On 31 May 1987 they saw her off from Watling Street, near St Paul's Cathedral, her three panniers filled with clothes, documents, maps and dictionaries as well as Horace's *Odes* and letters of introduction to be presented along the way.

After crossing to Boulogne, she found the routine of fifty miles a day, five days a week, hard going, but was encouraged by friends who came out from England to visit her en route.

Her adventures prompted more than just curiosity from those she encountered, and Anne Mustoe found herself being propositioned by a young French cyclist in knickerbockers, a suggestive father who had to be restrained by his grown-up sons in Italy, and four separate suitors in Salonika, Greece. Outside Ankara she was greeted by a university friend: 'You must be Anne. There can't be two mad women on bicycles on the Eskisehir road.'

By the time she arrived in Karachi, Anne Mustoe had covered 4,000 miles and was conscious of being light years away from the headmistress in a Hardy Amies suit.

Unaccompanied women were considered unusual and even provocative, but her bicycle attracted constant interest. She rode up the Khyber Pass until stopped by heavily armed Pathans and politely sent back to Peshawar. Many hotels had only basic amenities and, in one, she had to contend with an amorous waiter who appeared at the window saying: 'My love, my love, open this door.'

In India her main problem was gangs of young cyclists who jeered, jabbed at her, pulled her hair and grabbed the handlebars. Mounting hysteria one day outside a school brought out the headmistress of old: 'I glared around with a steely eye and, controlling the pitch of my voice with great effort, said slowly and authoritatively: "Will you kindly step back and let me pass through?" It worked a charm. Whether or not they understood what I said, they recognised the magisterial tone.' Only at a safe distance did she lean against a tree 'until the trembling had stopped'.

From there Anne Mustoe progressed through Malaysia and then America with an aplomb that overcame all setbacks until her return to Watling Street. In *A Bike Ride* (1992) she recorded that she had cycled 11,552 miles in 14 countries over 439 days, in which £4,898 had been spent on food, accommodation and sundries and £1,127 on fares. She had lost 23lb in weight.

The daughter of a shopkeeper and bookmaker, Anne Revill was born in Nottingham on 24 May 1933 and educated at the High School before reading Classics at Girton College, Cambridge. She first worked as a personal assistant in a management training department of GKN engineers in London, then was secretary to Nelson Mustoe, QC, whom she married in 1960, before teaching classics and economics at Francis Holland School in Kensington under Heather Brigstocke. She next became deputy head at Cobham Hall, Kent, before arriving at Saint Felix in 1978.

The success of *A Bike Ride* led her to write *Escaping the Winter* (1993), a practical guide for those planning long holidays abroad.

But Anne Mustoe was keen to get back on her bike. *Lone Traveller* (1998) was an account of her second global tour, this time an east–west journey from Rome, via Lisbon to South America, across China (where she was arrested on the Great Wall and spent two days in jail) and home again.

Two Wheels in the Dust (1998) concerned several trips in the Indian subcontinent in which she followed the trail of the *Ramayana*, the Hindu epic poem; and *Che Guevara and the Mountain of Silver* (2007) was the tale of a visit to South America along the route of the revolutionary on his motorcycle ride from Buenos Aires. There were also other, shorter trips, which took in the Baltic and the Santiago de Compostela way.

Anne Mustoe set off on what was to be her last ride in May 2009, still riding her trusty Condor, and was in Aleppo, Syria, when she fell ill and died in hospital.

⊰ 11th ⊱

Yasser Arafat, b. 1929, d. 2004

Yasser Arafat, who has died aged seventy-five, was the unchallenged leader of the Palestinian people and their movement for statehood over more than thirty years.

His Machiavellian grasp of political bargaining, an uncanny talent for personal and political survival, and an ability to work harder and sleep less than his rivals bore fruit in 1993 with an agreement with Israel that laid the shaky foundations of a Palestinian state in scraps of land prised from the grip of the occupying power.

But that high point (in 1994 he was jointly awarded the Nobel Peace Prize with the Israelis Yitzhak Rabin and Shimon Peres) was followed by a decade in which Arafat presided over a politically stagnant and corrupt administration in the West Bank and Gaza, and his people's lives declined into penury, repression and anti-Israeli violence.

Muhammad Abd al-Rahman Abd al-Raouf Arafat al-Qudua al-Husseini was born in Cairo on 24 August 1929, the sixth of seven children. (He assumed the forename Yasser, after a companion of the Prophet Mohammed, in the 1940s.) His father was a respectable wholesale foodstuffs merchant of modest means who had moved the family from Gaza.

Growing up in Cairo, Arafat showed a precocious aptitude for leadership. He would organise neighbourhood boys into regiments, which he would drill in the streets and lead in demonstrations against British rule in Egypt. Too hyperactive to attend school regularly, he was fascinated by politics.

When the first Arab-Israeli war broke out in 1948, he joined a unit of irregular soldiers which fought in southern Gaza. Arafat earned a reputation as a fearless fighter at this time, though he would later greatly embellish his accounts of his own exploits.

After the Arab defeat, and the establishment of the state of Israel, Arafat enrolled at the University of Cairo as an Engineering student. He became active in the militant Egyptian Students' Union and, as a student activist, met three men who were to be his closest political colleagues for more than thirty years: Khalil al-Wazir, Salah Khalaf and Faruq al-Qaddumi. This group later founded the Palestinian independence movement Fatah and formed its core leadership. In later years, as top officials of the PLO (Palestinian Liberation Organisation), they represented the only effective check on Arafat.

In 1957 he left Egypt for Kuwait, joining the public works department as an engineer and afterwards starting a profitable construction firm. His political activities also prospered in Kuwait's more liberal atmosphere, and with his colleagues from Cairo University he founded Fatah, which was based on the principle of Palestinian political independence. In 1963 he moved to Damascus to organise Fatah in Syria, Lebanon and Jordan. More hot-headed than his colleagues, he led a faction impatient to begin guerrilla attacks on Israel, and worked feverishly to organise armed groups. Attacks began in early 1965.

After the defeat of the Arab forces in the 1967 Six Day War, Arafat entered the West Bank, basing himself at Nablus with a team of thirty men. But the guerrillas were no match for the new Israeli military administration in the West Bank, which promptly rounded up hundreds of Palestinian fighters; Arafat fled to Jordan. Undeterred, he established guerrilla bases in the Palestinian refugee camps that had sprung up there.

The high point of his success as a guerrilla leader came in March 1968, when the Israeli Defence Forces launched a retaliatory attack on the Jordanian village of Karamah, where Arafat had established the core of Fatah's command network. Supported by the Jordanian army, Fatah put up a bold defence; though the Israelis won, Fatah inflicted considerable losses, and the battle was seen as a victory for them.

The world first heard of Arafat at this time. Fatah's popularity and its membership soared after Karamah, and Arafat, its hero, was named its spokesman. His bearded face, hidden by raffish black glasses, appeared on the cover of *Time*.

The next year he was elected chairman of the executive committee of the PLO. It was an umbrella organisation, and holding its factions together in a single coalition was to be Arafat's biggest political headache for much of his career. He never seemed to be trying hard enough to rein in the excesses of his radical fringe to satisfy Israel or the West.

It became clear to Arafat by the early 1970s that a military victory over Israel was impossible, and that the only realistic way forward was to accept the existence of Israel and to use diplomacy to secure a Palestinian state in what was left of the original Palestinian territory. Bringing the Palestinian people and the PLO behind such a policy was to take many years, but would prove a major political accomplishment.

In 1970 he was expelled from Jordan for unsettling the regime there, only to move to Beirut, where in 1982 Fatah fighters were again defeated by Israel. Arafat then experienced the lowest point of his political fortunes in exile in Tunis. In October 1985, in retaliation for an attack on an Israeli-owned yacht, six Israeli F-15 fighter bombers swooped over PLO headquarters in the city, reducing the buildings to rubble and killing seventy-three people. Arafat was in one of his safe houses and was unharmed, though he assumed he was the raid's target.

In December 1987 a popular Palestinian uprising against Israeli rule broke out in the impoverished Gaza Strip and quickly spread to the West Bank. The intifada (as it came to be known) caught Arafat by surprise, but he moved quickly to harness the worldwide sympathy it generated.

Then, in November 1988, he persuaded the Palestinian National Congress, the Palestinian parliament in exile, to support his plan for statehood alongside Israel. He then announced the PLO's acceptance of Israel's existence at a special session of the UN General Assembly in Geneva. The immediate result of his speech was an American decision to open a 'substantive dialogue' with the PLO. But his success was short-lived. Within a few months, America abruptly ended talks after Arafat failed to denounce a seaborne terrorist attack on the Israeli coast by the Palestine Liberation Front, a radical group.

In 1991 the United States invited Jordan and Israel to take part in peace talks in Madrid, on condition that the Palestinians involved were not members of the PLO. But it was an open secret that Israel was now, for the first time, negotiating with Arafat.

Never one to see much virtue in simplicity, Arafat authorised the opening of a second, secret channel of negotiations with Israel while the Washington-sponsored talks were still under way. In the end, it was these talks, held in Oslo under the auspices of the Norwegian government, that produced the breakthrough. At the end of August 1993 the Israeli cabinet approved the Oslo plan, which provided for the establishment of Palestinian local government in Gaza and a tiny enclave around the isolated oasis town of Jericho. On 13 September, President Clinton oversaw the signature of the agreement between Israel and the PLO at a ceremony on the White House lawn. Arafat shook hands with the Israeli prime minister, Yitzhak Rabin.

In conducting the Oslo negotiations, Arafat was interested above all in acquiring the symbols of statehood (uniformed guards at the borders, his own face on the new Palestinian Authority postage stamps) and securing Israel's recognition of the PLO. But Palestinians found themselves still humiliatingly subordinate to Israel.

Arafat was elected President of the Palestinian Authority in 1996, at the same time as the establishment of a legislature that he eventually neutralised. He prized loyalty above competence, or even honesty, in his deputies.

By 2000, the promise of the Oslo Agreement had all but withered, and Arafat's position in negotiations with Israel hardened. At a summit with Israel and America at Camp David in July, Arafat rejected the offer of a larger area of land than the Palestinians had ever been offered until then, a stand that he later acknowledged was a grave mistake.

When a new uprising broke out later that year, more violent than the original intifada, he did little to discourage his police and security units from engaging in gun battles with the Israeli military forces that were sent into Palestinian areas to suppress it. By 2002 Israeli forces were besieging the Palestinian Authority compound in Ramallah in which Arafat was living. At the time of his death, he was a virtual prisoner in a single, windowless room, protected by a small core of loyalists, surviving on bread and olives. His only value to his people was as a symbol of stubborn resistance to Israeli domination.

⊰ **12**th ⊱

Dolores Ibarruri, b. 1895, d. 1989

Dolores Ibarruri, better known as La Pasionaria, who has died aged ninety-three, was one of the moving spirits behind the Republican forces in the Spanish Civil War and the most famous Spanish woman of her generation.

Although a committed Communist from an early age, La Pasionaria ('the Passion Flower') inspired people as much by her undoubted courage, the power of her oratory and her presence – she was very tall and always dressed in black – as by her belief in revolution.

In the first months of the war no face or voice on the Republican side was better known than hers. The posters in Madrid portrayed Lenin, Stalin and La Pasionaria, rather than the president or any other politician; it was she who led the recruiting campaign for the Republican army in rousing, often fanatical, speeches on the wireless and at mass rallies. A battalion was named after her.

The name of La Pasionaria is most often associated with her rallying cry at the beginning of the war, '*No pasaran!*' ('They shall not pass') – echoing Pétain at Verdun. No less memorable were her exhortations to Republican troops to 'die on your feet rather than live on your knees'.

Dolores Ibarruri was born on 9 December 1895, the eighth of eleven children, to a mining family in the Basque country. Her upbringing was harsh, and at fifteen she went to work for a seamstress, then as a domestic servant, resentful that women could not work in the mines.

Dolores's marriage, at twenty, to a miner, and the birth of a daughter, did nothing to alleviate her poverty; she began to lose her previously strong religious convictions and to read Marx and Engels. Her husband was often in prison, and three of her five children were to die in infancy.

Shortly after the Russian Revolution, writing in a journal called *The Class Struggle*, Dolores signed her article Pasionaria, and the name stuck. She joined the Basque Communist party in 1920, and was elected to the Central Committee of the Spanish Communist party (PCE) ten years later.

In 1939, at the end of the Spanish Civil War, La Pasionaria left the 'rats of capitulation' for exile in Russia. When she returned to Spain after Franco's death – having slavishly followed Moscow for sixty years, with only one public protest at the time of the invasion of Czechoslovakia in 1968 – La Pasionaria found herself out of touch with the new generation of young 'Eurocommunists'. For their part they found her an embarrassment and restrained her from speaking too often in public.

But she was acclaimed by artists and writers. Picasso dedicated more than one work to her, and used to visit her; she is also widely believed to have inspired the character

502

Pilar in Ernest Hemingway's *For Whom the Bell Tolls* – Ingrid Bergman played the part in the film.

H.R. Haldeman, b. 1926, d. 1993

H.R. Haldeman, who has died aged sixty-seven, was the hard man in Richard Nixon's White House – which meant that he was very hard indeed.

If the grubbiest work was allotted to 'Chuck' Colson, and the more subtle insinuations were left to John Ehrlichman, Haldeman had no rival in administering the face-to-face humiliation. Where Nixon disliked confrontation, Haldeman proclaimed his talent for 'chewing people out'. Theirs, as Ehrlichman remarked, was a 'true marriage'.

❦ 13th ❦

Commander W.A. 'Biffy' Dunderdale, b. 1899, d. 1990

Commander W.A. 'Biffy' Dunderdale, who has died in New York aged ninety, was a member of the Secret Service for thirty-eight years and was sometimes spoken of as the prototype of James Bond.

The son of a Constantinople ship-owner, Wilfred Albert Dunderdale was born in Odessa on Christmas Eve 1899. He was studying to be a naval architect in St Petersburg when the Russian Revolution broke out in 1917.

His father sent him to Vladivostok to take delivery of the first of a new class of submarines, built in America, and deliver it to the Black Sea. To transport a submarine, still in five separate sections, thousands of miles by rail across a country in the throes of a revolution was asking a good deal of a seventeen-year-old boy – but young Biffy accomplished it.

The submarine was completed too late to serve in the Imperial Navy and was eventually scuttled at Sebastopol in April 1919. By then the political situation in the region was of literally Byzantine complexity. In 1920 British warships operated in the Black Sea and the Sea of Marmara, bombarding shore installations and sending ashore parties of sailors and marines. With his knowledge of naval engineering – and of Constantinople and the Black Sea ports – his businesslike pretext and his fluent Russian, German and French, Biffy Dunderdale made a superb undercover agent.

Still only nineteen, operating under the nom de guerre of 'Julius', he was twice mentioned in despatches. In 1920 he was promoted honorary lieutenant RNVR and appointed MBE.

Dunderdale joined the Secret Service in 1921 and in 1926 joined the SIS station in Paris, where he worked with the Deuxième Bureau and established good relations with the French – particularly with Colonel Gustav Bertrand, head of the French Intelligence Service.

Dunderdale was also on good terms with the Poles, which led to a major intelligence coup. The Poles were pioneers in breaking the Enigma machine cyphers which all three German armed forces were using, so it was imperative that British Intelligence obtain an example.

Dunderdale was 'the Third Man' at the celebrated meeting under the clock at Victoria Station on 16 August 1939 – which might have come straight out of a spy thriller – when 'C' himself (head of the British Secret Service) met Bertrand, a member of the Paris embassy staff, and Dunderdale, who had an Enigma machine in his valise. 'C' was on his way to a dinner and cut a conspicuous figure as he strode away, in evening dress, with the ribbon of the Legion d'honneur in his buttonhole and the Enigma under his arm.

The day before war was declared Dunderdale was given the rank of Commander RNVR. He was one of the last Englishmen to leave Paris when the Germans entered the city in June 1940.

When he reached Bordeaux an RAF Avro Anson was sent to make sure he escaped. During the war he kept his links with the Poles and was in contact by radio with Bertrand in Vichy France, and with other members of the Deuxième Bureau who had stayed behind.

Dunderdale served with the SIS in London after the war until he retired in 1959, but his influence had declined. Perhaps he knew too many secrets, and realised that his life in espionage had been an elaborate game; but he was an excellent host at his apartments in Paris and New York and his house in Surrey.

He let the occasional detail of his career slip. In the autumn of 1922 British and Turkish troops had confronted each other at Chanak in the Dardanelles, a crisis which brought the exile of Sultan Mohammed VI, who was taken to Malta in the battleship *Malaya*.

Dunderdale's part in these events was domestic rather than epic. He was responsible for arranging and paying for the repatriation of ex-members of the Sultan's harem who were not Turkish nationals – including one houri from Leamington Spa, packed off home on the Orient Express.

Jamie Pierre, b. 1973, d. 2011

Jamie Pierre, who has been killed by an avalanche aged thirty-eight, was known as 'skiing's most dangerous man', 'the Gravity Research Skier' or 'The King of Big Air' for his delight in skiing off clifftops; his most lunatic escapade saw him fall 255ft, the height of a 24-storey office block.

It was, he admitted, an all too literally death-defying stunt. Having skied towards the precipice, at Grand Targhee Resort in the Teton Mountains of Wyoming, Pierre tucked his skis underneath him in an attempt to remain upright. 'I prefer to land in the slouch position so you spread out the impact,' he said afterwards. But about halfway through his four-second free fall he lost control, and footage of the jump shows him plunging headfirst into the powder snow at the cliff's base.

As his support crew rushed to extricate him from the ten-foot impact crater, it was unclear whether he was still alive. Then a voice crackled over the radio: Pierre was unscathed but for a cut lip. It had, he admitted, been 'way scary landing on my back', but moments later he was celebrating a world-record-breaking feat that – even in the adrenalin-soaked world of extreme sports – won him plaudits for unparalleled daring. His wife Amee, at home with their baby daughter, took a dimmer view, and refused to speak to him for several days.

≈ 14th ≈

Quentin Crewe, b. 1926, d. 1998

Quentin Crewe, the travel writer and restaurant critic who has died aged seventy-two, attacked life with a vivacity and strength of spirit all the more remarkable for the fact that he had suffered since birth from muscular dystrophy.

On Fleet Street in the 1950s he helped to launch *Queen* magazine, before taking up the restaurant column and earning himself the nickname 'Meals on Wheels' as he raced about London's nightspots in a wheelchair.

Meanwhile, he wove his way in and out of three marriages. 'It has never taken me more than a weekend to fall in love,' he wrote in his autobiography, and indeed, cupid's arrow often struck the girls as quickly. Crewe's physical disability lent no apparent barrier to his legendary success with the opposite sex. 'People used to wonder,' he wrote, 'how it was that a man in a wheelchair could manage to have any physical success with girls. I had no intention of enlightening them, then or now.'

His love of women was almost equalled by his wanderlust. The more his physical condition deteriorated, the more he felt the urge to roam. In 1966 he was inspired by Wilfred Thesiger's book *Arabian Sands* to cross the Empty Quarter of Saudi Arabia, the bravest in a catalogue of odysseys – across America, to Japan, around the whole of Europe – that he undertook with extraordinary enthusiasm and energy.

With his habitual gusto he took to the road again and again. *In Search of the Sahara* (1983), his acclaimed account of a trip through the Sahara Desert in a Land Rover, made little of malaria and land mines, and much of the nature of Africa. A 24,000-mile journey around South America was described in *In the Realms of Gold* (1989). 'In some ways,' he said, 'I sought to demonstrate what people in wheelchairs can do.'

⊰ 15th ⊱

James Watts, b. 1904, d. 1994

James Watts, the American neurosurgeon who has died aged ninety, was with his colleague the neurologist Walter Freeman responsible for popularising the pre-frontal lobotomy, one of the most contentious and macabre practices in the history of medicine.

The pre-frontal lobotomy was an operation in which the 'leukos', or white fibres connecting the frontal lobes to the rest of the brain, were severed to relieve symptoms of anxiety in psychiatric patients. At first prescribed as an operation of last resort, it was soon being promoted as a remedy for all human sadness, and even a means for social control.

'Society can accommodate itself to the most humble labourer,' observed Freeman, 'but justifiably distrusts the thinker ... lobotomised patients make good citizens.'

Egas Moniz had developed the leucotomy in Portugal in the early 1930s, and in 1936 Freeman and Watts began practising the operation in Washington, renaming it the lobotomy.

By the end of the year they had performed twenty lobotomies with Moniz's method, cutting holes in the top of the skull and inserting an instrument modelled on the apple corer. Later they modified the technique, making holes on either side of the head and using a steel probe with its end flattened rather like a butter knife; this was the pre-frontal lobotomy.

Although Freeman was a brilliant neurologist and neuropathologist, he had never qualified as a surgeon, and ostensibly needed Watts to perform the lobotomy under his guidance. After once being caught operating, and reprimanded, Freeman would sit in front of the patient, using his remarkable knowledge of the brain's geography to guide Watts' hands.

Surgery was performed under local anaesthetic, and the pair monitored the progress of the operation by engaging the subject in conversation, reckoning from the response how much matter had yet to be destroyed. The weird transcripts of the patients' failing utterances often pinpointed the moment at which some aspect of personality vanished.

Freeman, Watts recalled, was 'a ham actor with a flair for the dramatic', and guests would be invited to watch operations in which Watts fiddled away inside the head while Freeman urged the subject to sing 'God Bless America' or 'Mary Had a Little Lamb'. He might join in the chorus. In one exchange, Freeman asked a patient, 'What's going through your mind now?' to which came the reply: 'A knife.'

By late 1945 traumatised war veterans were causing the asylums of America to overflow; nearly half the 1.5 million beds in public hospitals were occupied by psychiatric patients. Freeman wanted to work faster, and believed that if he developed a sufficiently simple technique he might operate independently of Watts.

Secretly he carried out a transorbital lobotomy. For this the patient was anaesthetised by ECT shocks; the eyelids were lifted and a sharp stiletto-like leucotome was hammered through the orbital bone to a depth of 2.5 inches, one incision through each eye socket.

The leucotome was then vigorously flexed. Freeman limited his post-operative advice to, 'Wear a pair of sunglasses.' The operation took ten minutes and was first performed with an ice pick taken from Freeman's kitchen drawer.

Watts thought the technique degrading and too freely administered. In 1946 he threatened to break off their association, and Freeman promised not to perform the operation in Washington. But in 1948 Watts caught Freeman performing transorbital lobotomies at their joint practice in the city.

'He asked me to hold the icepick,' Watts recalled, 'while he photographed the patient and the angle of the instrument. I said, "I'd rather not", and pointed out the risks of transorbital lobotomy as an office procedure.' They could not be reconciled, and Watts walked out.

Freeman repeatedly traversed America promoting his technique. Between 1945 and 1955, the peak years, at least 40,000 Americans were lobotomised, many by psychiatrists using the ice pick. On occasion Freeman himself would perform more than twenty in a day, developing a conveyor belt system, the sight of which caused hardened soldiers to faint.

In the early 1960s the arrival of antidepressants and growing public suspicion brought about a rapid decline in the use of the lobotomy. Before Freeman and Watts split they had performed at least 700 pre-frontal lobotomies, on patients as young as four. Watts had ethical doubts about only one, a young female schizophrenic who loved to play the harp.

James Winston Watts was born at Lynchburg, Virginia, on 19 January 1904, and educated at Virginia Military Institute and Virginia University, where he studied Medicine. By 1930 he was a resident in neurosurgery at Chicago University, and two years later he became a research fellow at Yale.

He published an influential paper in which he argued that the large frontal lobes in humans were more concerned with basic animal urges and functions than previously thought, and that the mind did not function independently of the body – the frontal lobes could affect cardiac rate and kidney function. This brought him to the attention of Freeman.

The first patient they lobotomised was a 63-year-old woman who Freeman described as a 'typically rigid, emotional, claustrophobic individual ... a past master at bitching who really led her husband a dog's life'. At the last minute she backed down, fearful that her head would have to be shaved. She was promised that her curls would be spared; this was a lie, but after the operation she no longer cared.

Patient No. 10 sued the duo for paralysis; patient No. 18, an alcoholic lawyer suffering from paranoia, absconded from his bed after the operation, and was found drunk in a bar, the lobotomy having cured his paranoia but having left his addiction intact. Patient No. 20 had eighteen cores made in her brain, and became the first fatality. Freeman remarked that he and Watts learned much more from their failures than their successes, because failures could be subjected to autopsy.

After leaving the partnership with Freeman, Watts continued to live and work in

Washington, practising privately and at the George Washington University hospital. He briefly experimented with the trans-orbital lobotomy, later forsaking it for more orthodox forms of neurosurgery. He retired in 1969.

⊰ 16th ⊱

Rosemary Brown, b. 1916, d. 2001

Rosemary Brown, who has died aged eighty-five, was a medium specialising in communication with dead composers; her clairvoyant contact with, among others, Liszt, Chopin, Beethoven, Schubert and Rachmaninov resulted in hundreds of piano miniatures which the composers 'dictated' to her.

In 1964, as a widow with two children, Rosemary Brown was working in a school kitchen at Balham, south London, when she was forced to take time off work after breaking two ribs in a fall. It was then that she was 'visited' by Liszt as she sat in front of a piano. 'I could stumble through an easy tune,' she said, 'but this was like automatic playing. I began to play virtuoso-style pieces, and it grew from there.'

Liszt became her spiritual guide. He spoke English, but with a strong accent, so she took evening classes in German in order to communicate with him. He visited her often and even watched television with her. Through Liszt she claimed that she met Bach, Beethoven, Chopin and many others. Each composer would dictate to her, sometimes at the piano, sometimes preferring her to take musical notation.

Bach, she recalled, tended to be rather stern and impatient, and Beethoven was no longer deaf. Schubert was good-humoured but 'still a little shy', had lost some weight, given up his spectacles and learned to speak English. The composers would also wear contemporary clothes. 'Debussy has wonderful things – sheepskin coats and so on. The others are more or less orthodox, though Liszt and Beethoven both have long hair.'

Her composers did not confine themselves to purely musical messages. On one occasion, when her daughter had turned on the bath without Rosemary Brown's knowledge, Chopin came to the rescue: 'Suddenly he stopped giving me music and appeared to be quite agitated. He started speaking in French. Eventually I realised that he was saying *"Le bain va etre englouti"*.' She came to regard Liszt as a friend. 'He is,' she claimed, 'a very generous, very cultured, very devout man.'

Intrigued by her claims, numerous musicians, composers and critics clamoured to meet her and hear her work. In 1969 Richard Rodney Bennett interviewed her for BBC TV's *Music Now* programme, although he was noncommittal as to the authenticity of the compositions. 'Whether she really has Debussy in her drawing room,' he said, 'I don't know.' A number of musical experts agreed that Rosemary Brown's music bore many similarities to the work of the composers she purported to represent, although many attributed this to a knack for musical mimicry; the tunes themselves, though recognisably influenced by individual composers, were somewhat slight. Some observed that if the great composers had wanted the world to hear them from the grave, they might have dictated music that was a little more inspirational.

There was no doubt, however, as to Rosemary Brown's dedication and belief in her gift. A devout Christian, she made no money from her work, and sponsors helped to pay for records and recitals. 'Writing the music down takes hours,' she explained. 'It's very hard work, and I never know how it is going to sound until it is played. Don't think that it is easy going for me. I didn't ask to be chosen.'

She was born Rosemary Dickenson on 27 July 1916 at Stockwell, south London. She had ambitions to be a dancer but, after leaving school aged fifteen, she joined the Post Office and worked in various office jobs until her marriage.

Throughout her youth she had experienced psychic phenomena, but did not become directly involved in spiritualism until 1961 after the deaths of both her mother and her husband.

In the early 1970s Rosemary Brown appeared regularly on television and in public. She played at the New York City Hall and appeared on the *Johnny Carson Show* in America, where her talents were embraced. In Britain, however, she had a mixed reception.

Indeed, Rosemary Brown encountered many 'viperish attacks' on her credibility. She accepted that dishonest mediums had given spiritualism a bad press, but was adamant that clairvoyance was a genuine gift. 'I suspect,' she wrote in 1971, 'that many individuals highly gifted with extra sensory aptitudes keep silent about their abilities, fearing that to reveal them would invite persecution from religious bigots and otherwise biased people, as well as from the ill-disposed, envious and ignorant.'

❧ 17th ❧

John Wimber, b. 1934, d. 1997

John Wimber, the American evangelist who has died aged sixty-three, brought renewed zeal to the charismatic movement in the Church of England.

His influence in England dated back to 1981, when he first preached at St Andrew's, Chorleywood, Hertfordshire. He adopted a friendly man-in-the-street approach – 'I'm just a fat man trying to get to heaven' – and encouraged his congregation to put themselves on the same kind of terms with the Almighty.

In the 1960s Wimber had been involved with the Righteous Brothers pop duo; and twenty years later his religious services gave prominence to guitar, keyboard and repetitive community singing. To his followers, Wimber was tapping fresh springs in an arid desert; to his opponents he was purveying the kind of enthusiasm that Dr Johnson denounced as 'a vain belief of private revelation, a vain confidence of divine favour or communication'.

The time-honoured procedures of the Church of England began to be interrupted, as in the days of John Wesley, by members of the congregation speaking in tongues, or fainting in ecstasy. At Holy Trinity, Brompton, which became associated with Wimber's American churches, the congregation were instructed that 'Jesus blows your mind'.

Ferenc Puskas, b. 1927, d. 2006

Ferenc Puskas, who has died aged seventy-nine, was among the greatest footballers ever to play the game. Over eighty-four international appearances he scored eighty-three goals, a return that has been bettered only by Pele.

He was also the architect of England's first defeat at home by a foreign side.

In November 1953 the Hungarian team arrived at Wembley in the middle of a run that would see them beaten only once in forty-eight games, and that in the World Cup Final. But in England an insular football establishment scorned the Continental passing game, believing still that the old-fashioned English style of play, based on running with the ball, was superior. The visitors thrashed the home side 6–3.

A goal up after ninety seconds, the Hungarians' third was scored by Puskas, their captain and inspiration. Puskas calmly dragged the ball away from Billy Wright with the sole of his left boot and swivelled to lash a shot inside the near post. Billy Wright's sliding tackle was, wrote one reporter, 'like a fireman racing to the wrong fire'.

❧ 18th ❧

Lady Heathcoat Amory, b. 1901, d. 1997

Lady Heathcoat Amory, formerly Joyce Wethered, who has died aged ninety-six, was arguably the greatest woman golfer of all time.

Indeed, when Bobby Jones was asked if there had ever been a better woman player, he replied: 'I am very doubtful if there has ever been a better player, man or woman.' He had come to this conclusion after playing Joyce Wethered at St Andrews in 1931, the year after he had won the professional and amateur Opens of both Britain and the United States. They drove from the same tees, and Joyce Wethered was two up with three to play. Though she lost the last three holes she was still round in 71. But for his greater strength, Jones acknowledged, he was 'utterly outclassed'.

Joyce Wethered was born at Brook, Surrey, on 17 November 1901, and educated privately, having been adjudged too frail to go to school. She first hit a golf ball at the seaside town of Bude, in Cornwall, where she received her one and only lesson, from Tom Lyle, the professional there.

Her swing was a model of balance and grace. Ideally, she used to say, nothing on earth could dislodge her from her right foot at the top of the back swing, or from her left at the finish of her follow-through. The most remarkable feature of her game was her accuracy with iron shots.

Yet Joyce Wethered never thought of playing championship golf until 1920, when Molly Griffith, a leading Surrey player, suggested she should come with her to the English Ladies' Championship at Sheringham, in Norfolk. Joyce Wethered proceeded to play her way to the final, in which she encountered the formidable 'Cecil' Leitch. Soon she found herself well down. But wrapping herself into a cocoon of concentration she managed to retrieve the situation and win 2 and 1 on the seventeenth green. Had she not been disturbed, she was asked afterwards, by the train that whistled as she was bending over her winning putt? 'What train?' she returned.

Not only did she hold on to the English Ladies' Golf Championship for the next four years; in 1922, 1924 and 1925 she also won the Ladies' Open Amateur Championship. Her defeat in the semi-final in 1923 seemed like a departure from the natural order of things.

By 1932 her family was on its uppers, and the next year she took a job advising customers about golf equipment at Fortnum & Mason. In 1935 she undertook a tour of America, to publicise Wanamaker's golf supplies with a series of exhibition matches. At first things did not go well, at least by her standards. But, she told reporters, she would do better when she became acquainted with American greens and with the coarser sand in the bunkers ('I fancy a heavier niblick might help').

Five months later, she had played fifty-three matches in all parts of America, and established thirty-six new records, notwithstanding the vast distances travelled and her lack of knowledge of local conditions. She also made herself a tidy £4,000 – perhaps £100,000 in today's money.

In 1937 she married Sir John Heathcoat Amory, 3rd Bt. He was the elder brother of Derick Heathcoat Amory, who was Chancellor of the Exchequer from 1958 to 1960 and created Viscount Amory.

It is said that Sir John had refused to propose to Joyce Wethered until he had beaten her at golf – a rash undertaking even for a fine games player, with a handicap of two. As a pair, they seemed less happy on the golf course than off it.

❧ 19th ❧

Basil D'Oliveira, b. 1931?, d. 2011

Basil D'Oliveira, the cricketer who has died aged at least eighty, was a Cape Coloured South African subjected in youth to the full rigour of apartheid; through supreme natural talent and quiet determination, however, he was able to transform himself into an England Test player.

This achievement was all the more striking because D'Oliveira reckoned that he was already past his prime by the time that he reached England in 1960. 'In terms of eyesight, co-ordination, instinct and fitness,' he wrote in his autobiography *Time To Declare* (1980), 'I was at my peak when playing with non-whites in the Fifties.'

It was also his fate that his success as a Test cricketer, far from liberating him from the injustice of apartheid, once more enmeshed him in its toils.

From the moment D'Oliveira made his debut for England in 1966, he set his sights on returning to South Africa on MCC's tour scheduled for 1968–69. And after he had averaged more than 50 over the three series against West Indies, India and Pakistan in 1966 and 1967, his place in the side seemed assured.

He did less well in the West Indies in 1967–68, when he succumbed rather too easily to parties, and showed no distaste for rum. By contrast, in the first Test against Australia in 1968 he was the only batsman to put up much resistance, scoring 87 not out (the only English innings of more than 50 in the match) as his team tumbled to defeat. In the fifth Test at the Oval he scored a brilliant 158 and took a vital wicket as England won handsomely. The next day the selectors announced the party to tour South Africa. D'Oliveira's name was absent.

Earlier in the year John Vorster, Prime Minister of South Africa, had privately informed Lord Cobham, a past President of MCC, that England's tour would have to be cancelled if D'Oliveira were selected.

Privately, D'Oliveira wept in disappointment and disbelief. Now, though, the selectors were under pressure. The press accused them of appeasing South Africa; various MCC members resigned; and the Rev. David Sheppard formed a protest group.

In September, when injury forced Tom Cartwright to drop out of the tour party, the selectors thought it wise to replace a bowler who could bat a bit with D'Oliveira, a batsman who could bowl a bit. Shortly afterwards the South African government publicly announced that an England side containing D'Oliveira would be unacceptable. MCC, having exhausted the last resources of appeasement, called off the tour.

The only person who emerged well from this sorry saga was D'Oliveira himself, whose dignity was always proof against histrionics and bitterness. But then he had been well trained in the school of adversity.

Basil Lewis D'Oliveira was born into a strict Roman Catholic family which lived at the bottom of Signal Hill, a precipitous suburb on the east side of Cape Town. Wisden states that the date was 4 October 1931.

The year of his birth, however, proved to be variable. In 1964, when D'Oliveira joined Worcestershire, he claimed to have born in 1934. In fact he may have been three years older, not three years younger, than Wisden's official date. After he established himself in county cricket he put the date back to 1931; and in his autobiography he hinted that he was older than that, having masked his true age to prevent being overlooked by the England selectors. 'If you told me I was nearer to forty than thirty-five when I first played for England in 1966,' he wrote, 'I would not sue for slander.'

Basil was still a toddler when his family moved to a house on the top of Signal Hill. There could be no hope, however, of any social ascent in a system increasingly dedicated to the maintenance of white supremacy.

The D'Oliveiras were classified as 'Cape Coloured', a term used to designate those who were neither Indian nor African, but a combination of either Indian and white, or African and white. Even among non-whites, cricket in South Africa suffered from odious distinctions. Africans, Coloureds, Malays and Indians generally played in separate leagues. Lewis D'Oliveira, Basil's father, was captain of St Augustine's, which turned out, simultaneously with up to twenty other clubs, on a tract of patchily grassed wasteland known as Green Point, two miles from Signal Hill.

Lewis D'Oliveira sought no favours for his son. Basil had no coaching, and learned his cricket almost entirely in the streets of Signal Hill, where the uncertain bounce on the cobbles demanded razor-sharp reactions. It was soon clear that Basil possessed this talent to the point of genius.

At sixteen he began playing for St Augustine's where, rather to the disapproval of his father, who favoured a more classical approach, he sought to smash every ball out of sight, and very often succeeded.

His lithe physique generated awesome power, notwithstanding a short backlift. In the season of 1950–51, he succeeded his father as captain of St Augustine's. By this stage he was already a legend, albeit one studiously ignored by the white population. Aged nineteen, he scored 225 in under seventy minutes, an innings which began with five consecutive sixes. In 1954 he hit 46 in a single eight-ball over.

This policy of all-out attack, to which he remained faithful when selected for West Province, did not preclude consistency. In nine years between 1951 and 1960, D'Oliveira notched up eighty-two centuries in club and representative cricket. Arguably, this was the most astonishing part of his career, the more so when it is remembered that he was playing on uneven matting wickets against fast bowlers who considered it as much of an achievement to hit the batsman as the wicket.

In 1956–57, D'Oliveira captained a black South African team which demolished an XI representing Kenya. In 1958, he led a tour of East Africa and Kenya which again conclusively proved that the outcasts of the apartheid system were more than a match for first-class opposition.

But in 1959 the last-minute cancellation of a projected tour by a West Indian team to be led by Frank Worrell against black South Africa brought home to D'Oliveira that, if he was ever to do justice to his extraordinary talent, he must seek to play in England.

To this end he wrote to John Arlott, the cricket commentator, who in turn contacted John Kay, a Manchester journalist closely concerned with the Lancashire League. Kay, hearing in 1960 that Wes Hall was unable to take up the position of professional at Middleton, secured the post for D'Oliveira. When D'Oliveira sought advice on playing conditions in England from a former Nottinghamshire professional called Tom Reddick who was coaching in Cape Town, it was the first time he had ever been inside a white man's house.

He was, therefore, overwhelmed when received as a star in England. Notwithstanding the kindness of his landlords and fellow players in Middleton, it took this shy and socially diffident man some time to overcome the culture shock inevitable in one who had never even seen television before.

More seriously, D'Oliveira had not previously batted on a grass pitch. After a testing start, however, he rose to the challenge, ending the season at the top of the Central Lancashire League averages, ahead even of Gary Sobers.

In his four seasons with Middleton (1960–63) he scored 3,663 runs at an average of 48.20, and took 238 wickets at 14.87 apiece. Stories of his prowess spread, and in 1962 he was invited on a tour of East Africa with a team of international stars.

In such company D'Oliveira ceased to be a teetotaller. Nevertheless, at Nairobi he hit a century in sixty minutes – an innings which Everton Weekes considered one of the best he had ever seen. Tom Graveney, who became a close friend on that tour, also took notice. It was through Graveney's influence that D'Oliveira signed up with Worcestershire, for whom, in 1965, he made a century in his first county championship match.

In 1966, D'Oliveira was called up to England colours. Though unluckily run out at Lord's on his debut when going well, he then reeled off scores of 76, 54 and 88 (including four sixes) against a fearsome West Indian attack that included Wes Hall, Charlie Griffith, Gary Sobers and Lance Gibbs.

Next year, against India, he made his first Test century, though he was never a man to take much pride in flogging tired and inadequate bowling. By contrast, he considered that his 114 not out against Pakistan in Dacca in 1969, on a pitch pitted with holes – as unpredictable in bounce as those on which he had learned to play in South Africa – was the greatest innings of his life.

By the winter of 1970–71, when MCC toured Australia under Ray Illingworth's captaincy, D'Oliveira's joints were beginning to creak. Yet he played an important part in winning back the Ashes, notably with an innings of 117 at Melbourne. Going on to New Zealand he hit his fifth and last Test century on a bad wicket at Christchurch.

In 1971, he enjoyed an excellent run of form against Pakistan, and next year performed usefully enough against Australia. England, however, retained the Ashes only after drawing the series, and D'Oliveira's Test career was extinguished by the cry for younger talent. He continued to play for Worcestershire until 1979, when he was conceivably over fifty.

In his forty-four Test matches D'Oliveira scored 2,484 runs at an average of 40.06, and took 47 wickets at 39.55 apiece. In 362 first-class matches he made 18,919 runs (including forty-three centuries) at an average of 39.57, and took 548 wickets at 27.41 each.

After his retirement from first-class cricket, D'Oliveira was the Worcestershire coach from 1980 to 1990. In 1980, he was a member of a Sports Council Delegation which visited South Africa; typically, he saw 'much that was extremely encouraging'. He and his wife, though, were completely at home in England, and never ceased to declare their gratitude to the English people.

Basil D'Oliveira was appointed OBE in 1969 and CBE in 2005.

Group Captain Ken Gatward, b. 1914, d. 1998

Group Captain Ken Gatward, who has died aged eighty-four, carried out a daring raid over occupied Paris on 12 June 1942.

According to information from SOE, the Germans held a daily parade in the Champs-Elysées between 12.15p.m. and 12.45p.m. So Gatward's orders, received in strictest secrecy, were to appear over Paris at that time and strafe the German soldiers. Failing that, he was instructed to attack the Kriegsmarine Headquarters, on the north side of the Place de la Concorde.

Gatward piloted a Coastal Command Beaufighter and his navigator was Sergeant George Fern, a former schoolmaster from the Forest of Dean. While the two men were making their plans, they were sent a large tricolour flag, which they were told to drop over the tomb of the Unknown Warrior at the Arc de Triomphe.

Four times in early June 1942 the raid was aborted due to inadequate cloud cover. By the time Gatward took off from Thorney Island a fifth time on 12 June, he was determined to press on whatever the risk.

As the aircraft proceeded towards Paris at a height of thirty feet (occasionally rising to avoid electricity cables), the French countryside was bathed in brilliant sunshine. Even so, there was no challenge when Gatward and Fern flew over the Luftwaffe aerodrome at Rouen. Thirty miles from Paris they recognised the Eiffel Tower 'sticking up like a matchstick', and at 12.27 approached the Arc de Triomphe.

The tricolour which they carried had been cut into two pieces, owing to its size. After Fern had released the first section over the Arc de Triomphe, Gatward banked to port and headed down the Champs-Elysées at roof-top height, disappointed to note that there were no German soldiers to fire at. Having picked out the Ministère de la Marine in the Place de la Concorde he swept round to starboard, circling over the Opera.

He flew south over the Seine and then headed north again, holding the Ministère de la Marine in his gunsight. He raked the building with 20mm shells, smashing several windows, and had the pleasure of watching the terrified sentries running for their lives, while Fern dropped the second part of the tricolour.

Gatward cleared the top of the building by just a few feet and, pursued by streams of tracer, headed back to England. They landed unharmed at Northolt.

Sir Edward Ford, b. 1910, d. 2006

Sir Edward Ford, who has died aged ninety-six, was assistant private secretary to the Queen from her accession in 1952 until his retirement in 1967, and found unexpected fame at eighty-two when he wrote to commiserate with her on what he called her 'annus horribilis'.

The year was 1992, which saw the collapse of the marriages of three of her four children and culminated in the partial destruction by fire of Windsor Castle. A few days later, at a Guildhall luncheon to mark the fortieth anniversary of her reign, she quoted Ford's Latinity to poignant effect and the phrase passed into the history books.

⊰ 20th ⊱

Frank Steele, b. 1923, d. 1997

Frank Steele, who has died aged seventy-four, was the MI6 officer who set up talks between William Whitelaw and the Irish Republican Army in 1972.

One of the IRA's conditions for talks was that among its delegates should be Gerry Adams. When Steele, who had formally been seconded to the Home Office, spoke to Adams, he was surprised to find that instead of the aggressive tough he had been briefed to expect, Adams was 'a very personable, intelligent, articulate and self-disciplined man'.

The secret talks were agreed for 7 July 1972; only those members of the Cabinet who sat on its Northern Ireland sub-committee were to know of them. The IRA delegation met Steele at a pre-arranged spot in Co. Londonderry, and were driven in a minibus with brown paper over the windows to a waiting helicopter.

During the flight to Belfast, Martin McGuinness was nervous lest they prove a tempting target for IRA gunmen on the ground. From there they flew to RAF Benson in Oxfordshire and were then driven in two cars to the house in Chelsea belonging to Paul Channon, the Northern Ireland Minister.

It was a fine summer morning. On the way, at Henley, Steele stopped to buy some apples. 'I got back in the car,' he recalled later, 'and handed the apples to the three IRA men who were sitting in the back seat. They all looked at each other. "My God," I thought, "perhaps they think they're drugged!" So I took one at random and took a great bite out of it. Then I handed the bag to the Special Branch driver and he did the same. I then passed it to the back. I think they were satisfied.'

⚜ 21st ⚜

Quentin Crisp, b. 1908, d. 1999

Quentin Crisp, who has died aged ninety, was the author of *The Naked Civil Servant* (1968), which told of his adventures and ordeals as a self-proclaimed – indeed exhibitionist – homosexual before during and after the Second World War.

Crisp never attempted to disguise the tragedy of his life; he did, however, know how to face it with both courage and humour. Witty, intelligent and cynical, he described how, in a period when most men 'searched themselves for vestiges of effeminacy as though for lice', he had dyed his hair red, put on lipstick and mascara and painted his finger and toenails.

'I wore make-up at a time when even on women eye shadow was sinful,' he related. 'From that moment on, my friends were anyone who could put up with the disgrace; my occupation, any job from which I was not given the sack; my playground, any café or restaurant from which I was not barred, or any street corner from which the police did not move me.'

The televising of *The Naked Civil Servant*, in 1975, starring John Hurt, launched Crisp at the age of sixty-six as 'one of the stately homos of England' and into a new career as an actor.

In the spring of 1978, he appeared in his own one-man show at the Duke of York's theatre, London. The production, which Crisp described as 'a straight talk from a bent speaker', received rapturous reviews, transferred to the Ambassadors, and was later taken to Australia and many cities in America, including New York, where he took up residence on Lower East Side in 1981.

But Crisp enraged militant homosexuals in America by refusing to align himself with their cause. The more that homosexuals insisted on their 'rights', he thought, the more they distanced themselves from the heterosexual world – 'and this is such a pity'. For himself, he had always been conscious of being alone, and of having to invent his own happiness.

Denis Charles Pratt – he did not adopt his more effervescent name until his early twenties – was born at Sutton, Surrey, on Christmas Day 1908, the third son of a somewhat ne'er-do-well London solicitor and a former governess with mild social and artistic pretensions.

Denis's effeminacy was evident from an early age; his only boyhood ambition, he recalled, was to be a chronic invalid. Frail, pale and hopeless, he was 'an object of mild ridicule from birth'.

Leaving Denstone College in 1926, he took a course in journalism at King's College, London, but failed to get a diploma. He also attended art classes in Battersea and at the Regent Street Polytechnic.

His high heels and red hair failed to allure prospective employers, and by the age of nineteen he had fallen upon the seedier side of Soho – and more particularly the Black Cat café in Old Compton Street. The proprietor was later involved in a murder case; and many of his customers were male prostitutes. Crisp himself was 'on the game' for six months.

Already thirty years old at the outbreak of the Second World War, Quentin Crisp lied about his age and attempted to enter the Army, only to be declared 'totally exempt, suffering from sexual perversion', after a searching physical examination.

In the summer of 1940, Crisp moved into the first-floor front bed-sitting room at 129 Beaufort Street, Chelsea, which was to remain his home until the end of the 1970s and which he never attempted to clean. 'The dust doesn't get any worse after three years,' he observed.

His attempts at writing were unsuccessful, though his poem about the Ministry of Labour, *All This and Bevin Too* (1943), appeared in pamphlet form.

The Naked Civil Servant grew out of a radio interview in 1964 conducted by the off-beat Third Programme personality Philip O'Connor, which happened to be heard by the then managing director of Jonathan Cape. It was followed by *How To Have A Life Style* (1974) and an autobiographical sequel *How To Become A Virgin* (1981), which told of his love affair with New York.

In later years, drawn into 'the smiling and nodding racket', he was to be seen at some of the flashiest parties in New York and London, and was also much in demand as a chat-show guest and as an actor. He played Lady Bracknell in a Greenwich Village production of *The Importance of Being Earnest*, and a laboratory assistant in Sting's film *The Bride* (1985).

In 1993, at the age of eighty-five, he appeared as an over-rouged and voluptuously becurled Queen Elizabeth I in Sally Potter's film of Virginia Woolf's *Orlando* – though his acting showed considerable dignity and finesse. He also delivered an Alternative Queen's Christmas Message to the British nation from a suite in the Polaza Hotel,

New York. 'Towards the end of the run you can overact appallingly,' he remarked in justification of such extravagances.

Crisp's views remained both unpredictable and independent. He described sex, psychiatry and other people as 'a mistake'. He hated Oscar Wilde, worshipped the Kray twins, and described *Death in Venice* as a crashingly boring film. Although his West End show attracted distinguished admirers – John Betjeman, the Pinters, Lady Diana Cooper – he never clung to their coat tails. 'Never try to keep up with the Joneses,' he recommended. 'Drag them down to your level. It's cheaper.'

22nd

Mary Kay Ash, b. 1918, d. 2001

Mary Kay Ash, who has died aged eighty-three, founded the largest cosmetics direct-sales empire in America and was known to her fans as 'The High Priestess of Pink'.

She was forty-five when she started her company in 1963 and beginning to feel her age. She once explained: 'From fourteen to forty, a woman needs good looks; from forty to sixty, she needs personality; and I'm here to tell you that after sixty, she needs cash.'

Captain Charles Upham, b. 1908, d. 1994

Captain Charles Upham, who has died aged eighty-six, twice won the Victoria Cross.

Only three men have ever won double VCs, and the other two were medical officers: Colonel A. Martin-Leake, who received the decoration in the Boer War and the First World War; and Captain N.G. Chavasse, who was killed in France in 1917. Chavasse's family was related to Upham's.

For all his remarkable exploits on the battlefield, Upham was a shy and modest man. In a television interview in 1983 he said he would have been happier not to have been awarded a VC at all, as it made people expect too much of him. 'I don't want to be treated differently from any other bastard,' he insisted.

When King George VI was conferring Upham's second VC he asked Major-General Sir Howard Kippenberger, his commanding officer: 'Does he deserve it?'

'In my respectful opinion, Sir,' replied Kippenberger, 'Upham won this VC several times over.'

A great-great-nephew of William Hazlitt, and the son of a British lawyer who practised in New Zealand, Charles Hazlitt Upham was born in Christchurch on 21 September 1908.

Upham was educated at the Waihi Preparatory School, Christ's College and Canterbury Agricultural College, which he represented at rugby and rowing. He then spent six years as a farm manager, musterer and shepherd, before becoming a government valuer in 1937.

In 1939 he volunteered for the 2nd New Zealand Expeditionary Force as a private in the 20th Battalion and became a sergeant in the first echelon advance party. Commissioned in 1940, he went on to serve in Greece, Crete and the Western Desert.

Upham won his first VC on Crete in May 1941, commanding a platoon in the battle for Maleme airfield. During the course of an advance of 3,000 yards his platoon was held up three times. Carrying a bag of grenades (his favourite weapon), Upham first attacked a German machine-gun nest, killing eight paratroopers, then destroyed another which had been set up in a house. Finally he crawled to within fifteen yards of a Bofors anti-aircraft gun before knocking it out.

When the advance had been completed he helped carry a wounded man to safety in full view of the enemy, and then ran half a mile under fire to save a company from being cut off. Two Germans who tried to stop him were killed.

The next day Upham was wounded in the shoulder by a mortar burst and hit in the foot by a bullet. Undeterred, he continued fighting and, with his arm in a sling, hobbled about in the open to draw enemy fire and enable their gun positions to be spotted. With his unwounded arm he propped his rifle in the fork of a tree and killed two approaching Germans; the second was so close that he fell on the muzzle of Upham's rifle.

During the retreat from Crete, Upham succumbed to dysentery and could not eat properly. The effect of this and his wounds made him look like a walking skeleton, his commanding officer noted. Nevertheless he found the strength to climb the side of a 600ft-deep ravine and use a Bren gun on a group of advancing Germans.

At a range of 500 yards he killed twenty-two out of fifty. His subsequent VC citation recorded that he had 'performed a series of remarkable exploits, showing outstanding leadership, tactical skill and utter indifference to danger'. Even under the hottest fire, Upham never wore a steel helmet, explaining that he could never find one to fit him.

His second VC was earned on 15 July 1942, when the New Zealanders were concluding a desperate defence of the Ruweisat ridge in the 1st Battle of Alamein. Upham ran forward through a position swept by machine-gun fire and lobbed grenades into a truck full of German soldiers.

When it became urgently necessary to take information to advance units which had become separated, Upham took a Jeep on which a captured German machine-gun was mounted and drove it through the enemy position. At one point the vehicle became bogged down in the sand, so Upham coolly ordered some nearby Italian soldiers to push it free. Though they were somewhat surprised to be given an order by one of the enemy, Upham's expression left them in no doubt that he should be obeyed.

By now Upham had been wounded, but not badly enough to prevent him leading an attack on an enemy strong-point, all the occupants of which were then bayoneted. He was shot in the elbow, and his arm was broken. The New Zealanders were surrounded and outnumbered, but Upham carried on directing fire until he was wounded in the legs and could no longer walk. He was awarded a Bar to his VC.

Taken prisoner, he proved such a difficult customer that in 1944 he was confined in

Colditz Castle, where he remained for the rest of the war. His comments on Germans were always sulphurous.

After his release from Colditz in 1945 Upham went to England and inquired about the whereabouts of one Mary ('Molly') McTamney, from Dunedin. Told that she was a Red Cross nurse in Germany, he was prepared, for her sake, to return to that detested country. In the event she came to England, where they were married in June 1945.

Back in New Zealand, Upham resisted invitations to take up politics. In appreciation of his heroism the sum of £10,000 was raised to buy him a farm. He appreciated the tribute, but declined the money, which was used to endow the Charles Upham Scholarship Fund to send sons of ex-servicemen to university.

In 1946 Upham bought a farm at Rafa Downs, some 100 miles north of Christchurch beneath the Kaikoura Mountains, where he had worked before the war. There he found the anonymity he desired.

In 1962, he was persuaded to denounce the British government's attempt to enter the Common Market: 'Britain will gradually be pulled down and down,' Upham admonished, 'and the whole English way of life will be in danger.' He reiterated the point in 1971: 'Your politicians have made money their god, but what they are buying is disaster.' He added: 'They'll cheat you yet, those Germans.'

⊰ 23rd ⊱

Mary Whitehouse, b. 1910, d. 2001

Mary Whitehouse, who has died aged ninety-one, battled for more than thirty years against the liberal orthodoxy which was loth to acknowledge that sex and violence on television might produce any harmful effect.

The Clean Up Television Campaign, which she founded in 1964 – a year later it became the National Viewers' and Listeners' Association – denounced 'the propaganda of disbelief, doubt and dirt that the BBC projects into millions of homes through the television screens'.

The determination with which Mrs Whitehouse pressed home her attack earned her vilification from all quarters of the permissive society. Students bellowed obscenities, intellectuals affected a lofty disdain, satirists pilloried her, lunatics sent death threats, and for four years the BBC (always her prime target) refused to allow her to appear on its programmes.

This last infliction seemed to rankle more than the others. The only person who moved her to bitterness was Sir Hugh Greene, Director General of the BBC from 1960 to 1969 – 'the devil incarnate', as she once called him.

There was, indeed, something pathological in Sir Hugh's attitude towards Mrs Whitehouse. He purchased a naked portrait of her, adorned with six breasts, by Lawrence Isherwood and (it was said) would amuse himself by throwing darts at it, squealing with pleasure as he made a hit.

By comparison Mary Whitehouse seemed well-adjusted and good-humoured. 'I never had any hang-ups about sex,' she claimed. 'As for being sexually repressed, nothing could be further from the truth. There are more hang-ups now than ever there were when I was growing up.' She was, she protested, amusing and full of fun. 'I am not narrow-minded or old-fashioned. But I am square, and proud of it, if that means having a sense of values.'

Yet, as far as cleaning up television was concerned, her campaign failed. In the 1960s she had found matter for objection in such programmes as *The Man from Uncle* and *Doctor Who*; by 1993 she was not even bothering to object to the late-night screening of *The Good Sex Guide*.

Latterly her attention was increasingly absorbed by satellite television – 'our greatest challenge yet'. An Italian programme called *Strip Poker* had sounded the alarm in 1989: 'If that came over here I would want to tackle it at source – via the Vatican.'

She was born Mary Hutcheson, the second of four children, on 13 June 1910. Her Scottish father had dreamed of being a professional artist; necessity made him a gentleman's outfitter and later a cattle food sales representative in Cheshire. Her mother, a resourceful and energetic woman, kept the wolf from the door by dressmaking.

Young Mary was educated at Chester City Grammar School and studied art at the County Training College, and from 1932 to 1940 taught at Wednesfield School, Wolverhampton.

When she was twenty she fell in love with a 36-year-old married man – though, as she stressed, 'there was no misbehaving'. The affair, such as it was, ended when Mary Hutcheson saw the man's wife looking desolate. 'I just knew,' she recalled, 'that if I was the cause of so much unhappiness, our relationship could not be right.'

By that time she had become involved in the Moral Rearmament movement, through which, in 1932, she met Ernest Whitehouse, a sheet-metal worker whom she married in 1940. For the next twenty years Mrs Whitehouse was busy bringing up a young family in Wolverhampton.

In 1960 she returned to teaching as senior mistress and senior art mistress at Madeley School in Shropshire, where she gave sex education classes that laid emphasis on the conjugal bond as the sole permitting factor.

Her own pupils gave her the final push into campaigning. 'The girls I taught would be waiting for me at the school gate the morning after a programme on sex. I remember after a particular one on premarital sex, one girl enthusiastically came up to me to say, "I know what's right now, Miss. I can have intercourse when I'm engaged, can't I?" That's what the programme had done for her.'

The possibility of adolescent irony did not strike Mary Whitehouse. With another housewife, she called a meeting in Birmingham Town Hall and formed the Clean Up Television Campaign.

Within a year she claimed to have won the support of 'half a million housewives, the Chief Constables of Britain, MPs, bishops, leaders of all Churches, city councils and people of standing throughout the country'. The postman delivered 250 letters a day.

There were, however, programmes that Mary Whitehouse liked, notably *Dixon of Dock Green*, which she presented with a special award in 1967. She also enjoyed the

Wimbledon fortnight on television, snooker tournaments, nature programmes and *Neighbours*.

24th

The 3rd Lord Moynihan, b. 1936, d. 1991

The 3rd Lord Moynihan, who has died in Manila aged fifty-five, provided, through his character and career, ample ammunition for critics of the hereditary principle.

His chief occupations were bongo-drummer, confidence trickster, brothel-keeper, drug-smuggler and police informer, but 'Tony' Moynihan also claimed other areas of expertise – as 'professional negotiator', 'international diplomatic courier', 'currency manipulator' and 'authority on rock and roll'.

If there was a guiding principle to Moynihan's life, it was to be found on the wall of his office in Manila, where a brass plaque bore the legend, 'Of the 36 ways of avoiding disaster, running away is the best.'

Moynihan learned this lesson at an early stage. The first time he ran away was in 1956, to Australia. There were two reasons for his flight. The first was to elude his father's fury over a liaison with a Soho nightclub waitress.

The second was to escape his wife, an actress and sometime nude model; they had married secretly the previous year, and she had now taken out a summons against him for assault. Her father had made a similar complaint – 'I regret to say I gave him a swift right upper cut,' Moynihan announced from Australia.

The idea was that he should work on his uncle's sheep farm in the bush, but after five days he ran away to Sydney, where he made his debut as a banjo-player and met the Malayan fire-eater's assistant who was to become his second wife.

The next year he returned to London, where he effected a reconciliation with his first wife and found a job as manager of the Condor, a Soho nightclub. The job did not last, and in 1958 he married the former fire-eater's assistant, by now a belly-dancer working under his management.

'Of course,' Moynihan explained, 'it means I shall have to become a Mohammedan first.' To this end, at dusk each day he kneeled to the setting sun with a cloth draped over his head.

After he succeeded his father in the peerage in 1965 Moynihan took the Liberal Whip in the House of Lords, where he was principally concerned in arguing that Gibraltar be given to Spain. The House was not impressed.

In 1968 Lord Boothby interrupted one of Moynihan's speeches: 'My Lords, the noble Lord has bored us stiff for nearly three-quarters of an hour. I beg to move that he no longer be heard.'

Moynihan's business career and personal finances had meanwhile given rise to a number of complications. By 1970 he faced fifty-seven charges – among them fraudulent trading, false pretences, fraud against a gaming casino and the purchase of a Rolls-Royce motor-car with a worthless cheque. To avoid disaster he fled once more, this time to Spain.

'I knew of my impending arrest forty-eight hours in advance,' he claimed. 'I'd been approached by a CID man who told me that for £50,000 the case against me would be dropped. Because I believe in God and England I told him to get stuffed.'

His extradition was sought from Spain, but he disappeared, to resurface the next year in the Philippines.

In 1968 he had married for a third time – another belly-dancer, this one a Filipino – and the new Lady Moynihan's family had a chain of massage parlours in Manila, where Moynihan remained for much of the rest of his life. At the Old Bailey in 1971 he was named in his absence as 'the evil genius' behind a series of frauds. 'This is a case of *Hamlet* without the Prince of Denmark,' declared the judge. 'The prince figuring behind all these offences is Lord Moynihan.'

As the 1970s wore on Moynihan found employment in the narcotics trade, as well as in fraud and prostitution. The first hint of this came in 1980, when he was named by an Australian Royal Commission as an associate of Sydney's 'Double Bay Mob', engaged in the import of heroin from Manila.

No charges were brought, however, and Moynihan continued his life as a Filipino pimp under the patronage of President Marcos – 'my drinking chum', as he called him. At one stage he ran a brothel within 100 yards of the British Ambassador's residence.

After the coup against Marcos in 1986, Moynihan's position became exposed, and the next year he was forbidden to leave the Philippines pending investigations of his links with drugs and prostitution.

Moynihan was thus vulnerable to pressure from Scotland Yard and the American Drugs Enforcement Agency to help them catch Howard Marks, a Balliol man who at that time controlled an estimated sixth of the global market in marijuana, and with whom he was already on friendly terms. He approached Marks with a bogus offer to sell him an island in the Philippines, on which he could grow marijuana; and in return for his own immunity agreed to wear a secret tape-recorder to ensnare his friend.

Marks was duly convicted in Florida, with Moynihan as chief witness for the prosecution. The DEA gave him refuge and protection in the United States for a time, and hailed him as 'a hero, one of the good guys'. Marks saw things differently. 'I feel terribly betrayed,' he said. 'He's a first-class bastard.'

Antony Patrick Andrew Cairne Berkeley Moynihan was born on 2 February 1936, the elder son of Patrick Moynihan, a barrister and stockbroker who succeeded to the Barony of Moynihan later that year.

Tony was educated at Stowe and did his National Service with the Coldstream Guards; it was his last contact with respectability, and he was inclined to reminisce over it in his cups.

In Manila, to which he returned after his sojourn in America, Moynihan lived in the suburbs in a heavily fortified house with a swimming pool, and had as his base in the city a brothel named the Yellow Brick Road. 'I just sit back and collect the money,' he said. 'The girls do all the work.'

❧ 25th ❧

His Tremendousness Giorgio Carbone, b. 1936, d. 2009

His Tremendousness Giorgio Carbone, who has died aged seventy-three, was the elected prince of Seborga, a self-proclaimed principality on the Italian Riviera.

Carbone claimed the sovereignty of Seborga (pop. 364) from the Italian government in 1963 and took the title His Tremendousness. A former flower-grower, he produced documents from the Vatican archives to prove that the village was never the property of the House of Savoy and therefore not part of the Kingdom of Italy after 1861. He insisted that Seborga had been a sovereign state since 954, a principality from 1079, and minted its own coins after 1666.

The villagers of Seborga, which lies near the picturesque Ligurian town of Bordighera, were enchanted by Carbone's quirkiness and he won 304 of a possible 308 votes to represent them. He was re-elected in 1995.

As His Highness Giorgio I, Prince of Seborga, Carbone did not draw a salary, but he could help himself to cheese and ham from the village shop without paying.

He was born in 1936, the son of a local flower grower who followed his father into the trade. His grand plans for the principality involved a Cabinet of fifteen ministers, a dozen members of parliament, and minting a currency, the Luigino. Seborga has its own flag, a white cross on a blue background, a patron saint, St Bernard, and a Latin motto: *Sub Umbra Sede* (Sit in the shade).

Carbone managed to convince around twenty states to recognise Seborga. 'The first state to step forward and recognise us was one of those revolutionary ones: Burkina Faso,' he said. Consular representation was maintained in ten countries.

Perhaps tiring of his role, Carbone announced in January 2006 that he would retire upon reaching the age of seventy. But a challenge to his authority a few months later appeared to re-energise him.

A woman calling herself Princess Yasmine von Hohenstaufen Anjou Plantagenet wrote to the newly elected Italian President, Giorgio Napolitano, claiming that she was the true heir to Seborga's throne and offering to hand it over to Italy. Carbone gruffly dismissed her claim, voicing doubts over her lineage: 'I have never seen her,' he said. 'We call her the internet princess'.

George Best, b. 1946, d. 2005

George Best, who has died aged fifty-nine, was the outstanding British footballer of any generation; the mercurial Manchester United and Northern Ireland forward possessed a genius that bears comparison only with the trio of modern masters, Pele, Johann Cruyff and Diego Maradona.

The originality of Best's play was breathtaking, encompassing a repertoire of feints and swerves, sudden stops and demoralising spurts which left opponents slack-jawed and bewildered. He reacted to scoring chances with a deadliness that made goalkeepers dread him. His skill was the epitome of natural, intuitive talent; he made it seem easy. It was Best's tragedy that he ultimately became as famous for his unsuccessful attempts to conquer his alcoholism as for his exploits on the football field.

Despite his slight frame, he had tremendous physical strength and resilience, along with an almost unnatural elasticity of limb and torso which led the midfield player Paddy Crerand, Best's Manchester United team-mate, to declare that he gave opponents 'twisted blood'.

Along with this – no small factor in the course that his career took – were Best's striking good looks. With vivid blue eyes set wide in a dark, mischievous face framed by luxuriant black hair, he possessed a physical grace and attractiveness which made him the first British sportsman to be accorded pop star status.

Throughout the 1960s his photograph was as likely to be seen in the music press as on the sports pages. He became an icon, his irresistible combination of devil-may-care rebelliousness and effortless flair ensuring that there was never a shortage of beautiful girls more than willing to accompany him on the late nights which came to overshadow his career. Though never vain, Best knew the price he paid: 'If I had been born ugly,' he once said, 'you would never have heard of Pele.'

⊰ 26th ⊱

James Frere, b. 1920, d. 1994

James Frere, who has died aged seventy-four, was a picturesque and eccentric character on the fringes of the old Establishment.

As Bluemantle Pursuivant of Arms and Chester Herald, he played an important ceremonial role in many great State occasions, and at the Coronation in 1953 was stationed closer to the throne than all but the Great Officers of State.

He later claimed that he had stocked a nearby oak chest with cold duck, Perigord pie and black cherries in port wine but, to his great regret, could not gain access to them during the long ceremony.

⊰ 27th ⊱

Alan Freeman, b. 1927, d. 2006

Alan Freeman, who has died aged seventy-nine, was a disc jockey who, as host of *Pick of the Pops* in the 1960s, established himself as one of the most prominent broadcasters to emerge from popular music radio.

Faced with the apparently tedious task of listing the country's twenty best-selling records, Freeman assumed an urgent gravity reminiscent of a Movietone news reader. As he neared the number one single, his voice took on a note of mounting frenzy.

This potent formula was instantly appreciated by younger listeners, many of whom listened to the later stages of Alan Freeman's countdown with the expectant zeal of a bingo player one number short of house. He would begin the programme with the ritual exclamation, 'Greetings, pop pickers!' This affectionate term for his listeners, which Freeman employed throughout his subsequent career, would be repeated at regular intervals during the show, rather as the narrator of *Just So Stories* makes reference to his 'Dearly Beloved'. Freeman, who was famously generous in his praise of most of the records he introduced, liked to acknowledge outstanding achievement with the cry: 'Not 'arf!'

In the late 1980s he experienced a remarkable renaissance when, at the age of sixty-one, he returned to Radio One as host of his own late-night rock show. Unfettered by the requirements of the station's play-list, Freeman would intersperse heavy metal records – his preferred genre once he reached pensionable age – with even more ancient styles of music such as opera and orchestral works. He confessed that he was 'a bit of a nutter for Russian symphonies'.

Alan Leslie Freeman was born in Melbourne on 6 July 1927, the son of a foreman in a timber yard. His ambition was to be a professional footballer, but, immoblised by asthma, he acquired a taste for the American popular songs he heard on Melbourne radio.

It was at the age of twenty, while he was presenting a three-hour request programme on a local station, that he acquired his nickname, 'Fluff'. The origin of his peculiar nom de guerre was the subject of considerable speculation, sometimes exotic. The truth, Freeman explained, was prosaic. 'Someone gave me a white submarine sweater as a pressie,' he said. 'I used to wear it all day and sleep in it at night. Eventually after a go at the dry-cleaner's, it turned fluffy like a sheep. People started calling me Fluff.'

Freeman arrived in Britain in 1957, and did holiday relief on Radio Luxembourg before joining the Light Programme in 1960, presenting *Housewives' Choice*. The BBC's tone was altered irreversibly when, in 1962, Freeman began presenting *Pick of the Pops*. After the first week, he recalled, he received a warning from his superiors. 'They didn't like the pace, you see,' Freeman said. 'So the next week, I went even harder.'

Freeman left Radio One in 1978, and joined Capital Radio the following year. He returned to the BBC in January 1989, at the age of sixty-one, and stayed for four years. A popular figure with his fellow disc jockeys, he had, amazingly, managed to sustain a rapport with teenage listeners, who shared his interest in Def Leppard, Led Zeppelin and Gong. His own demeanour was somewhat removed from the strident machismo of most of the guitar-wielding artistes whose careers he furthered, and there was speculation that the disc jockey's sexuality might not be quite so uncomplicatedly heterosexual as that of his heroes. 'If I was gay I would say so,' said Freeman, who preferred to describe himself as 'neuter'.

Freeman was a dedicated Royalist and was thrilled to have shaken hands with the Princess Royal; Princess Margaret; Diana, Princess of Wales; Prince Philip and Prince Charles. His great ambition was to meet the Queen. He also enjoyed watching *The Cook Report* on television.

'If God said, "OK, Fluff, the moment you die you can come back and do it all over again,"' he once remarked, 'I'd honestly have to say, "No thanks." I've enjoyed my life. But once is enough. When the time comes I would like to bow out suddenly in the middle of a broadcast. The headline will be simply: "Fluff snuffs it".'

⋇ 28th ⋇

Flight Lieutenant William Reid, b. 1921, d. 2001

Flight Lieutenant William Reid, who has died aged seventy-nine, won a Victoria Cross in 1943 for his heroism on a bombing expedition to Germany.

On the night of 3 November 1943, Reid was serving with 61 Squadron as captain of a Lancaster bomber on the way to Düsseldorf when it was attacked by a Messerschmitt 110 night-fighter as it crossed the Dutch coast. His windscreen was shattered, the plane's gun turrets, steering mechanism and cockpit were badly damaged, and Reid himself sustained serious injuries to his head, shoulders and hands. The plane dived 200ft before he managed to regain control.

Saying nothing about his injuries, Reid called his crew on the intercom for a damage report and proposed that they forge ahead regardless. As the Lancaster continued on its mission, it was soon attacked again, this time by a Focke-Wulf 190, which raked the plane with gunfire, killing Reid's navigator, fatally wounding the wireless operator and knocking out the oxygen system. Reid sustained further injuries to his right arm, but still refused to turn from his target.

Sustained by bottled oxygen from a portable supply administered by his flight engineer, Sergeant J.W. Norris, Reid pressed on for another fifty minutes. He memorised the course to his target and continued in such a normal manner that the bomb aimer, cut off from the cockpit by the failure of the plane's communications system, had no idea his captain was injured. After reaching Düsseldorf, he released his bombs right over the centre of the target – a ball-bearing factory – then set course for home.

Semiconscious at times, freezing cold because of his broken windscreen, and half blinded by blood from a head wound which kept streaming into his eyes, Reid, assisted by flight engineer Norris, somehow kept the plane in the air despite heavy anti-aircraft fire over the Dutch coast and the physical effort required to hold the control column steady.

As they crossed the North Sea, all four engines cut out and the plane went into a spin. Luckily Norris remembered in the nick of time that he had forgotten to change over the petrol cocks to a full tank, and swiftly rectified the fault.

They managed to find their way home, taking their bearings from the Pole Star and the moon. As he came in to land at Shipdham air base, Reid had to use an emergency pressure bottle to hand-pump the undercarriage down, and this exertion and the aircraft's descent into warmer air reopened his wounds. As the Lancaster touched down, the undercarriage collapsed and the bomber skidded along the runway for sixty yards before coming to a halt.

William Reid was born at Baillieston, Glasgow, on 12 December 1921, the son of a blacksmith. He was educated at Coatbridge Secondary School and studied metallurgy for a time, but then applied to join the RAF.

After a period in hospital, Reid went to C Flight 617 ('Dambuster') Squadron at Woodhall Spa in January 1944 and flew sorties to various targets in France. In July 1944, 617 Squadron was linked with 9 Squadron for a 'Tallboy' deep-penetration bomb attack on a V-bomb storage dump at Rilly-la-Montagne, near Rheims. As Reid released his bomb over the target at 12,000ft, he felt his aircraft shudder under the impact of a bomb dropped by another Lancaster 6,000ft above. The bomb ploughed through his plane's fuselage, severing all control cables and fatally weakening its structure, and Reid gave the order to bail out.

As members of his crew scrambled out, the plane went into a dive, pinning Reid to his seat. Reaching overhead, he managed to release the escape-hatch panel and struggled out just as the Lancaster broke in two. He landed heavily by parachute, breaking his arm in the fall.

Within an hour he was captured by a German patrol and taken prisoner. After various transfers, he ended the war in Luckenwalde PoW camp, west of Berlin.

Reid left the RAF in 1946 and resumed his studies, first at Glasgow University and later at the West of Scotland Agricultural College. In 1950, he became an agricultural adviser to the MacRobert Trust, Douneside. From 1959 to his retirement in 1981, he was an adviser to a firm of animal feed manufacturers.

When he married Violet Gallagher in 1952, he did not tell her of his VC. She was, he confessed, 'a wee bit impressed' when she found out.

⇜ 29th ⇝

Giant Haystacks, b. 1946, d. 1998

Giant Haystacks, the wrestler who has died aged fifty-two, may have been, as friends testified, 'a real gentleman' outside the ring; as a fighter, however, he experienced no difficulty in appearing as a vicious brute, intimidating in bulk and terrifying of visage.

He stood 6ft 11in, and in his later days would weigh in at as much as fifty stone. Opponents were thrown out of the ring with such force that it seemed impossible they should ever rise again. Lest there should be any lingering doubt about his status as a baddie, he sported a black beard and mane, and wrestled for a time in a vest and breeches that seemed to be sewn together from pieces of old sacking.

After one disqualification in 1978, he attacked and jumped on the referee. And in a bout against Kendo Nagasaki, the masked wrestler, he even pulled off his opponent's mask – the very depths of bad form.

The climax of many a bill was the arrival of Big Daddy (who died in 1997) to rescue some smaller wrestler from the attentions of Giant Haystacks. Being on the receiving end of Big Daddy's 'splashdown' (he weighed twenty-eight stone) might not have been a comfortable way of earning a living, but it was certainly lucrative. On Saturday afternoons around 1980 wrestling attracted a television audience of some 10 million. 'You'd be surprised who watches it,' he told a journalist. 'We had Roy Jenkins down at the Albert Hall one night.'

Much of Giant Haystacks' background remained a mystery, though he was certainly of Irish origin. Like his wife, Rita, he was a devout member of the Roman Catholic Church, attending Mass at every opportunity and refusing to wrestle on Sundays. He liked to keep his real name to himself, proclaiming himself at different times as Luke McMasters or Martin Ruane.

'I come from a family of giants,' he once volunteered. 'My grandfather was 7ft 5in. I've been wrestling since 1967, when I was thirteen. I've wrestled all over the world – China, Western Samoa, Africa. I'm an honorary citizen of Zimbabwe, and that can open a lot of doors.'

It is said that in his youth, when he weighed only twenty-six stone, he worked as a bouncer. His break into big-time wrestling came through Max Crabtree, Big Daddy's brother and one of the sport's chief promoters.

At the end of his career, Giant Haystacks ran a debt collection agency in Manchester, and occasionally wrestled under the name of the 'Loch Ness Monster' in America, where the sport became immensely popular on television in the 1990s.

When cancer struck, he confessed to being terrified. 'In my career I've had both kneecaps fractured, elbows smashed, crushed all my ribs and broken most of my bones. I've been covered in bruises and had gashes requiring 500 stitches. But nothing prepared me for my fear of dying on the operating table, powerless to fight back.'

⇥ 30th ⇤

Tiny Tim, b. 1930, d. 1996

Tiny Tim, the American pop singer who has died aged sixty-six, specialised in horrendous falsetto vocalisations of sentimental songs, and cultivated an appearance of utter ghastliness to match.

In a way he was always consistent. 'As a singer only one thing stands between him and success,' it was observed: 'Complete and utter failure.'

Tiny Tim was born Herbert Buckingham Khaury in New York on 12 April 1930, the son of a Roman Catholic Lebanese father and a Polish Jewish mother. He was never a handsome boy, and his looks were not improved when, on a school outing, he slipped and broke his nose on a cannon that had once belonged to George Washington.

As a young man he gained some notoriety in the homosexual clubs of Greenwich Village with his cracked falsetto renderings of classic songs. 'Why'd you gotta sing like a fairy?' his mother demanded.

After a career which at its height had seen him earning $50,000 a week at Caesar's Palace, in 1975 he was back in Greenwich Village, living in the spare room of his mother's apartment. 'Why'd you gotta look like a nut?' she remonstrated.

The 2nd Lord Milford, b. 1902, d. 1993

The 2nd Lord Milford, who has died aged ninety-one, was the only professed Communist in Parliament.

In 1962, on succeeding his father, the 1st Lord Milford, in the peerage, he chose to take his seat in the Lords. In his maiden speech he called for the abolition of the Upper House.

He condemned the Lords as 'an undemocratic anachronism composed of the inheritors of wealth and privilege and bent on their protection, an indefensible obstacle to progressive legislation and the forward march of world socialism'.

The new Lord Milford, who was not an 'inheritor of wealth' as his father had disinherited him, was heard in frosty silence by their lordships. It fell to the leader of the Labour peers, Earl Attlee, to offer the customary congratulations on a maiden speech.

'There are many anomalies in this country,' observed Lord Attlee. 'One curious one is that the views of the Communist Party can only be heard in this House. That, of course, is an advantage of the hereditary principle.'

Wogan Philipps was born on 25 February 1902 into a remarkable family which produced a clutch of twentieth-century peers. He was educated at Eton and Magdalen College, Oxford, and began life in a conventional enough manner. He attended debutante dances, drove lorries in the General Strike and joined the family shipping firm in the City of London.

Surveying his brief career as a capitalist, he said: 'I felt the resentment of the staff in the company when I joined. They must have felt "Who's this little bugger?" During the General Strike I saw men lying about the street, down and out, and I began to wonder what it was all about.'

In 1928 Philipps married the novelist Rosamond Lehmann and entered enthusiastically into bohemian life.

He joined the Labour Party in the 1930s and during the Spanish Civil War served with the International Brigade as an ambulance driver. After being badly wounded himself, when a shell hit his ambulance, Philipps helped to organise shipping supplies and to assist refugees.

During the Second World War he volunteered for service in the Merchant Navy but was rejected on medical grounds. Instead he worked as an agricultural labourer at a government farm in Gloucestershire, and subsequently started his own small farm near Cirencester. It was in the course of the war that Philipps joined the Communist Party.

His telephone was bugged by the local police; when he exclaimed, 'Oh come on, Constable, get off the line,' a voice would reply: 'Sorry, Sir.'

DECEMBER

⚜ 1st ⚜

Sir Frank Bowden, b. 1909, d. 2001

Sir Frank Bowden, 3rd Bt, who has died aged ninety-two, was an eclectic cheetah-owning private collector of Japanese swords, spears, halberds and spiked poles, known as 'sleeve entanglers'.

The swords ranged from a blade by the great thirteenth-century smith Ichimonji Norifusa of Bizen to others made for twentieth-century Japanese officers; one came with a note explaining that it had been tested on a malefactor's neck.

All were displayed first on the walls and later on flat racks in what had been the refectory of Thame Park, Bowden's 100-room Oxfordshire home, which had been a Cistercian monastery before the Reformation. Visitors would receive an even greater thrill on encountering Chui, the cheetah whom Bowden had obtained from a big-game hunter in Kenya. This friendly beast, which was allowed into the house along with a dog fox, had a purr like windscreen wipers.

Chui had his own heated chamber in an outhouse with a specially made window so he could see outside on cold days. Although stouter than the average cheetah on the plains, he was still so fast that a BBC television crew was disappointed to discover that a van dragging a rabbit as bait could not go fast enough to stretch him fully.

Bowden liked to take him out in the passenger seat of his car, but gave this up because too many drivers immediately pulled off the road on seeing them.

Frank Houston Bowden was born on 10 August 1909, grandson of Sir Frank Bowden, 1st Bt, who on returning home from Hong Kong in poor health had taken up bicycling and built up the Raleigh Cycle Company. Young Frank was educated at Rugby and Merton College, Oxford, where he read Modern Languages and was a winter sports enthusiast.

On the outbreak of war in 1939, he served first as a ciphers officer in the cruiser *Shropshire*, which captured a small freighter in the South Atlantic. As the only German speaker aboard, Bowden interrogated the captain and discovered that his dog had been left in the freighter; a rescue operation was immediately mounted. Bowden spent the remainder of the war in Britain, training sailors to man defences on merchant ships.

With the return of peace, he was involved in a variety of commercial ventures, but it was after he inherited the remains of his grandfather's weapons collection, when he came into the baronetcy on the death of his father in 1960, that Bowden's great passion for swords developed.

Bowden's interest in Japan led him to become president of the Kendo Society and a vice-president of the Japan Society. Last year he was awarded the Order of the Gold Sun, Golden Rays with Rosette, by the Emperor of Japan.

⋙ 2nd ⋘

Big Daddy, b. 1930, d. 1997

Big Daddy, the fighting name of Shirley Crabtree, who has died aged sixty-seven, was the star attraction of the professional wrestling circuit during its televised heyday in the 1970s and 80s.

Weighing in at twenty-eight stone and clad in spangled top hat and overburdened leotard, Big Daddy was a portly avenging angel in a comic-book world of heroes in white trunks and villains in black masks.

At its peak, wrestling drew Saturday afternoon audiences of 10 million, attracted not so much by the finer points of the hammerlock and Boston Crab as by its unvarying rituals. These began with the commentator Kent Walton's welcome – 'Greetings, grapple fans' – and climaxed with the entry of Big Daddy into the ring, usually to save a small wrestler from the attentions of his *bête noire*, Giant Haystacks.

His arrival was accompanied by chants of 'Ea-sy, ea-sy' from stout matrons in the crowd, in manner the spiritual descendants of the *tricoteuses* who sat by the guillotine. For Big Daddy's vast belly easily held opponents at bay before he despatched them with his speciality – the 'splashdown'. This was a manoeuvre in which he mounted the ropes, leapt on top of his stupefied opponent, and squashed him flat to the canvas.

These antics brought Big Daddy notable fans, among them the Queen, whose interest in the sport was first recorded in Richard Crossman's diaries, and Margaret Thatcher, who found the wrestler a useful topic of conversation in Africa, where he was a household name.

Richard Todd, b. 1919, d. 2009

Richard Todd, the actor who has died aged ninety, was one of the first British officers to land in Normandy in advance of the main D-Day landings and went on to become Britain's highest earning matinee idol of the post-war years; his most memorable role was that of Wing Commander Guy Gibson, VC, in *The Dam Busters* (1955).

Handsome, blue-eyed and with an erect military bearing, Todd enjoyed the unusual distinction of appearing in films about D-Day in which the role of his wartime self was played by other actors.

As an officer in the 7th (Light Infantry) Parachute Battalion, he had not only been one of the first to land in Normandy, he had also been among the first to meet the glider force under the command of Major John Howard defending Pegasus Bridge, a scene memorably recreated in two epic films in which Todd later starred. In *D-Day, the Sixth of June* (1956), he played the commanding officer of his unit who vies for the affections of Dana Wynter with his Yank rival Robert Taylor.

In *The Longest Day* (1962), which was based on the book of the same name by the *Telegraph* special war correspondent Cornelius Ryan, Todd took the role of Howard, performing one scene opposite the actor playing himself. 'I was, in effect, standing beside myself talking to myself,' he noted. At a cost of $8 million, *The Longest Day* was the most expensive black-and-white film made until *Schindler's List*.

Emmanuel de Margerie, b. 1924, d. 1991

Emmanuel de Margerie, a former French ambassador to London and to Washington, who has died aged sixty-six, was as resolute an Anglophile as anyone could be, charged with representing the interests of France.

No one could doubt 'Bobbie' de Margerie's concern for the Entente Cordiale. Yet he possessed to the full the sprightliness and wit with which the French delight to confront the stolid Anglo-Saxon mind. A small, bespectacled man with fluffy grey hair, de Margerie made many English friends as ambassador between 1981 and 1984. Through no fault of his own, however, the *rapprochement* suffered a severe reverse during President Mitterrand's visit in 1984.

After the President had been entertained at Buckingham Palace, the French made lavish preparations for the return fixture at their embassy, jetting in carpets, tapestries, china, silver and cooks.

Unluckily, though, one of Mitterrand's guards took it upon himself to test the efficacy of the security services by planting two lumps of dynamite in the garden, and then inviting the British police to search for them.

The wheeze, presumably, was to complain when the officers failed to find the explosive. But it never does to underestimate the British dog. Olive and Lucy, two labradors, effortlessly sniffed out the ruse, and the President's bodyguard was hauled off to Scotland Yard.

The British put on a fine display of outrage. The French riposted, with a scarcely less impressive display of effrontery, that Scotland Yard had suggested the whole scheme, and that the English had demonstrated a marked lack of humour. Eventually the Quai d'Orsai announced that it 'regretted the misunderstanding', which was reckoned to be as close to an apology as a French government is capable.

The son and grandson of ambassadors, Emmanuel Jacquin de Margerie was born on Christmas Day 1924. His early years were spent in London, where his father was posted and where young Bobbie acquired his faultless command of English.

He was educated at the Lycée Francais in Kensington, at the Universite Aurore in Shanghai, at the Sorbonne, and at the Ecole Nationale d'Administration.

In 1951 he entered the Ministry of Foreign Affairs; his first posting, from 1954 to 1959, was in London. Subsequently de Margerie served in Moscow, Tokyo and Washington, before becoming director of the European Department at the Quai d'Orsai from 1972 to 1974. It was under Giscard d'Estaing's presidency that de Margerie was appointed to London in 1981 – but, ever the perfect civil servant, he proved no less loyal to Giscard's socialist successor.

En poste in London de Margerie was a diligent student of English politics. In 1983 he attended the Liberal, Labour and Tory party conferences. In the case of the SDP, however, it sufficed to stay with the Duke of Devonshire at Chatsworth.

3rd

Diana Gould, b. 1926, d. 2011

Diana Gould, who has died aged eighty-five, became famous overnight in 1983 when she confronted Prime Minister Margaret Thatcher about the sinking of the Argentine warship *General Belgrano* during the Falklands War.

The cruiser was sunk on 2 May 1982 by the British submarine *Conqueror*, with the loss of 323 lives. This caused controversy because she was sunk outside the 200-mile exclusion zone around the Falklands, and at a time when some thought that a peace deal was still possible.

Diana Gould, a teacher from Cirencester in Gloucestershire, challenged the Prime Minister on the current affairs television programme *Nationwide* in May 1983, during the election campaign of that year.

Mrs Thatcher: 'Mrs Gould, when the orders were given to sink it, when it was sunk, it was in an area which was a danger to our ships. Now, you accept that, do you?'

Gould: 'No, I don't.'

Thatcher: 'One day, all of the facts, in about thirty years' time, will be published.'

Gould: 'That is not good enough, Mrs Thatcher.'

Afterwards, the Prime Minister's husband Denis remarked that the episode had confirmed his view that the BBC was run by 'a load of pinkos'.

Diana Gould was born Diana Sydney Prigg on 18 April 1926 at Clifton, Bristol. When she was five her family moved to Cardiff, where she attended Howard Gardens Grammar School. She won a scholarship to Newnham College, Cambridge, where she took a double first in Physical Geography. After joining the WRNS she served as a meteorological officer in Cornwall. In 1950 she married Clifford Gould, a lieutenant in the Fleet Air Arm.

Both Diana and Clifford Gould left the Navy to become teachers. In 1955 Diana became a part-time PE teacher at the comprehensive school in Cirencester. In 1984 she published a book, *On the Spot*, about the Belgrano affair.

⟪4th⟫

Stanley Green, b. 1915, d. 1993

Stanley Green, who has died aged seventy-eight, paraded Oxford Street for twenty-five years with a placard warning against the dangers of protein, and sold thousands of hand-printed leaflets (at 12p each) explaining why lustful feelings were induced by 'fish, bird, meat, cheese, egg, peas, beans, nuts and sitting'.

'Protein makes passion,' he said. 'If we eat less of it, the world will be a happier place.'

Stanley Owen Green was born on 22 February 1915 and worked in the civil service before launching his campaign against lust in 1968. He had learned from experience, he said, that 'passion can be a great torment'.

He produced his leaflets on a press in his small council flat at Northolt, west London; the tenants below often complained about the relentless thumping on printing days.

Until he qualified for a free travel pass, Green would bicycle to Oxford Street each day in his raincoat, cap and wire-rimmed spectacles. His own diet comprised porridge, fruit, steamed vegetables, lentils, home-baked bread and barley-water mixed with milk powder. He took his lunch in 'a warm and secret place' near Oxford Street – 'I think it is justified,' he said, 'because I am doing a public service and I need to be warm.'

The campaign was not without its hazards. Green was twice arrested for causing an obstruction, and wore green overalls as protection against spit. But he held no grudges, explaining that people attacked him only because they mistook him for a religious man.

He liked nothing better than to distribute leaflets in Leicester Square on a Saturday night. He would home in on cinema queues, using such opening gambits as 'You cannot deceive your groom that you are a virgin on your wedding night,' and often sold fifty leaflets in an evening.

⟪5th⟫

Karlheinz Stockhausen, b. 1928, d. 2007

Karlheinz Stockhausen, who has died aged seventy-nine, was the leading pioneer of electronic music and regarded by many avant-garde musicians as the most significant German composer since Richard Wagner, but his appeal to the general public was more restricted.

Some of his works attained a rapt kind of beauty. In *Gesang der Jünglinge* (Song of the Young Boys), the taped voice of a Cologne Cathedral chorister singing the Benedicite is altered by echo-effects, filters and other means and combined with electronic sounds.

But in *Aus dem sieben Tagen* (From the Seven Days), each of the fifteen sections has a verse of text to suggest the mood the players must create. One of them is inscribed: 'Live completely alone for four days, without food in complete silence, without much movement. After four days, late at night, without talking beforehand, play single sounds without thinking what you are playing. Close your eyes. Just listen.'

It was this kind of thing which prompted Sir Thomas Beecham to reply to the question whether he had heard any Stockhausen: 'No, but I think I've trodden in some.'

Karlheinz Stockhausen was born in Burg Mödrath, near Cologne, on 22 August 1928, the son of a village schoolmaster. He began to play piano, violin and oboe aged five.

His mother suffered from severe depression and went into an institution when her son was four. She was later murdered in the Nazis' euthanasia experiments. His father joined the Nazi Party in the 1930s, enlisted in the army at the outbreak of war and was killed in 1945.

Between 1944 and 1947 Stockhausen paid for his education by working as a stretcher-bearer in a military hospital, as a farmhand, as an assistant to a travelling magician and as a jazz pianist in clubs.

He was at Cologne High School for Music from 1947 to 1951, when he began composing, mainly choral pieces. Listening to the first 'total serialist' work (the application of Schoenberg's twelve-note rules to all aspects of a composition) he found it 'terribly exciting to discover that there was music of which I could not make sense'. It inspired him to write his *Kreuzspiel* (Cross Play) for oboe, bass clarinet, piano and percussion in which extreme high and low sounds 'crossed over', hence the title. He likened it to the architecture of Le Corbusier.

In 1952 Stockhausen went to Paris to study with Messiaen for fourteen months. There he composed several works, of which the instrumental *Kontra-Punkte* (Counter-Points) became his first published work. On his return to Cologne, he went to work in the new radio electronic studio creating, with *Studie I* (1953) the first composition to be constructed entirely from sine-waves.

Stockhausen then evolved a theory of 'parameters' or dimensions of sound – pitch, intensity, duration, timbre and spatial position – and serialised each parameter. The culmination of this phase was *Momente* (1961–64) for soprano, four choral groups and thirteen instruments, which was said to be a portrait of his second wife Mary Bauermeister. Its text comprised extracts from the Song of Songs, letters and personal names, passages from Malinowski's *Sexual Life of Savages* and samples of audience reaction. Besides singing, the chorus clicked, clapped and stamped and played small percussion instruments.

He also intensified the element of chance in his work, whereby the performer had a large say in what was performed. Thus in *Zyklus* (Cycle, 1959), for solo percussionist, the performer may start at any of its seventeen pages of score and go on until returning to the starting-point. He or she may read from left to right or turn over the score and go from right to left. In the score, graphic signs represent instruments in addition to giving directions for performance.

In 1964 Stockhausen formed his own ensemble to perform live electronic works, with himself at the mixing desk. The first piece he wrote for it was *Mikrophonie I*. This featured the tam-tam. Using microphones and electrical filters, it was made to produce a rich range and variety of sounds.

In *Kurzwellen* (Short Wave, 1983) the players imitate and improvise on sounds they have picked up from short-wave receivers.

In the mid-1970s Stockhausen directed all his creative energies to his cycle of operas, *Licht: die sieben Tage der Woche* (Light: the Seven Days of the Week), composed, like Wagner's operas, to his own librettos. The cycle has three principal characters: Michael the hero, Eva the mother and lover, and Luzifer the father and antagonist. Each is also represented by an instrument and a dancer. Michael is tenor and trumpet, Eva soprano and clarinet, and Luzifer bass and trombone.

Stockhausen's operatic week began on a Thursday with *Donnerstag aus Licht*, premiered at La Scala, Milan, in 1981 and performed at Covent Garden in 1985. The autobiographical element is obvious: in the first opera Michael's mother is taken to an asylum and the father goes off to war. What some, even among his admirers, regarded as an act of gigantic egomania has not established itself in any opera house's repertory.

Nor, since the heyday of the 1960s, has most of Stockhausen's music. It has its fanatical advocates still who regard him as a visionary pathfinder, but most of the next generation of composers looked to Pierre Boulez before Stockhausen or to Gyorgy Ligeti before both.

As for the mass of the general public, when not repelled it remained baffled, convinced that this was not music and suspecting that the man was a charlatan or an opportunist playing a vast hoax on the whole world of music.

There can be little doubt, though, that Stockhausen believed in everything he did.

6th

Tommy Gould, b. 1914, d. 2001

Tommy Gould, who has died aged eighty-six, won the Victoria Cross, the only Jewish recipient of the Second World War, while serving in the submarine *Thrasher* in February 1942.

At about midday on 16 February, *Thrasher*, on patrol off Suva Bay, on the north coast of Crete, torpedoed and sank an Axis supply ship of some 3,000 tons, escorted by five anti-submarine vessels.

The escorts counter-attacked, with support from aircraft, and dropped thirty-three depth-charges, some of them very close indeed. *Thrasher* survived the attacks and, that evening after dark, surfaced to recharge batteries.

In the early hours of the morning, when *Thrasher* altered course across the swell and began to roll heavily, banging noises were heard from above, as though some heavy object were loose and rolling about. It was found that there was a bomb, probably weighing about 100lb, lying on the submarine's casing (a free-flooding structure, erected on top of the submarine's pressure hull) in front of the four-inch gun mounting.

Lieutenant Peter Roberts, the First Lieutenant, and Petty Officer Gould volunteered to go on deck and remove the bomb. But it was too heavy to be thrown clear, so they manhandled it 100ft forward to the bows and dropped it overboard, while *Thrasher* went full astern to get clear.

Looking more closely at the casing, they found a jagged hole and inside, another bomb, resting on the pressure hull. It was not possible to handle the bomb up through the hole it had made. The only way was through a hinged metal grating about twenty feet away. The two men lowered themselves through the opening and wriggled on their stomachs to where the bomb lay. If it exploded, the submarine would be lost.

Furthermore, *Thrasher* was off an enemy coast, and the enemy knew there was an Allied submarine in the area. If a surface vessel or aircraft were sighted, *Thrasher*'s CO, Lieutenant (later Vice Admiral Sir Hugh 'Rufus') Mackenzie, would have to dive, and the two men would be drowned.

Gould lay flat on his back with the bomb in his arms. Roberts lay in front of him, dragging him by the shoulders as he crawled along. By the faint light of a shaded torch, the two of them worked the bomb through the narrow casing, easing it up through the grating. The bomb made a disconcerting twanging noise whenever it was moved and it was forty minutes before the two men had it clear and could wrap it in a sack, carry it forward and drop it over the bows.

'I never expected to get the VC,' Gould said. 'When we came down from the casing that night, we were soaking wet.' All the Captain said was: "You'd better get yourselves dried".'

Mackenzie did not make much of the 'bombs incident' in his patrol report, merely commending Roberts and Gould for their 'excellent conduct'. The incident was virtually forgotten until several months later, when, as Mackenzie recalled, he was 'shaken by the news that Roberts and Gould had each been awarded the Victoria. A great personal honour to themselves and, as they and I felt, also to their fellow submariners.'

The VCs were awarded on the recommendation of the C-in-C Mediterranean, Admiral Sir Andrew Cunningham, but were opposed by the Honours and Awards Committee in London, which argued that the acts of bravery had not been performed in the presence of the enemy, as VC Warrants stipulated, and that the George Cross would be more appropriate. Cunningham, however, retorted that two large enemy bombs, in a submarine off an enemy coastline, constituted quite enough enemy presence.

Thomas William Gould was born at Dover on 28 December 1914. His father, Reuben Gould, was killed in action in 1916. His mother married a second time, to Petty Officer Cheeseman.

From St James's School, Dover, Gould joined the Navy on 29 September 1933, and served in the cruisers *Emerald* and *Columbo*. He joined submarines in 1937 and was rated Acting Petty Officer on 17 August 1940. Later in the war, he was mentioned in despatches after the submarine *Truculent* sank *U-308* off the Faroes on 4 June 1943.

As a VC hero, Gould was interviewed by the Marquess of Donegal, who asked him what he was thinking while busy with those bombs. 'I was hoping,' Gould replied, 'that the bloody things would not go off.'

Christabel Leighton-Porter, b. 1913, d. 2000

Christabel Leighton-Porter, who has died aged eighty-seven, was the model for the *Daily Mirror*'s wartime strip cartoon 'Jane'; the character's lightly clad adventures with the Security Service were credited with maintaining the morale of the Forces and even, on the morning in 1944 when she first appeared nude, with inspiring the 36th Division to advance six miles through Normandy in a single day.

'Jane' had first begun in 1932 as 'Jane's Journal – The Diary of a Society Girl', a pocket cartoon drawn by Norman Pett, who used his wife Mary as the model. But by the late 1930s the *Mirror* wanted to use it in panel form and with more risqué content, and when Mary Pett's attention suddenly turned to golf, her husband began to look for a new model. In late 1939, on a visit to his old art school in Birmingham, he found her when he saw the blonde Christabel Leighton-Porter posing for a life class.

Christabel Leighton-Porter liked to believe that the character's popularity was due to her healthy, girl-next-door appeal, but in truth Jane's admirers (as ever with the British male) were won over by the amount of flesh on view.

Jane was forever shutting her skirt in doors, reaching for her towel in the bath, or romping unclad in tropical ponds. Even the slightest breeze could reduce her to a bra and frilly camiknickers.

In the early 1940s, she began to tour in a burlesque stage show based on the cartoon. This proved very popular with wartime audiences, although the Lord Chamberlain, as the official censor, was concerned about the amount of clothing removed. Christabel Leighton-Porter tried to persuade him that in a bikini scene she could remove her top with her back to the audience and then cover herself with her hands before turning round.

'I see,' said the Lord Chamberlain, looking sceptically at her *embonpoint*. 'You must have very large hands.'

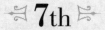

7th

Peter Langan, b. 1941, d. 1988

Peter Langan, the erratic Irish-born restaurateur who has died aged forty-seven, was celebrated more for the eccentricity and extravagance of his behaviour than for the real merits of the restaurants with which he was associated.

Among the tales he did not deny was that of the cockroach which a distraught customer had found in the ladies' room. 'Madam,' he exclaimed after studying it closely, 'that cockroach is dead. All ours are alive.' He then apparently swallowed it, washing it down decorously with a glass of vintage Krug.

Sunny von Bülow, b. 1932, d. 2008

Sunny von Bülow, who has died aged seventy-six, spent the last twenty-eight years of her life in a coma, unaware that she had played a central role in one of the most sensational trials of the twentieth century.

Her life during the fifty years prior to her falling into an irreversible coma could be said to have resembled a film script, and indeed her story was the subject of a movie, *Reversal of Fortune* (1990), which secured an Oscar for best actor for its star, Jeremy Irons.

She was born Martha Sharp Crawford at Manassas, Virginia, on 1 September 1932, the daughter of George W. Crawford, founder of Columbia Gas, Lone Star Gas and Northern Natural Gas. He died when Sunny (as she was always known for her cheerful disposition) was only four years old, leaving her his enormous fortune. She attended Chapin School in Manhattan and St Timothy's, Maryland, but elected not to go on to university.

A brief first marriage was ended in 1965 by a quick divorce and was followed in June the next year by marriage to the Danish man-about-town Claus von Bülow – a graduate of Trinity College, Cambridge, and a barrister from Lord Hailsham's chambers.

Sunny von Bülow's wealth and beauty combined with her husband's charm and wit to make them a glittering couple. In July 1967 they gave a sumptuous ball at his old bachelor home in Belgrave Square, after which they settled down at 960 Fifth Avenue in New York. For the next thirteen years the von Bülows were counted among America's most socially glamorous couples. Later, however, Sunny's friend Truman Capote was to describe her as 'very pretty, but a psychological wallflower', and it was said that she had taken refuge in drink and drugs.

Then, on the night of 21 December 1980, Sunny von Bülow was found unconscious on the marble floor of the bathroom of their house in Rhode Island. She was in an irreversible coma, and six months later her husband was indicted on two counts of attempted murder by insulin injection.

The prosecution claimed that he stood to gain £14 million from his wife's will, and that her death would have left him free to marry his mistress, an actress called Alexandra Isles. The defence said that Sunny's coma had been self-induced by a binge of drugs and sweets, including a 'sugar bomb' of eggnog, twelve fresh eggs and a bottle of bourbon.

It was the start of an international media circus that was to last for five years. The story had every prerequisite for newspaper sales and television ratings: enormous wealth, adultery, and allegations of attempted murder in high society.

The von Bülow case was the first major criminal trial to be televised in the United States. And the network executives soon discovered that real-life courtroom drama – in which the sets and the actors came gratis – generated higher ratings than even the most popular soap operas.

At the first trial, held between February and April 1982, the court was told by Sunny von Bülow's maid, Maria Schrallhammer, that when her mistress had fallen ill on a previous occasion, in 1979, Claus von Bülow had been slow to send for a doctor; and that she had found a bag belonging to Claus containing a hypodermic needle encrusted with insulin and a bottle marked 'insulin'. Von Bülow was found guilty and sentenced to thirty years' imprisonment.

At a retrial, which began in May 1985, Von Bülow assembled a leading legal team, which found no fewer than nine experts who established that her coma had been caused by factors including barbiturates, alcohol, beta-blockers, hypothermia and aspirin. Claus von Bülow was acquitted, and there was even a suggestion that there had been an attempt to frame him.

Despite the verdict, some newspapers and television stations still sought to cast doubt on his innocence, something *Reversal of Fortune* (starring Glenn Close as Sunny) tended to reinforce. The marriage between Sunny and Claus von Bülow was dissolved, and he abandoned all claims to her fortune. In the late 1980s he moved to London, where he is a popular figure in society.

Sunny von Bülow lived out the rest of her life in a Manhattan hospital, and latterly in a nursing home, at an estimated cost of more than $500,000 a year; twice a week a hairdresser came in to dye her hair and attend to her make-up.

⊰ 8th ⊱

Nicholas Polunin, b. 1909, d. 1997

Nicholas Polunin, who has died aged eighty-eight, was the botanist on an expedition which in 1948 discovered the last islands to be added to the map of the world.

Polunin was then Macdonald Professor of Botany at McGill University, Montreal. It was a time when the Canadian Arctic was being photographed from the air and mapped for the first time, and he took full advantage of the opportunity to make extensive plant collections.

Having claimed a place as botanist on the Canadian Air Force and Geodetic Survey of Canada, he was involved in the discovery of new islands in Foxe Basin, north of Hudson Bay. They were later named Air Force Island, Prince Charles Island (Prince Charles having been born on 14 November 1948) and Foley Island (after the navigator of the aircraft that identified it).

⊰ 9th ⊱

Cecil Williamson, b. 1909, d. 1999

Cecil Williamson, one-time 'Witch Protector to the Royal House of Windsor', who has died aged ninety, collected information on more than 1,000 incidents of witchcraft including a sensational case of alleged human sacrifice.

Williamson was a strange mixture of showman, investigator and convinced witch. A friend of Aleister Crowley and Gerald Gardner, both notorious exponents of magic, he enjoyed varied careers including clairvoyant's oracle, silent film-maker, tobacco farmer and spy.

In 1930 he began collating material for an 'index file on the craft of the witch'. By his own account, he worked with eighty-two wise women, participated in 1,120 cases of witchcraft and recorded a success rate of 60 per cent, which he considered 'not bad going'.

Not least of these cases was a 'human sacrifice' at a barn near Glastonbury in the early 1930s. Williamson recalled that the assembled group of about eighty, locked in the outbuilding, witnessed an elaborate ritual culminating in what they were led to believe was the death of a child.

The 'infant' was passed around the circle in a hessian bag. At one point in the ceremony, Williamson grasped a pair of trotters, and discovered the bag contained a suckling pig from the local butcher's shop. 'Nobody did this sort of kick-up for nothing,' he recalled, 'because it needed quite an outlay. I believe it was to get the bite on people who thought they had taken part in human sacrifice. It was something you couldn't talk about. It was a form of blackmail.'

Williamson also claimed to have witnessed a large-scale magical ceremony in Ashdown Forest during the Second World War, organised by Aleister Crowley. 'The purpose,' he said 'was to undermine Hitler's power.' Williamson remembered seeing 'forty Canadian airmen draped in blankets embroidered with symbols from the Key of Solomon'. During the exercise the fire brigade had to be called when 'a burning effigy of Hitler got out of control'.

Cecil Hugh Williamson was born on 18 September 1909 in Paignton, Devon, into a naval family. His first brush with magic took place when he was six and staying with his uncle, the rector of North Bovey, Devon. Williamson attempted to save an elderly woman from a mob of drunken farm workers who had accused her of being a witch. 'Auntie May', as he came to know her, befriended Williamson, taught him country lore and how to tickle trout.

Bullied at prep school, Williamson hid in kitchens or wandered the woods where, aged eleven, he met another wise woman who taught him a witch's 'swing spell' for turning away evil. Williamson claimed to have mastered it so successfully that his principal bully suffered a crippling accident and never returned to school.

Still in his teens, Williamson bluffed his way into a job in silent films and worked throughout the remainder of the 1920s as a film-maker. In the early 1930s, with the advent of the talkies, Williamson left the film business and emigrated to Rhodesia, where he managed a tobacco plantation. He soon annoyed local white people by treating black workers as equals.

At the outbreak of the Second World War, Williamson was, by his own account, recruited by MI6 to set up a research centre cataloguing the activities of Nazi occultists. He later hinted that he had had some involvement in Rudolf Hess's visit to Britain.

After the war, Williamson made his first attempt to run a museum of witchcraft. He chose Stratford-upon-Avon, but local people objected so strongly that he decided to move to the Isle of Man. There, in 1950, he opened the Folklore Centre of

Superstition and Witchcraft, in Castletown. He also founded the Witchcraft Research Centre, funded by his wife's restaurant, the Witches' Kitchen.

In the early 1950s Cecil Williamson moved to Windsor and opened a second witchcraft museum, but with little financial success. While there, he was approached by Rosa Woodman, who introduced herself as an 'hereditary witch'. She claimed her role was to protect the Royal Family by performing a 'wild, leaping, galloping dance culminating in the tossing of an acorn necklace into the air'.

Rosa Woodman knew she was dying, and passed on her tools, rituals and the duty of 'Witch Protector to the Royal House of Windsor' to Williamson. Her accessories included her familiar, a large toad called Tim.

Williamson never undertook the ritual fully and after a year was asked to vacate his premises by 'two gentlemen of the Royal Household', who told him it was 'embarrassing that witchcraft was flourishing on the doorstep of the Royal residence'.

⊰ 10th ⊱

The 11th Earl of Egmont, b. 1914, d. 2001

The 11th Earl of Egmont, who has died aged eighty-seven, became one of the peerage's most romantic figures at the age of fifteen when he reluctantly moved from a two-room prairie shack to Avon Castle, Hampshire, on his father's inheritance of the earldom.

Members of a junior branch of the Perceval family which had emigrated to Iowa and then Alberta in the late nineteenth century, the boy and his widowed father 'batched' together on a 600-acre ranch at Priddis, near Calgary. Wearing chaps, boots and Stetsons, they contentedly built up a herd of cattle, chopped their own wood and cooked their own meals.

Then on 12 January 1929 Lord Beaverbrook ordered a *Daily Express* reporter in London to inform the father of his good fortune. 'This is the first I have heard of it,' replied the 56-year-old 10th Earl when he was brought to a telephone station. 'I have been out with a bunch of cattle for the past few days and have just got in.'

His son Frederick George Moore Perceval, who was born at Calgary on 14 April 1914, now had the courtesy title Viscount Perceval. After a sale of their effects in which the boy's two mongrels, Jack and Rummy, made 25 cents each and his saddle pony, Pat, $3.25, they set off. As the pair boarded ship at Montreal, father and son swapped their Stetsons for caps.

When they landed in England an estate agent worked out that around £300,000 went with the Irish Earldom of Egmont, the Viscountcy of Perceval of Kanturk and the Barony of Arden of Arden, Co. Cork, as well as the Barony of Lovel and Holland in the United Kingdom. The inheritance came through their descent from Spencer Perceval, the Prime Minister assassinated at Westminster in 1812 who was the seventh son of the 2nd Earl.

The new Earl and his son moved into Avon Castle, with its private railway halt and 1,300 acres at Ringwood, Hampshire, seven months after their arrival. By then the

Earl was thoroughly bemused by the England he had not seen since the age of six, and his son was firmly for returning to Priddis. Instead, they dismissed the servants and moved into the huge kitchen to re-create their Albertan self-sufficiency.

The gates were closed; the house shuttered; overtures from county neighbours were rebuffed. The new Earl got on well enough with the villagers he met in the pub and local shop, though he didn't care for the way they always called him 'sir'.

The young Lord Perceval occasionally played with other boys in Ringwood but was more often to be seen riding alone on his bicycle; later he bought a motorcycle which he enjoyed riding late at night along deserted roads at 85mph. The Earl continued to be of abiding interest to the press, which dubbed him 'the loneliest peer in England'; then fate intervened when he was killed in a motor accident in Southampton.

The 18-year-old new Earl immediately set out for Canada. On encountering a Calgary journalist on the train at Winnipeg his first questions were about the present owner of his saddle pony.

That afternoon, he borrowed a horse and set off for a ride. A few months later Egmont married his cousin, Geraldine Moodie, a dental nurse who had been his childhood sweetheart. The honeymoon involved the usual pursuit by newsmen, who remained fascinated by 'the only member of the House of Lords who could rope, throw and brand a steer'.

Egmont hardly fulfilled normal expectations of a belted earl when encountered on his ranch in bib overalls and a dusty hat, with six days' beard. He liked his neighbours to address him as 'Fred', but they called him 'the Earl' behind his back.

Settling down to develop some of the finest stock in the West on the Priddis ranch, Egmont resisted his wife's promptings that they go to England until 1938, after he had rescued their son from a fire which destroyed their ranch-house.

He bought a car in London, toured the country and talked about sending his son to Eton. Instead, he put Avon Castle on the market and returned to Priddis where he built a 26-room ranch-house, complete with solid oak floors that had to be supported by twelve-inch steel girders in the basement.

When the farm was sold twenty-one years later he used his handsome profit to buy the 5,000-acre Two-Dot Ranch at Nanton, forty miles south of Calgary, which had once belonged to the Earl of Minto, Canada's Governor-General from 1898 to 1904.

Egmont is survived by his heir – Thomas Frederick Gerald, Viscount Perceval, who was born on 17 August 1934 – and a younger son and two daughters.

❧ 11th ❧

Eddie Chapman, b. 1914, d. 1997

Eddie Chapman, who has died aged eighty-three, was known under the codename Zig-Zag as one of the most colourful of the double cross agents run by British Intelligence during the Second World War.

He was born in 1914 and brought up in Sunderland, where he found work in the shipyards and at eighteen showed his mettle by rescuing a man from drowning off Roker. Chapman then served in the Coldstream Guards until the mid-1930s, when he embarked on a second career as a safecracker. He enjoyed some success until 1939, when the police discovered him trying to blow open a safe in Glasgow.

While awaiting trial, he broke out of jail and made his way to Jersey, where he was arrested. He was about to be returned to Scotland when the Germans occupied the Channel Islands. Chapman always claimed that his offer to carry out sabotage for the Germans in Britain, using his knowledge of explosives, was motivated by a desire to return home.

But one of the British Intelligence officers who later handled him was probably closer to the mark when he suggested that it was at least in part because Chapman 'loved an exciting life'.

After training by the Abwehr military intelligence organisation, he was given the codename Fritzchen. On the night of 20 December 1942 he was dropped by parachute near Ely, equipped with a wireless, an automatic pistol, a cyanide suicide pill and £1,000. His mission was to blow up the De Havilland aircraft factory at Hatfield, Hertfordshire, where the new Mosquito fighter-bomber was being built.

The Germans promised him that, if he succeeded, he would be given £15,000 and sent to America to carry out further acts of sabotage. But by now MI5 had set up the double cross system, whereby German agents arriving in Britain were intercepted and offered the stark choice of facing execution or working for the British.

Immediately after landing, Chapman telephoned Wisbech police station – but had some difficulty persuading the police that he was a former safecracker turned German spy who now wanted to work for the British.

MI5 rechristened him Zig-Zag and allowed him to radio to the Abwehr that he had arrived safely. The double cross committee then set about creating the illusion that would allow him to claim that his mission had been accomplished. The first problem, a legitimate explanation of how he acquired the necessary explosives, Chapman solved by returning to a quarry near Sevenoaks with which he was familiar from his previous career.

On the night of 29 January 1943, Zig-Zag and an MI5 officer scaled the fence of the Mosquito factory and laid a series of notional charges around the power plant. Jasper Maskelyne, a celebrated magician and illusionist, then used a controlled explosion to blow out part of the roof. At the same time, he released smoke bombs and scattered pieces of transformer around the plant to give the impression of a much greater blast.

The explosion was reported in *The Daily Telegraph* and other national newspapers and Chapman's Abwehr controllers sent him a message of congratulations. They told Chapman to make his own way back to Germany from where he would be sent on the second mission to America.

Hoping to use him to take similar control of this operation, MI5 put him on a British ship bound for Lisbon, having firmly declined his numerous offers to assassinate Hitler. On arriving in the Portuguese capital, Chapman reported to the local Abwehr representative who gave him a piece of 'coal' and offered him a large sum if he would go back to the ship and place it in its coal store.

MI5 was horrified to discover from the intercepts of Abwehr traffic that the coal was explosive designed to detonate when placed in a fire, but Chapman had handed it to the ship's master and asked him to give it to the War Office.

The mission to America never materialised and Chapman spent the next year blowing his Abwehr pay on an extended holiday in Norway before being recalled to Germany.

Chapman was now given a series of briefings on Abwehr operations. Before being sent back to Britain on another mission he was awarded the Iron Cross. He was then dropped on to the main road at Six Mile Bottom, Cambridgeshire, in the early hours of 27 June 1944. When he reported to the nearest police station and told his story, the duty officer replied: 'Don't be silly. Go to bed.'

Chapman's response was: 'That's exactly what they told me last time. Ring up your station in Wisbech. They'll remember me.'

After giving MI5 a breakdown of Abwehr operations, he was installed in a flat in Kensington. But the temptations of the £6,000 that the Abwehr had given him proved too much. Chapman was less than discreet to his friends among the criminal fraternity about the source of his new-found wealth, and MI5 was forced to abandon him.

After the war, he wrote an account of his wartime experiences, which was serialised in a French newspaper. He again found himself in court, this time on a charge of breaching the Official Secrets Act. A second attempt at publication was thwarted by a D-Notice, but, as MI5 had found out during the war, Zig-Zag was not easily discouraged, and *The Eddie Chapman Story* eventually appeared in print. A film, *Triple Cross*, in which Chapman was played by Christopher Plummer, came out in 1967.

❧ 12th ❧

Antonio Ordonez, b. 1932, d. 1998

Antonio Ordonez, who has died aged sixty-six, was perhaps the greatest matador of the twentieth century; certainly he was the finest exponent of the bullfighter's art during the 1950s and 1960s, when his rivalry with Luis Miguel Dominguin was celebrated by Ernest Hemingway in his paean to machismo, *The Dangerous Summer*.

Hemingway's admiration for Ordonez began in 1953 when he first saw him fight; in 1959 he spent most of the bullfighting season travelling with the fighter from one corrida to the next. This was the year of what Hemingway called 'the duel', as Ordonez strove to assert his mastery over his own brother-in-law, Dominguin, who had come out of retirement to prove his continued right to the appellation Numero Uno.

While Dominguin fought in the proud and flashy manner of Seville, Ordonez belonged to the antithetical Ronda tradition, whose classical style has a melancholy edge to it. Like Manolete, he was noted for the fluency of his fighting, often drawing the bull past his body as if in slow motion.

This gave his performances an emotional charge none of his contemporaries could match; Kenneth Tynan described his talent as 'wholly lyric', while Hemingway wrote that he 'used the cape as no one alive has ever used it'.

Day after day through the Spanish summer, the two matadors fought on the same sand, bringing bullfighting to its highest pitch for a decade. The pressure began to tell on Dominguin, though Hemingway exaggerated in describing the contest as 'the gradual destruction of one person by another'.

On 30 July, Dominguin was badly gored in Valencia when a gust of wind blew his red cape to one side. Just three weeks later, fighting before he had fully recovered, he was again severely wounded in Bilbao. But Ordonez too had been hurt, and by the time Hemingway published his account of that summer in *Life* magazine in 1960, their dispute had still not been resolved.

Because of the financial problems of both Ordonez and Dominguin, the two men agreed not to fight on the same bills in 1960, much to the relief of Ordonez's wife, Carmen, the sister of Dominguin. At the end of a season fighting in different rings, Dominguin had collected forty-one bulls' ears in forty-two fights, while Ordonez had been awarded a superior eighty-two ears in fifty-six fights.

Antonio Jimenez Ordonez was born on 16 February 1932 in the southern town of Ronda, where modern bullfighting first evolved in the early eighteenth century.

He made his debut in the ring in 1948, became a professional torero in 1951 and soon established a reputation as a fighter in the best classical style. When Dominguin retired from the ring, Ordonez remained to champion the best aspects of a controversial sport and in 1961 won the biggest contract in the history of the ring – £3,500 a fight for five nights in the Plaza de Toros, Madrid.

In 1966, Ordonez suffered one of his most serious injuries, when a bull caught him and left a ten-inch gash in his left thigh. Ordonez struggled to his feet to make another six passes and despatch the bull before being carried semi-conscious from the ring.

There was no doubting Ordonez's courage, although out of the ring he could be hot-tempered. He was not averse to beating up a newspaper critic who gave him a bad notice or claimed that he was developing a paunch.

By the early 1980s, having fought more than 2,000 bulls, Ordonez began to dedicate his time to breeding them instead. He bought a ranch outside Ronda, where the ashes of his friend Orson Welles are buried.

The ashes of Ordonez himself were scattered at the bullring in Ronda, which he owned.

⇒ 13th ⇒

Lord Grade, b. 1906, d. 1998

The Lord Grade, universally known as Lew, who has died aged ninety-one, was a founding father of independent television and always played the exuberant role of an old-time showbiz mogul.

With his nine-inch cigars, his Phantom VI Rolls-Royces, his extravagant self-publicity and his constant readiness to close multi-million-dollar deals over the transatlantic telephone, he became the closest Britain could get to a Sam Goldwyn. A good day in the life of Lew Grade was one on which he got up (as usual before 6 a.m.) with an idea for a new television series, sold it to an American backer by noon, and informed his partners of the deal over lunch.

In his long career he exploited an unrivalled network of contacts among fellow entrepreneurs and international stars, calling in favours from one when negotiations with another flagged. His idea of purgatory, he once said, was 'sitting on a beach in the south of France, sunning myself, with no phone calls to make'.

The Grade brothers – Lew, Bernie (later Lord Delfont), and Leslie – controlled between them a huge slice of the entertainment world. It was not quite rags-to-riches – Lew's autobiography, *Still Dancing* (1987), revealed that his Jewish-Russian parents had in fact been relatively prosperous. But their progress from East End immigrants to the most powerful show-business family in Europe was extraordinary.

Many of the stories about Lew Grade are apocryphal. A true one he told against himself concerned the time he was watching a comedy act in the second half at the Metropolitan Theatre in the Edgware Road. He thought it was top of the bill material and rushed backstage. 'I'm Lew Grade. Your act was amazing. How much are they paying you?' '£25 a week, Mr Grade.' 'Ridiculous, absurd, outrageous. I could get you £200. Who's your agent?' 'You are, Mr Grade.'

Many former employees and colleagues, especially those fallen on hard times, could attest to Grade's generosity. But the image of 'Lovable Lew' (a phrase coined by one of his long-serving publicity aides) did not fit his ruthlessness in business.

Louis Winogradsky was born in the Ukrainian town of Tokmak in 1906. His father was a genial jack-of-all-trades with little business acumen, though he appears once to have owned a small private cinema. It was Lew's formidable mother, a matriarch in the richest Jewish tradition, who in 1912 masterminded their emigration to London, where her brothers were doing well as cabinet makers.

At Rochelle Street School in Bethnal Green, Lew discovered a talent for figures and a strong memory. He put these to use in the family embroidery business, but early visits to the East Ham Palais confirmed that he had also inherited an aptitude for dancing. By the time he was nineteen he had changed his name to Grad (later Grade) and become a professional entertainer. His speciality was doing the Charleston on a tiny table top.

Dancing across Europe, he realised there was more money to be made as an agent. One of his first bookings was a juvenile troupe, Beams' Breezy Babes, led by fourteen-year-old Kathleen Moody, a prodigy with a Gracie Fields voice. Seven years later, when the Grade Agency was on its way to becoming the largest in Europe, she became Mrs Grade. 'The best deal,' Lew liked to say, 'that I ever made.'

In the 1950s, as independent television got off to a shaky start, Grade and his partner Val Parnell effectively took over an under-financed franchise, newly named Associated Television, from Norman Collins and Sir Robert Renwick. For nearly twenty-five years he exploited his ATV franchise, granted to supply the Midland region, in order to produce populist 'action-adventure' series aimed at the American market.

At the same time he kept a shrewd eye on those in high places who needed placating with judicious doses of 'culture'. As boss of ATV, he sold Eugene O'Neill's *Long Day's Journey Into Night* to an unconvinced ABC Network. 'Think of the prestige,' he urged.

Far outweighing such achievements was an unending string of long-running audience-pullers like *The Saint, Danger Man, The Power Game, The Persuaders, The Prisoner* and *Robin Hood*. The unlikely *Thunderbirds* was later to become a cult favourite.

Grade's ATV gave British viewers *Crossroads*, which ran four evenings a week until the IBA cut it back to three. It gave the world the *Muppet Show*, which sold to a record 112 countries.

At the height of his television fame, Grade decided to diversify into feature films, with notably less success. *Raise the Titanic* flopped so badly that Grade joked ruefully: 'It would have been cheaper to lower the Atlantic.'

Grade's career as a television tycoon ended after the Independent Broadcasting Authority decided that their Midland franchise should go to Central Independent Television. Undaunted, in 1985 Grade launched The Grade Company, which he ran until his death. Its products – including a series based on novels by Barbara Cartland – were less than distinguished. But they staved off the lack of occupation that Lew most dreaded.

⤞ 14th ⤝

John Arlott, b. 1914, d. 1991

John Arlott, who has died aged seventy-seven, turned the routine business of cricket commentary into something approaching an art form, so that for thirty-four years his rich and mellow Hampshire tones became an integral part of the English summer.

His style was instantly recognisable not merely by the accent but also by an incomparable blend of poetic imagination, verbal resource, shrewd judgment of character, and ready humour. Arlott was essentially an impressionist, with an eye for the telling irrelevancy; he never descended into mere punditry.

As a phrase-maker he was unmatched. 'Consider Lillee in the field,' he once observed. 'He toils mightily but he does not spin.' Lillee, incidentally, claimed that it was listening to Arlott that had first made him interested in cricket: 'He really made me want to play.'

Apart from the quality of his broadcasts, in sheer volume of output no one approached him. From the first Test of 1946 against India at Lord's he covered an unbroken succession of Tests at home until he retired after the Centenary Test against Australia in 1980. He also commentated on Sunday League games for television, although he never seemed quite at home in a medium that obviated the necessity for word painting.

Arlott the wireless commentator signed off for the last time as though it were a normal occasion – 'and now, after comment by Trevor Bailey, it will be Christopher Martin-Jenkins'. But first his fellow commentators, then (after a loudspeaker announcement) the fielding Australian side and the entire Lord's crowd stood and applauded him – a gesture that was almost too much for this deeply emotional man.

Arlott's contribution to cricket profited from his sense of proportion about its place in the general scheme of things. 'Anybody for whom cricket was everything,' he said, 'wouldn't half be a limited chap.'

He himself was a man of letters, a passionate collector of books, aquatints and glass, a Liberal candidate (at Epping in 1955 and 1959), a lover of France, and, above all, an oenophile strong on theory and even stronger in practice.

Leslie Thomas John Arlott was born on 25 February 1914 at Basingstoke, in the lodge of the cemetery where his grandfather had been registrar, and won a scholarship to Queen Mary's Grammar School. Here he nurtured a deep loathing for the caning headmaster.

In 1926 he went to the Oval to watch the first day of the Test Match against Australia, conceiving his devotion to Jack Hobbs. He began his working career, however, as office boy to the Basingstoke town planning officer, and then became diet clerk at the local mental hospital. In 1934 he joined the police force, and, after a spell in the tough training school at Birmingham, went on the beat in Southampton.

He watched Hampshire play whenever he could, and on one occasion his wildest fantasies were fulfilled when, in an emergency, he was asked to field (in borrowed flannels) for the county against Worcestershire.

During the Blitz he was appointed to the War Emergency Department, and then – having acquired a smattering of Norwegian and German to go with his French – he found himself translated into Detective Constable, Special Branch.

In plain clothes, and out on inquiries, he formed the plan of producing a book of topographical verse, and tried unsuccessfully to engage John Betjeman as a co-editor. The anthology, *Landmarks*, was published in 1943; and next year a book of Arlott's own verse, *Of Period and Place*.

Arlott's breakthrough came when Betjeman mentioned the phenomenon of the 'policeman-poet' to Geoffrey Grigson, then a talks producer with the BBC at Bristol, who proceeded to commission a talk from the prodigy.

Arlott huffily replied that he was not prepared to be exhibited as a freak, but agreed, nevertheless, to present himself for an audition. Grigson noted in his report: 'This man is a natural broadcaster and should be encouraged.' Required to give further evidence of his abilities, Arlott wrote a piece entitled 'The Hampshire Giants', about Hambledon cricket club. Its broadcast constituted Arlott's debut alike as a broadcaster and as a cricket expert.

Arlott was put in charge of two weekly programmes, one of poetry and one of prose. Then, in January 1946, Donald Stevenson, head of the BBC Eastern Service, asked Arlott to broadcast short (and unpaid) reports of the Indian touring team's first two matches. These transmissions were deemed so successful that Arlott was commissioned to persist with them throughout the summer.

At his first Test Match, at Lord's, some of his colleagues did not trouble to disguise their doubts about his cricketing knowledge. But by the end of the season Arlott was firmly established as a specialist broadcaster on the game.

'I have listened to your broadcasts last summer,' 'Lobby' de Lotbiniere, head of outside broadcasts, told the new find, 'and while I think you have a vulgar voice, I think you have a correspondingly interesting mind – would you like to broadcast on next summer's South African tour?' The years after the Second World War were a vintage era for cricket, in particular 1947, when Compton and Edrich indulged in feasts of run-making, and 1948, the year of the all-conquering Australians, a summer that would live in Arlott's memory as the golden season.

After 1950 journalism went hand in hand with his BBC work, most notably as chief cricket correspondent for the *Guardian*. He also covered football for the *Guardian*, and had a lucky escape when he volunteered to cover Manchester United's game against Belgrade in February 1958. In the event the paper's main soccer correspondent decided to go himself, only to be killed at Munich on the return journey.

In 1980 Arlott retired to Alderney, together with his fine collection of wine. This hobby had taken wing after he had provided the editor of the *Evening News* with a sparkling Languedoc for a party. The wine was successfully passed off as champagne, and Arlott became the newspaper's wine correspondent. Thereafter the cellars in his Alresford home – a former pub – began to fill rapidly. He learned as he drank, and the head of Christie's wine department judged that he had never handled a finer collection, which included every first growth of the 1970 clarets.

⊰ 15th ⊱

Christopher Hitchens, b. 1949, d. 2011

Christopher Hitchens, who has died aged sixty-two, described himself as an 'essayist and a contrarian' and, as a journalist, critic, war correspondent and bon vivant, enjoyed a forty-year career as one of the world's most ubiquitous and provocative public intellectuals.

He began as a leading iconoclast of the left and, during the 1970s, was a voluble member of a talented and raffish gang, with Julian Barnes, Martin Amis, Ian McEwan and James Fenton, which gave the *New Statesman* magazine its glittery literary edge. But he got tired of British politics and, in 1981, moved to America where his repeated assaults on such hate figures as Ronald Reagan and Henry Kissinger continued to guarantee him a welcome in radical circles.

All this changed after the 9/11 terrorist attacks on New York and Washington, an event he interpreted as a turning point in 'a war to the finish between everything I love and everything I hate'. He became an outspoken opponent of 'Islamofascism', forging a breach with the left which became a permanent rift after the invasion of Iraq in 2003. While his erstwhile colleagues were out on the streets proclaiming 'Not in Our Name' (a slogan he found nauseating in its 'unstinting self-regard'), Hitchens emerged as one of the fiercest cheerleaders for George W. Bush's strategy of 'regime change'. To the inevitable accusations of betrayal (George Galloway described him as the 'first ever metamorphosis of a butterfly back into a slug'), Hitchens responded with characteristic gusto: such attacks, he said, washed off him 'like jizz off a porn star's face'.

But, as Hitchens confessed in his memoir *Hitch-22* (2010), there had always been a 'Janus-faced' side to his personality. He acknowledged that alongside the donkey-jacketed revolutionary 'Chris' of his student years, there was the suave, good-looking and socially ambitious 'Christopher' – 'Hypocritchens', as he was known at Balliol – who enjoyed the company of 'confident young men who owned fast cars' and frequented the Union and the Gridiron Club.

The young man spraying pro-Vietcong slogans on car plant walls or marching the streets toting some insurgent flag might, the same evening, be found at a right-wing dining club happily gobbling up a pudding called 'bombe Hanoi'. Friends later joked that the sentence least likely to emerge from Hitchens' mouth was: 'I don't care how rich you are, I'm not coming to your party.'

Though he claimed to keep 'two sets of books' when it came to political purpose and social ambition, his 'Mr Both Ways' approach was as much intellectual as social. He took pride in 'asking annoying questions at every opportunity' and found it difficult to see a sacred cow without lobbing a hand grenade. His more eminent targets included Mother Teresa (whom he portrayed as a fundamentalist Catholic bigot who glad-handed totalitarian regimes); Bill Clinton (the subject in 1999 of *No One Left to Lie to: The Triangulations of William Jefferson Clinton*); and God (the target in 2007 of *God Is Not Great: How Religion Poisons Everything*).

The elder of two sons (his younger brother is the journalist and author Peter Hitchens), Christopher Eric Hitchens was born on 13 April 1949 in Portsmouth, where his father, a naval officer, was stationed.

His mother, Yvonne, a glamorous but tragic figure whose carefully concealed Jewish ancestry Christopher would discover only when he was in his forties, eventually left her husband for an unfrocked vicar, with whom she became a devotee of the Maharishi Mahesh Yogi ('the sinister windbag who had brought enlightenment to the Beatles in the summer of love'), and with whom she died in a suicide pact in an Athens hotel when Christopher was twenty-four.

At the Leys School in Cambridge, Christopher discovered a passion for literature, dabbled in homosexuality and was introduced to the pleasures of Marxism by the headmaster who, in a vain attempt to inoculate him against such a heresy, presented him with a copy of the Communist Manifesto.

He developed all three interests at Balliol College, Oxford, where he went up ostensibly to read PPE, but devoted more energy to sit-in and picket-line duties (as well as joining the Labour Party, he became a member of the Trotskyist International Socialists) and to cultivating friendships among a camp and reactionary circle of students and academics.

After graduating with an inevitable Third, Hitchens launched his career in journalism as 'social science correspondent' at *The Times*, a 'Gogol-like ghost job which I held for six months before its editor said something to me that made it impossible for me to go on working for him'. (In a footnote in his memoir, Hitchens noted that the exact words were: 'You're fired.')

In the 1970s, as well as working as a freelance, he took various 'mainstream' jobs, from being a researcher for the Insight team at the *Sunday Times* to working as a foreign correspondent for the *Daily Express*, before joining the *New Statesman* as a staff writer and editor under Anthony Howard. At the same time he became a regular at the famous Bloomsbury 'Friday lunches' at which such luminaries as Clive James, Peter Porter, the Amises (*père et fils*), Craig Raine and others would swap jokes and gossip. But by the 1979 election (in which, for the first time, he did not vote Labour) he was starting to feel 'the strong gravitational pull of the great American planet'.

Hitchens' decision to settle in the United States was a turning point in his life, both personally and politically. As a columnist for *The Nation*, he continued to fulminate against familiar targets – American imperialism, military fascism, religious fundamentalism – but his rightward political odyssey rolled inexorably on, driven by a disgust with the empty pieties of the left and an appreciation of the dynamism of the American political tradition.

Hitchens' ideological shift was driven also by a concern at the growing threat of Islamic extremism to Western freedoms. He was appalled by the 'tepid reaction' of the European left following Ayatollah Khomeini's issue of a fatwa against his friend Salman Rushdie, and also by the events of 11 September 2001 which, in his view, opened up a 'whole new terrain of struggle'.

Among other causes, Hitchens, a heavy smoker and drinker for much of his life, had been a vocal defender of smoking, and staunch opponent of smoking bans. When commentators pointed out that smoking and drinking are also the main causes of squamous-cell carcinomas of the kind with which he himself was eventually diagnosed, Hitchens was honest enough to admit that he had 'been in denial for some time, knowingly burning the candle at both ends and finding that it often gives a lovely light'.

Though notorious for his view of religion as 'a terrible fetter on the mind, and a maker of slaves', he claimed to be touched by the number of Christians who were praying for his soul.

⇜ 16th ⇝

The 4th Earl Russell, b. 1921, d. 1987

The 4th Earl Russell, who has died aged sixty-six, was the eccentric elder son of the philosopher Bertrand Russell and caused the occasional sensation in the House of Lords with his outrageous speeches.

In 1978, during a debate on aid for victims of crime, Lord Russell referred to modern society and the effects of automation in factories. Then he said: 'There should be universal leisure for all, and a standing wage sufficient to provide life without working ought to be supplied ... so that everybody becomes a leisured aristocrat – aristocrats are Marxists.'

Peers seemed startled as he continued: 'In a completely reorganised modern society, women's lib would be realised by girls being given a house of their own by the age of twelve and three-quarters of the wealth of the State being given to the girls so that marriage would be abolished and the girl could have as many husbands as she liked ...'

Finally Russell told the House of Lords: 'Mr Brezhnev and Mr Carter are really the same person'.

⇜ 17th ⇝

Kim Jong-il, b. 1942, d. 2011

Kim Jong-il, the North Korean dictator, who has died aged sixty-nine, presided over the systematic impoverishment and starvation of millions of his people, while enjoying the life of a spoiled playboy – fast cars, fast women, cellars of vintage French wines, and a passion for *Rambo* and Daffy Duck videos.

The son of North Korea's self-styled 'Great Leader' Kim il Sung, Kim Jong-il (known as 'Dear Leader') became the first ruler of a Communist state to gain power through inheritance – on his father's death in July 1994. A pudgy, unprepossessing figure with bouffant hair and platform shoes, Kim Jong-il was initially thought to lack the elder Kim's low cunning and populist flair. Many predicted that his tenure would be short-lived. Yet after his accession, it became clear that he was his father's son – unpredictable, wily and ruthlessly determined to sustain his power by any means.

Officially, Kim Jong-il was born in 1941 on the slopes of Mount Paektu – the mythical birthplace of the Korean people. In search of miracles with which to deify the young Jong-il, state hagiographers borrowed heavily from Christian tradition. It was said that a bright star shone over Jong-il's nativity, although instead of a stable he was born in a log cabin. The humble abode stands to this day – as it should, since it was in fact built only in 1986.

The reality is that Kim was born on 16 February 1942 close to Khabarovsk, Siberia, where his father had taken refuge from the Japanese, then occupying Korea. He had a troubled upbringing: a younger brother drowned in childhood, and his mother died when he was seven years old, shortly after his father had been installed as Stalin's puppet in North Korea. In 1950 the Korean War broke out, and Kim was sent to Manchuria, not returning home until three years later when the war ended.

Of Kim's life before 1994, little is known for certain. His ascent to power began in 1975, when he was reportedly made a member of North Korea's politburo and put in charge of the cultural scene. The six operas he composed during a period of two years were said to be 'better than any mankind had ever created', though, sadly, no recordings appear to have been allowed out of the country.

One thing that was never in question was Kim's passion for the cinema. In 1978 he ordered the abduction of a South Korean director, Shin Sang Ok, and his wife, an actress. They were brought to Pyongyang, locked up for five years in prisons and re-education camps, then released to 'assist' with the development of the North Korean film industry. They escaped after eight years, and their account of their time in the North represents one of the best sources of information about Kim. On their first meeting, Kim asked the director: 'What do you think of my physique? Small as a midget's turd, aren't I?'

In 1980 Kim was officially designated 'Dear Leader' and his father's acknowledged heir; coincidentally, the North Korean Academy of Social Sciences expunged the definition of hereditary rule as 'a reactionary custom of exploitative societies' from its Dictionary of Political Terminologies.

Even after he had been publicly anointed as successor, Kim kept a low profile. Indeed, so complete was the secrecy that it was only in 1992 that the CIA learned that Kim had two children, already grown up. Meanwhile, direct evidence of his continued existence derived from Thai and Swedish prostitutes who had apparently been flown in especially for the Dear Leader. There were stories of his arranging parties and then watching the entire proceedings in private on video monitors.

The news of Kim il Sung's death in 1994 was accompanied by wild scenes of public mourning in North Korea. After his father's elaborate public funeral, Kim Jong-il dropped out of sight and it was some time before it was clear that he had established his grip on power. Then it quickly became clear that Kim was no more prepared to expose his country to foreign scrutiny to save his people than his father had been. The few foreign aid workers who received visas were kept penned up in Pyongyang while Kim proclaimed that 'Imperialist aid is a noose of plunder and subjugation'.

It is estimated that between two and three million North Koreans succumbed to starvation in Kim's first decade in power – a tenth of the population. Escapees spoke of scavenging bands of skeletal orphans gnawing on bark and leaves, and human flesh being sold for meat in the country's depleted markets.

Meanwhile Kim was widely credited with masterminding the country's weapons programme. If so, he played his cards well, demanding trade concessions and diplomatic recognition, and winning time during which the programme could develop.

Yet a few years later Kim the warmonger was replaced by Kim the peacemaker, intent on seizing the olive branch held out by South Korea, which had adopted a policy of engagement. In 2000 he embraced the cause of reunification between the two countries in a historic meeting with its President Kim Dae Jung, but the two sides were subsequently unable to agree on any substantial improvement in their relations.

More promisingly, a visit by President Clinton's Secretary of State Madeleine Albright to Pyongyang in the same year extracted a promise that North Korea would not pursue its nuclear weapons programme if America would agree to pay for a nuclear energy facility. After the visit Madeleine Albright said she did not find Kim as weird as his reputation suggested, describing him as 'perfectly rational, isolated but not uninformed'.

But Kim's apparent willingness to engage in dialogue faded with the arrival of the new Bush administration and the President's declaration in his 2002 State of the Union address that North Korea, Iran and Iraq made up an 'axis of evil'. Angered by the apparent reversal in American policy, Kim reverted to his eccentric persona again, openly boasting that, contrary to previous assurances, North Korea had not halted its nuclear weapons programme after all and that a project to produce highly enriched uranium had been under way since 1998. Washington promptly cut off heavy-fuel shipments and food aid, plunging the North Koreans into further misery, while leaving the regime unscathed.

Later there were signs of a thaw in relations between Kim and his detractors in the West. In 2007 he announced that his nation would disable its main nuclear reactor. He also held a summit meeting with Roh Moo-hyun, President of South Korea, at which the two leaders agreed to seek a peace treaty that would formally end the Korean War.

Away from high politics, Kim Jong-il was said to take pleasure in caviar, Hennessy Cognac and his troupe of 2,000 dancing girls, recruited from the country's high schools as teenagers to perform in 'pleasure groups' in the dictator's 32-odd villas and palaces – before being pensioned off at twenty-five. Each pleasure group was composed of three teams: a 'satisfaction team', which performed sexual services; a 'happiness team', which provided massage; and a 'dancing and singing team'. Visitors were treated to choreographed stripteases, though only Kim was allowed to avail himself of the other services.

In 2008 it was suggested by a Japanese historian that Kim Jong-il had actually died in 2003, and had, since that point, been replaced by four body doubles for public appearances.

≋ 18th ≋

Susan Travers, b. 1909, d. 2003

Susan Travers, who has died in Paris aged ninety-four, was the only woman to have joined the French Foreign Legion; English by birth, she came to regard the Legion as her true family and played a key part in the breakout by its troops from Rommel's siege of the desert fortress of Bir Hakeim in 1942.

When war came in 1939, Susan Travers was living in the south of France, where she had grown up, and joined the French Red Cross. Hitherto she had led the rather inconsequential life of a socialite, but the challenges that now faced her gave her a purpose. Although her dislike of blood and illness made her a less than ideal nurse, she soon realised her ambition to become an ambulance driver, and in 1940 accompanied the French expeditionary force sent to help the Finns in the Winter War against the Russians.

France fell to the Nazis while she was in Scandinavia, and so she made her way to London, where she volunteered as a nurse with General de Gaulle's Free French forces. She was attached to the 13th Demi-Brigade of the Legion Etrangère (about half the Legion had stayed loyal, the others throwing in their lot with Vichy) and sailed for West Africa, where she witnessed the abortive attack on Dakar.

She was then posted to Eritrea and took on the hazardous job of driving for senior officers. The desert roads were often mined and subject to enemy attack, and she survived a number of crashes, as well as being wounded by shellfire.

Her dash and pluck quickly endeared her to the legionnaires, who nicknamed her 'La Miss'. For her part, she admired the Legion's code of '*honneur et fidelité*', and formed good friendships with many of her comrades, among them Pierre Messmer, later Prime Minister of France.

She also enjoyed several romantic liaisons, notably with a tall White Russian prince, Colonel Dimitri Amilakvari, but none of these proved lasting. Then, in June 1941, her world was transformed. The cause was Colonel Marie-Pierre Koenig, her commanding officer, whose new driver she became.

Although he was married, they quickly fell for each other – he wooing her with roses when she was in hospital with jaundice – and although it was impossible to show affection for one another in public, they enjoyed a happy few months together while posted to Beirut.

This idyll was ended when their unit was attached to the 8th Army and, in the spring of 1942, sent to hold the bleak fort of Bir Hakeim, at the southern tip of the

Allies' defensive line in the Western Desert. At the start of May, Italian and German forces attacked in strength, Rommel having told his men that it would take them fifteen minutes to crush any opposition; the 8th Army hoped the fort would last a week. Instead, under Koenig's command, the 1,000 legionnaires and 1,500 other Allied troops held out for fifteen days, and Bir Hakeim became for all Frenchmen who resisted the Nazis a symbol of hope and defiance.

With all ammunition and – in temperatures of 51C – all water exhausted, Koenig resolved to lead a breakout at night through the minefields and three concentric cordons of German panzers that encircled Bir Hakeim. Susan Travers was to drive both him and Amilakvari.

With tracer lighting up the night sky and tank shells hurtling towards her, Susan Travers pressed the accelerator of her Ford to the floor and burst through the German lines, blazing a trail for the other Allied vehicles to follow. Although her car was struck by a score of bullets, and on one occasion she drove into a laager of parked panzers, she reached the British lines.

Of the 3,700 Allied troops who had been at Bir Hakeim, more than 2,400 escaped with her, including 650 legionnaires, and Koenig became the hero of France. Susan Travers was awarded the Croix de Guerre for her feat.

With Koenig's career in the ascendant, he ended his affair with Susan Travers soon afterwards, much to her grief. Nevertheless, she remained with the Legion until the end of the war, acting as both a driver and a nurse to the wounded and the dying. By May 1945, 'I had become the person I'd always wanted to be' and, not wanting any other life, she applied to join the Legion officially.

She took care to omit her sex from the form, and her application was accepted. She was appointed an officer in the logistics division, and so became the only woman ever to serve with the Legion.

Susan Travers was born in London on 23 September 1909. During the First World War her father, a naval officer, had been put in charge of marine transport at Marseilles (where his own father had once been British Consul), and in 1921 he decided to move the family to Cannes.

Being a girl, she had been more or less ignored by her father and her only brother, and by her late teens had developed a craving for male company: 'Most of all,' she wrote later, 'I wanted to be wicked.' Sent to a finishing school in Florence, she succumbed at seventeen for the first time to the blandishments of a man, a hotel manager named Hannibal.

By her own admission, she spent the next decade in a rather vapid, if enjoyable, round of skiing and tennis parties all over Europe, thinking nothing of travelling to Budapest or Belgrade for a week's entertainment.

With her gamine figure, striking features and blue eyes, she was a constant and willing object of male attention. It was a careless approach to life brought to an abrupt halt by the onset of conflict in 1939.

After the war she served for a time in Indo-China, but resigned her commission in 1947 to bring up her children from her marriage that year to a Legion NCO, Nicholas Schlegelmilch. He contracted an illness in the tropics in 1949 and, after spending eighteen months in hospital, was never the same as before. Nevertheless, they remained together; after his death in 1995 she continued to live in France.

In 1956, Susan Travers was awarded the Medaille Militaire in recognition of her bravery at Bir Hakeim. The medal was pinned on her by Koenig, by then Minister of Defence.

His Honour James Pickles, b. 1925, d. 2010

His Honour James Pickles, who has died aged eighty-five, was for many years the most notoriously outspoken member of the bench.

His sentencing policy – or rather lack of it – was thought deficient even by the tolerant standards of the English judiciary. Pregnant women and mothers of tiny babies were sent down for minor offences while more serious offenders were released to walk the streets.

Meanwhile, he was liable to offer ammunition to *Private Eye*'s vision of the out-of-touch Mr Justice Cocklecarrot with observations in court such as: 'Who are the Beatles?' Of the Spice Girls, he once said: 'They arrived on the scene breasts first, but I don't know their names.'

Never short of an outrageous opinion, at various times Pickles described the Duchess of York as a 'scrubber' and Freddie Mercury as a 'greedy bisexual'. Meanwhile the former Lord Chief Justice Lord Lane was a 'dinosaur'.

❧ 19th ❧

David Lloyd, b. 1940, d. 2010

David Lloyd, who has died aged seventy, was a colonial officer and big-game hunter turned conservationist; having dissipated his inherited wealth in an uncompromising pursuit of pleasure, he eventually set about saving Kasanka, a neglected game reserve which he re-established as Zambia's first privately funded national park.

Edward David Mortimer Lloyd was born at Llangoedmor, Cardigan, to Captain Edward Lloyd and his wife Ella (née Phillips) on 15 May 1940. Educated at Cheltenham College, Lloyd joined the Colonial Service in 1960 and was posted to Northern Rhodesia, now Zambia.

Lloyd resigned from the Colonial Service shortly after Zambian independence and embarked on an estate management course at London University. The following year, 1966, his father died.

With his new-found independence, Lloyd swiftly abandoned his studies and departed once again for Africa. He spent a season as a professional hunter with Norman Carr in Zambia's Luangwa Valley and then joined the Kenya Wildlife Department as a ranger. Posted to the Northern Frontier District, where the Shifta War had descended into disorganised banditry and a high level of violence, Lloyd was involved in more than one shoot-out and decided it was not suitable employment for a man with a fortune still to enjoy.

During the 1970s he was involved in various hunting ventures, more often as gentleman adventurer than professional hunter, and also travelled extensively in South America and the Far East. His hunting activities could be erratic. On one occasion he was hired to take some French dignitaries on safari in Zaire. Having arrived in Kinshasa, he promptly disappeared. When another member of the team arrived some days later, his first task was to track Lloyd down. Armed with a passport photo and $500, he wrote: 'I began my first hunt in Zaire through the red-light district of Kinshasa; often getting close to my quarry as he remained just one drink ahead of me.' When Lloyd was finally run to ground enjoying a well-earned breakfast at the Holiday Inn, he was relieved of command but, typically, proceeded with the trip anyway, as a client.

By this time he had collected a band of followers, many of whom were sustained by his extraordinary generosity and severe lack of commercial discipline. Towards the end of the decade, he was said to have charged more than £200,000 – around one million in today's money – to American Express alone. The income from his estates could not support such expenditure, and sales (Lloyd was said to be running through 'a farm a year') were inevitable.

When his mother moved out of Coedmore House he finally attempted to do something with the estate. Teaming up with the wildlife biologist Peter Moss, he set aside a parcel of land on the banks of the River Teifi to create a nature reserve. The Cardigan Wildlife Park, which featured bison, deer, wild boar and wolves alongside rare breeds of sheep, cattle and horse, proved to be a success when it opened in 1978, picking up awards and attracting 50,000 visitors a year.

Four years later it achieved national notoriety when eight wolves escaped. For ten days the beasts created fear and havoc in the surrounding area, killing some thirty animals until all were hunted down and shot by police and local marksmen.

Lloyd's African ventures were not faring any better. Then, while flying back to Lusaka from Zambia's Northern Province, he passed over Kasanka, a small national park bordering the Congo Pedicle that was in danger of closure due to rampant poaching. Out of curiosity, he decided to visit; there were no roads or bridges, and no tourists had penetrated the park for many years, but he managed to explore a little on foot. On hearing the crack of gunshots he concluded that, if there was still poaching, there must be animals. Impressed by the wide variety of habitats, he decided to try to save the park from total depletion and the threat of losing its national park status.

He and Gary Williams, a local farmer who had also explored the park a little, used their own resources to employ scouts and build roads, bridges and temporary camps. The Zambian government, which had been unable to manage the park itself, encouraged their efforts. Crucially, they secured the backing of local communities and of Chief Chitambo IV, whose great-grandfather, the first chief Chitambo, had received David Livingstone in 1873, when the explorer was on his deathbed. Livingstone's heart was buried under a tree at a spot a few miles outside the park, a place now marked by a simple stone monument.

The Kasanka Trust was set up to formalise their position and help raise funds, and soon attracted attention from conservationists. Tourism then started to bring in a little money and, by 1990, the Zambian authorities were sufficiently impressed by progress to sign an agreement allowing the Trust officially to manage the park. Lloyd's understanding of, and affection for, local Zambians – he had a firm grasp of four tribal languages and apparent immunity to threats of witchcraft – was crucial to this success.

Today the populations of hippo, elephant, sable antelope and hartebeest are recovering. The puku antelope, once reduced to a few hundred, now exceed 5,000 and there are sizable herds of the swamp-dwelling sitatunga, reedbuck and waterbuck, as well as groups of the rare blue monkey.

Kasanka was Lloyd's home for the last two decades; the bank had forced the sale of his last bolt-hole in Britain, a flat in Chelsea's Flood Street, after Lloyd stood as guarantor for yet another failing safari business. His friends were now getting old, or had died, and he no longer had the money to 'play'. He was happiest at his rondavel in the park surrounded by the community he had helped support.

Kim Peek, b. 1951, d. 2009

Kim Peek, who has died aged fifty-eight, was the model for the autistic character Raymond Babbitt in the 1988 film *Rain Man*, starring Dustin Hoffman.

Hoffman's portrayal of a middle-aged savant's complex interaction with the world through astonishing mental facilities and childlike emotions earned him an Oscar for best actor. But it was Peek, who suffered from agenesis of the corpus callosum (a condition similar to autism), whom Hoffman and Barry Morrow – *Rain Man*'s writer, who also won an Oscar – acknowledged as the inspiration behind the performance.

Kim Peek was born on 11 November 1951 in Salt Lake City, Utah – both his parents were Mormons. Despite his mother's uneventful pregnancy, Kim's head was 30 per cent larger than normal at birth. He was a sluggish baby who cried frequently, and doctors soon discovered that he had a blister inside his skull that had damaged the left hemisphere of his brain, which controls language and motor skills.

By the time he was nine months old he was expected to be mentally impaired for life. His parents were advised to place him in an institution, but they dismissed the idea, deciding to bring him up normally alongside their other son and daughter.

They were soon astounded by his progress. At the age of sixteen months Kim taught himself to read children's books. When he was three he consulted a dictionary to clarify the meaning of the word 'confidential'; it was then that his parents realised that he could also read newspapers. Yet for all his brilliance, his oversized head required physical support because of its weight; and, unusually, he was unable to walk until he was four.

When Kim was six, a visit to Utah by the renowned brain surgeon Peter Lindstrom resulted in his being offered a lobotomy. His parents declined, and Kim went on to memorise the entire Bible before his seventh birthday. At this point he was sent to a local school, but was expelled on his first day for being disruptive. By the time he was fourteen, Kim had completed the high school curriculum.

Before the release of *Rain Man* – by which time he was thirty-seven – Peek had an insular existence, knowing only about twenty people. Unable to describe his condition, or to dress himself, cook, shave or brush his teeth without help, he was looked after by his mother, Jeanne, until 1981, when his parents divorced. Thereafter his father provided the supervision he required.

At eighteen he had been given a job working in the accounts department of a community centre. Spare time was devoted to absorbing literature. He read and immediately memorised thousands of texts, including the complete works of Shakespeare. He used telephone directories for exercises in mental arithmetic, adding each column of seven-digit numbers together in his head until he reached figures in the trillions.

On a rare excursion away from home in 1984, he attended the national conference of the Association of Retarded Citizens in Arlington, Texas, and it was there that he was 'discovered' by Barry Morrow. After spending four hours with Peek, the screenwriter approached Fran Peek, asking him if he realised that his son knew every postcode, area code, and road number in every state across America. He urged Fran to share his son with the world.

Not wishing Kim to become part of a freak show, Fran ignored the request. Two years later, however, Morrow contacted him to explain that a film studio had just bought a script he had written.

The story of a selfish yuppie who discovers that an autistic brother he never knew existed has inherited their father's fortune outright, *Rain Man* put Dustin Hoffman's acting skills to the test in the lead role. It was Peek's rapid monotone, rocking motions, ability to count cards and childlike emotions that Hoffman copied for the part.

Neuroscientists who conducted tests discovered that Peek had no corpus callosum, the membrane that separates the two hemispheres of the brain and filters information. This meant that Peek's brain was effectively the equivalent of a giant databank, giving him his photographic memory. He was also the only savant known to science who could read two pages of a book simultaneously – one with each eye, regardless of whether it was upside down or sideways on. His ability to retain 98 per cent of the information he absorbed led to his designation 'megasavant'.

Never having any romantic inclinations, Kim Peek did not marry and had no children. His favourite possession was the Oscar which Morrow won for writing the Best Screenplay at the 1989 Oscars. Morrow gave it to Peek, who took it with him whenever he travelled.

⪦ **20**th ⪧

Professor Carl Sagan, b. 1934, d. 1996

Professor Carl Sagan, the American astronomer who has died aged sixty-two, was zealous in his belief that science, and the stars, could be explained to everyone. He made his academic discipline seem a thrilling quest and his conviction that intelligent life existed elsewhere in space gripped the public imagination.

His contribution to the study of the planets was enormous. For most of his career he was Professor of Astronomy at Cornell University, New York. He was also an adviser to many of Nasa's space projects, briefing the Apollo crews, during the 1960s and 1970s. Above all, he strove tirelessly, through books and television, to popularise the study of the universe.

Carl Edward Sagan was born in New York on 9 November 1934, the son of a Russian immigrant tailor. The family moved to New Jersey, where Carl was educated at Rahway High School. He graduated from the University of Chicago in 1954, and gained his MSc in Physics there in 1956.

In March 1961 he published a paper in the journal *Science*, re-evaluating existing information about Venus. Sagan suggested that the planet could be made habitable for humans by seeding the upper atmosphere with algae, which would live off water vapour and survive the strong ultraviolet light and high temperatures. Absorbing carbon dioxide and steam, the algae would reduce the temperature and produce oxygen.

He went on to prove that life could survive in the thin, oxygen-free atmosphere of Mars, though he proposed that markings on the planet surface had nothing to do with life. Mariner 9, which mapped the planet in 1971, proved his thesis correct. He also showed that life could not have travelled to Earth from anywhere else in space – the distances were too great and the radiation too intense.

In 1968, Sagan became director of the Laboratory for Planetary Studies at Cornell. There he first turned his attention to Jupiter, the biggest planet, using the Orbiting Astronomical Observatory to look for signs of organic molecules – more clues to the origin of life. Jupiter has a deep atmosphere, and somewhere in it, at moderate temperatures, with the water and organic compounds known to exist, Sagan thought life might exist.

Although some astronomers remain sceptical, Sagan was convinced that intelligent life is abundant elsewhere in the universe, even if not in our solar system. It was his idea to affix images of the human body to the outside of the Jupiter probes Pioneer 10 and 11, together with a map of where they came from, in case any being should meet them once they left the solar system. In 1995 Pioneer 11 left the solar system for the 'shoreless sea' of interstellar space, where it is expected to offer its clues to all-comers for some 100 million years.

But he had concerns about life on earth. In 1983, Sagan and the biologist Paul Ehrlich began a long-running debate by proposing the 'nuclear winter' theory. They pointed out that if, in a nuclear war, only 10 per cent of existing nuclear weapons were used, enough matter would be blown into the stratosphere to initiate an artificial 'wintry night' that would last several months at least – long enough to put human life on Earth in serious danger of extinction.

In the mid-1970s Sagan complained that NASA was allowing public interest in space to die because it was unable to explain it simply. 'There's nothing that can't be explained to a layman,' he said. He duly became a national figure in 1980 when he presented a television series called *Cosmos*, which he co-wrote with his second wife. The series was watched by 500 million people worldwide – the greatest audience ever recorded for a science programme – and the accompanying book sold over two million copies in twenty countries. His numerous other books included the novel *Contact* (1986), which focuses on the first contact with extraterrestrial intelligence.

⇥ 21st ⇤

Stanley Flashman, b. 1930, d. 1999

Stanley Flashman, who has died aged sixty-nine, styled himself 'King of the Ticket Touts'; he subsequently enjoyed a colourful spell as chairman of Barnet Football Club.

In the 1960s and 70s, 'Fat Stan' reckoned to be able to get hold of any ticket for a price. Although he normally handled such events as Wimbledon, the FA Cup final and West End premieres, he also claimed to have obtained – 'from a public servant in a high position' – invitations to Princess Anne's wedding.

'I call myself a ticket broker,' said Flashman. 'Some people call me a tout and some people call me a spiv. They can call me what they like if the colour of their money is right.'

For many years, his 'office' was a council flat in King's Cross, to which he commuted by Mercedes from a substantial mock-Tudor house in Hertfordshire. He was evicted from the former in 1981 after a High Court judge described the purpose to which he put the flat as an 'absolute outrage'. Nevertheless, the judge found Flashman an 'endearing personality'.

Stanley Flashman was born in 1930 in east London, the son of a tailor. Educated locally, he began his trading career in Houndsditch, selling pots and pans and sheets and ties, making a healthy £35 a week.

It was while supporting Tottenham Hotspur football team at White Hart Lane in the early 1960s that he spotted an even more profitable alternative. 'I saw the boys selling tickets outside the ground. I bought a couple, sold them to a punter and made £10. In a couple of hours, I'd made £40.'

By the end of the decade, Flashman ran the biggest ticket touting business in the country. Although many disapproved of his activities – a Labour MP unsuccessfully attempted to have touting banned – Flashman's connections among football players ensured a constant supply of tickets for big games.

In 1985, Flashman was approached by Barnet Football Club, then languishing in the Vauxhall Conference League with debts of £80,000. Although discouraged by his accountant, Flashman promptly bought the club, whose fortunes then steadily began to improve.

Crowds increased tenfold to more than 3,000, and the club finished second in the league three times during the late 1980s. Yves Saint Laurent – with whom Flashman had 'done a bit of business' – provided slacks and blazers for the players to wear to their away matches. The club also raised £1 million in transfer fees over five years and began to pay its own way.

Things, however, soon started to go wrong. In 1992 the players, complaining that their wages had not been paid, asked to be transferred en masse. Later that year, Barnet were found guilty of breaching accounting regulations and fined £50,000. One 9,000 crowd had, for example, been put down in the books as 4,881.

Flashman resigned as chairman in 1993 and shortly afterwards was declared bankrupt. He was succeeded as chairman by an accountant.

⇜ 22nd ⇝

Jacques Mayol, b. 1927, d. 2001

Jacques Mayol, who has died aged seventy-four, was one of the most remarkable divers of his generation; in 1983, aged fifty-six, he set the world record by diving 347 feet (105 metres) with a single breath.

Mayol was able to hold his breath for five minutes when motionless, and four minutes when active. Believing free diving to be a matter of retaining oxygen in the bloodstream, he used meditation techniques and yoga to slow his heart rate and oxygen consumption. To the astonishment of the medical establishment, his pulse would drop from seventy to twenty beats per minute while diving – something which would cause most people to pass out.

In 1984, the director Luc Besson approached Mayol about making a film centred on his rivalry with fellow freediver Enzo Maiorca. The film, *The Big Blue* (1988), starred Jean-Marc Barr as Mayol. But where the hero of *The Big Blue* saw freediving as a sport, for Mayol it was inextricably linked to his understanding of the human condition and to his love of the ocean and of dolphins.

'The sea is my lover,' the Frenchman often told interviewers. 'I make love to her when I dive.'

Born in Shanghai in 1927 to French parents, Jacques Mayol spent the first thirteen years of his life in Asia. He first became interested in diving on family holidays in Japan, and was undeterred when his father died in a diving accident.

As a young man, Mayol won several European contests among freedivers, who would cling to weighted, falling sleds, and were judged purely on how deep they were able to fall. The contests were suspended after a number of participants died.

With his Italian rival, Enzo Maiorca, Mayol continued to extend the boundaries of freediving, descending 60 metres (197 feet) off the coast of Miami in 1966, then 100 metres (330 feet) ten years later – the first freediver to plunge so deep.

It was in Miami that, in 1955, Mayol met the dolphin Clown (the mother of Flipper, of the 1960s television series) at the Miami Seaquarium. He later said, 'I learned everything from her,' and earned the sobriquet 'dolphin man'.

⇥ 23rd ⇤

Lieutenant-Colonel Eric Wilson, b. 1912, d. 2008

Lieutenant-Colonel Eric Wilson, who has died aged ninety-six, was awarded a Victoria Cross for his gallant defence against a large Italian force during the East African campaign in August 1940; the award was originally posthumous since Wilson was thought to have been killed in action.

When the Italians, with 350,000 troops in Abyssinia and Eritrea, invaded British Somaliland, which was defended by 1,500 men, they threatened control of the entrance to the Red Sea and British positions from Aden to Suez. As they headed for Berbera, on the coast, a meagre Allied force began to search for a defensive position. Most of the terrain was flat, but parallel to the sea lay the rugged Golis Hills, with an 8,000ft pass, where the Allies chose to make their stand.

Wilson, an acting captain with the Somaliland Camel Corps, was given the vital task of siting the corps' machine guns on four small hills of the Tug Argan Pass – named Black, Knobbly, Mill and Observation – though they were too widely separated to cover their entire vista. He placed himself on Observation, which commanded the widest arc of fire, but was tremendously exposed.

As two battalions of Blackshirts, with three brigades of colonial troops and artillery, appeared on all sides on the morning of 11 August, Wilson's machine gun received a hit which knocked it off its mounting – though he and his three Somali gunners soon had it back in action. Then another shell came straight into the embrasure of their post, killing the Somali sergeant standing next to Wilson, and severely wounding Wilson in the right shoulder and left eye; his spectacles were broken, and the fragments could be seen under his skin ever afterwards.

Repairing and remounting the gun, he poured down fire on enemy troops advancing on Mill Hill in the afternoon. This inflicted such heavy casualties that the Italians brought up a pack battery to within 700 yards which fired back over open sights until it was hit in turn by the defenders' only artillery, the 1st East Africa Light Battery.

A heavy downpour brought a respite. But next morning the Italians began to work their way in small parties up through the scrub, concentrating their field artillery on Wilson's position. On 13 August the enemy overran the artillery position on Mill Hill. An order to withdraw was sent to Wilson's company but never arrived. Next day, two of the other machine-gun posts were destroyed, yet Wilson, now suffering from malaria as well, kept his own post in action until finally overrun at 5 p.m.

When news of the action reached London, Wilson was believed to have been killed in the final assault, and his VC was gazetted two months later. But after medical treatment, he was put in a prison camp at Adi Ugri in Eritrea. Four months later a captured RAF officer was surprised to meet the 'late' Captain Wilson, and informed him of his award.

Wilson received his medal from King George VI at Buckingham Palace. A tall, shy, nervous man, his mother described him as 'such a dear boy and so timid'.

Eric Charles Twelves Wilson, the son of the rector of Hunsdon, Hertfordshire, was born on 2 October 1912 at Sandown on the Isle of Wight and educated at Marlborough.

In 1937 he volunteered for the King's African Rifles, supporting the colonial administration upcountry in Tanganyika; he became a Nyassa speaker.

After recovering from his wounds at Tug Argan, Wilson served in North Africa as adjutant of the Long Range Desert Group, demonstrating a knowledge of the desert which greatly aided its work behind German lines.

Wilson retired from the Army in 1949 and became a colonial officer in Tanganyika (now Tanzania), where he became fluent in four Bantu languages. Above all, however, he remained greatly attached to the Somali people, whom he would 'back against all-comers for cheerful toughness'.

His youngest son, the photographer Hamish Wilson, maintained the family link with the Somalis, fighting in 1991 in the war to establish a separate state of Somaliland in the north of the country. He was the only European present at the liberation of its capital, Hargeysa. He made a television programme about it, visiting and fighting at the same places as his father, and fighting alongside the children of men his father had known and fought with.

❧ 24th ❧

Walter Hudson, b. 1945, d. 1991

Walter Hudson, who has died aged forty-six, was once listed in *The Guinness Book of World Records* as the heaviest man on earth.

About 6ft tall and 9ft around, with cherubic features set off by pigtails braided in the Cherokee style, he long devoted himself to the pleasures of the table.

In 1987 Hudson – then tipping the industrial scales at his top weight of eighty-five stones – gained worldwide notoriety (as 'Whopping Walter') when he became stuck in his bedroom door. He was wedged there for some four hours; it took eight firemen to free him.

Walter Hudson was born at Brooklyn in 1945 and, as he recalled, 'began gorging at the age of six'. At fifteen he was so obese his legs collapsed underneath him and he was confined to bed. Indeed, except for the time when his family moved in 1970 and he was transported by motor-car (his then forty-two stones broke the seat), he remained inside. 'I'm just a foodaholic,' he once confessed, 'I have no excuse.'

Hudson's eating habits were fuelled by food brought in by members of his family. He would generally start his day with a breakfast of two pounds of bacon, thirty-two sausages, a dozen eggs, a loaf of bread, jam and coffee.

For luncheon Hudson favoured four Big Macs, four double-cheeseburgers, eight boxes of fried potatoes, six pies and six quarts of Coca-Cola. He would dine off six corns-on-the-cob, three ham steaks, half a dozen yams and another six or seven baked potatoes, ending with a whole apple pie.

Between these principal repasts he would despatch a fowl or two, chased by macaroni, string beans, six large bottles of soda, not to mention colossal sandwiches and copious snacks such as Ring-Dings, Yodels, Yankee Doodles, Twinkies and assorted candy. 'All I cared about,' he recalled, 'was food, food, FOOD.' When not eating and sleeping he would watch television. Hudson, though, was advised against sitting up for longer than five minutes because of the risk of being smothered by flab. The only exercise he engaged in was when he attended to his ablutions; it took him an hour to negotiate the six yards to the bathroom from his bedroom.

Then, in 1987, he found himself wedged in the doorway. 'The day I got stuck in that door,' he recalled, 'that's when the Lord got me the help I needed.' The help to which he referred was offered by Dick Gregory, a comedian who masterminded the Slim Safe diet scheme.

Gregory placed Hudson on a 1,200-calorie-a-day diet of raw fruit and orange juice. For exercise he was advised to lie in bed waving his arms about like a conductor.

Hudson soon lost some four inches off his knees, and within three months had shed twenty-eight stones. It began to look as if he might fulfil such ambitions as visiting his mother's grave, riding on the New York subway, driving into the country – and even flying to a clinic in the Bahamas, from which he envisaged emerging as a sylph of thirteen stones.

But it was not to be. At the time of his death, of an apparent heart attack, Hudson reportedly weighed eighty stones. Rescue workers had to cut a large hole in the wall of his bedroom to remove the body.

❧ 25th ❧

Hugh Massingberd, b. 1946, d. 2007

Hugh Massingberd, who has died aged sixty, always used to insist, during his time as obituaries editor of *The Daily Telegraph*, that understatement was the key to the form.

It is by no means an infringement of that principle to begin his own obituary with the declaration that those who worked for him – and indeed everyone who came to know him properly – considered him one of the most extraordinary and lovable Englishmen of his time.

He was also one of the most complex. A gentleman to his roots, he was nevertheless delighted to be guyed as 'Massivesnob' in *Private Eye*. The supreme master of fact, he revelled in daydreams. Shy and diffident, he at the same time exhibited a strong theatrical streak, holding forth masterfully as public speaker or broadcaster.

Above all, the man seemingly content to be taken as a Woosterish bumbler and bon vivant possessed a prodigious capacity for hard work. This professed amateur of journalism – he would type with two fingers – matched any professional in practice.

It was as obituaries editor of *The Daily Telegraph* from 1986 to 1994 that he found the perfect fulfilment for his gifts. First, though, he had to reinvent the whole concept of the form, substituting for the grave and ceremonious tribute the sparkling celebration of life.

Before his arrival at the *Telegraph*, obituaries had been regarded as an inferior branch of News, and afforded minimal space. As far back as 1969, however, Massingberd had discerned the immense potential that lay in this disregarded cranny of journalism. The moment of illumination had come when he went to see Roy Dotrice's rendering of John Aubrey's *Brief Lives* at the Criterion Theatre.

Picking up a dusty tome, Dotrice/Aubrey read out a dreary entry about a barrister (Recorder of this, Bencher of that, and so on). Suddenly he snapped shut the volume with a 'Tchah!' and turned to the audience: 'He got more by his prick than his practice.'

There and then, Massingberd later wrote, 'I determined to dedicate myself to chronicling what people were really like through informal anecdote, description and character sketch.' Laughter, he added, would be by no means out of place.

In 1986, Max Hastings gave Massingberd his opportunity. Immediately, *Telegraph* readers found themselves regaled by such characters as Canon Edward Young, the first chaplain of a striptease club; the last Wali of Swat, who had a fondness for Brown Windsor soup; and Judge Melford Stevenson, who considered that 'a lot of my colleagues are just constipated Methodists'.

The column made a speciality of tales of derring-do from the Second World War. The foibles of aristocrats proved another fertile source. Part of the fun lay in the style which Massingberd evolved to pin down the specimens on display. Liberace, readers were gravely informed, 'never married'. Hopeless drunks were 'convivial'. Total shits 'did not suffer fools gladly'. Financial fraudsters seemed 'not to have upheld the highest ethical standards of the City'.

But this man, who delighted so many people, never satisfied himself. Supersensitive, he registered every slight, however effectively his feelings were concealed. Just occasionally hints of vulnerability would slip through the guard, in a waspish review, or an uncharacteristically sharp aside. He had been a thwarted and insecure young man, whose early history inclined him towards a romantic view of aristocracy.

He was born Hugh John Montgomery at Cookham Dean, in Berkshire, on 30 December 1946. His father was in the Colonial Service and later worked for the BBC; his mother was a 'leftward-leaning schoolmistress'.

His remoter background, however, was distinctly grand, even if it promised a great deal more than it delivered. The Montgomerys, seated at Blessingbourne in Co. Tyrone, were a Protestant Ascendancy family. In his youth Hugh stayed at the Montgomerys' pseudo-Elizabethan (actually 1870) pile in the full expectation that one day it would be his. It was, therefore, a shattering blow to be told in his mid-teens that a cousin who intended to be a farmer would inherit Blessingbourne; this youth, it was judged, would be better qualified than Hugh to return the estate to order after years of benign neglect.

Hugh's relative mediocrity as a games-player inspired the first of his fantasy creations, that of Sir John Julian Bruce, Bt, MA, OBE, VC, the great all-rounder – 'As England's opening bowler, I found that wickets fell like apples from a tree' – universally adored for his good looks, modesty and charm. Hugh filled countless exercise books with accounts of his prowess.

Hugh left Harrow a year early, in 1964. The only promise in his life at this period was his discovery of the satire boom. In no time he had the sketches from *Beyond the Fringe*, which opened at the Fortune Theatre in 1961, off by heart; and he was also an early aficionado of *Private Eye*, first published in the same year. 'At last,' wrote his form master after Hugh had written an essay on satire, 'you have found a subject which really interests you.'

He seemed in particularly self-destructive mode at this time, rejecting any notion of Oxford or Cambridge on the grounds that he could bear neither the student radicals nor the Brideshead poseurs with their teddy bears. And so, masochistically, he chose the Law. Still only seventeen, he began to commute from Cookham to solicitors in Lincoln's Inn. By the afternoon on the first day, having been condemned to a windowless cell and instructed to add up the assets of some peeress, he was shaking with silent sobs.

He lasted three dreary years before snapping one afternoon and walking out of the office for good.

Considering the option of taking up a place at Selwyn College, Cambridge, in the autumn of 1968, he attended a crammer at Oxford to gain the necessary qualifications. Fate intervened, however, when he heard about a job as an assistant at *Burke's Peerage*.

He obtained the post, and for the first time in his life found himself totally focused and committed. Thoughts of Cambridge were dismissed as he applied himself with astounding industry and grasp to the genealogies of the landed gentry, and then moved on to produce, single-handedly, a new edition of *The Peerage, Baronetage and Knightage*. The standards he set have never been matched since.

Suddenly, in 1971, as a result of an office coup organised by Christine Martinoni, whom he would marry the next year, Massingberd found himself appointed editor of all the firm's publications. As he later observed, for the first time in his life fantasy had collided with reality.

He drew up a list of projects, some of which came to fruition. Financial support for Massingberd's schemes, however, soon withered, although he did not finally resign from Burke's until 1983. He now sought to build another career as a freelance writer and columnist. *The Spectator* and *The Field* proved particularly amenable. Within two years he had found fulfilment at the *Telegraph*.

Eventually, however, Massingberd became a victim of his own success. The *réclame* of his obituaries' page gave him the opportunity to write other pieces for the paper – a Heritage column on country houses, continuing his work for *The Field*; interviews with stars (in one of which he confessed to a desire to kiss Hugh Laurie); scores of book reviews; and – not conducive to good health – articles as restaurant critic.

The pressure of work was already feverish when, in 1992, he accepted an invitation to add the editorship of the Peterborough column to that of obituaries. This proved a step too far, and even after he had given up the post, he found his confidence drained. As if in acknowledgment of his fall, which, in truth, hardly existed outside his own mind, he reduced his by-line from the efflorescent Hugh Montgomery-Massingberd to plain Hugh Massingberd. Early in 1994 he suffered a near-fatal heart attack.

He recovered a measure of health, wrote a superb article on his brush with death, and for two years worked from home as *The Daily Telegraph*'s television critic. Again, though, the insecurities surfaced, and in 1996, as the pressure became intolerable, he wisely resigned the post.

He continued to write both books and book reviews, as authoritative and sparkling as ever. At last, though, he had some spare time to enjoy.

What could he not have done? His books alone, something of a sideline notwithstanding their excellence, might have constituted a lifetime's work for an ordinary mortal. Among them were six books of *Telegraph* obituaries.

26th

Sean Collins, b. 1952, d. 2011

Sean Collins, who has died aged fifty-nine, brought the light of scientific inquiry to bear on one of modern sport's most mystical quests – the surfer's search for the perfect wave.

The veneration of surfers for the ideal cresting swell, and their dedication to tracking it down, is legendary. But for decades after surfing's popular rise in the post-war era, such waves usually proved elusive. Flat calm oceans frustrated surfers everywhere, including Collins, who had grown up on the beaches of California.

Determined to maximise his productive surfing time, he began to scrutinise meteorological data and maritime charts. But instead of using them to predict what effects weather might have on shipping, he investigated what the consequences of offshore storms might be for surfers in Hawaii, or Mexico. 'I was obsessed,' he once said.

His predictions would have counted for little had they not been accurate, but they almost always came up trumps (Collins himself estimated a 5 per cent failure rate). Instead of being forced to drop everything and rush to the beach as news spread of great waves, surfers were able to plan their trips. Soon Collins was being besieged by 'friends of friends' calling up for forecasts, and realised that his insight could become a money-spinner. In 1984 he co-founded the telephone tip service Surfline, before leaving in 1986 to found his own company, Wavetrack, which soon bought out Surfline.

Such were his predictive powers that Collins became known as surfing's 'Alan Greenspan'. Surfline's proprietary swell model, known as LOLA, is now so well regarded that it is used by America's Coast Guard.

Sean Collins was born on 8 April 1952 in southern California. He started surfing on Seal Beach, California, at the age of eight and competed in sailing races with his father.

The combination of sailing and surfing helped him to find the best waves. 'I've been in storms a hundred miles out at sea, then surfed the same swells the next day,' he said. 'I was always looking at charts to plan my surfing and sailing, and developed a keen sense about the ocean, which is at the core of what I live for.'

Sean was educated at Wilson High School in Long Beach, California, and took a few lessons in meteorology at Long Beach Community College. But after leaving full-time education he mostly dedicated himself to surfing, taking odd jobs to fund his perpetual quest for the perfect wave. That changed in 1983, with the birth of his first son. 'I had to get a real job,' he confessed, and when he was asked the following year to help found Surfline, he seized the opportunity.

The eventual success of the business allowed Collins to devote much of his time to chasing waves, and he would happily leave the office at a moment's notice to go surfing in Mexico; he took trips as far away as China.

In 1999 he was named one of the '25 Most Influential Surfers of the Century' by *Surfer Magazine*.

27th

Fanny Cradock, b. 1909, d. 1994

Fanny Cradock, the irascible *grande dame* of the kitchen who has died aged eighty-five, rejoiced in her singular combination of haute couture and haute cuisine.

In her various television series in the 1950s and 1960s Mrs Cradock eschewed aprons and appeared in Hartnell ball gowns while roaring gravel-throated orders – 'More wine, Johnnie! More butter! Don't stint!' – at her forbearing companion, a kindly-looking cove sporting a monocle.

It was easy to make fun of Fanny Cradock and the much-put-upon Johnnie – she was, for instance, guyed as 'Fanny Haddock', the husky-voiced harridan in the wireless comedy shows *Beyond Our Ken* and *Round the Horne* – but she did much to awaken British regard for cooking after the war, and to improve the standards of commercial catering.

Her aim was to make good cookery easy and fun for the post-war generation of housewives, who had grown up during the years of food shortages. But she was dedicated to classical cookery, and refused to cut corners.

Latterly Mrs Cradock became as celebrated for her bad temper as for her cooking. She recalled one contretemps with some youths outside a hotel who refused to move their car: 'I went in kicking low. I can still remember how exhilarating was the slosh of handbag on fleshy nose.' The youths fled.

She was born Phyllis Pechey in the Channel Islands on 26 February 1909. Her father, Archibald Pechey, was a butterfly collector. At the age of one, the infant Fanny was given to her grandmother as 'a birthday present', and remained with her until she was ten. She later claimed to have learned almost everything about food and wine from her grandmother. 'All the food was pink,' she recalled of one of their elegant soirees, 'pink mousse on pink glass plates chilled in pink ice into which pink moss rosebuds had been frozen'.

She was sent to board at the Downs, which she described as 'the hell pit'. At fifteen she was expelled for encouraging other girls to contact 'the spirit world'.

Although her parents wanted to send her to a finishing school Fanny was determined to stay with her grandmother. She earned her keep by cooking dinner each evening: 'They insisted I was in evening dress and in my place by the time the fish was served. To save time I wore my Schiaparelli beaded frock and slave bangles in the kitchen – that's how I learned to cook in ball gowns.'

At seventeen she eloped with her first husband to Brighton, but he died a few months later in an accident, leaving Fanny a pregnant widow. After her father went bankrupt in 1928 she was reduced to earning a living by washing up at a Roman Catholic canteen.

She pawned some clothes in order to place an advertisement for a dress-making service in a local newsagent's window. Another source of income was selling vacuum cleaners door to door. She also made a second marriage, though it is not mentioned in her memoirs, *Something's Burning*.

In 1939 she met Johnnie Cradock, an amiable Old Harrovian, and began an association which lasted until his death in 1987; they did not marry until 1977. Initially they lived in a house which was celebrated for both its ghosts and its hospitality. 'Our cooking used to amaze our friends,' Fanny Cradock recalled. 'They thought we had black market supplies from Fortnum's.'

Locally available food would be ingeniously disguised: 'Bracken shoots were asparagus and I used liquid paraffin for my pastry. We caught and cooked sparrows from the garden and often ate baked hedgehogs (rather like frog's legs).'

While Johnnie Cradock served in the Army during the Second World War, Fanny spent her time writing novels. She had some success with such bodice-rippers as *The Lormes of Castle Rising* and *Storm Over Castle Rising*, under the name Frances Dale. After the war she turned to cookery writing, publishing *The Practical Cook* (1949) and *The Ambitious Cook* (1950).

In 1954 the Cradocks toured Britain lecturing on cookery for the Brains Trust. Two years later they gave the first live televised cookery demonstration. Before the show Mrs Cradock was so nervous that she had to leave the set, run to the nearest church and pray for twenty minutes before she could face the cameras.

She went to enormous lengths in the service of television. She dieted rigorously and even had plastic surgery on her nose when technicians told her it was 'too big' and was 'casting shadows over the food'.

But as the years advanced she became increasingly eccentric and temperamental. In 1964 she was charged with careless driving, and fined £5; the arresting officer described her as 'abusive and excited'. When he asked her to move her Rolls-Royce (parked across the stream of traffic) she called him a 'uniformed delinquent' and told him to wait while she finished her conversation.

By the 1970s her memory for detail – always somewhat unreliable – seemed to be failing. When, in 1977, she finally married Johnnie Cradock at a registry office there was confusion over both her age and her name. Mrs Cradock claimed she was fifty-five, even though her elder son was then fifty and her second son forty-eight.

Meanwhile country neighbours of the Cradocks used to complain of Mrs Cradock's erratic behaviour, especially of her distressing tendency 'to lash out with her walking stick at those who got in her way'.

⊰ 28th ⊱

R.F.B. Letts, b. 1928, d. 2010

R.F.B. Letts, who has died aged eighty-two, was a West Country headmaster of the old order, cherishing cricket, classics and the cane; for thirty years he ran Oakley Hall in Cirencester, instilling in pupils not only the merits of fair play and patriotism but also the more subtle attractions of a quirky intransigence.

Some considered Letts an eccentric – a charge he cheerfully cultivated by zipping around in a Sinclair C5 electric buggy and by continuing to calculate boys' pocket money in shillings and pence long after decimalisation.

Richard Francis Bonner Letts was born on 15 May 1928, just a few hundred yards from Oakley Hall. Four months after his birth, the school was bought by his father, Major C.F.C. Letts, whose temperament, after a Great War in which he was thrice wounded, was perpetually sunny.

Dick was educated at Oakley Hall and at Haileybury and, after National Service, joined the staff at the school to 'see if he liked' teaching. In 1962 he succeeded his father to the headmastership. Although Letts was a vehement critic of the comprehensive schools introduced by the Wilson government – he called them 'apprehensives' – the closure of grammars was a boon to private education and numbers swelled.

It was a place of chalk dust, mortar boards and flogging. Letts would sweep into Sunday chapel in a gown to take services according to the Book of Common Prayer, complete with responses sung to a wheezing harmonium. Swimming was conducted without trunks and boys had to declare daily details of their bowel movements. After that it was into a curriculum of Ovid, Homer and English kings and queens.

Letts was a painfully shy man and left much of the organisation of the school to his mercurial wife, who had arrived at Oakley Hall as an under-matron. Their courtship became a matter of keen debate among older boys, some of whom placed bets on how long it would take Letts to pop the question.

Letts had little truck with teaching trends and would deal with schools inspectors by giving the visitors two large gins before lunch. His methods brought Oakley Hall a high number of classics scholarships to public schools. Alas, his application to the business side of things was less rigorous and there were many instances of fees not being paid or (in deserving cases) being waived. Letts retired in 1992 and Oakley Hall closed two years later.

In 1991 he had made the national press after brawling with a visiting parent on the rugby field touchline. Letts felt that the man had been voicing unnecessarily coarse support for his team. The fight, he later conceded, had been a lot more entertaining than the game itself.

⇜ 29th ⇝

Bob Monkhouse, b. 1928, d. 2003

Bob Monkhouse, the comedian who has died aged seventy-five, became synonymous with television game shows, playing the unctuous host to more than thirty different programmes that, like him, seemed to many to exemplify all that was most superficial about television.

His oozing charm, lacquered tan and hovering eyebrow attracted a measure of critical loathing that was markedly at odds with the popularity of his shows. But this perception changed late in Monkhouse's career, when his brilliance as a stand-up comedian – he had instant recall of many thousands of one-liners – led to a reappraisal of his talents. Off-stage, as interviewers discovered, Monkhouse possessed a warm intelligence and self-awareness that eluded many of his peers. 'By the age of twenty-eight,' he once said, 'it was clear to me that I had no talent. What I had was a certain facility, that was all.' It was a perceptive, if overly harsh, judgment.

Just as the tan, though regularly topped up in Barbados, was mostly make-up needed to disguise a severe pigmentation disorder – he suffered from vitiligo, which made him, beneath his underpants, 'a riot of polka dots and moonbeams' – Monkhouse's smug fluency masked considerable technical skill and dedicated preparation; he was devastated when two books containing years of material were stolen in 1995. (They were recovered eighteen months later.)

In fact, he was a remarkably brilliant gag writer. 'They laughed when I said I was going to be a comedian,' ran one of his best lines. 'They're not laughing now.'

Robert Alan Monkhouse was born at Beckenham, Kent, on 1 June 1928. His grandfather was a custard-powder tycoon whose death the nine-year-old Bob took so hard that he was unable to speak for three months.

He was a lonely, fat child who felt unloved by his parents and consoled himself by writing jokes. At Dulwich College, where he was known as 'The Oil', because of his predilection for hair cream, he began selling gags to children's comics, including the *Beano* and the *Dandy*. Soon he was knocking out racy pulp novels for the troops under names such as Ramon Le Croix.

He did his National Service with the RAF and by 1948 had conned his way into an audition for the BBC – getting an RAF neurologist, for whom he acted as secretary, to sign, unread, a letter that attested to Corporal Monkhouse's need for therapy in the form of a studio test. Within a few weeks he was, with Terry Scott, the BBC's first contracted comedian. Graduating rapidly to top billing, Monkhouse maintained a ferocious rate of work throughout the next two decades.

He and his writing partner Denis Goodwin wrote up to seven radio scripts a week, as well as material for Bob Hope and Dean Martin. He continued to be a mainstay of radio comedy for decades, and starred in several, mostly forgettable, films, including the first of the *Carry On* series and *Dentist in the Chair*. He also appeared on stage. New routines were relentlessly polished on the cabaret circuit.

Yet by 1967 his career had stalled as he fell out of favour with the BBC.

Then, on safari in South Africa, he received a cable asking him to compere the next *Sunday Night at the London Palladium* for ITV. Booked for one edition only, Monkhouse's vigorous invention revived the ailing show and saw his contract extended weekly thirteen times. It led in 1967 to perhaps his best-known role, as host of *The Golden Shot*, a hugely popular if ludicrous show in which contestants directed by telephone a blindfolded crossbowman to score a bullseye. In 1972, Monkhouse was quietly replaced after too blatantly endorsing a new razor on the programme.

The genially bland persona he had cultivated made him the obvious choice for a welter of subsequent game shows, among them *Family Fortunes*, *Celebrity Squares*, *Bob's Full House*, *Bob's Your Uncle* and a revival of *Opportunity Knocks*.

Each made little demand of his talents while offering him easy scope for well-rehearsed quips. He remained among the highest-paid television entertainers into the mid-1990s, betraying a slight self-loathing with a favourite remark: 'I'm a hard man to ignore, but well worth the effort.'

Yet beneath the outward success ran a broad seam of pain and potential disaster. A particular sadness was his first marriage in 1949, to a Belfast WRAF, Elizabeth. Disapproving of his career, his mother threatened to cut him off without a penny and advised Elizabeth to turn her attentions instead to his older brother, an accountant. She attended the wedding in black.

Monkhouse and his mother did not speak again for twenty years, though they were reconciled shortly before her death. Anthony Clare, in a 1992 episode of his radio programme *In the Psychiatrist's Chair*, prompted Monkhouse to break down at the suggestion that his mother's possessiveness indicated her love for him.

He dealt bravely with the inoperable prostate cancer with which he was diagnosed in 2001, and never abandoned the opportunity to crack jokes. 'I still enjoy sex at seventy-four,' he said last year. 'I live at seventy-five, so it's not far to go.'

⚞ **30**th ⚟

Julius Epstein, b. 1909, d. 2000

Julius Epstein, the scriptwriter who has died aged ninety-one, was largely responsible, with his twin brother Phil, for writing *Casablanca* (1942).

The story derived from a play called *Everybody Comes to Rick's*, by Murray Burnett and Joan Alison. Although many lines from the play were incorporated into *Casablanca*, the Epsteins succeeded brilliantly both in enhancing the wit and snap of the dialogue, and in re-imagining the characters.

Most fundamental were the changes made to the leading woman. In the play she is Lois Meredith, an American of doubtful morals, and such she remains in the Epsteins' first draft. They were, however, perfectly willing to fall in with the suggestion that she should be transmogrified into a European.

'You try and get a foreign girl for the part,' wrote 'Julie' Epstein accommodatingly to the studio. All the same, he could not resist adding: 'An American girl with big tits will do.' The role went to Ingrid Bergman.

⚜ **31**st ⚜

Geoffrey Van-Hay, b. 1937, d. 2009

Geoffrey Van-Hay, who died on New Year's Eve aged seventy-two, was the celebrated figure who presided over El Vino, the drinking place of journalists in the high old days of Fleet Street.

Always impeccably dressed in white collar and dark jacket with striped trousers, Van, as he was always known, maintained order among the often unruly clients with a combination of wit and charm.

The banning of journalists for unsuitable, drink-fuelled antics was strictly enforced by Van-Hay. Hugh Cudlipp and the famous columnist Cassandra, both of the *Daily Mirror*, got their marching orders – as did many less distinguished hacks – for antisocial behaviour. Vicky, the left-wing cartoonist, was also expelled. All three claimed that they had barred themselves because they disliked the snobbery of the place, in which men were compelled to wear suits and ties.

That view was shared by many others. Charles Wintour, editor of the *Evening Standard*, rarely visited the bar. On one occasion that he did go there, his proprietor Lord Beaverbrook tracked him down by telephone to reproach him: 'You will find no news stories in El Vino's public house.'

The son of a London policeman from the Elephant and Castle, Geoffrey Van-Hay was born on 7 September 1937 and was educated locally. He made his debut in Fleet Street working behind the counter of an electrical goods shop a few doors down from El Vino.

His vocation as the Jeeves of the wine bars began when Christopher Mitchell, whose grandfather founded the El Vino wine shipping business, talent-spotted Van-Hay selling light bulbs over the counter and decided to train him to manage his flagship bar. 'He had charm, personality and a positive attitude,' Mitchell recalled.

So began Van-Hay's stewardship of one of the most famous bars in London. It could be a wild place. Maurice Richardson, the *Guardian*'s arts critic, boasted about his boxing skills, almost knocked Mitchell down when he was told to quieten his drunken behaviour. Mitchell and Van-Hay, both big men, then threw him into the street and banned him for ever.

Eventually Van-Hay decided to establish his own wine bar in a cellar in nearby Carmelite Street. At first named the Girder Club, it was partly financed by loans from journalists. It later flowered as Scribes. When the warring newspaper tribes finally abandoned their base in Fleet Street, Van-Hay folded his tent and followed. He set up a basement bar near the new *Daily Mail* headquarters in Kensington and called it Scribes West. There he recreated something of the old El Vino atmosphere, also welcoming journalists from other papers who happened to stray into that part of London.

Among the 2,000-odd journalists who signed up as members of the new club was Carol Thatcher. One evening, as she sat at the bar, Van-Hay came up with a bright idea. In the camp theatrical voice he sometimes used when unsure, he said to her: 'I say, my dear, do you think you could ask your mother to open our new club?'

She promised to try. Van-Hay boldly thrust a telephone at her, and to everyone's surprise she was soon talking to the Prime Minister. 'Will you do me a real favour and personally open a jolly club friends of mine are starting in Kensington?' She listened to the instant answer and then hung up.

'Well?' stuttered Van.

'Mum said "Yes".'

INDEX